THE V&A BOOK OF COLOUR IN DESIGN

On p. 4 C.F.A. Voysey, textile design, watercolour and pencil, London, 1918
E.207-1974. Given by Courtauld Ltd

First published in the United Kingdom in 2020 by Thames & Hudson Ltd,
6–24 Britannia Street, London, WC1X 9JD in association with the
Victoria and Albert Museum

This paperback edition published 2025

The V&A Book of Colour in Design © 2020 and 2025 Victoria and Albert
Museum/Thames & Hudson Ltd, London

Text and V&A photographs © 2020 Victoria and Albert Museum, London
Design © 2020 Thames & Hudson Ltd, London
Designed by Here Design

EU Authorized Representative: Interart S.A.R.L.
19 rue Charles Auray, 93500 Pantin, Paris, France
productsafety@thameshudson.co.uk
interart.fr

A CIP catalogue record for this book is available from the British Library

ISBN 978-0-500-29867-1
02

Printed and bound in China through Asia Pacific Offset Ltd

Be the first to know about our new releases,
exclusive content and author events by visiting
thamesandhudson.com
thamesandhudsonusa.com
thamesandhudson.com.au

Colour has been used to exclude and discriminate, and is bound up with
narratives around race. We have tried to signal here where an object's colour
might divide or exclude people – though these important histories are not
the primary story of this book.

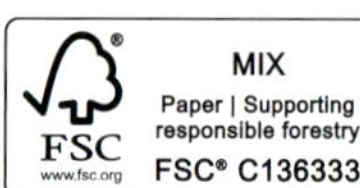

V&A Publishing

Supporting the world's leading
museum of art and design,
the Victoria and Albert
Museum, London

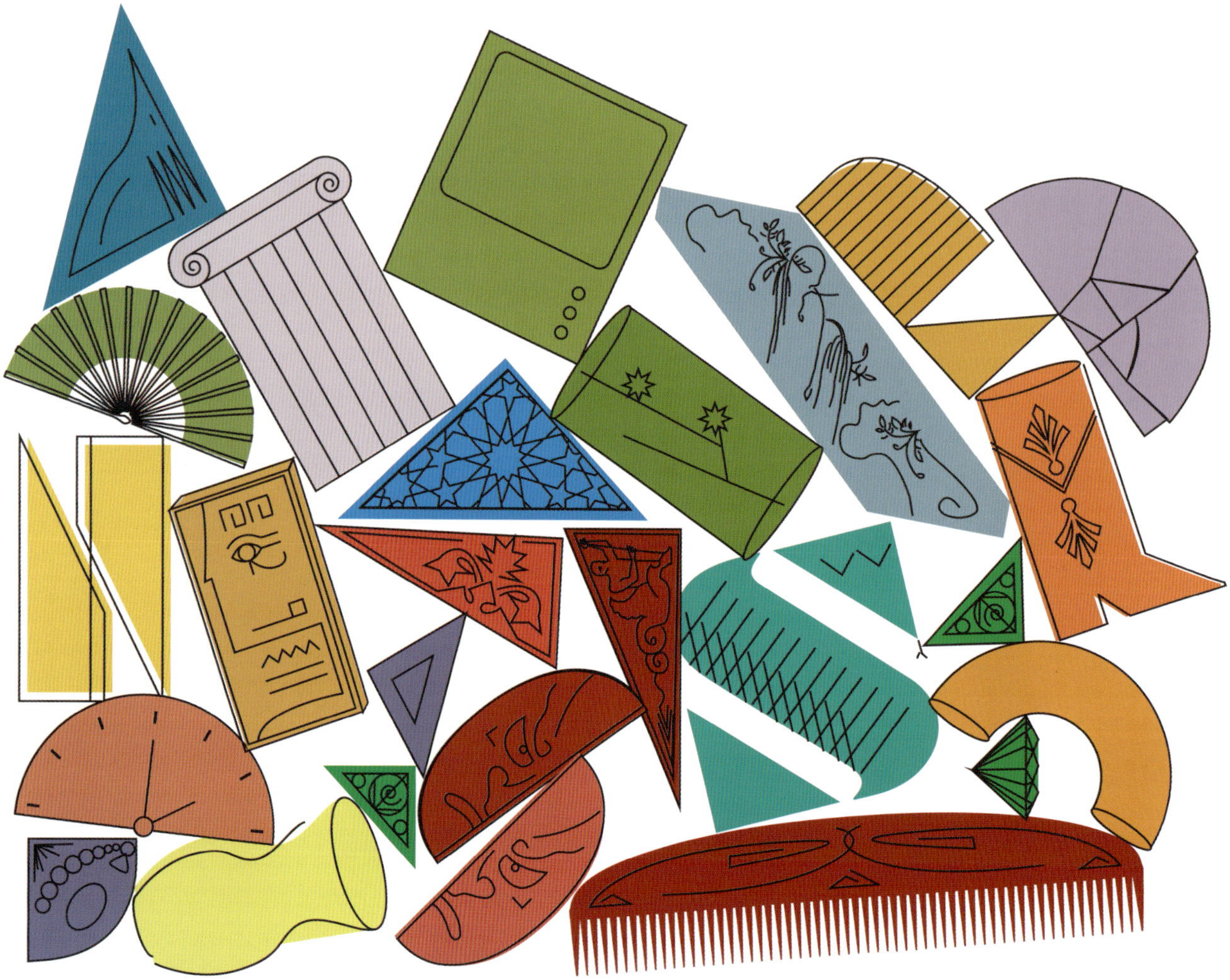

THE V&A BOOK OF COLOUR IN DESIGN

Edited by Tim Travis

Over 450 illustrations in colour

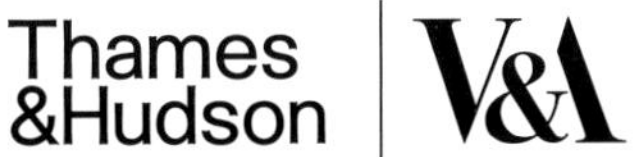

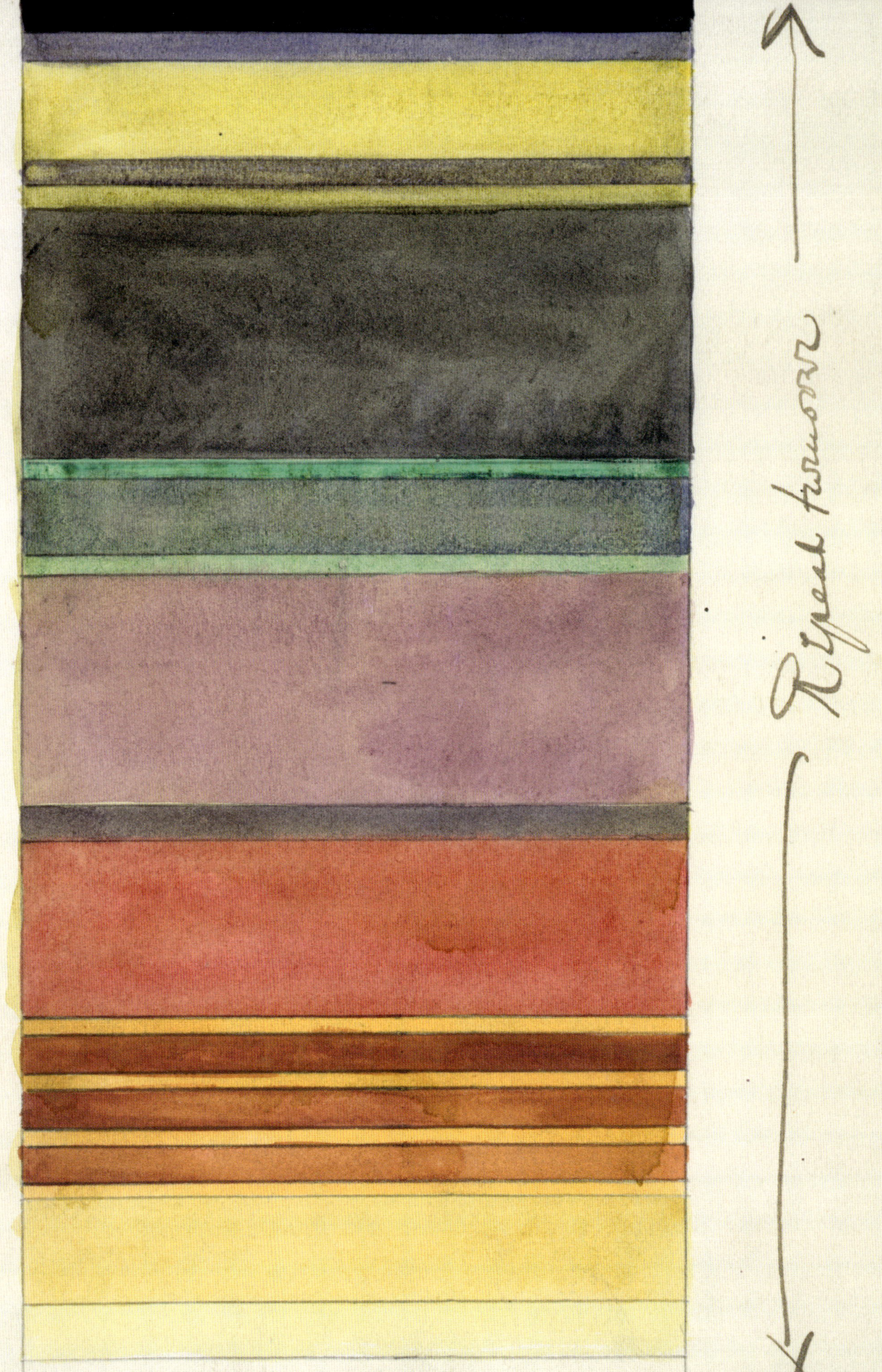

CONTENTS

INTRODUCTION

In H.P. Lovecraft's 1927 short story 'The Colour Out of Space', a meteorite lands on a farm in Massachusetts and sinks into the earth, glowing with an unearthly colour that none of the witnesses can describe and that defies scientific analysis. The next harvest yields a bumper crop of unusually large fruit and vegetables, but they are foul-tasting and inedible, crumbling into grey dust. Subsequently, the surrounding vegetation, wildlife, farm animals and eventually the farmer and his family are all affected too. The humans succumb to psychosis, then a mysterious wasting disease and finally a horrible death, all in the lurid glow of the now dreaded 'colour'. Abundance turns to monstrosity, and what seemed a natural wonder becomes a menacing blight, reducing the whole district to a grey dust-filled desert abandoned by the local population and passing into lore as 'the blasted heath'.

Like most horror stories, 'The Colour Out of Space' and its subsequent incarnations in film speaks to the anxieties of its time, but it also taps into a long-standing ambivalence about colour, historically regarded with a mixture of fascination, fear and disdain. The artist David Batchelor, in *Chromophobia* (2000), traces an aversion to colour running through western culture from ancient Greece to modernity. Colour is regarded either as an attribute of the alien other, 'usually the feminine, the oriental, the primitive, the infantile, the vulgar, the queer or the pathological', or is dismissed as subjective, unstable and secondary, 'relegated to the realm of the superficial, the supplementary, the inessential or the cosmetic'. When societies are convulsed by iconoclastic episodes of reform or revolution, decadent colour is usually one of the first candidates for purging.

One source of this ambivalence may be the relative imprecision of colour vocabulary. Two people sharing a common language and perfectly capable of distinguishing between one shade and another can still disagree about the basic colour term for it. The same shade of maroon may be called red, purple or brown by different observers. Queen Elizabeth II's outfit for the State Opening of the UK Parliament after the 2019 General Election sparked a lively debate in the press and on social media about whether her coat was green or blue (incidentally, some languages have only one word for green and blue, which anthropologists render in English as 'grue').

Since at least the seventeenth century, philosophers have debated whether colour even exists as an objective phenomenon, or is just an arbitrary way of organizing subjective experiences. For much of the twentieth century, many anthropologists subscribed to a theory of 'linguistic relativity' – the idea that language shapes our perceptions such that we cannot recognize a colour as distinct unless we have a word for it. Experiments by cognitive psychologists in the 1950s, comparing the ability of English speakers to remember shades of yellow and orange with Native American Zuni speakers, who had one word for both colours, seemed to back up the theory. But studies of a wider pool of cultures and language groups by the anthropologists Paul Kay and Brent Berlin, published in *Basic*

René-Henri Digeon (active 1855–1872), plate from *Des Couleurs et de Leurs Applications aux Arts Industriels* (On Colours and their Applications to the Industrial Arts) by Michel Eugène Chevreul (1786–1889), aquatint, 1864

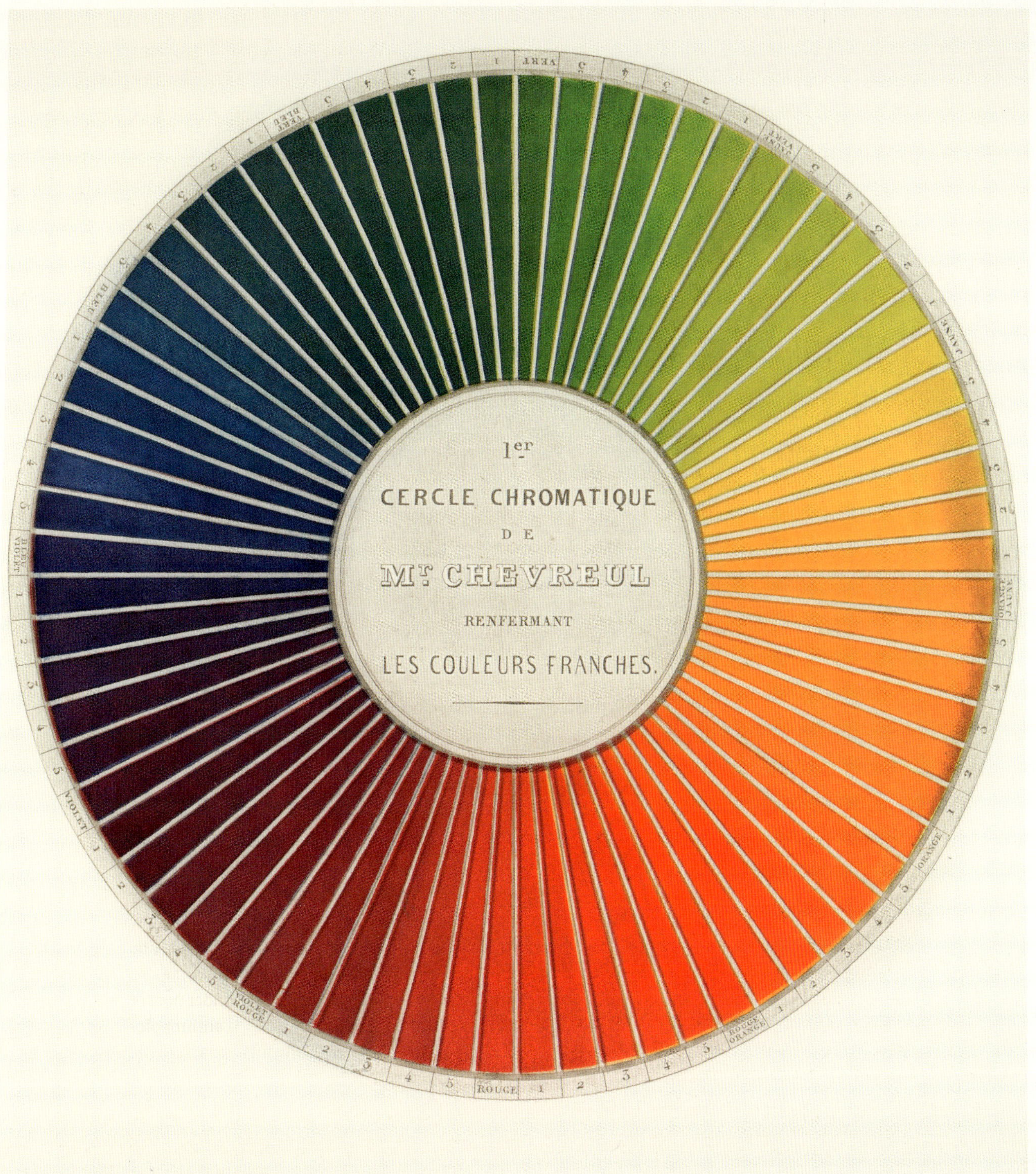

1er
CERCLE CHROMATIQUE
DE
Mr CHEVREUL
RENFERMANT
LES COULEURS FRANCHES.
VERT
VERT BLEU
BLEU
BLEU VIOLET
VIOLET
VIOLET ROUGE
ROUGE
ROUGE ORANGE
ORANGE
ORANGE JAUNE
JAUNE
JAUNE VERT

Colour Terms: Their Universality and Evolution (1969), revealed surprising similarities between the groups, both in the number of basic colour terms used and the evolution of the colour vocabularies.

More recently, cognitive psychologist Anna Franklin's studies at the University of Sussex seem to indicate that we can categorize colours long before we can speak. Franklin works with infants before they have learned to talk. Attracted by novelty, when shown different colour swatches they will stare for longer at a colour they perceive as different from the preceding one. It seems that even without a colour vocabulary, they compartmentalize the visible spectrum in a similar way to adults – but with an interesting difference. Infants are quicker to recognize new colours seen in the left visual field, which is processed on the right side of the brain, while in adults the right visual field and therefore the left side of the brain dominates. The left side is where language is processed. As language develops, people's recognition of colour categories somehow passes from the right to the left of the brain. The chicken-and-egg/nature-versus-nurture debate about colour continues.

A more practical reason for ambivalence about colour may have been its sheer natural mutability. Sky and sea catch fire at sunset; fruit ripens; flowers fade; leaves turn brown in autumn; hair turns grey with age – all constant reminders and allegories of death. Early pigments were derived from natural sources – extracts of minerals, plants and insects – and were often fugitive, fading over time, or unstable, reacting unhelpfully with underlying surfaces or neighbouring pigments. The range of available colours was limited and some of the most desirable, such as Tyrian purple or ultramarine blue, were labour-intensive to produce, traded over long distances and prohibitively expensive, reserved for imperial or ecclesiastical use or procured as a luxury by the most ostentatiously wealthy patrons. Rudimentary synthetic pigments such as lead white and vermilion had existed since antiquity, but the plentiful supply of light-fast, chemically stable pigments in a wide range of colours did not become a reality until the scientific and industrial revolutions of the eighteenth and nineteenth centuries. The first modern synthetic pigment, Prussian blue, was discovered by accident in about 1706, when a Berlin colourman, Johann Jacob Diesbach, was trying to produce red cochineal dye. His potash (a salt used in dyeing) was contaminated with blood, which reacted with the iron sulphate in the cochineal recipe to produce a deep blue.

The growth of mass-production after the industrial revolution meant that products could be made available in a novel choice of colours. Systems were needed to standardize colours and colour terms for industry, design and commerce. In the mid-nineteenth century, the French chemist Michel Eugène Chevreul published a series of enormously influential 'atlases' of colour for artists, designers and manufacturers, including the 1864 *Des Couleurs et de Leurs Applications aux Arts Industriels* (On Colours and their Applications to the Industrial Arts), a large-format volume illustrated with twelve magnificent colour plates by René-Henri Digeon (see p. 7). Each shows a circle divided into seventy-two colours. The first two plates show bright, fully saturated colours, with subsequent circles growing progressively darker with the gradual addition of black. The last plates have only the subtlest nuance of colour. As well as a resource for designers and manufacturers, the book was a masterpiece of nineteenth-century colour printing.

Throughout the nineteenth and twentieth centuries, printers and manufacturers of products including paper, textiles, paints, ceramics and plastics have published their own colour charts as both a form of advertising and a tool to help consumers make choices. Some companies, more ambitiously, have set out to devise colour-matching systems across different products and media. The best-known is Pantone, founded in 1963 by Lawrence Herbert and originally a colour printing company. The Pantone Matching System, reference-numbered and presented as colour chips, revolutionized graphic design and printing, and is now used internationally for 'colour management' across a range of industries. Since 1986 the Pantone Colour Institute has published research on the role of colour in design, commerce, consumer taste and psychology. Colour-coding is now used for everything from pharmaceuticals to transport systems, from electrical wiring to wayfinding, safety information, political allegiance or sexual preference. It has become an international visual language, disseminated by global trade and travel and the explosion of digital media.

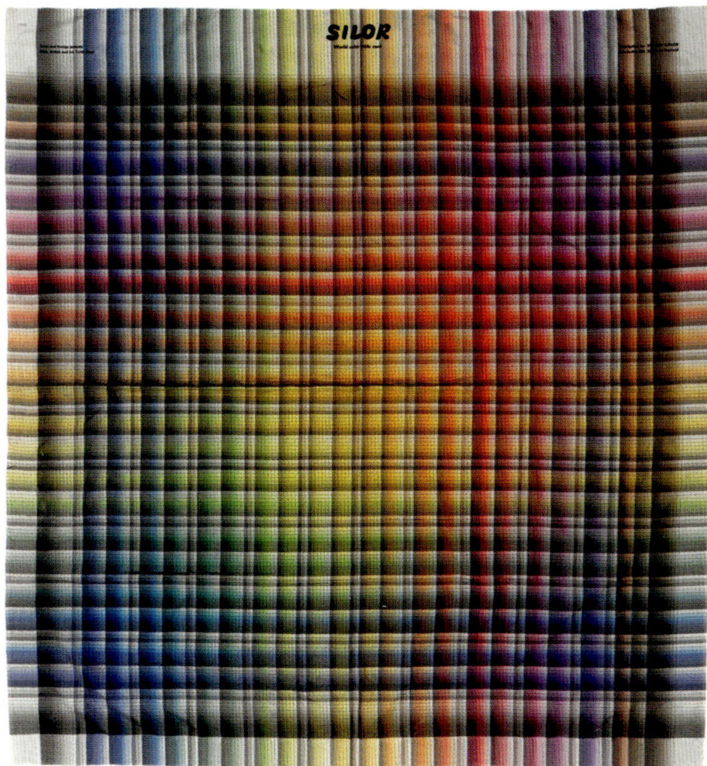

Silor World Colour Cable Card, distributed by Studio Colour, Zurich, silk mounted on card, 1950–70

In fact, the entire visible spectrum – the whole world of colours we see around us and by which we navigate our lives – represents just a tiny sliver of the electromagnetic spectrum, sandwiched between the vast invisible worlds of ultraviolet, x-rays and gamma rays on one side and infrared and radio waves on the other. In the 1660s, Isaac Newton passed a beam of white light through a glass prism to break the light up into its constituent colours, and then through another prism to refract the colours back together into white light. He published his findings in *Opticks: or, A Treatise of the Reflexions, Refractions, Inflexions and Colours of Light* (1704). It had previously been thought that the spectrum effect was caused by impurities in the glass distorting and colouring white light, and for centuries the mixing of pigments to create new colours had been regarded as unnatural and even unethical. Newton's proposition that white light, freighted with religious and moral associations, was an admixture of symbolically less pure colours was profoundly countercultural.

The idea was also counterintuitive: as any painter knows, the more pigments you add to a mixture the murkier and muddier the result. This is the difference between additive and subtractive colour mixing. The former is what Newton was doing when he refracted the coloured rays back together into white light. Each colour transmits light waves in a different wavelength, which when combined produce the total of all visible wavelengths: white. But when a painter mixes oils on a palette, each pigment reflects all the light wavelengths but one – the colour of the pigment. As more colours are added to the mix, fewer light waves are reflected and the colour of the mixture darkens. This effect may also have reinforced the historical disapproval of mixing colours.

Newton divided the visible spectrum arbitrarily into seven (red, orange, yellow, green, blue, indigo and violet), influenced by the number's cultural and religious significance. Later scientists reduced this to six – three primary and three secondary colours – but the seven-coloured spectrum has proved remarkably resilient in symbolic and literary treatments of the subject. Equally resilient has been Newton's colour wheel, a device to demonstrate the sequence of the colours and

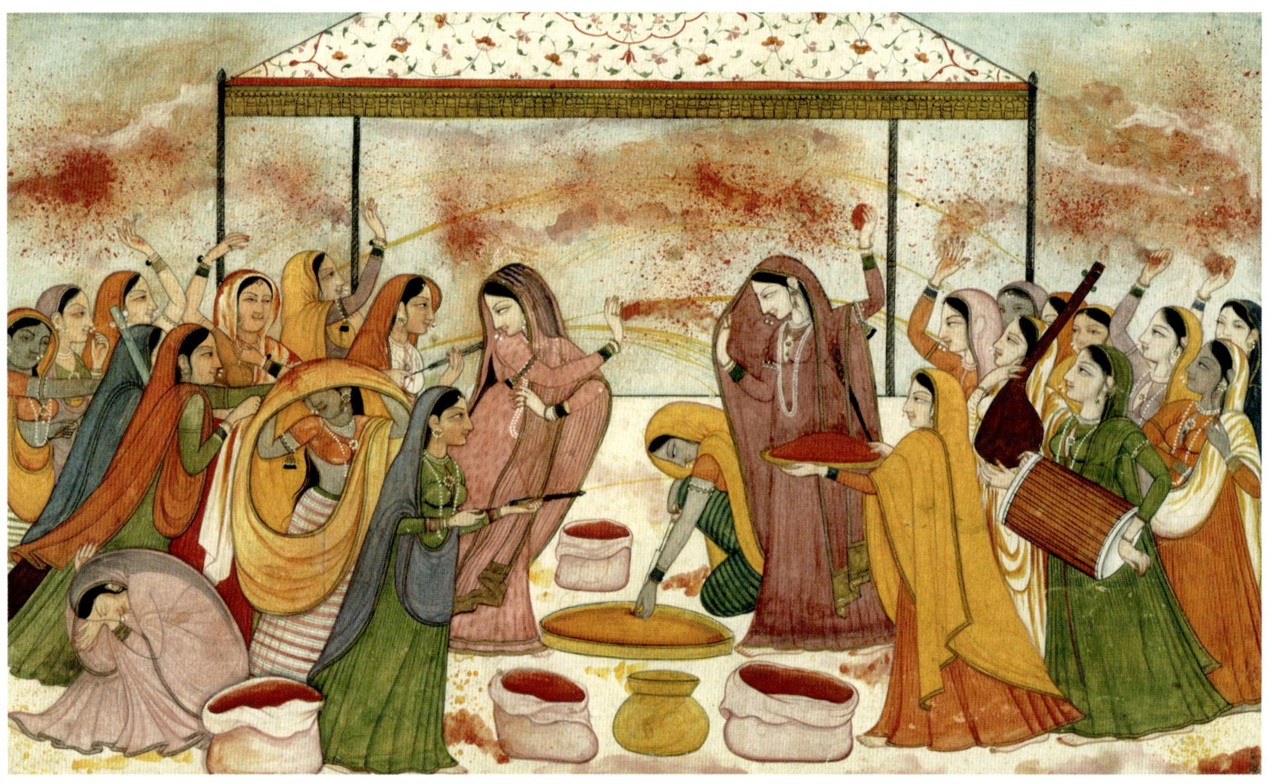

Radha celebrating the Holi festival, Kangra, India, opaque watercolour, 1788

their relationships with one another. Three centuries of published treatises and manuals of instruction on colour for naturalists, artists, designers, decorators and educators adopt or adapt the wheel, as well as spheres and globes, triangles and pyramids, to map a colour universe of harmonizing, contrasting or complementary, primary, secondary and tertiary hues, shades and tints.

A century after Newton, the German writer and scientist Johann Wolfgang von Goethe published his three-volume treatise on colour *Zur Farbenlehre* (On the Doctrine of Colours). He took issue with many of Newton's theories, arguing that colour was produced by the interaction of light and darkness, the latter being an active component and not the mere absence of the former. Though Newton is taken more seriously by physicists, Goethe's ideas about the interaction of colours, subjectivity in colour perception and the emotional effects and cultural associations of colours remains of interest to philosophers and artists.

In 2001, British astronomers Karl Glazebrook and Ivan Baldry, studying star formation at Johns Hopkins University, surveyed light from over 200,000 galaxies and found that the 'average' colour of the universe seen from earth was a bland-sounding off-white or pale beige. This is the real 'colour out of space': dull but not deadly. After an online poll, the colour was christened with the catchier 'Cosmic Latte', partly in recognition of caffeine's role in so much scientific research.

At the opposite end of Goethe's light–dark spectrum, the research and development laboratory Surrey NanoSystems developed Vantablack, a material so dark that it absorbs over 99.9 per cent of visible light. An object coated in Vantablack appears as a black void, only revealing its form when turned around. 'Vanta' is an acronym for 'vertically aligned nanotube arrays'. The material is formed by chemically growing a forest of infinitesimally tiny carbon tubes onto a substrate. Light is trapped between the tubes so that almost none is reflected back to the viewer's eye. Originally formulated for use in the space and defence industries,

Vantablack was controversially licensed for artistic use exclusively to British artist Anish Kapoor – much to the disapproval of other artists including Stuart Semple, who launched an 'open source' rival to Vantablack, an acrylic paint called Black 3.0 that is, he says, 'not available to Kapoor'. Black 3.0 was used as the backdrop to several of Rembrandt's portraits in the Dulwich Picture Gallery exhibition *Rembrandt's Light* (2019–20). Later versions of Vantablack have been developed as a spray coating that has been applied to luxury goods including a BMW car and the face of a wristwatch by Swiss watchmaker Moser & Cie.

The earliest human use of pigments was probably not functional, but rather for ritual body painting and cave paintings. In the 1990s, archaeologist Lawrence Barnham discovered pigments preserved in an undisturbed layer of sediment at the Twin Rivers cave, Zambia, dating to between 200,000 and 400,000 years old. Minerals had been ground to produce powders in brown, red, yellow, purple, blue and pink, in large quantities and over a long period of time. The distances over which they had been gathered and the painstaking extraction and processing activity pointed to the 'sumptuary destructions' of effort and resources that philosopher and anthropologist Georges Bataille associated with religious rather than economic motives.

Colour is still sacred. The Hindu festival of Holi celebrates the beginning of spring and the triumph of good over evil. It is a time to forgive past wrongs, heal relationships and make a fresh start. Along with music, feasting and visits, the day is marked with a joyful ritual of colour, as worshippers douse family, friends and passers-by with coloured water or dry coloured powders (*gulal*). Traditionally the colours were derived from natural sources, especially the extracts of medicinal plants, bestowing the additional benediction of health. Synthetic dyes have added scintillating new colours to the proceedings, but are not without their drawbacks. In February 2018, *Asia News International* warned readers of the health risks posed by chemicals such as lead oxide, mercury sulphite and copper sulphate used in some of the colours. Side effects include skin and eye irritation and respiratory problems brought on by inhaling the powder. The news agency's health and beauty expert provided tips to repair or prevent damage and called for a return to natural ingredients – a marketing opportunity readily taken up by suppliers, who now emphasize the non-toxic and eco-friendly credentials of their *gulal* as well as its chromatic range.

From the celestial blue sacred to the Virgin Mary, 'the sapphire' who, as Dante wrote, turns all of heaven blue, to the gold background of icons, representing the heavenly Jerusalem, Christian iconography is saturated with colour symbolism. Different coloured vestments and hangings indicate the changing seasons of the church year; in Catholic churches, purple is used for the penitential seasons of Lent and Advent, white for Easter and the feast days of virgins and confessors, red for Pentecost and the feasts of martyrs, and green for ordinary time. Colour also denotes affiliation to different religious orders of monks and nuns: black habits for the Benedictines, brown for the Carmelites, grey for the Franciscans, white for the Carthusians, and so on. In an echo of the medieval sumptuary laws that codified materials and colours of dress proper to one's social station or profession, clerical rank is denoted by colour: black for priests, purple for bishops, red for cardinals and white for popes.

Cultural and religious beliefs and customs intersect most forcefully with the business of everyday life during the rites of passage surrounding childbirth, marriage and death. Life's phases and milestones are often symbolically associated with colours. Mourning has been expressed in different cultures and periods by wearing black, white, purple or red. In Edgar Allan Poe's short story 'The Masque of the Red Death' (1842), Prince Prospero entertains the local gentry sheltering from the eponymous plague at a lavish masked ball in the seven great halls of his fortified Gothic abbey, each decorated and lit in a symbolic colour corresponding to the seven stages of human life, arranged from east to west: blue for birth, purple for childhood, green for adolescence, orange for adulthood, white for old age, violet for senescence and black (lit with red) for death. The festivities end abruptly when a sinister red-stained figure, the Red Death in person, slips in among the revellers and they succumb to the disease. At the end of Roger Corman's 1964 film adaption, shot in Pathécolor by Nicolas Roeg (his first colour film), the symbolism is reinforced when the Red

Death figure is met by his six brothers: the White Death, the Yellow Death, the Golden Death, the Blue Death, the Violet Death and the Black Death. They compare their toll of victims before setting off in grim procession to their next reaping ground.

Poe's macabre fiction pales beside the real horrors of the First World War and subsequent 1918 influenza pandemic, which brought death and bereavement on an overwhelming scale. One of the war's cultural effects was the growing popularity of spiritualism, the occult and esoteric religions, as survivors tried to make sense of the cataclysm. Theosophy was founded in the USA in the late nineteenth century by Helena Blavatsky, and in the early twentieth century its theories about colour mysticism were developed by Charles W. Leadbeater, Annie Besant and Rudolf Steiner. Their descriptions and classifications of the colourful 'thought forms' and 'human auras' visible to clairvoyants, illustrated with charts and diagrams ascribing colours to different emotional and spiritual states, influenced pioneers of abstract art such as Wassily Kandinsky and Piet Mondrian.

As the artistic spat over Anish Kapoor's monopoly on Vantablack demonstrated, colour is a serious business. The International Colour Association was founded in 1967 to support research about colour and encourage innovation in the arts, sciences, design and industry. Since 2009, it has celebrated International Colour Day on 21 March. The date was chosen to coincide with the Spring Equinox, when night and day are of equal length, which is reflected in the association's choice of logo: two concentric colour wheels with half of the segments in the colours of the visible spectrum and the other half in black. Also in 2009, David McCandless, designer and founder of 'Information is Beautiful', devised 'Colours in Culture', a colour wheel to help creative directors and brand managers negotiate the meanings and associations of different colours across a global marketplace. The circle's circumference is divided into segments numbered from one to eighty-four, representing concepts or associations. These are mostly positive (joy, gratitude, good luck, peace) with a few negatives (death, unhappiness). The radius is divided into ten bands, lettered A to J, corresponding to ten cultural groupings or geographic regions. Using the wheel, one finds black, for example, at 76/A and B, corresponding to style in America/the west and

Japan; 74/E and G, self-cultivation in China and Eastern Europe; F/46, intelligence in Asia; and so on. Inevitably market-led and broad brush in approach (there is one band for the whole African continent), it nonetheless proposes a visual model for organizing the complexities of colour associations across cultures that could be refined and expanded to accommodate new or alternative data.

Every year, trend spotters and style gurus from companies such as Pantone, Dulux and the World's Global Style Network (WGSN) announce their pick for the forthcoming year's Colour of the Year, with suitable fanfare and discussion in the design press. For 2020 Pantone selected its Classic Blue (PANTONE 19-4052), described in publicity as 'elegant in its simplicity' and 'suggestive of the sky at dusk', a reflection of 'our desire for a dependable and stable foundation on which to build as we cross the threshold into a new era'. The design journal *Dezeen* reviewed the choice as a safe bet after the 'debacle' of naming Living Coral as 2019 Pantone Colour of the Year. Paint company Dulux has chosen a pale grey–green called 'Tranquil Dawn' for 2020, 'a colour inspired by the morning sky, to help give homes the human touch. This versatile shade of green can be used to create spaces for care or for play, to find meaning or for creativity.' As early as May 2018, WGSN identified a cool pastel green called 'Neo Mint' as the colour to watch in 2020, 'a gender-neutral colour with an oxygenating, fresh tone that aligns science and technology with nature'. The marketing of colour, especially for domestic interiors, with its breathless prose and inventive nomenclature, is satirized by John Dilnot in his print *Map* (2004). Evocatively-named colours from commercial paint charts form a map of Britain, the shades loosely configured around the places inspiring their names in a wry comment on consumer nostalgia for a fondly imagined rural idyll. In 1994, the Victoria and Albert Museum licensed a range of heritage paints by the tile and decorating company Fired Earth, targeting the discerning decorator with a collection of eighteen 'Traditional Colours' including 'Oxford Ochre' and 'Better Class Red'.

The Victoria and Albert Museum is among the most colourfully decorated museums in Britain. From the outset its first director, Henry Cole, conceived of the museum as a showcase for the best

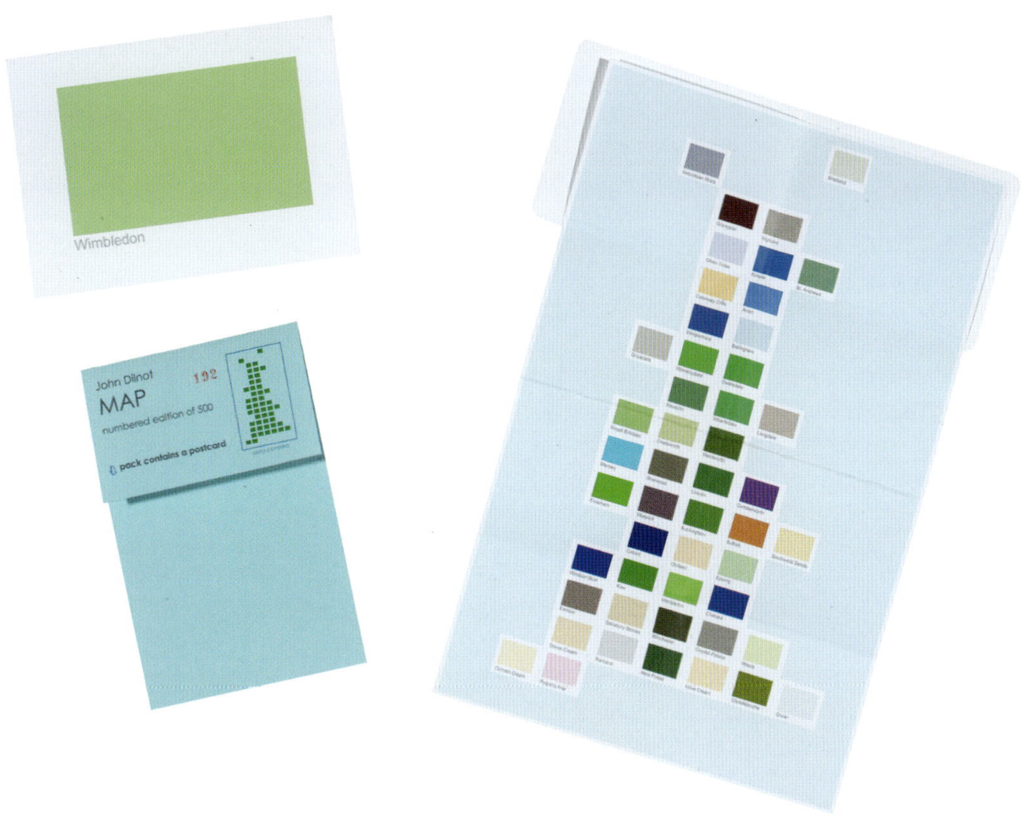

John Dilnot, *Map*, multiple consisting of a cover, a folding colour
chart map and a single colour card, UK, inkjet print, 2004

of British art and design, not only through its collections but also in its fabric. One of the ways in which this vision was realized was in its interiors, which were commissioned from leading designers including William Morris and Owen Jones. Morris's scheme for the Western Refreshment Room, later known as the Green Dining Room and now called the Morris Room, has been cited as an early example of the 'greenery-yallery Grosvenor Gallery' style of interior decoration satirized in Gilbert & Sullivan's *Patience* (1881). The painted tiles lining the walls of the nearby Dutch Kitchen or Grill Room (now the Poynter Room, after its designer Edward J. Poynter) anticipated the Aesthetic Movement craze for blue-and-white porcelain. Owen Jones designed eastern-inspired schemes for the Oriental Courts, evoking the cultures of Asia with rich ornament and vivid colours. The Architectural Courts (now the Cast Courts) were painted in deep purple-red and olive green to act as a foil to the exhibits, which

consisted of relatively drab plaster casts, architectural models, electrotypes and photographs. The original Paintings Galleries were also relatively undecorated, painted in sage green above a grey dado so as not to distract from the paintings. The colour scheme was chosen by the painter Richard Redgrave, the museum's Director for Art.

Between 1910 and 1914, much of the interior decoration of the museum was covered up, as taste turned against the rich Victorian style and palette. Under the directorship of Sir Cecil Harcourt-Smith, interiors were simplified to 'be like the setting of a fine gem, dignified, harmonious and self-effacing'. After the Second World War, the Victoria and Albert Museum's new director Leigh Ashton oversaw the reinstallation of the collections returning from safe storage. He too believed the museum was 'over-decorated, architecturally', and was particularly fond of 'the loveliest light grey, a dawn-mist tone'. Taste changed again in the 1970s, with a new appreciation of Victorian art and design and the restoration of many of the museum's original colour schemes under the direction of Roy Strong, a process that continues today.

The theorist Mikhail Epstein describes three kinds of museum, inhabited by three kinds of objects: the 'museum-as-treasury' filled with rare, beautiful or valuable objects; the 'systematic museum' with objects organized to represent entire classes or categories of similar objects; and the 'museum-memorial', whose objects are not unique or typical themselves, but are interesting because of their association with a historically important individual or event. Most museums, he suggests, belong to one or sometimes more of these three types. The Victoria and Albert Museum is arguably all three at once, but it is also a contender for another, novel type proposed by Epstein: the 'lyrical' museum. That is a museum of objects chosen not for their uniqueness, typicality or proximity to celebrity, but for what Epstein calls their 'lyrical' quality, which he defines as their 'individuality of existence marked by the habits and ideals of their owners', to which we could add their makers, custodians and visitors, the meanings, associations and possibilities that they express, and the stories they tell. As Epstein says: 'The world is articulated, uttered through things … To hear the voice, contained in things and prophesying from within their depth, is to understand them and oneself.'

Whether by accident or design, taxonomies of conventional museumship such as place, period or materials meet as haphazardly in an ever-evolving institution like the Victoria and Albert Museum as in Jorge Luis Borges' apocryphal Celestial Emporium of Benevolent Knowledge, discussed in his essay 'The Analytical Language of John Wilkins' (1942). Epstein might call it 'museum-as-category-mistake'.

Perhaps, then, it would not be so great a departure to consider the collections rearranged by less conventional, more 'lyrical' qualities like colour. What would the visitor to such a museum experience? A succession of galleries of saturated hues, like the livid halls of colour through which Prince Prospero and his doomed guests dance their way to a Red Death, or a suite of soothing neutrals like Ashton's 'dawn-mist tone', setting the objects free to 'prophesy'? The British artist Cornelia Parker adopted something like the latter approach to curate her 2011 exhibition *Richard Of York Gave Battle In Vain*, the title a familiar English mnemonic she was taught as a child to recall the seven colours of Newton's spectrum. Parker selected works from the British Government Art Collection and hung them in floor-to-ceiling bands of colour, organized in the order of the spectrum on the white walls of the Whitechapel Gallery. This resulted in unexpected and thought-provoking juxtapositions, conversations between objects that might not otherwise have met and spoken to each other, 'random clashes of old masters rubbing shoulders with YBAs (Young British Artists)'.

This book, the result of a close creative collaboration between design consultancy Here Design, publisher Thames & Hudson and the Victoria and Albert Museum, is another such exercise in curating by colour. It is also a visual source book for practitioners, and a collection of stories about colour, told through the Victoria and Albert Museum's centuries-worth of colourful objects by some of the museum's archivists, curators and librarians. The book is divided into twelve colours, and its twelve introductory essays are followed by pages of museum objects captured by the museum's photographers, brought together not only by colour but by symbolic and thematic associations: love, death, divinity, serenity, danger…. The themes sometimes overlap; sometimes contain objects with an obvious material or visual affinity; and sometimes create unexpected juxtapositions, as the stories they tell weave in and out of materials, places, styles and cultures. The 'spectrum' of the book, like Goethe's light-to-dark vision, begins with white and ends with black, but it can be read in any order, starting at any point. Perhaps choose your favourite colour, or least favourite, or any colour at random, and see where it takes you – to Dante's sapphire heaven or a Lovecraftian blasted heath.

A Diagram to Illustrate the Harmonious Relations of Colour, published by Chapman & Hall, lithograph mounted on card, c. 1853

A DIAGRAM TO·ILLUSTRATE

THE HARMONIOUS RELATIONS OF COLOUR.

Prepared for the Ufe of Schools in connexion with the

DEPARTMENT OF PRACTICAL ART.

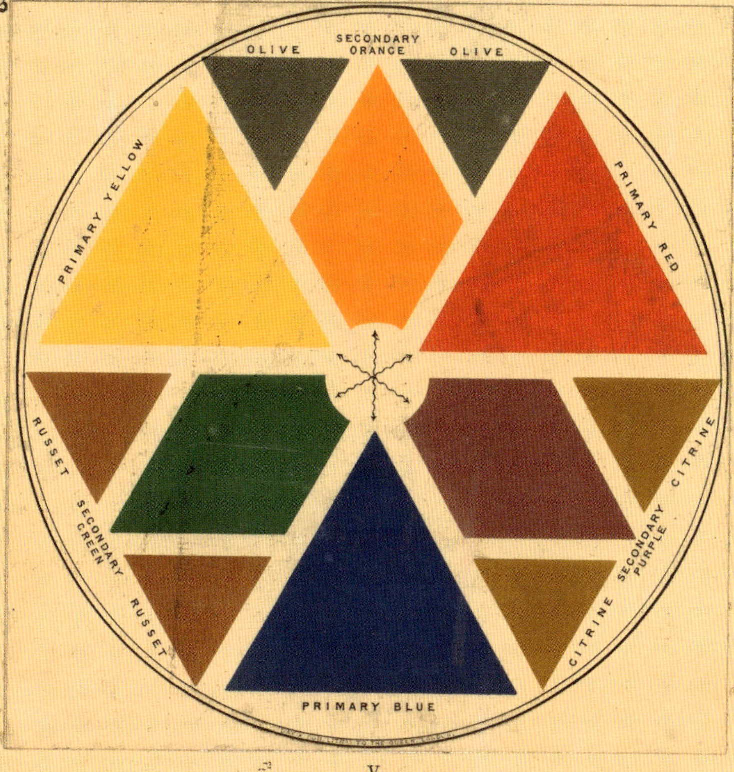

Laws of Harmonious

I.

THERE are three fimple or primary Colours which cannot be produced by mixture :—namely, YELLOW, RED, and BLUE. From thefe three in various proportions all other Colours are compofed.

II.

TWO primary Colours being mixed a fecondary Colour is the refult. Thus RED and YELLOW produce the fecondary ORANGE: BLUE and YELLOW, GREEN : and RED and BLUE, PURPLE.

Relations of Colour.

III.

THE mixture of SECONDARY Colours produces the *tertiary* Colours. Thus ORANGE and GREEN, produce *Citrine:* PURPLE and GREEN, *Olive:* ORANGE and PURPLE, *Ruffet:* each tertiary therefore is compofed of two fecondaries, and is in harmony with the third, or that which does not enter into its own compofition : thus Citrine is in harmony with Purple, Olive with Orange, and Ruffet with Green.

IV.

ALL thefe are called *hues* of Colour which may be diluted into *tints* by White, or deepened into *fhades* by Black.

V.

TO fatisfy the eye and produce Harmony of Colour, the prefence of all the three primaries is required, either pure or in combination : thus RED when not fupported by due quantities of pure YELLOW and BLUE is harmonized by the fecondary GREEN, which is a union of thofe two primaries: and which is therefore called the complementary colour of RED; for the fame reafon PURPLE is complementary to YELLOW, and ORANGE to BLUE.

N.B. *The arrowheads in the centre of the Diagram point back to the oppofite complementary or harmonizing Colour of the primaries.*
The tertiary colours are in harmony with the fecondary with which they are grouped in the diagram.

Some Qualities and Properties of Colour.

VI.

YELLOW is of all Colours the neareft allied to light, whilft its complementary PURPLE is the darkeft of all *hues :* they contraft therefore as to light and dark.

VII.

RED is the moft exciting and pofitive of all colours, its complementary, GREEN, the moft grateful and foothing. RED and GREEN are non-contrafting as to light and dark, but they are contrafting as to their power of exciting the eye and as to power of Colour.

VIII.

BLUE is the coldeft and moft retiring of all Colours : its complementary ORANGE the warmeft and moft advancing. Their contraft is both as to advancing and retiring, and as to hot and cold.

IX.

WHILST the union of two primaries refults in a new and perfect hue, every mixture of the three has a tendency to neutralize or deftroy Colour : from this caufe the tertiary compounds are far more neutral than the fecondaries.

The full neutralizing power of the primaries is in the proportion of three YELLOW, five RED, and eight BLUE, fince fo mixed they completely deftroy one another.

X.

IT fhould be remembered that as any one of the primary colours, by mixture with either of the others, lofes its purity and becomes *in a degree* fecondary, the fecondary which is complementary to it muft contain more of the remaining primary : thus if RED tends towards *Scarlet,* which is an *Orange-Red,* (a Red with Yellow in it) the GREEN to be truly complementary fhould incline towards the remaining primary BLUE, and be a *Blue Green;* when the RED

C5 M4 Y5 K3 — C6 M6 Y4 K1 — C2 M3 Y5 K4 — C5 M3 Y5 K3 — C4 M2 Y5 K2

C6 M4 Y4 K1 — C1 M2 Y4 K5 — C4 M4 Y3 K1 — C5 M5 Y4 K6 — C0 M1 Y4 K4

C4 M4 Y7 K0 — C5 M4 Y4 K0 — C1 M3 Y5 K1 — C4 M4 Y3 K4 — C0 M2 Y3 K7

C3 M4 Y3 K5 — C4 M5 Y3 K2 — C3 M0 Y0 K3 — C3 M3 Y3 K0 — C0 M0 Y4 K2

C0 M0 Y2 K8 — C5 M3 Y4 K2 — C4 M5 Y6 K4 — C5 M3 Y3 K3 — C4 M2 Y5 K5

C4 M0 Y5 K0 — C4 M4 Y5 K2 — C6 M5 Y5 K2 — C5 M4 Y4 K7 — C1 M3 Y3 K4

C4 M1 Y5 K6 — C4 M0 Y7 K2 — C6 M5 Y6 K0 — C6 M4 Y4 K4 — C0 M0 Y6 K6

C4 M0 Y0 K4 — C0 M2 Y4 K6 — C4 M4 Y5 K0 — C0 M4 Y4 K3 — C4 M6 Y6 K2

C4 M3 Y3 K2 — C0 M0 Y6 K0 — C0 M4 Y4 K1 — C5 M5 Y3 K1 — C4 M6 Y7 K0

C4 M4 Y8 K5 — C6 M4 Y6 K2 — C2 M0 Y7 K2 — C0 M0 Y0 K10 — C5 M2 Y10 K0

C6 M3 Y6 K0 — C3 M2 Y4 K5 — C5 M3 Y4 K0 — C2 M3 Y4 K6 — C3 M6 Y0 K0

WHITE

In the 1660s, English physicist Isaac Newton discovered that colours are not inherent to objects. Instead, an object appears to be a particular colour because its surface reflects certain wavelengths of light in the visible spectrum while absorbing others. We see an object as white when all the colours in the spectrum are reflected into our eyes. White, therefore, might be thought of as a lack of colour, or non-colour; yet it is also the visible sum of all colours.

Herman Melville recognized the contradictory nature of white in his 1851 novel *Moby Dick*. Ishmael, the tale's narrator, astutely observes that 'whiteness is not so much a colour as the visible absence of colour, and at the same time the concrete of all colours'. To Ishmael, white is characterized by a 'dumb blankness full of meaning', and it is true that though white is not technically a colour at all, throughout history people have perceived it as such and imbued it with significance. Much of that meaning is born out of its physical properties: it is the embodiment of light, paler than all other colours and often seen in opposition to them, especially black. Because of this, white has been put on a pedestal, considered a flawless and exclusive marker of moral and physical purity, wealth and civility.

The dichotomies of white and black, good and evil, light and darkness, day and night, order and chaos have been central to creation myths throughout human history. For many cultures, light brought life into the world where previously there was only darkness and oblivion. As a symbol of new beginnings, white is worn to mark important rites of passage in people's lives, from birth to coming of age ceremonies and marriage. Since as early as the sixteenth century, Christian babies have traditionally been baptized in white garments such as the lace christening set on p. 27, made between 1650 and 1700, to mark the beginning of their life with Christ. Maasai men mark their transformation into senior warriors by decorating their bodies with white chalk designs recalling their accomplishments. And in Japanese wedding ceremonies, brides wear an entirely white ensemble known as the *shiromuku* (*shiro* meaning 'white' and *muku* meaning 'pure'), symbolizing purity and clarity. The ensemble consists of a white silk outer kimono, known as an *uchikake*, with a lighter white silk kimono underneath (see p. 27) and worn with a hood called a *watabōshi*.

White is also one of the oldest and most widespread colours for mourning, and has been worn to mark the death of a loved one in many parts of the world including China, India, Korea and areas of Africa and Europe. Today in much of Europe the colour black is so closely associated with death and funerals that it is almost impossible to imagine white being used to mourn the dead. But it has been a colour of mourning in parts of Europe since ancient times, symbolizing innocence, simplicity and purity of the soul. White was the colour of mourning for French queens and women of the aristocracy until the sixteenth century. Known as *deuil blanc* (white mourning), the women typically wore a white linen hood and veil like the one worn by an unidentified lady of the French court in the sixteenth-century enamel miniature on p. 27. Although black became increasingly popular after it was worn by Anne of Brittany to mourn the death of her husband Charles VIII in 1498, white long remained an appropriate colour for mourning children, as a symbol of their purity and innocence. To commemorate the death of his young daughter Lydia in 1674, John Dwight, founder of John Dwight's Fulham Pottery, had a white salt-glazed stoneware likeness of her made (p. 27).

White has a physical purity. Colour is often seen to corrupt that purity, leaving behind marks and stains on a white surface. Although white light is made by all the colours in the visible spectrum blending together, mixing coloured pigments cannot create white. When colour is added to white pigment it darkens it, on a one-way path towards black. Because of this corruptibility, white is often considered a virtuous colour, and has been used to represent morality and ritual purity. It is the colour of the unsullied and the immaculate, often symbolizing a person's virginity or chastity. Many of the highest-ranking religious and cult figures have worn white to symbolize their moral purity: in Ancient Egypt priests would wear white linen; in ancient Rome the priestesses of Vesta wore white to symbolize the vows of chastity they took; in the Bible angels clad in perfectly white linen praise God; and in Shintō rituals, white cloths, or more usually paper strips, are folded into zigzag streamers as offerings to the gods.

Elizabeth I, also known as the 'Virgin Queen', is another figure known to have worn white to indicate her morality and virginity. Aware of the power clothing had in the sixteenth century to convey messages about a person's social status, the unmarried queen used dress to manipulate her public image. In portraits – such as the exquisite miniature on p. 22, created by Nicholas Hilliard between 1595 and 1600 – she is often portrayed wearing white clothes and adorned with pearls, also symbolic of purity and virginity. By presenting herself to her subjects as chaste, projecting an image of sexual virtue, she demonstrated her ability to control the realm.

Being lighter than other colours, white shows up dirt and so has also become associated with sanitization. A modern obsession with cleanliness has led to a proliferation of hygienic white objects, from bed linens to washing machines, toilets to tableware – but this connection between the colour and its ability to keep us clean and healthy is certainly not new. For many western Europeans in the sixteenth, seventeenth and eighteenth centuries, fully immersing the body in water to keep clean was not common practice. Bodily secretions were thought to provide a layer of protection against disease, so doctors warned people against washing with water. Instead, people wore white linen undergarments: shirts and underdrawers for men (see p. 24) and chemises for women. Not only was the material practical, as it would not lose its colour when washed at high temperatures, it was actually thought to clean the body by attracting and absorbing sweat. The stains the material collected appeared to be empirical evidence of this happening. Wealthy people bought their linen undergarments in the dozens and changed them regularly, and so the wearing of clean white shirts and chemises became a show of wealth. It was fashionable to reveal these white undergarments as an indication of status, so collars tended to be high and sleeves long, often trimmed with fine white lace. Long after people renewed the practice of regularly washing with water, white continued to be a popular choice for underwear. In the 1980s, white Y-fronts (see p. 25), also known as 'tighty whities', were a fashionable underwear choice for men, although they have waned in popularity today.

While white linen was believed to have cleansing properties and has been used specifically because it shows dirt, white is essentially a very impractical colour because it is difficult to keep completely clean. Because of this, it has long been considered a colour of luxury reserved for the rich and powerful. For much of history, only the elite in society would have worn white, as they were able to employ the staff to keep their garments clean. Even today, when white clothes are worn by people of all classes, they can make a statement about a person's social status. Donning an expensive white outfit might suggest that a person does not have to engage in manual labour or take public transport. On the other hand, they might be making a political statement. In the USA, during the 2019 State of the Union Address, the women of the Democratic party in Congress wore white as a show of solidarity and to highlight their visibility, their white outfits sharply contrasting with the sea of black, blue and grey suits.

White's associations with purity, morality, rationality, cleanliness and the elite have also informed a prejudicial opposition to colour in western culture, from the classical world to today. In the late 1990s, artist David Batchelor explored this endemic distaste for colour in his book *Chromophobia*. He suggested that the west sees colour as 'other', considering it feminine rather than masculine, primitive rather than civilized, eastern rather than western and infantile rather than adult. It is a distraction from high culture: superficial, cosmetic, inessential and ornamental. This insidious idea that white is superior to colour works within the system of racist and prejudicial regard for people and cultures defined as 'other' by a Eurocentric viewpoint.

Nowhere is this more apparent in art history than in the myth that the buildings and sculptures of ancient Greece and Rome were of bare white marble. This misconception of the classical world, which began during the Renaissance and still prevails in the popular imagination today, is based on error and wilful misunderstanding. Small traces of pigment remain on the surface of many ancient sculptures and architectural fragments, which prove that they were in fact painted in vivid colours. Although the artists of the Renaissance may have been ignorant of this, the fact that classical sculptures were polychromatic was known by the nineteenth century, and inspired artists and designers such as Lawrence Alma-Tadema and Owen Jones to create work inspired by a colourful classical world. Others refused to believe it, or chose to ignore it. Auguste Rodin is reputed to have beaten his chest in sorrow and exclaimed, 'I feel it here that they were never coloured.' He continued to create works in gleaming marble that perpetuated the idea that pure, white sculpture was the epitome of beauty and civility (p. 39) . Even to this day the myth holds sway in the contemporary imagination, perpetuated through popular representations of the classical world.

Conversely, white has also been considered the most neutral of all the colours: a white flag raised in battle signifies surrender, and the white dove has become a symbol of peace. White makes the perfect background colour. It is a blank surface full of anticipation and possibilities.

This neutrality has meant that white has often been adopted in reaction to colour. It has been widely used by some of the most ardent contemporary minimalist designers. In 2001, with the launch of the original iPod, Apple Inc. started to make all their consumer products white. The colour choice was the idea of Jonathan Ive, Apple's lead designer, who chose the colour in a quest for simplicity. He described it as '… brutally simple. It's not just a colour. Supposedly neutral – but just an unmistakable, shocking neutral.' This desire for neutrality was in part a reaction to the design of Apple's iMac G3, a personal computer that came in a range of bright colours from Bondi Blue, to Grape, Tangerine, Lime and Strawberry. But it was also a reaction to other consumer electronics available at the time, most of which were dull off-white, grey or black.

Blank, minimalist, neutral and spotlessly clean, yet rich in religious and cultural symbolism, white is a complex colour, a quality perhaps epitomized by its place as both the sum of all colours, and a non-colour, impossible to recreate by mixing pigments.

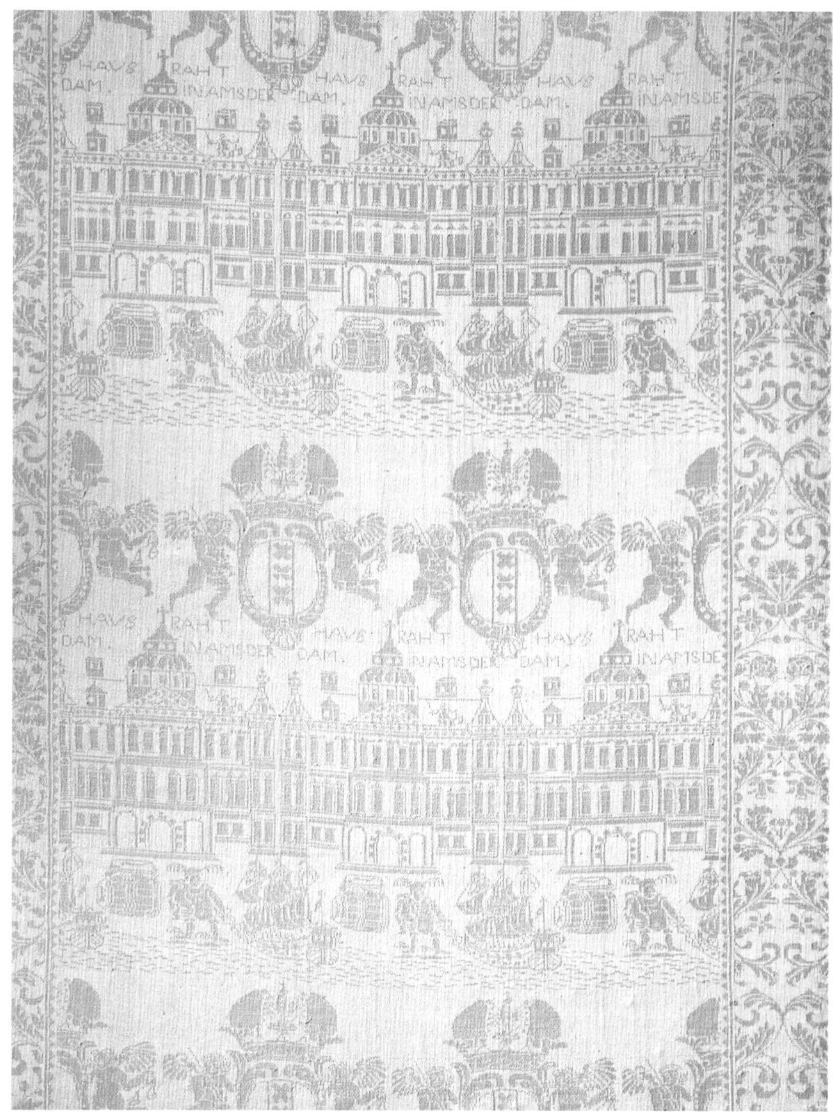

For the first half of the 18th century, the Dutch were the European experts on bleaching, and produced the whitest high-quality linen. The Dutch textile industry flourished in cities such as Haarlem, which had large bleaching fields where cloth was laid on the ground and exposed to sunlight as a method of whitening the fabric. Damask table linen, such as this napkin made in the Netherlands between 1680 and 1720 (left), was prized for its elaborate reversible patterns. The two textures in the fabric reflect the light differently.

Artist Christopher Bucklow also harnesses the power of sunlight in *Guest, 1.56 p.m., 4th November, 1995* (1995; opposite). White light, long associated with spirituality and ethereality, here evokes a sense of otherworldliness. To create the image, Bucklow drew onto foil before puncturing it with thousands of pinholes. Stretched over a box camera and exposed to the sky, each hole focused the sunlight onto photographic paper to create a glowing, dream-like effect.

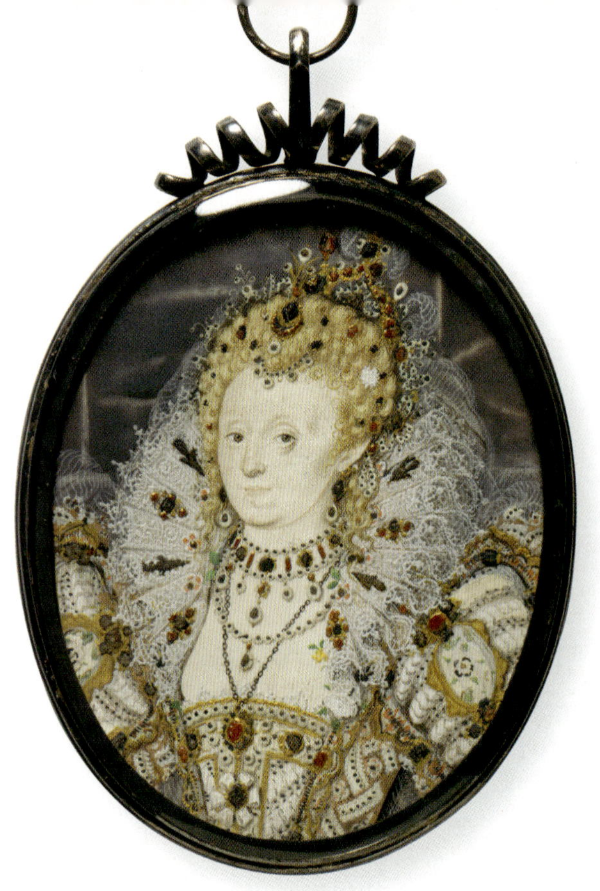

Symbolizing virginity, chastity and innocence, pristine white has long been associated with the unsullied. In this portrait miniature painted by Nicholas Hilliard (1595–1600; left), white pearls adorn the clothes of Elizabeth I as a symbol of her purity and virginity. This Gothic statuette of the Virgin and Child (below left), made around 1280–1300, is carved from ivory. The whiteness, firmness and lucidity of the material evoke the Virgin's purity and chastity.

In the medieval and Renaissance periods the unicorn was a symbol of chastity; legend had it that unicorns could be caught only by a maiden. They frequently appeared in manuscripts, paintings and tapestries such as this example from Flanders (1500; opposite). It was also believed that unicorn horn could purify water. 'The Danny Jewel', made from narwhal horn (below right), which was believed at the time to be that of a unicorn, may have been worn as an amulet to protect the wearer from poisoning.

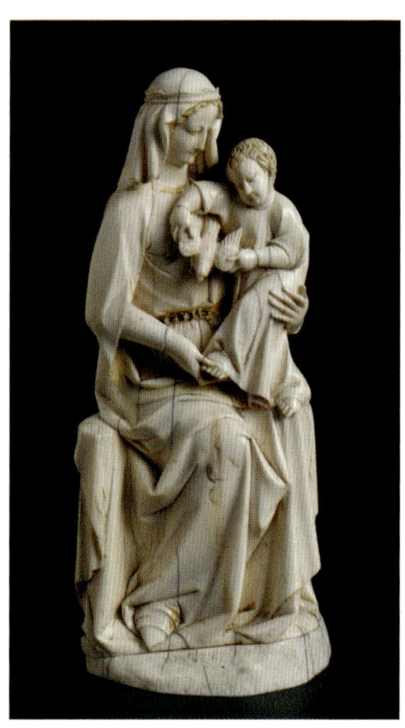

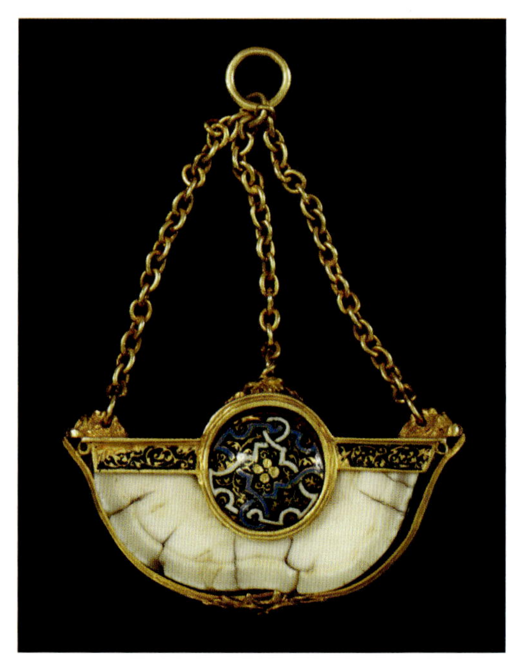

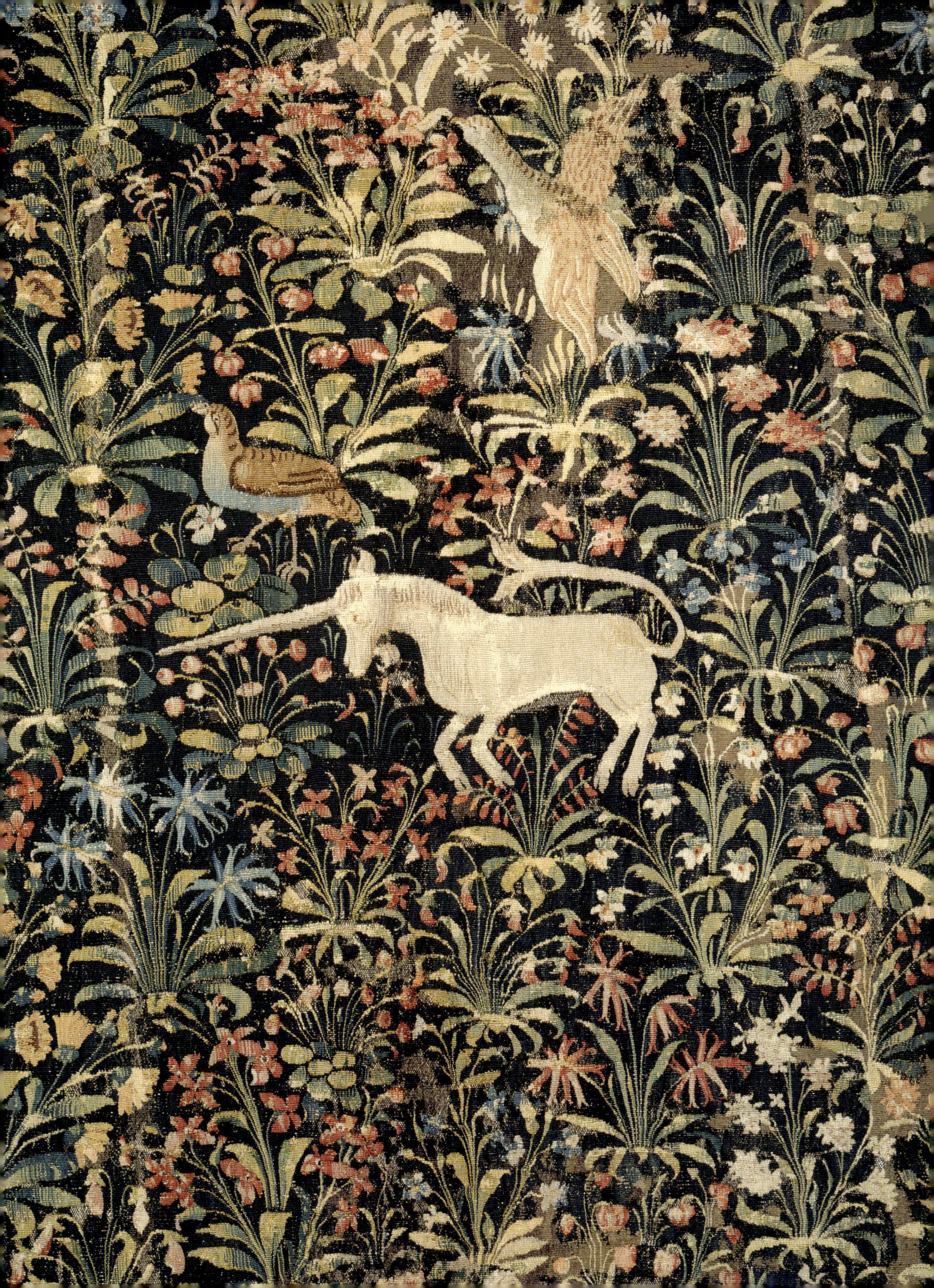

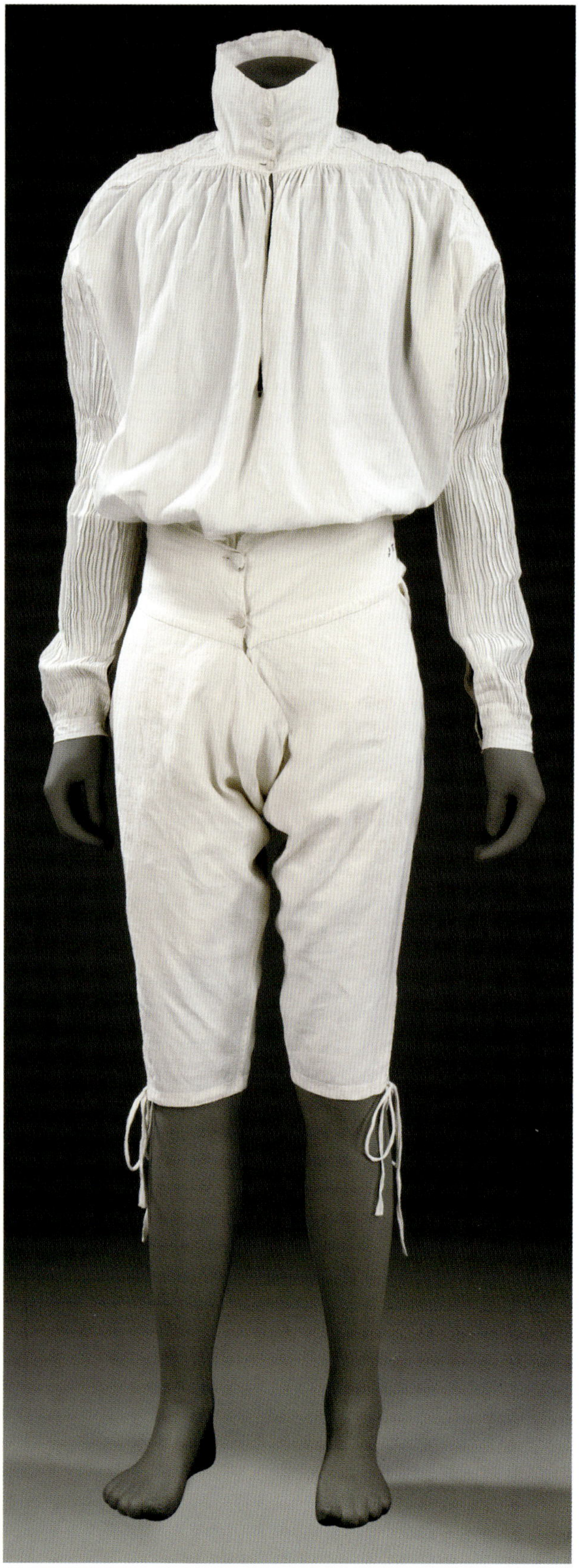

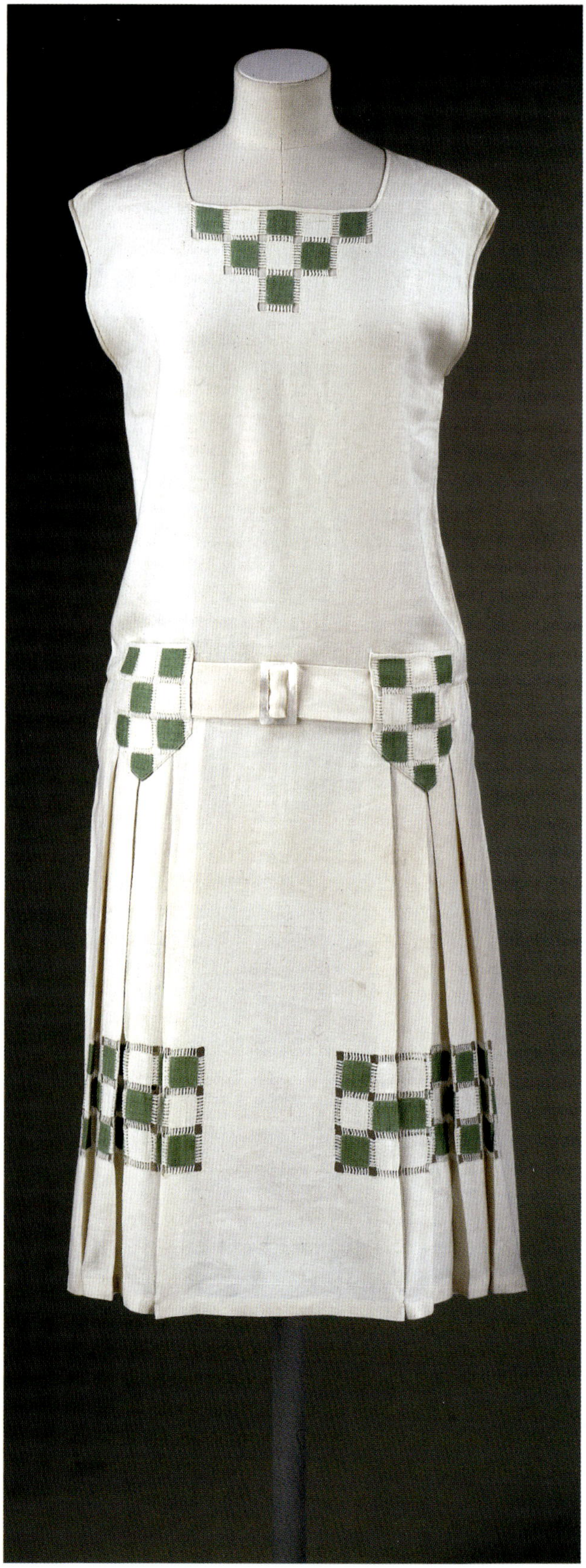

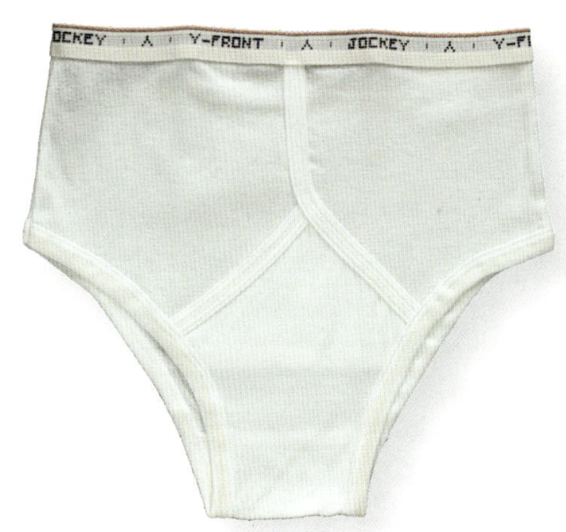

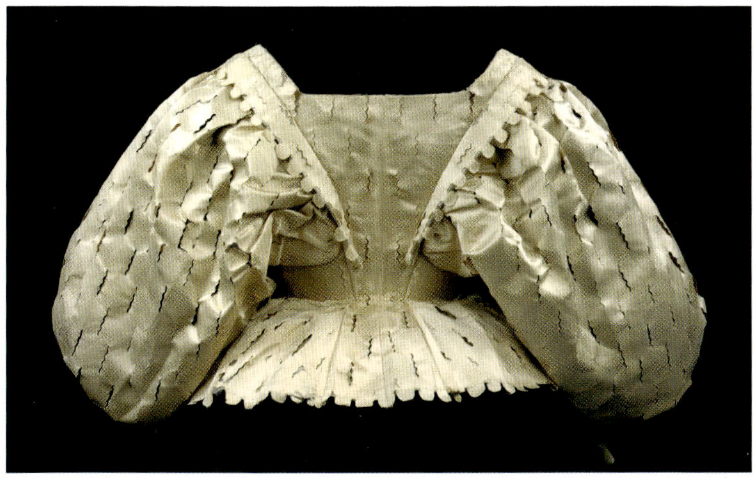

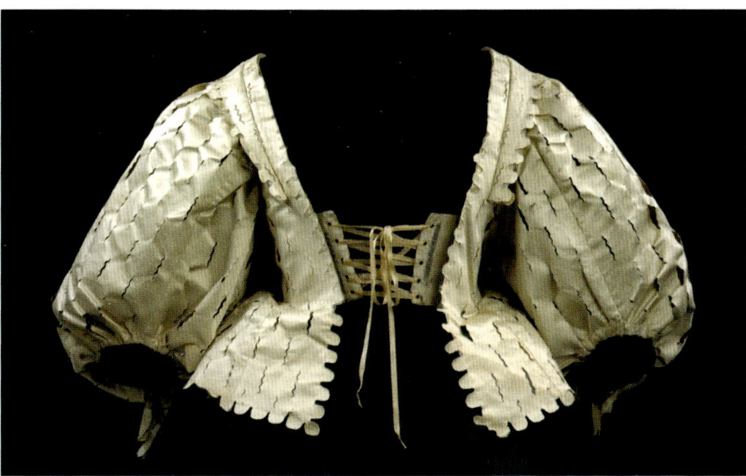

In Europe in the 16th, 17th and 18th centuries, it was widely believed that white linen clothing could cleanse the body. Instead of bathing, people wore linen undergarments such as this man's shirt (1780-95) and underdrawers (1775-9) next to their skin (opposite, left). White remained a popular choice for underwear - such as this pair of Y-fronts made in the 1980s by Jockey (above) - long after people started washing again.

Until the invention of modern washing machines, keeping white clothing clean was costly. Because of this, items such as this slashed silk satin bodice (left), hand-sewn in the 1630s, were a luxury exclusive to the elite. From the 19th century white became a popular colour for summer sportswear - particularly tennis clothing - for the leisured classes, as it was thought to uphold decorum by hiding the perspiration of the genteel players. This linen tennis dress (opposite, right) was made by its wearer Hepburne Scott in the 1920s, when white prevailed as the most popular colour for tennis attire.

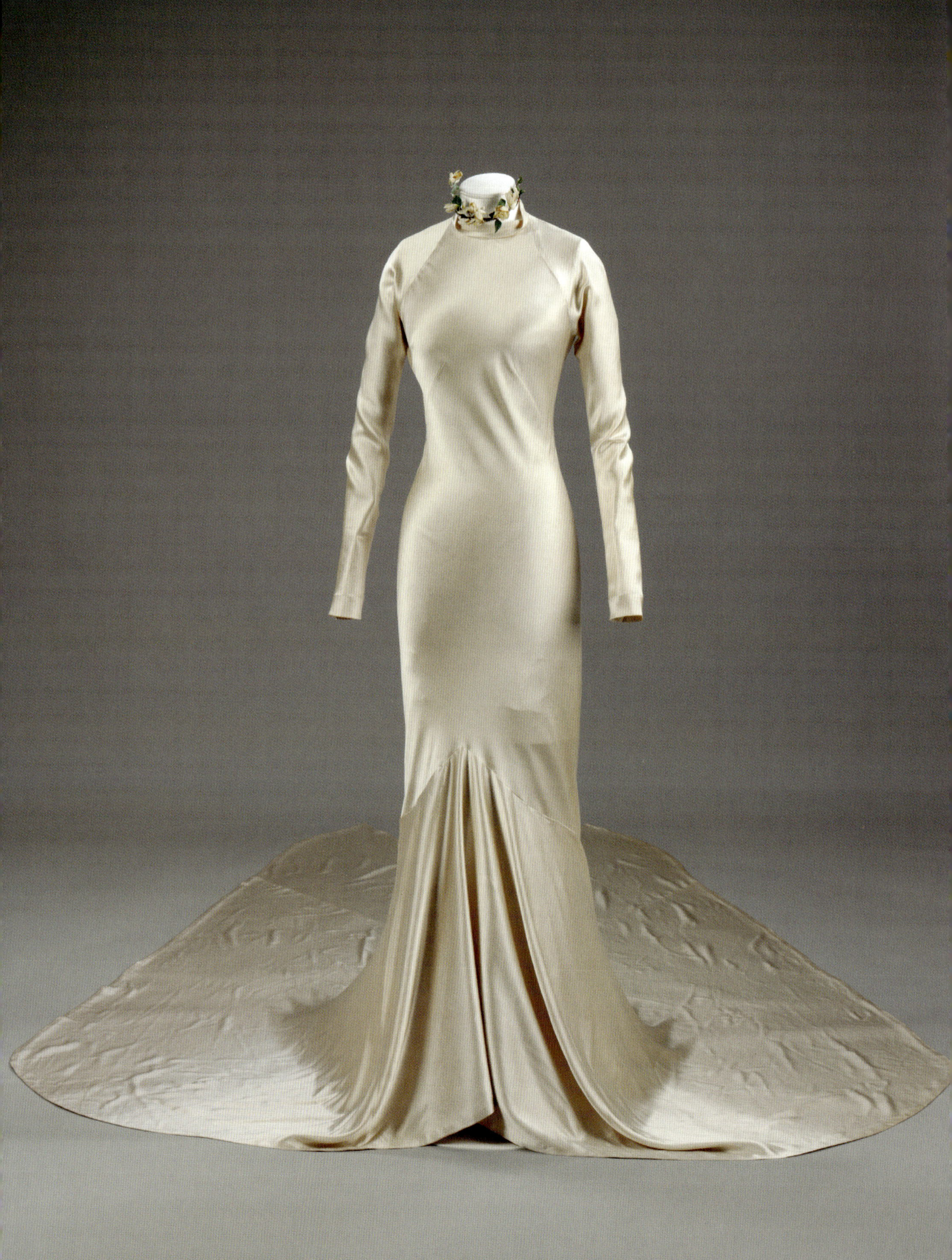

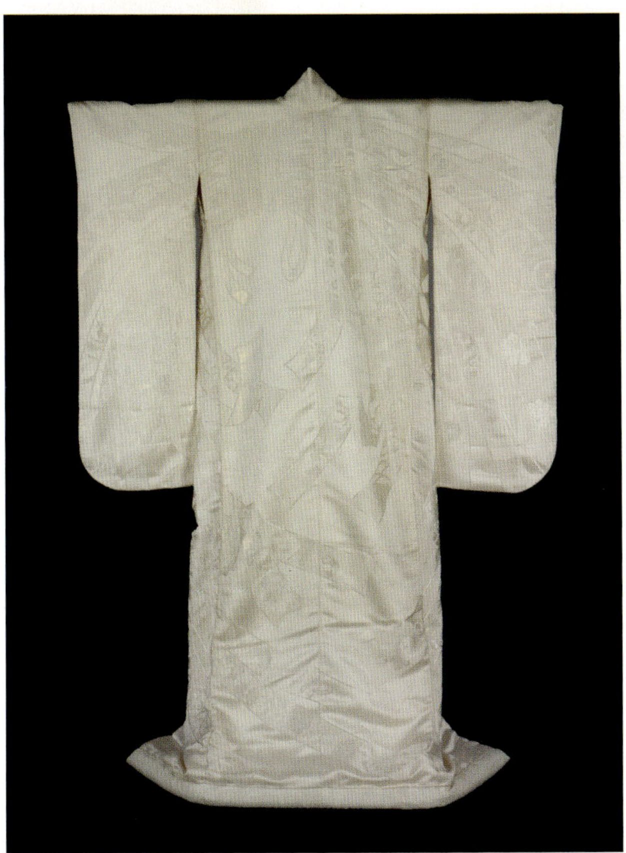

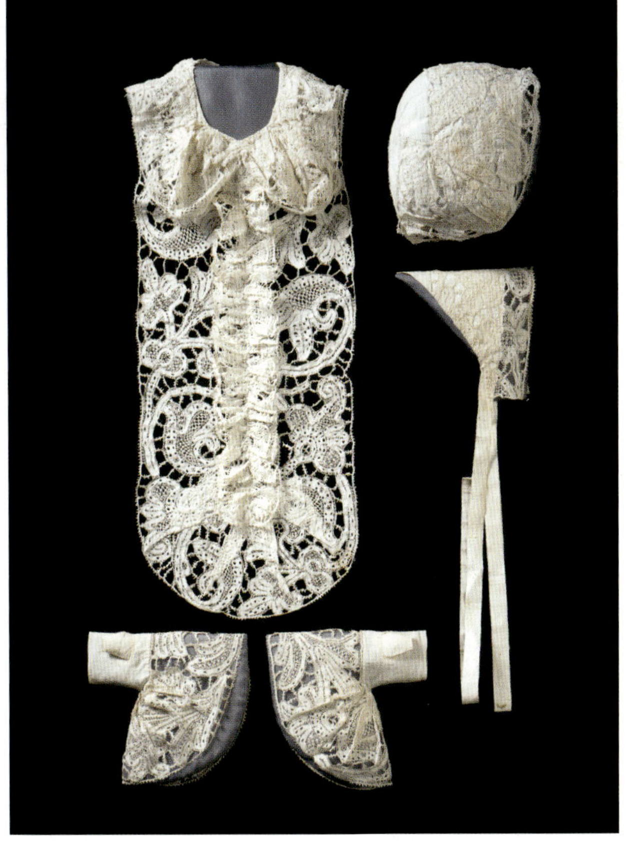

White is worn to mark important rites of passage, as a symbol of new beginnings and purity. Christian babies are traditionally baptized in white garments such as the christening set (1650–1700; above right), elaborately crafted from bobbin lace and linen. This silk outer kimono (1980–2000; above left) is part of a Japanese wedding ensemble known as *shiromuku*, meaning pure white. When she married in 1840, Queen Victoria set a royal precedent by choosing an ivory satin wedding dress, helping to popularize the fashion for bridal white evident in this silk satin wedding dress designed by Charles James in 1934 (opposite).

White is also a colour of deep mourning. *Deuil blanc* (white mourning), shown in the enamel medallion (1530–40; left) by Léonard Limousin, was a 16th-century French custom. Signifying innocence, the use of white is particularly poignant in this white-glazed ceramic sculpture (far left) commissioned in 1674 by the founder of John Dwight's Fulham Pottery to capture the likeness of his young daughter after her death.

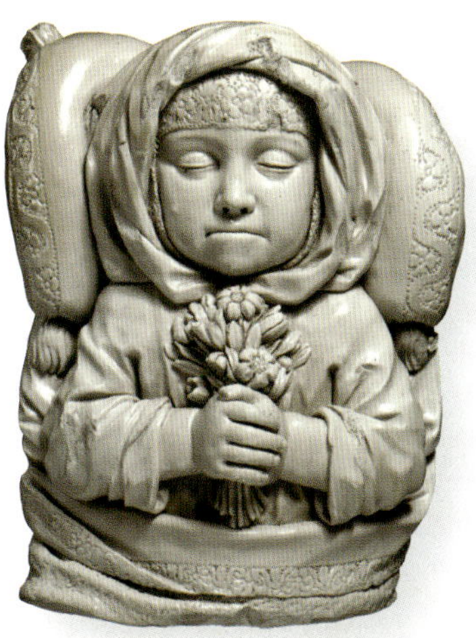

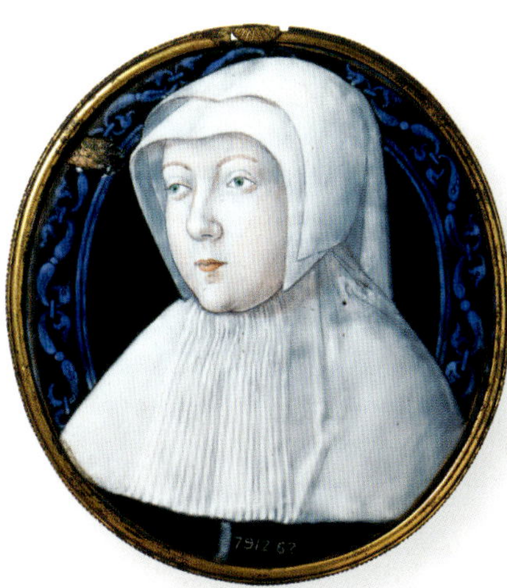

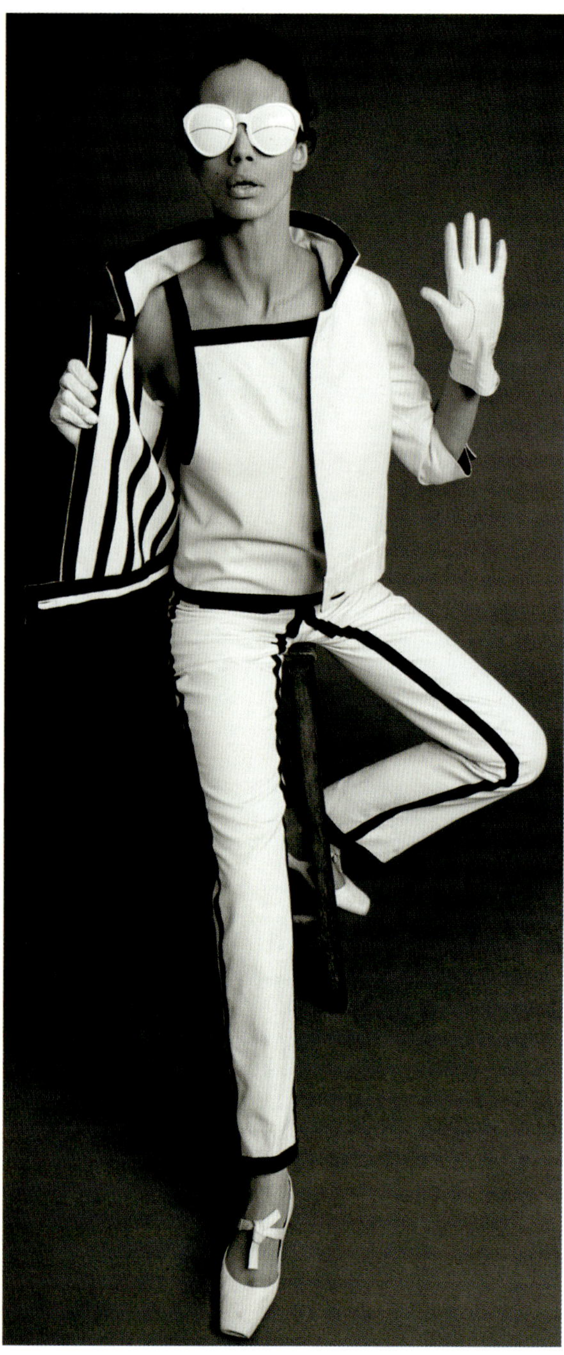

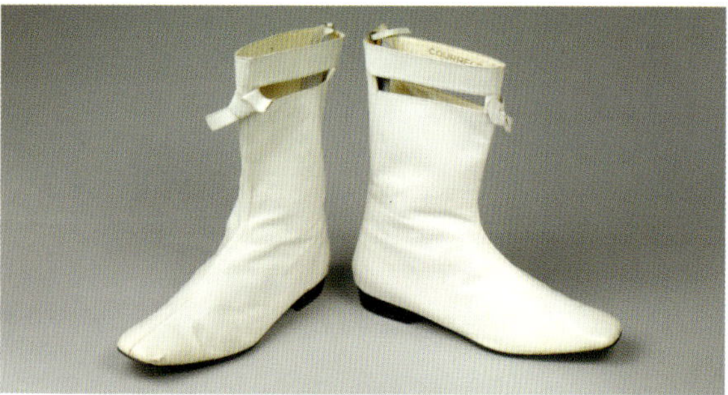

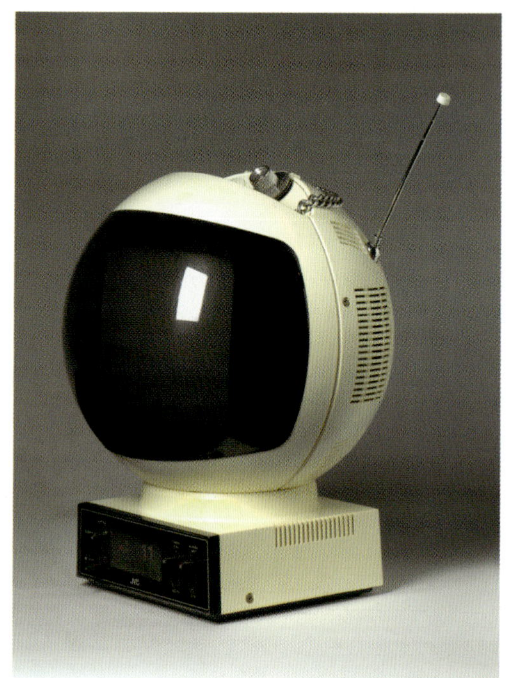

A marker of modernity and progress, white has been used in design to espouse a bright view of the future. The Trylon and Perisphere, captured in Gordon Gilkey's etching (opposite), were the centrepieces of the 1939 New York World's Fair. Occurring at the end of the Great Depression of the 1930s, the fair sought to promote a sense of optimism by presenting a utopian vision of the 'World of Tomorrow'. Designed in the Streamline Moderne style, the towering structures, painted in gleaming white, became symbols of hope for the future.

Resembling an astronaut's white helmet, the JVC Videosphere (1971; above) was inspired by the moon landing in 1969, an era when space travel captured the public imagination and influenced design. French couturier André Courrèges created clothing that was both functional and liberating for women living in the modern world of the 1960s, such as these elegant yet practical flat leather boots (pre-series, 1965; left) and a white cotton gabardine trouser suit, as photographed by John French for the *Daily Mail*, London in 1965 (above left).

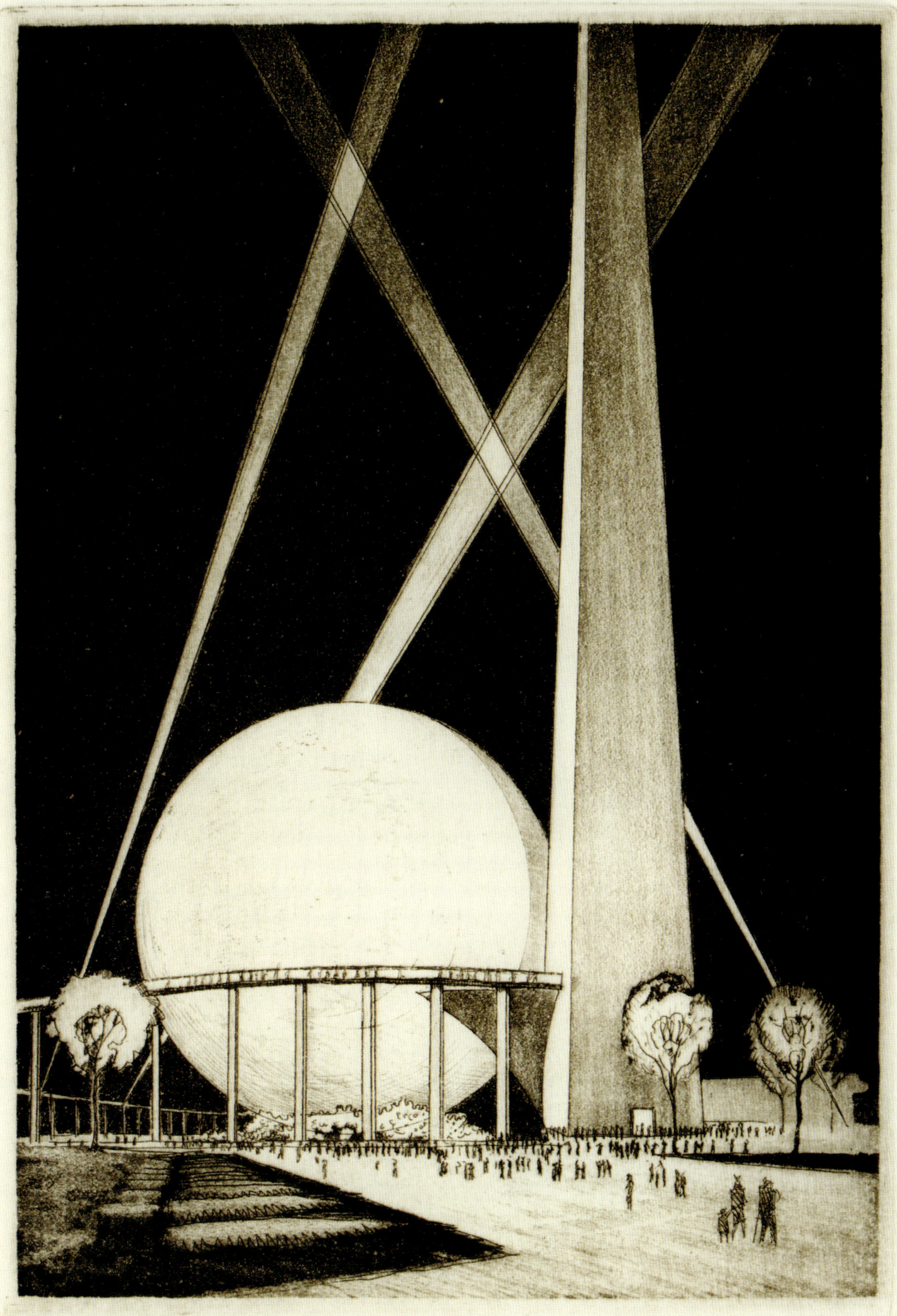

The Theme Center - N.Y. World's Fair (13)
Gordon Gilkey

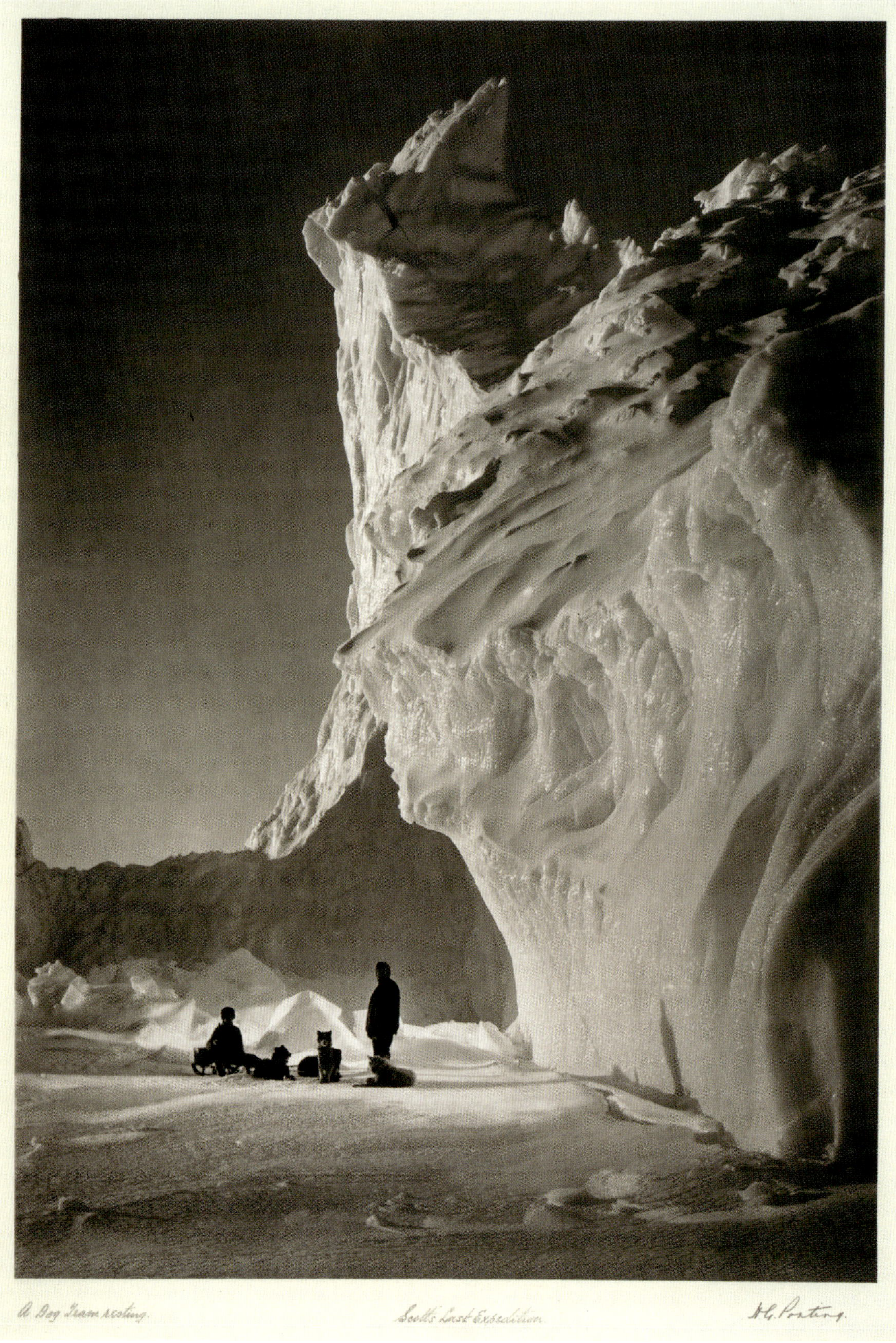

A Dog Team resting.
Scott's Last Expedition
H.G. Ponting.

Bright white is often considered pristine, indicative of an unsullied and natural state. George Herbert Ponting was the official photographer for Captain Scott's final expedition to the Antarctic. His 1910 photograph (opposite), taken in the uncharted territory of the South Pole, encapsulates the idea of an immaculate and unspoilt landscape, while E. Shubin's poster design *To The Purity Of Our Nature* (1989; right) uses the stark image of a white feather dripping in oil to draw attention to the threat of pollution in rivers, lakes and seas.

The demand for ivory as a luxury material has tragically resulted in the endangerment of several animal species around the world. This necklace (1920–40; below) was made to resemble ivory – the beads are carved with a pattern of stained cracks in imitation of aged ivory – but it is actually casein, a plastic produced from another natural white material: milk.

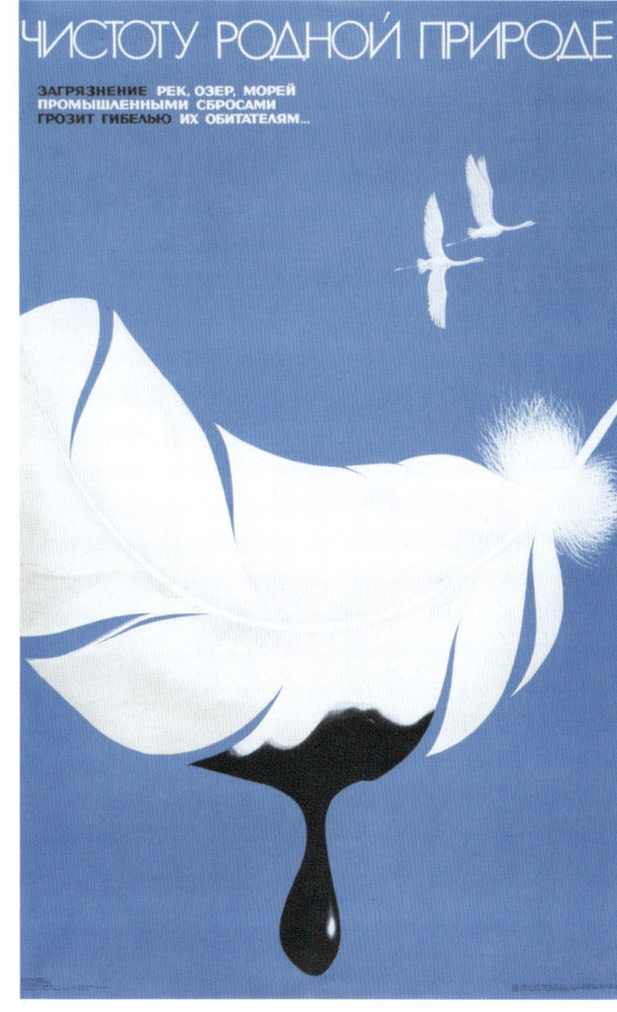

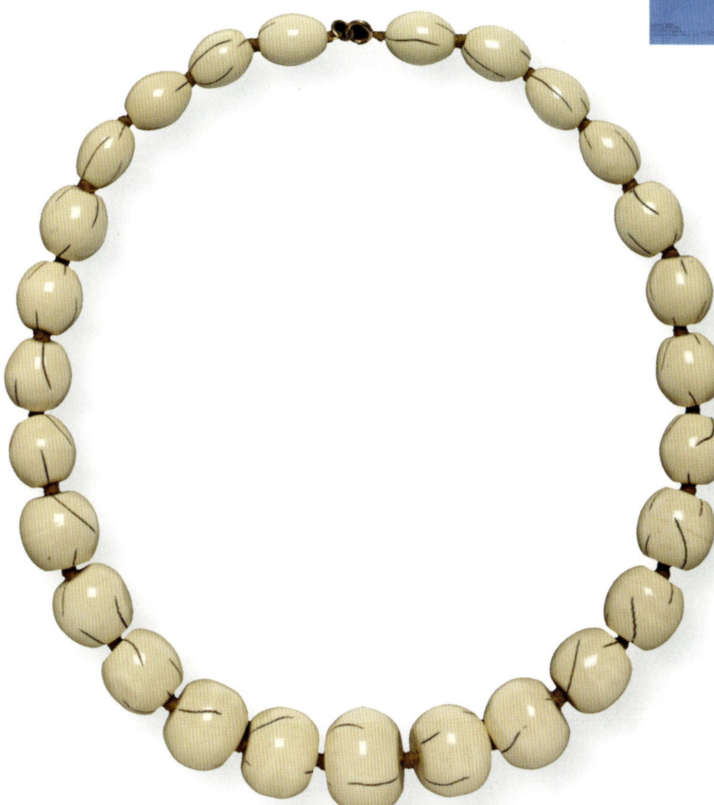

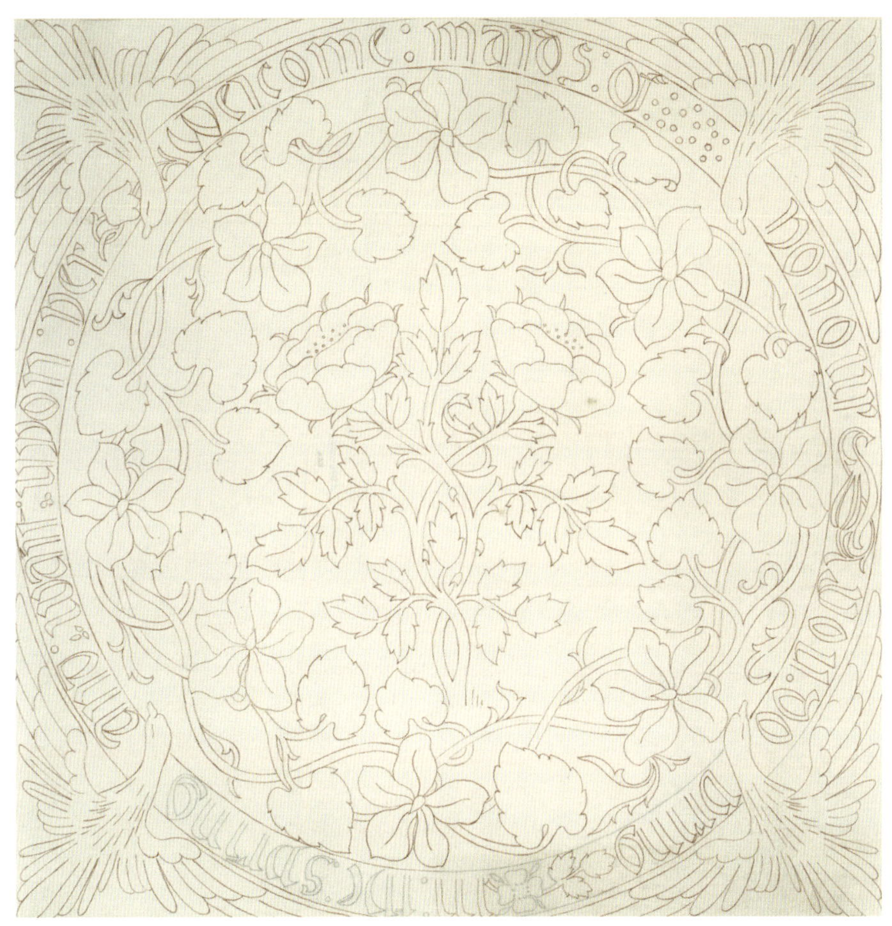

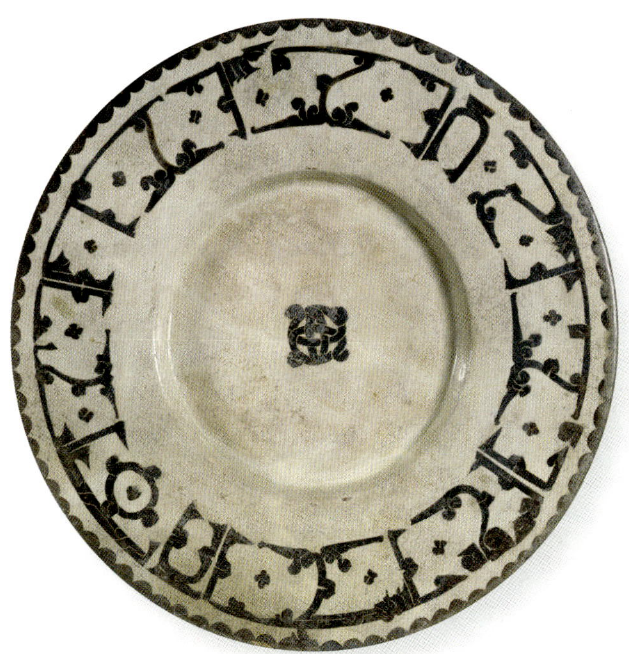

White is a colour full of anticipation: a blank sheet of paper waiting to be filled, or a malleable piece of porcelain clay moulded into form. It makes the perfect background for writing and mark-making, as coloured pigments stand out against its starkness. The calligraphic design on this 10th-century earthenware dish (left) is reminiscent of ink on white paper. Made in Nishapur or Samarkand, the moral message and the clarity of the text is enhanced by the white background, achieved by applying a white slip. The same can be said for the 19th-century embroidery design by May Morris (above), drawn in pencil on white paper, ready for pouncing: a technique for transferring the design onto a textile. In *Orchid*, from the series *Face* (2004; opposite), contemporary Chinese artist Huang Yan uses the human body as a canvas, painting it in imitation of the white paper used in traditional Chinese landscape painting, onto which ink is applied to create an image.

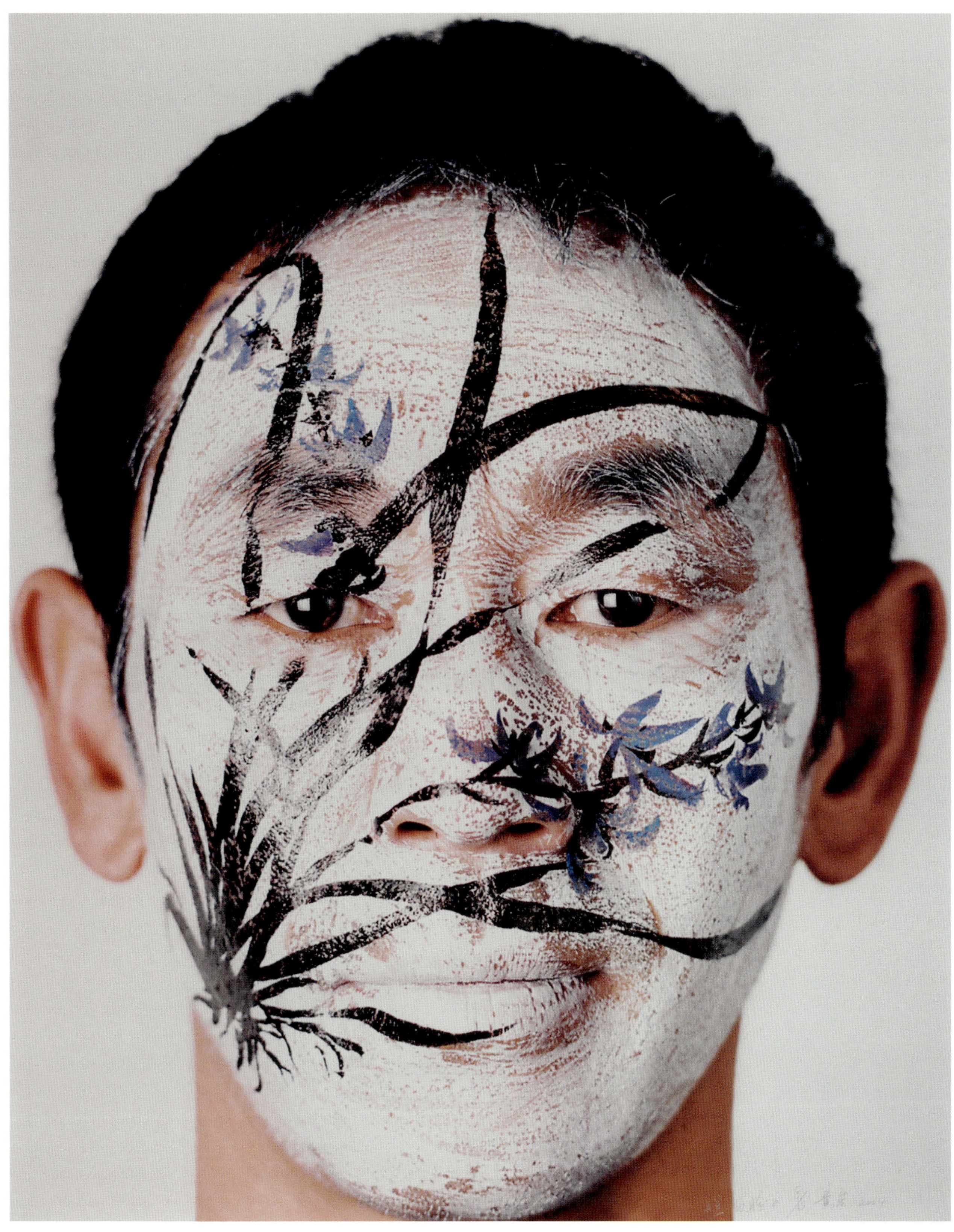

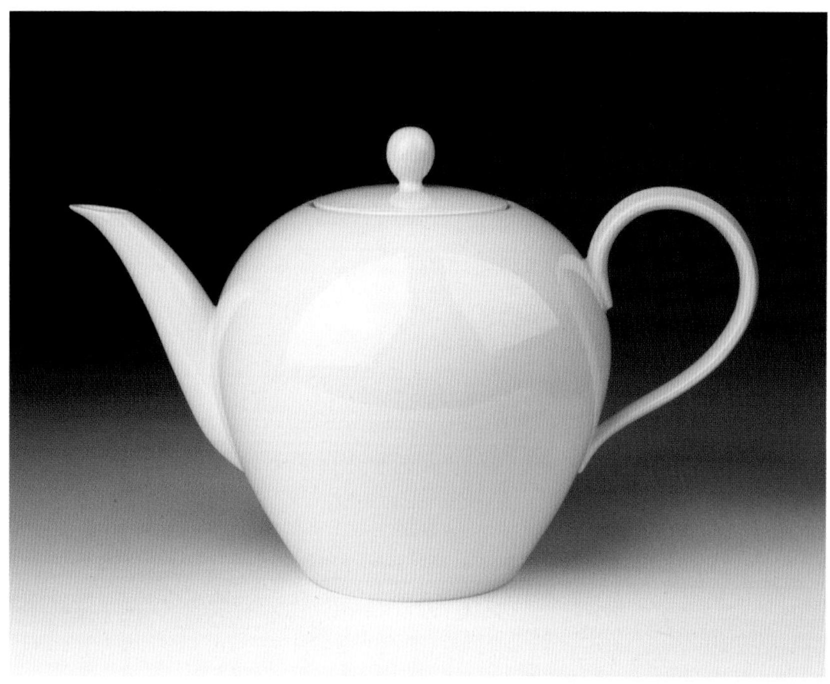

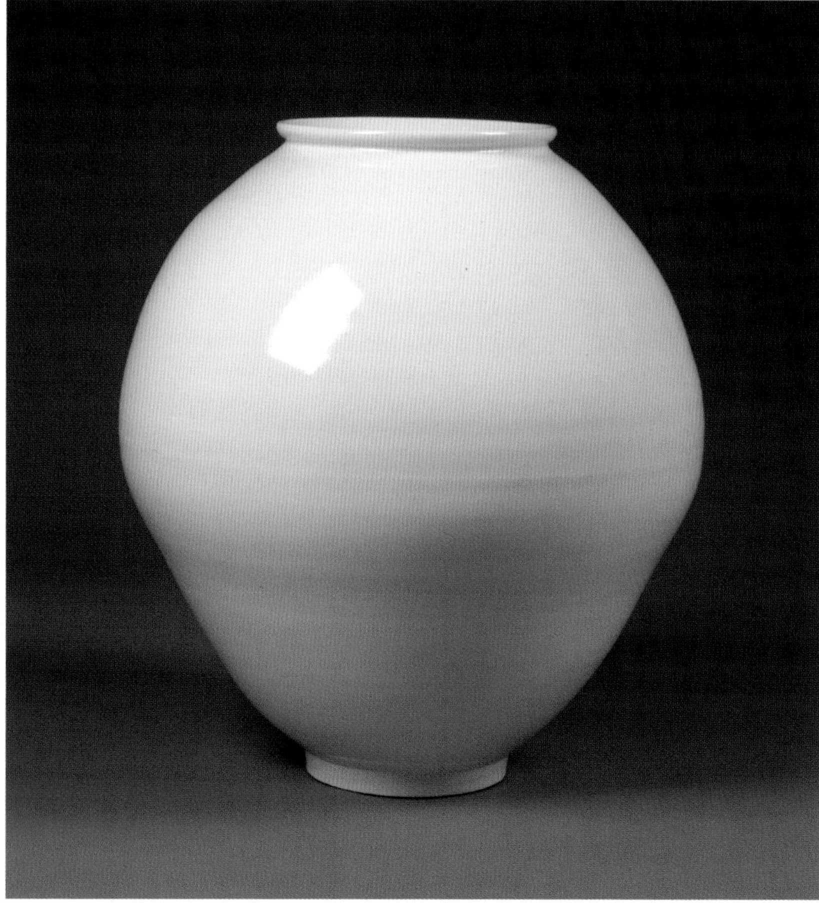

In contrast to colour, white has been seen as honest, elegant and free from distractions. This porcelain jar (left), made in about 2008 by Korean artist Young Sook Park, recalls the form of similar ceramics made in Korea in the 17th and 18th centuries. Known as moon jars, they were sought after in Korea for their elegant simplicity.

Modernist designer Trude Petri-Raben's simple porcelain teapot (above left) expresses the ethos of Modernist style in its banishment of ornament in favour of functionality.

This *kamiko* (paper clothing) ensemble (right) was designed by Issey Miyake for his 1982 Autumn/Winter collection, and is made predominantly of *washi* paper handmade in Shiroishi, Japan. Exuding a soft glow, the garment remains honest to the natural state of this traditional material. Warm and durable, *kamiko* have been worn in Japan since the 10th century, but have now been replaced by cotton, wool and synthetic materials.

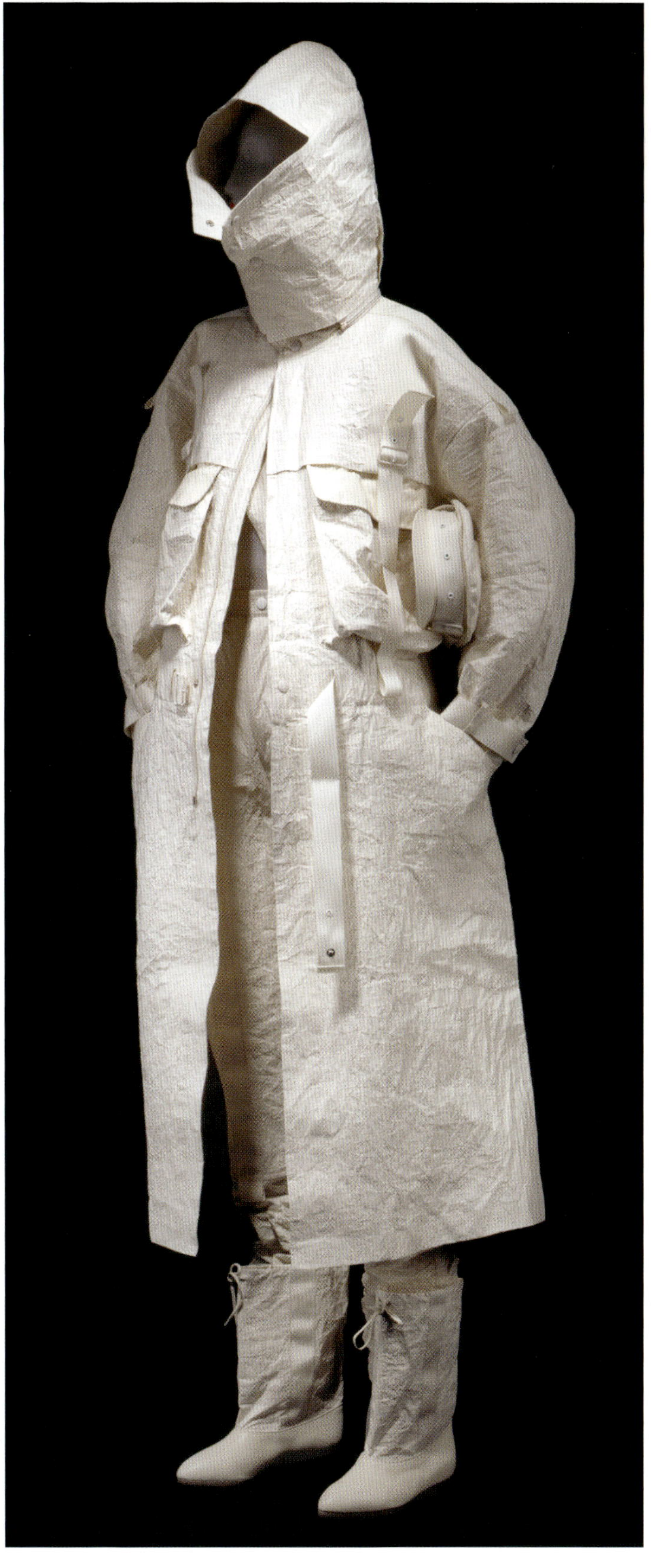

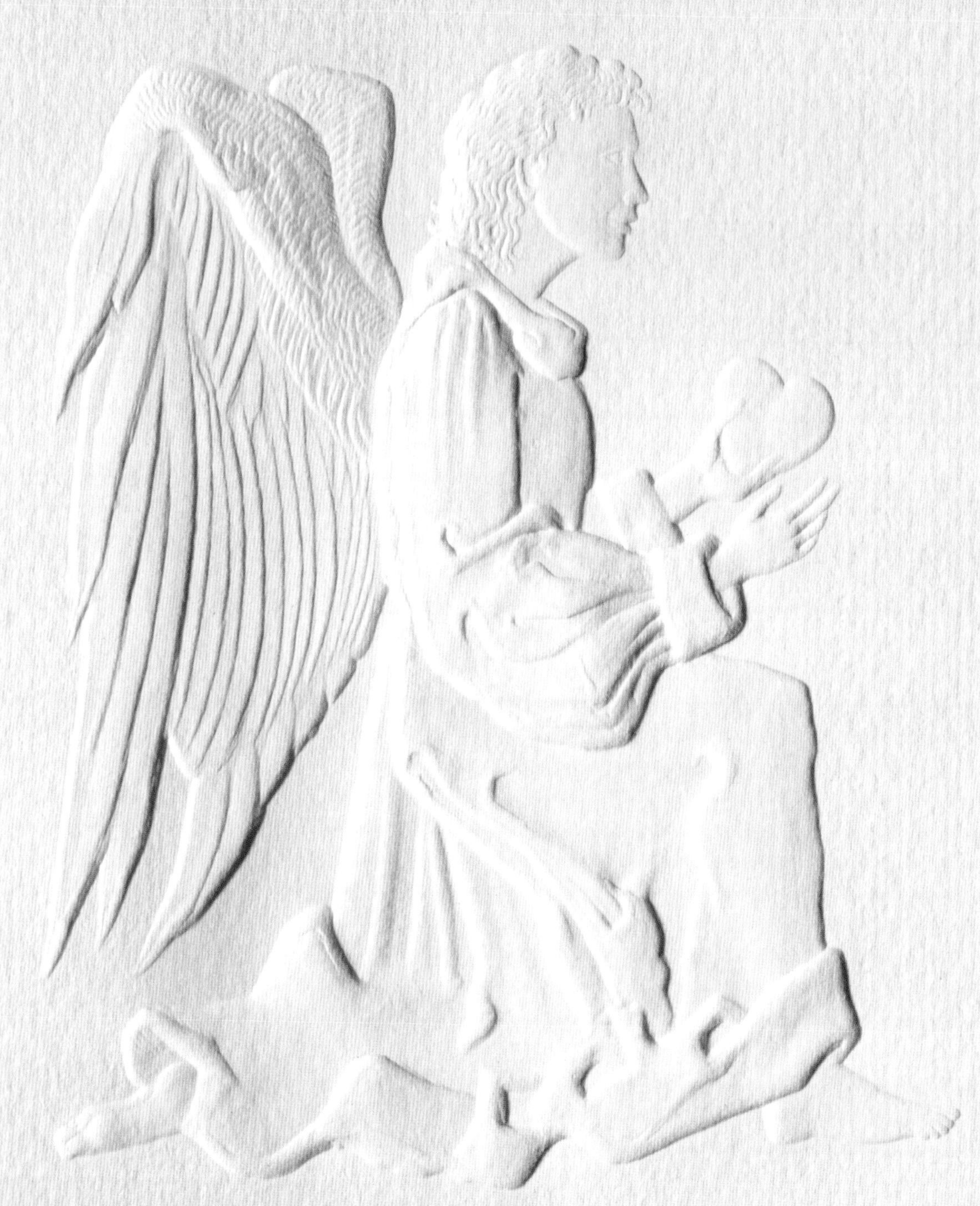

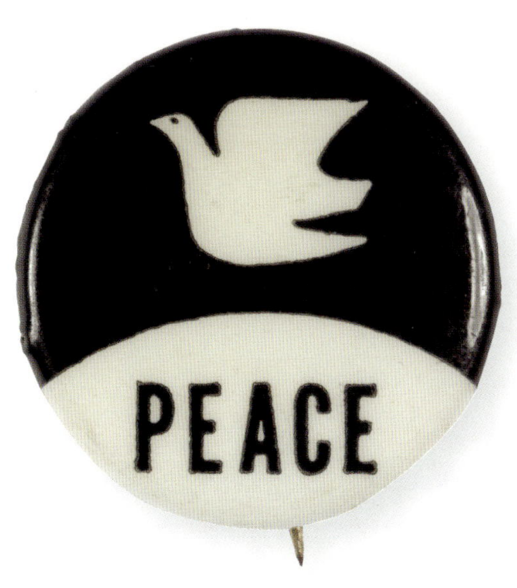

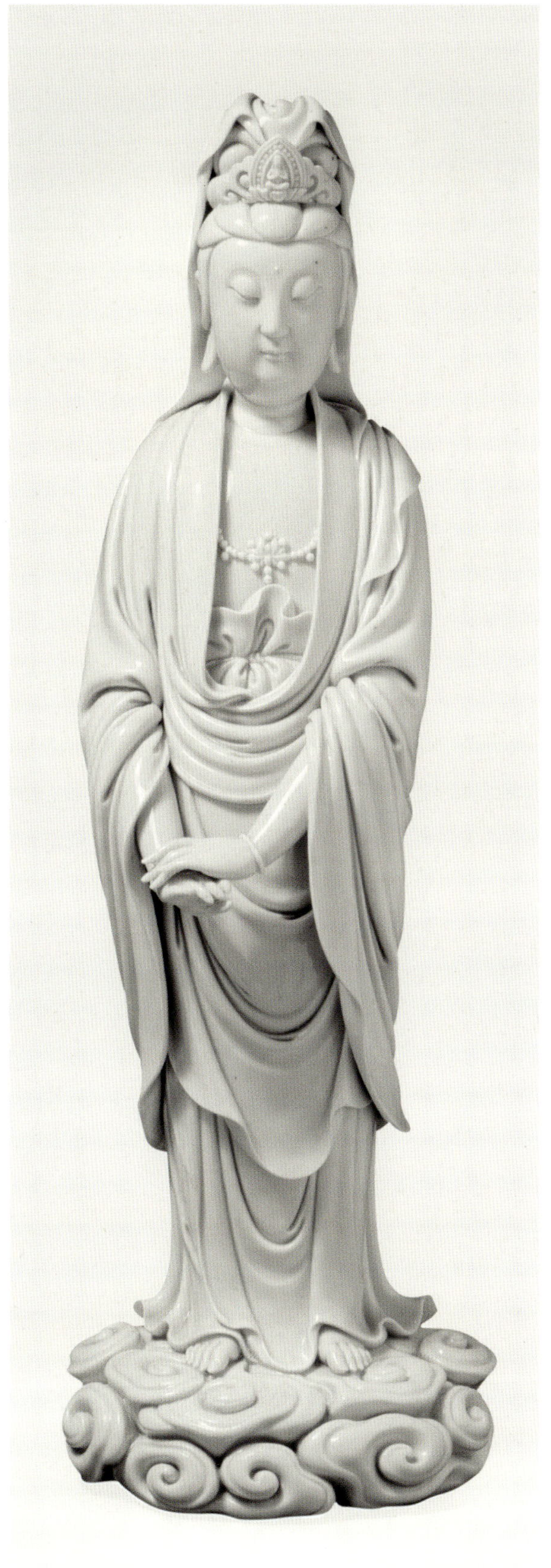

Suggesting peace and serenity, white is imbued with a sense of hope. The white dove is an internationally recognized symbol of love and harmony; this badge, made in about 1960 (above), promotes the widespread mid-20th-century peace movement.

Whiteness is also associated with divinity and kindness. Images of white-winged angels, such as the one on this blind-embossed greetings card (c. 2000; opposite), are often used to convey messages of goodwill. In Buddhism, Guanyin is the *bodhisattva* associated with compassion. She is most often represented as a beautiful, white-robed woman. This glazed porcelain figure, made by Chaozong He between 1580 and 1650 (right), was produced in the town of Dehua in Fujian province, south-east China. Dehua porcelain was prized for its association with purity; in the west it was known as 'Blanc de Chine', or 'white from China', and inspired European potters to develop their own hard-paste white porcelain.

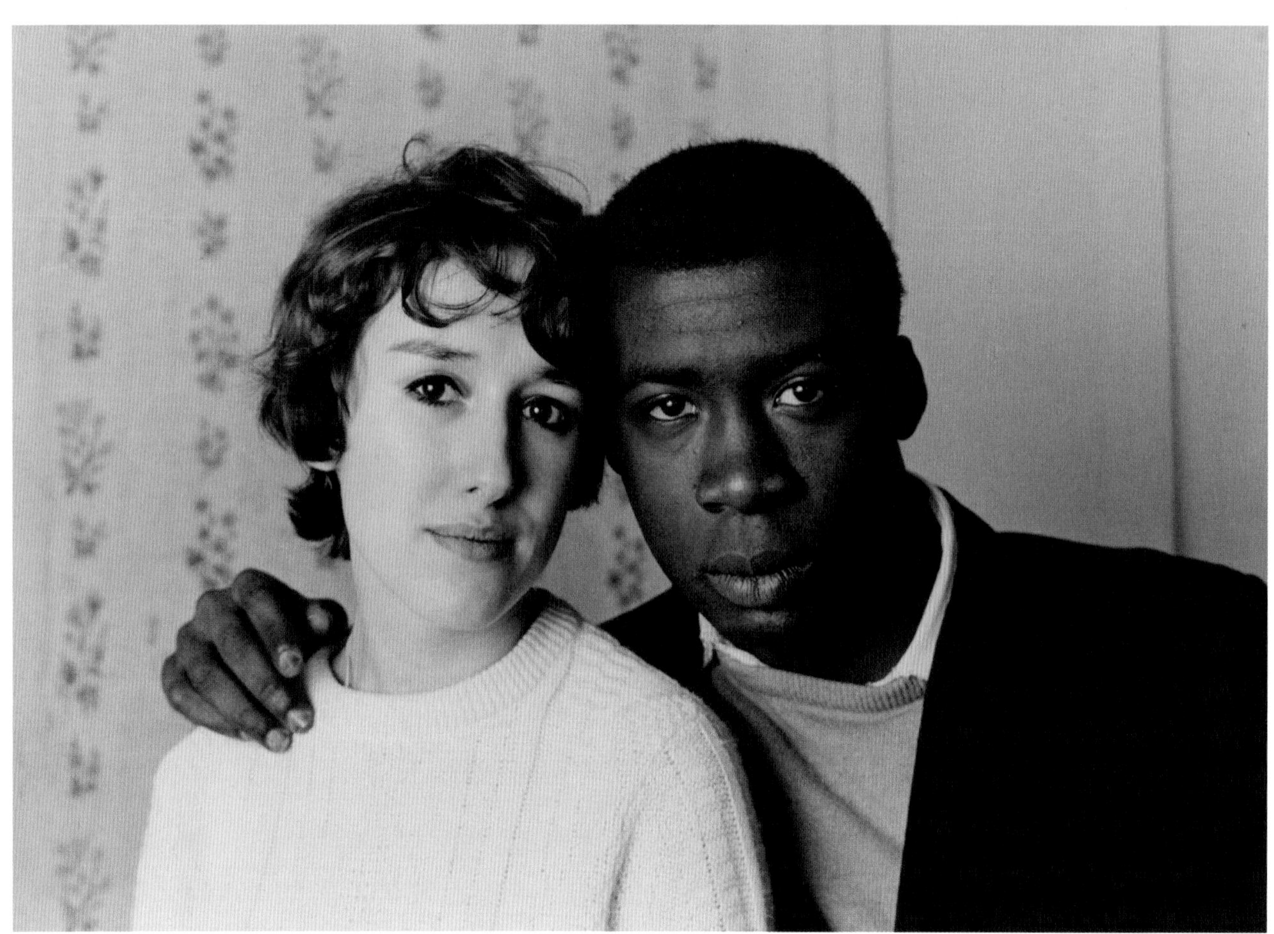

White has long been associated with power and privilege. It is the divisive, austere colour of exclusivity and cultural elitism, underpinned by assumptions of race and aesthetics. Auguste Rodin perpetuated the idea that white sculpture was the epitome of taste, beauty and civility. He drew inspiration from classical sculpture, but objected to evidence proving such objects were originally coloured. His *Cupid and Psyche* (c. 1898; opposite), was made in gleaming white marble.

While Rodin's couple reinforce an idea of white as the colour of perfection, *Notting Hill Couple* (1967; above) by Ronald 'Charlie' Phillips challenges such views. The value attributed to white is often cast in binary opposition to black, but this portrait is one of unity – both partners hold the viewer's gaze with equal weight. Shot in black and white, the title situates the couple in an area of London where, in the late 1950s, the interracial community had experienced a series of violent attacks.

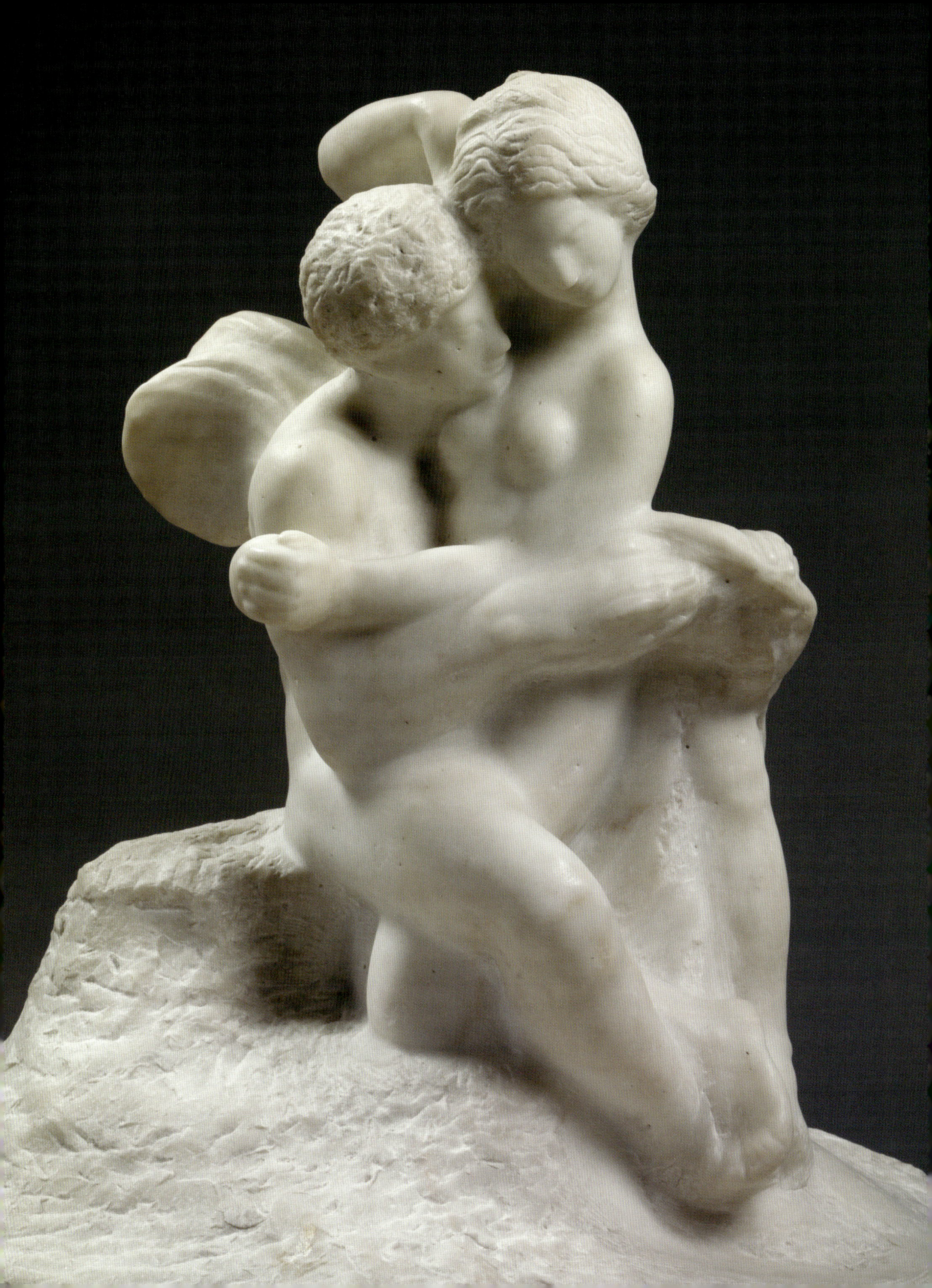

C9 M9 Y15 K18

C7 M5 Y6 K13

C5 M13 Y16 K38

C37 M34 Y33 K11

C8 M13 Y11 K30

C13 M6 Y9 K16

C10 M8 Y8 K9

C12 M6 Y4 K16

C48 M45 Y45 K20

C50 M42 Y41 K43

C14 M15 Y7 K28

C5 M0 Y10 K27

C0 M0 Y8 K58

C11 M14 Y17 K28

C7 M5 Y6 K8

C27 M24 Y25 K11

C22 M17 Y23 K34

C10 M10 Y9 K15

C3 M3 Y3 K70

C9 M10 Y10 K19

C14 M16 Y17 K55

C8 M6 Y7 K29

C8 M7 Y9 K9

C15 M11 Y17 K8

C10 M13 Y4 K28

C7 M8 Y8 K13

C6 M7 Y7 K14

C20 M19 Y19 K42

C36 M26 Y35 K0

C14 M6 Y4 K43

C11 M11 Y10 K20

C36 M30 Y32 K10

C20 M20 Y18 K21

C6 M7 Y10 K20

C0 M0 Y6 K43

C5 M16 Y23 K57

C7 M0 Y0 K30

C8 M2 Y2 K18

C40 M31 Y34 K17

C22 M21 Y15 K14

C15 M16 Y14 K43

C13 M9 Y5 K25

C11 M11 Y5 K37

C5 M5 Y0 K14

C15 M14 Y15 K12

C34 M35 Y32 K55

C7 M10 Y8 K27

C11 M12 Y14 K41

C24 M25 Y22 K41

C14 M13 Y12 K44

C15 M8 Y15 K13

C17 M14 Y11 K56

C8 M6 Y8 K17

C0 M3 Y4 K30

C8 M8 Y12 K74

GREY

Mutable, nebulous, ephemeral, grey is a fugitive colour, defying definition. Conventionally associated with neutral or even negative qualities and attributes, grey describes a low mood, a dull day, anything lacking clearly defined characteristics – a 'grey area'. It is considered bland, boring, lifeless, old. So negligible is grey, so indecisive and uncertain, that many books on the history and meaning of colours leave it out altogether.

Yet a number of artists have embraced the peculiar qualities of grey, finding something positive and useful in its outcast state. For the Minimalist sculptors of the 1960s and 1970s, materials such as lead and thick grey felt were valuable not only for their 'ready-made' industrial aesthetic but also for the lack of emotion, metaphor and affect embodied by their greyness. For American artist Jasper Johns, grey was the cool antithesis of the vivid chromatic agitation of Abstract Expressionism that he reacted against early in his career. The negatives of grey were for Johns a useful corrective, devoid of symbolic power: 'Grey drained the work of the excitement that colour afforded.' After a period of working with vibrant colours, in the 1970s the German artist Gerhard Richter made a series of monochromatic grey paintings. For him, grey is 'the ideal colour for indifference, fence-sitting, keeping quiet, despair'. He has claimed that 'it does not trigger off feelings or association, it is actually neither visible or invisible ... it has the capacity that no other colour has, to make "nothing" visible'.

In real-world applications the visibility (or otherwise) of grey can be problematic, while for the superstitious, it may be considered unlucky. Statistics show that after black, grey and silver cars are the most likely to be involved in accidents.

In the 1995–6 football season, Manchester United launched a new all-grey away strip. At half-time in a match against Southampton they were 3-0 down, and their manager, Alex Ferguson, had the team change into a blue and white kit, after which they scored a goal. Ferguson believed that the grey kit rendered his team invisible to one another on the pitch; they did not win a single game while wearing it and it was dropped before the end of the season.

There is a slipperiness to grey, a resistance to being pinned to a simple definition. As such, grey is rarely just itself, but, as G.K. Chesterton put it in his essay 'The Glory of Grey', 'always seems on the eve of changing to some other colour'. Indeed, it is often qualified and hyphenated: Vincent van Gogh wrote of grey's endless variety, listing 'red-grey, yellow-grey, blue-grey, green-grey, orange-grey, violet-grey'. Bridget Riley's suite of screenprints, *Coloured Greys* (1972), plays with these nuances, with undulating bands of modulated colour tinted with green, blue and pink to produce optical sensations that read as 'grey' (p. 46).

These subtle shifts in the grey spectrum are perhaps most evident in the pencil, that most commonplace and familiar of art materials. Graphite (from the Greek *graphein*, 'to draw or write') was so-named in the 1780s. It was previously known as 'plumbago', a misnomer suggested by its resemblance to lead. 'Plumbago' persisted, and gave its name to miniature portraits made with graphite on vellum in the seventeenth and eighteenth centuries, a fashion derived from the preparatory drawings made for portrait engravings in the influential sixteenth-century Netherlandish print trade and later imported to Britain (see pp. 58–9).

Pure graphite was discovered in Borrowdale, Cumbria, and by the seventeenth century graphite rods were being encased in wood to make drawing implements. But today's pencils are the result of experiments in 1795 by French painter and inventor Nicolas-Jacques Conté, who added various amounts of clay to powdered graphite, which was then hardened by firing, producing a wide tonal range. By varying the choice of pencil, using it sharpened or blunt and applying more or less pressure, the artist could produce faint silvery traces or dark dense grey-blacks, and everything in between.

The dictionary describes grey simply as a colour between black and white, 'a neutral hue'. It may be 'dark, dismal or gloomy', or 'dull, dreary and monotonous'. All these adjectives are regularly applied to the English weather, and indeed Chesterton's essay was written as a defence of that climate, with its grey skies, and sombre moods. He vigorously refutes the idea of grey as 'colourless', declaring grey to be 'a very powerful and pleasing colour'. He claims 'the doubt of grey' as a positive virtue, while also praising it as an effective foil to the vivid 'decision' of colours such as scarlet.

But for all Chesterton's fond arguments in its favour, grey indisputably belongs to a world of fogs and mists, drizzle and haar, overcast days and dull skies. Rain gives a grey cast to landscapes urban and rural, veiling the view, blurring slate, stone and clouds in a drear harmony of what Tennyson called a 'doleful' grey. Grey is the colour of November, with John Ruskin bemoaning a 'Grey, blackish, damp, wretched morning' on 2 November 1857, and of February, with Nathaniel Hawthorne in Lancashire (also 1857) lamenting four years 'spent in a gray gloom' of English mists.

Grey is the colour of smoke and shadows, the essence of the atmosphere at dusk along the misted banks of London's River Thames, where James Abbott McNeill Whistler found the defining subject for scenes he called 'Nocturnes' (pp. 62–3). These near-dark, atmospheric views are symphonies of grey in which, in Whistler's words, 'the evening mist clothes the riverside with poetry, as with a veil and the poor buildings lose themselves in the dim sky, and the tall chimneys become campanili, and the warehouses are palaces in the night ….' His exaggeratedly poetic description glosses over the fact that the dim sky and veils of mist were caused in part by noxious emissions from factories sited along the river banks. Smoke and fumes generated by industry and domestic fires were also the cause of the impenetrable fogs and smogs common in towns and cities, before the advent of Clean Air legislation in Britain. Charles Dickens sets the scene in the opening paragraphs of *Bleak House* (1852–3) by describing London and its environs on a November day, enveloped by a dense dirty fog rolling and flowing indoors and out, choking and disorientating the city's inhabitants.

By contrast, grey is also the colour of the world seen by moonlight, where it creates a mood of magic and mystery. In paintings and prints, moonlight imparts a colourless monochrome to the landscape and conjures up an atmosphere of seclusion, silence and secrecy. A softly glowing moon seems to cast a silvery hue over the autumnal scene decorating the silk kimono on p. 44. In poetry and prose, science and art, the moon itself appears as a luminous grey – a colour also characteristic of the precious mineral moonstone. The gemstone has been used in jewellery since Roman times, and was believed by the Romans to be formed from frozen moonlight. Ghosts and apparitions, insubstantial misty wraiths which mostly appear after dark, are often described as being grey. A 'Grey Lady' from the time of Queen Elizabeth I famously haunts Rufford Old Hall in Lancashire, but her namesakes have been seen in many historic houses in Britain and beyond.

Just as cloud, rain, fog, mist and smoke are seen or experienced as grey, so too is the urban landscape. Though towns and cities are animated by billboards, neon light and shop windows, cars and buses, their fundamentals are grey – from the concrete and steel of Modernist architecture to cement and tarmac, slate-tiled roofs and stone walls. There is grey beneath our feet, too, colouring cobbles, paving stones and the cast-iron drains, manhole covers and gratings that punctuate gutters and pavements.

Coming indoors, grey has been a fashionable feature of interior design schemes since the eighteenth century: *grisaille* wallpapers and other papers imitating plaster and stucco mouldings were printed in contrasting shades of grey, as were the Gothic Revival papers of the early nineteenth century, with their patterns of architectural stonework. In the later nineteenth century the palettes of Aestheticism and Arts and Crafts design also tended towards muted, low-key tones, with William Morris just one of several designers to choose greys for wallpaper and textiles. This was reflected in dress, with so-called 'art' colours, including 'drab' (a common synonym for grey), coming into fashion. Traditionally worn by Cistercian monks and Franciscan friars to symbolize their vows of poverty and chastity, grey clothing had long been seen as modest, self-effacing and calm, also associated with Puritanism and Quakerism. This character-defining association is frequently referenced in nineteenth-century literature: in George Eliot's *Middlemarch* (1871–2), for example, the serious, dutiful and virtuous Dorothea Brooke dresses in 'Quakerish grey'. To wear grey was seen as evidence of high-minded seriousness and the refusal of a showy femininity. When Mr Rochester takes Jane Eyre to buy dresses before their marriage he selects silk in 'brilliant amethyst' and 'pink satin'. Jane, determined to assert herself, persuades him to buy instead 'a sober black satin and pearl-grey silk'. Jane had first come to Rochester's home as a governess, a figure of uncertain in-between status in Victorian society, belonging neither with the masters or the servants. Such women were expected to dress plainly so as not to draw attention to themselves.

Regarded as practical and utilitarian, grey has long been associated with tailoring – the ubiquitous business suit, or the plain and functional 'utility clothing' of the 1940s (p. 54), designed in response to rationing. It has been popular for workwear, overalls and uniforms. But there is a sophisticated elegance to the restrained understatement of grey that has also made it a regular choice for haute couture in everything from suits, shoes and gloves to evening dresses and jewellery. Christian Dior launched his 'New Look' in 1947, characterized by an exaggeratedly feminine hourglass figure. Perhaps in a nod to post-war austerity and the uniforms many women had worn during wartime service, he included a grey wool flannel jacket that referenced military styling in its clean lines and lack of ornament (p. 56). For Dior, grey

was 'the colour of luxury'; he and the designers who succeeded him have used shades including dove grey, pearl grey, smoke grey and silver grey in every couture collection since 1947, and he also chose it for the facades and interiors of the Dior boutique on the Avenue Montaigne, Paris. In 2013, the fashion house issued a new perfume, the smoke-coloured 'Gris Montaigne', in celebration of Dior grey.

In the late twentieth and twenty-first centuries grey has come to suggest efficiency and a neutral functionality, represented by mobile phones, equipment such as typewriters and early desktop computers, as well as office carpets, filing cabinets and desks. In Edwin Morgan's poem *Grey* (2002), grey is an accumulation of absences – 'of movement, colour, contrast' that creates a mood of uniformity and aesthetic self-denial.

Grey is everyday and colour is an aberration, a fantasy, as the film *The Wizard of Oz* (1939) suggests when Dorothy is whisked from the flat grey landscape of her Kansas home and set down in the saturated Technicolor world of Oz; when the adventure comes to an end, the grey, uneventful security of home enfolds her once again. But grey also stands for desolation; in Cormac McCarthy's dystopian novel *The Road* (2006), colour has leached from the world after environmental catastrophe has precipitated a nuclear winter. It is bitterly cold, each day 'more grey than the last', with even the snow a tainted grey.

Grey is a colour of contradictions – hard and soft, dark and light, dull and lustrous, poetic and prosaic, authoritative and humble. In general, the negatives of grey – old age, fading, obscurity – are balanced by positives: the wisdom and authority of the 'grey beard', the analytic and creative powers to be found in the 'grey matter' of the human brain. Grey may be gloomy – think of Eeyore, the perennially pessimistic donkey in the *Winnie the Pooh* stories – but it is also modest, practical, calm and gentle, as embodied in Alison Uttley's *Little Grey Rabbit* (p. 54).

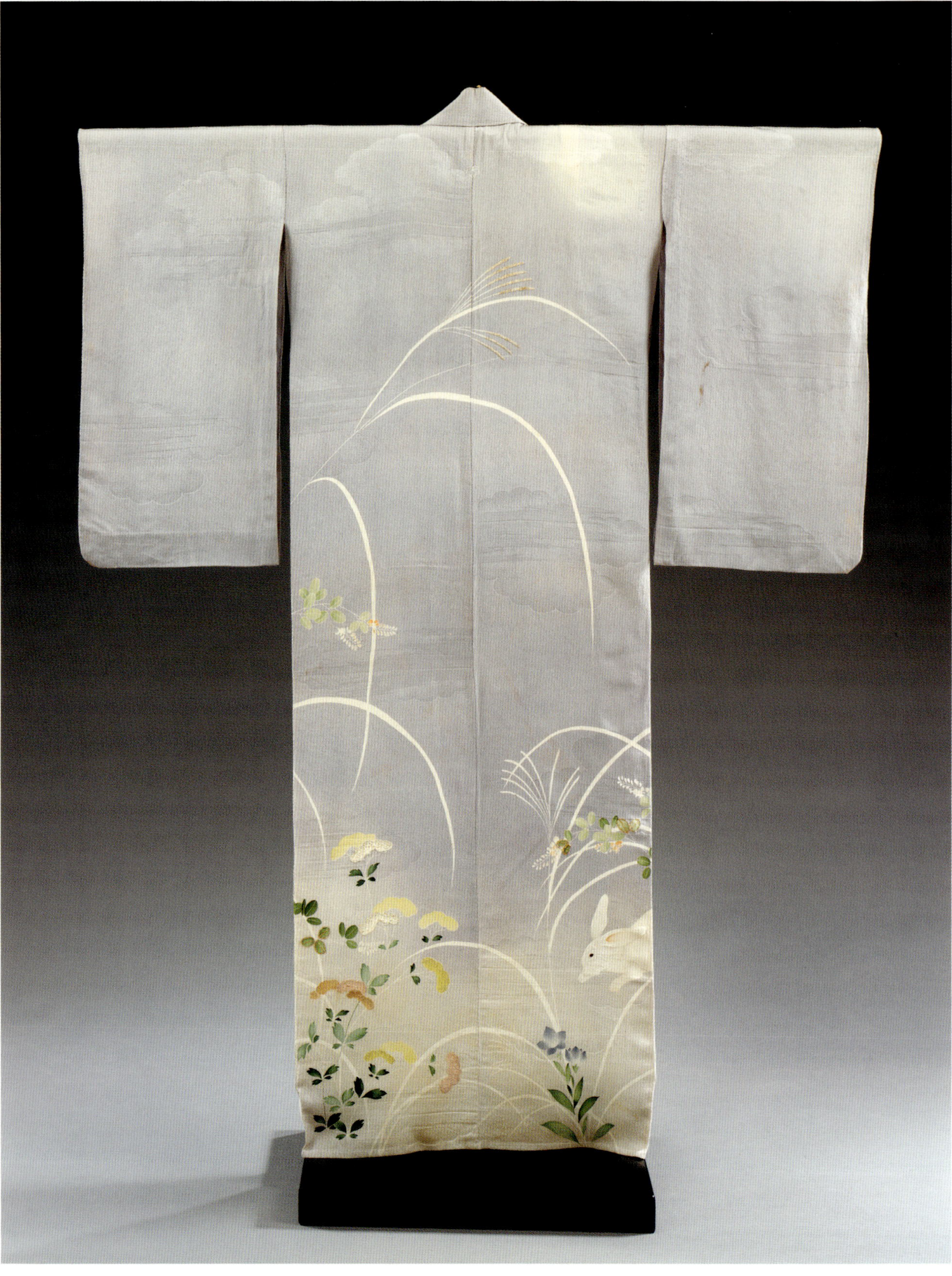

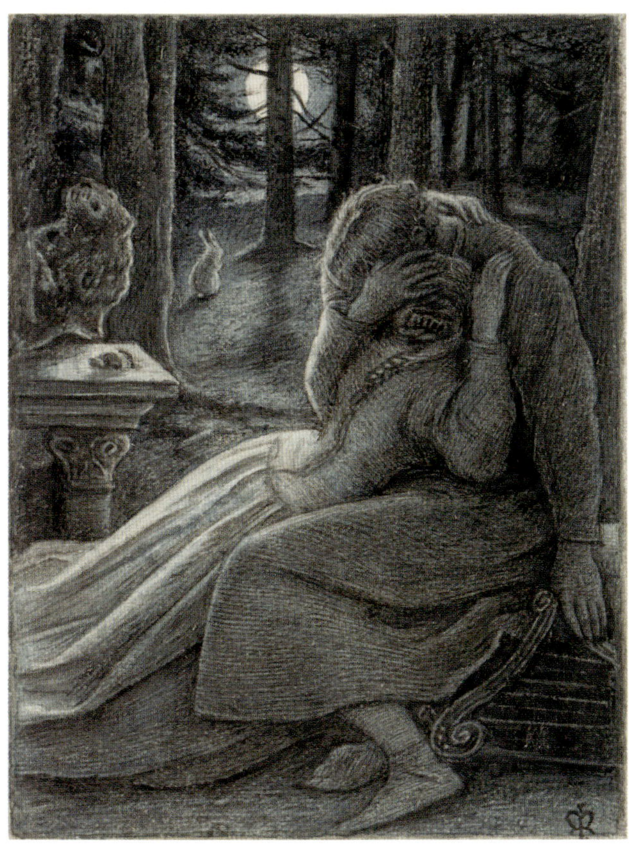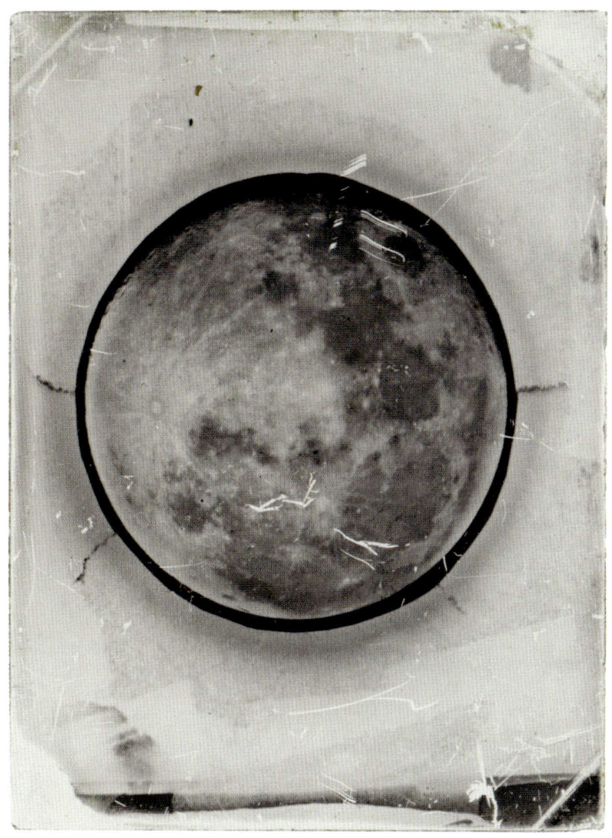

Moonlight sets the scene for romance, mystery and magic. Under a silvery moon, bluish-grey shadows shroud the anonymous lovers in John Everett Millais's watercolour *Love* (c. 1862; above left) in a poetic mood of stillness, secrecy and silence. In scenes printed on a cotton fabric produced in Manchester in 1911 (right), polar bears roam an icy wasteland, coloured by grey shadows cast from a clouded moon. With its flat areas of muted colour, the design is clearly influenced by Japanese woodblock prints. Enhanced by the sheen of the fabric, a full moon glows softly from the shoulder of a luxurious silk kimono (c. 1912–26; opposite). Perhaps made for a geisha, it is further embellished with clouds to suggest a moonlit night sky. The moon itself appears as a dark grey globe, photographed on glass plate negatives by William Crookes in 1855 (above right), almost luminous against a black void.

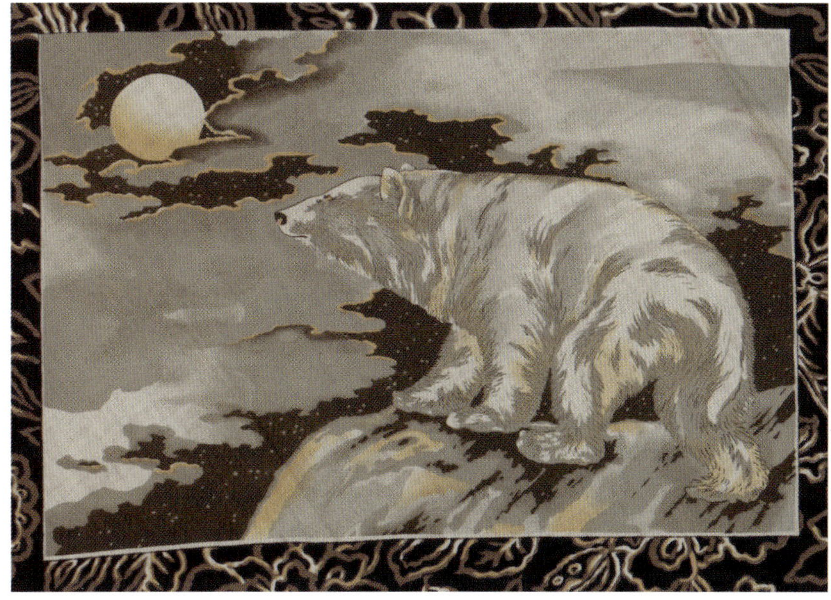

As an 'in-between' colour, grey is often combined with black and white to create optical tricks, as seen in a ceiling paper from 1769 (opposite), printed to give the illusion of three-dimensional moulded decorations. Grey has also been an effective tool for exploring perceptions of colour. In one of many works on this theme, *WIS-II* from *White Line Squares (Series 1)*, 1966 (below right), Josef Albers printed three shades of grey as nested squares; by printing a white line 'frame' in the second square, he created the illusion that the greys on either side are subtly different, though they are not. In Bridget Riley's *Coloured Greys I* (below left), one of three screenprints grouped as *Coloured Greys* (1972), muted tones of lilac, green and terracotta are woven together, with the effect that the eye sees shades of grey. The rhythmic geometric patterns that characterize the painted surfaces of Elizabeth Fritsch's pots, as in *Saxophone and Piano Duo* (1978; right), have a correspondence with music, and create an optical effect that moves the object towards the insubstantial.

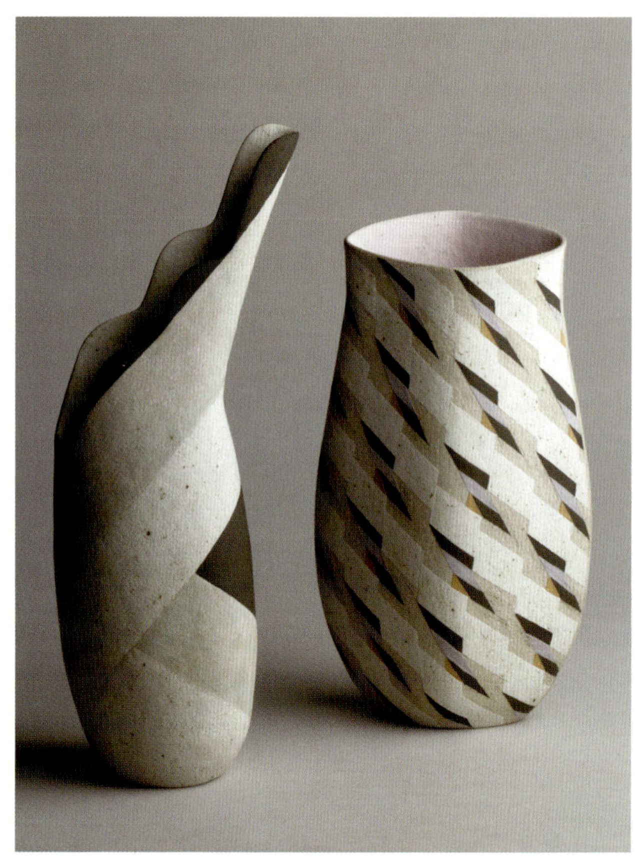

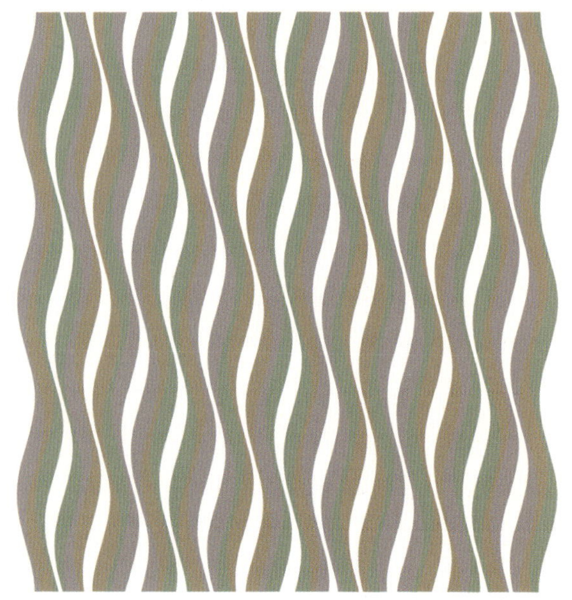

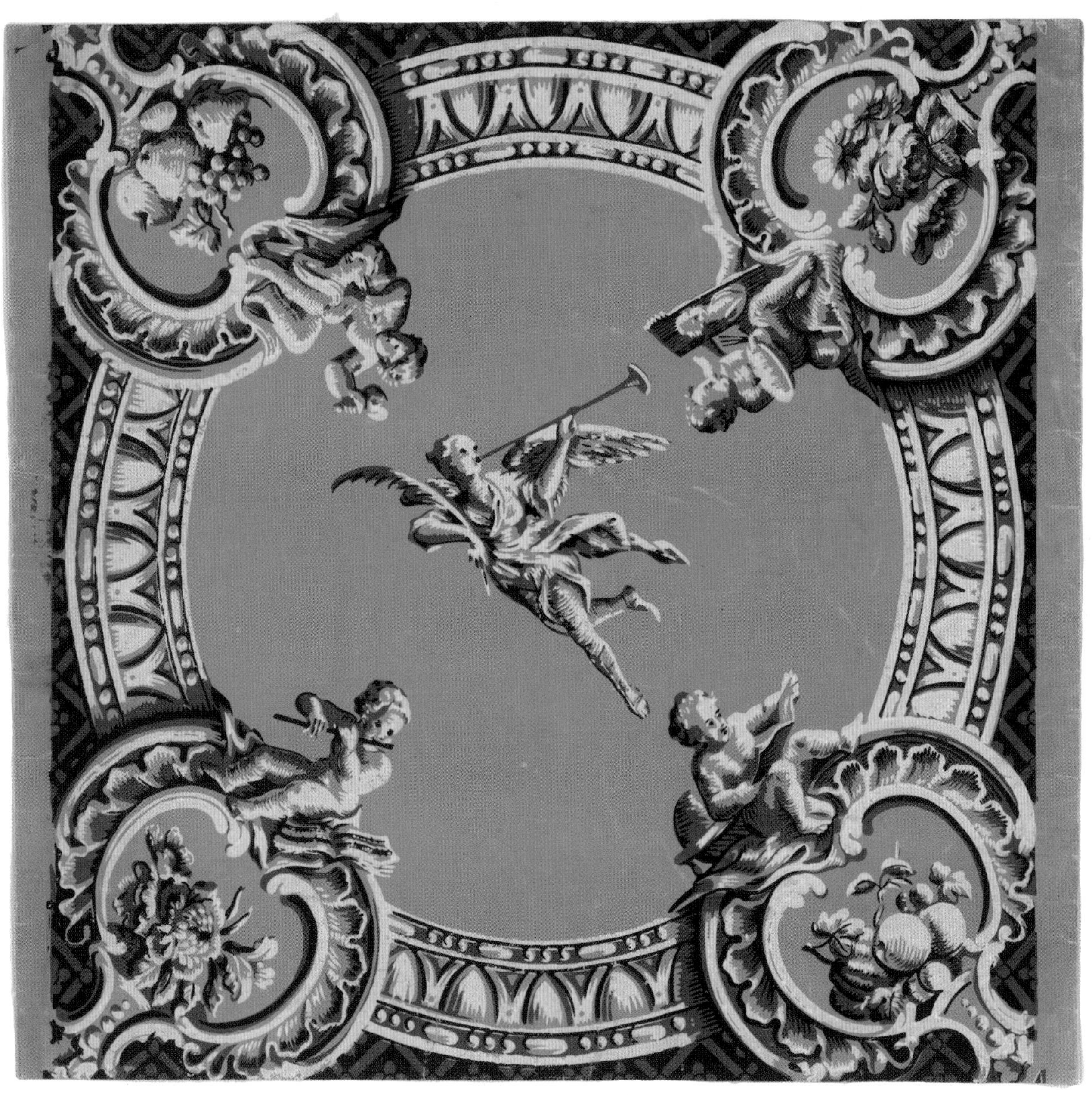

In nature, grey signifies camouflage, stealth and predatory power. In a watercolour by Ji Biao (1819; right), a prowling grey cat moves like a stealthy shadow to ambush its prey. The grey heron (*Ardea cinerea*) takes its Latin name from the colour of its plumage – *cinerea* meaning 'ash-grey'. This helps to hide the bird as it stands motionless in the shallows of rivers and lakes, hunting for fish and frogs, as we see in a colour woodcut by Allen W. Seaby (1900–8; opposite, bottom). The harrier hawk, another powerful predator (painted in 1918 by Edward McKnight Kauffer, opposite, top left), is disguised by its mottled grey and buff feathers.

Imitating nature, grey is also deployed in a military context, where camouflage and stealth are all-important. Two construction toys (opposite, top right) – a naval destroyer made of LEGO (2011) and a model of a Skybusters stealth jet (1989) – demonstrate how battleships and bombers are painted grey to escape enemy detection and hide their approach.

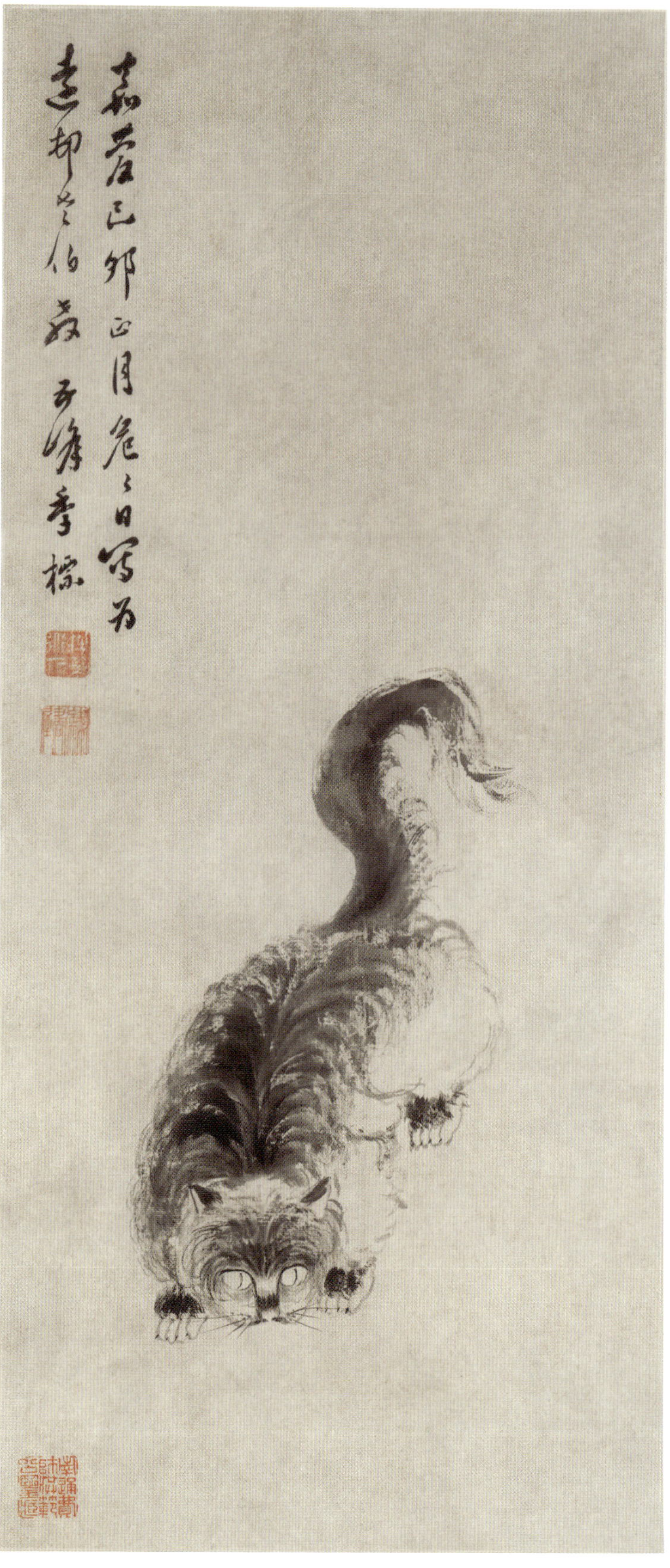

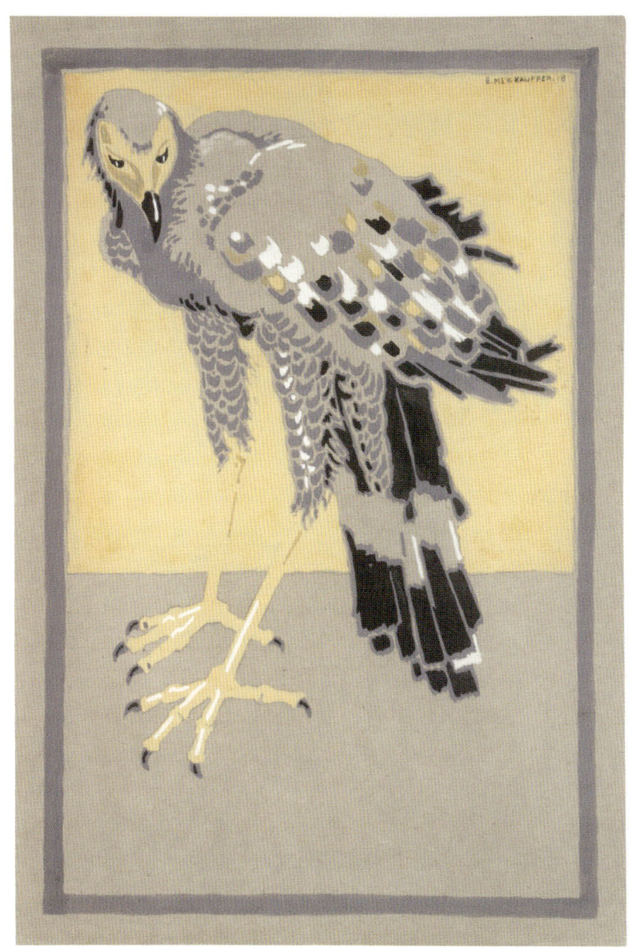

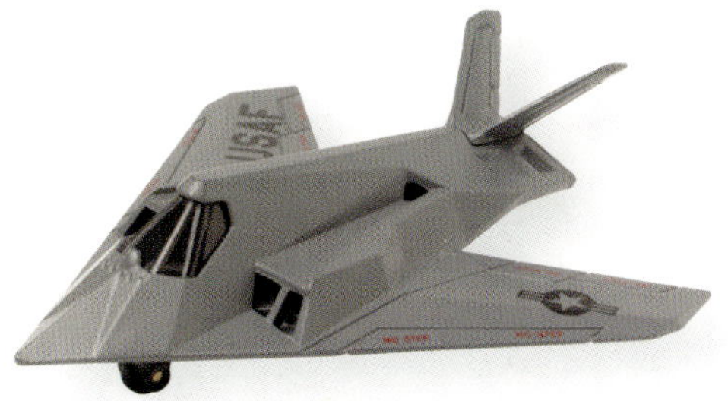

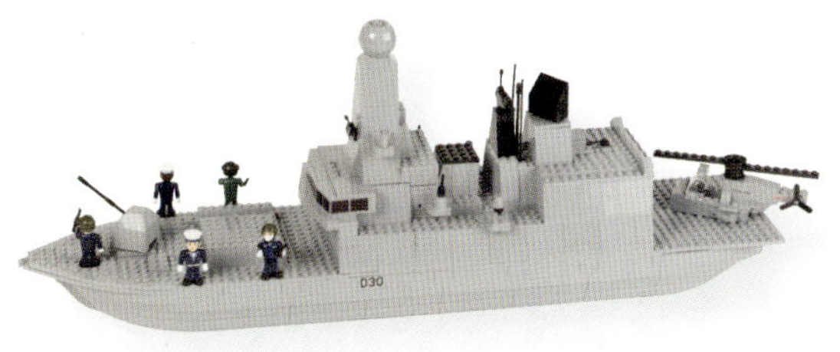

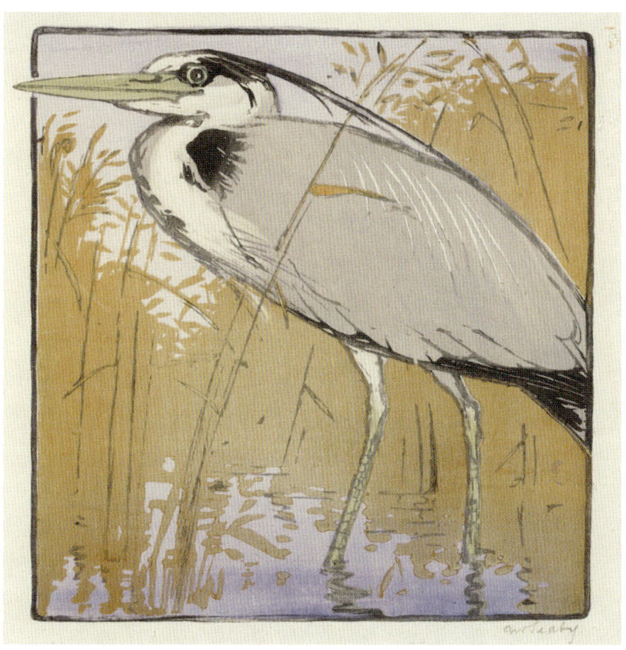

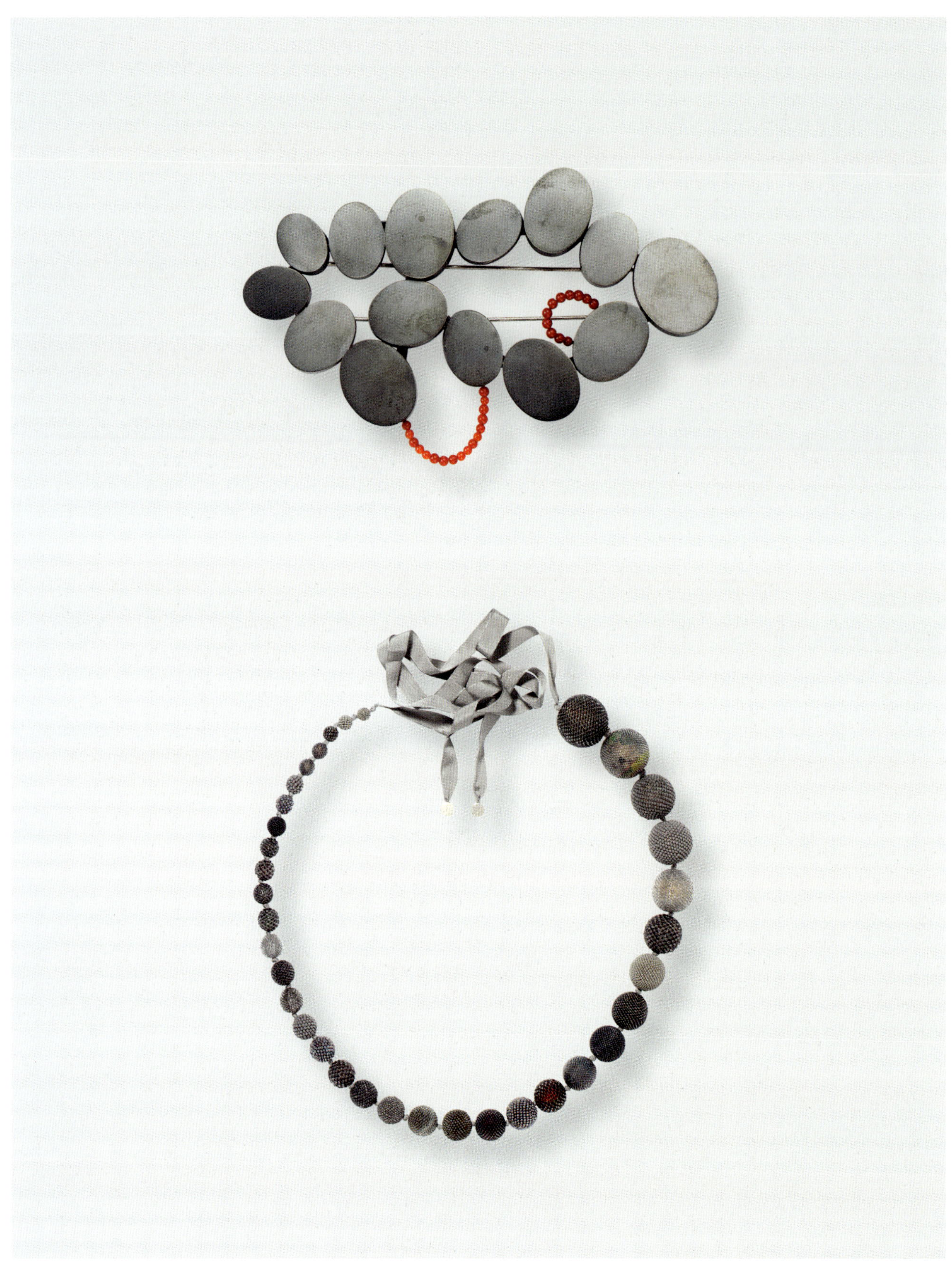

Sombre grey is often associated with decay or ageing, reflected in works relating to mourning and death. Many 18th-century designs for funerary monuments were drawn with grey watercolour wash, as in John Flaxman's tomb design with figures representing Memory and History (below). Artists have often used grey tones for *memento mori* compositions, in which fragile objects symbolize the fleeting pleasures of life. Ann Carrington's sculpture *Devil's Trumpet* (2016; right) is a bouquet inspired by Dutch 17th-century flower paintings, crafted from worn, tarnished metal cutlery. Likewise, the silver pieces in Dorothy Hogg's 'Artery' brooch (2008; opposite, top), oxidized to a dark grey, allude to the physical effects of ageing, while a necklace (1995–9; opposite, bottom) by German jeweller Axel Russmeyer, with glass and metal beads and grey freshwater pearls strung on a grey ribbon, has the air of a time-worn heirloom.

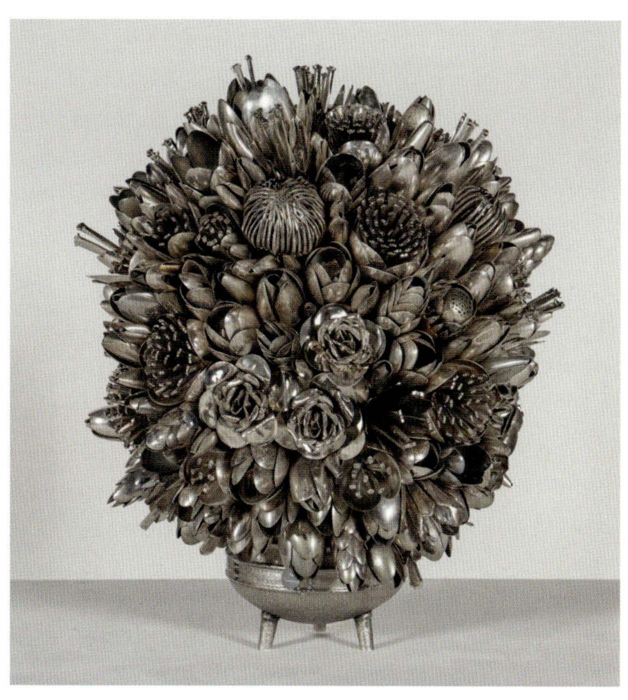

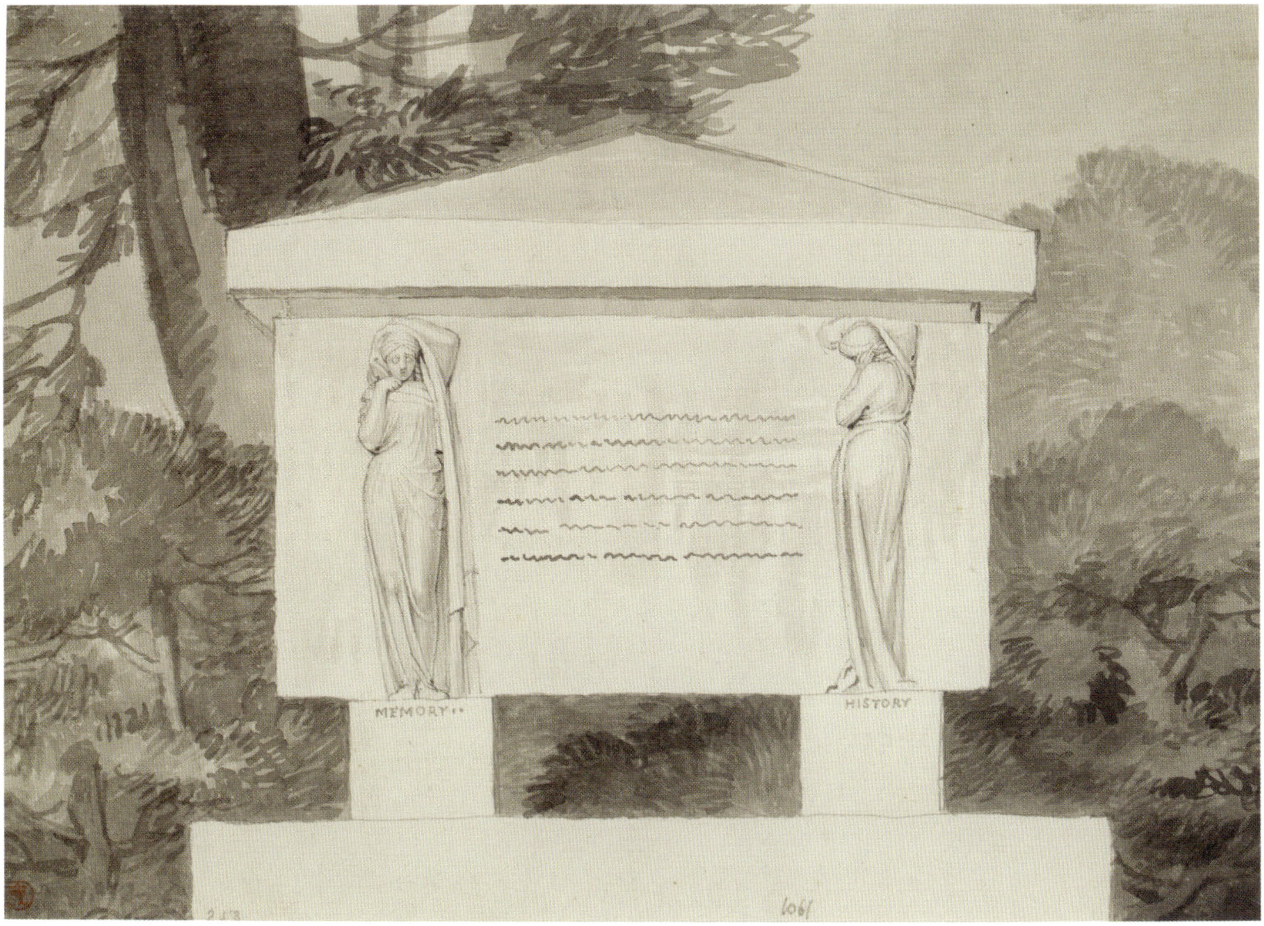

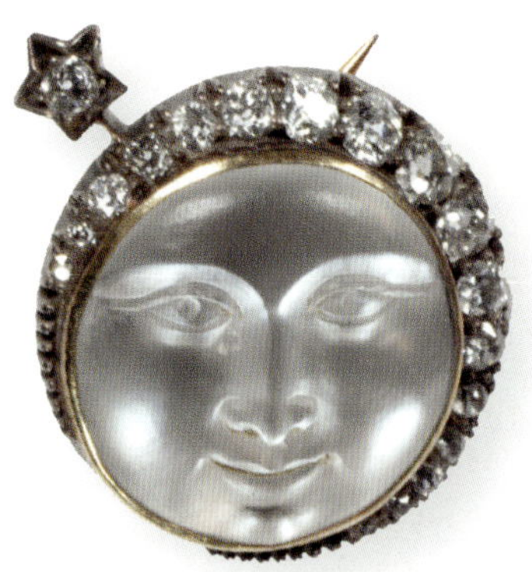

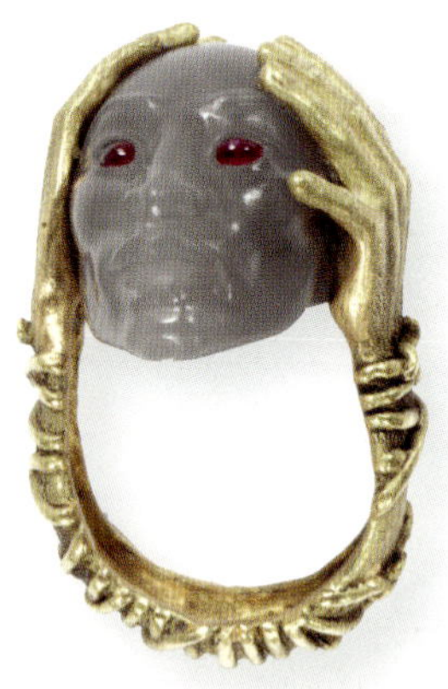

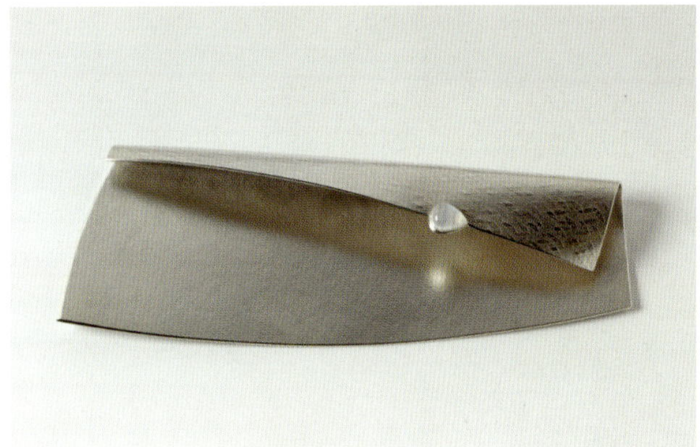

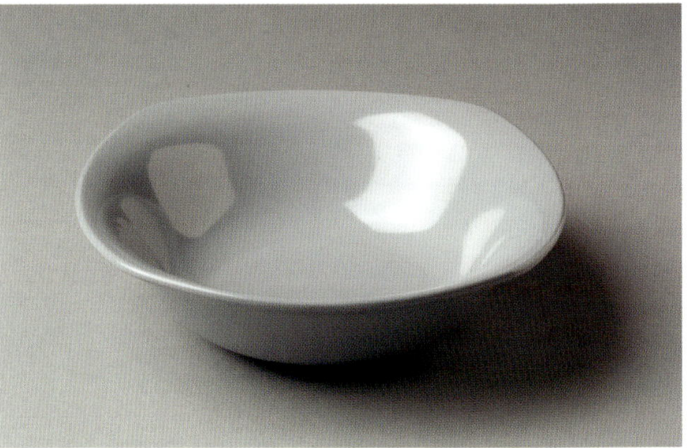

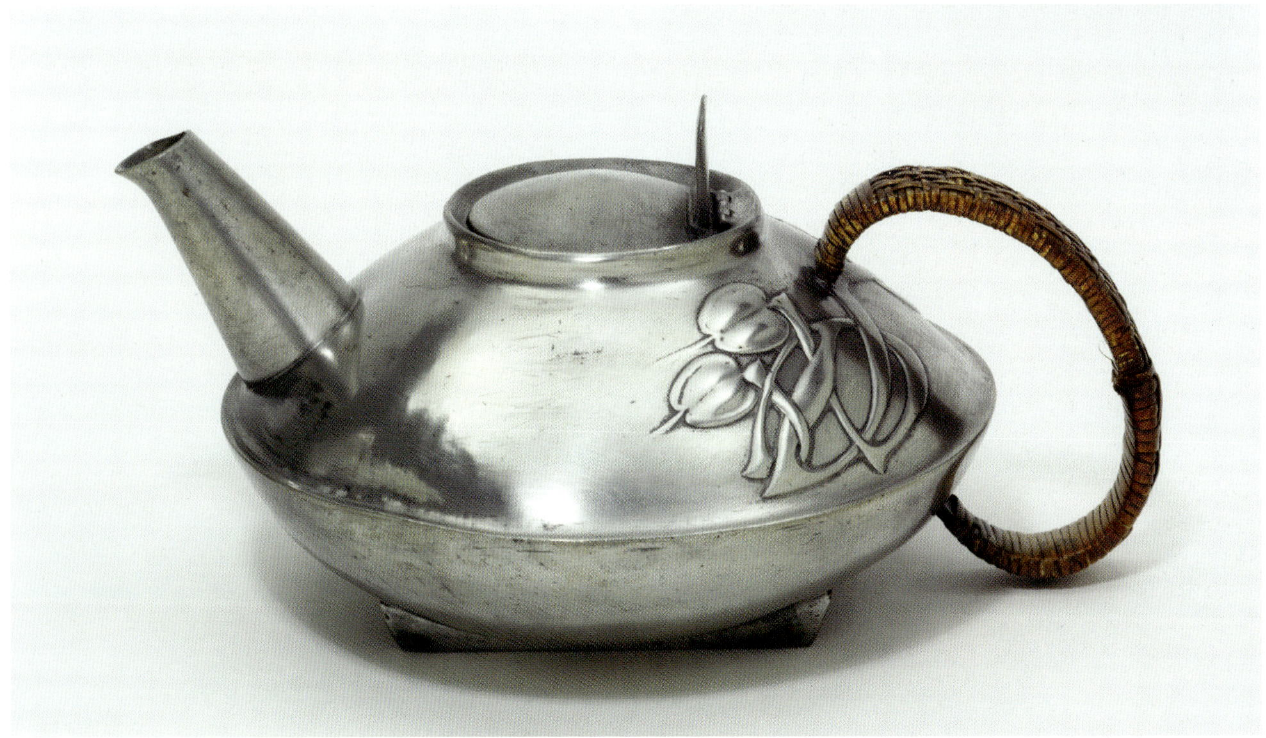

Many grey materials are characterized by a surface sheen. Pewter, a soft greyish-silver metal alloy, was nick-named 'poor man's silver' because when polished it resembles the more valuable metal. This is evident in an 18th-century cast-pewter dove (right), representing the Holy Spirit, and in tablewares, such as Liberty's 'Tudric' range (1903–4; opposite, bottom) designed by Archibald Knox. Gleaming silver is combined with the mineral moonstone in a fish-slice by the jeweller Jacqueline Mina, made in 1999 (opposite, centre left). A folded sheet of silver suggests a wave, and the gem evokes the glint of sun on sea. A polished storm-grey moonstone is the centrepiece of the 'Caliban' ring (1985; opposite, top right) by Kevin Coates, and a silvery-white moonstone adorned with diamonds forms the face of a 'Man in the Moon' brooch (c. 1888; opposite, top left). A surface lustre gives an air of preciousness to everyday materials – see the pearly gloss of a melamine bowl from the 'Midwinter Modern' range (1957; opposite, centre right) designed by A.H. Woodfull and John Vale, and the shiny plastic of the Tekno Robot Puppy (2000; below), designed to mimic metal.

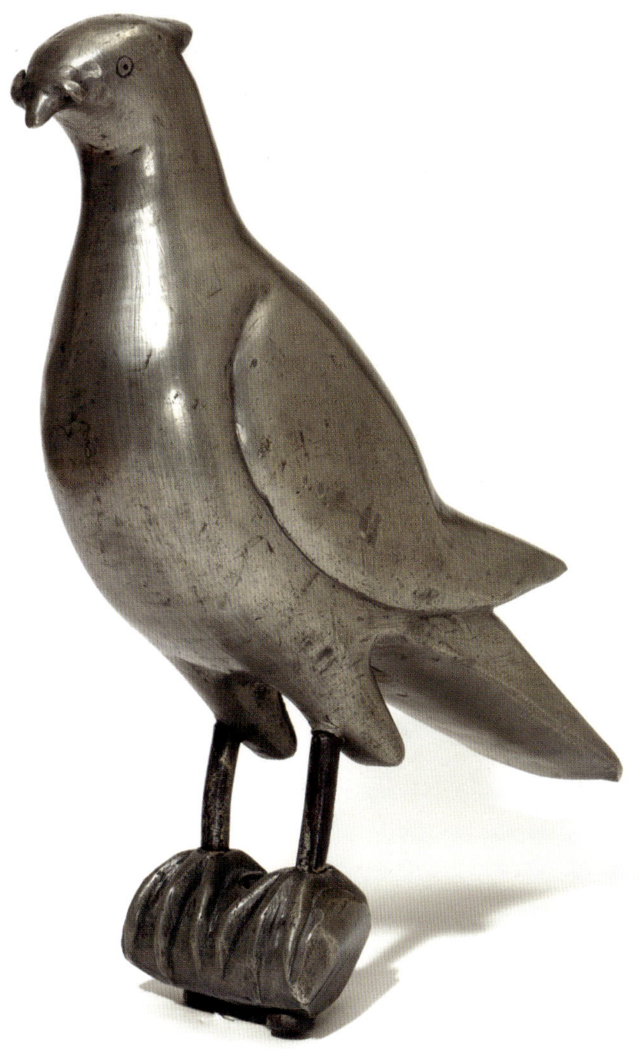

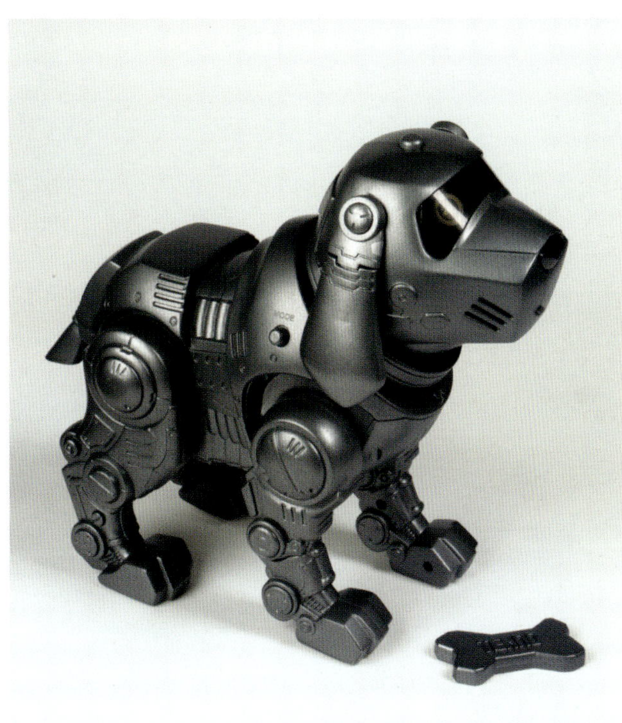

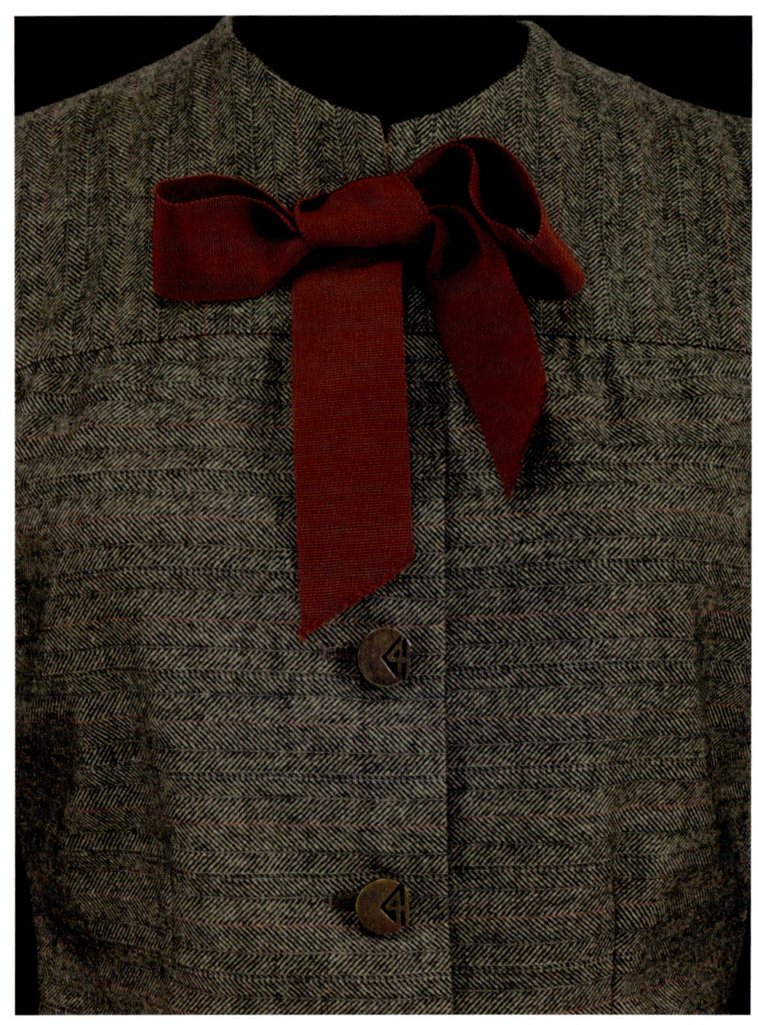

The positive virtues of grey – modest, self-effacing and practical – are embodied in the character and dress of Little Grey Rabbit, the protagonist of Alison Uttley's children's books, first published in 1929 (below right). Aprons, overalls and workwear have often been made of grey materials to disguise dirt or wear. In 1922, Russian artist Alexander Rodchenko designed a work suit; this reproduction was made by Aio Morishita in 2005 (opposite, left). The original, made by Rodchenko's wife, Varvara Stepanova, from a grey wool fabric, was both protective and practical. Grey cloth, hard-wearing and unostentatious, was also popular for the civilian 'Utility' clothing produced in Britain during the Second World War, when fabrics were rationed. A grey herringbone wool skirt suit (1942; left) is typical. Grey also stands for practical utility in industry and in offices. Plain forged steel underlines the elegant minimalism of these scissors made in Germany in 1928 (opposite, right), clearly influenced by Bauhaus design. Likewise, the grey casing of the Olivetti Lexicon 80 typewriter (1942–68; below left), designed by Marcello Nizzoli, emphasizes its unadorned functionality.

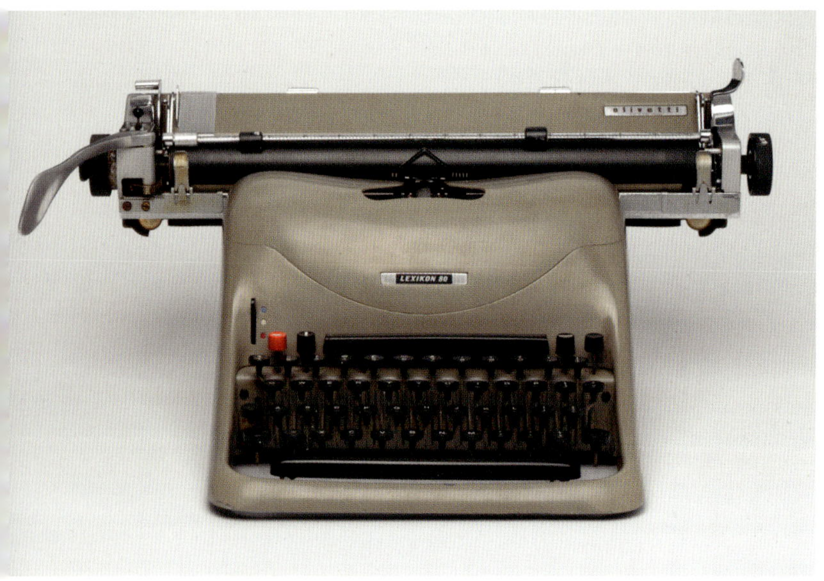

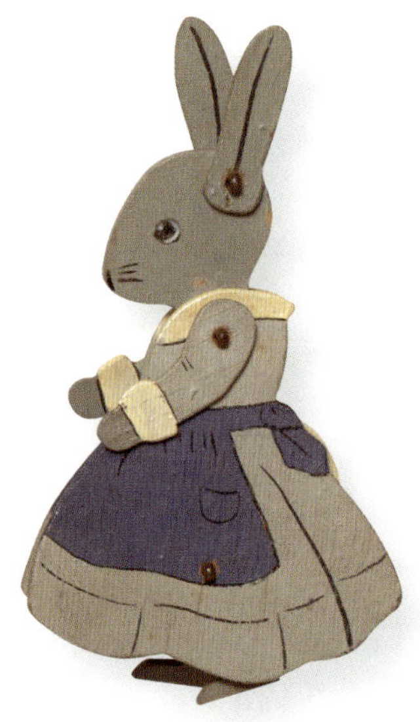

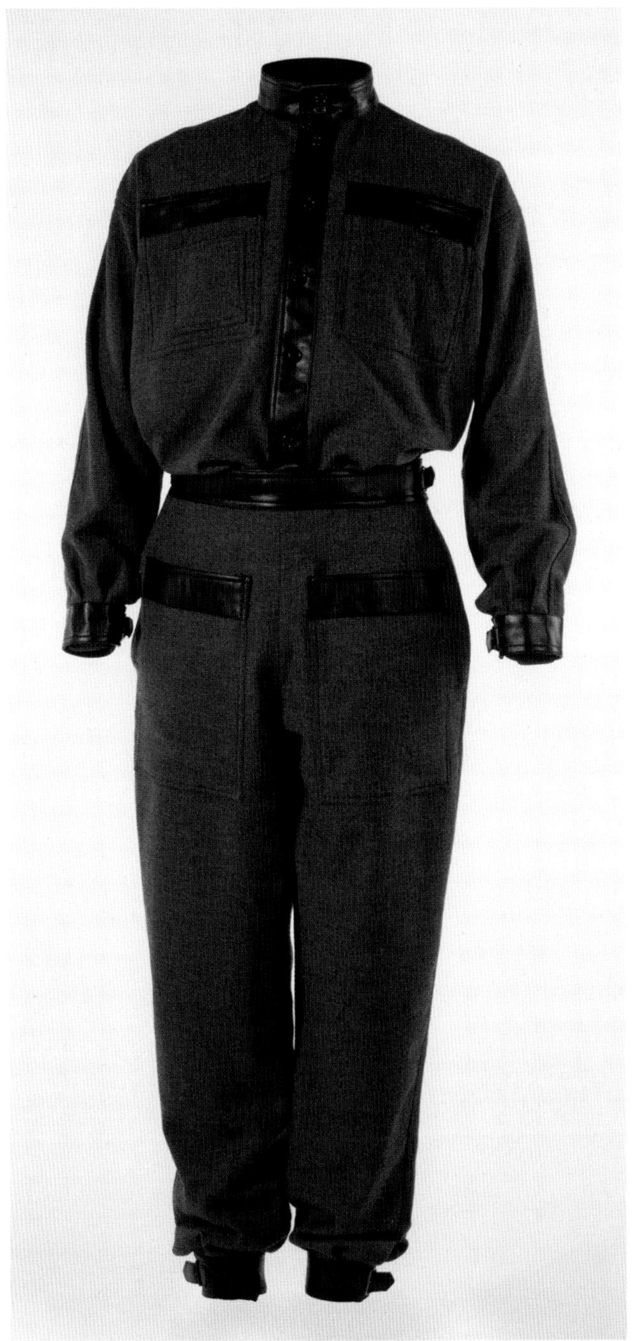

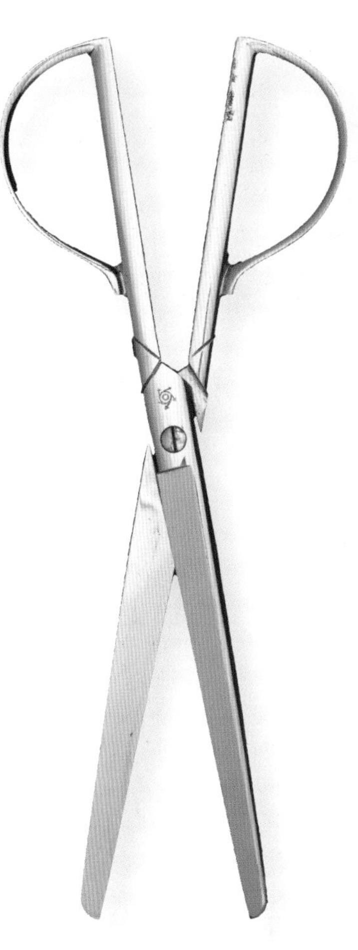

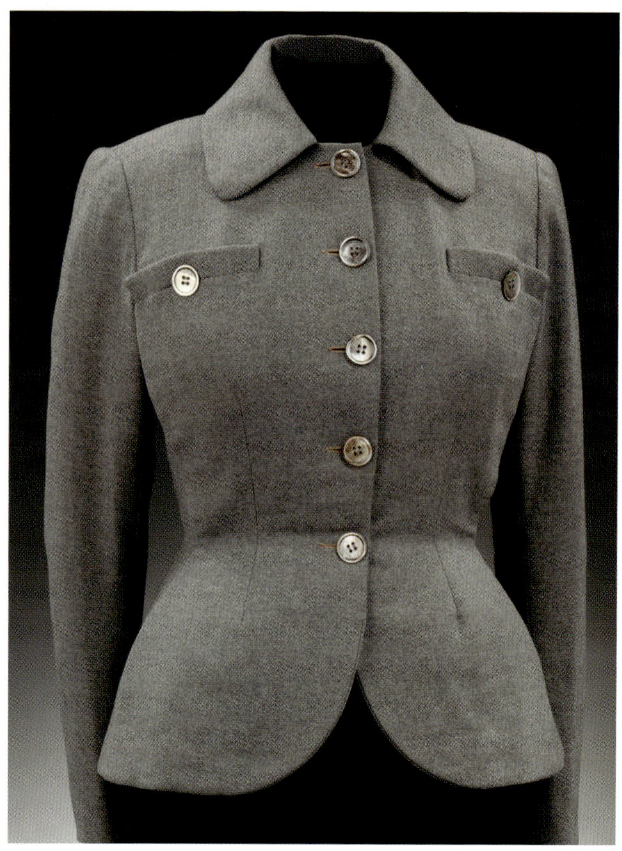

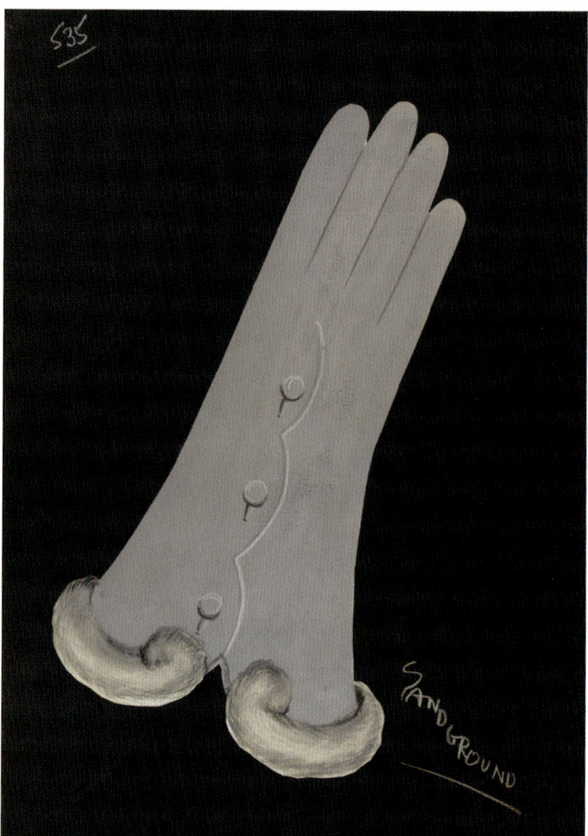

In fashion, grey has long been a hallmark of luxury and elegance, not only for suits and dresses but also for accessories such as gloves, as seen in a 1930s design by leather-goods specialist Ruby Estelle Sandground (above right). In couture, grey became a signature colour for Christian Dior. The severe tailoring of his grey flannel 'New Look' jacket (1947–8; above left) references military uniform, but with an exaggerated, feminine silhouette. In the same period, screen-printed silk dress fabrics, characterized by a restrained palette and designed by artists such as Julian Trevelyan for the British company Ascher Ltd (opposite), were popular with British, French and Italian couturiers. Another luxury material, the dense, soft grey fur of the chinchilla, has been used for coats and stoles as well as for an opulent trim for Manolo Blahnik's embroidered grey felt 'Poirete' mules (1998/9; far right). The richness and value of the animal's fur is suggested by Carl Fabergé's jewelled grey chalcedony model (1910; right).

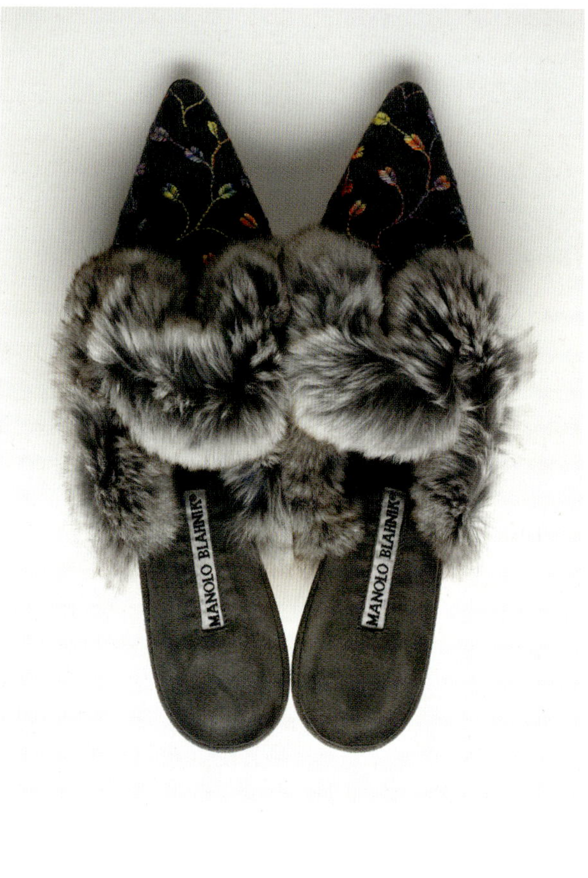

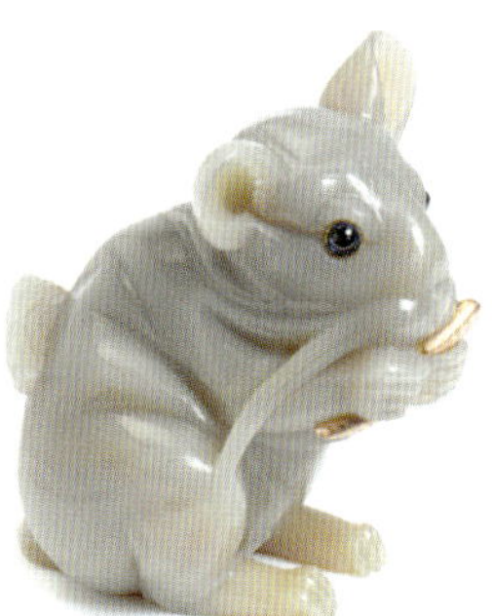

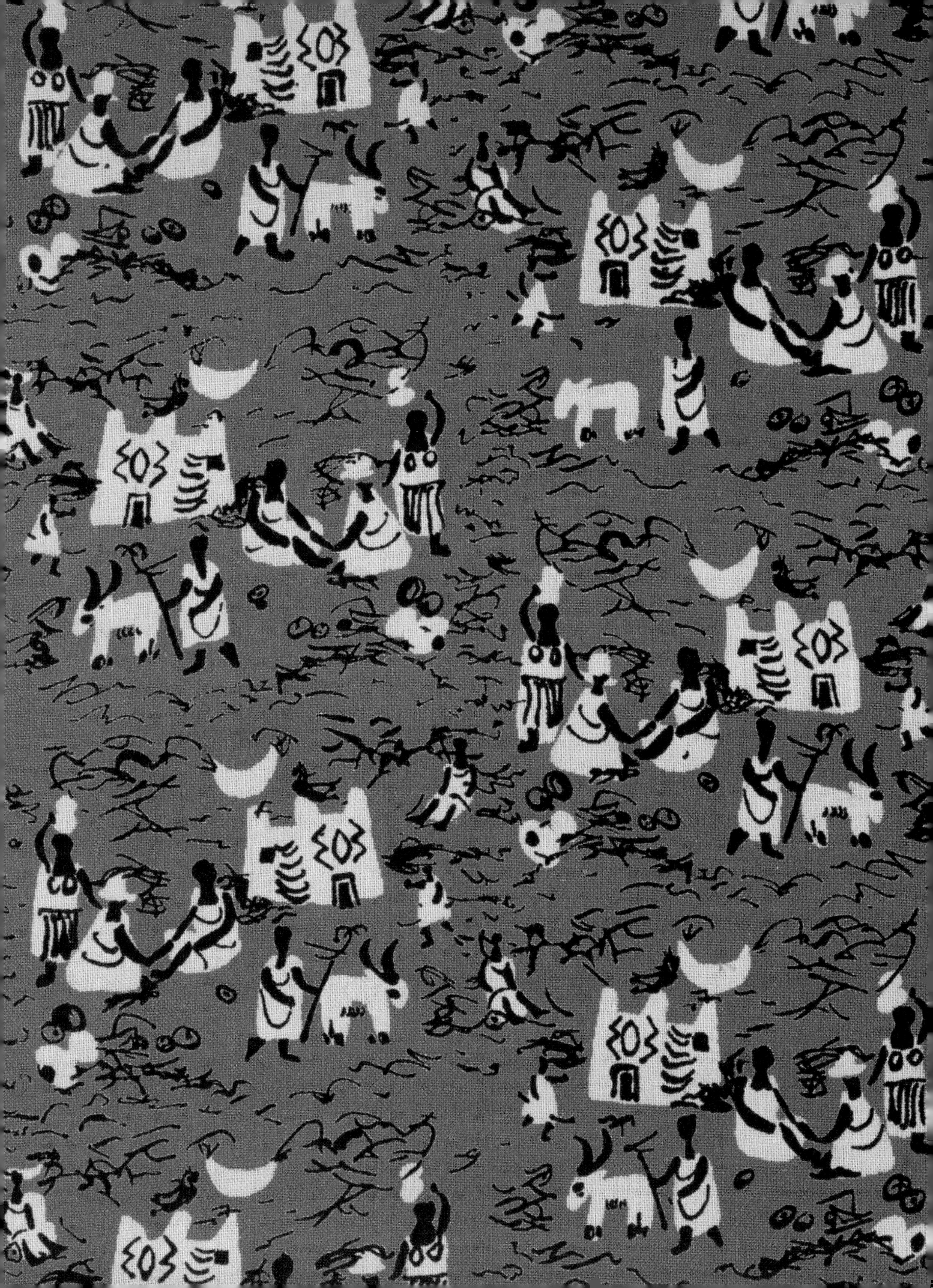

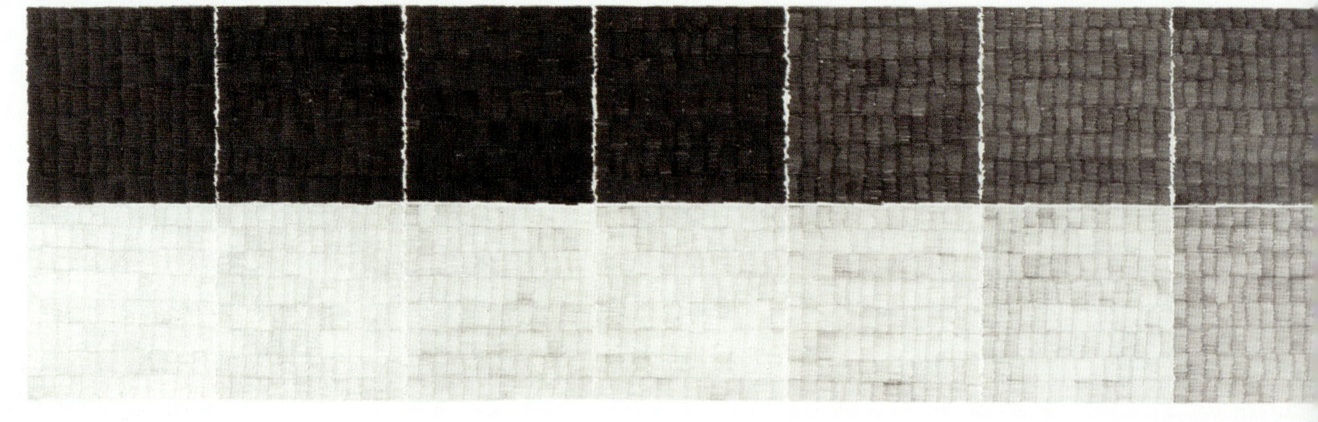

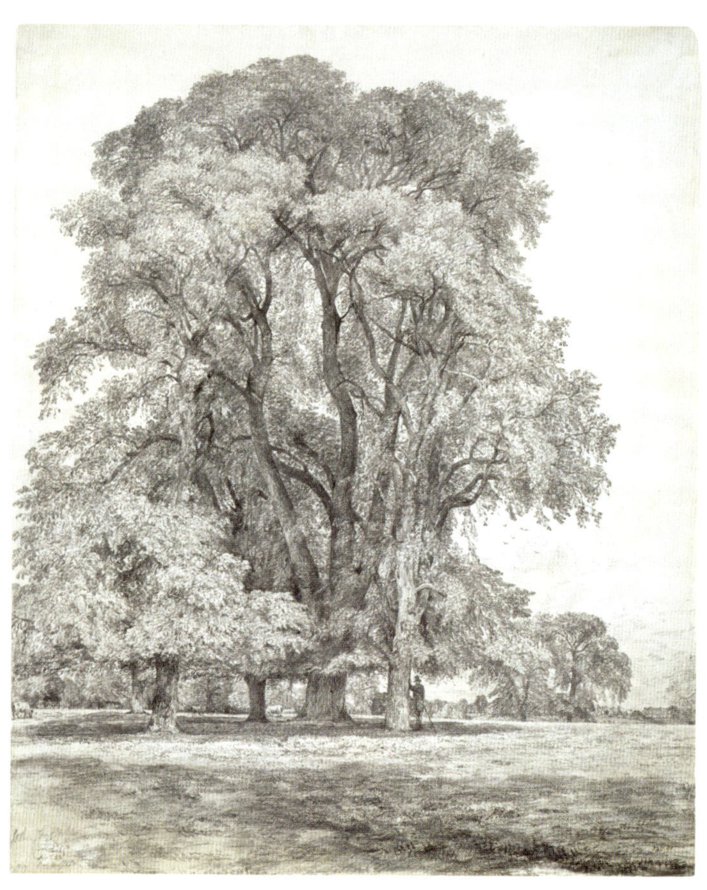

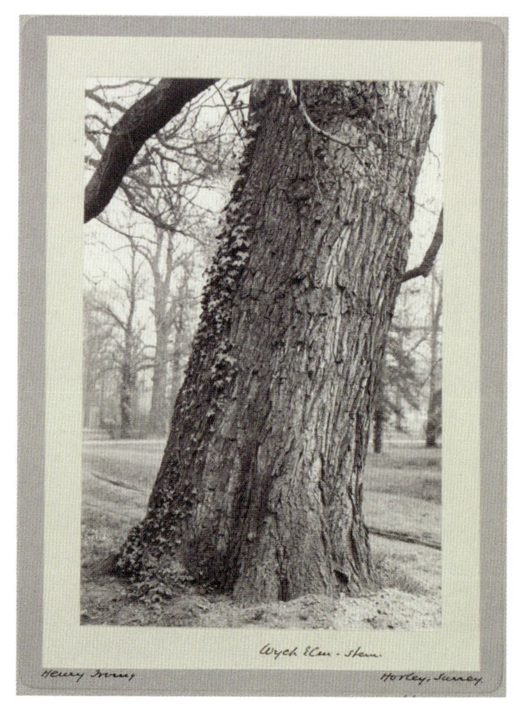

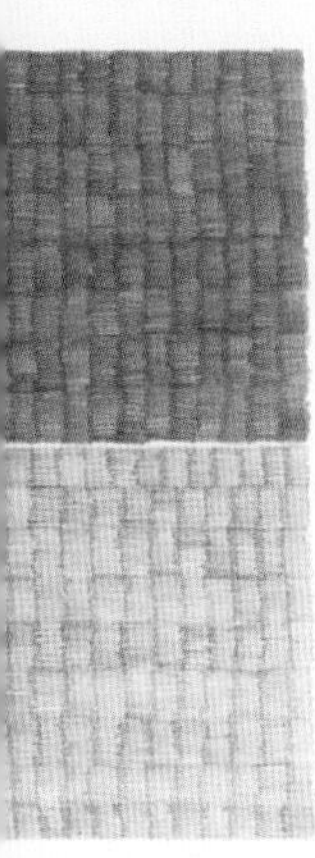

The pencil, a commonplace drawing tool used in western art since the 17th century, can produce a wide range of grey tones and subtle, nuanced marks. John Constable's drawing of elms, dated 1817 (opposite, bottom left), shows how versatile pencil could be in describing delicate masses of foliage, the silvery tones of bark and the darker greys of the trees' shadowed trunks. Similar variations of tone and contrasting textures can be seen in 'plumbago' (graphite on vellum) portraits by David Loggan (*James Butler, 2nd Duke of Ormonde*, 1682; below left) and Lewis Pingo (*Penelope Pingo*, 1770s, below right). Maria Lalić's 1992 drawing *8B-B/H-8H* (left) is a minimalist tabulation of the various pencil grades, from the palest silvery grey of 8H to the dark near-black of 8B. Silvery-grey midtones are also characteristic of platinum prints, a type of photographic process demonstrated to exquisite effect in Henry Irving's early 20th-century records of trees and tree trunks, such as *Wych Elm – Stem* (c. 1900; opposite, bottom right).

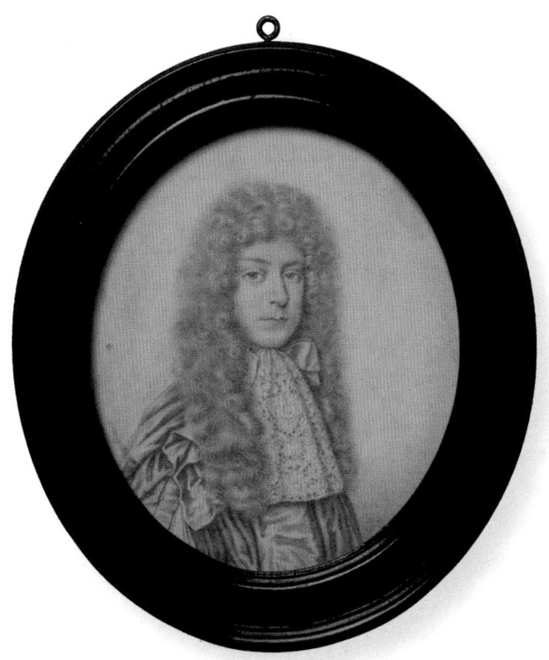

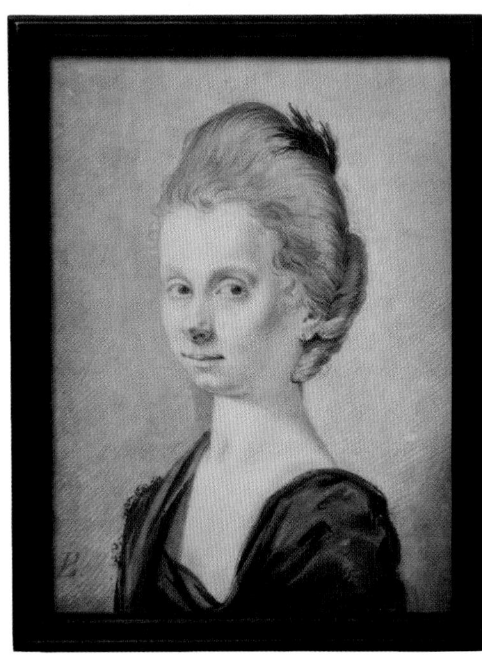

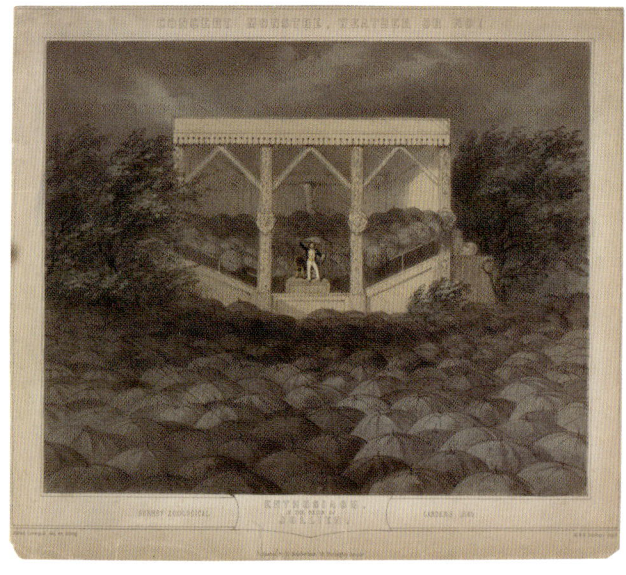

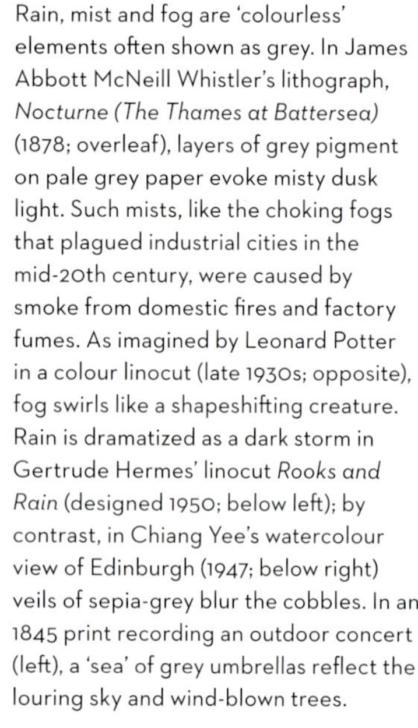

Rain, mist and fog are 'colourless' elements often shown as grey. In James Abbott McNeill Whistler's lithograph, *Nocturne (The Thames at Battersea)* (1878; overleaf), layers of grey pigment on pale grey paper evoke misty dusk light. Such mists, like the choking fogs that plagued industrial cities in the mid-20th century, were caused by smoke from domestic fires and factory fumes. As imagined by Leonard Potter in a colour linocut (late 1930s; opposite), fog swirls like a shapeshifting creature. Rain is dramatized as a dark storm in Gertrude Hermes' linocut *Rooks and Rain* (designed 1950; below left); by contrast, in Chiang Yee's watercolour view of Edinburgh (1947; below right) veils of sepia-grey blur the cobbles. In an 1845 print recording an outdoor concert (left), a 'sea' of grey umbrellas reflect the louring sky and wind-blown trees.

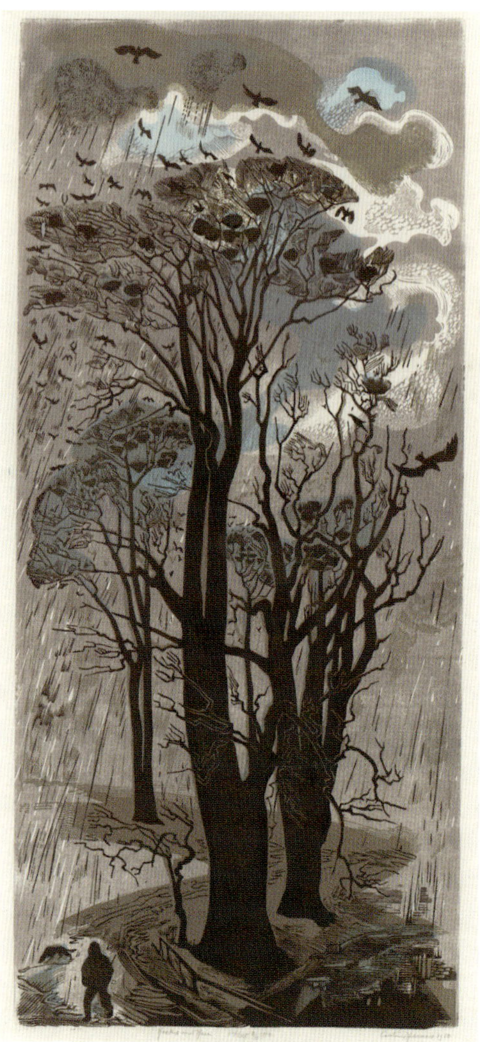

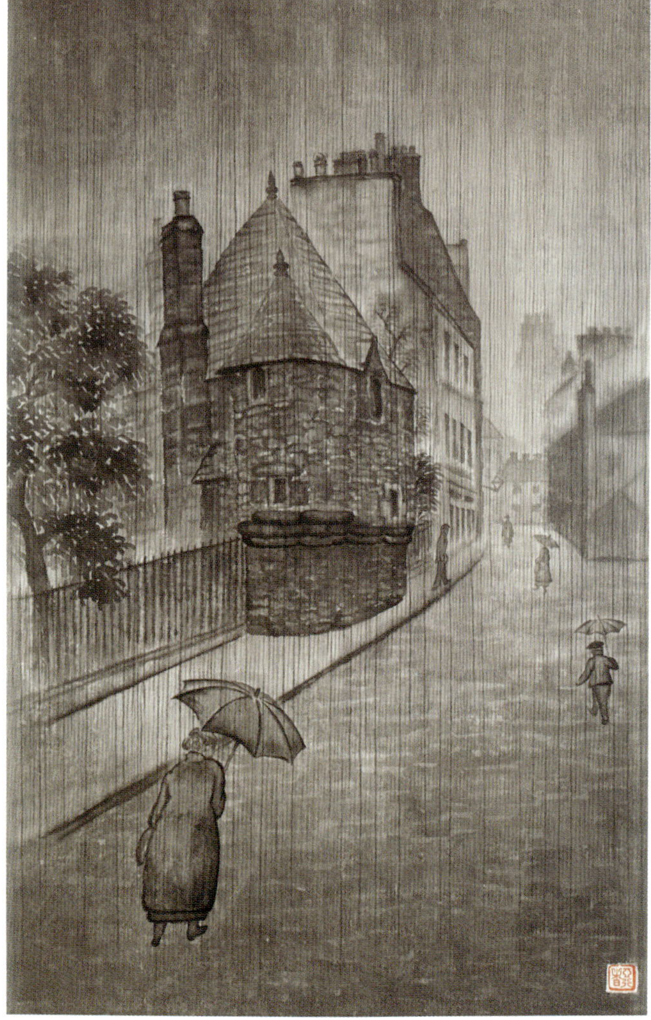

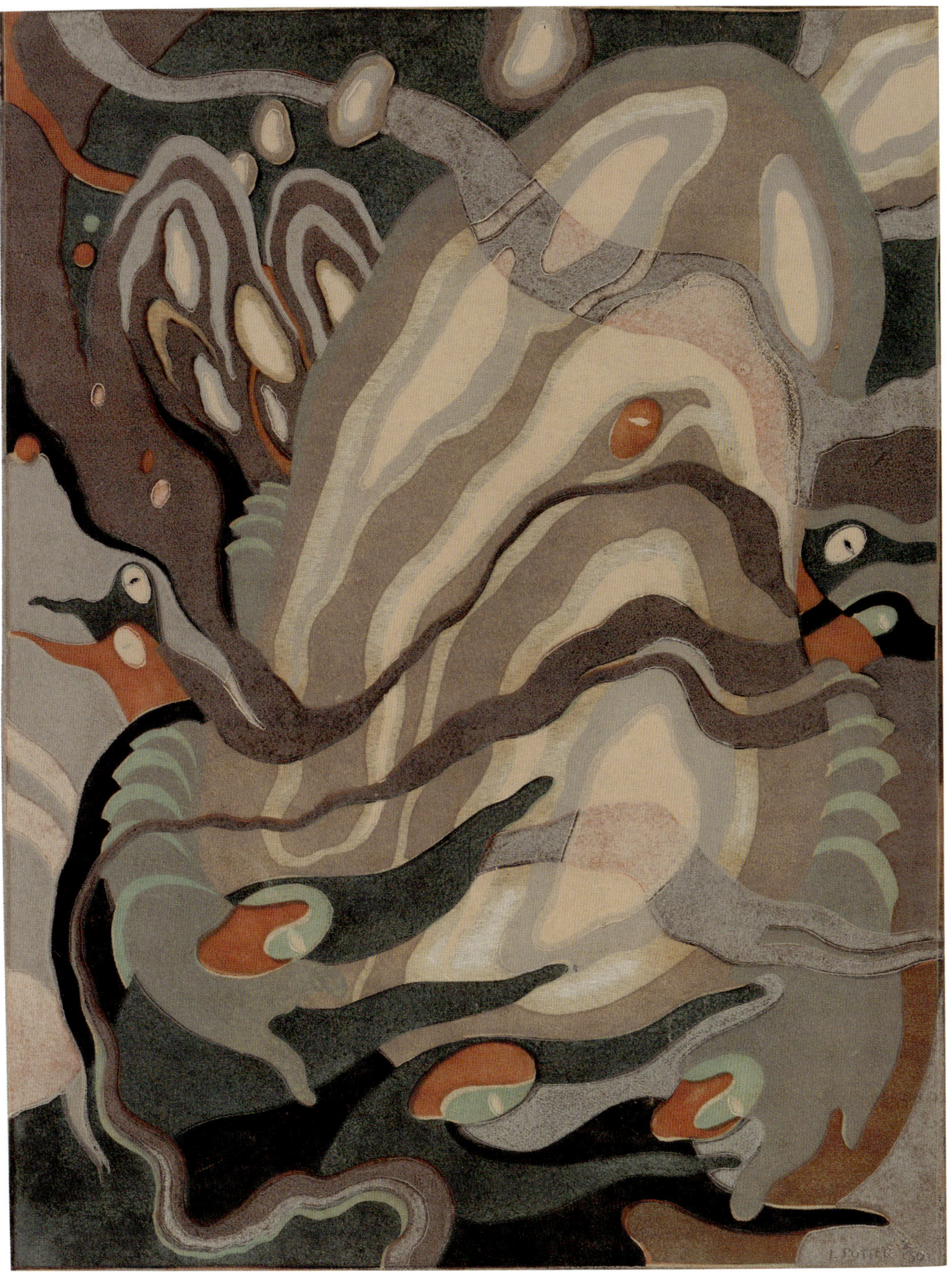

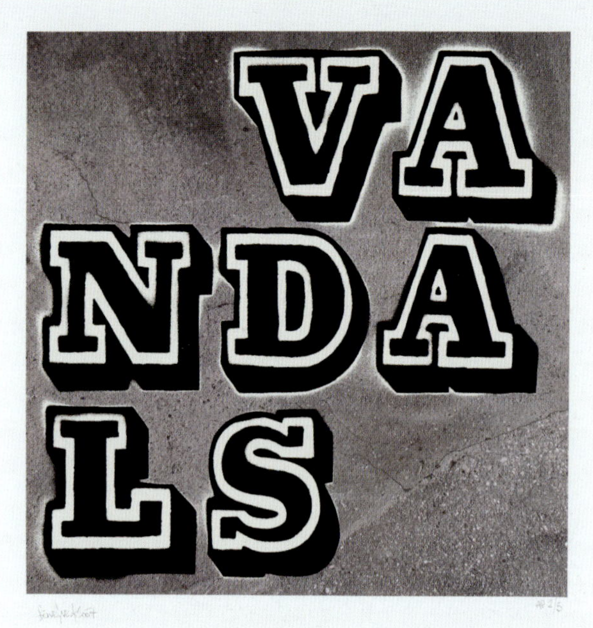

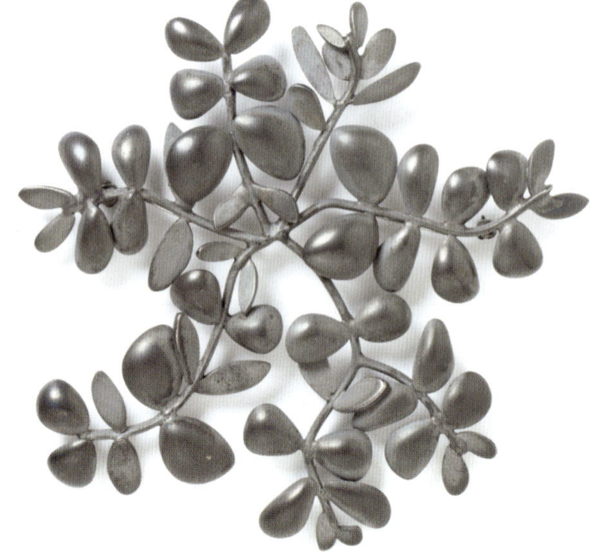

Concrete, cement, stone, tarmac – these are the materials that colour the urban landscape. Street artist Ben Eine, best known for his stencilled and painted lettering on walls and hoardings in east London, used grey to suggest concrete in his screenprint *Vandals* (2007; above left). It is concrete, too, that is the key element in much modern architecture, as pictured in a mixed-media print (2011; right) by Claire Hynds, one of several in which she explores the iconography of new towns and utopian urban spaces. In his suite of screenprints, *A Walk to the Studio* (1976–7; opposite), Tom Phillips recorded commonplace things seen en route, such as the worn and weathered stopcock box lids that punctuate the pavements with skull-like motifs. In city streets even the wayside weeds are grey with dust, as implied by Jan Yager's use of dark grey silver for her 'American Sidewalk' brooch (1999; above right), based on the tenacious drought-tolerant plant purslane.

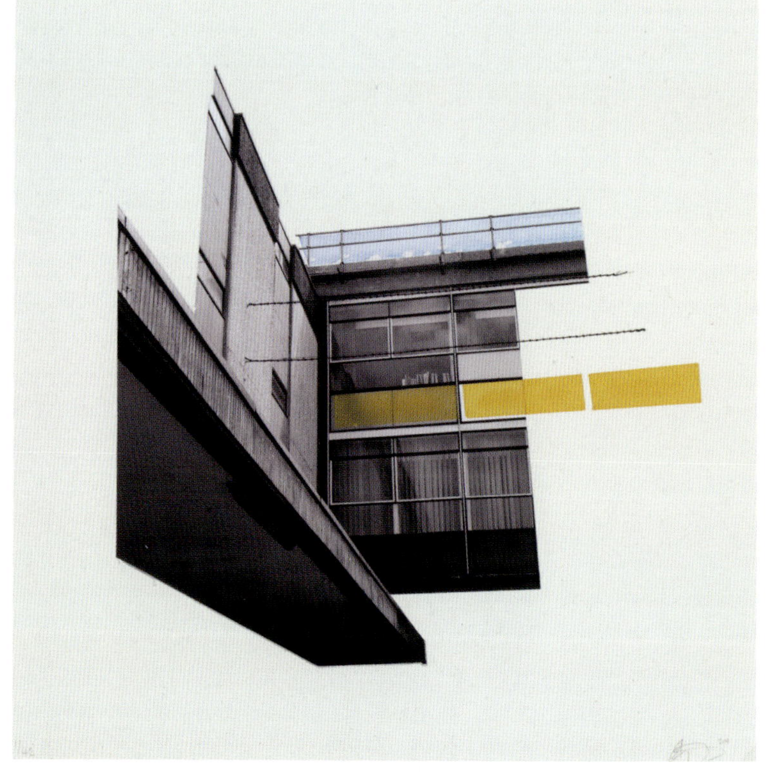

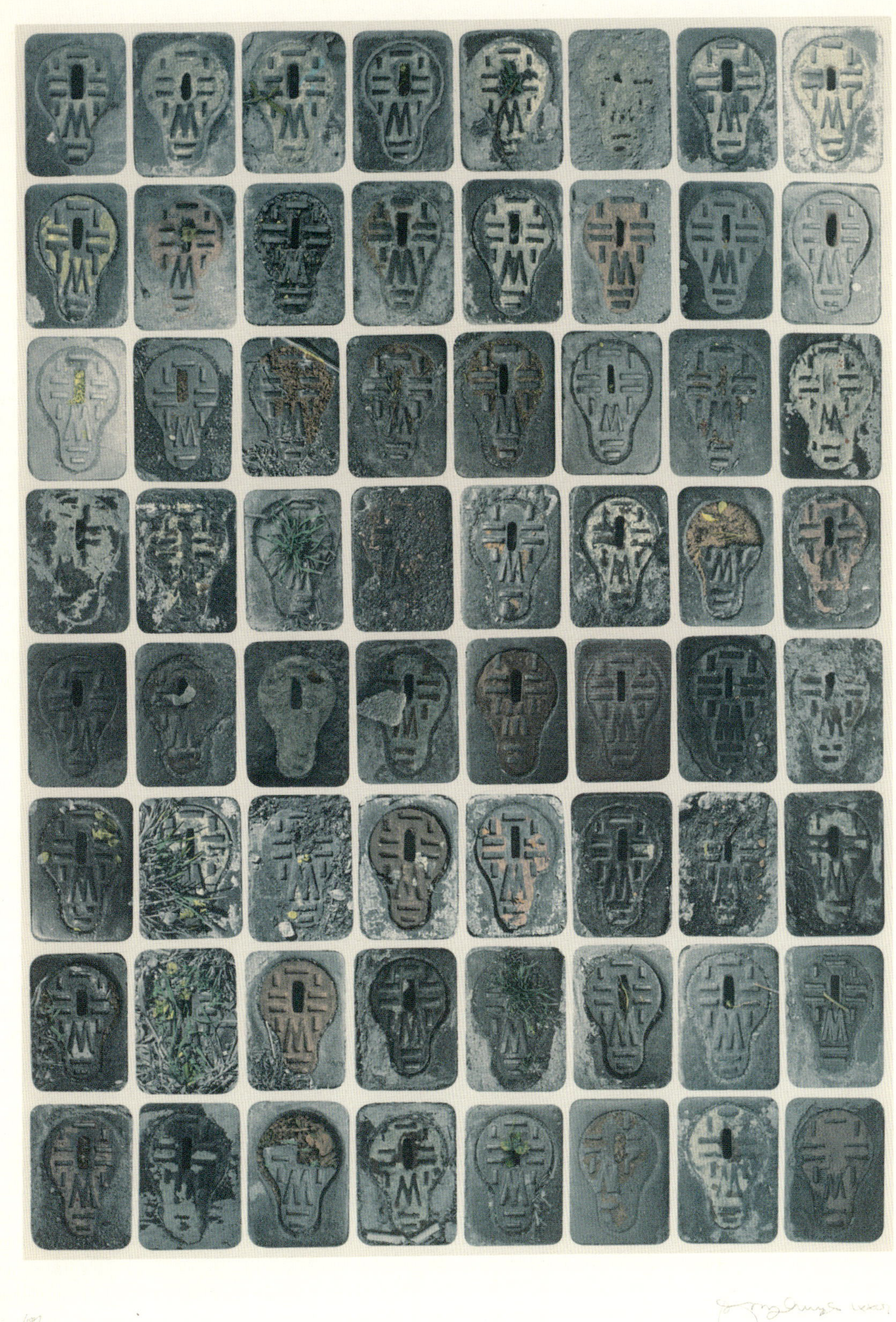

C9 M0 Y89 K0 | C14 M0 Y60 K0 | C2 M8 Y88 K0 | C19 M15 Y95 K0 | C3 M0 Y70 K0

C6 M0 Y71 K0 | C1 M13 Y79 K0 | C0 M28 Y84 K0 | C3 M7 Y90 K0 | C7 M31 Y94 K0

C21 M8 Y100 K9 | C12 M11 Y89 K0 | C5 M0 Y51 K0 | C0 M25 Y85 K0 | C7 M11 Y91 K0

C13 M0 Y57 K0 | C5 M0 Y58 K7 | C7 M0 Y72 K0 | C12 M7 Y92 K0 | C5 M0 Y68 K0

C4 M0 Y86 K0 | C5 M10 Y67 K0 | C8 M0 Y87 K16 | C0 M24 Y88 K0 | C10 M0 Y94 K0

C2 M2 Y60 K0 | C4 M11 Y92 K0 | C10 M0 Y95 K0 | C19 M1 Y93 K0 | C0 M20 Y88 K0

C9 M0 Y93 K0 | C11 M16 Y84 K1 | C3 M0 Y70 K0 | C7 M0 Y71 K15 | C6 M0 Y91 K24

C11 M17 Y100 K0 | C7 M0 Y55 K0 | C14 M0 Y90 K0 | C0 M16 Y90 K0 | C7 M28 Y93 K0

C13 M0 Y73 K0 | C14 M0 Y87 K0 | C10 M0 Y70 K20 | C9 M5 Y91 K0 | C11 M1 Y91 K0

C4 M0 Y44 K0 | C8 M0 Y78 K0 | C8 M22 Y73 K20 | C10 M0 Y36 K0 | C13 M17 Y79 K0

C8 M0 Y69 K0 | C9 M16 Y55 K0 | C13 M9 Y67 K0 | C9 M0 Y84 K0 | C12 M0 Y67 K0

YELLOW

In March 1888, when Vincent van Gogh first arrived in southern France, he wrote to his brother Theo: 'The sun dazzles me and goes to my head, a sun, a light that I can only call yellow, sulphur yellow, lemon yellow, golden yellow. How lovely yellow is!'. Deriving its pigment from clay, yellow is thought to have been one of the first colours used in prehistoric cave art, over 17,300 years ago. Yellow has embodied many emotions and ideas, falling in and out of favour throughout history depending on its shade, its application and its connotations. At times the colour of the natural world, of the sun gods and Imperial China, symbolizing warmth, wealth and status, yellow gained a new visual vocabulary in the modern age, as a transgressive, attention-grabbing colour.

Language has not always been kind to this colour. To yellow is to age and wither. In English slang, 'yellow-bellied' refers to a coward, and 'yellow journalism' describes fake news. In French and Italian, a yellow person ('jaune', 'giallo') is deemed a traitor, while in German 'gelbe laune sein' means to be jealous. Jaundice, yellow fever and bubonic plague are all linked to the colour, and some sources of yellow pigments, such as cadmium, lead and chrome, can be toxic. But when yellow turns to gold, it becomes positive and valuable: we talk of a golden age, a golden handshake, a golden child.

Yellow clothing is burdened by its past association with dishonesty, jealousy and discrimination. Xanthophobia, fear of the colour yellow, is evident in numerous Christian depictions of Judas Iscariot, the yellow-clad disciple who betrayed Christ, while iconography of the Middle Ages often portrayed executioners dressed in yellow.

In Nazi-occupied parts of Europe, persecuted Jewish people were forced to wear the yellow Star of David on their clothing as a demeaning marker of their religious identity.

But wearing yellow can also represent hope. During the First World War, women in Canada would wear a yellow ribbon as they waited for loved ones to return from battle. In 1979, at the beginning of the Iran hostage crisis, many Americans revived the tradition to support those held in Tehran. Since 2004, Singapore's Yellow Ribbon Project has promoted the rehabilitation of ex-convicts and encouraged integration and re-employment.

A link between yellow and the sun was established early. For the Greeks and Romans, Apollo, the sun god, was typically depicted as a young man of radiant beauty (pp. 86–7) and considered a beneficial healer, dispelling darkness and bringing harmony to the mortal world. Sunshine is often associated with good health; it is a positive source of vitamin D, and the slightest ray of sunlight can uplift the gloomiest of days. Because of its affiliation with the sun, yellow has become a symbol of warmth, positivity and joy. The sixteenth-century King Henry VIII of England certainly agreed, and famously wore yellow each of the six times he married, demanding that his new queen and all the court wear it too.

Yellow's happy hue is found in children's toys and cartoons, notably Pokémon's Pikachu and Winnie-the-Pooh. In 1963, Harvey Ross Ball was commissioned to create an image to raise the morale of employees at the State Mutual Life Company in Massachusetts, and came up with the beaming yellow smiley face symbol that would become a widespread emblem of radiant joy. Yellow's association with happiness has led to its frequent use by brands that want to be seen as upbeat and cheerful. Fashion designer Mary Quant tapped into this dynamic trend with her playful plastic 'Quant Afoot' boots from 1967 (p. 78), in a brilliant chrome yellow.

Yellow has also, conversely, been a marker of transgression and sexuality. *The Yellow Book* was a periodical published in London from 1894 to 1897 (p. 76), containing work from a wide range of avant-garde literary and artistic genres. It had an enormous impact on late-Victorian culture in its short life, and even lent its name to the 'Yellow Nineties'. The 1890s coincided with the peak of the Aesthetic Movement, which saw sunflowers and yellow chrysanthemums bloom across paintings, wallpapers and textiles. *The Yellow Book*, meanwhile, took its bright cover from a tradition of nineteenth-century French erotic novels. Such books were wrapped in yellow paper, both hiding and signalling their illicit contents. In April 1895, at the height of his fame, Oscar Wilde was arrested with a yellow book under his arm. He was later found guilty of gross indecency and jailed for two years. After Wilde's arrest, a mob stormed the Bodley Head publishing house where *The Yellow Book* was printed, believing them responsible for the book in Wilde's possession. He was in fact holding a copy of French writer Pierre Louÿs's yellow-bound, particularly racy novel *Aphrodite* (1896).

This was not the first time yellow had been associated with sensuality. In nineteenth-century Europe, sex workers were required to wear a visible yellow sign, and in modern China, adult films are still referred to as 'yellow movies'. Blonde hair has been perceived as an indicator of both beauty and provocation. In Greek and Roman mythology, blonde hair was highly prized – as is apparent in Sandro Botticelli's painting *The Birth of Venus* (1485–6). The goddess of love stands in a colossal scallop shell, her nude body framed by billowing, blonde hair, which Botticelli accentuated by weaving gold leaf through it. Considered the original blonde bombshell, Venus has since been referenced in music, poems, theatre and souvenirs worldwide. The James Bond film *Dr. No* (1962) pays homage to the painting with an iconic scene in which the blonde, bikini-clad Honey Ryder emerges from the sea holding two seashells. Blonde women have often been cast in the role of the seductress. The Bible's first female sinner, Eve, is widely depicted with golden locks coiling around her nude body, echoing the serpent that persuaded her to eat forbidden fruit. When 'Miss Clairol' hair dyes introduced home hair-colouring kits in 1956, they used enticing slogans such as 'Is it true blondes have more fun?' and 'If I have only one life, let me live it as a blonde.'

The high visibility of this bold, attention-seeking colour has long made it a useful feature of designs that demand to be seen. Yellow is used for warning signs and emergency vehicles. During the Second World War, the British Royal Air Force introduced a thick yellow outline to its tricolour roundel of blue, white and red to help it stand out against the dark paint of frontline aircraft. On the football field, a yellow card alerts the player to the threat of a disqualifying red card, while the yellow jersey donned by the winner of the Tour de France, introduced in 1919, highlights the leader among the pack of cyclists. The 1930s ushered in huge technical advancements in colour photography, and fashion photographer Horst P. Horst used dazzling colours like yellow as a new, eye-catching way to promote stylish products (p. 81) after the Depression years in the United States.

In the 1980s, attention was refocused on yellow by rave culture. Electrifying, intense colours injected excitement and energy into the nightclubs that bathed revellers in fluorescent lights. 'Acid' came to reference the house music played at clubs such as London's Shoom and Manchester's Haçienda, as well as the drugs that fuelled the scene. In 1988, Shoom subverted the joyful yellow smiley face for their flyers. The beaming icon became ravers' informal mascot, appearing on t-shirts and badges everywhere, a symbol of unbridled euphoria and hedonism – but after a series of ecstasy-related deaths in the late 1980s, the smiley also became a mark of danger and excess.

Yellow has long been a colour of devotion and worship. In India, during the springtime Vaisakhi festival, Sikh worshippers often wear yellow to reflect the flowers growing in the fields (p. 82). But it is yellow's metallic incarnation as gold that is most often used to inspire awe among worshippers. The medieval Christian church, with its glinting gold altarpieces, directed the gaze towards the figure of Christ. Russian Orthodox icon paintings such as *The Virgin of Vladimir* (c. 1131) show glowing halos against backgrounds made entirely of gold leaf. In Bangkok, a forty-six-metre-long golden reclining Buddha lies at the entrance of the Wat Pho temple, attracting thousands of worshippers and tourists each year.

Gold's affiliation with splendour and richness has made it the clear choice for valuable, enduring objects. For centuries, glittering trinkets made from the precious metal have been cherished and coveted. Archaeologist Howard Carter, who uncovered the tomb of Tutankhamun in Egypt, summarized its awesome effect in his diary on 26 November 1922: 'details of the room within emerged slowly from the mist, strange animals, statues, and gold – everywhere the glint of gold … I was struck dumb with amazement, and when Lord Carnarvon, unable to stand the suspense any longer, inquired anxiously, "Can you see anything?" it was all I could do to get out the words, "Yes, wonderful things."' Gold's allure lies in part in its rarity and expense, qualities that have caused it to be associated with greed and hoarding. The cautionary tale of King Midas warns of the dangers of avarice; his foolish wish to turn anything he touches into gold proves fatal when contact changes food and liquid into inedible metal.

Gold and yellow are frequently associated with natural wealth and abundance. They are the colours of honey, grain, lemons, wheat and oil, and enjoy positive connections with light, warmth, fertility and prosperity. John Constable painted idyllic images of lush golden landscapes; *The Wheat Field* (1816) depicts workers gathering abundant sheaths of wheat, with vast fields of golden grain and green rolling hills promising successful future harvests. Drawing on its unique range of natural resources, an astonishing array of yellows for textiles and paints has been developed in India. The term 'Indian Yellow' has various origins, and is thought to be an extract prepared from the urine of cows fed exclusively on mango leaves and water, known as *gaugoli*. It was used extensively in Indian paintings from the late sixteenth to the nineteenth century,

and came in the form of dried brown lumps with deep yellow on the inside. Brilliant yellow textile dyes have also been created with natural materials such as pomegranate rind, saffron flower and the rich-toned turmeric root.

In China, yellow was the imperial colour. In the Qing dynasty (1644–1911), the emperor and members of the imperial family wore garments of different shades of yellow, which were assigned according to their individual rank. Influenced by Chinese art and design, yellow also enjoyed a period of popularity in Europe. This was particularly true in eighteenth-century dress, where *chinoiserie* motifs of wildflowers, feathers and bamboo were adopted by European artisans to adorn sumptuous yellow garments (p. 70). Western designers Balenciaga, Dior and Christopher Kane all included dazzling yellows in their Spring 2018 collections, and off the runway, in what fashion magazines dubbed 'Gen Z yellow', brilliant bucket hats and vivid platform sneakers began to appear on high streets everywhere.

The colour has also been used to denote contemporary civic or social status, as seen in 2019 when yellow resurged onto the political palette and into the streets. The French 'Gilets Jaunes' protest movement, sparked by rising fuel prices and high living costs, expanded to include wider issues of socio-economic inequality. The yellow safety jacket, chosen as a symbol of unity because of its visibility, ubiquity and association with working-class industries, came to be seen as a beacon of rebellion and solidarity with the protestors.

Yellow is constantly evolving and adaptable – its role in design, politics, dress, religion and art remains in a paradigm of contradictions; fluid yet solid, glorious and dangerous, accessible but unattainable. This enigmatic colour of gods, emperors, traitors and activists continues to intrigue, provoke, delight and inspire, carrying the weight of its past, with a hopeful glance towards the future.

During the Qing dynasty in China, yellow was reserved for the residents of the imperial household. Every year, the Emperor would perform rituals at the Altars of the Sun, the Moon, Heaven and Earth. Porcelain vessels of different colours such as this one (below left) were placed at the different altars, yellow being the symbolic colour for earth. The Chinese emperor wore opulent court robes of yellow silk; the 19th-century example opposite is richly embroidered with five-claw dragons.

By the 18th century, when trading relationships had been established between China and Europe, the European elite had come to see yellow as indicative of the country's prosperity, and it began to appear more prominently in western clothing and decoration. This satin man's waistcoat from the 1730s (right) imitates the motifs of Chinese court dress with lavish leaves and exotic wildflowers. Feather fans were popular accessories for men and women in China. This example (below right), owned by fashionable expatriate Alexandra Comnÿne-Everts, who travelled in China in the 1910s and 1920s, maintains its regal roots with its bright yellow shade.

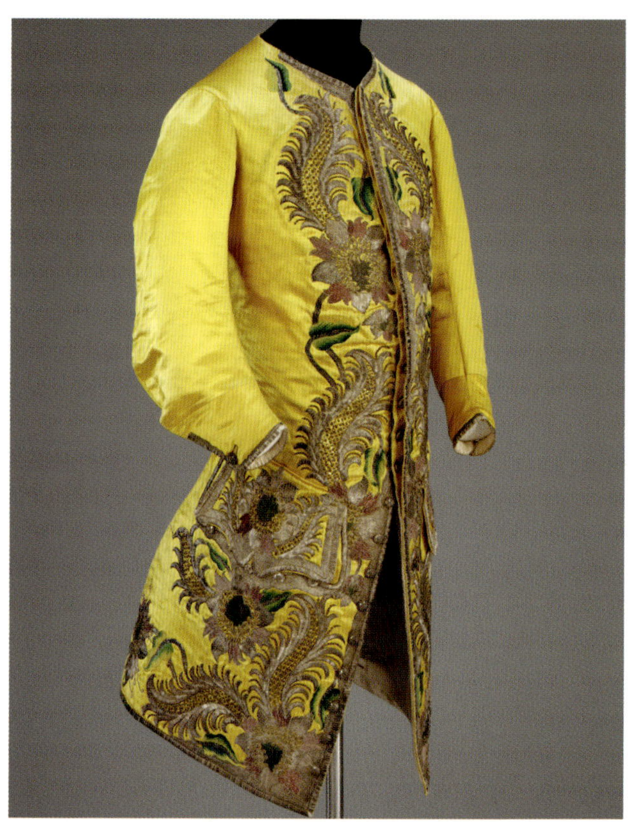

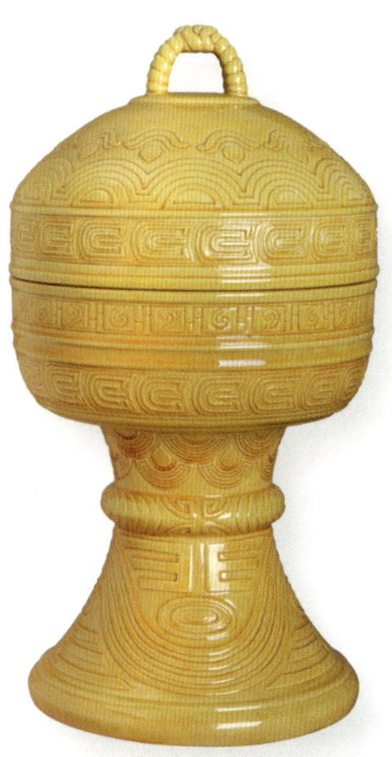

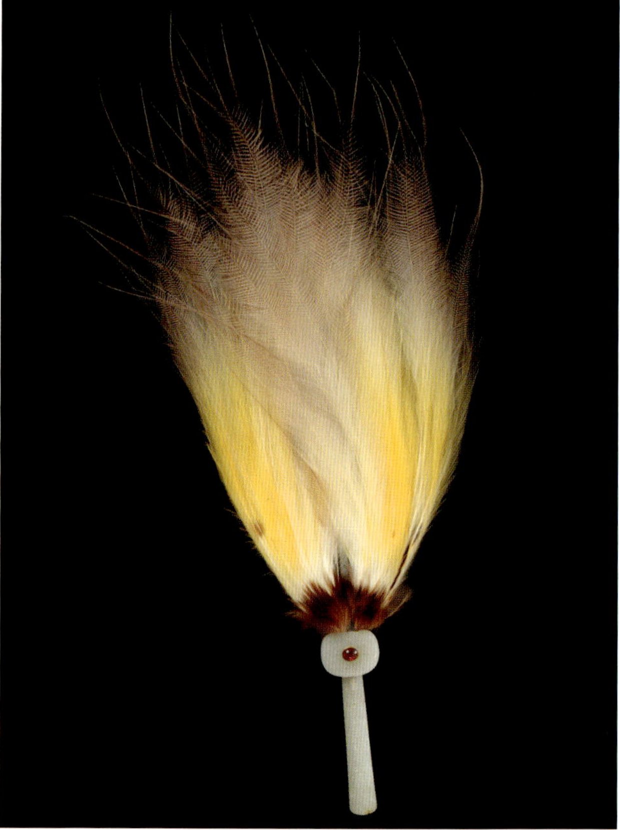

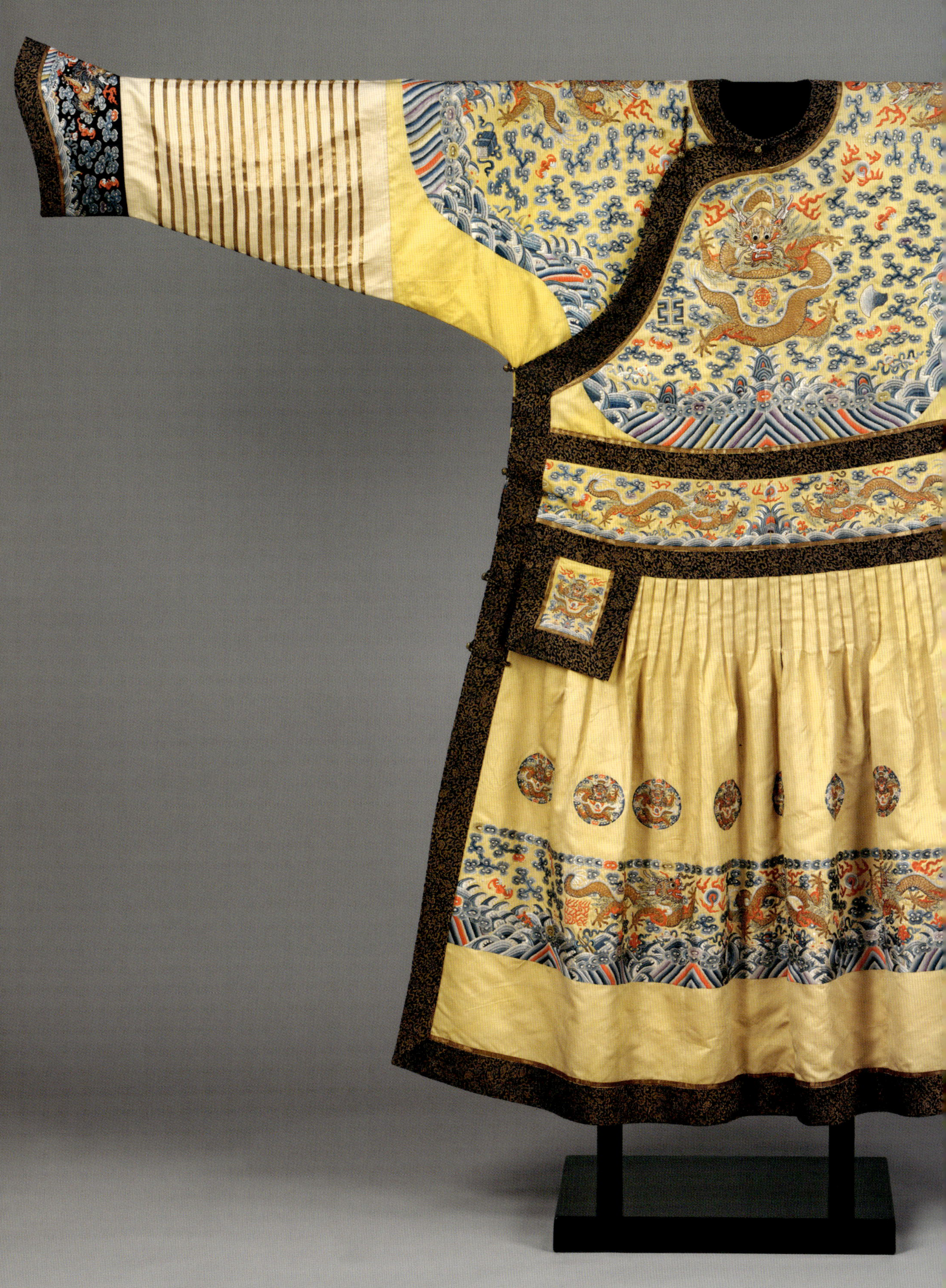

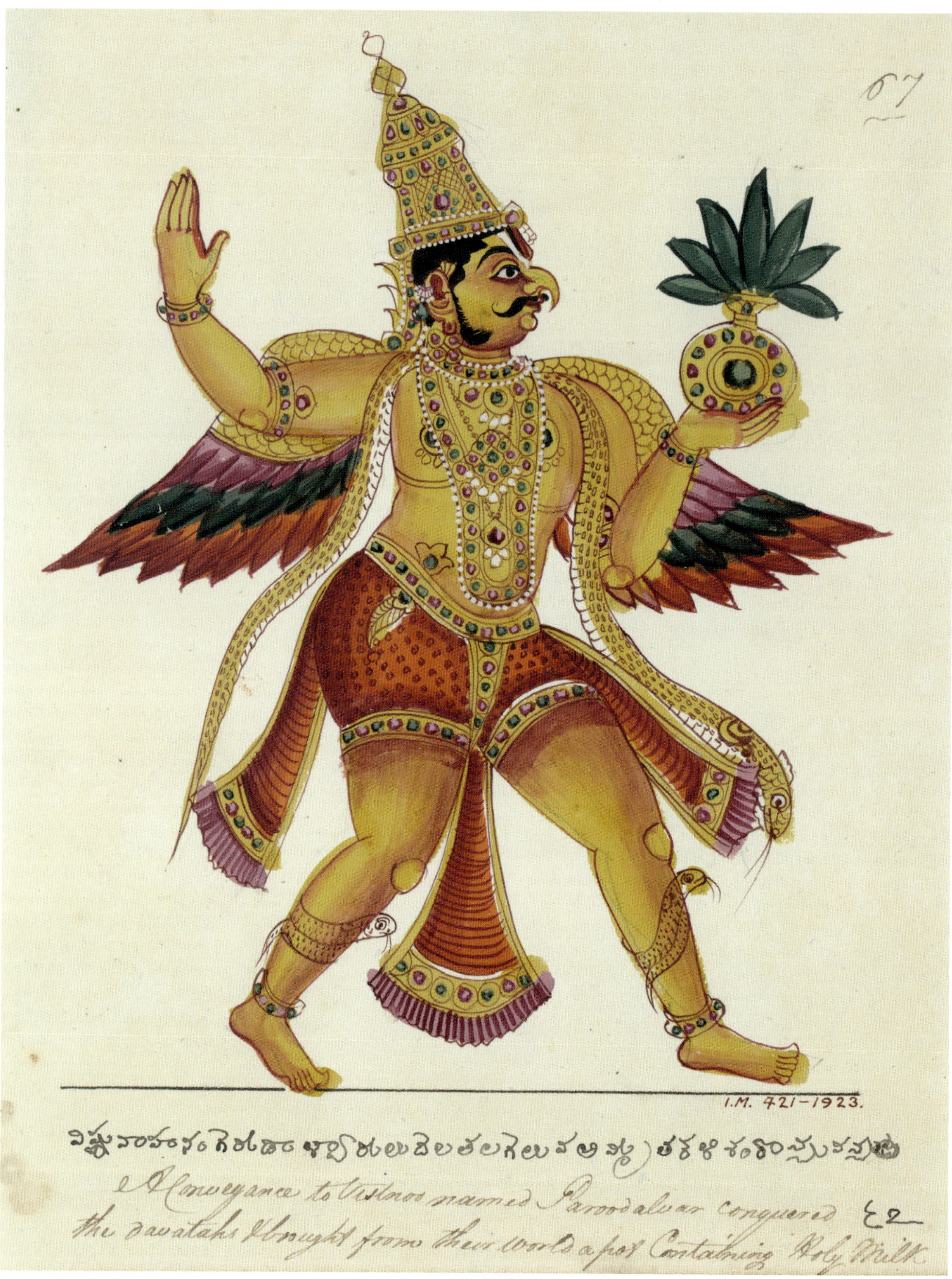

I.M. 421-1923.

A Conveyance to Visnoo named Paroodaluar conquered the savatahs & brought from their World a pot Containing Holy Milk

೬೨

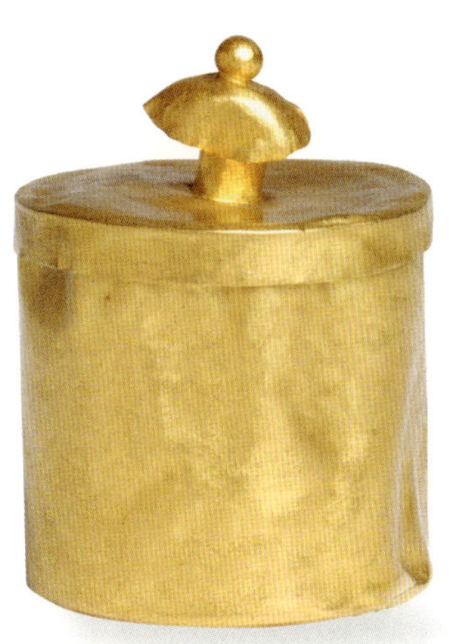

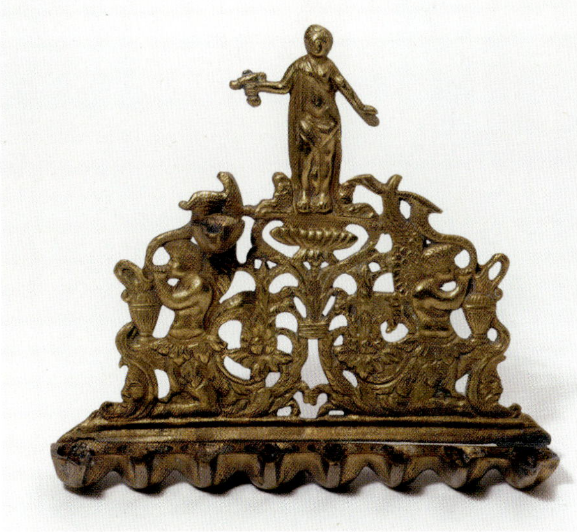

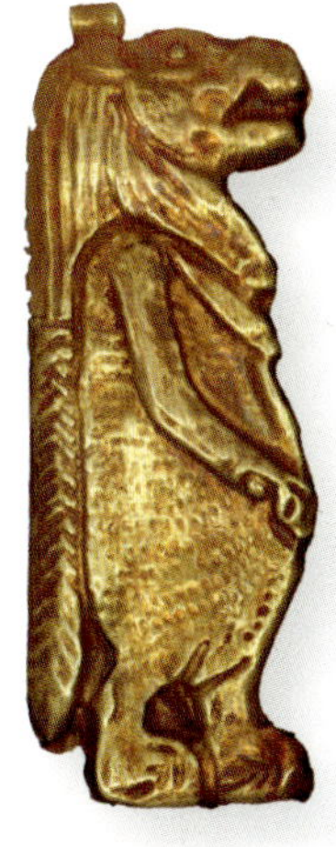

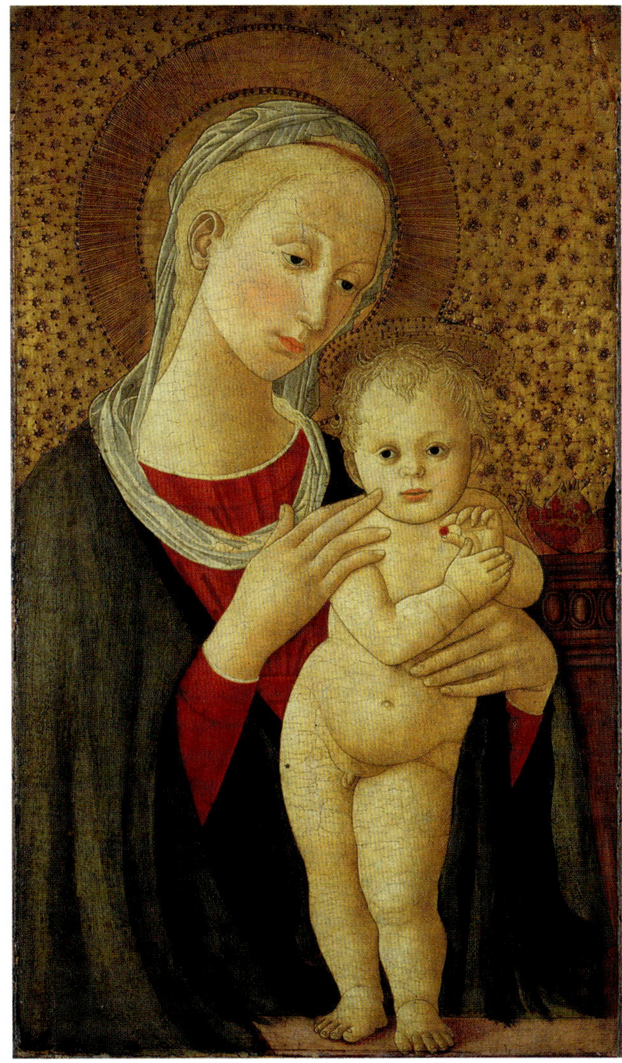

Yellow and gold have long been colours of divinity. In Hindu mythology, the eagle-like deity Garuda is the vehicle of Vishnu. In this painting (c. 1825; opposite), he is depicted as golden yellow. Egyptian amulets were worn for their protective properties. This golden example from 1400–400 BC (above left) represents Taweret, goddess of maternity, and was believed to ensure fertility and heal souls in the afterlife. The worship of relics became significant to Buddhist ritual. This small gold reliquary casket (2nd–5th century, above centre), preserving the bone fragments of a distinguished religious teacher, was excavated from the great Indian monastery of Takht-i-Bahi. Gold also surrounds the Virgin Mary and Christ-child in this Renaissance painting (right), lending its colour to their glowing halos and blonde hair. A brass menorah (c. 1600; above right) celebrates the Jewish festival of Hanukkah; sword in hand, Judith stands atop this lamp, referencing the Torah story in which she saves Israel from the siege of Holofernes.

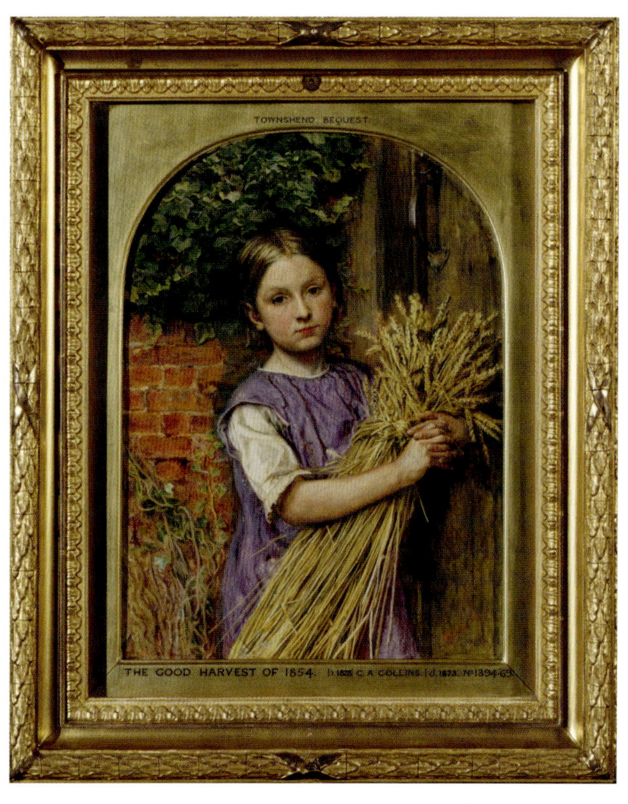

As the colour of light and warmth, yellow is associated with abundance and natural wealth. This dazzling dress by Norman Hartnell (below left) was worn by Queen Elizabeth II of the United Kingdom in Paris in 1957. Richly embroidered with pearls and gold thread, the gown diplomatically depicts French natural motifs, including daisies, crossed wheat sheaves and Napoleonic bees. Similarly naturalistic motifs of honeysuckles and rosebuds decorate this sumptuous yellow silk sack dress from the 1760s (below right). Pre-Raphaelite painter Charles Allston Collins conveys abundance through the hefty bunch of golden wheat in the arms of a young girl in *The Good Harvest of 1854* (1854; left).

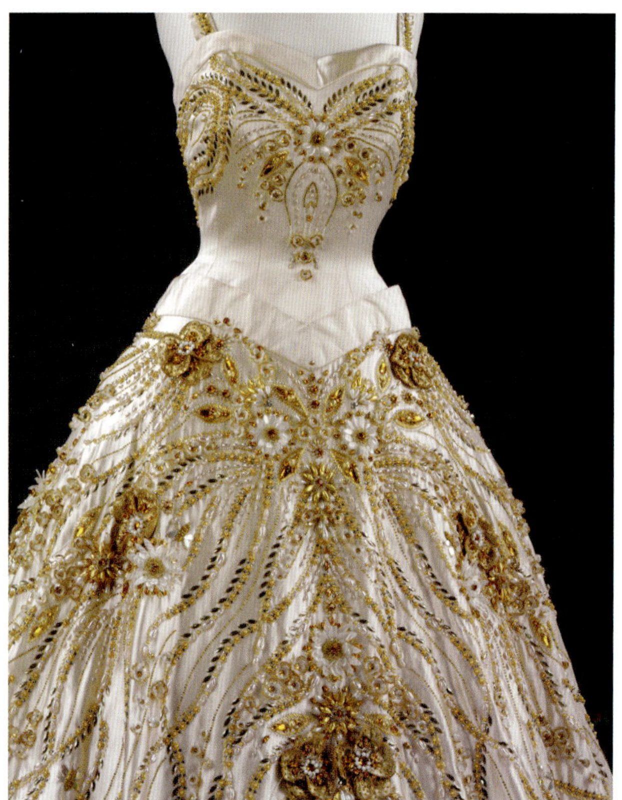

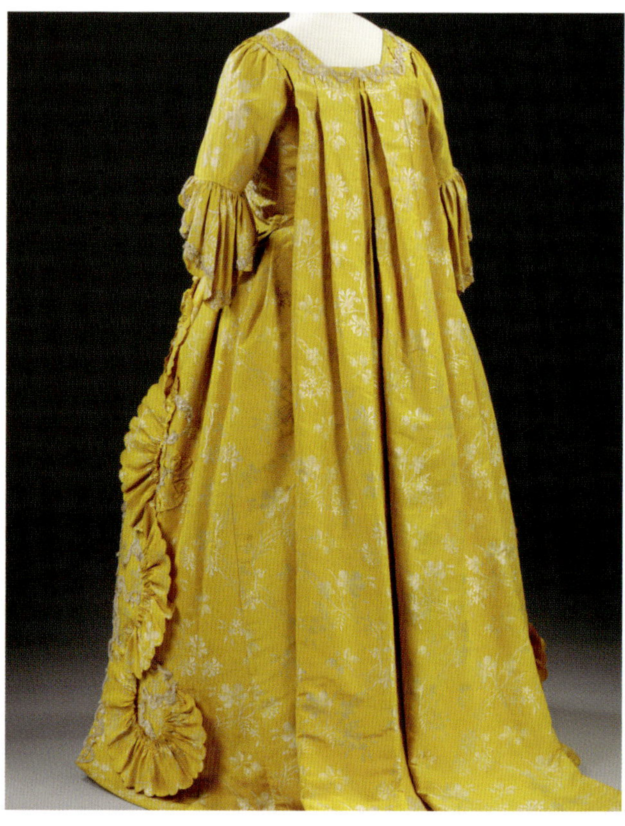

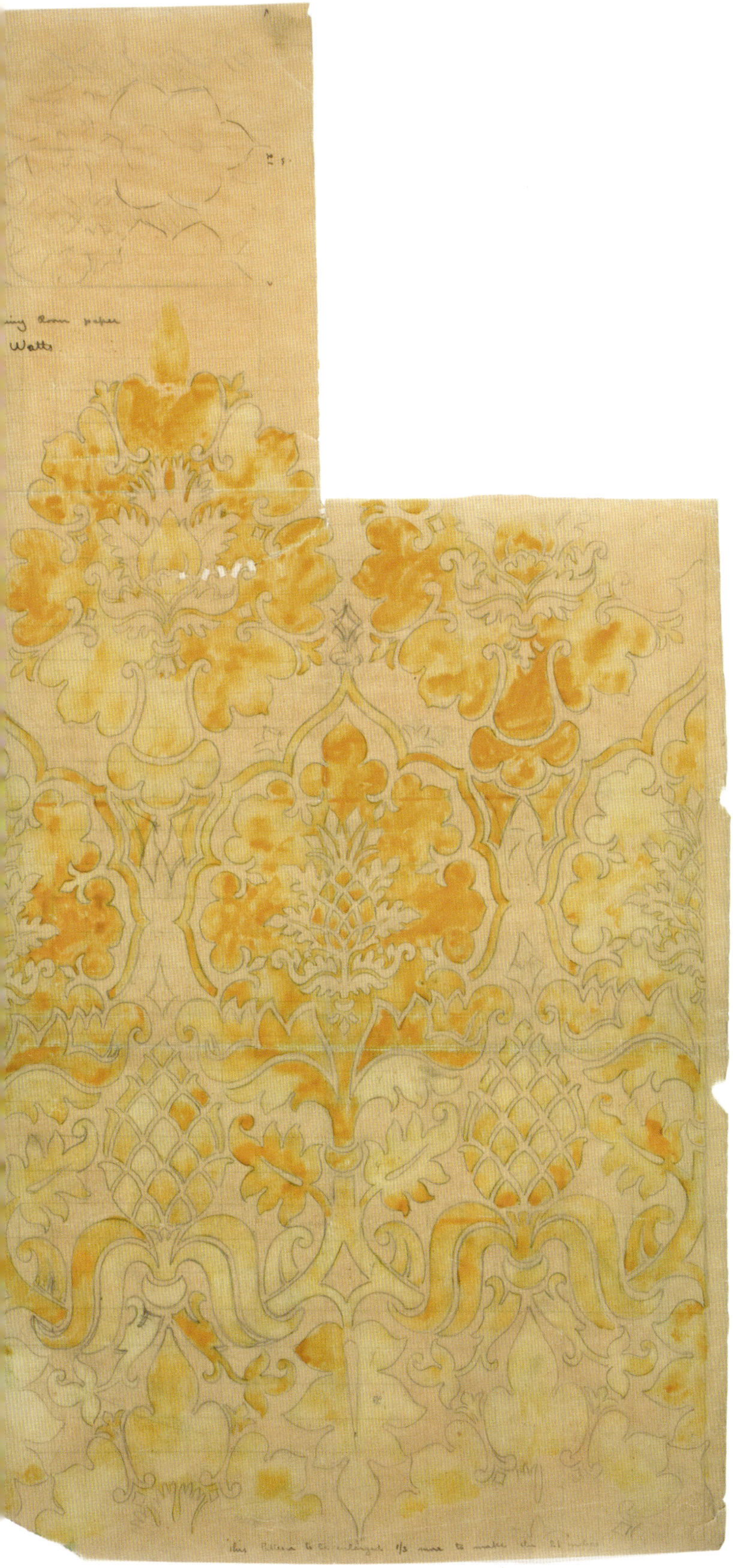

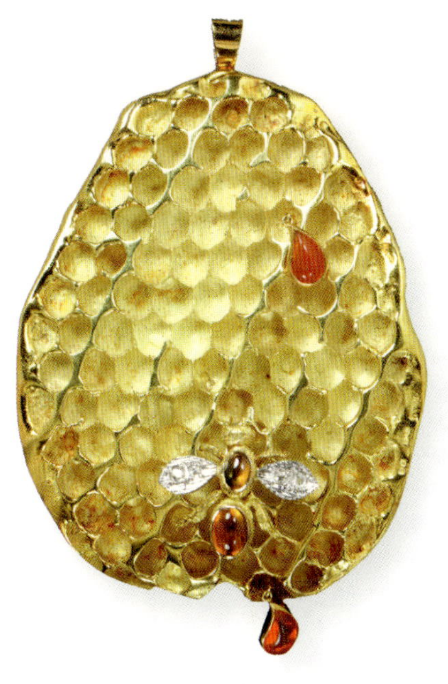

A.W.N. Pugin's wallpaper design from 1852 (left) playfully portrays pineapples as a symbol of natural and financial wealth. This fruit, once available only to the wealthy elite, was flaunted as an exotic status symbol at the courts of Louis XV and Catherine the Great. To create this brilliant brooch-pendant (above) in 1969, John Donald replicated the honeycomb's intricate geometry in solid gold, with jewelled honey drops and a bee with diamond-set wings.

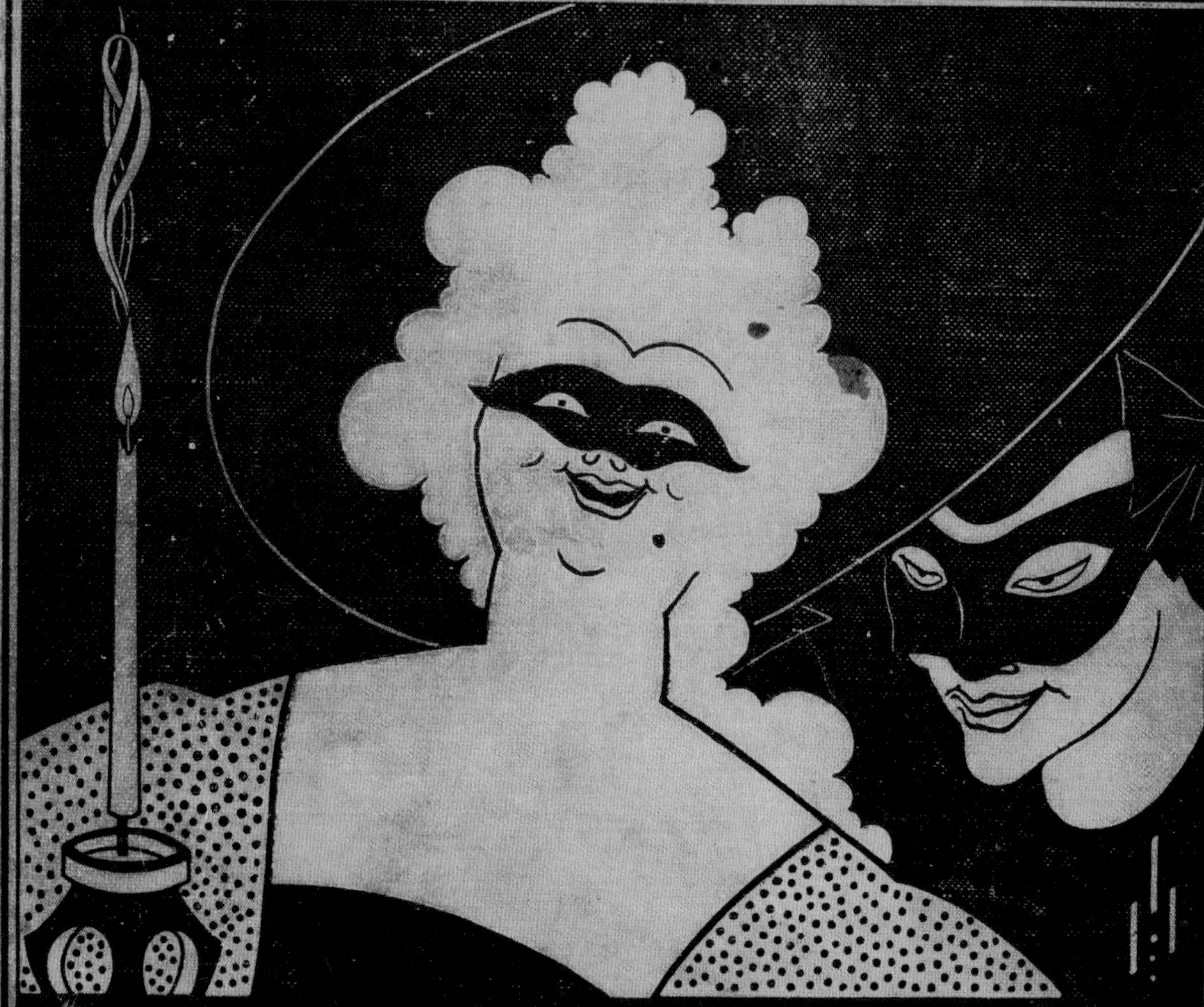
The Yellow Book
An Illustrated Quarterly
Volume I April 1894
London: Elkin Mathews & John Lane
Boston: Copeland & Day
Price
5/-
Net

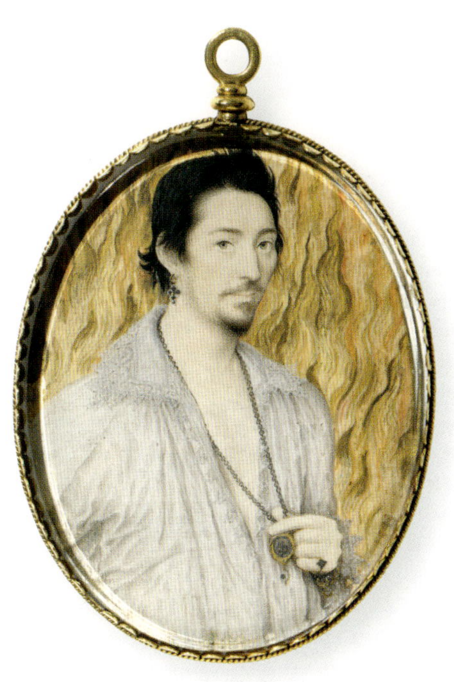

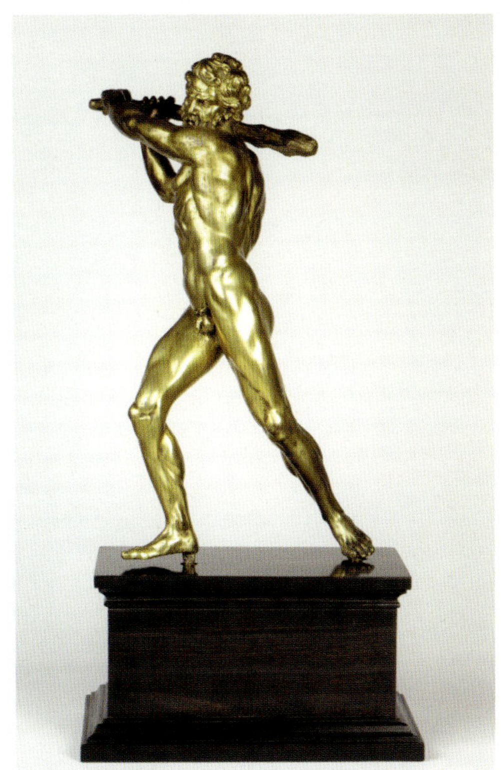

Yellow has been an early marker of transgression and sexuality. In Greek and Roman mythology, Hercules embodied strength and was known for his fluid sexuality. This homoerotic golden statuette (late 16th to early 17th century, above right), made in Italy, depicts a nude Hercules launching himself into battle. His muscular body illustrates the physical ideal of male beauty and references his depiction as the attractive lover of Abderus and Hylas. The Victorian periodical *The Yellow Book* (opposite) took its brilliant cover from French erotica, which used yellow to alert to the texts' illicit content. Aubrey Beardsley was the publication's first art director and mocked the conservatism of the Victorian artistic model with his whiplash lines and lascivious illustrations. During the 1890s, Henri de Toulouse-Lautrec visited the cabarets of Paris and London and produced eye-catching advertisements. In this poster for the Palace Theatre's can-can dances (right), yellow signals the sensual nature of the performances. In Nicholas Hilliard's intimate portrait miniature (c. 1600; above left), golden flames frame the sitter, symbolizing his passion and perhaps even his lust.

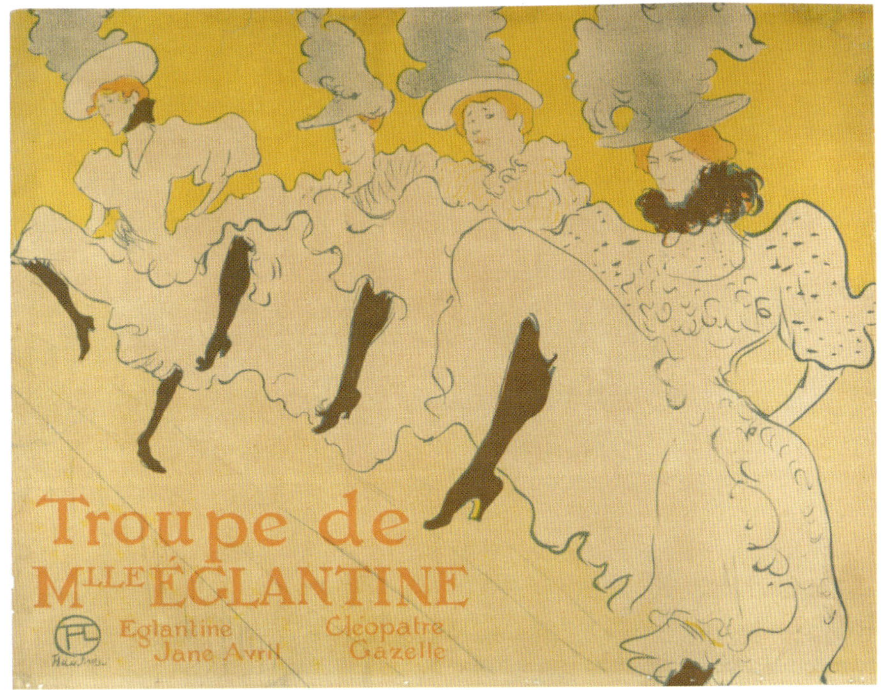

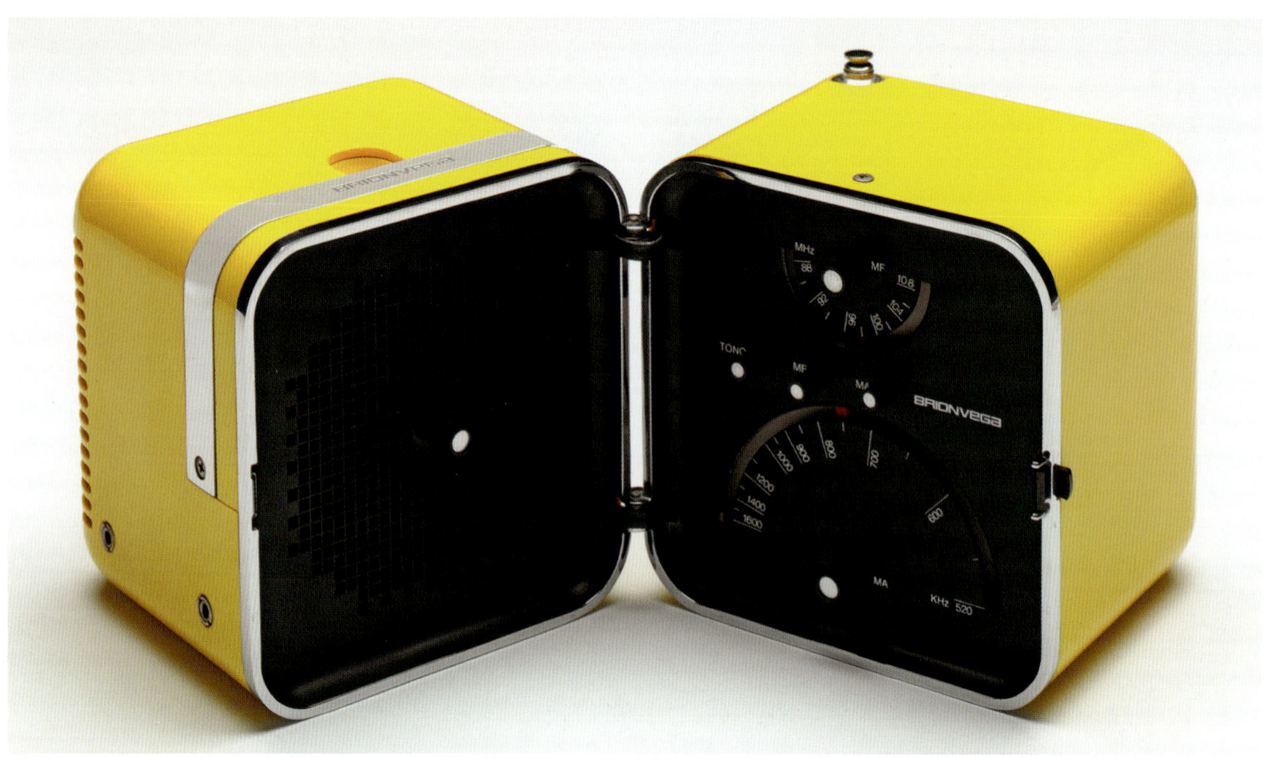

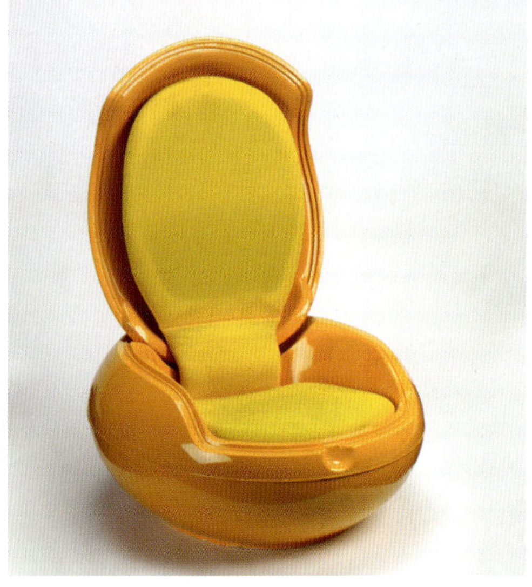

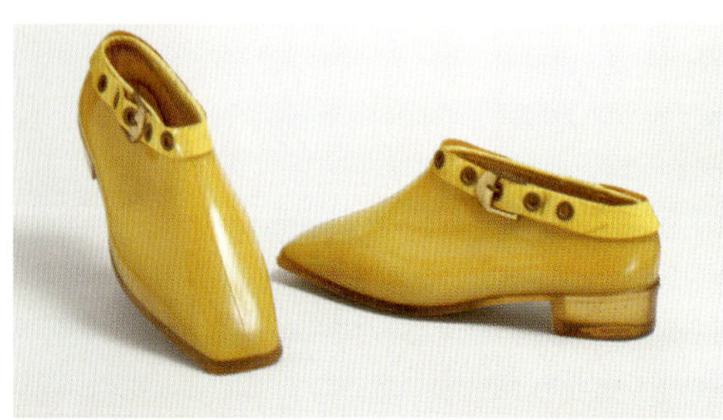

A symbol of warmth, light and positivity, sunny yellows have long been linked with joy and happiness. In this square tile from the 1950s (opposite), artist Peggy Angus used simplistic lines reminiscent of a child's drawing, and personified a glowing sun as a smiling and friendly yellow face. Radical British fashion designer Mary Quant created lively looks when she stepped on to the fashion scene in the 1960s. Her practical, playful products came in an array of vibrant colours, including these yellow PVC weatherproof boots for her 'Quant Afoot' range (left below). In the same period, household objects and furniture characterized by a sense of fun were popular on the European market. Cheery, energetic yellows brightened up everyday products such as this box-like Brionvega TS502 radio from 1963 designed by Richard Sapper and Marco Zanuso (above) and Peter Ghyczy's futuristic 'Garden Egg' chair (left centre), which combines a tangerine plastic lacquer shell with electric yellow cushions in line with the bold, bright 'pop' interiors of the 1960s.

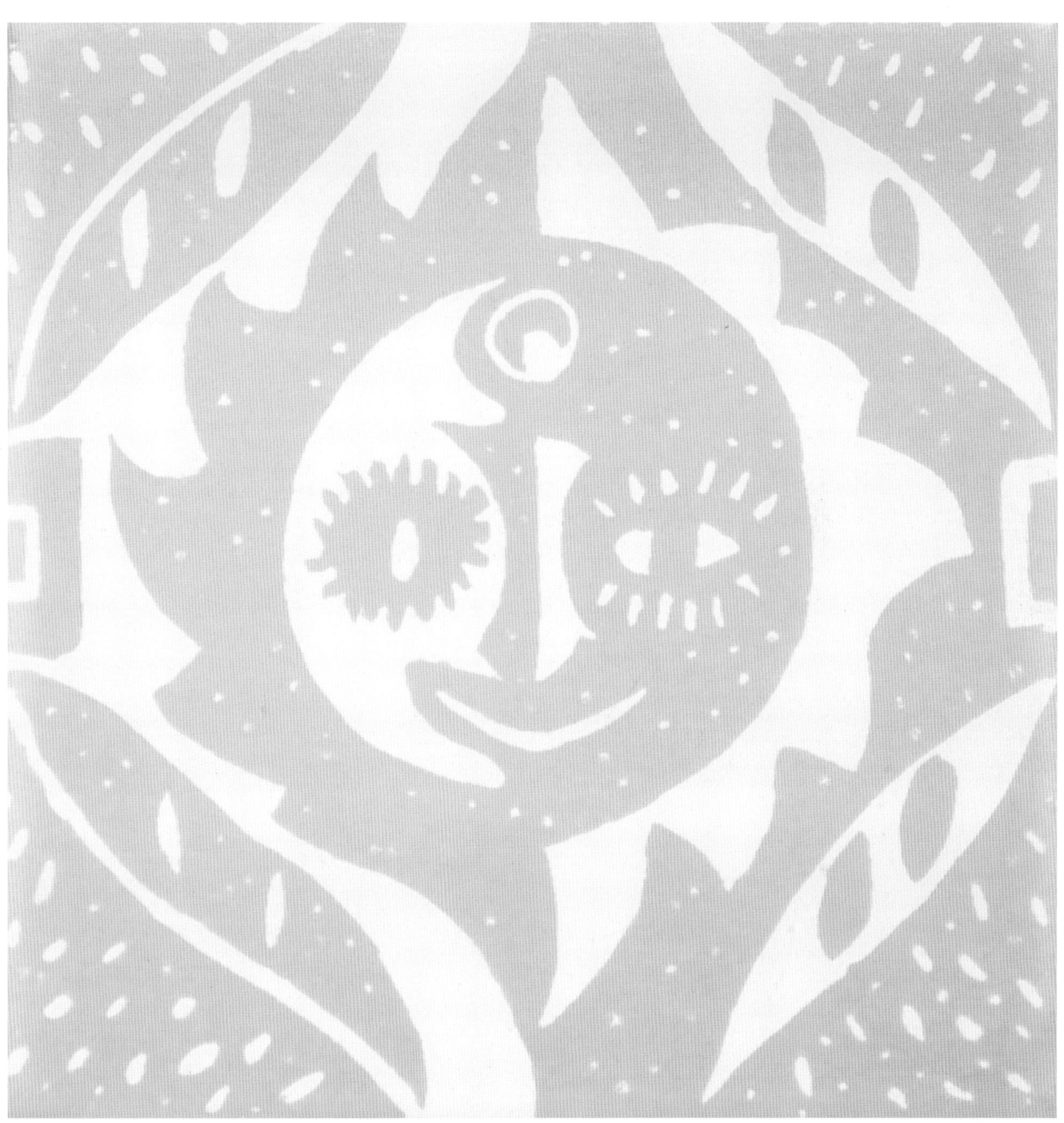

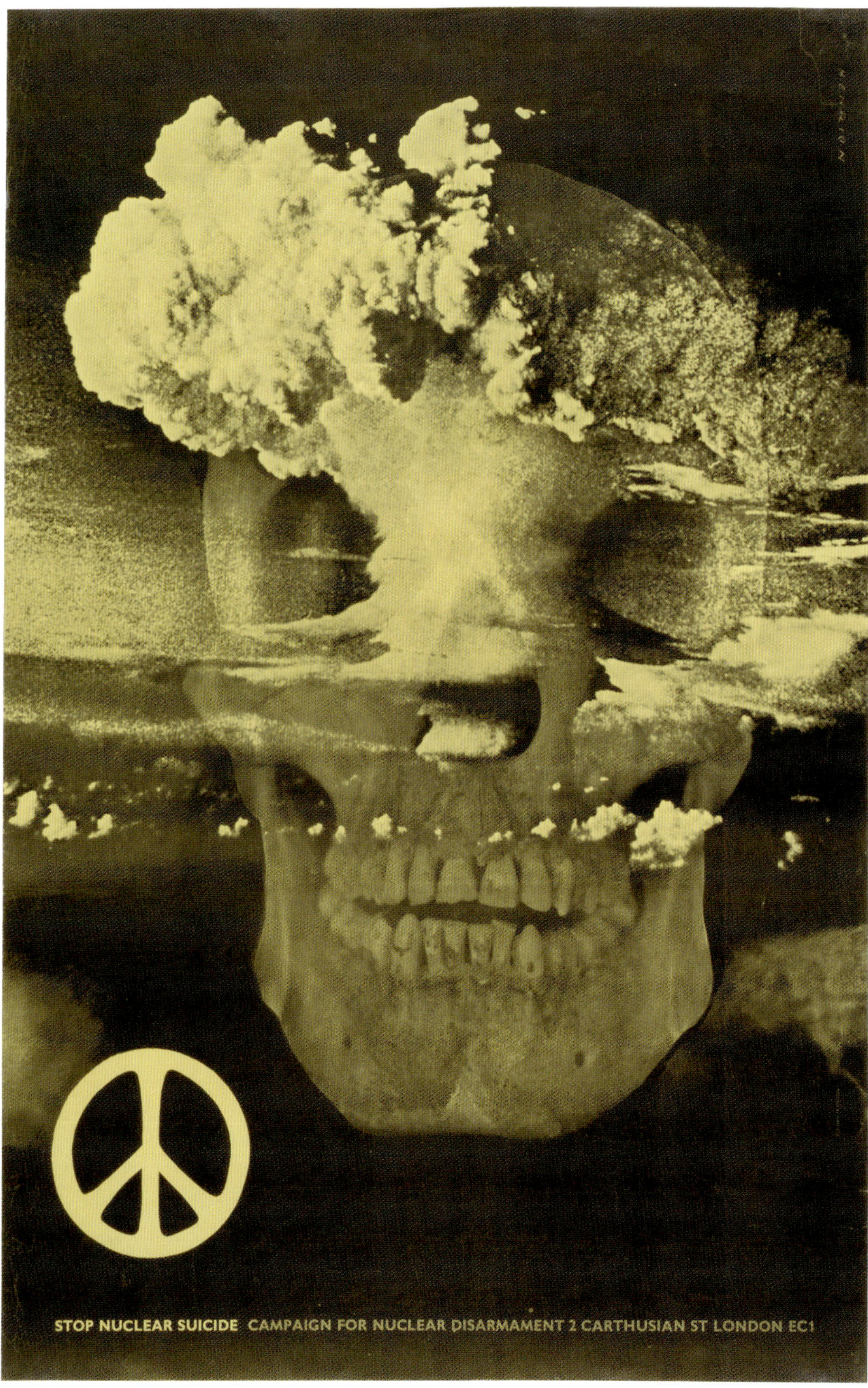
STOP NUCLEAR SUICIDE CAMPAIGN FOR NUCLEAR DISARMAMENT 2 CARTHUSIAN ST LONDON EC1

Bold and eye-catching, yellow undoubtedly attracts attention. Fashion magazines of the 1940s used bright colours to engage readers; Horst P. Horst created some of *Vogue*'s most striking photographs, often prioritizing a single, vivid shade. In this picture (below left), dramatic lighting frames a yellow hat and handbag. Yellow has also been a popular choice for thought-provoking protest posters, such as this yellow skull overlaid on a mushroom cloud (1963; opposite), produced by the Campaign for Nuclear Disarmament to highlight the looming threat of nuclear weapons. Jamie Reid's t-shirt (1978; top right) chronicles the sensation surrounding punk band The Sex Pistols. Against a punchy yellow, Reid's trademark cut-and-paste aesthetic records the media attention the band – and punk's anti-establishment views – attracted. Neon yellow frequently features in sportswear; Nike's 'Magista Obra' boots (2014; centre right) are easily spotted on the field and on television screens. Likewise, Schwan's 'Stabilo Boss' fluorescent highlighters (below right) accentuate yellow's vibrancy, marking out the important parts of a page, as advertised on this plastic bag from 1988.

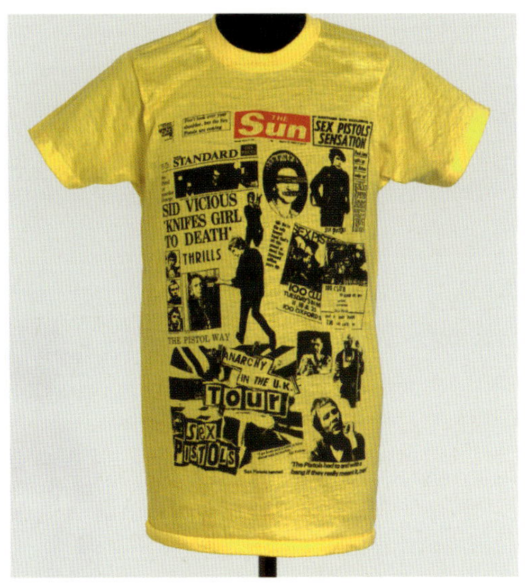

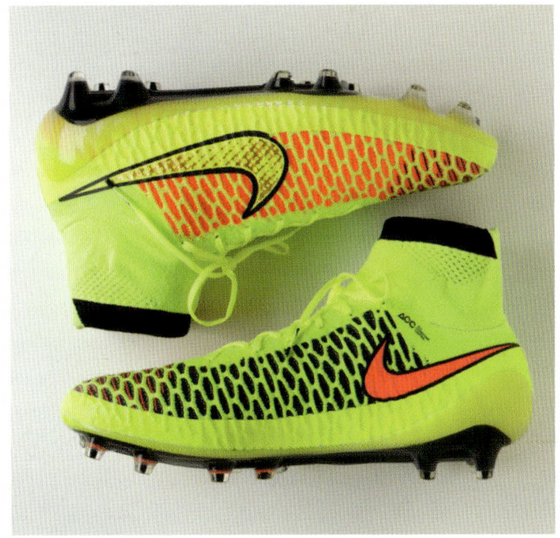

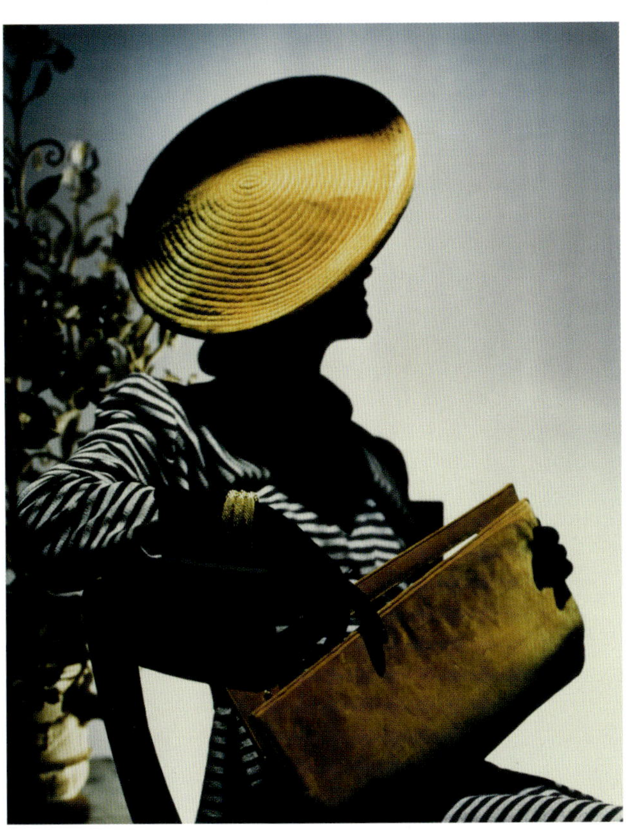

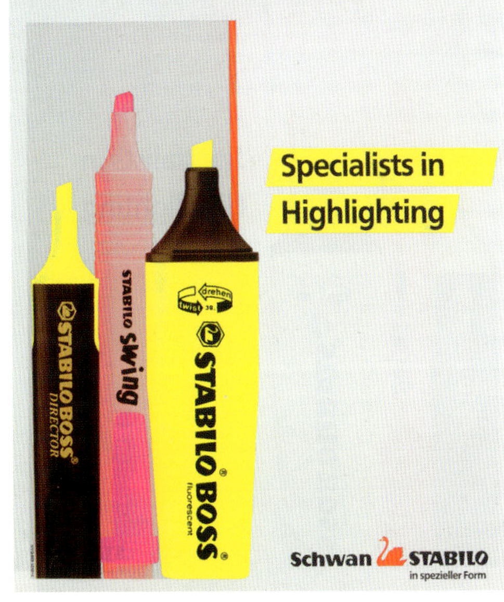

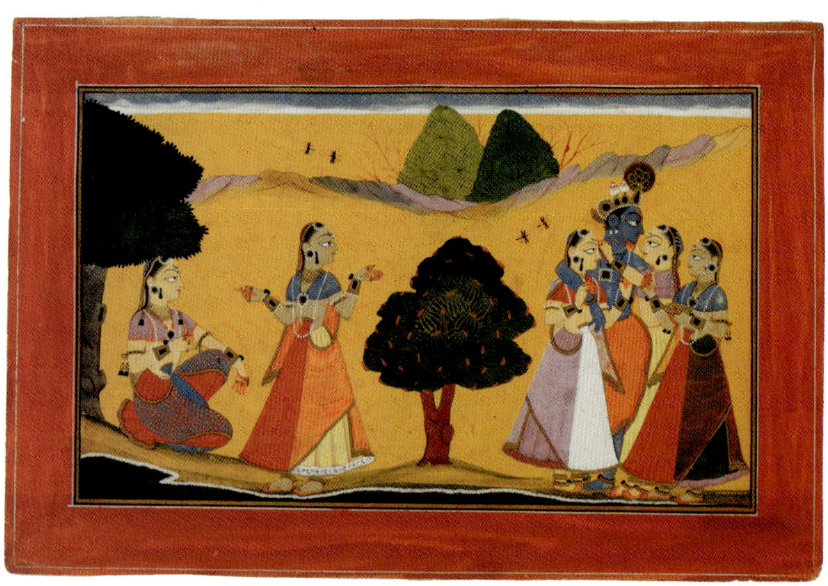

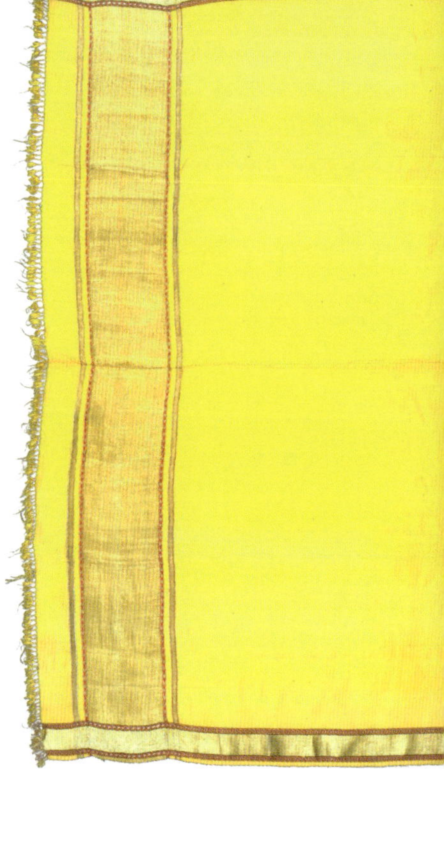

Yellow has long been part of the Indian colour palette. In this Pahari painting (c. 1760; opposite), Hindu gods Shiva and Parvati sit under a mango tree with their sons Karttikeya and Ganesh, each draped in splendid yellow fabric. In another painting (c. 1730–5; above left), a blue-skinned Krishna, adorned in gold jewels, is surrounded by female devotees against a brilliant yellow background. This painting is part of a bigger group illustrating the *Gita Govinda*, the story of Krishna's youth. Kalighat paintings, characterized by their bold, graphic impact, were made cheaply for the mass market. In this example (below left), of a courtesan holding a peacock, yellow takes centre stage against a plain background.

The deep yellow in this red-bordered sari (1950–60; below right) owes its tone to turmeric root, a plant widely found across India. This fine example of a *lungi*, a man's garment, was made in Lahore of vibrant yellow silk (1855; above right). Swati Kalsi's lemon-yellow sari from 2011 (below centre) suggests that this colour remains a fashionable choice.

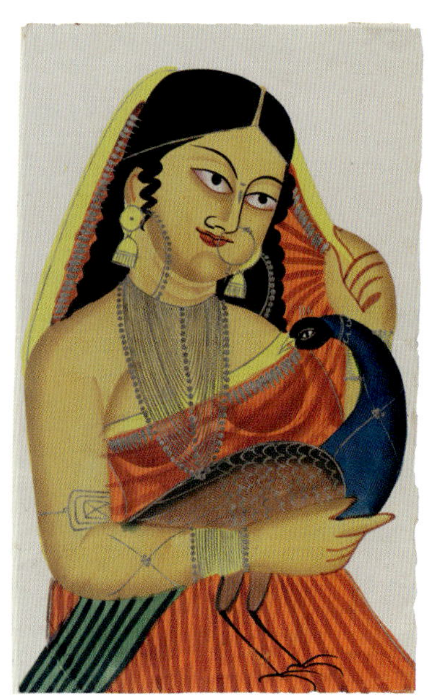

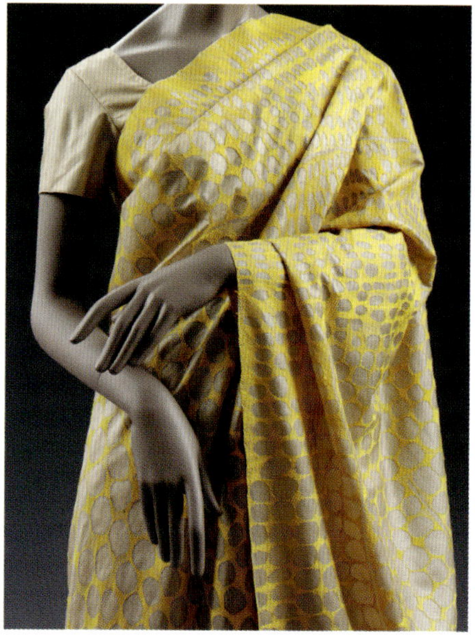

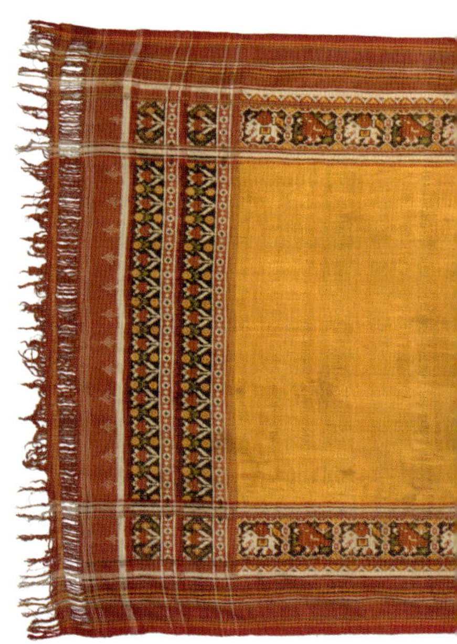

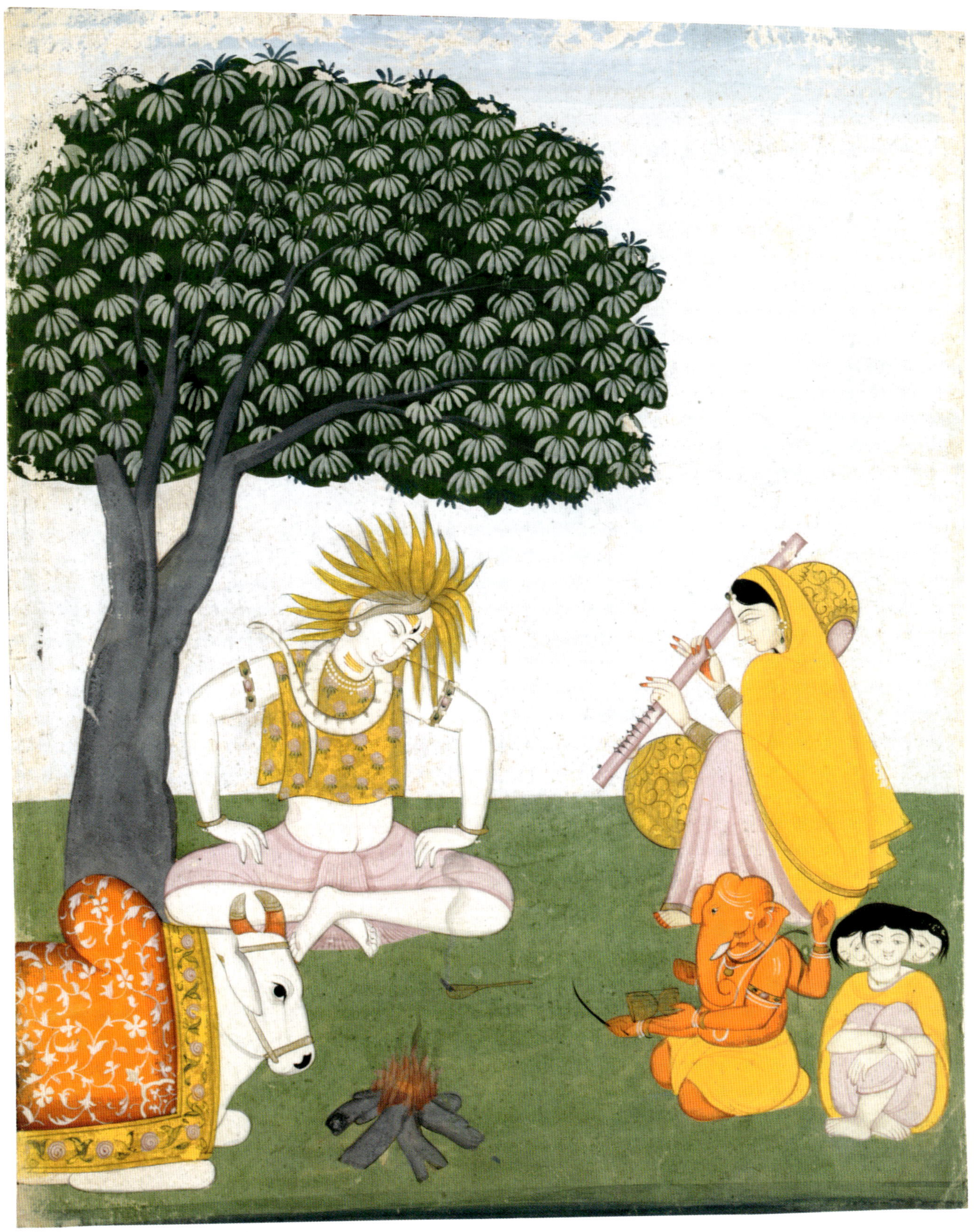

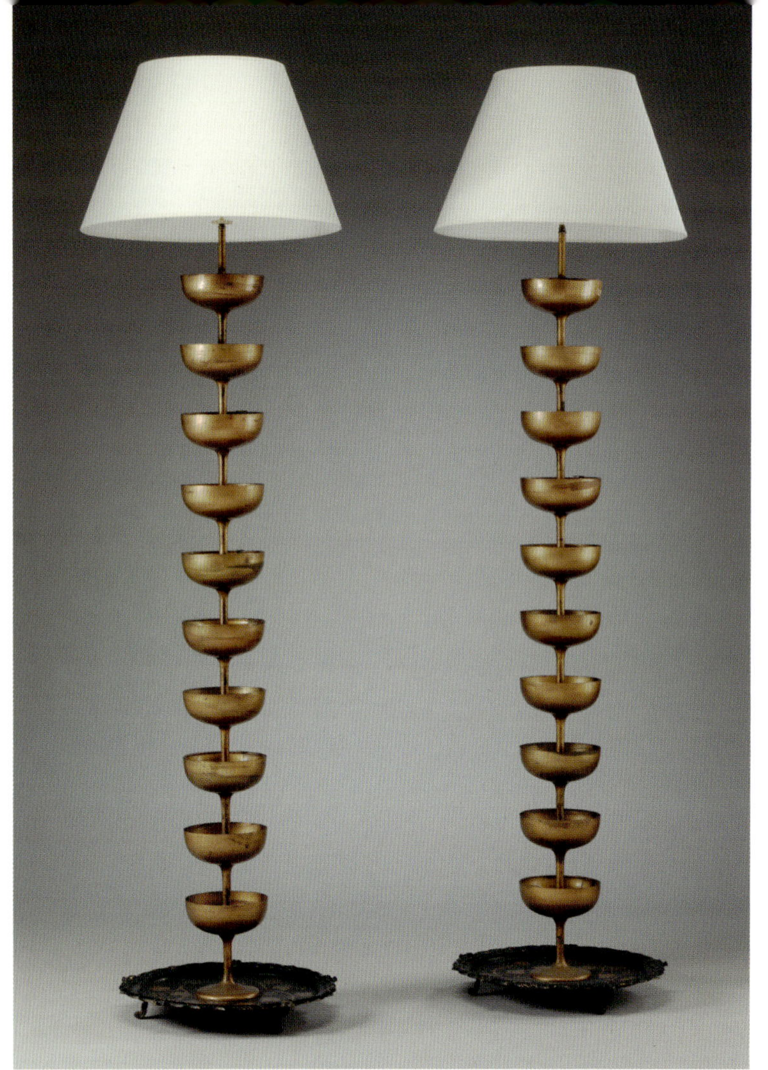

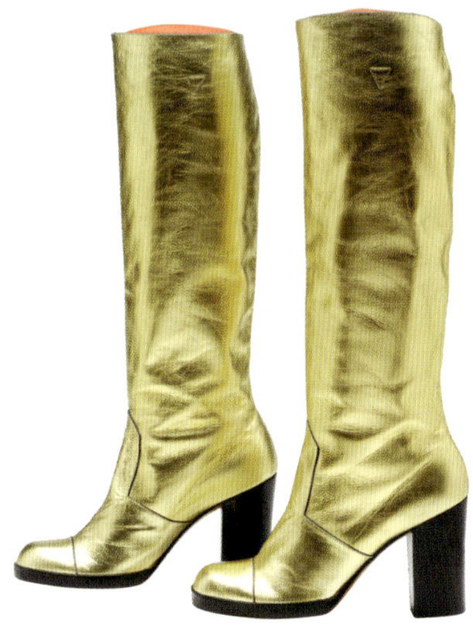

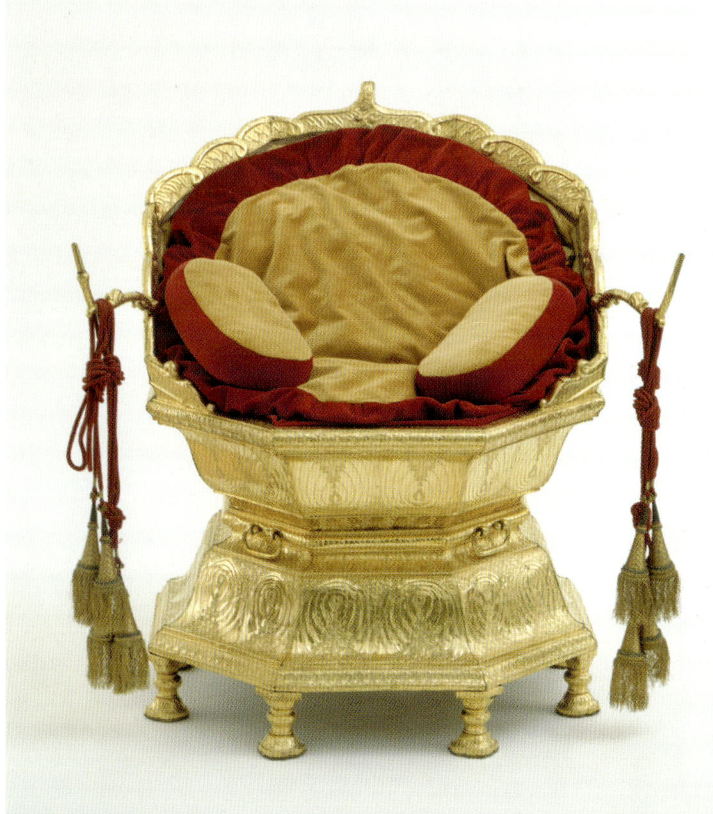

Rich yellows and glorious golds are synonymous with opulence and wealth. The 19th-century Sikh ruler Maharaja Ranjit Singh was famously modest in person, but renowned for the splendour of his court. His throne (left), of thick, heavily ornamented sheet gold took centre stage. Its distinctive cusped base is composed of two tiers of lotus petals. In 1938, surrealists Salvador Dalí and Edward James challenged the domestic display of wealth when designing a pair of standing lamps shaped like a stack of golden champagne coupes (above left).

The opening of Liberty's department store in 1875 popularized the taste for brilliant, lavish fashion. This late 19th-century gown's luxurious layers feature plush velvet edgings, voluminous sleeves and embroidered sunflower motifs (right). This curved ring by Ute Decker (2015; below), made from ethically sourced Peruvian gold, was the first piece in the Victoria and Albert Museum collection to bear the Fairtrade hallmark, which was introduced to jewellers in 2011. Extravagant metallic footwear stepped onto the fashion scene in the 1970s, as shown by these Yves Saint Laurent leather boots (opposite, right).

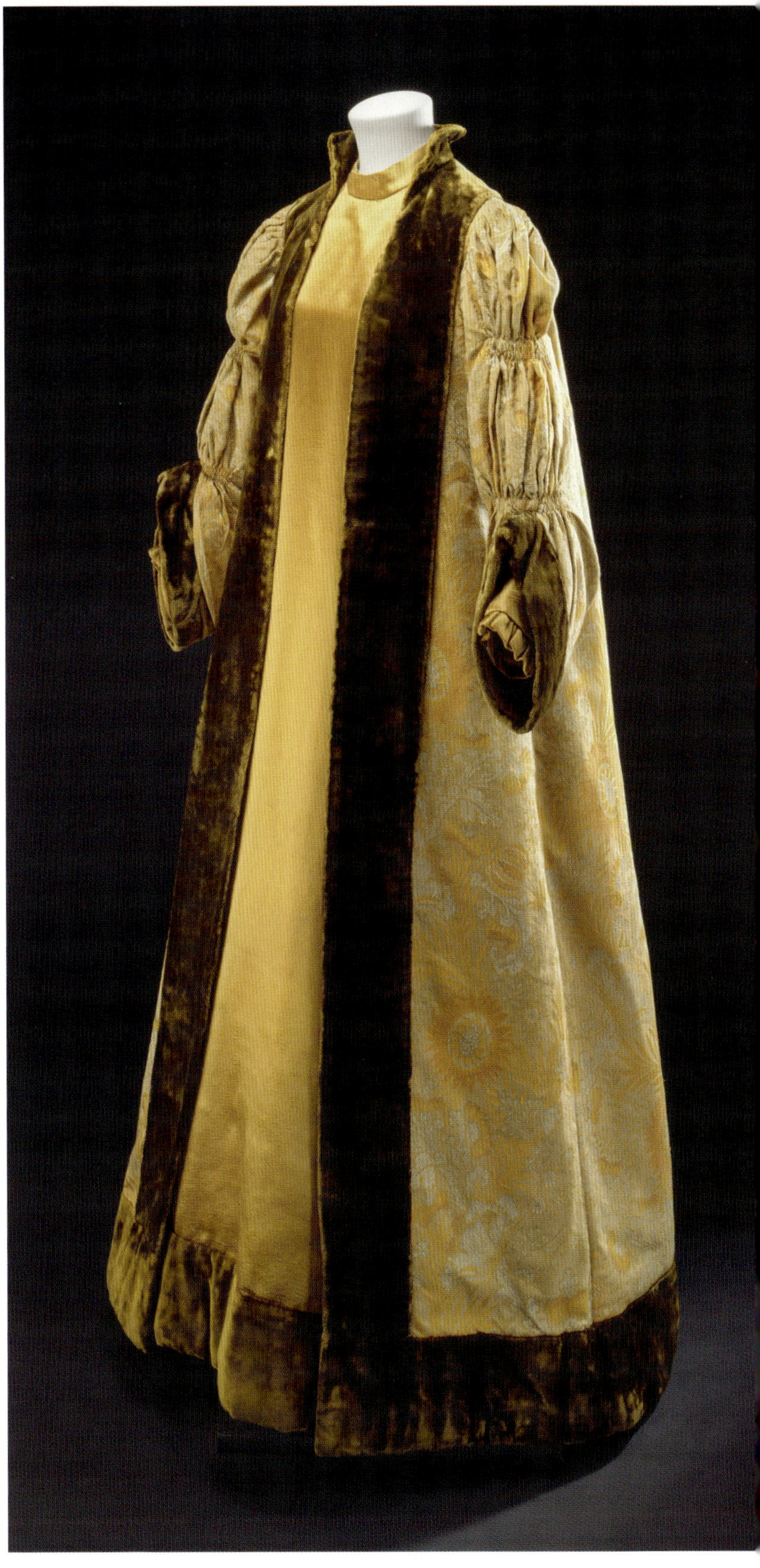

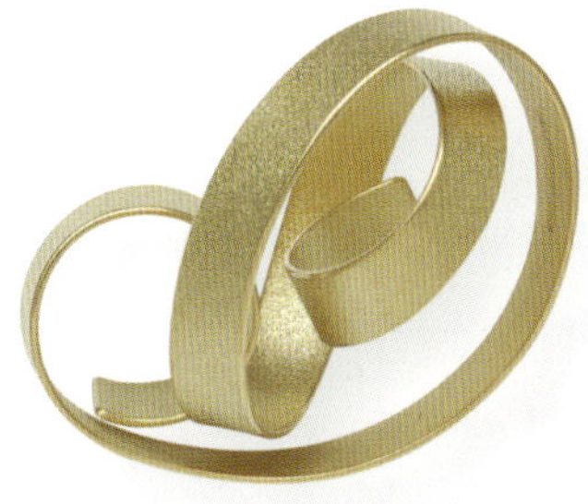

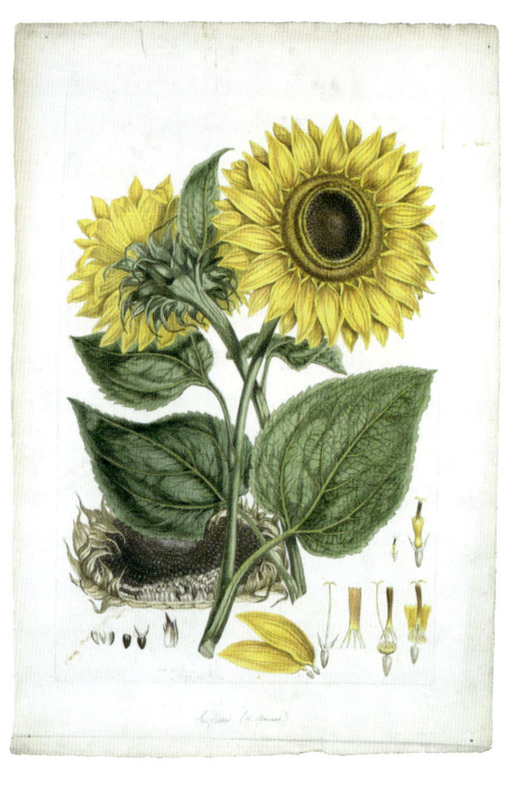

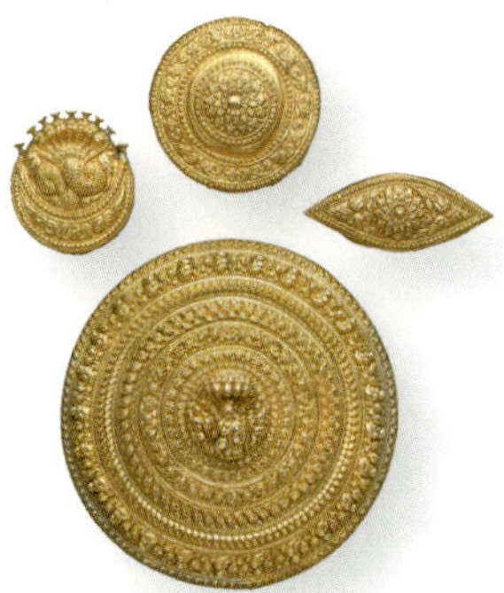

Brilliant and warm, yellow has long been associated with sunshine. This early 16th-century gilt-bronze plaque (opposite) depicts a musical contest between the satyr Marsyas and the Greek and Roman sun god Apollo. As the bringer of light and harmony, Apollo is portrayed as a strong, radiant young man. David Walker's humorous take on Apollo for a ballet costume (1969; below right) pairs a gold lurex bodysuit with an extravagant crown of sun rays, referencing both mythology and the court of the 'Sun King', French monarch Louis XIV. In India, gold ornaments worn on the head, such as these examples (left) from the 1870s, often symbolized celestial bodies including the sun. Sun worship also occurs in the natural world, as John Miller's botanical study (far left) from the 1770s suggests. Miller offers a complete view of the sunflower's life cycle, from seed pods to the blooming yellow petals that follow the sun throughout the day. In 1930s Britain, sunbathing was a popular activity. This vibrant yellow jersey two-piece (below left) by Finnigans Ltd is typical of the luxury swimwear available at the time.

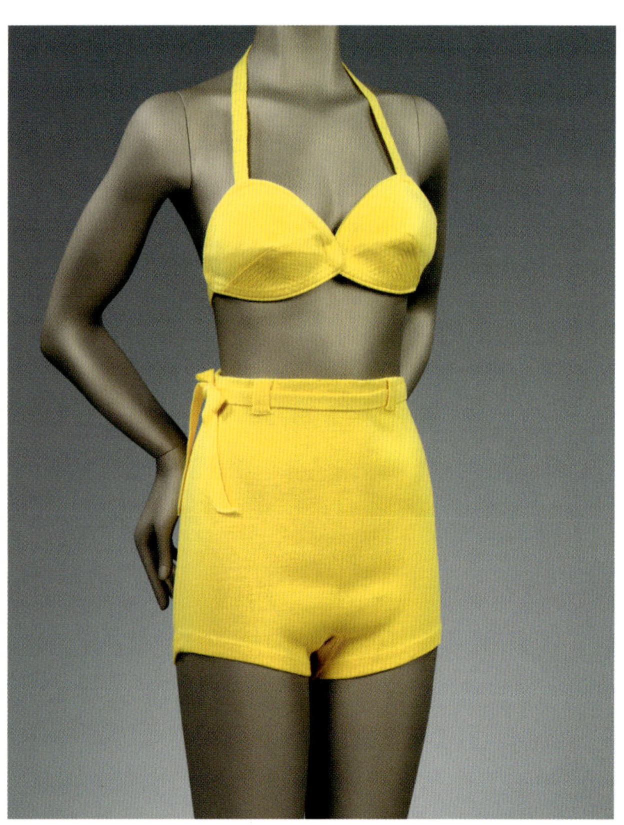

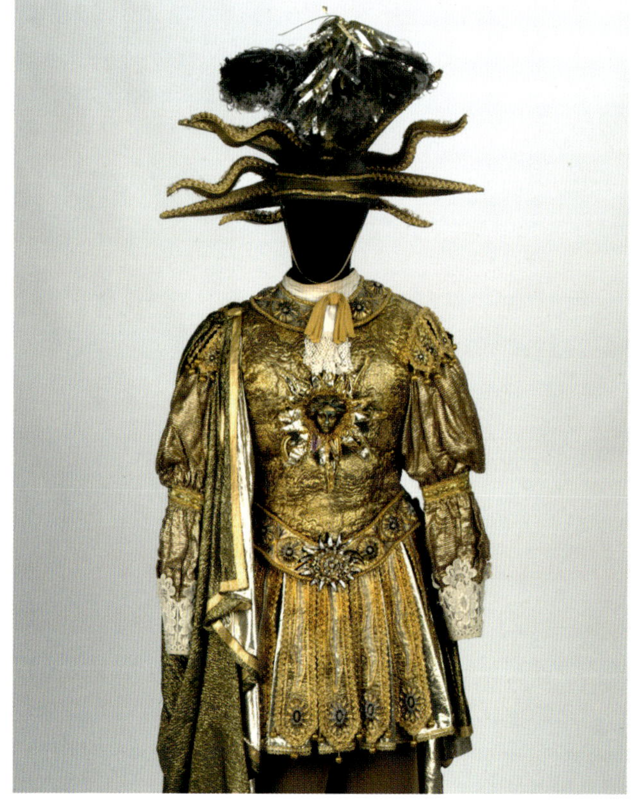

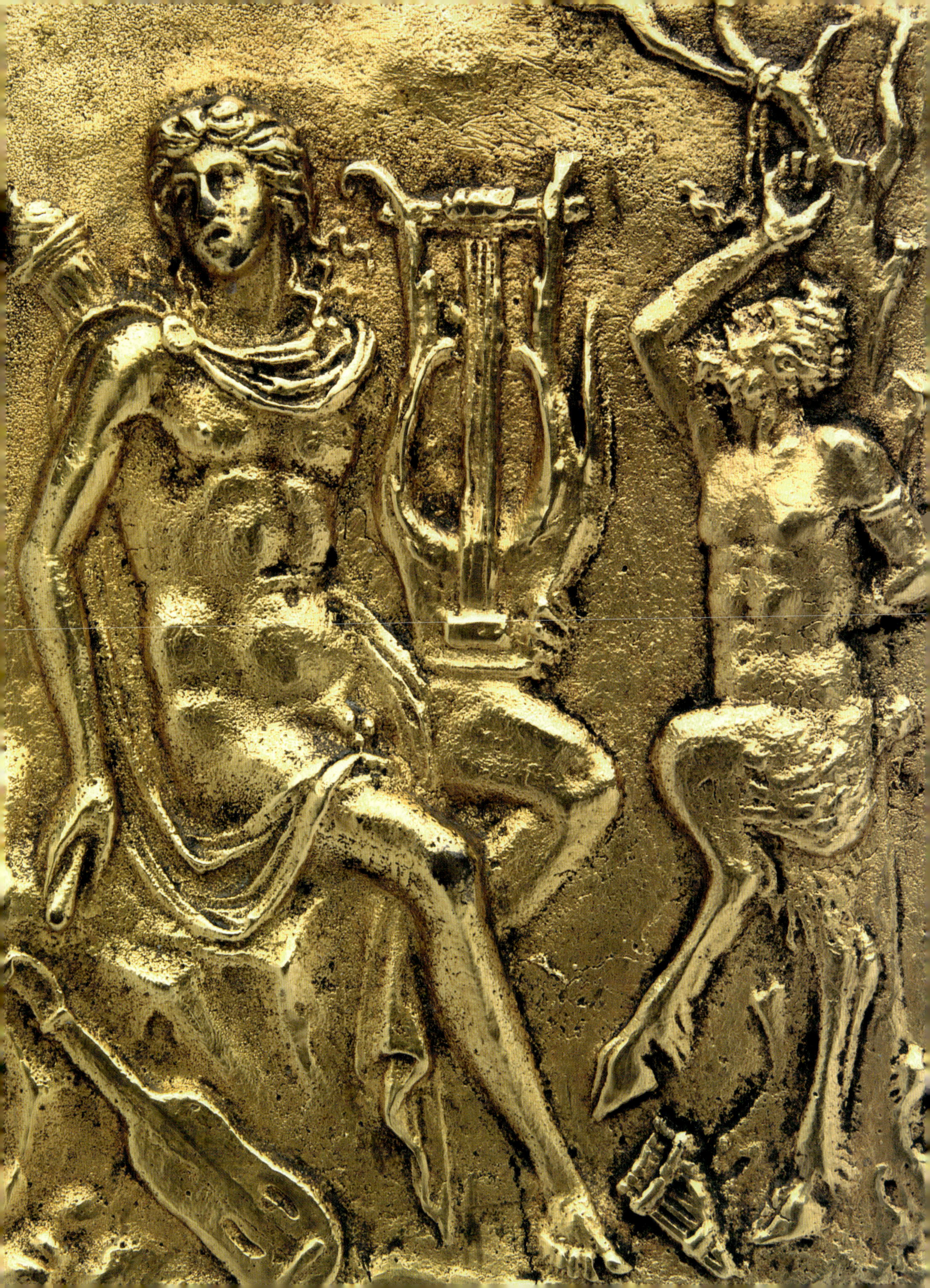

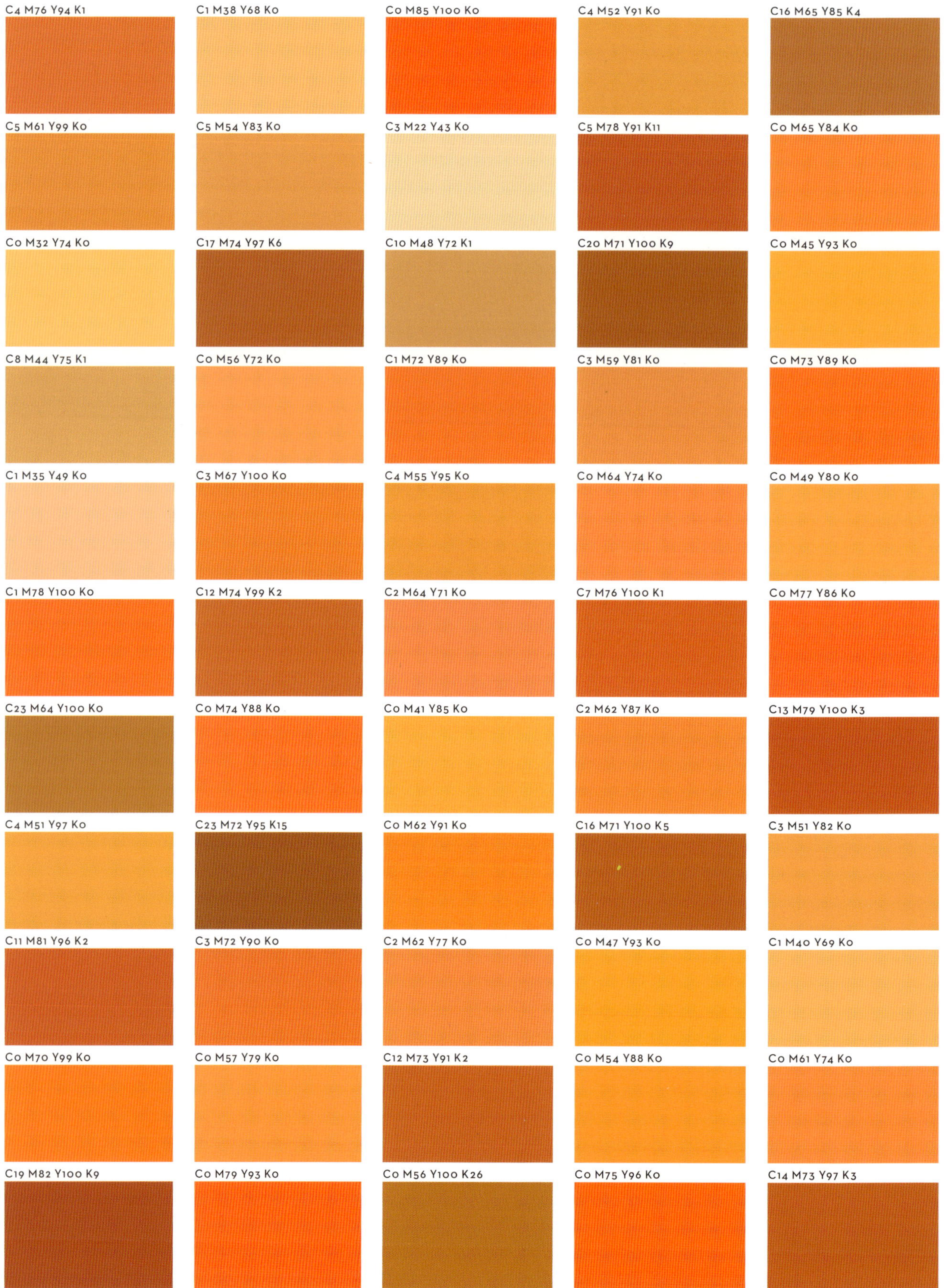

C4 M76 Y94 K1
C1 M38 Y68 K0
C0 M85 Y100 K0
C4 M52 Y91 K0
C16 M65 Y85 K4
C5 M61 Y99 K0
C5 M54 Y83 K0
C3 M22 Y43 K0
C5 M78 Y91 K11
C0 M65 Y84 K0
C0 M32 Y74 K0
C17 M74 Y97 K6
C10 M48 Y72 K1
C20 M71 Y100 K9
C0 M45 Y93 K0
C8 M44 Y75 K1
C0 M56 Y72 K0
C1 M72 Y89 K0
C3 M59 Y81 K0
C0 M73 Y89 K0
C1 M35 Y49 K0
C3 M67 Y100 K0
C4 M55 Y95 K0
C0 M64 Y74 K0
C0 M49 Y80 K0
C1 M78 Y100 K0
C12 M74 Y99 K2
C2 M64 Y71 K0
C7 M76 Y100 K1
C0 M77 Y86 K0
C23 M64 Y100 K0
C0 M74 Y88 K0
C0 M41 Y85 K0
C2 M62 Y87 K0
C13 M79 Y100 K3
C4 M51 Y97 K0
C23 M72 Y95 K15
C0 M62 Y91 K0
C16 M71 Y100 K5
C3 M51 Y82 K0
C11 M81 Y96 K2
C3 M72 Y90 K0
C2 M62 Y77 K0
C0 M47 Y93 K0
C1 M40 Y69 K0
C0 M70 Y99 K0
C0 M57 Y79 K0
C12 M73 Y91 K2
C0 M54 Y88 K0
C0 M61 Y74 K0
C19 M82 Y100 K9
C0 M79 Y93 K0
C0 M56 Y100 K26
C0 M75 Y96 K0
C14 M73 Y97 K3

ORANGE

Orange sits between red and yellow on the colour spectrum. By the early eighteenth century, Isaac Newton's *Opticks* (1704) included it as one of seven colours – red, orange, yellow, green, blue, indigo and violet – in his basic colour wheel. He had initially identifed just five; the secondary colours of orange and indigo were added to the list so that the number of colours matched the number of notes in a musical scale. Indigo is sometimes dropped, but orange continues to feature in most depictions of the rainbow – the iconic album cover for Pink Floyd's *Dark Side of the Moon* (1973), for example, shows white light passing through a prism to produce a six-colour rainbow. In the six-colour version of the LGBTQ+ rainbow flag, orange stands for healing.

The enduring popularity of the colour is hard to measure, but orange has been going in and out of fashion ever since it was first named after the citrus fruit. The English word comes from the Old French *orenge* or French *pomme d'orange*, which derives from *arancia*, from the Arabic *nāranj* and Sanskrit *nāraga*. According to the Oxford English Dictionary, the first known use of the term in English was in the early 1500s. Until then the colour had been rather clumsily described as yellow-red, or *giolureade*.

Oranges are not the only fruit to lend a name to a colour, but they are the most popular. First cultivated in ancient China, around 82 million tonnes of oranges are now harvested annually, with Brazil by far the biggest producer and Spain the largest in Europe. Seville oranges were first cultivated in the tenth century and have played a vital part in the Spanish economy for decades. Some sweeter varieties are grown in the Valencia region, much of which is covered in orange groves and filled with the scent of orange blossom in April and May.

Werner's Nomenclature of Colours (1814; second edition by Patrick Syme, 1821) includes six shades of orange, ranging from yellowish to reddish – Dutch Orange, Buff Orange, Orpiment Orange, Brownish Orange, Reddish Orange and Deep Reddish Orange. Syme also lists examples of the colour in the animal, vegetable and mineral worlds. Dutch Orange, for example, is the colour of the Common Marigold (see p. 97), while Orpiment Orange apparently features on the belly of the Warty Newt. He says that 'Orpiment Orange, the characteristic colour, is about equal parts of gamboge yellow and arterial blood red'. Orpiment is a deeply coloured orange-yellow mineral that contains arsenic sulphite and is thus highly toxic.

Most colour experts would probably agree that gamboge is more yellow than orange, but some might claim that orpiment is yellower too; it is said to have the deep colour of saffron, the spice derived from tiny crimson filaments that appear in the flowers of the Crocus sativus. Highly prized for its delicate flavour and dyeing properties, saffron has been harvested for over three thousand years. For centuries, orange – and in particular, saffron orange – has been associated with religion and spirituality. The first Buddhist monks used spices such as turmeric or saffron to dye their robes, which were traditionally made of discarded rags. Theravada Buddhists continue to wear saffron-coloured robes today. Saffron is also the most sacred colour for Hinduism, and features in the national flag of India.

William of Orange led the sixteenth-century Dutch revolt against the Catholic Spanish and is known in the Netherlands as the 'founder of the fatherland'. His grandson William III, an ardent Protestant, invaded Britain in 1688 and overthrew the Catholic king, James II of England and Ireland. William and his wife Mary reigned jointly until her death in 1694. The colour orange is associated with Protestantism to this day; Orangemen still, controversially, hold marches in Northern Ireland and elsewhere.

Like saffron, amber is seen as a luxurious material because of its rarity and consequent expense. Prized for its translucence, amber is made of fossilized tree resin that frequently contains plant and animal materials. The colour can range from yellow, through orange, to brown. Some of the most sought after honey-coloured examples contain the remains of long-dead insects, trapped in liquid that solidified aeons ago. Amber has been used in jewellery for thousands of years, but it has also been employed on a much larger scale. A highly ornate Amber Room was installed in the Berlin City Palace at the beginning of the eighteenth century, and in 1716 was given to Tsar Peter the Great of Russia as a diplomatic gift. It was transported to Russia and reconstructed in the Catherine Palace near St Petersburg, where it remained for nearly 200 years. Sadly, the Amber Room was looted during the Nazi invasion of the Soviet Union during the Second World War, and its fate remains unknown.

Versatile, contrastingly cheap and readily available, clay is often a brownish-orange colour, though it can also be a creamy brown, yellow or grey. Ochre, an earth pigment that contains ferric oxide and varying amounts of clay and sand, can range from yellow to a deep orange or brown depending on the ingredients, while sanguine, or red chalk, is named after dried blood and can look rather more orange than red to the modern eye. A greater proportion of clay in the mix can produce a lighter orange colour, while more iron oxide produces a reddish-brown. In Britain, sanguine became an increasingly popular medium in portrait drawings from the mid-seventeenth century onwards. By the mid-nineteenth century, the chalk's orange-red colouring was an obvious choice for Dante Gabriel Rossetti, who used it to great effect in a portrait study of Alexa Wilding (*Head of Andromeda*, 1858). Rossetti's wife, Elizabeth 'Lizzie' Siddal, was one of several flame-haired women who featured in numerous artworks by the Pre-Raphaelite artists. Orange, and ginger or auburn hair in particular, is often still associated with vivaciousness or a fiery temper. For the Pre-Raphaelites, redheads were certainly in fashion. Orange drapery also features prominently in Frederic, Lord Leighton's *Flaming June* (1895) and Albert Moore's *Midsummer* (1887), among other late Victorian paintings. The Victoria and Albert Museum's Leighton corridor includes ceiling panels with similar orange-clad figures.

The orange tones of sunrise and sunset are influenced by a natural phenomenon called 'scattering'. When the sun is near the horizon, sunlight passes through more air in the earth's atmosphere. Blue and violet light is scattered, but the colours with longer wavelengths – yellow, orange and red – pass through. Francis Danby's view of the River Thames at sunset on p. 98 illustrates this nicely, with a yellow sky turning orange and becoming redder nearer the horizon. Another painting by Danby, *The Enchanted Castle* (*c*. 1841), shows the sun low in the sky, casting an orange glow over a dark, mystical landscape; among others, John Constable and J.M.W. Turner also famously exploited the drama of nature's atmospheric effects. Orange features prominently in many artworks and artefacts that make reference to sunrise, sunset or sunrays. The colour is particularly popular in art deco ceramics, notably in the work of Clarice Cliff (see p. 98).

Of course, orange occurs elsewhere in nature too, particularly in plants, animals and birds. The leaves of many deciduous trees turn orange, dark red or brown in the fall or autumn as the green chlorophyll in the leaves slowly degrades to reveal hidden pigments such as orange beta-carotenes. The orange appearance of selectively bred modern carrots is also down to carotenes, as is the characteristic colour of pumpkins and sweet potatoes. Orange pumpkins, hollowed-out and lit by candles, provide a warm glow at Halloween.

The petals of California poppies can feature shades of red, orange or yellow, but orange predominates. A sea of golden-orange flowers covers the Antelope Valley California Poppy Reserve each year, from late winter to early spring. Marigolds, daylilies and nasturtiums are also typically orange or orange-yellow, as is the perfectly named orange peel fungus, which looks like the discarded remains of the fruit. In some cases, though, names can be misleading. Goldfish are typically orange, rather than the colour of pure gold, while 'red' squirrels are more of a rusty orange-brown.

In modern times, orange is often associated with hazards – think flashing warning lights, or the green-amber-red sequence of many traffic lights. The colour is extremely useful where high visibility is required – for traffic cones, roadwork signs or construction sites. The American National Standard for Safety Colors even specifies the preferred shade for 'Safety Orange': Pantone 151C. The highly dangerous herbicide Agent Orange, used by the US army in the Vietnam War, was named after the orange band that appeared on its containers. As dramatized in the American TV series *Orange is the New Black,* prison jumpsuits are also often orange, presumably to facilitate the recapture of any escapees. Infamously, detainees at Guantanamo Bay were made to wear distinctive orange uniforms if they were deemed to be 'non-compliant'. Orange can also indicate a safety device, for example when used as a filter in safety glass (see p. 108).

Conversely, orange is often used in advertising and consumer products to suggest fun. EasyJet, the low-cost airline, markets its services using Pantone 021C, while the telecommunications company Orange utilized a similar shade, Pantone 151C. The two companies were locked in a trademark dispute for some years, both competing for the right to appeal to a younger, fun-loving clientele. The 'Easy' family of brands continues to use orange to promote a range of products and services.

Long before the Orange mobile phone brand appeared, telephone companies exploited orange's sleek, modern look – for example, in a trade catalogue from the 1930s, or Ericsson's upmarket handset for the British Post Office, marketed in the early 1980s (p. 104). A glossy orange chair by Joe Colombo on p. 104 still looks contemporary, and the Space Hopper toy, intended for use in the summer sun, has become iconic. Its original

designer, Aquilino Cosani, has explained that he wanted to avoid using gender-specific colours such as blue or pink. Orange's high visibility undoubtedly helped to sell the toy at a time when many children still played outdoors in the street.

Orange can also be portrayed as a strong colour – for example in the carbonated orange-coloured soft drink called Irn Bru, which claims to be 'made in Scotland, from girders'. Irn Bru (or 'iron brew') is sometimes described as 'Scotland's other national drink', after Scotch whisky – also orange-toned, though not quite so lurid. Of course, soft drinks aren't the only things that can make use of artificial colouring. Fake tans, like fake news, have been common for a long time; both have become associated with Donald Trump, elected to the US Presidency in 2016.

Like many colours, orange goes in and out of style. Despite its ups and downs, the colour has endured – thrived, even – in fashion, textiles and interior design. In late Victorian Britain, wallpaper designs incorporated warm orange patterns, blazing suns or cheerful flowers. Later, Arts and Crafts houses contained copper-orange artefacts such as fire screens, plates (p. 101) or light fittings. During the jazz era, flapper dresses came in flame orange, among other shades (p. 102). By the late 1960s and '70s, furnishing fabrics included swirling, psychedelia-influenced orange-brown motifs. Created in 2004, the artist John Dilnot's playful map of British paint chart colours features many shades of blue, green and cream, but only one that is recognizably orange (see p. 13). More recently, though, the name of Swedish psychedelic band The Orange Revival suggests yet another comeback for the colour. To quote the UK advertising slogan for the mobile phone company, 'The future's bright, the future's Orange'.

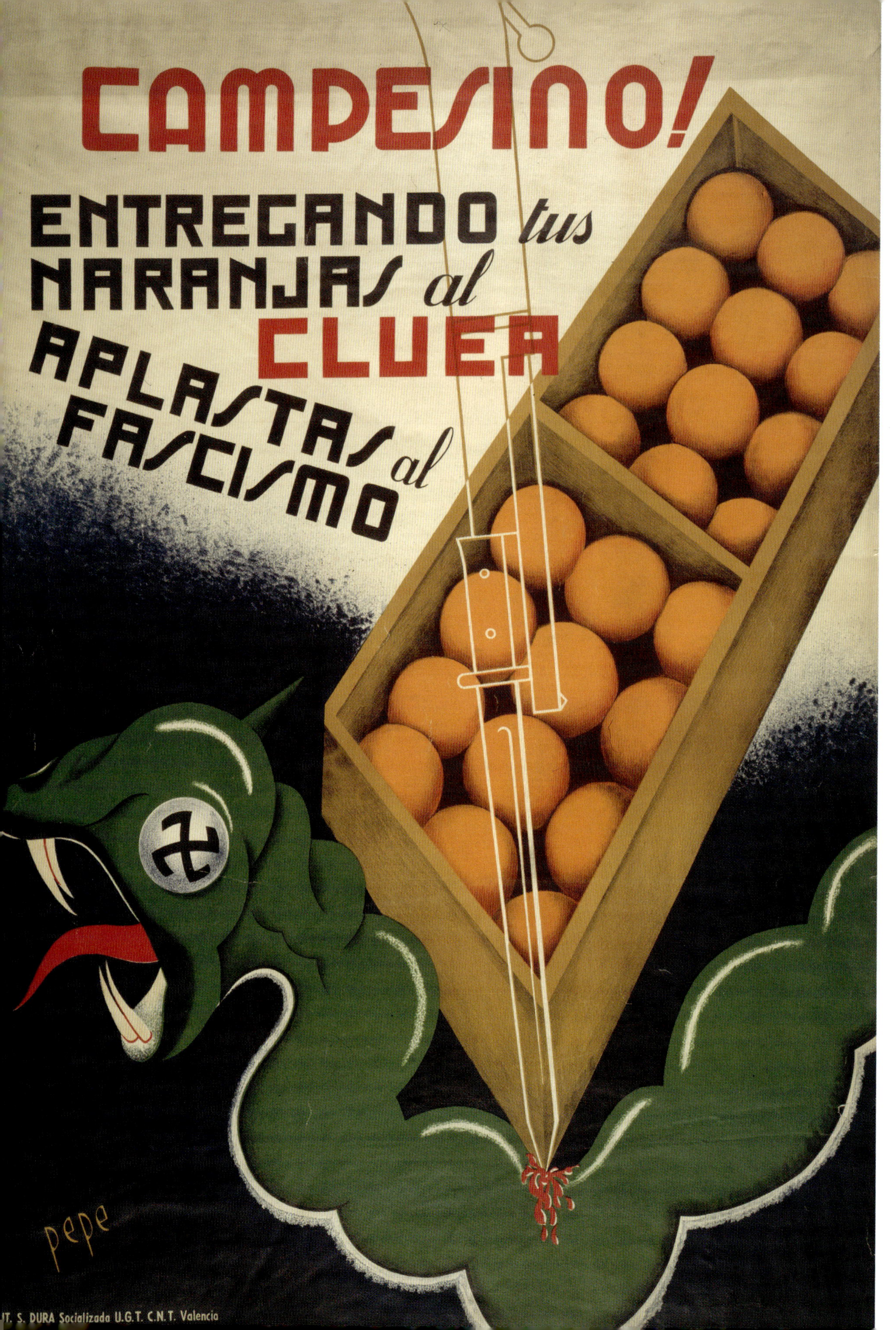

CAMPESINO!
ENTREGANDO tus
NARANJAS al
CLUEA
APLASTAS al
FASCISMO
pepe
IT. S. DURA Socializada U.G.T. C.N.T. Valencia

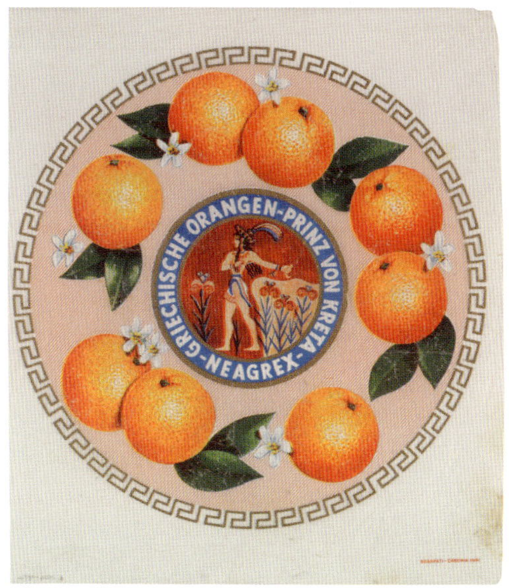

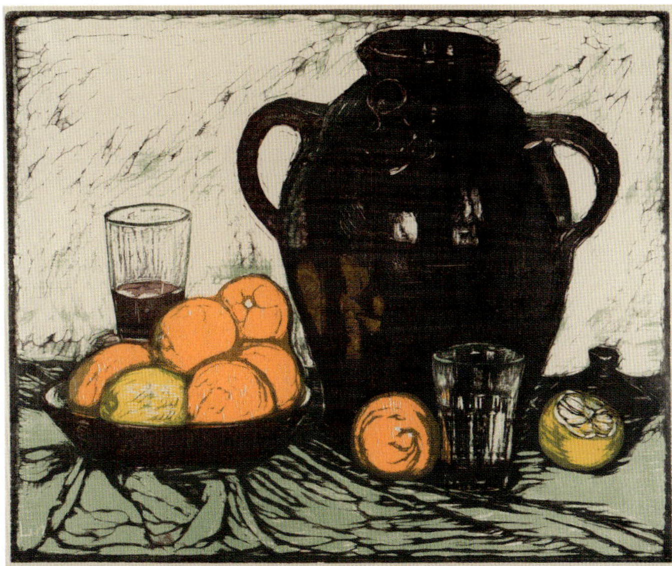

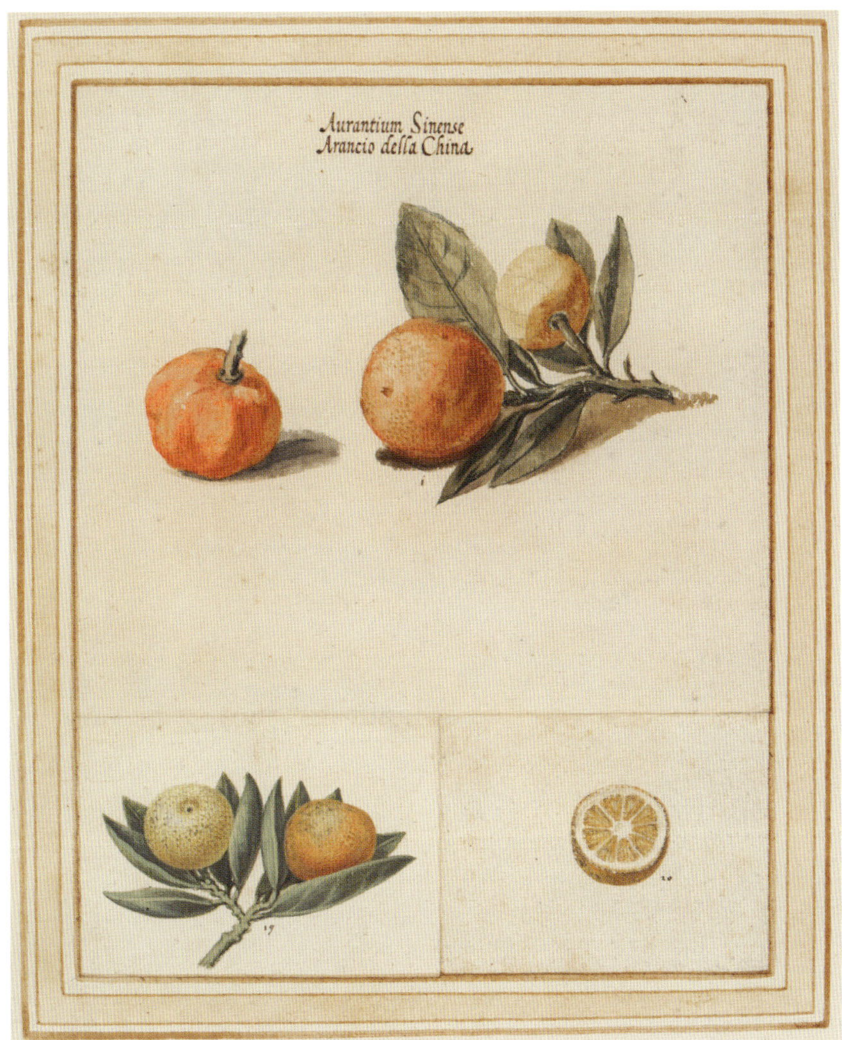

The preparatory studies for J.B. Ferrari's *Hesperides* (1646; left), the first scholarly work dedicated to citrus fruit, are highly detailed in order to help identification at a time predating the widespread availability of oranges. In the 20th century, brightly decorated orange wrappers, such as this Italian letterpress-printed example made by Griechische Oranges (above left), prevented one rotten orange spoiling a whole shipment, so that the fruit arrived safely on tables around the world – as depicted in German artist Wilhelm Laage's still life from 1917 (above right). A Civil War poster from Valencia (1937; opposite) depicts a freshly packed crate of oranges – an important Spanish export – crushing a swastika-eyed snake, urging farmers to align their export channels with their politics to quash the far right. In British artist Anya Gallaccio's installation *Tense*, oversized screen-printed oranges plastered the walls of a disused warehouse (1990; overleaf), while one tonne of the fruit was laid out on the concrete floor to decay during the show, conjuring a sense of contemporary excess.

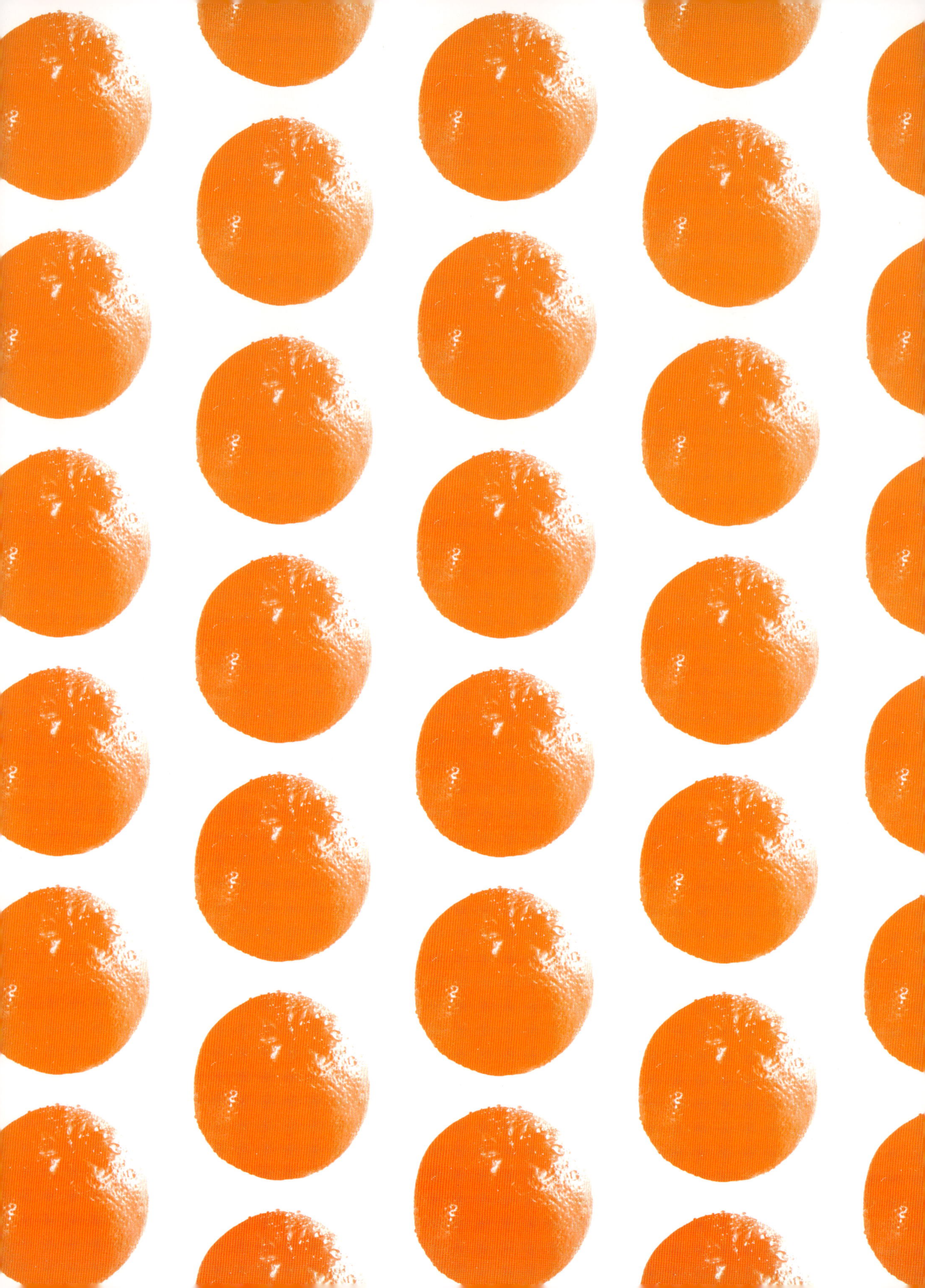

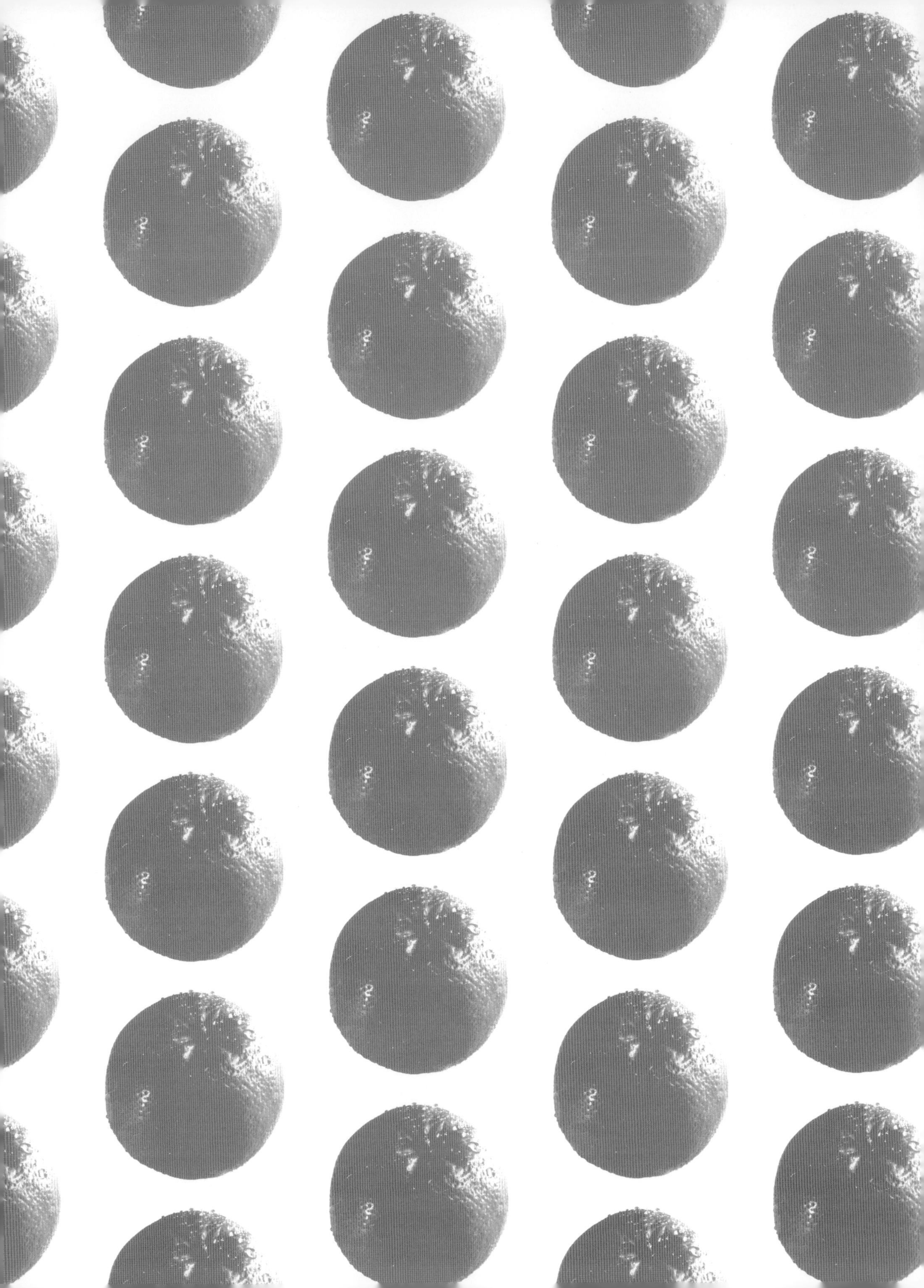

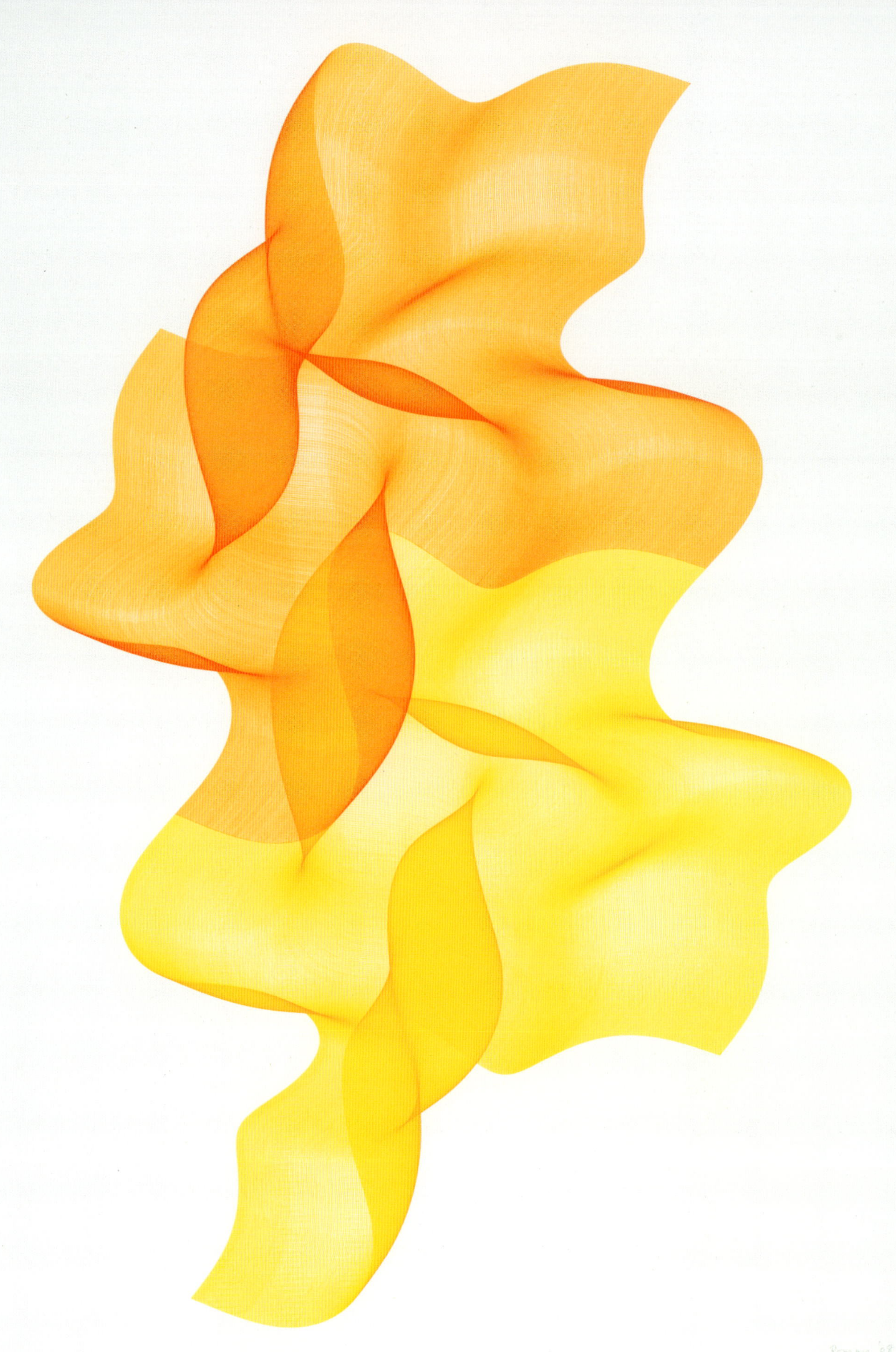

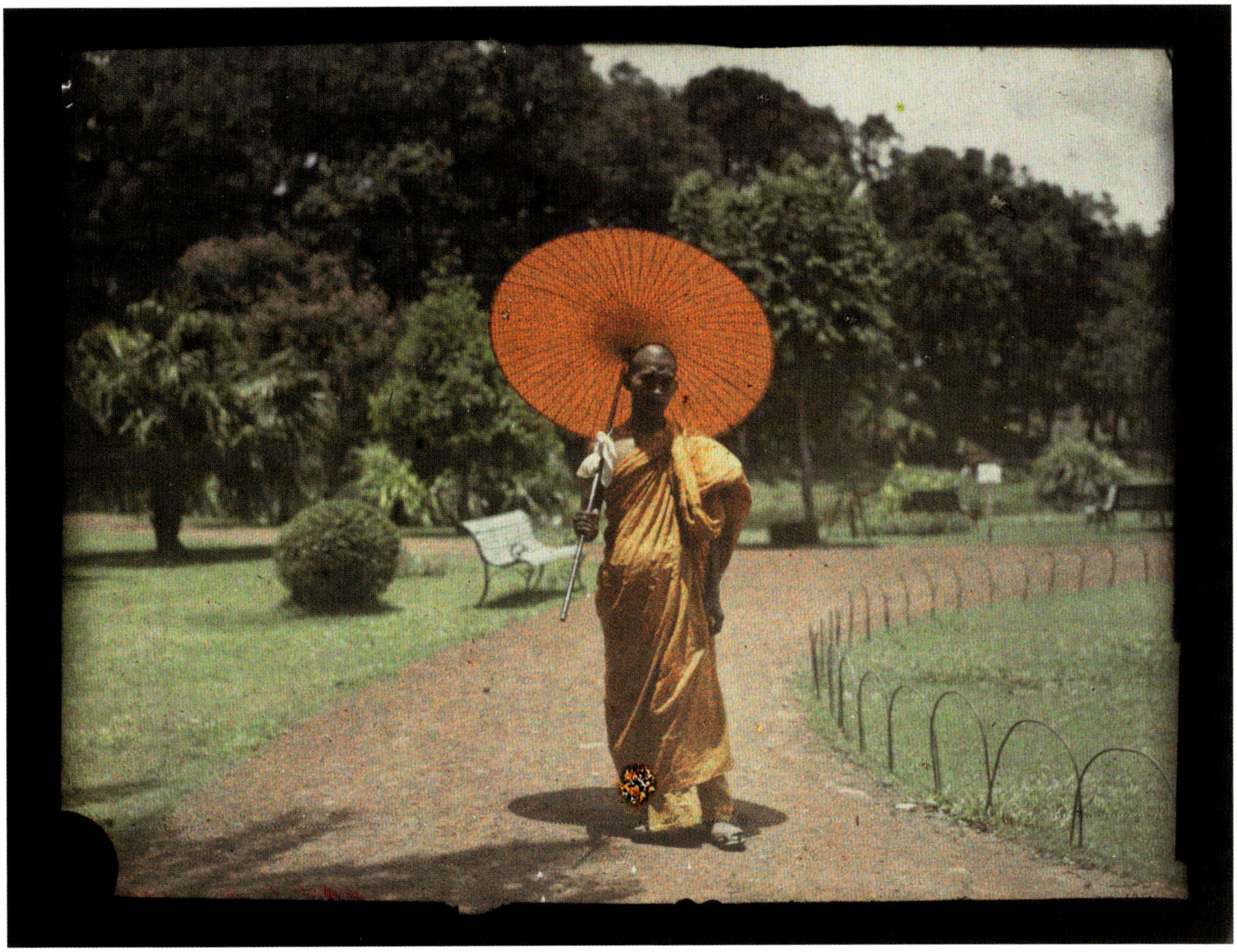

In Hinduism, the sun-like blooms of marigolds – as depicted in this 18th-century watercolour (right) – are strung into garlands to brighten life events from marriage or worship to mourning the dead. The colour is also prevalent in Buddhism. As instructed by the Buddha, monks originally wore robes of discarded ('pure') cloth stitched together and coloured using natural dyes of plant root or clay. Though today the fabric is often donated by the community, the warm orange colour continues to distinguish many monastic Buddhist traditions. In this vibrant autochrome photograph by Helen Messinger Murdoch (1914;

above), a robed figure poses under a bright orange parasol.

The work of pioneering algorithmic artist Roman Verostko, a former Benedictine monk, often embodies an element of philosophical inquiry. Verostko's intricate plotter-drawn designs explore the balance of control and chance in the human experience and spiritual journey. The forms in his *Cyberflowers* series (*Sunshine Version I*, 2008, is shown opposite) are the outcome of the repetition of a single curved line, imbuing the image with a meditative quality.

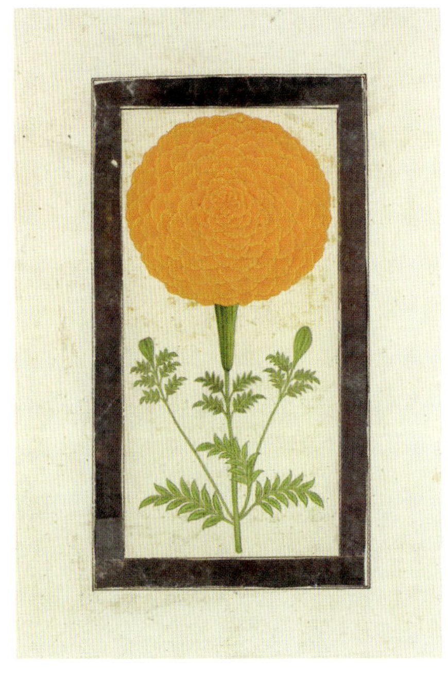

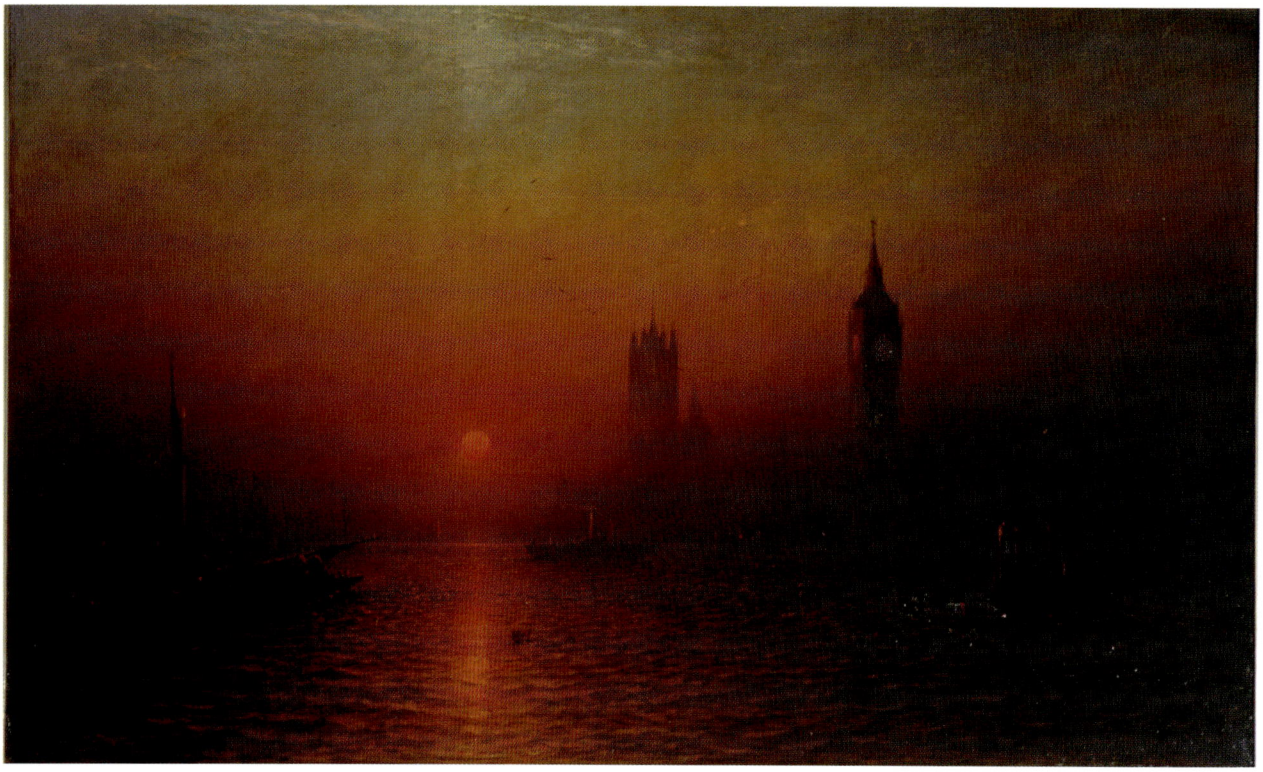

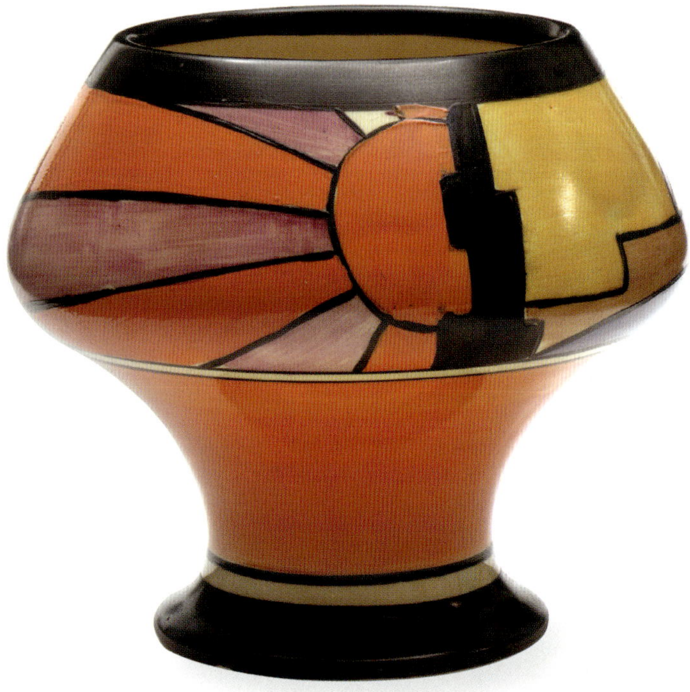

The vibrant colours that light up the sky at sunrise and sunset have mesmerized us for centuries. Francis Danby was celebrated for his skill in capturing early morning and sundown light, as in his oil painting *The Houses of Parliament from the River* (1864; above), bathed in a soft orange glow.

Sun rays are a popular Art Deco design motif, appearing on both architectural elements and home furnishings. Clarice Cliff used an abstracted version of the 'sunburst' to bold effect on ceramics for her popular 'Bizarre' range of the period (left), named as such for its dramatic departure from traditional designs. Textile designer Lucienne Day took inspiration from fine art objects, reinterpreting a Chinese sculpture in the Victoria and Albert Museum collection to produce the 'Horse's Head' (1939) textile print for her Royal College of Art degree show. She also worked with the trends around her, incorporating late 1960s tastes for large geometric patterns to capture a sherbet-coloured sky in the furnishing fabric 'Sunrise' (1969) shown opposite.

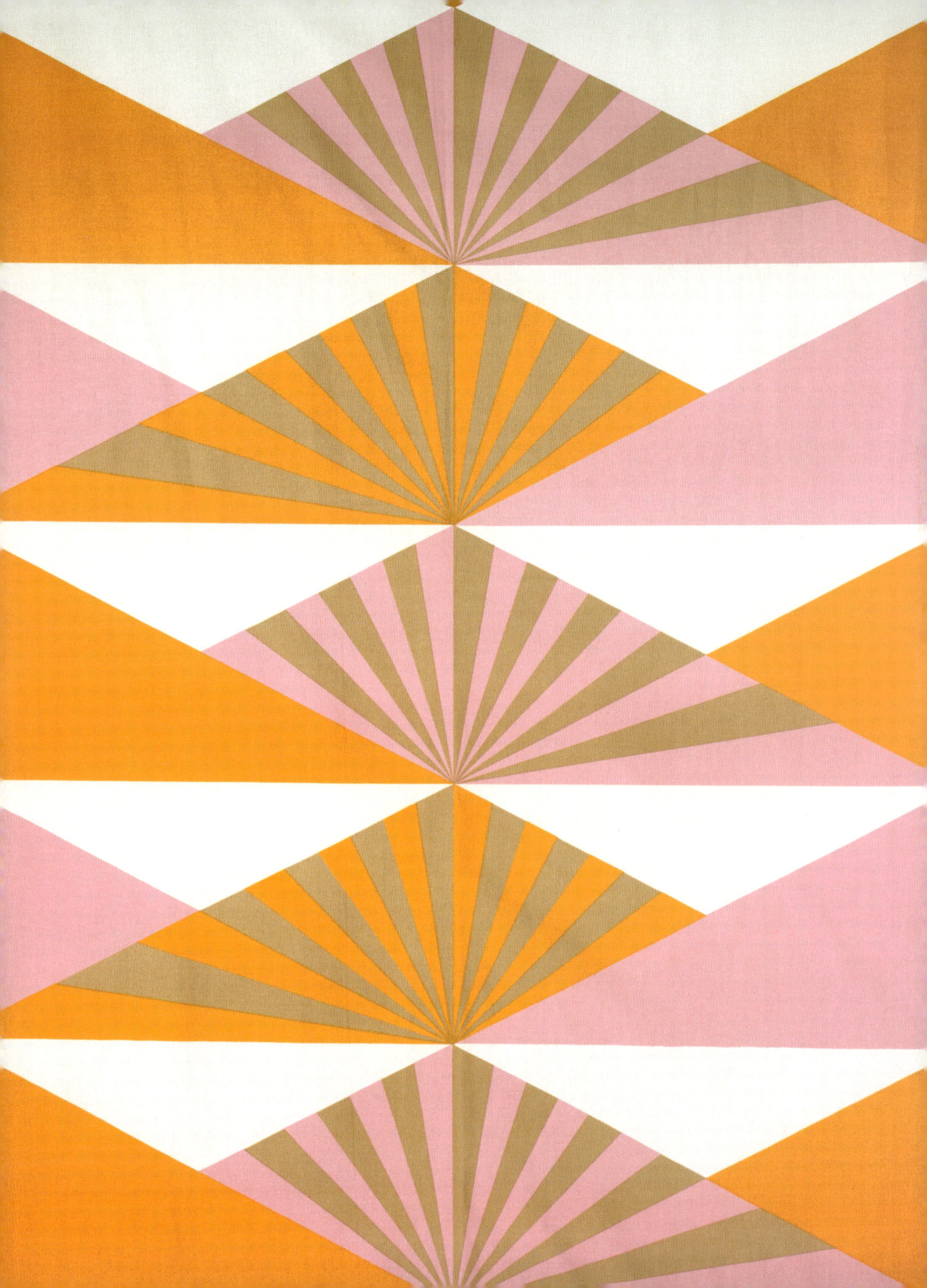

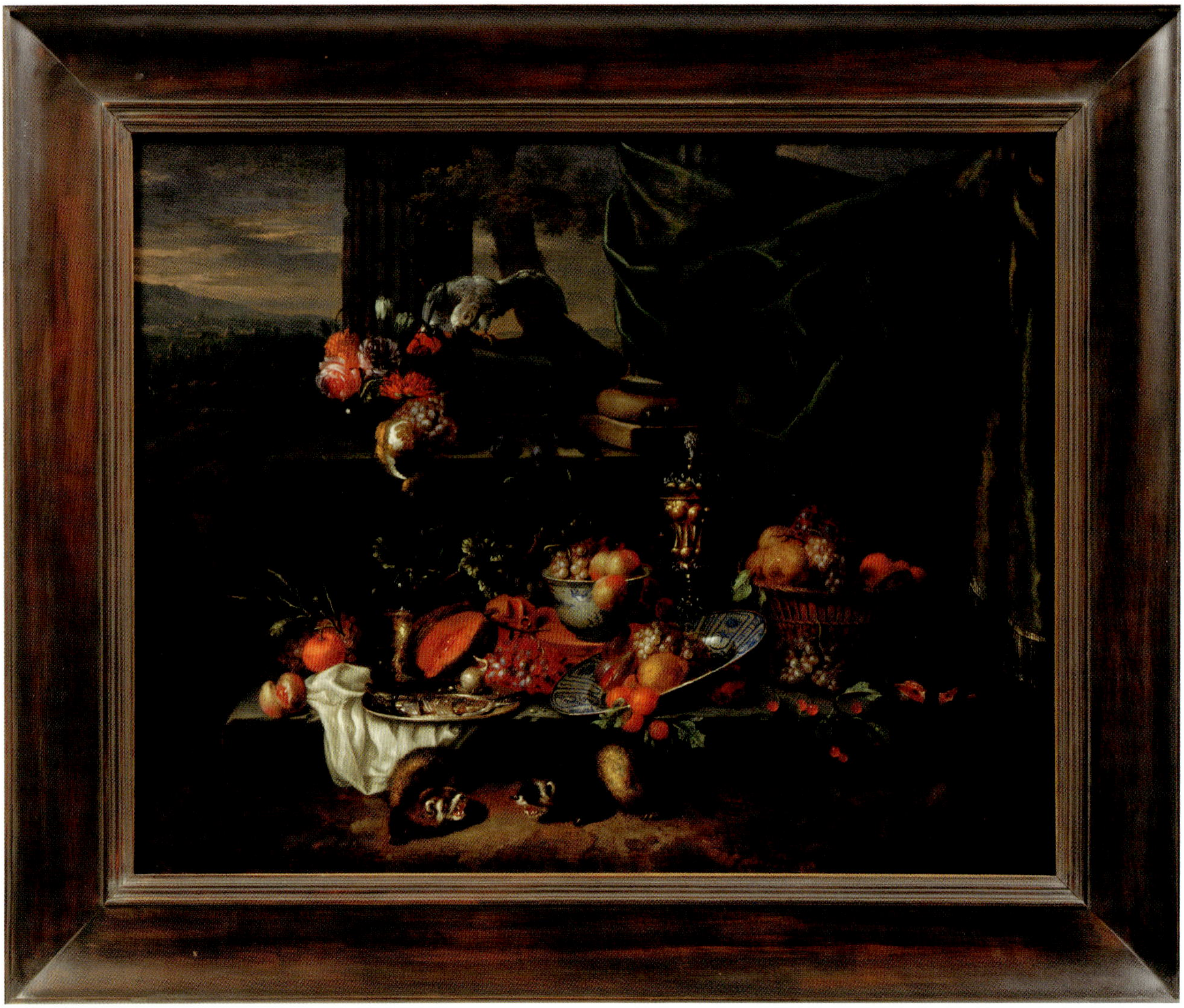

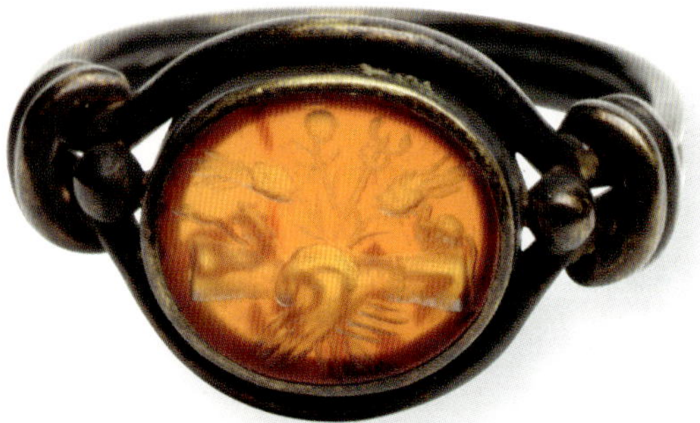

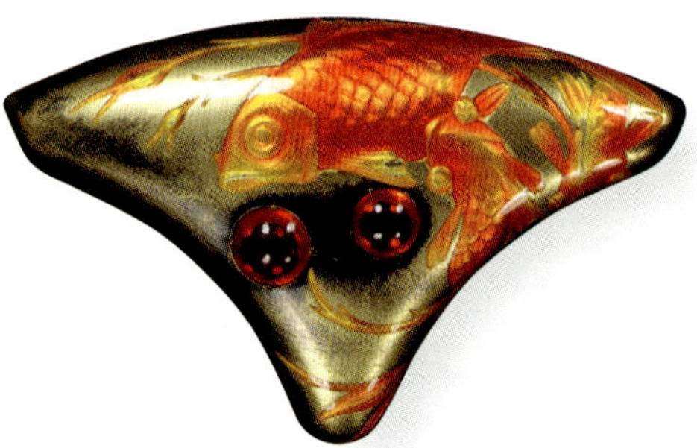

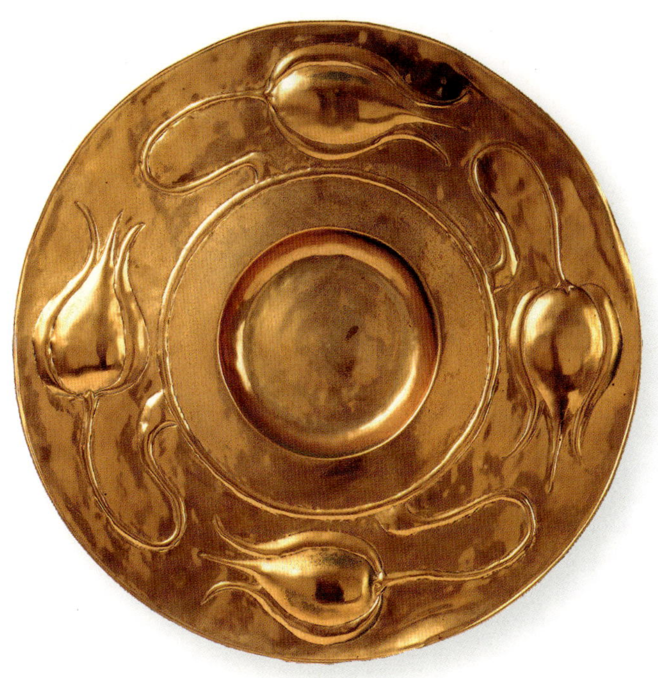

Glowing colour punctuates the dark tones of the 17th-century *Still Life with Fruit, a Parrot and Polecat Ferrets*, by Flemish painter Jan Pauwel Gillemans the Elder (opposite, top). The rich oranges and yellows of imported fruits arranged on decorative platters paint a scene of opulence matched by the alluring radiance of a 17th-century carved amber cup (below), probably collected for display in a Kunstkammer. An Art Nouveau brooch by celebrated jeweller René Lalique (1904–6) complements the vibrant colouring of a goldfish with inset fire opals (opposite, bottom right), and the highly polished copper sheen of Gustav Stickley's charger dish (c. 1905; left) fits in easily amid a display of decadence, despite its maker's Arts and Crafts sensibilities. A Roman engagement ring (200 BC– AD 199; opposite, bottom left) has outlasted more tokenistic displays of wealth. The carved brownish-orange carnelian stone displays emblems, including ears of corn, which symbolize the fruitfulness of the earth and give strength to the marriage.

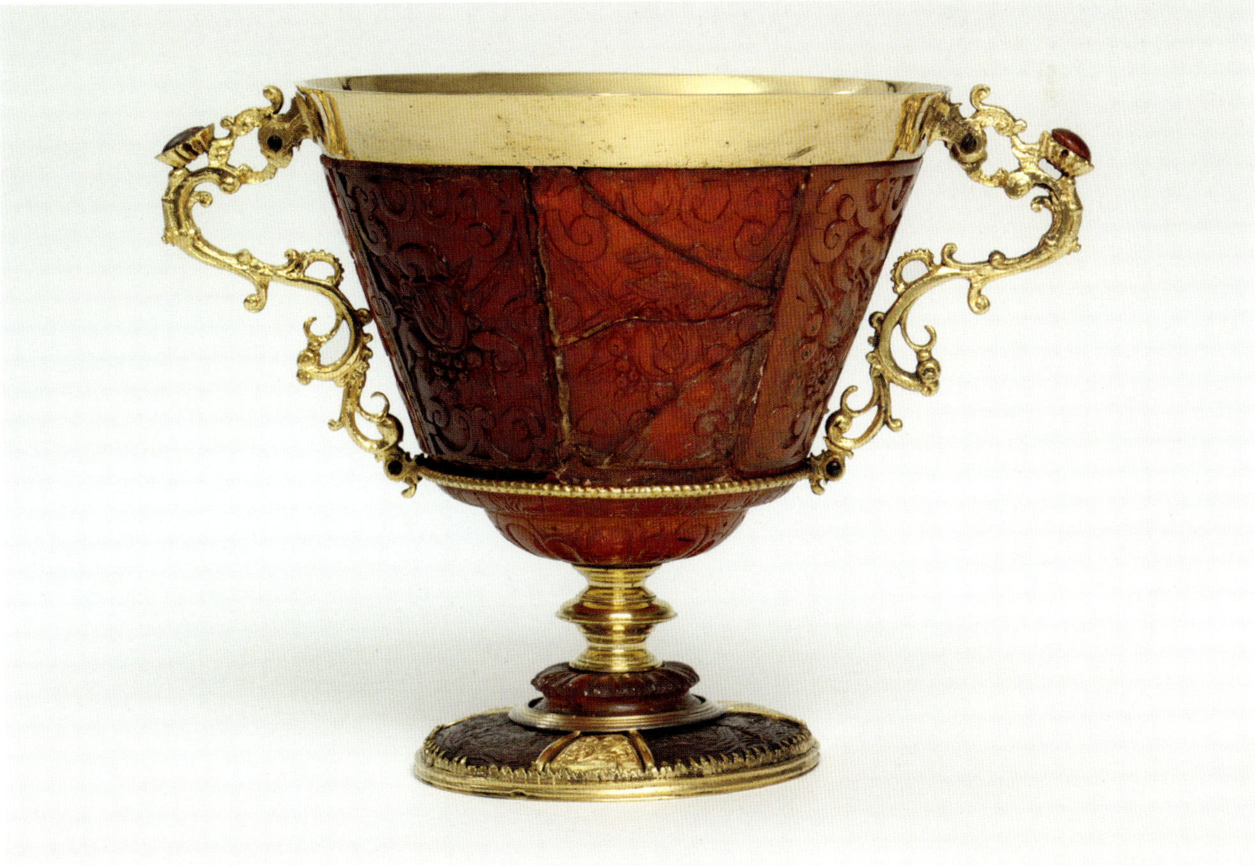

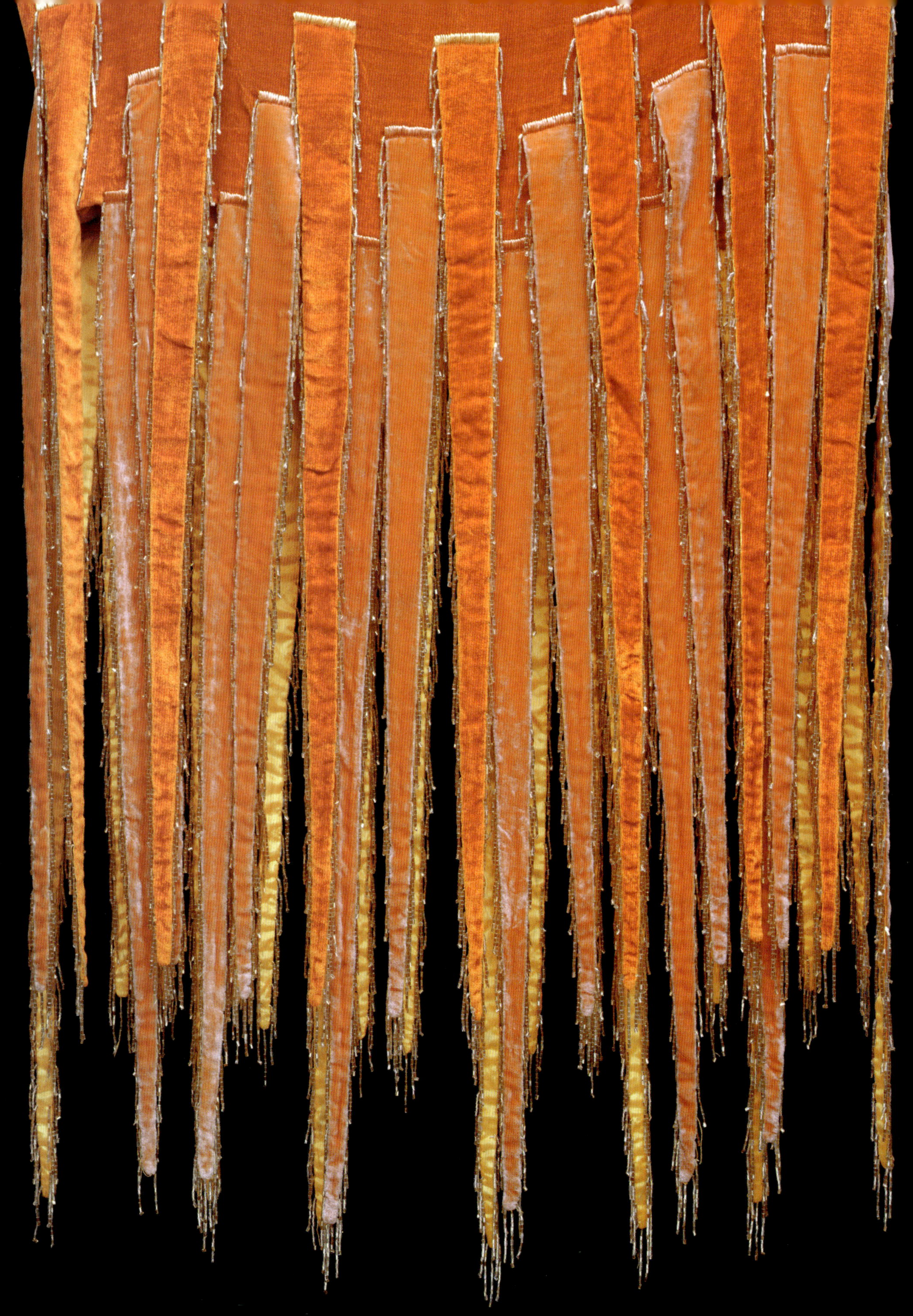

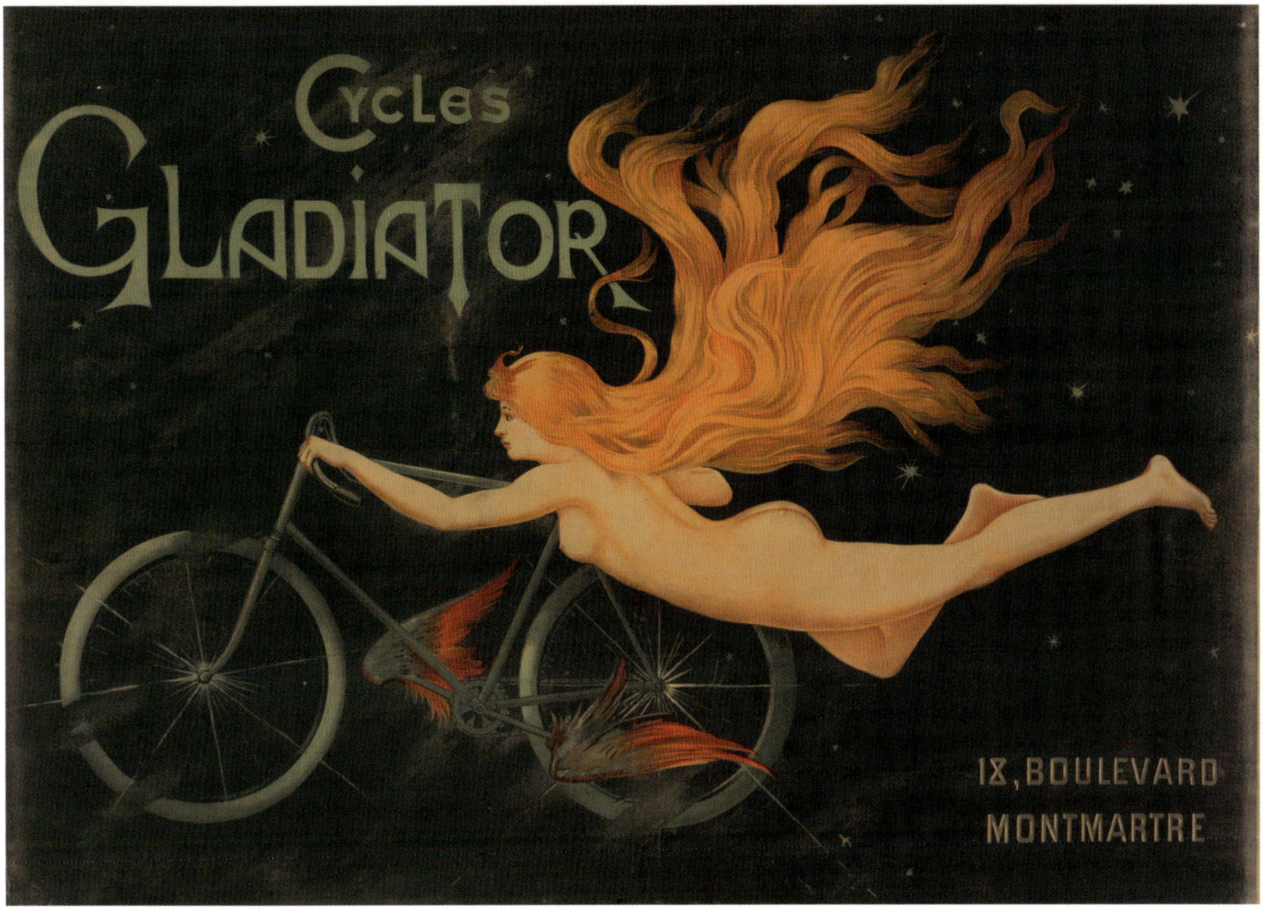

The bicycle's burgeoning popularity offered the 'New Woman' of the *fin de siècle* fresh independence. Advertising drew on Classical imagery to assuage societal disapproval; a flame-haired nude flies alongside a male-framed bicycle in this Gladiator Cycles poster (1898; above). Orange became a fixture of 1920s fashion, when heavy skirts and restrictive corsets gave way to the bolder freedoms of loose, drop-waisted outfits. Evening dresses, such as this silk velvet dress by Voisin (1925; opposite), accentuated the movements of rebellious new jazz and Charleston dances. The visibility and rarity of those with ginger hair has engendered many myths about their character, especially women. Cult film *Barbarella* (1968) stars a tangerine-haired Jane Fonda as the space-travelling heroine. The film was both lauded as indicative of the sexual revolution and criticized as exploitative; a man's hand grasps Barbarella's shoulder in this poster (right) based on Jean-Claude Forest's original comic.

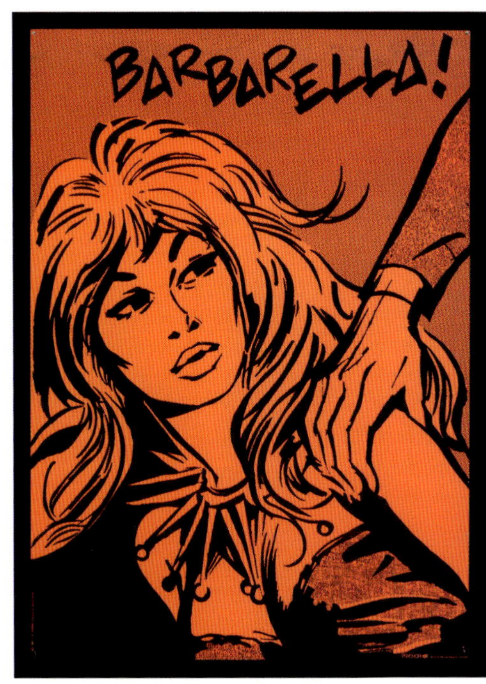

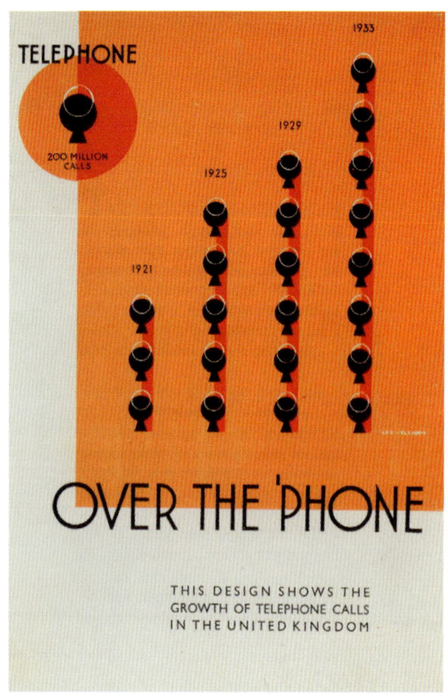

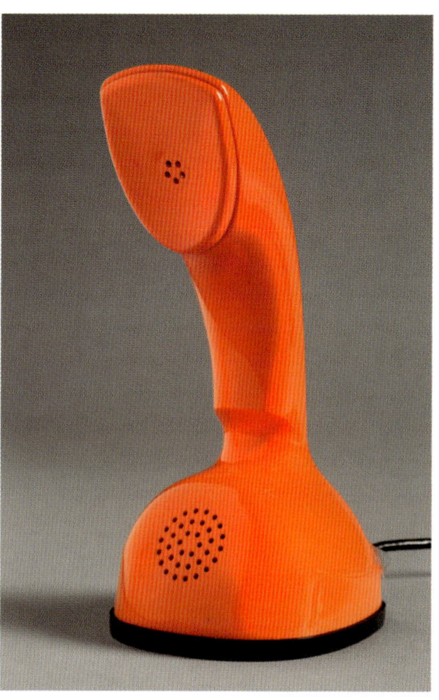

Bold oranges and reds convey positive and confident modernity, as in Theyre Lee-Elliott's *Over the 'Phone* poster (c. 1935; far left), which celebrates newly accessible telephone technology. Designed not long after, the futuristic Swedish one-piece 'Ericofon', designed in 1941 and manufactured from 1954 onwards by LM Ericsson Company (left) was still available as part of the British Post Office 'Specials' range in the 1980s. A glossy polyester varnish coats the surface of Joe Cesare Colombo's 1960s 'Model 4801' neon orange chair (below), to resemble the plastic from which much mass-produced seating of the time was made. It is, in fact, formed of three plywood elements slotted together. A bright cheerful orange, this playful Mary Quant jumpsuit (c. 1967; opposite, top) is based on a child's romper, while the cheeky face of the iconic 1970s Space Hopper (opposite, bottom) invites us to bounce away without a care.

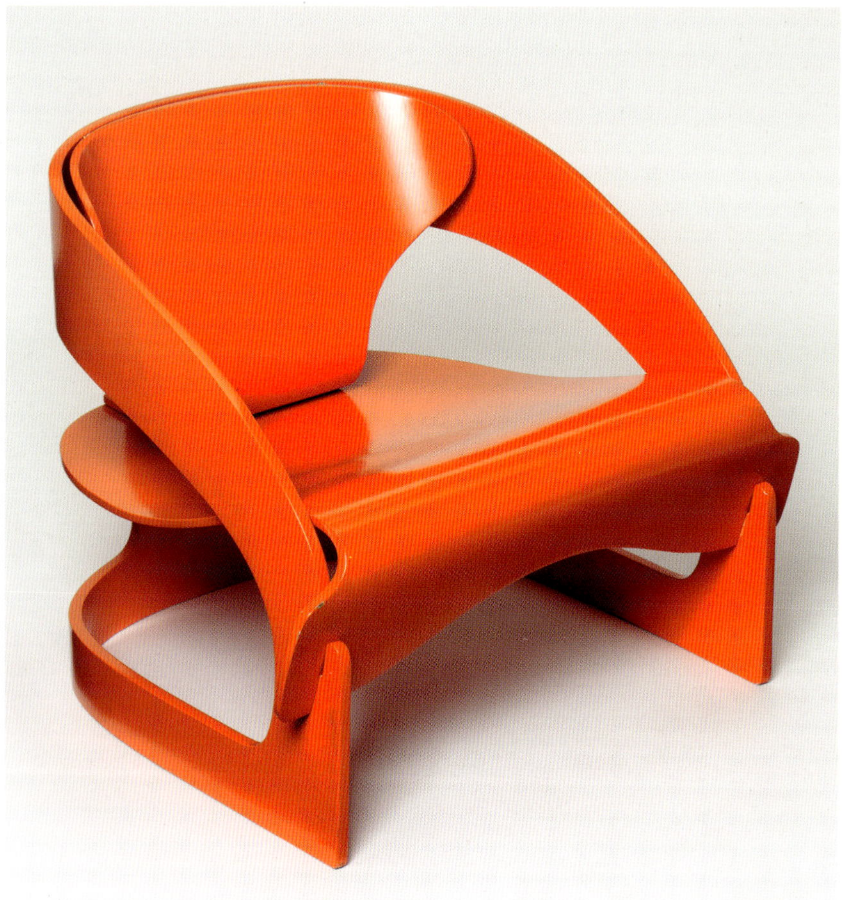

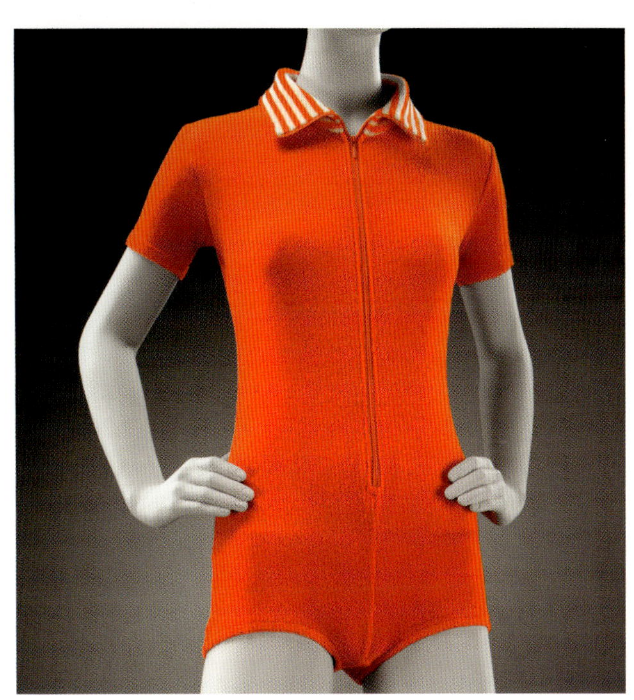

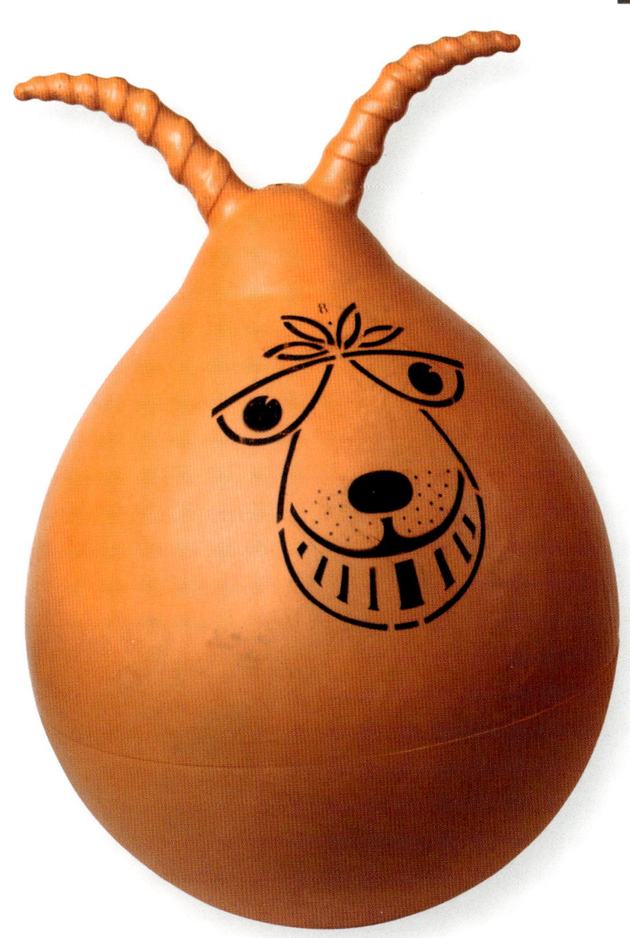

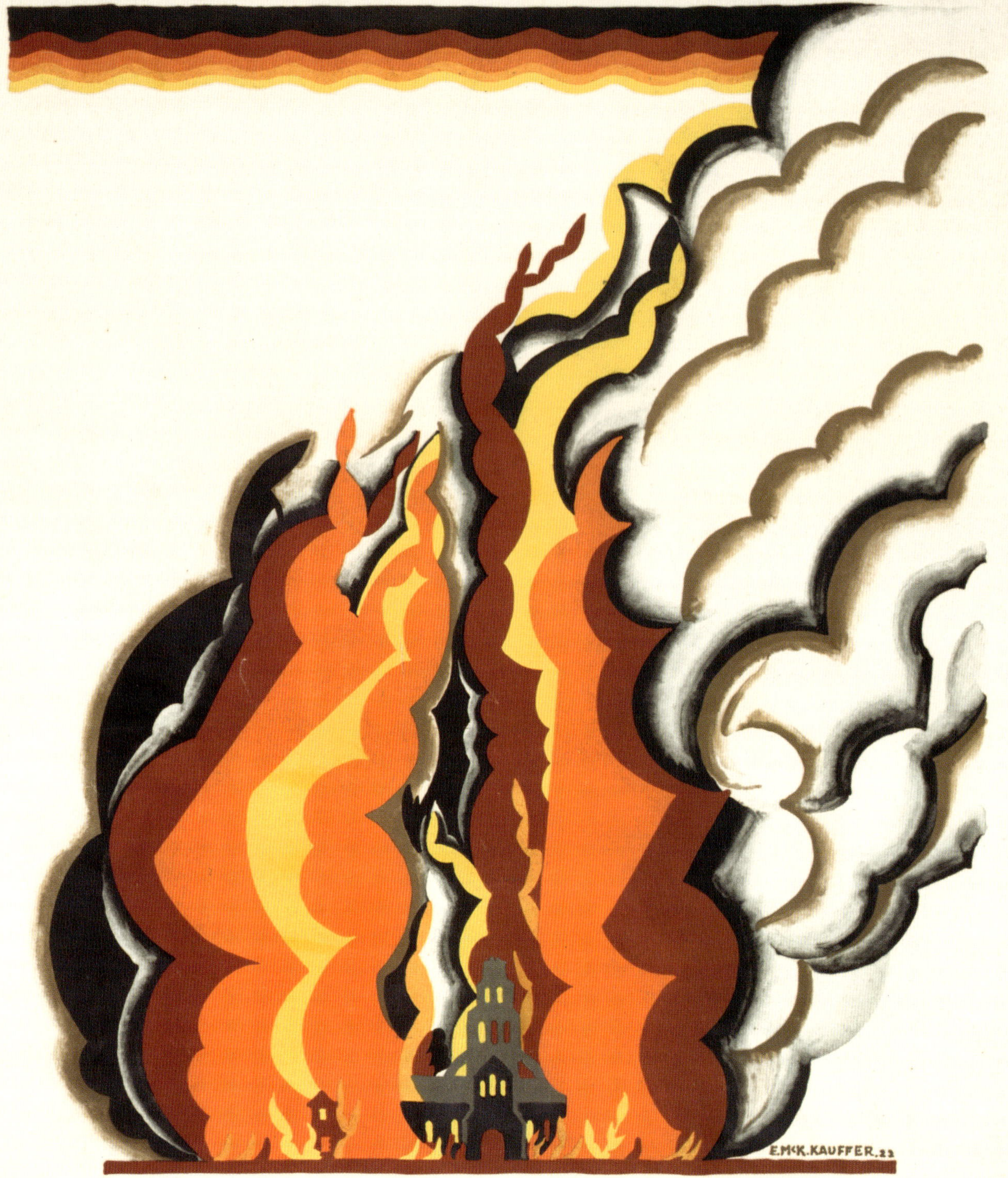

E.McK.KAUFFER.22
LONDON HISTORY AT THE
LONDON MUSEUM
DOVER STREET
OR ST. JAMES'S PARK STATION.

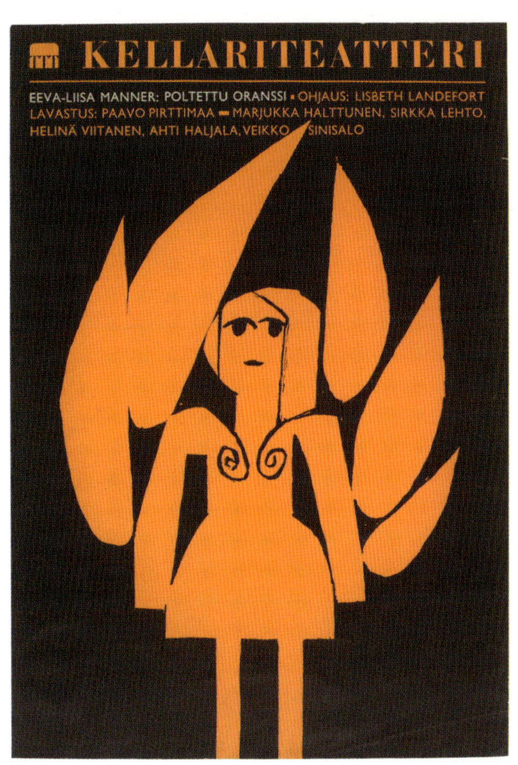

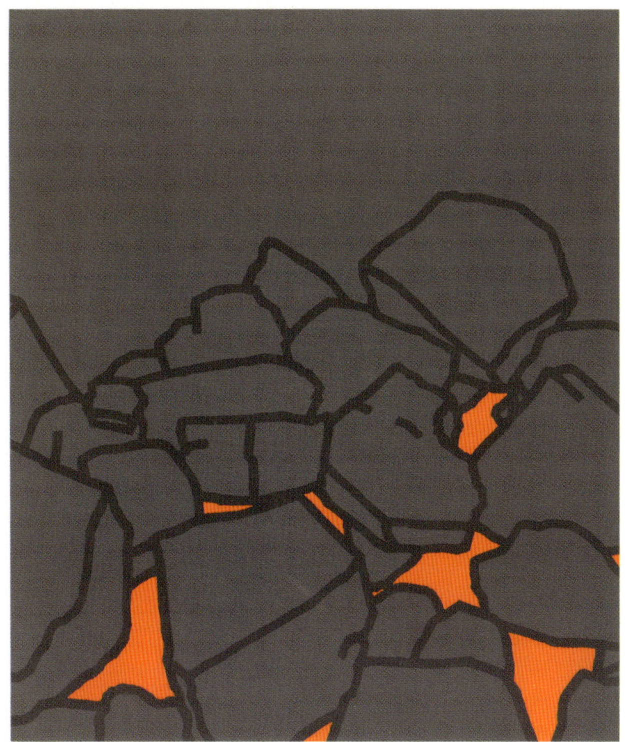

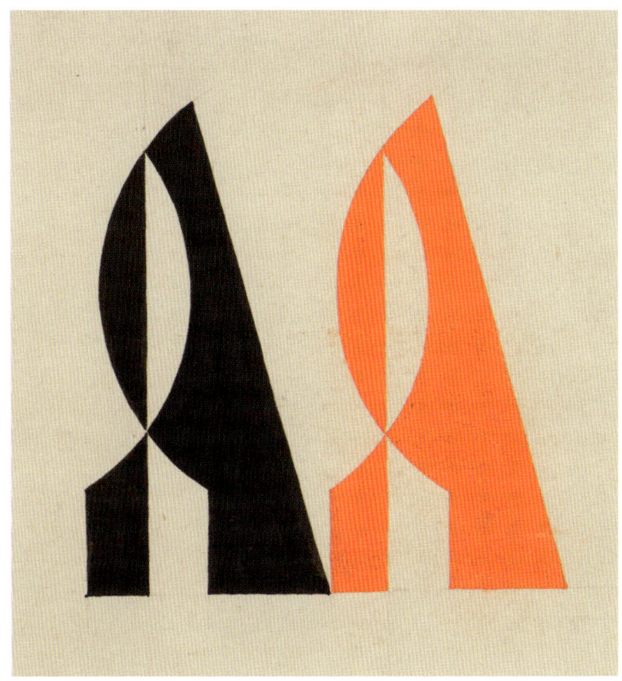

Fire is one of the most alarming displays of orange one might encounter. Edward McKnight Kauffer's poster *London History at the London Museum* (1922; opposite) portrays the ferocity of the mammoth flames that dwarfed the city during the Great Fire of London in 1666. The sense of chaos and destruction that comes with a blaze is more subtly evoked in the poster (1968; above left) for Finnish poet Eeva-Liisa Manner's play *Poltettu Oranssi* (*Burnt Orange*), which tells the story of Marina, a teenage girl experiencing hallucinations as she loses her grip on reality. Contained fire, on the other hand, can be a soothing presence. Theyre Lee-Elliott's 20th-century graphic resembling the geometric shadows cast by two candles (right) and Patrick Caulfield's muted screenprint *Coal Fire* (1969; above right) both attest to the peaceful, hypnotic experience of watching glowing embers or a steady flame.

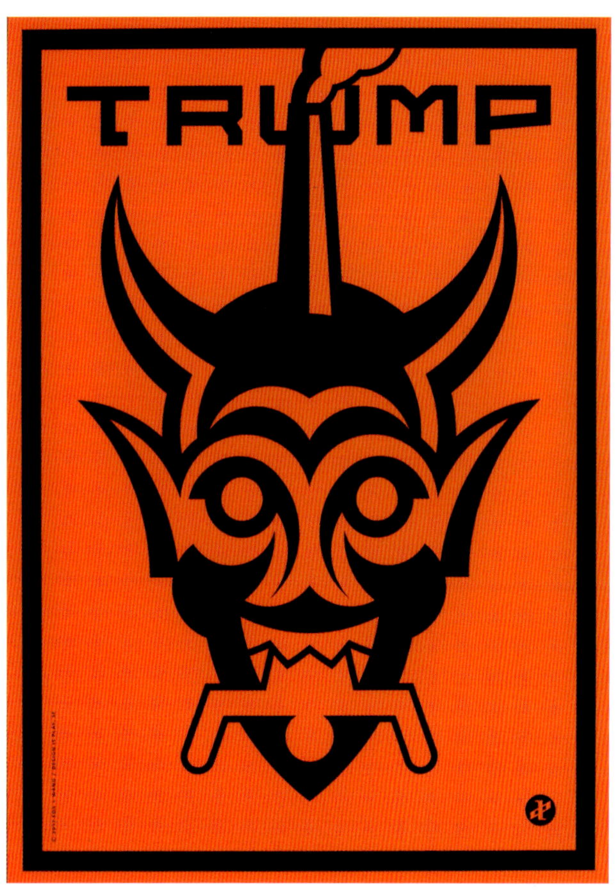

In nature, and consequently design, orange can be a colour of warning. Ori Gersht's photograph *Rear Window II* (2000; opposite) captures the unnatural, glowing orange of the London skyline, the result of atmospheric and light pollution. *The Faraday Chair* (1995; below), a conceptual work by Dunne & Raby, also focuses on environmental danger. Constructed in orange Perspex, as used in safety goggles and laboratory partitions to protect and warn of danger, the structure fits a single occupant connected to the outside by a breathing tube, shielding them from the electromagnetic energy given off by technological devices in homes and workplaces.

Borrowing the visual language of hazard symbols, Design is Play's poster *Trump (Moloch)* depicts the head of child-eating monster Moloch on a fluorescent background (2017; left). The screen-printed design was created in response to the US Republican party and President Donald Trump's 'anti-scientific, anti-environmental policies', the choice of colour perhaps also a tongue-in-cheek nod to Trump's famously not-so-natural skin tone.

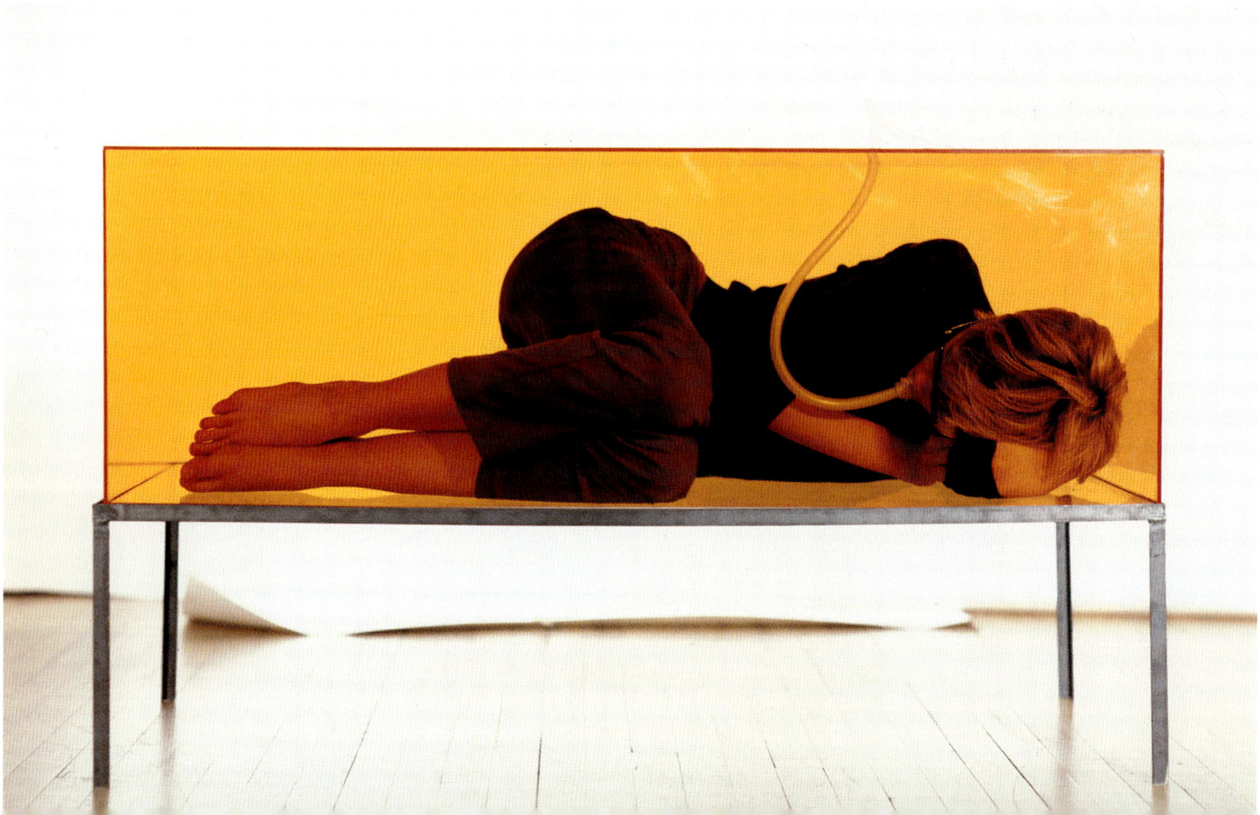

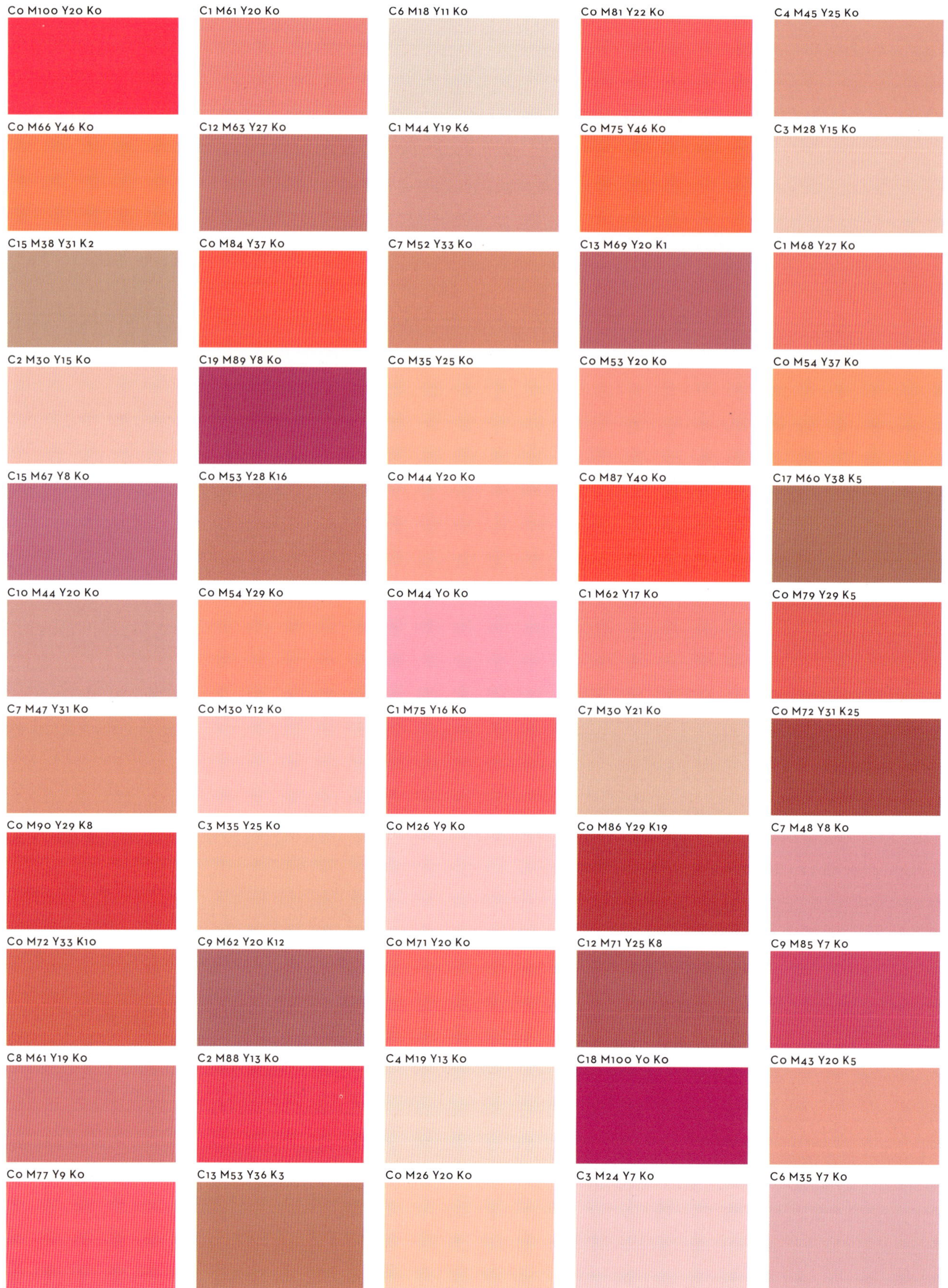

C0 M100 Y20 K0 | C1 M61 Y20 K0 | C6 M18 Y11 K0 | C0 M81 Y22 K0 | C4 M45 Y25 K0
C0 M66 Y46 K0 | C12 M63 Y27 K0 | C1 M44 Y19 K6 | C0 M75 Y46 K0 | C3 M28 Y15 K0
C15 M38 Y31 K2 | C0 M84 Y37 K0 | C7 M52 Y33 K0 | C13 M69 Y20 K1 | C1 M68 Y27 K0
C2 M30 Y15 K0 | C19 M89 Y8 K0 | C0 M35 Y25 K0 | C0 M53 Y20 K0 | C0 M54 Y37 K0
C15 M67 Y8 K0 | C0 M53 Y28 K16 | C0 M44 Y20 K0 | C0 M87 Y40 K0 | C17 M60 Y38 K5
C10 M44 Y20 K0 | C0 M54 Y29 K0 | C0 M44 Y0 K0 | C1 M62 Y17 K0 | C0 M79 Y29 K5
C7 M47 Y31 K0 | C0 M30 Y12 K0 | C1 M75 Y16 K0 | C7 M30 Y21 K0 | C0 M72 Y31 K25
C0 M90 Y29 K8 | C3 M35 Y25 K0 | C0 M26 Y9 K0 | C0 M86 Y29 K19 | C7 M48 Y8 K0
C0 M72 Y33 K10 | C9 M62 Y20 K12 | C0 M71 Y20 K0 | C12 M71 Y25 K8 | C9 M85 Y7 K0
C8 M61 Y19 K0 | C2 M88 Y13 K0 | C4 M19 Y13 K0 | C18 M100 Y0 K0 | C0 M43 Y20 K5
C0 M77 Y9 K0 | C13 M53 Y36 K3 | C0 M26 Y20 K0 | C3 M24 Y7 K0 | C6 M35 Y7 K0

PINK

Existing in shades between red and white, pink has not always been seen as a 'true' colour. In English, the earliest surviving record of the word used as an adjective is from 1607, much later than colours like blue and green. It is often claimed that the word for pink in the English language comes from *Dianthus plumarius*, a plant species with small pink flowers colloquially referred to as 'common pink' or 'wild pink'. Similarly, in many European languages, pink is known as rose or rosa, allied with the well-known flower.

Pink is a colour that feels intrinsically linked to nature, and in particular to flowers. Prized for their beauty, some pink flowers also have specific cultural or religious significance. In Japan, cherry blossoms are symbolic of spring and admired for their fleeting beauty. The arrival of the blossoms from March to early May is celebrated with a practice known as *hanami*, 'flower viewing'. Commonly depicted as pink in south Asian art, the lotus has spiritual significance in many religions. In Hinduism it is associated with a number of gods and goddesses including Brahma, god of creation. According to some traditions, Brahma was born out of a lotus that emerged from the navel of the god Vishnu, a scene we see occurring on p. 114, where the god is depicted rising from the open petals of a pink lotus. In European culture, pink roses often symbolize love, the flowers' delicate petals and sharp thorns representative of the challenges found in romantic pursuit.

Flowers are just one example of pink's abundance in the natural world. Tourmaline, pink topaz and rose quartz are all gemstones that occur in pink, their shades varying from delicate and gentle to bright and dazzling. Prized for their beauty, they are often used in jewellery to decorate brooches, buckles and rings, their natural attractiveness enhanced and celebrated by setting them alongside other stones or precious metals. Tiny pink tourmalines have been set into the centre of silver flowers on a 1920s pendant on p. 123, indicating the colours of the petals. The pink of the tourmalines picks up and amplifies the touches of pink running through the central heart-shaped opal, giving it a romantic feel.

With its bright pink feathers, the flamingo has also become emblematic of the colour, displaying its vibrant, alluring side. The word 'flamingo' comes from the Portuguese or Spanish word 'flamengo', which literally translated means 'flame-coloured'. Flamingos are not born with pink feathers, but take on the colour due to pigments consumed in their food – including brine shrimp and blue-green algae. They are at their brightest during mating season, to attract a partner.

Craftspeople have used both natural and synthetic pigments and dyes to replicate the many shades of pink, using it to colour everything from artwork to curtains. In Europe, pink gained prominence as a fashionable colour in the eighteenth century as part of the rococo style, and manufacturers developed a host of pink objects to cater to their customers' tastes. In 1757, a pink glaze known as rose was developed at the Sèvres factory in France and used to decorate their porcelain products, such as the tray on p. 120. Madame de Pompadour, official mistress of the French king Louis XV, was a well-known patron of Sèvres, and the new rose shade, rumoured to be her favourite, later became known in England as 'Rose

Pompadour' or 'Pompadour Pink'. Almost 250 years later, in 1990, the American artist Cindy Sherman produced her own rococo style porcelain, decorated with portraits of herself dressed as Madame de Pompadour. Available in a fitting shade of pink, Sherman's work illustrates the enduring connection between this colour and the rococo style.

Synonymous with style and luxury, the use of pink in the rococo period extended to all areas of design. This taste for pink is reflected in contemporary paintings such as those by François Boucher, which show elegant men and women draped in shimmering pink silks. Pink was not a gendered colour in the eighteenth century, and pink textiles were popular in both menswear and womenswear, with safflower and redwood dyes commonly used to create these hues. A man's waistcoat on p. 120, made from pink silk satin and embroidered with flowers, shows the pale pink shade that was favoured at the end of the century, as the rococo style gave way to neoclassicism.

The colour has also proved a popular sartorial choice in India, where pink has long been a colour embraced by both men and women. In 1956, fashion editor Diana Vreeland proclaimed pink 'the navy blue of India' in reference to its ubiquity. A painting of Maharaja Sir Sri Krishnaraja Wodeyar Bahadur, ruler of Mysore, southern India, made in about 1906 shows him dressed to impress in a light pink silk-satin coat and matching pink and gold turban (p. 122).

Bright pink is frequently associated with Mexican fashion and dress, and in the mid-twentieth century the phrase 'rosa mexicano' or 'Mexican pink' started to be used to describe the special variation of pink now synonymous with the country's art and culture. The shade was widely popularized by designer Ramón Valdiosera from the late 1940s onwards; when he died in 2017, *Vogue Mexico* described him as the 'father of Mexican pink'.

Despite its multitudinous meanings, since the early twentieth century pink has primarily become known for its binary gender associations; designated as a colour for women and girls, with blue its male counterpart. The many shades of pink are often used to evoke a range of stereotypical characteristics of femininity, from cute and meek to bold and sexy. At one end of the spectrum is pale pink, seen on p. 127 in a brassiere from the 1920s. Almost white, the shade evokes notions of gentility, softness and innocence. The colour has been cleverly paired with a thin, soft silk-satin material and floral lace inserts, both of which bolster similar notions of femininity. At the other end of the spectrum is bright pink, used to evoke thoughts of frivolity, sexuality and lust. This is perhaps epitomized by 'Shocking Pink', the shade famously associated with Italian fashion designer Elsa Schiaparelli (see p. 128), which she described as 'bright, impossible, impudent, becoming, life-giving, like all the light and the birds and the fish in the world put together' – yet again harking back to the natural world.

The idea of pink for girls and blue for boys took hold in Europe and America at the beginning of the century. The pink footwear set on p. 124 was sent to Princess Mary, the only daughter of George V, during her pregnancy in 1923. Following the birth of sons in both 1923 and 1924, the gift was returned. The message was clear: there was no use for pink shoes for a boy. But this codification of gendered colours was slow to solidify, and in the late nineteenth century pink was often still seen as a masculine colour, strongly associated with red, the colour of war. Blue, with its clear associations with the Virgin Mary, was a popular choice for girls. Marketing drives in the mid-twentieth century strengthened the 'pink for girls' trope, and companies increasingly produced pink product lines especially targeted at female consumers of all ages. In 1955 the American car manufacturers Dodge released the Dodge La Femme car, specifically targeted at female consumers. The car was painted 'Heather Rose' and 'Sapphire White', and featured pink interior upholstery and a pink purse to match. More recently, research has shown that products targeted at women are often more expensive than genderless or male equivalents, giving rise to the term 'pink tax' in critique of this inequality.

The meaning of pink is changing again. The colour is increasingly politicized, in a reflection and often subversion or rejection of the gendered characteristics with which it has been endowed. During the period of Nazi rule in parts of Europe, a pink triangle symbol was used to identify people classed as homosexual, drawing again on

'life-giving, like all the light and the birds and the fish in the world put together'
Elsa Schiaparelli, *Shocking Life* (1954)

the colour's association with femininity. In the 1970s, the pink triangle – and the colour pink more broadly – was reclaimed by the LGBTQ+ community. During the AIDS epidemic, LGBTQ+ activist group ACT UP, formed in 1987, adopted an upwards-pointing pink triangle alongside the slogan 'SILENCE = DEATH'. Pink is now worn and used for many LGBTQ+ campaigns. In the 1990s the fiscal pulling power of the community began to be referred to as the 'pink dollar' or the 'pink pound'.

Strongly associated with traditional twentieth-century ideas of femininity, pink has also been used in feminist activism. It was chosen as the colour for the 'Pussy Power' hat (p. 130) designed by Kat Coyle, which has become an internationally recognizable symbol of female power and protest. The hat was created as an open-source knitting pattern, intended for people to wear to protest the inauguration of US President Donald Trump at the Women's March in Washington in January 2017.

Whether used to subvert or celebrate, pink is a colour that inspires strong reactions. Childish, seductive, romantic, shocking, its meanings change depending on the cultural context in which it is used. Pink is the colour of the ballet, of Barbie dolls, of the city of Jaipur. It is prominent in pop art, punk and psychedelia. It has also become the colour of women and a colour of protest.

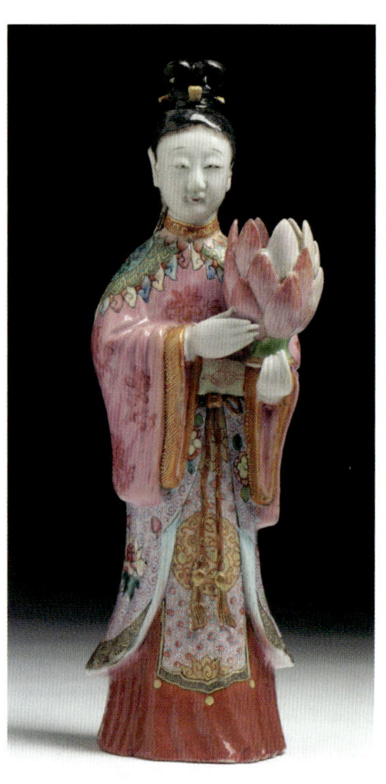

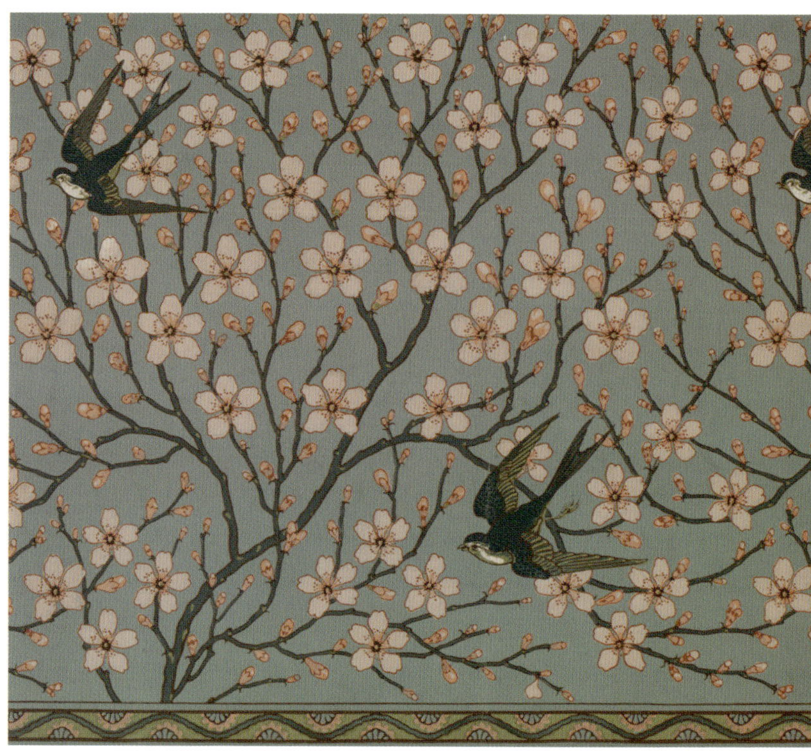

Symbolizing hope, divinity and rebirth, some of the most celebrated flowers are pink. Dressed in flowing robes, this 18th-century porcelain figure of a woman cradling a large pink lotus flower (above left) shows its historical importance in China. The lotus flower has spiritual significance in many religions including Hinduism and Buddhism. A key figure in the unending cycle of the creation and destruction of the universe, the Hindu god Vishnu can be seen in this 19th-century painting (right) with his wife, the goddess Lakshmi. A pink lotus emerges from Vishnu's navel, from which the god of creation, Brahma, appears.

Designed to be worn by a young unmarried woman, this exquisite pink silk-crêpe kimono (opposite), made between 1920 and 1940, is decorated with peonies, a symbol of good fortune, and peacock feathers. Walter Crane's wallpaper frieze from 1878 (above right), printed from wood blocks, depicts swallows flying through an abundance of pink almond blossom.

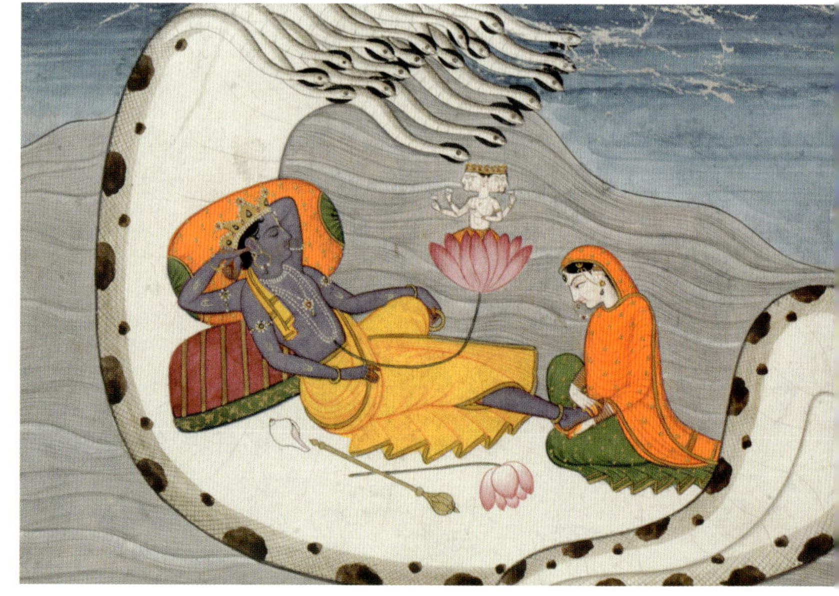

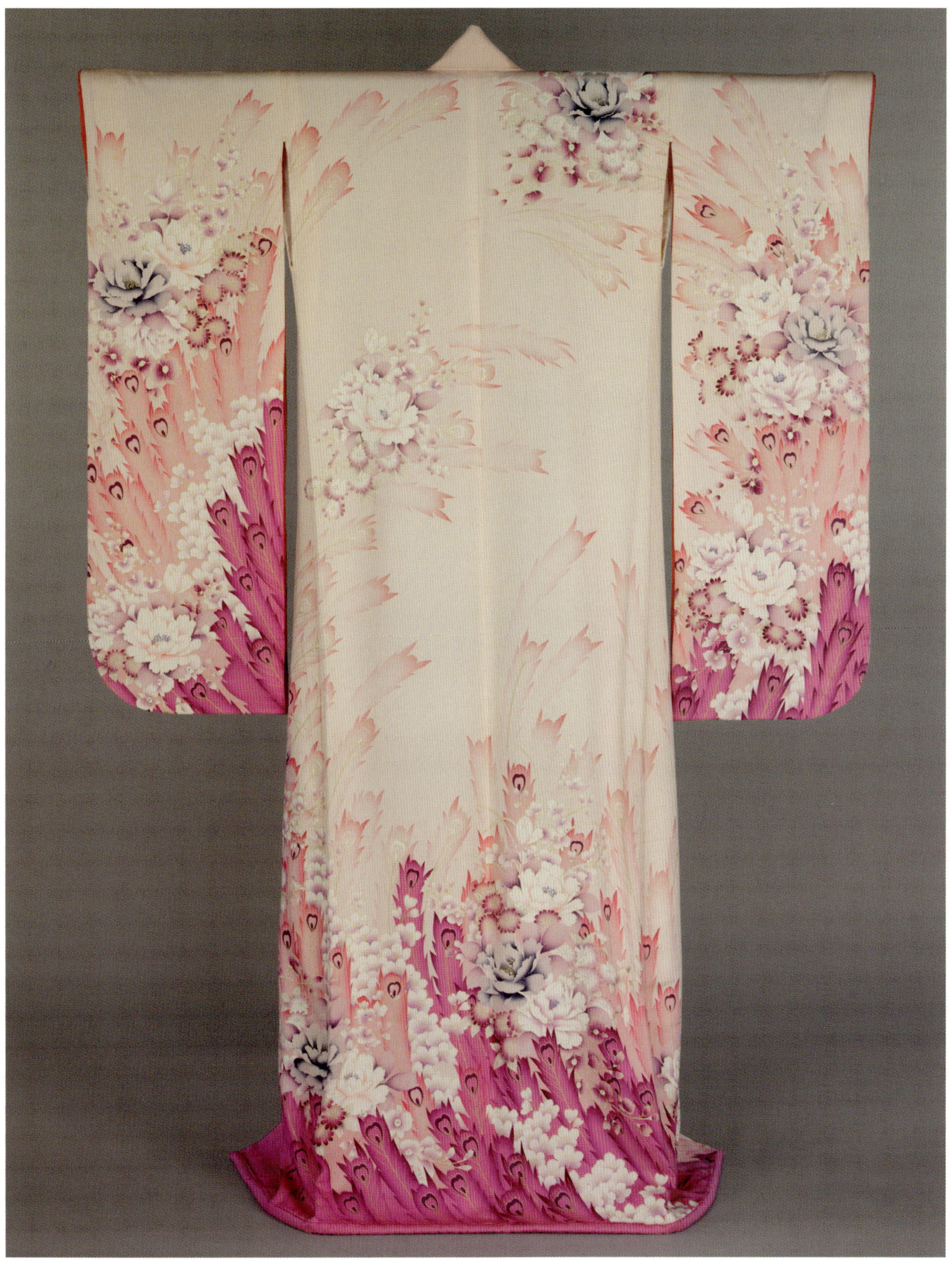

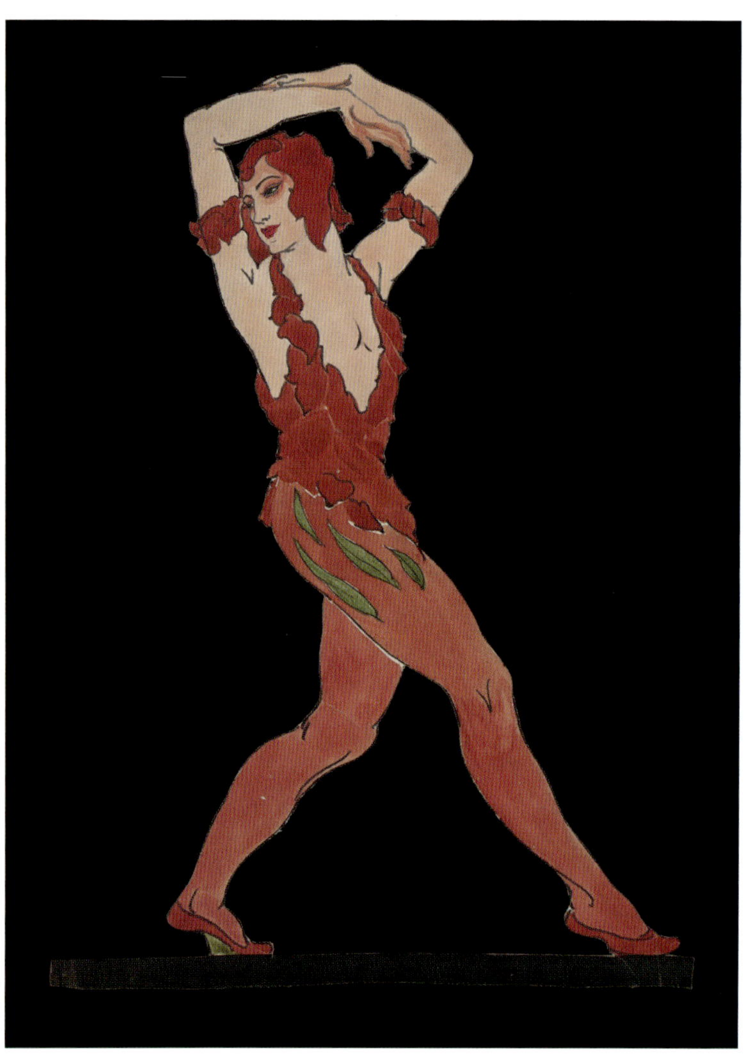

The pink rose is closely associated with romance. In this ring (c. 1830–60; below left), individually hinged panels hide secret messages. The enamelled pink roses, symbolizing love, would have clearly signalled that it was a lovers' token. Vera Willoughby's painted template for a plywood figure (1920s; left) portrays the iconic dancer Vaslav Nijinsky in the role of 'Le Spectre de la Rose' from Mikhail Fokine's famous ballet. Nijinsky wore a costume covered in silk petals to play the spirit of a young girl's romantic dreams.

Lucile (Lady Duff Gordon), wrote that she was 'the first dressmaker to bring joy and romance into clothes'. Her luxurious evening cloak (c. 1915; below right) of silk velvet, decorated with pink silk satin rosebuds, is fit for a heroine in a fairytale. Evoking imagery from a medieval romance, thorny yet sweet pink briar roses entangle themselves around dark green foliage in the classic wallpaper design opposite by John Henry Dearle for Morris & Co.

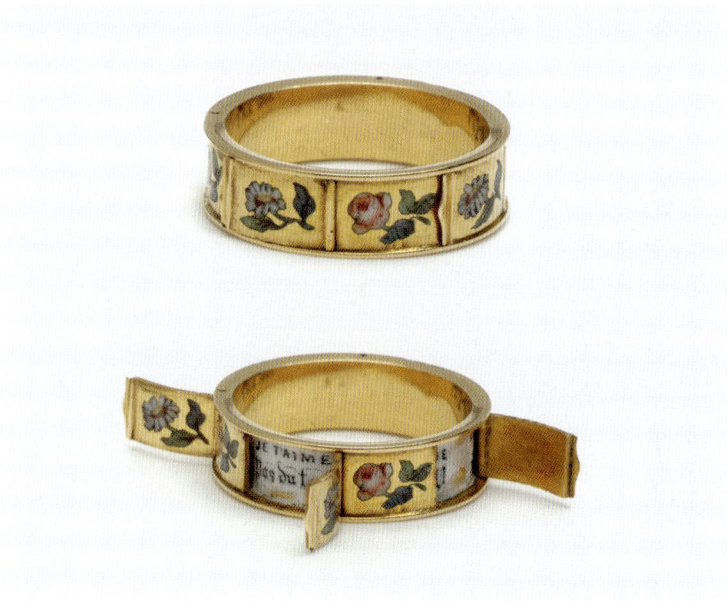

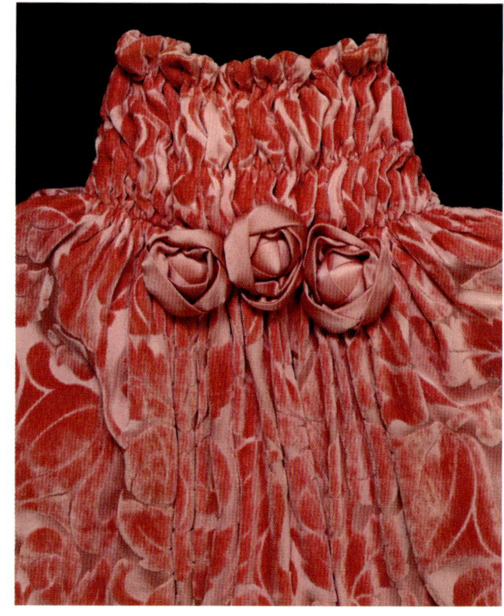

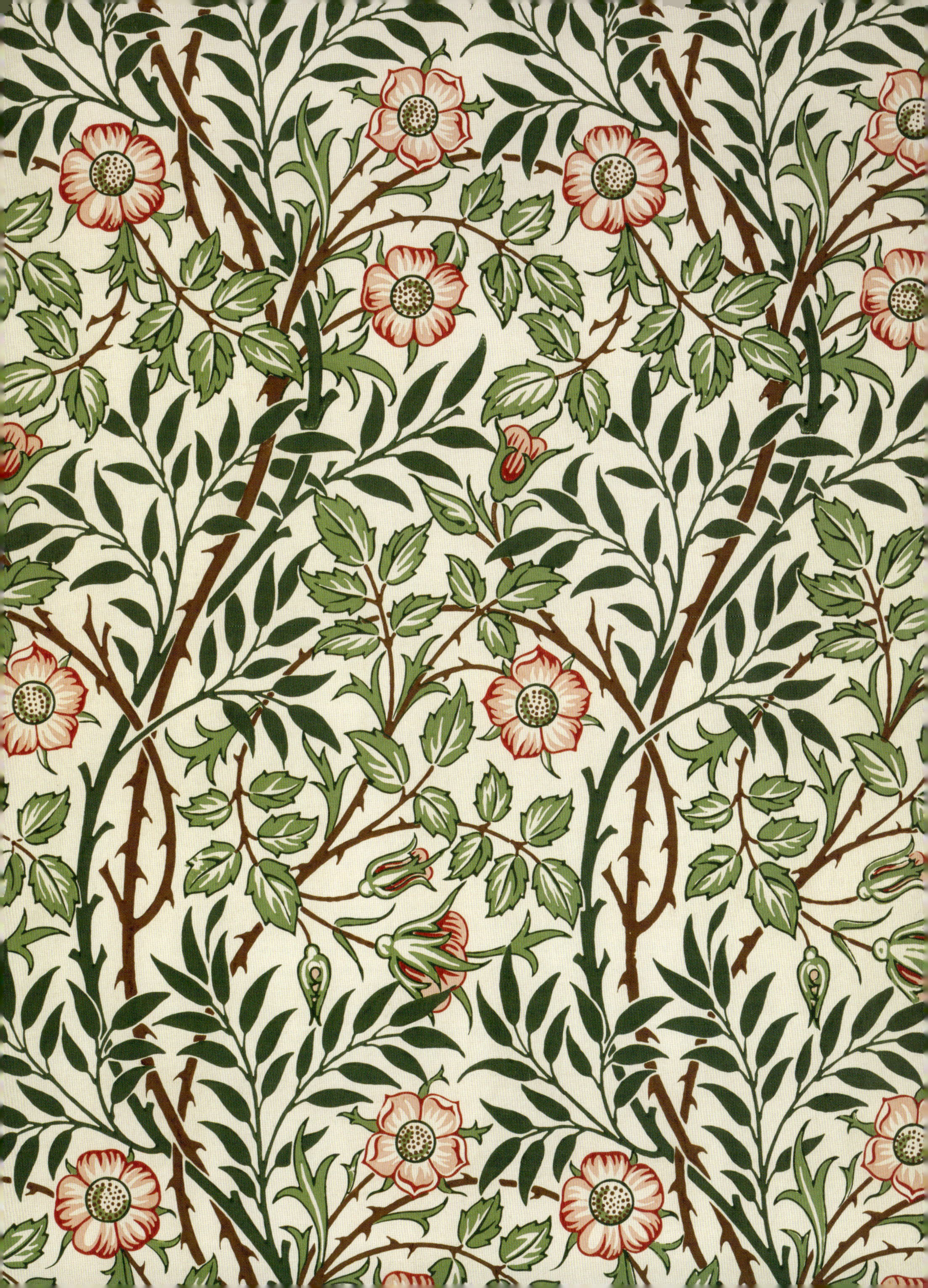

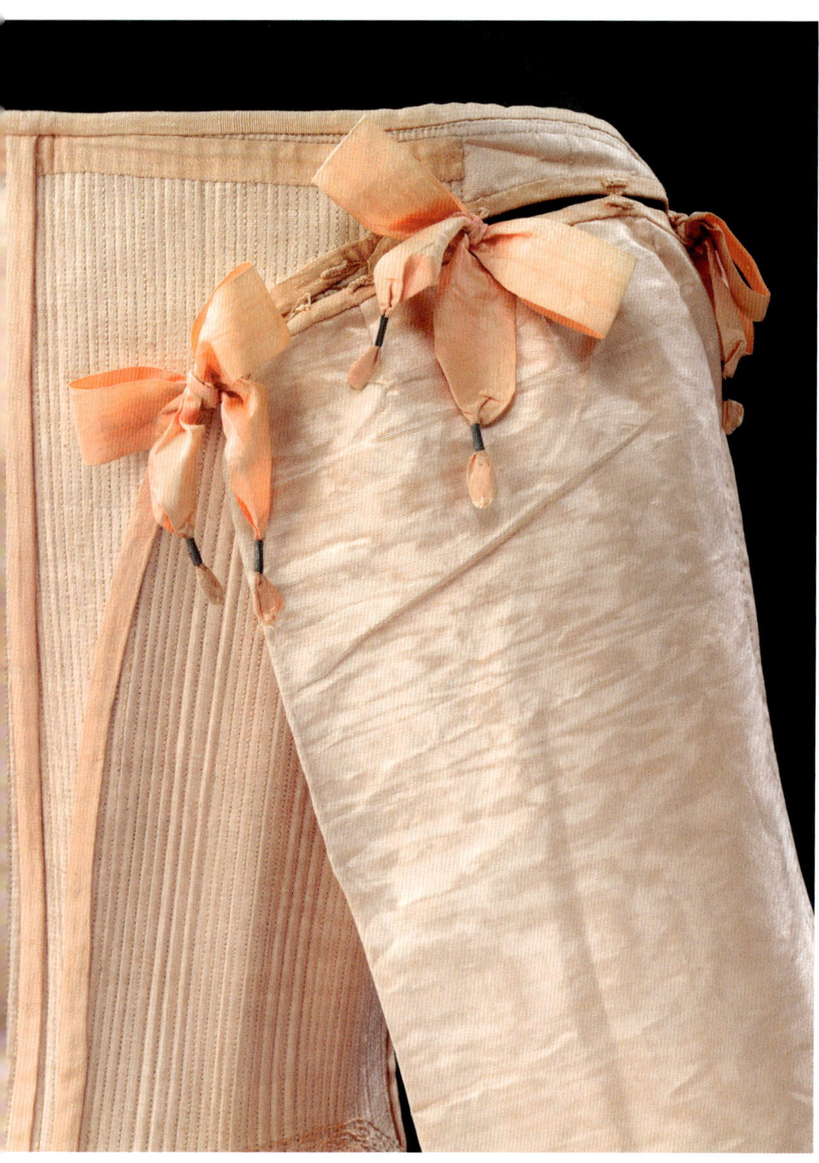

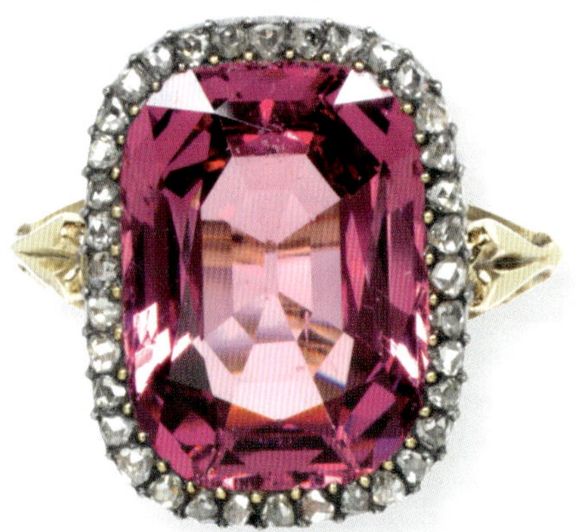

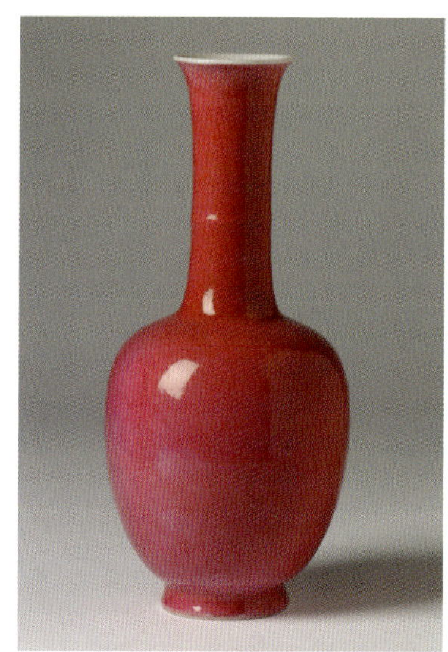

Austrian artist Julius Klinger chose the pink flamingo, so-coloured because of its diet, as the eye-catching focus for his 1910 poster (opposite) advertising the Zoological Gardens in Berlin. Organic pink dyes have been used by a wide range of artists and makers. Safflower petals were soaked in an alkaline solution to extract the pink colour for the ribbons on these stays (left), probably made in the Netherlands in the 17th century. The dye is unfortunately particularly light-sensitive and prone to fading.

The pure spinel gemstone is colourless, but the presence of a small amount of chromium when the stone is formed can turn it pink, one of the most prized colours for the gem. The spinel used for this ring (c. 1850; below left) is fittingly set within a border of brilliant-cut diamonds. The pink glaze of this 18th-century Chinese porcelain bottle (below right) was produced by mixing red copper with an opaque white enamel containing lead arsenic, a combination discovered by potters working in the kilns at Jingdezhen in the 1720s.

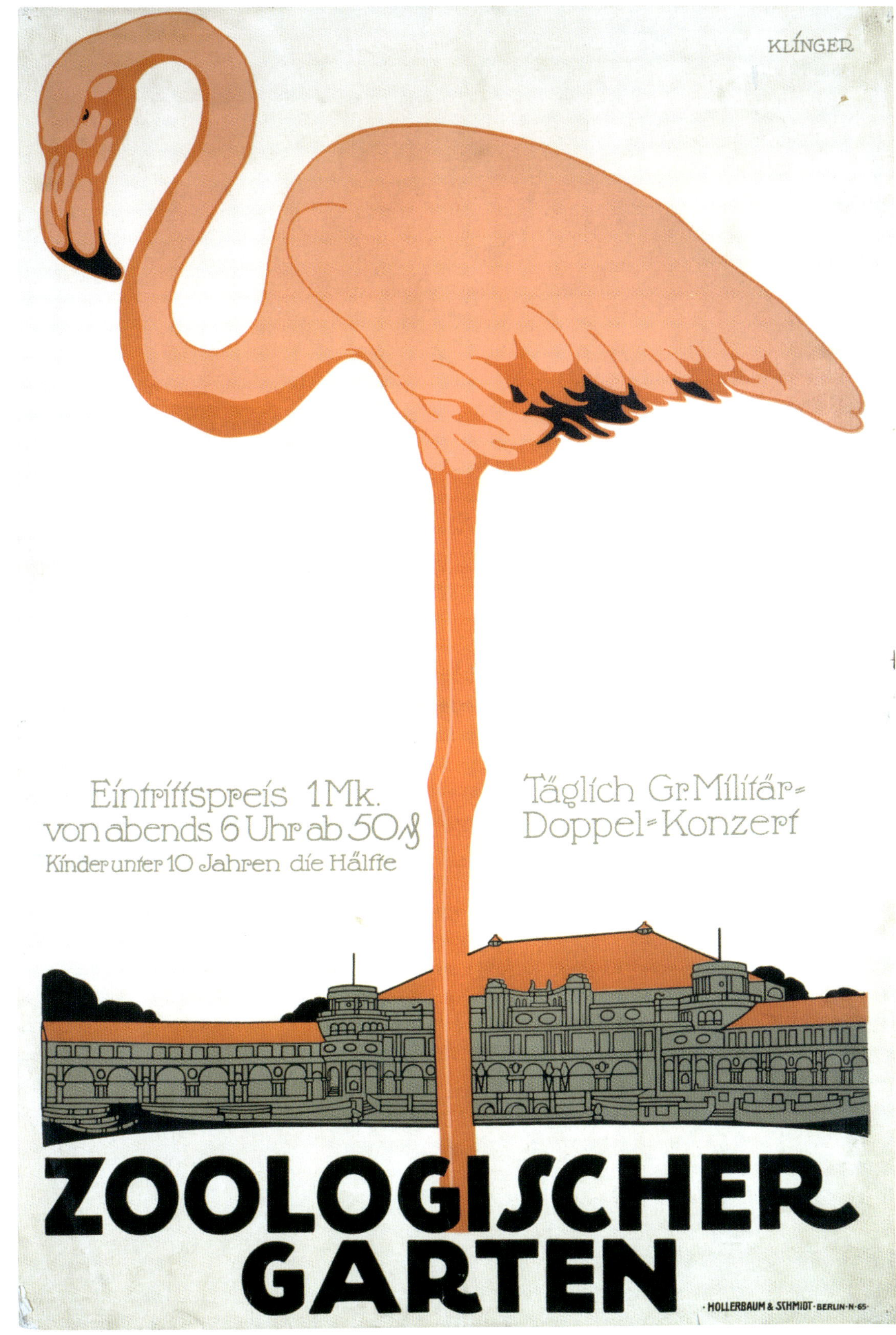

KLINGER
Eintrittspreis 1 Mk.
von abends 6 Uhr ab 50 ₰
Kinder unter 10 Jahren die Hälfte
Täglich Gr. Militär=
Doppel=Konzert
ZOOLOGISCHER
GARTEN
·HOLLERBAUM & SCHMIDT·BERLIN·N·65·

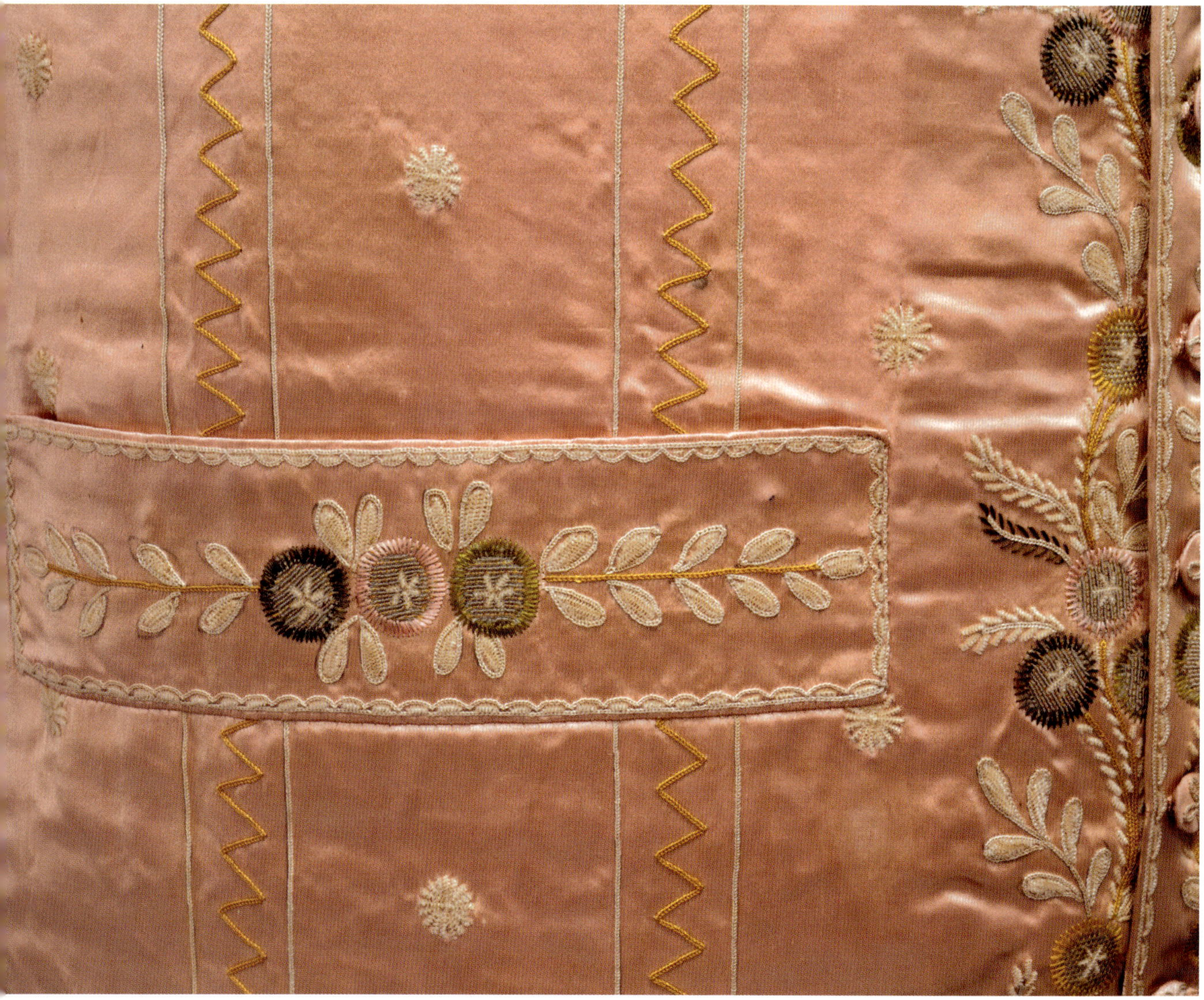

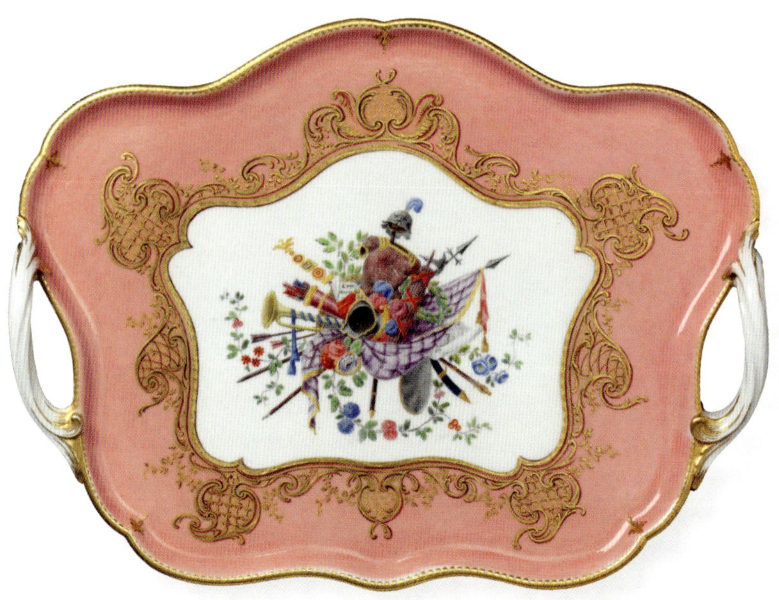

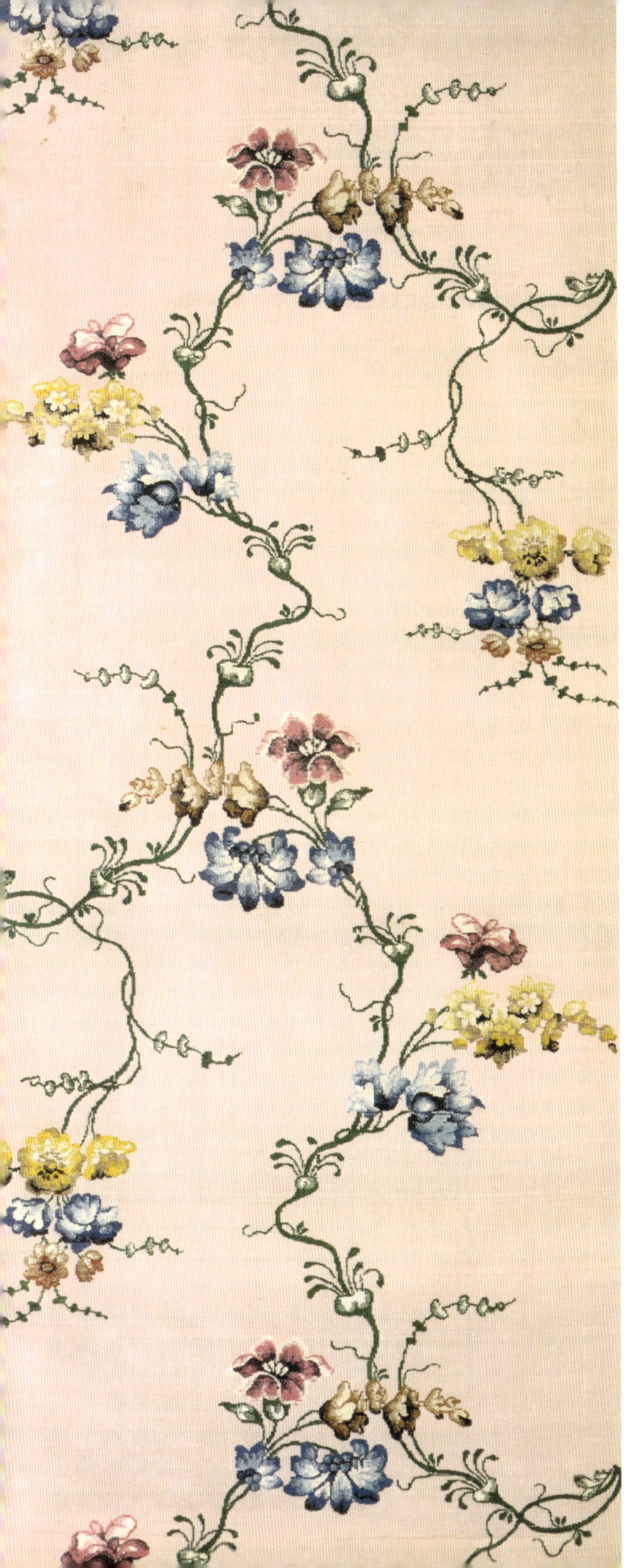

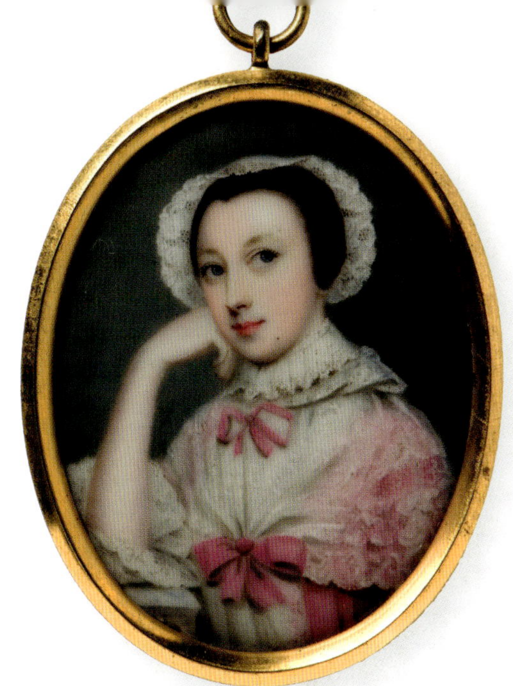

Among the favoured pastel tones of the 18th century, pink became highly fashionable. The colour is closely associated with Madame de Pompadour, official mistress to Louis XV. This tea tray (1761; opposite, bottom) is decorated with the pink ground colour rose, commonly known as 'Rose Pompadour'. The suggested links to Madame de Pompadour may have led its 19th-century buyer mistakenly to believe the service was once owned by this grand lady of fashion.

Woven in Spitalfields, London, Anna Maria Garthwaite's fabric of brocaded silk (1742; left) was intended to make fashionable ladies' gowns. The young girl in Gervase Spencer's enamel miniature (1752; above) is wearing a dress of white and pink, and a cape tied at the front with large bright pink ribbons. The choice of pink asserts the sitter's fashionable status. The colour was, however, genderless at this time, as shown by this man's waistcoat of pink silk satin (opposite, top) made towards the end of the same century.

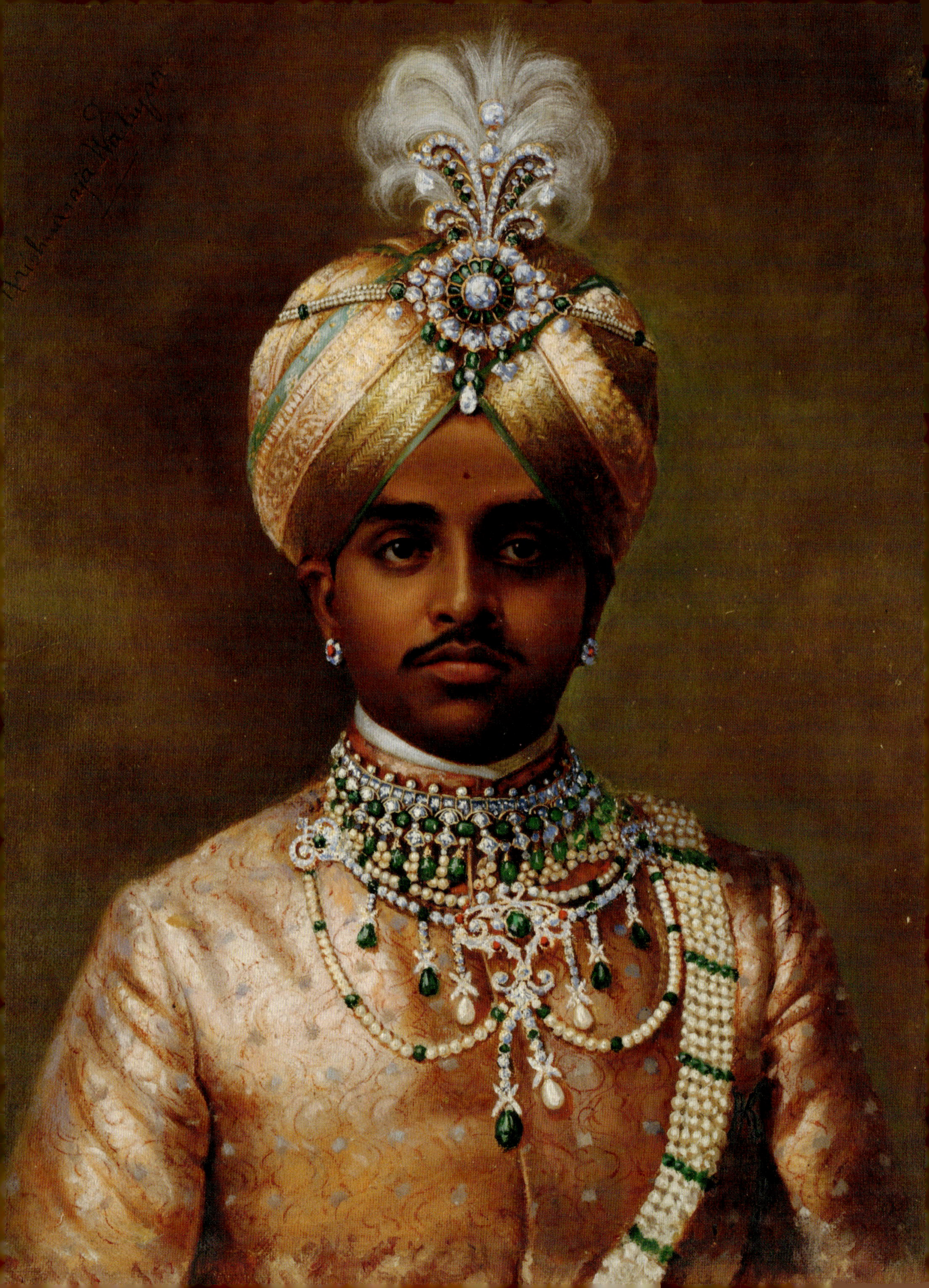

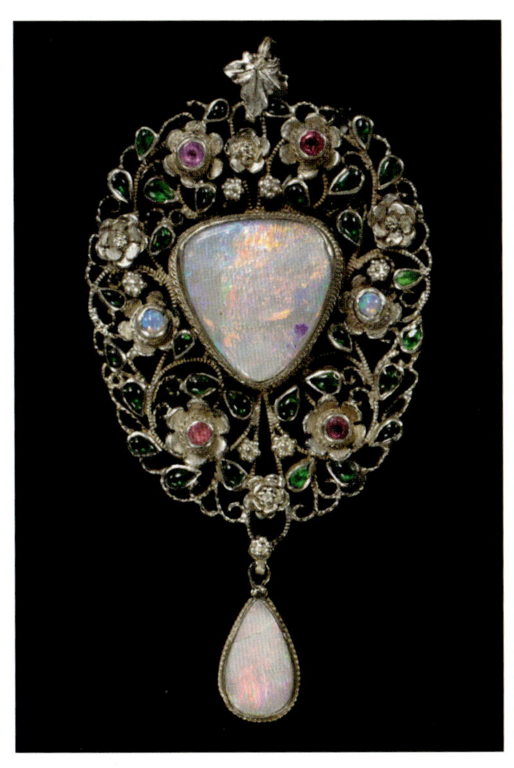

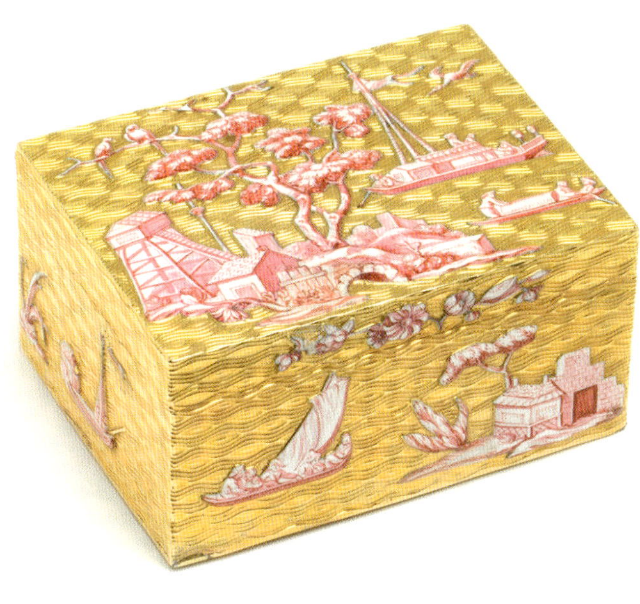

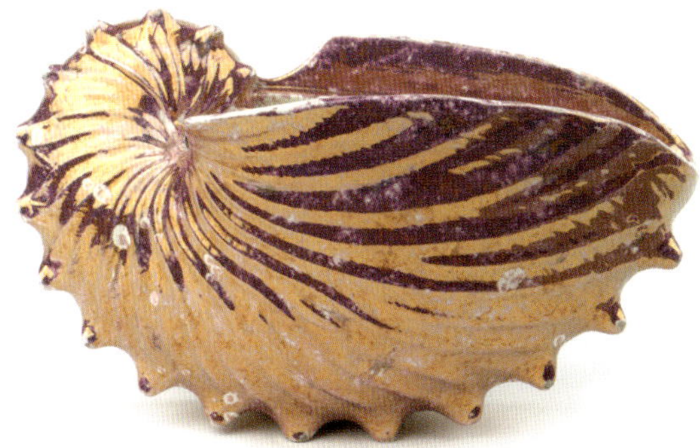

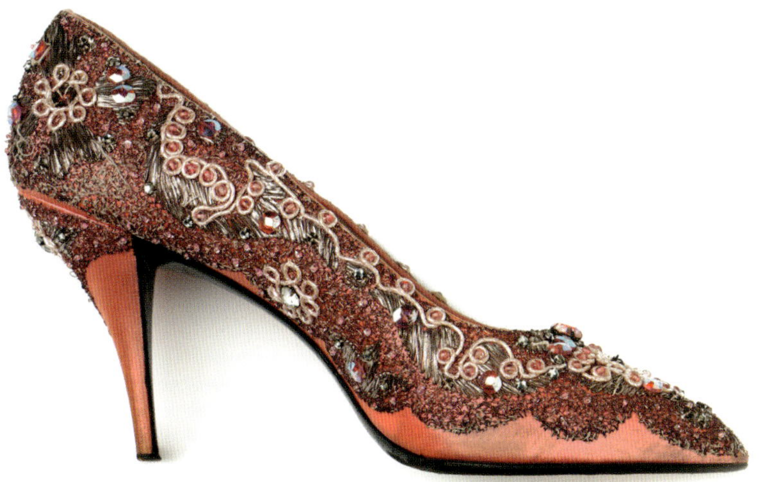

Used in tandem with metallics, or on sumptuous fabrics of silk and silk satin, pink can signal luxury. Dressed head to toe in pink and adorned with jewels, the status and wealth of Maharaja Sir Sri Krishnaraja Wodeyar Bahadur is evident in this oil painting of 1906 (opposite). Shimmering pinks and gilt threads have long been used to create fashion for the elite, such as these Roger Vivier for Christian Dior shoes (1958–60; below) owned by the famous socialite Gloria Guinness. Also using metallics in combination with pink, Josiah Wedgwood and Sons' iridescent, shell-shaped paper rack (left) brings extravagance into the everyday. The sheen was achieved by using a feather to brush pale earthenware with a liquid containing gold, tin and 'sweet wort', leaving a film of pink-hued metal once fired.

This elegant early 18th-century pink and gold snuffbox by Noël Léonard (above right) was designed to showcase the owner's fashion status. Made by Arthur and Georgie Gaskin, pink shimmers from the tourmaline-set silver flowers and large opal gemstones in this 1920s pendant (above left).

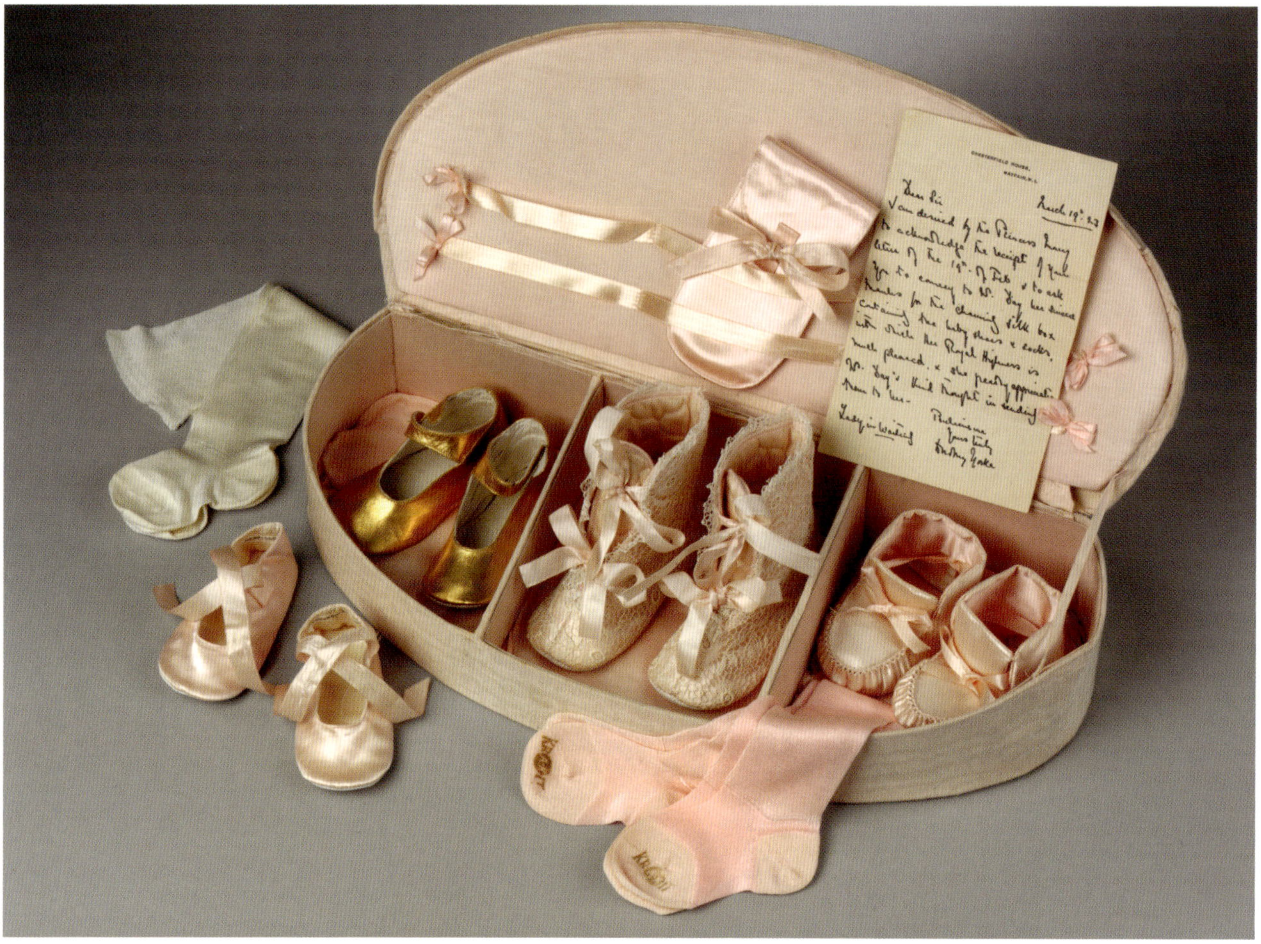

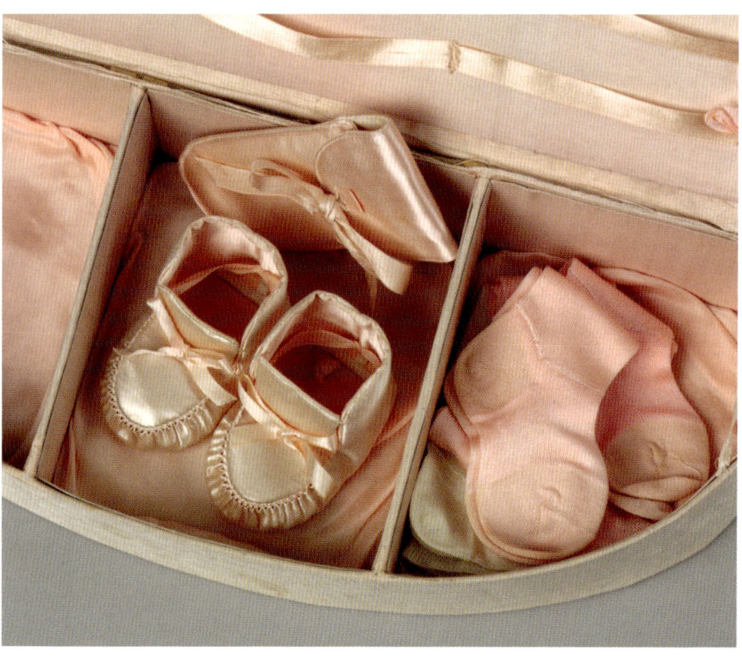

'Pink for girls' originated at the beginning of the 20th century in Europe and America, but took time to become ingrained in popular consciousness. This buster suit (1925–35; opposite, top right) was certainly thought appropriate for a boy, as was the delicate pale pink bonnet bought by a woman in 1920s Hungary expecting her first child (opposite, bottom left). But Princess Mary, following the birth of her second son in 1924, did not think a set of pink shoes in a pink ribbed silk box (above and left) was suitable for her royal prince, and returned the gift. Harringtons Baby Goods's mass-produced pink toy squirrel (1932–5; opposite, top left) was the favourite of a young boy called Lionel Hemsley, chosen from soft toys given to him when he was two or three years old. Clearly aimed at young girls, Kaye Gibson Ltd's birthday card (opposite, bottom right) shows how pink was becoming firmly established as a colour only appropriate for girls by 1963.

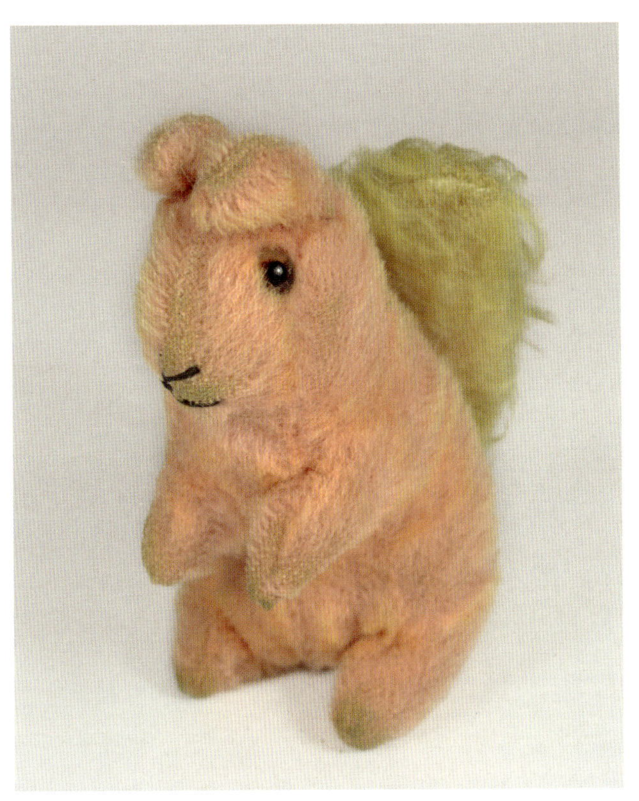

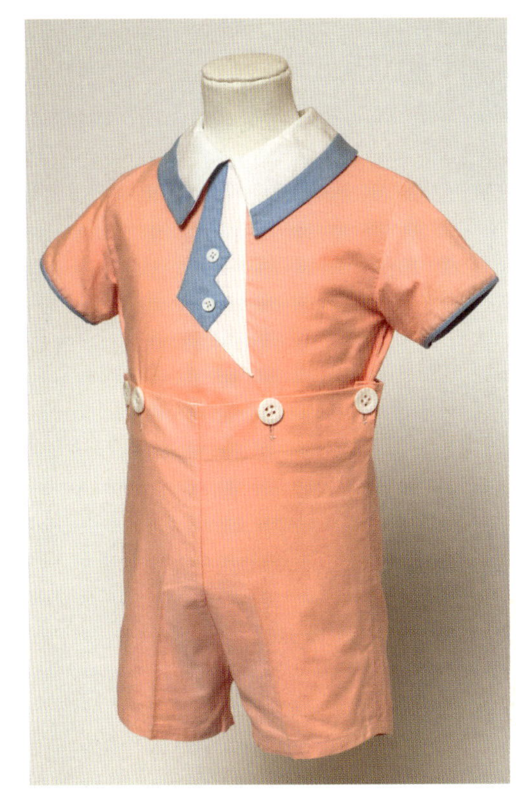

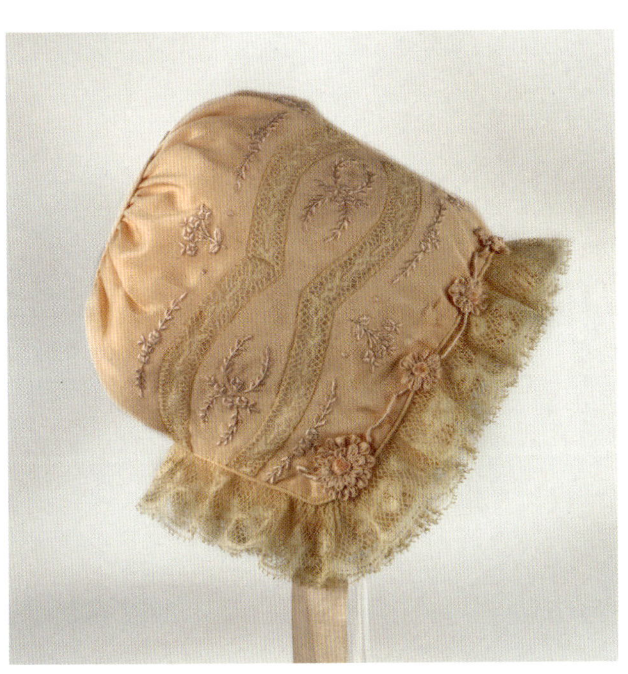

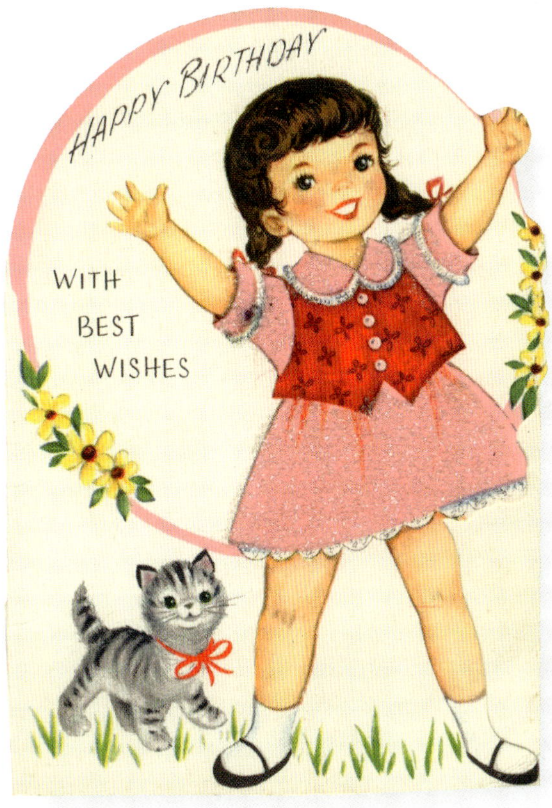
HAPPY BIRTHDAY
WITH
BEST
WISHES

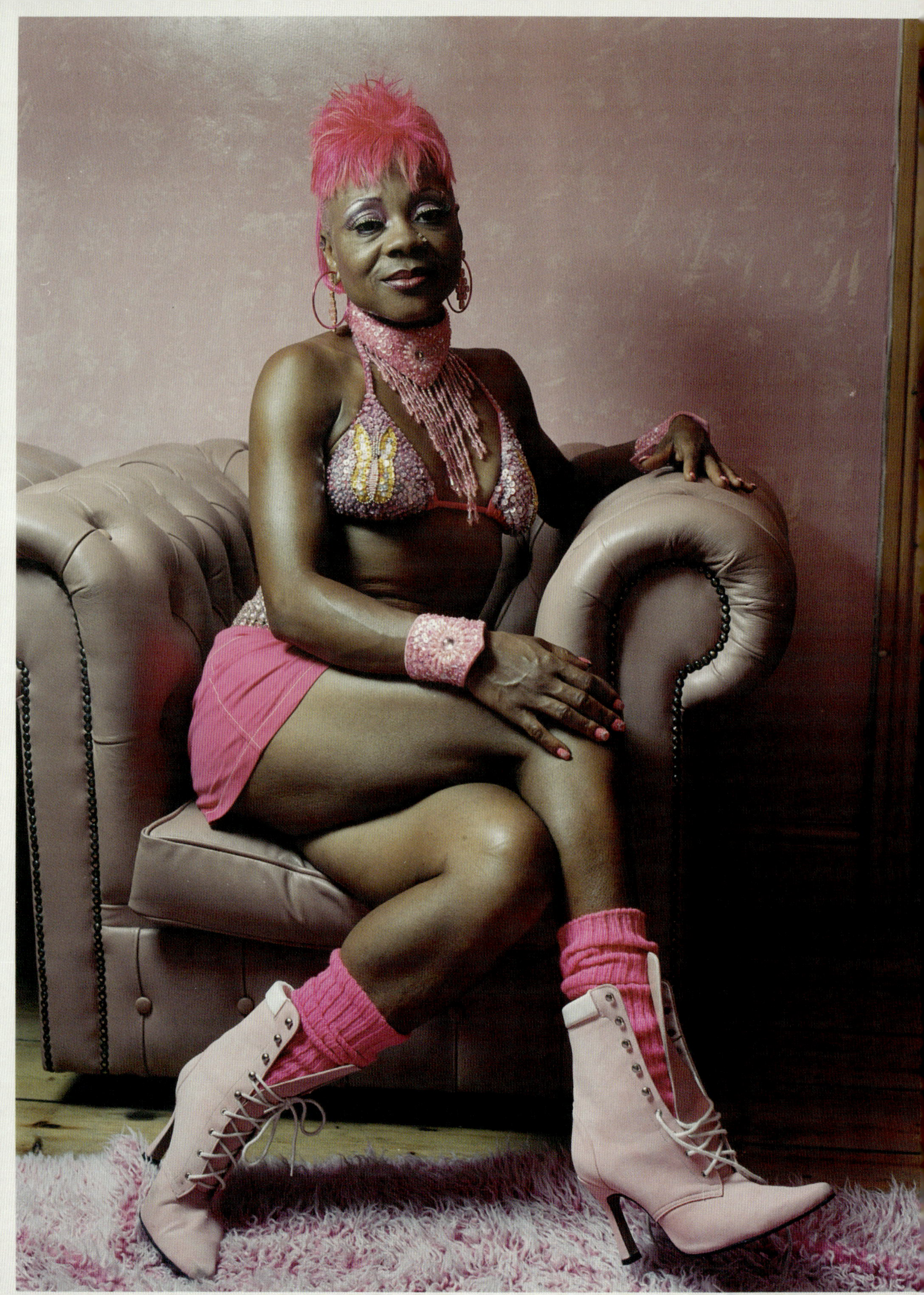

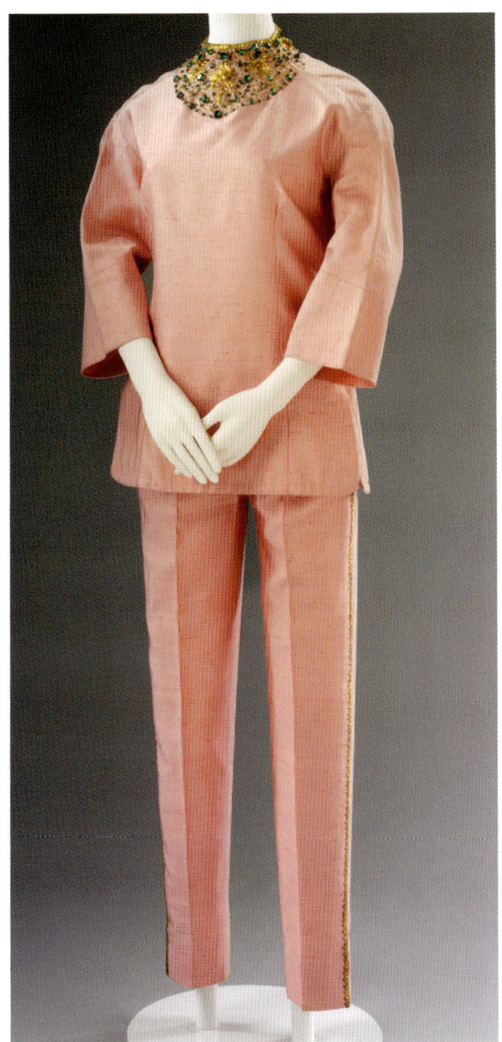

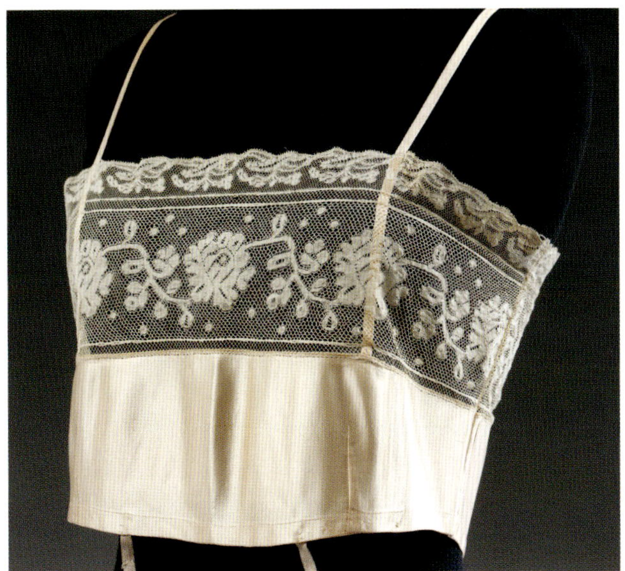

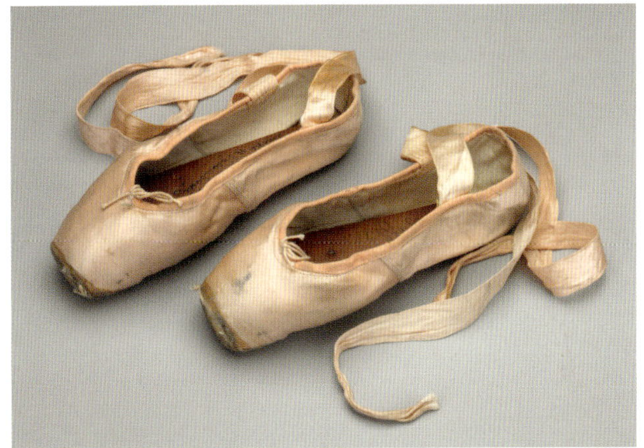

Wearing pink carries many – at times contradictory – connotations. Jennie Baptiste's photograph of Brixton Dancehall Queen Pinky (2001; opposite) captures the extravagant style of the sitter. Pinky sits proudly in her jewel-encrusted bikini top and pink lace-up boots, with bright pink hair, her striking use of colour empowering the character she has created. Irene Galitzine's two-piece pyjama evening suit (c. 1963; above left) epitomizes the chic style of the day, but the shimmering pink silk and bead and gold-coloured braid detail would have ensured that the wearer stood out from the crowd.

Conversely, this silk satin brassiere of soft pink (c. 1929; top right), made for a young woman by her mother, conjures notions of girlish innocence, reflecting the youthful fashions of the time. The pale pink colour of ballet shoes, such as this pair worn by Nina Vyroubova (above right), has come to be associated with delicacy and femininity, in contrast to the strength and resilience ballet demands. The association between pale pink and ballet is exclusionary. Ballet shoes were originally designed to create the impression of the dancer being barefoot, and the 'standard' nude skin tone echoes and reinforces ballet's lack of diversity.

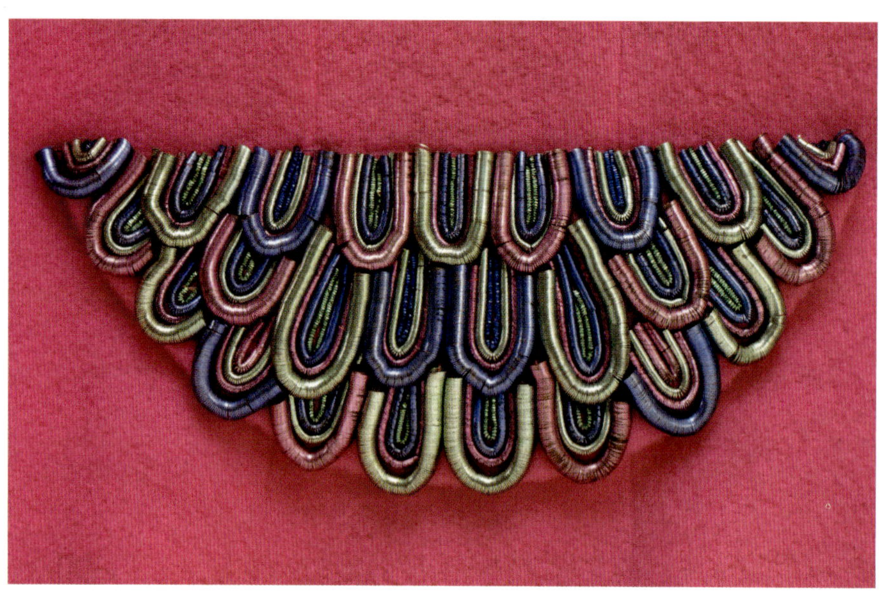

With its connotations of sexuality and promiscuity, shocking pink can be a bold fashion choice. Growth in the corset-manufacturing industries in the late Victorian era meant there was greater choice for women in terms of material, colour, size and fit. In contrast to the more muted tones of earlier years, colourful satin corsets became fashionable. Made of pink silk satin and decorated with handmade lace, this luxurious example from the early 1890s (right) would have been an expensive purchase.

Linked to the Surrealist movement, Elsa Schiaparelli was known for her eccentric designs and use of vibrant colour. Her evening jacket (1937) of bright pink woollen cloth, embellished with a highly decorative metallic braided collar and pockets (above), was designed to attract attention. Milliner Philip Treacy used a technique he calls 'painting with feathers' to create this hat (opposite), modelled by pop singer Kylie Minogue on the cover of *Tatler* magazine in July 1995. His use of shocking pink ensures that both hat and wearer make a bold statement.

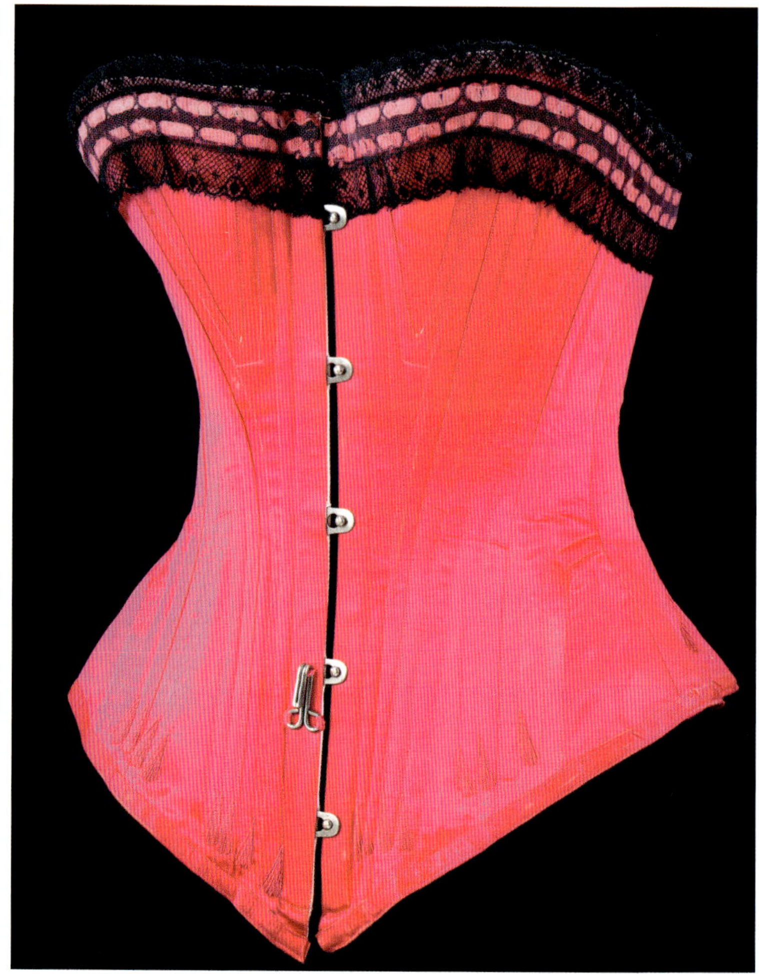

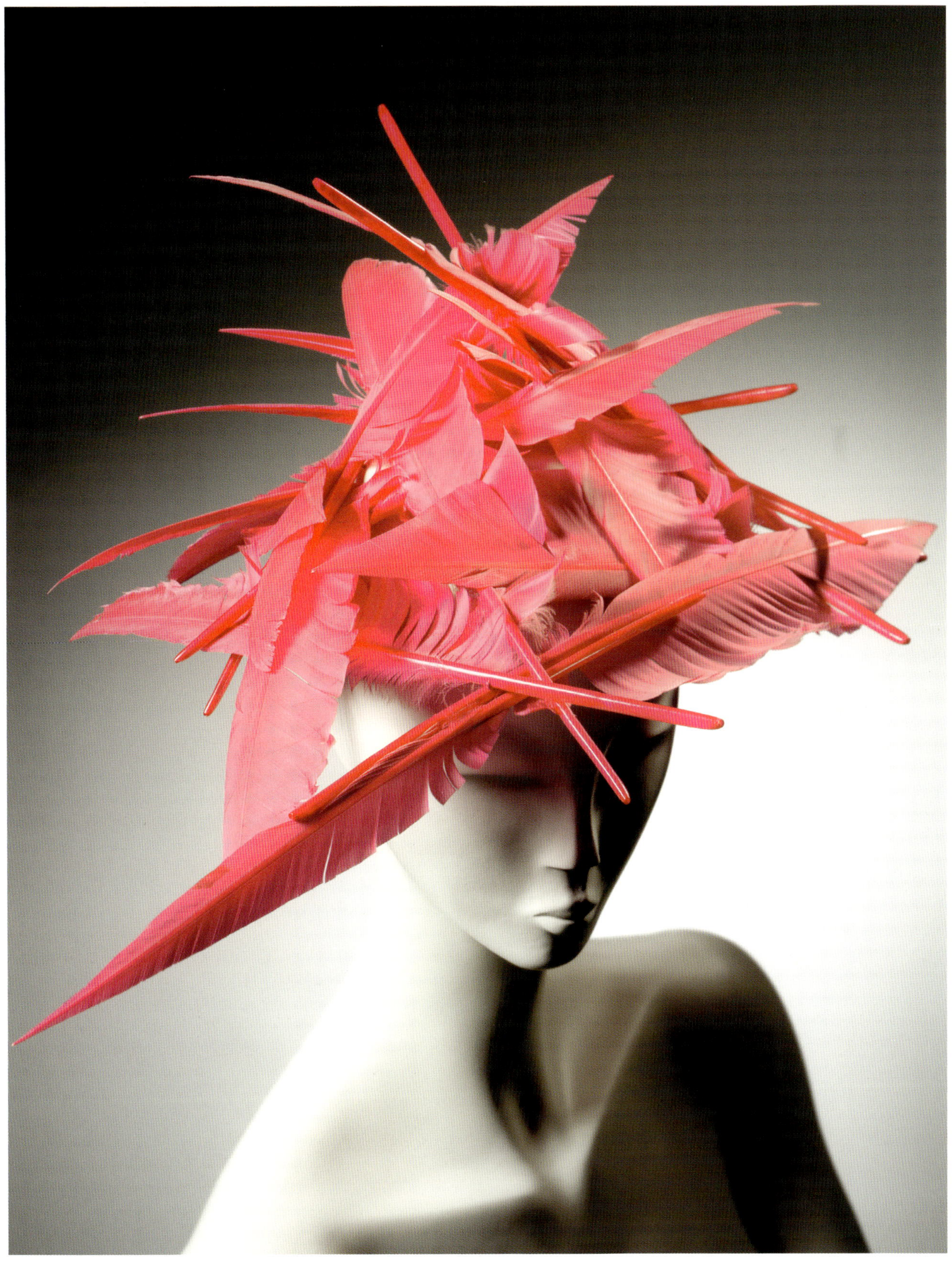

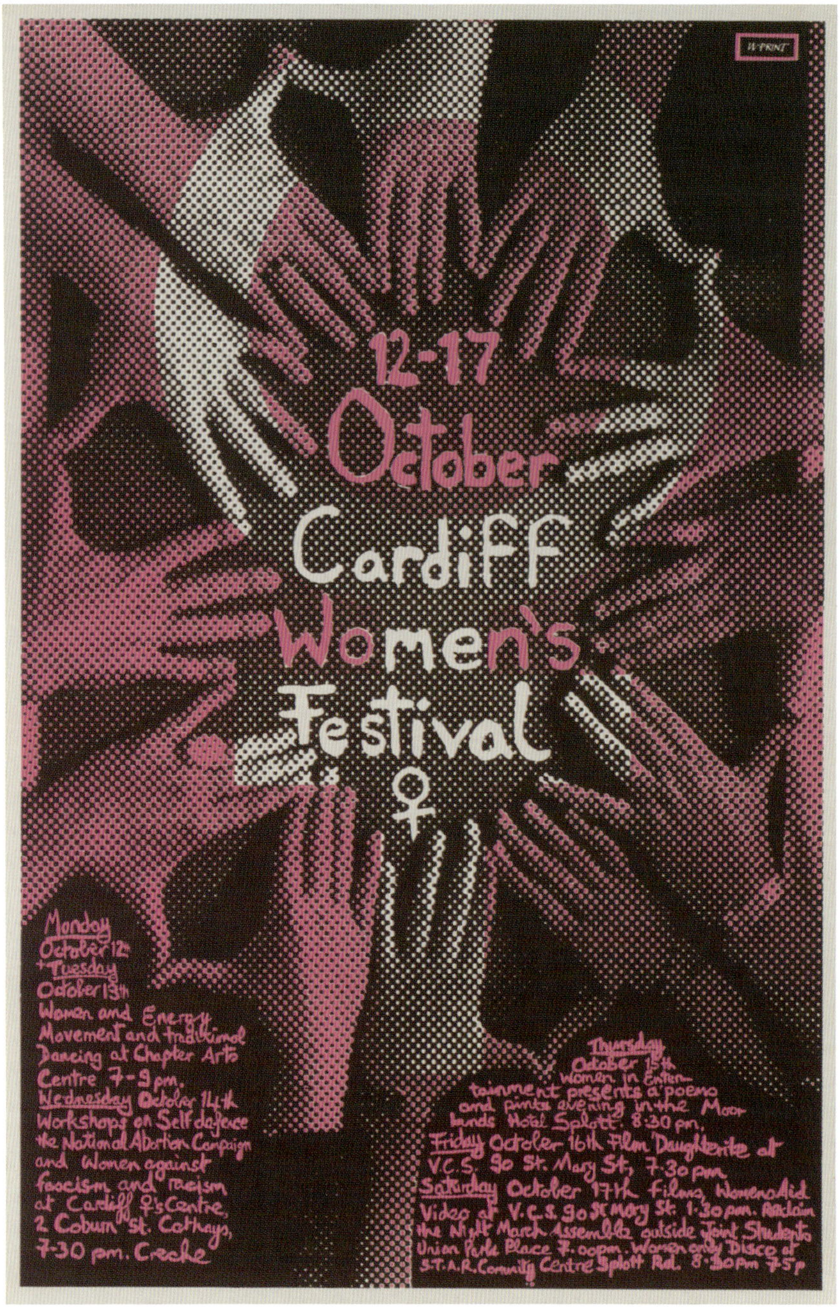

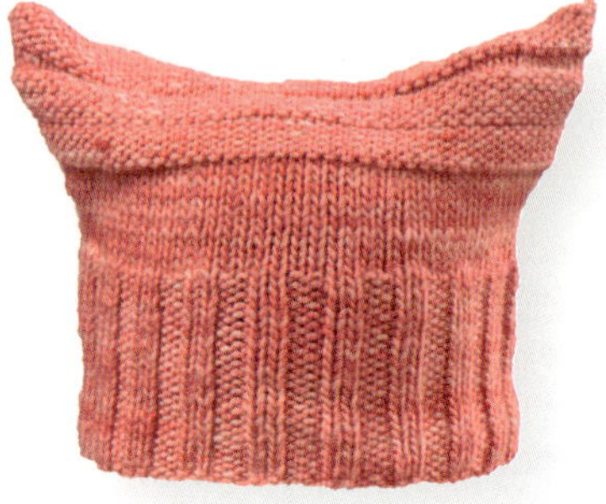

Subverting gendered associations, pink has become a symbol of protest and resistance. Used by the Nazi party as a badge of shame, the pink triangle has since been reclaimed by the LGBTQ+ community. Berkeley-based Inkworks Press's poster (1976; opposite) promotes a day of solidarity in memory of the Stonewall riots of 1969, widely regarded as the beginning of the gay rights movement.

Pink has also been used as a colour of defiance by women. The knitting pattern for the 'Pussy Power' hat (above), designed by Kat Coyle, was freely available online ahead of the Women's March in Washington, held the day after US President Donald Trump's inauguration in 2017. The pointed cat ears reference and challenge Trump's boast of grabbing women 'by the pussy'. Made for the Cardiff Women's Festival in the 1980s, U-Print Collective's predominantly pink poster (left) of a circle of connected hands is another example of how pink has evolved as a symbol of power and unity for women.

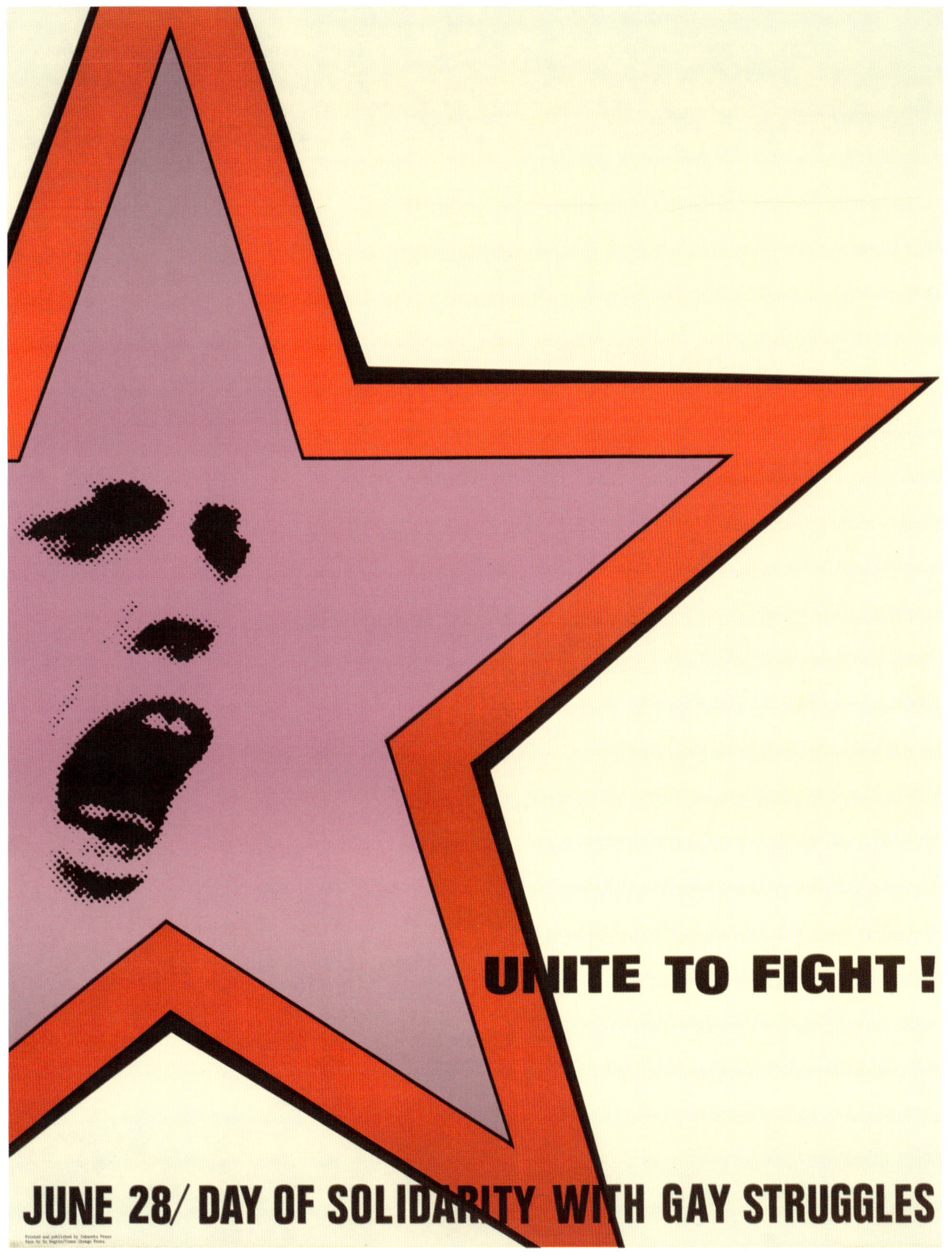

UNITE TO FIGHT !
JUNE 28/ DAY OF SOLIDARITY WITH GAY STRUGGLES

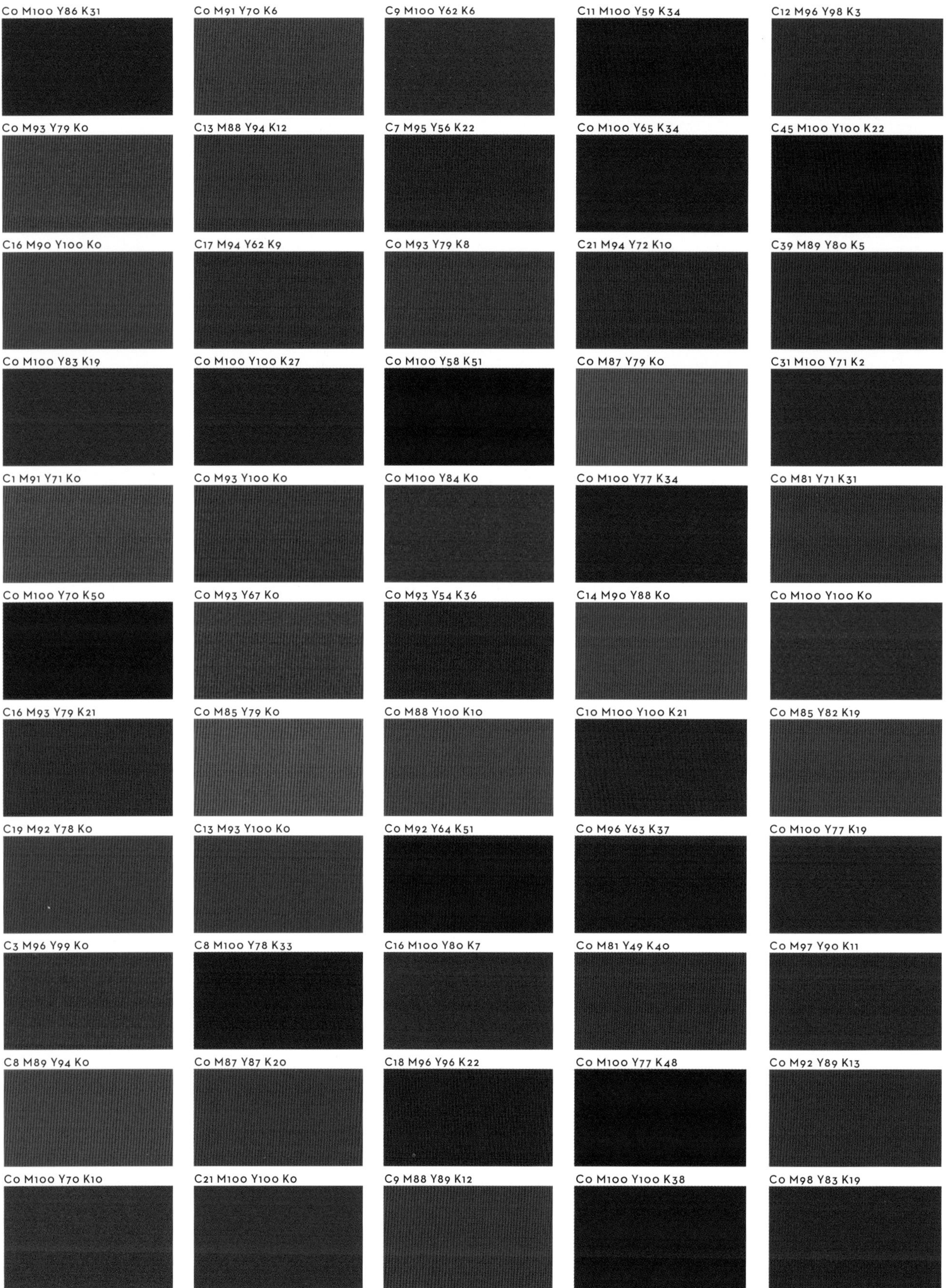

Co M100 Y86 K31
Co M91 Y70 K6
C9 M100 Y62 K6
C11 M100 Y59 K34
C12 M96 Y98 K3
Co M93 Y79 Ko
C13 M88 Y94 K12
C7 M95 Y56 K22
Co M100 Y65 K34
C45 M100 Y100 K22
C16 M90 Y100 Ko
C17 M94 Y62 K9
Co M93 Y79 K8
C21 M94 Y72 K10
C39 M89 Y80 K5
Co M100 Y83 K19
Co M100 Y100 K27
Co M100 Y58 K51
Co M87 Y79 Ko
C31 M100 Y71 K2
C1 M91 Y71 Ko
Co M93 Y100 Ko
Co M100 Y84 Ko
Co M100 Y77 K34
Co M81 Y71 K31
Co M100 Y70 K50
Co M93 Y67 Ko
Co M93 Y54 K36
C14 M90 Y88 Ko
Co M100 Y100 Ko
C16 M93 Y79 K21
Co M85 Y79 Ko
Co M88 Y100 K10
C10 M100 Y100 K21
Co M85 Y82 K19
C19 M92 Y78 Ko
C13 M93 Y100 Ko
Co M92 Y64 K51
Co M96 Y63 K37
Co M100 Y77 K19
C3 M96 Y99 Ko
C8 M100 Y78 K33
C16 M100 Y80 K7
Co M81 Y49 K40
Co M97 Y90 K11
C8 M89 Y94 Ko
Co M87 Y87 K20
C18 M96 Y96 K22
Co M100 Y77 K48
Co M92 Y89 K13
Co M100 Y70 K10
C21 M100 Y100 Ko
C9 M88 Y89 K12
Co M100 Y100 K38
Co M98 Y83 K19

RED

Imagine a pair of red shoes, glimpsed beneath a velvet gown; glo-boots splashing through a puddle; scarlet stilettos discarded after a night of seduction or ruby slippers primed with a magic that can take you home. In the 1948 film *The Red Shoes*, a young ballet star's passion for dancing ultimately leads to her violent death. As Yves Saint Laurent proclaimed: 'Red is a noble colour, the colour of a precious stone – rubies – as well as the colour of danger...it's the colour of blood...of royalty, Phaedra and so many other heroines... red is a battle between death and life.'

In contrast, Maiko Dawson's comfortable ballet-style red shoes (p. 137) convey the elegance of dance. The red gingham bows add a whimsical note. In Dawson's native Japan, the red and white combination – *kōhaku* – is celebratory and auspicious. In traditional Japanese dress red suggested youth, glamour and passion. The colour of the extravagant tie-dyed kimono on p. 136 came from *beni*, a very expensive dye made from safflowers. Red is also the colour of celebration in south India. Joyfully embracing a new phase of life, brides may choose saris in hues such as *kempu* (ruby red), *chemparuthi* (hibiscus red) or *thakkali* (tomato red). In some Hindu households a bride may step into the red powder *kumkum* before entering her new home, to create a trail of footprints indicating that the goddess Lakshmi has brought purity and prosperity to the home.

Fertility and love were assured for Roman brides who wore the fiery *flammeum* veil, a custom still followed in many European cultures, especially around the Balkans. In the Victoria and Albert Museum's 'World Dress' collection, red robes from nineteenth-century Bosnia are elaborately embroidered with floral motifs to signify and summon prosperity and plenty in marriage. Newlyweds in Anatolia are served pomegranates to ensure they will be blessed with a large family, and the skins are also used to make the red shade in the intricately patterned, hand-knotted carpets traditionally produced in the region. From Armenia to Israel and on to south-east Asia and China, the numerous seeds of this ruddy, glowing fruit are associated with abundance and good fortune. Both pomegranates and apples are at the core of many early creation myths. Basketfuls of rosy apples at Iranian weddings offer hope for a happy future and celebrate ancient Persian heritage. Apple orchards spread around the world, nurtured, the Romans believed, by the goddess Pomona, whose cornucopia brimmed with cherries, plums, berries and more.

Sunbirds and tanagers; snappers and starfish; damselflies and ladybirds; the shimmer of autumn foliage that belies the leaves' decay. The reds of nature can be fleeting, but they are also unmissable, possibly the reason why, after black and white, red is the first named colour in any language. The earth itself was the source of the earliest pigments; early reds came from red ochre, which takes its colour from the iron oxide hematite.

Other minerals also contribute to colouring the world red. Copper and lead compounds were used by ancient glassmakers to create rusty red tinted glass. The Romans later found that adding gold to molten glass yields a more intense roseate hue. The rediscovery of this technique generated a fascination for 'gold ruby' glass in seventeenth-century Europe. Gold and red have an affinity: gold leaf is applied to red clay on gilded frames, metallic thread is made by wrapping gold strips around red silk and gold coins were once known as 'red rogues'.

Copper is, however, significantly more affordable. Some of the most desirable and rare shades of red in porcelain come from the metal. In Japanese *ginbari* ware, the copper body of a vase is covered with an embossed foil coated with a translucent enamel called *akasuke* (pigeon's blood). In Europe in around 1900, *flammée* glazes – vitreous, stippled and often slashed with streaks of purple or turquoise – were the subject of intensive research. Ernest Chaplet, an influential French ceramicist, devoted his life to experimenting with this difficult and unpredictable technique, and jealously guarded its secrets. When he went blind in later life, he destroyed his recipes and notebooks.

Chaplet worked to re-create the Chinese *langyao hong* glaze, also known as *sang de boeuf* (ox-blood), which had been developed in Jingdezhen between 1705 and 1712, during the Qing dynasty (1644–1911). It was a revival of a red monochrome used in the preceding Ming dynasty (1368–1644), which was extremely difficult to make and sometimes referred to as a 'sacrificial' glaze because it was used on vessels for ceremonial temple offerings. Legend tells of the Ming Emperor Xuande (reigned 1426–35), who set his heart on red porcelain for the Altar of the Sun. He ordered the Jingdezhen kiln to produce it and threatened the craftsmen with death when they failed. Cuilan, the daughter of an elderly worker, was so enraged that she jumped into the fiery kiln. When it was opened two days later the porcelain inside was blood red.

Painstakingly applied layers of lacquer coloured orange-red with cinnabar were carved with intricate detail to produce furniture that was the privilege of the Chinese imperial court. Red lacquered pillars accentuated the grandeur of ceremonial buildings. In south Asia under Mughal rule (1556–1707), the Emperor Akbar's war elephants were caparisoned in scarlet and finest Burmese rubies, mined in modern-day Myanmar, glittered in turbans, ornaments and other possessions.

British royalty and power are represented by the red leather of the despatch box first used for parliamentary papers by Queen Elizabeth I in Tudor England. Elizabethan sumptuary laws decreed that crimson and scarlet were reserved for the highest nobility: 'dukes, marquises, earls, and their children, viscounts, barons, and knights being companions of the Garter, or any person being of the Privy Council.' In Renaissance Venice, subtle differences between red tones would also have revealed the substance and status of the wearer.

Similarly, King Louis XIV kept the influence of the French aristocracy in check by declaring that only those in royal favour could wear red heels dyed with carmine; the Spanish had a stranglehold on the South American trade in crushed cochineal beetles, making the dye a rare commodity at the time. Nowadays, those who can afford Christian Louboutin's red-soled shoes cherish the prestige of fame or wealth, rather than lineage and influence. Such stars walk to acclaim along a carpet that the Ancient Greek king Agamemnon was hesitant to tread, for fear that the gods might think he was trying to usurp them.

Red proclaims sovereignty and might, but the robes of Roman Catholic cardinals also signify a readiness to shed blood for their faith. Portrayed wearing a sanguine tunic in a fifteenth-century stained glass window, St Agnes, who made the martyr's choice of death over renunciation of her vows, personifies both suffering and strength (see p. 142). Symbolizing the wounds of Christ's sacrifice, rubies and garnets gleam from crucifixes like polished drops of blood.

In medieval lapidaries and modern crystal lore alike, red gems are imbued with the colour's mystical attributes: stimulating enthusiasm, increasing vitality and promoting courage. Coral, supposedly formed when blood from the severed head of Medusa dripped into the Ionian Sea, has been said to protect against the evil eye, while a red Kabbalah bracelet tied around the left wrist is believed to ward off misfortune. But in other traditions, red's magical properties manifest as evil, associated with demons, the devil and the fires of Hell.

In Christianity, the belief that Satan's influence is conquered by Christ's crucifixion and resurrection is made incarnate by the Christian cross, which has appeared in many forms through the ages. For Early Egyptian Coptic Christians, its shape was adapted from the *ankh*, the hieroglyph for 'life'. Centuries later, jeweller David Poston's 'The Real Thing' (see p. 145), a cross made from Coca-Cola bottle tops collected in a bar in Rwanda, challenges these positive associations. Evangelical Christianity offers life everlasting; Coca-Cola, its advertisements have claimed, 'adds life'. In the context of the 1994 Rwandan genocide, Poston asks, 'What does the cross mean? To the moral American Christians who run Coca-Cola, to the Christians in Rwanda? ... How great is the difference between the two symbols; do they both now represent brands?'

Nearly ninety per cent of Americans surveyed in 1987 associated the colour red with Coca-Cola. For brands including Transport for London, Virgin Media and HSBC, red's visibility has added power to branding – as it has to politics and propaganda. Chairman Mao's Little Red Book and the red flag of socialism are embedded in the modern psyche. Left-wing parties from UK Labour to the German SPD make use of red, which offers an immediately recognizable visual identity – though in the twenty-first century, the conservative US Republican party have also become associated the colour.

The flaming hair of Shiva's warrior aspect; Mars burning hotly over the battlefields; even the flush anger causes in our faces: danger, death and destruction can lie in red. But the shock of red has also been used to rail against brutality. In Britain and elsewhere, red poppies commemorate the broken bodies and senseless waste of war. The connection is made even more explicit in a provocative image advertising clothing brand Benetton, which depicts twelve test tubes filled with blood and labelled with the names of world leaders of differing political persuasion: Margaret, Yasser, Nelson, Fidel ... We are reminded that the apparent differences that lead to bloodshed are senseless, since we are 'red inside allee [all the] same as Queen Victoria' or, as the Iranians say 'Khoon-e- to az baghiyeh rangintar nist [your blood is no more coloured than others]'.

Surviving war demands strength from everyone, and during the First World War many women assumed new roles as bus conductors, ambulance drivers and factory workers. Though these opportunities were withdrawn in peacetime, the seeds had been planted. In 1912 in New York, suffragettes took to the streets wearing Elizabeth Arden's red lipstick, a form of rebellion that reverberates today with the painted lips of people affirming their power, unabashed and proud. Lipstick has a long and complex history, generally signifying privilege and glamour, sometimes vanity and even immorality. Historically, the blame for wanton behaviour has often been imposed on women by men. An embroidered sampler in the Victoria and Albert Museum testifies to this reality (p. 153), and the connection between sex and sin is still perceived as scarlet – though in more recent times the AIDS crisis has de-gendered sexual shaming.

The ingenue's ballet flats in the film *And God Created Woman* (1956), the drag queen's *Kinky Boots* (2005) and Agent Provocateur's cherry-red fluffy mules (1990s) represent shifting ideas about glamour, desire and debauchery. Paint a room claret or drape a dancer in cerise velvet and associations easily stray to carnality – and also to romance. Sensual and passionate, red is the colour of love. In the 1970s, Richard Burton was snapped at an airport with Elizabeth Taylor on one arm and, tucked under the other, a bright red Valentine typewriter (see p. 137), designed for writing poetry and love letters. Thirty years later, and Chris Ofili's *Afro Lunar Lovers* (see p. 157) shimmer with that moment when hearts pause and the world glows – before they dance into the red of dawn.

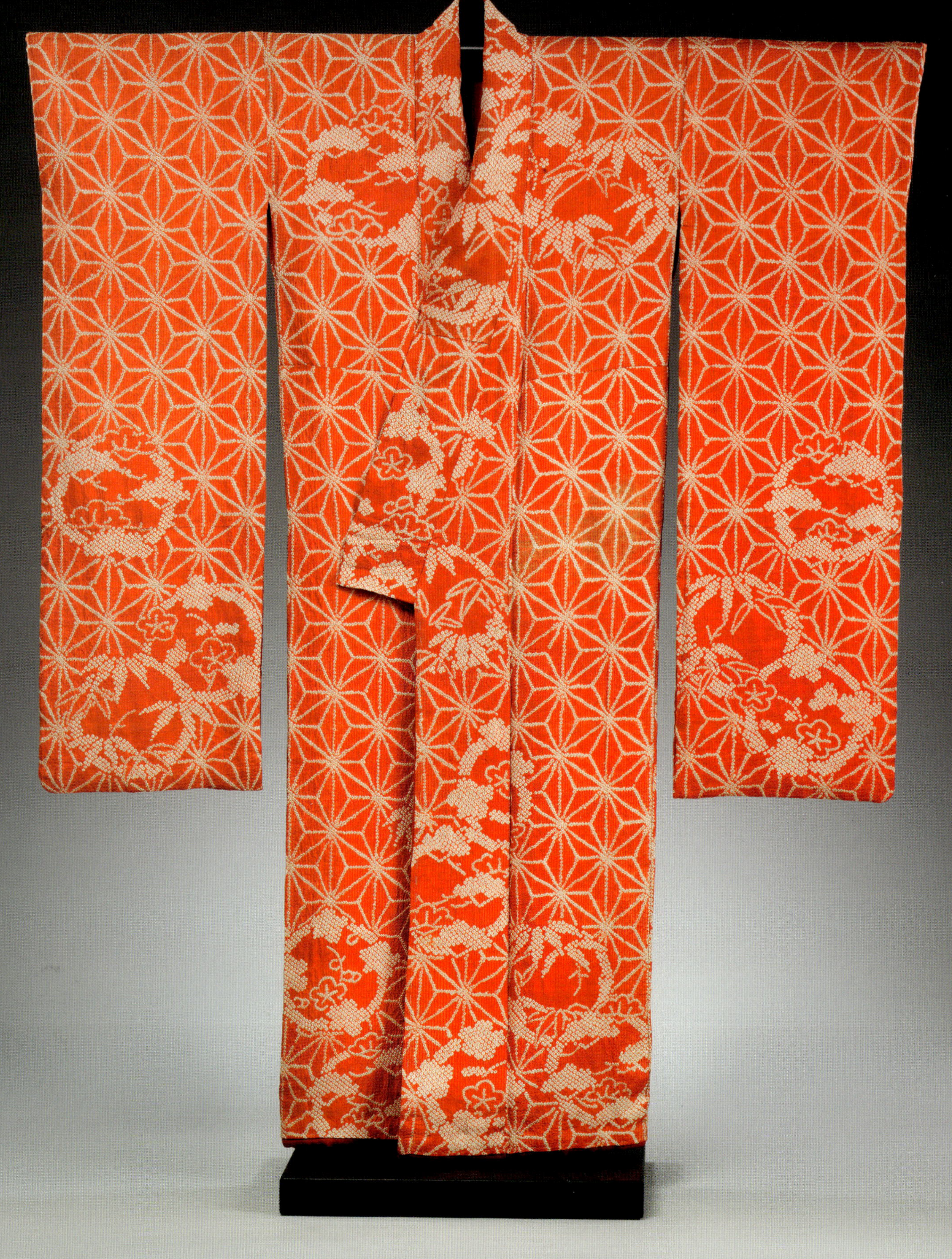

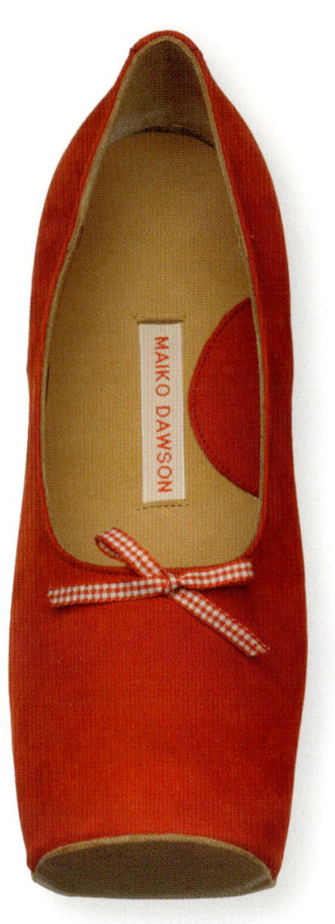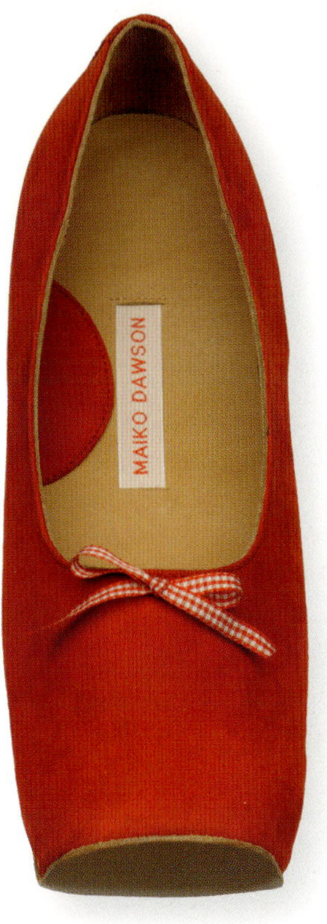

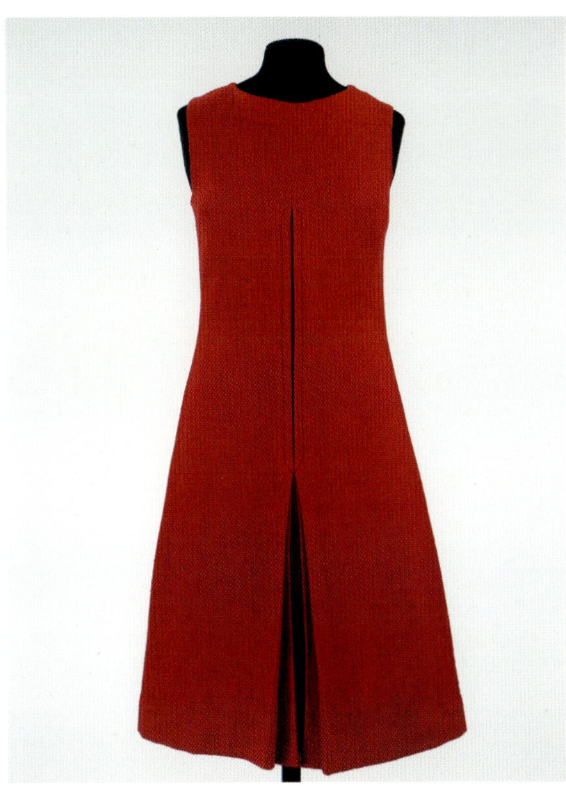

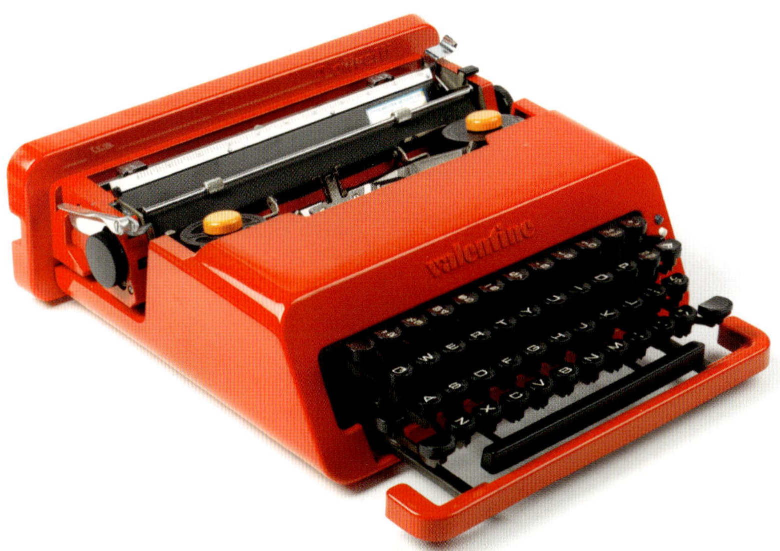

From the fresh face of a bouncing baby to the rosy-fingered dawn of a new day, red radiates all the vibrancy and promise of youth. In Japan, red is a popular colour for the *furisode* (swinging sleeves) kimono worn by unmarried girls, such as this early 19th-century example (opposite). The red gingham bows on Maiko Dawson's distinctive square-toed ballet shoes (2010; above left) evoke the same playful exuberance of a young heart running free.

In the Swinging London of the 1960s, fashion designer Mary Quant was in the vanguard of the 'youthquake'. With bright, informal designs such as this 'Peachy' dress (1962; above right), she allowed young adults to adopt their own unique style, distinct from that of their parents. The glossy 'Valentine' typewriter (left) designed by Ettore Sottsass and Perry King for Olivetti in 1969, was a product of the same movement; the 'it-bag' of its day even graced the bedroom of teenage tearaway Alex in Stanley Kubrick's *A Clockwork Orange* (1971).

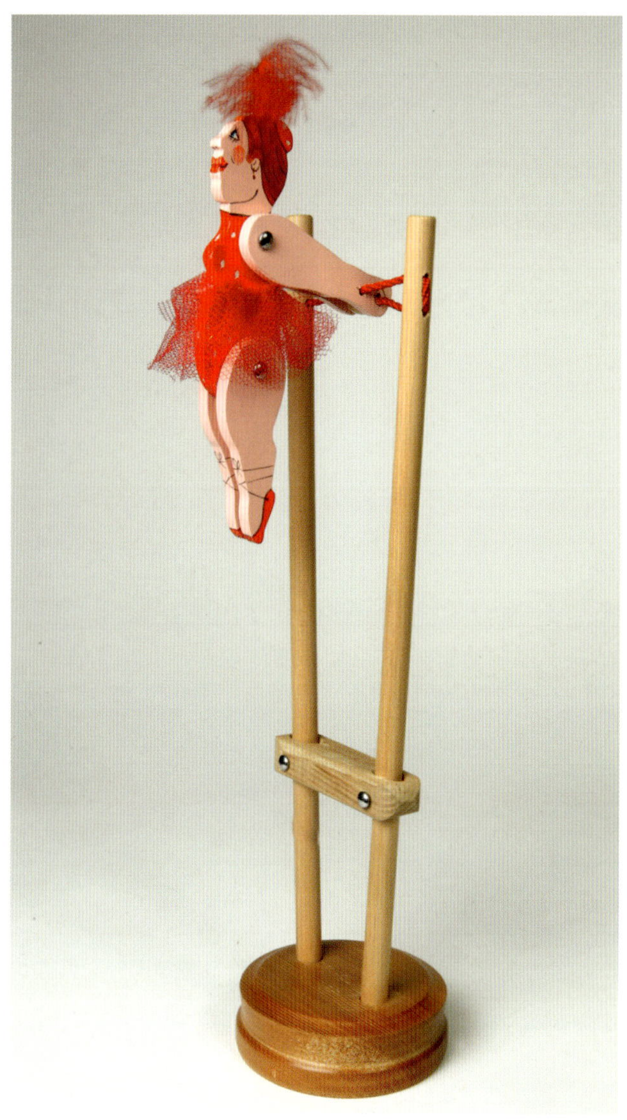

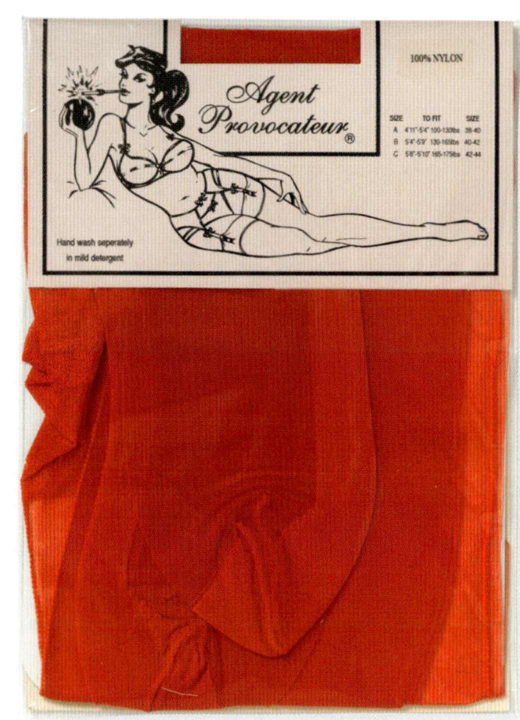

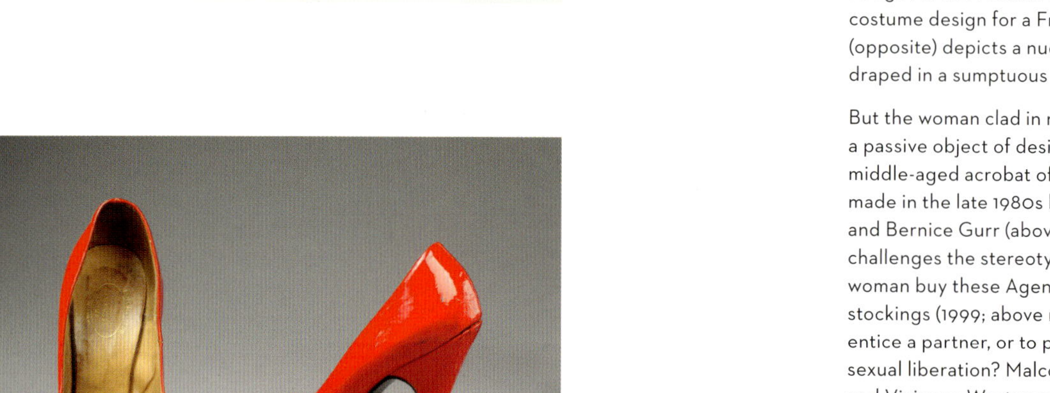

The woman in red – a smouldering seductress, a flirtatious *femme fatale*, the ultimate embodiment of sexual desire. From brothels to burlesque, red is the colour of the risqué; the world's most famous cabaret is called Moulin Rouge for this reason. This 1920s costume design for a French *revue* (opposite) depicts a nude showgirl draped in a sumptuous crimson robe.

But the woman clad in red is more than a passive object of desire. The plump, middle-aged acrobat of this torsion toy made in the late 1980s by Alan Jamieson and Bernice Gurr (above left) playfully challenges the stereotype. Does a woman buy these Agent Provocateur stockings (1999; above right) solely to entice a partner, or to proclaim her own sexual liberation? Malcolm McLaren and Vivienne Westwood's SEX stilettos (1974; left) – a riot of red PVC designed to provoke – unquestionably accomplish the latter, while on second glance, the showgirl subverts the dress of the Catholic cardinals who condemn her from the pulpit.

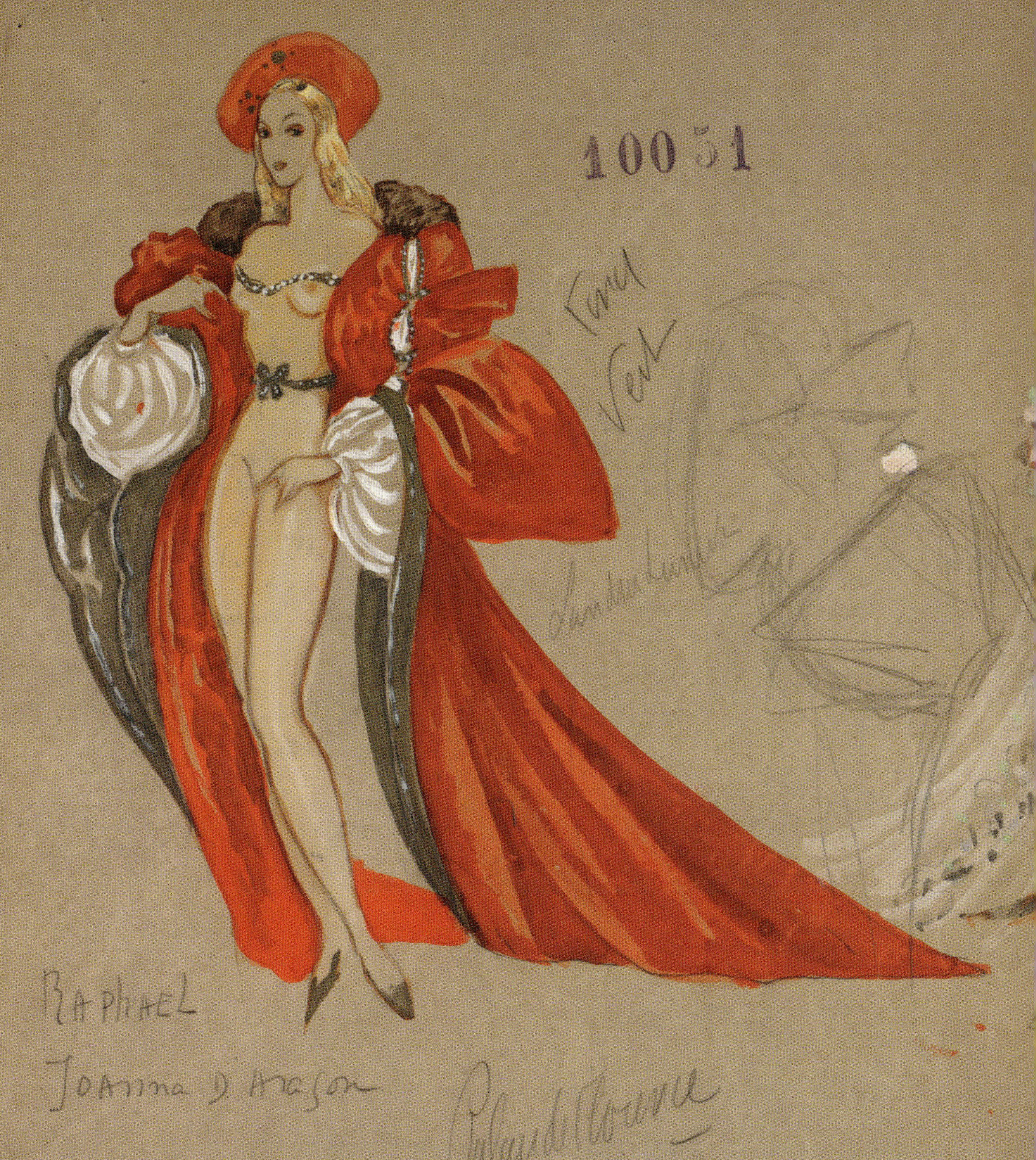

10051
RAPHAEL
JoAnna D'Aragon

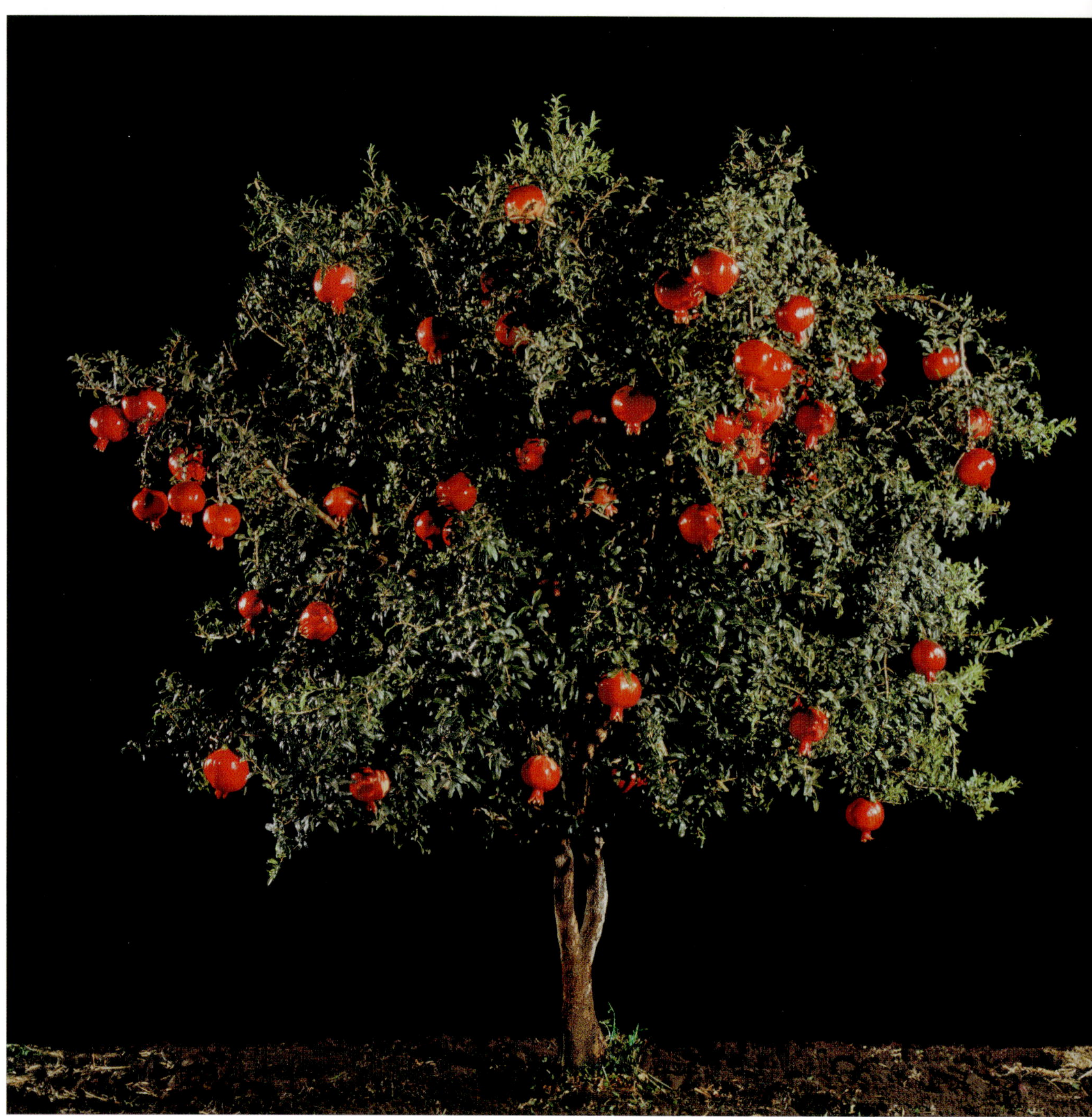

The pomegranate, containing hundreds of juicy red seeds waiting to burst into life, has long been associated with fertility. Set against a black background, the intense red of the tree's fruits is emphasized in Tal Schochat's photograph *Rimon (Pomegranate)*, made in 2010 (opposite). The word pomegranate derives from the Latin *pomum* (fruit), as does the name of Pomona, the Roman goddess of fruitful abundance. Designed by Edward Burne-Jones and John Henry Dearle and made by Morris & Co. around 1900, this tapestry (right) depicts Pomona cradling gathered fruit in the folds of her russet overdress.

Wedding dresses in many cultures are red. In the late 19th century Korean brides wore a predominantly red *hwarot* (over-robe) decorated with embroidered panels such as this example (below left) bearing auspicious images of flowers and phoenixes with their chicks. Red is often worn in south Asia at other festive occasions. These magnificent *jutti* slippers (below right) from the mid-19th century are lavishly lined with crimson velvet.

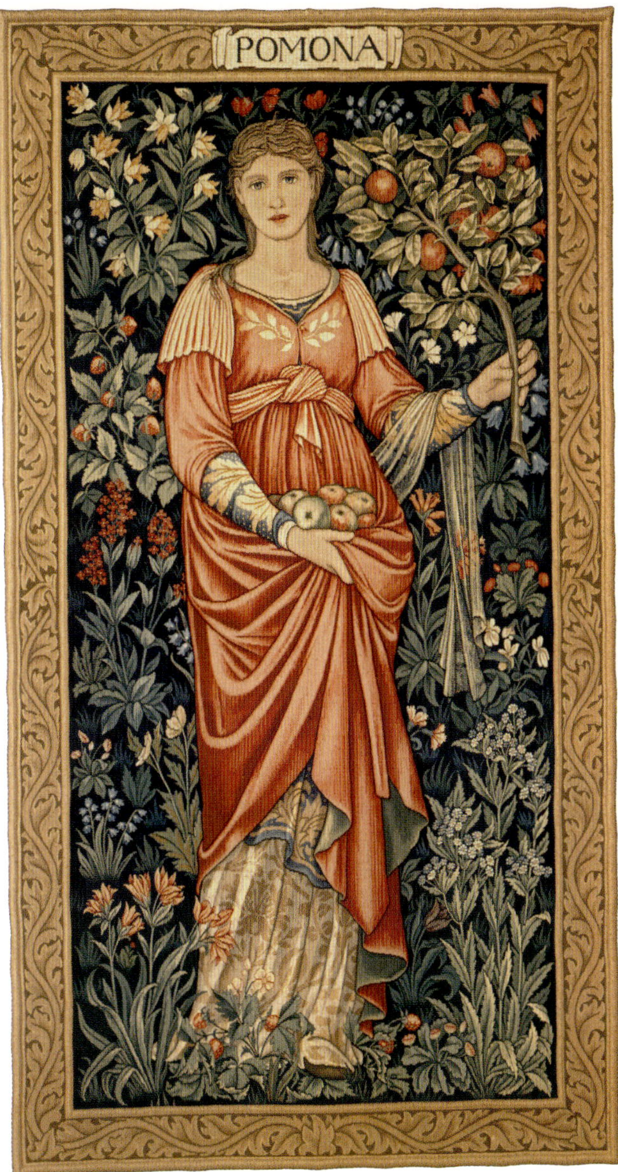

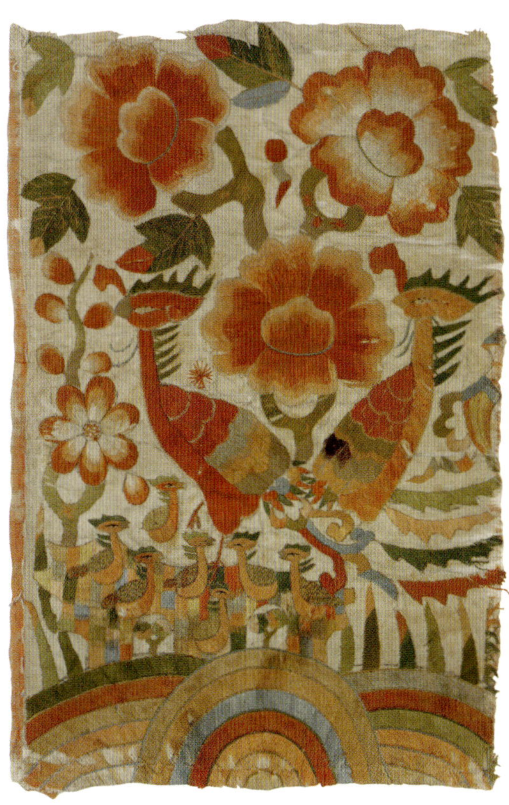

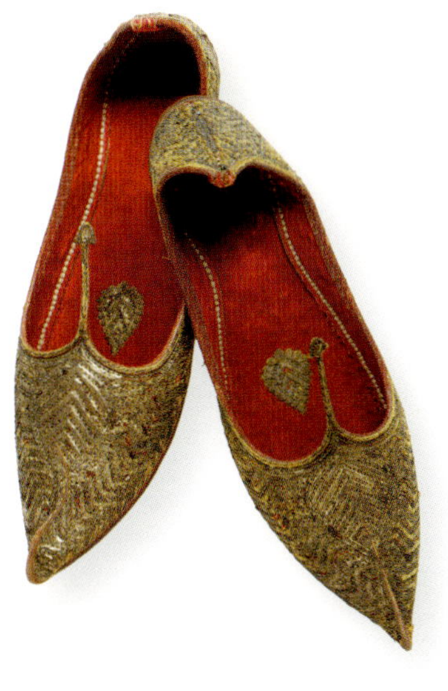

Since 1921, in the UK the red poppy has been a reminder of those who have died at war. Paul Cummins's public artwork *Blood Swept Lands and Seas of Red* (opposite), installed at the Tower of London by thousands of volunteers in 2014, was made up of 888,246 ceramic poppies, each representing a British or colonial casualty of the First World War. Red also speaks of sacrifices beyond Flanders' fields. This 15th-century English stained glass (below right) shows the Catholic martyr St Agnes. Her white dress is dyed with her own blood, spilt by the executioner's sword, while in this mid-16th-century Spanish pendant (below left) the popular symbol of the pelican piercing her breast to give life to her children symbolizes Christ's death for humanity's sins. The 'sacrificial' glazes of Chinese porcelain, such as this vase from Jingdezhen (1723–5; right), evoke the toil and tears spent in pursuit of the perfect lustre – and perhaps also a daughter's violent devotion.

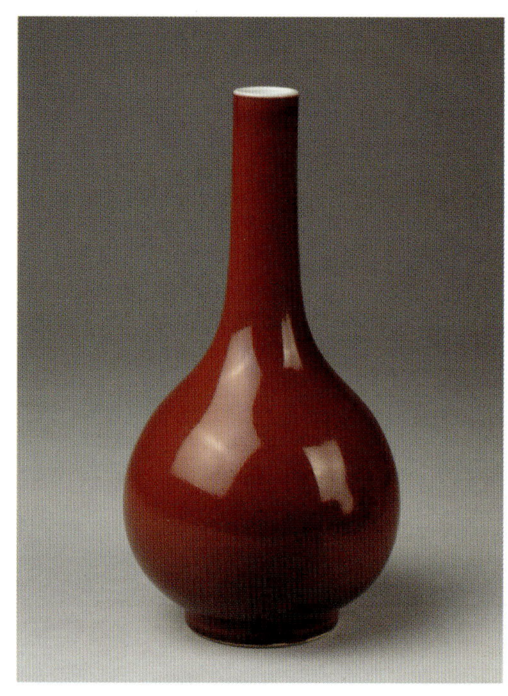

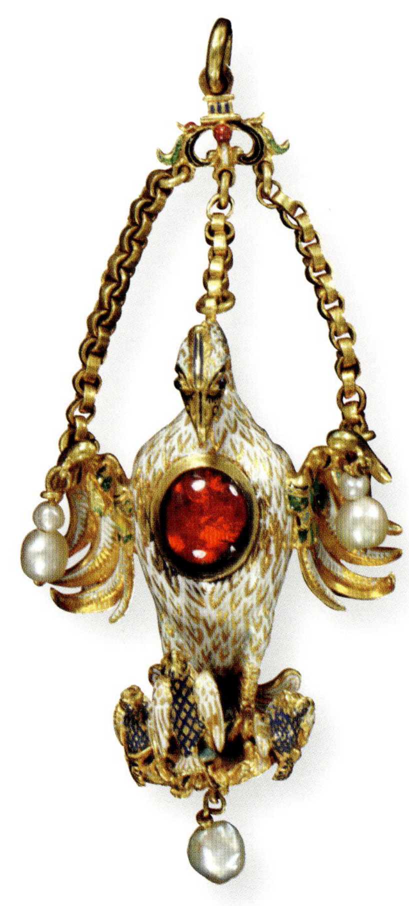

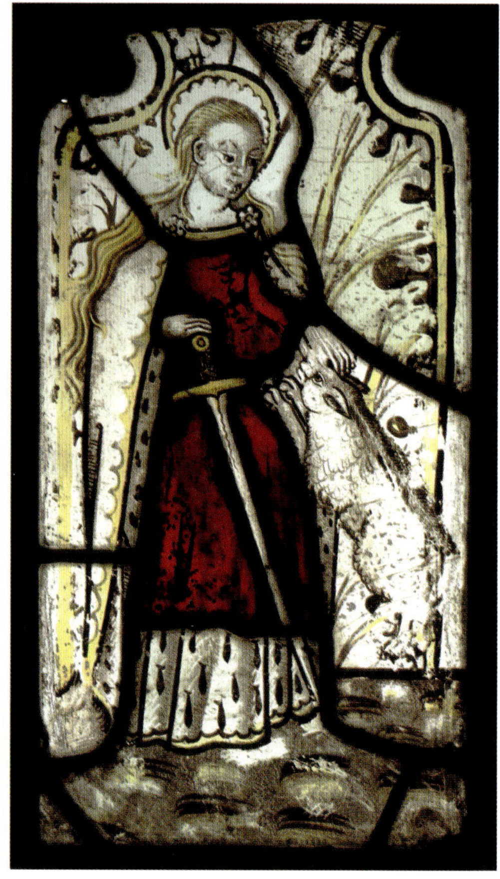

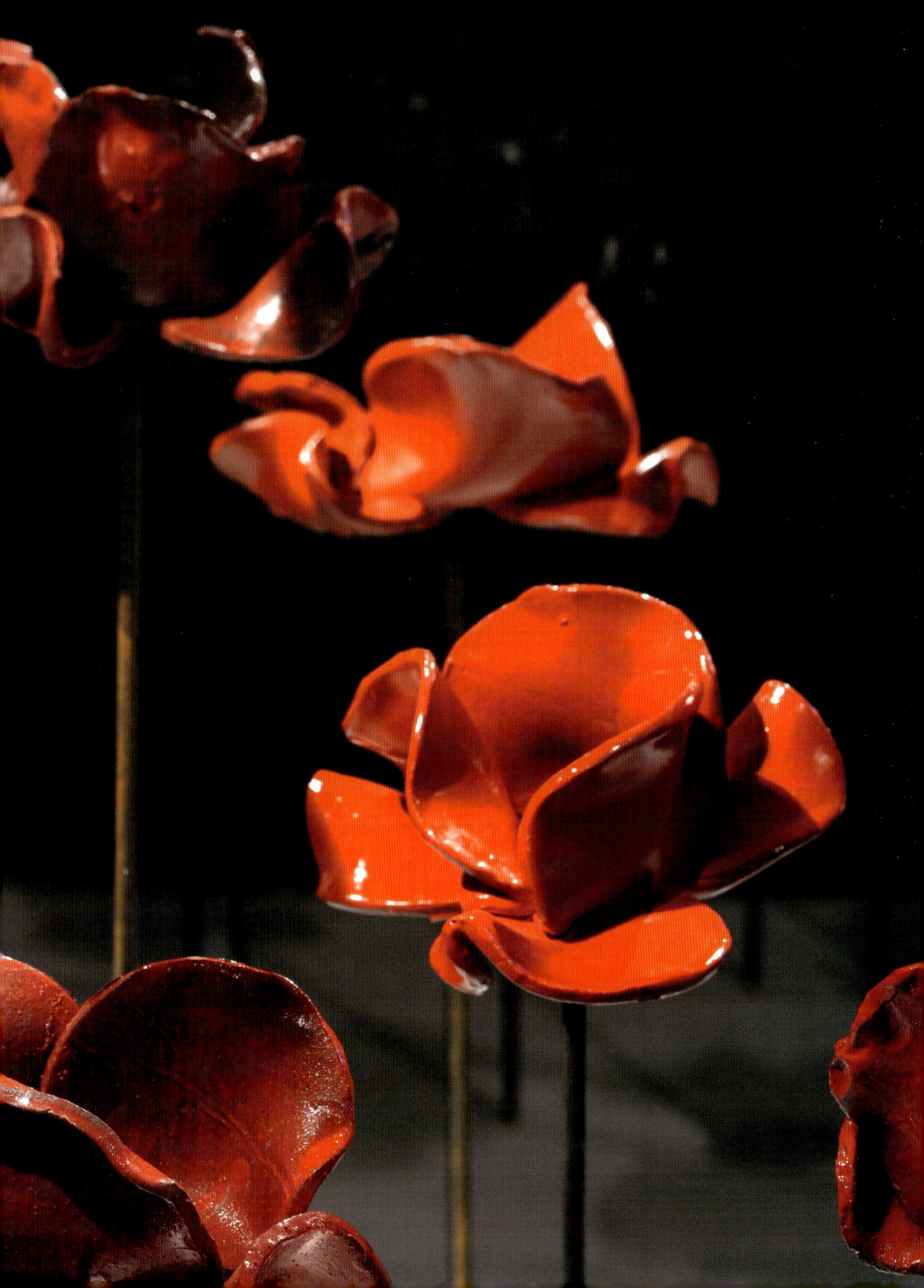

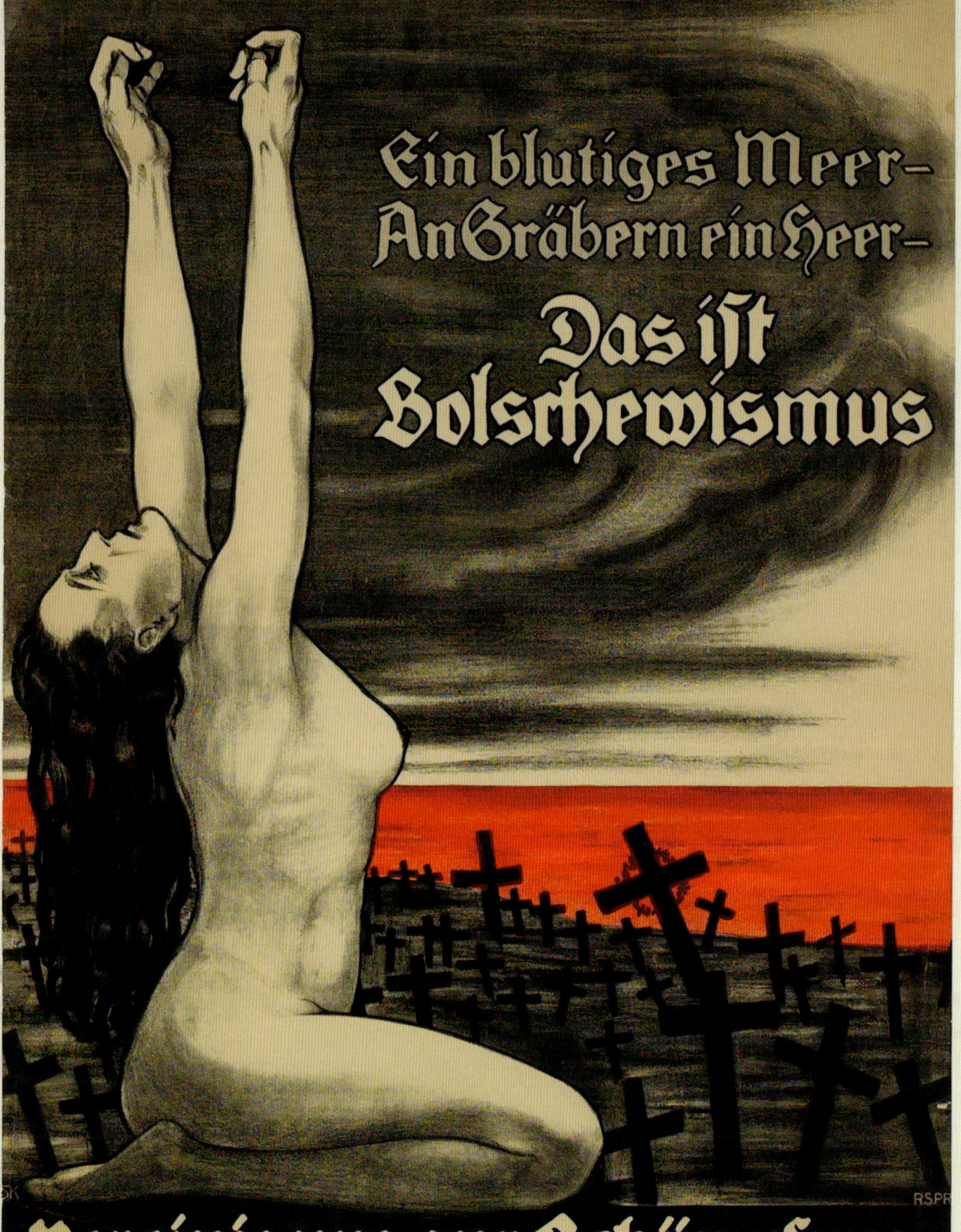

Ein blutiges Meer—
An Gräbern ein Heer—
Das ist
Bolschewismus
Vereinigung zur Bekämpfung
des Bolschewismus.
Berlin W. 9, Schellingstr. 2.

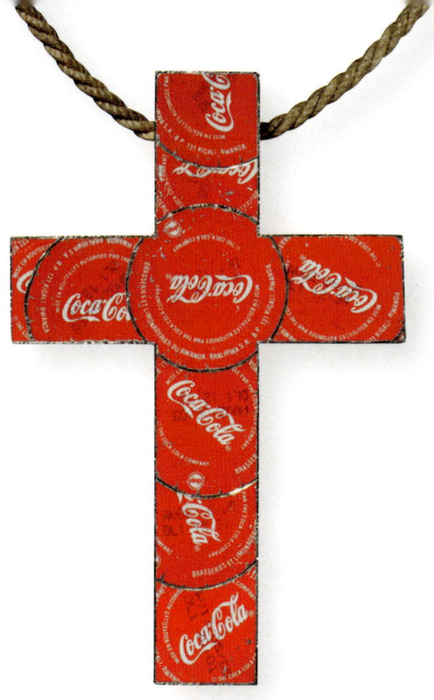

Historically, becoming a soldier was an economic alternative to urban poverty, though patriotism also played its part. The red uniform of the British army provoked the nickname 'redcoats'. Anger and fear, other emotions evoked by red, contribute to the propaganda that is intrinsic to war. Otto von Kursell's anti-Bolshevik poster (1919; opposite) twists the red of socialism into a sea of blood, inciting paranoia in interwar Germany. Ralph Steadman's poster for the Stop the War Coalition (2003; below), protesting Britain's involvement in the US-led war in Iraq, uses bloodstained newspaper strips to underscore the perils of modern warfare.

David Poston's pectoral cross 'The Real Thing' (2004; left) uses an iconic symbol and brand to ask questions about commerce and colonialism, and to convey the appalling senselessness of genocide. The red of Coca-Cola is instantly recognizable; here, it is also a reminder to stop and reflect on the costs of conflict.

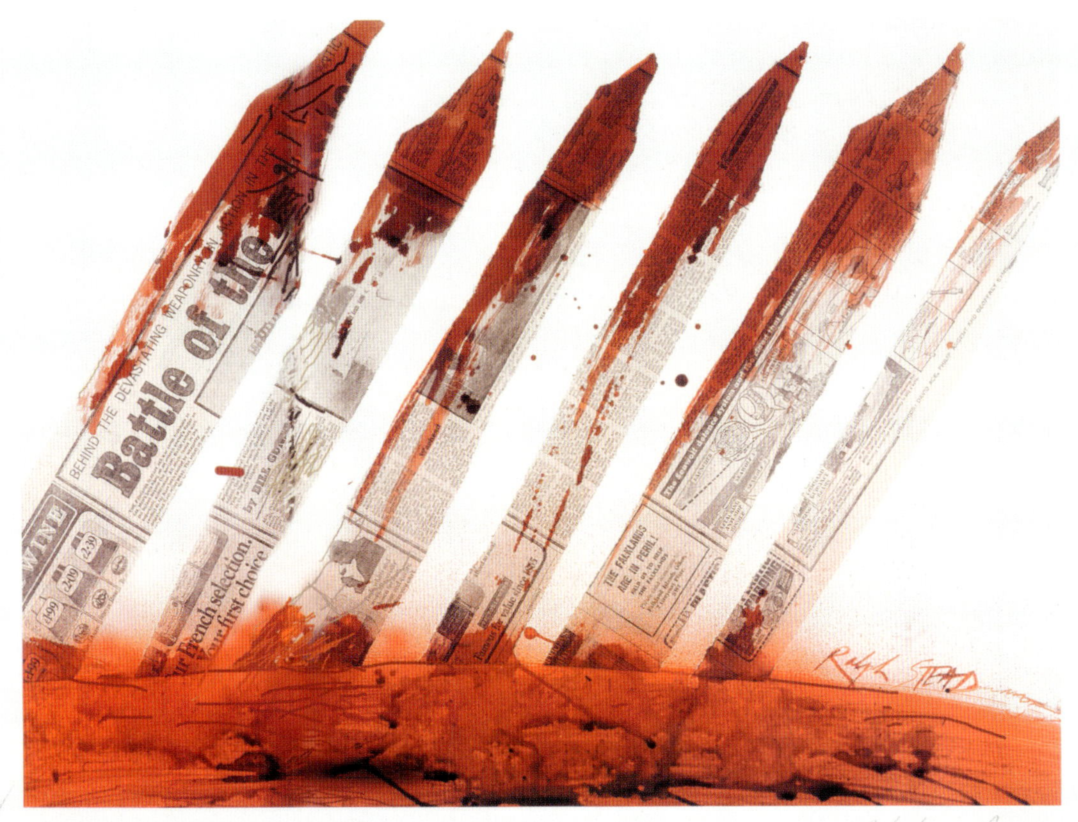

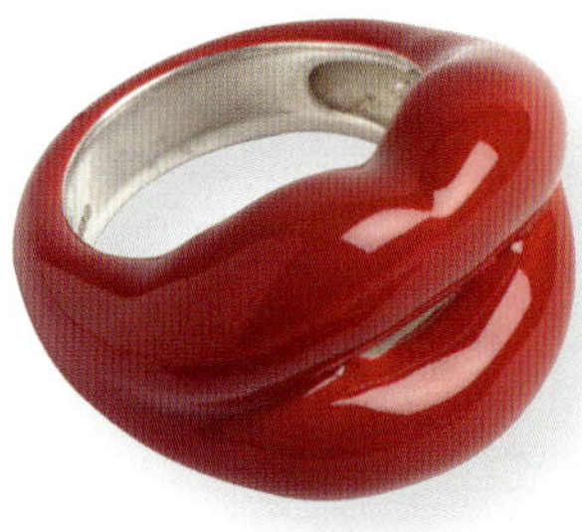

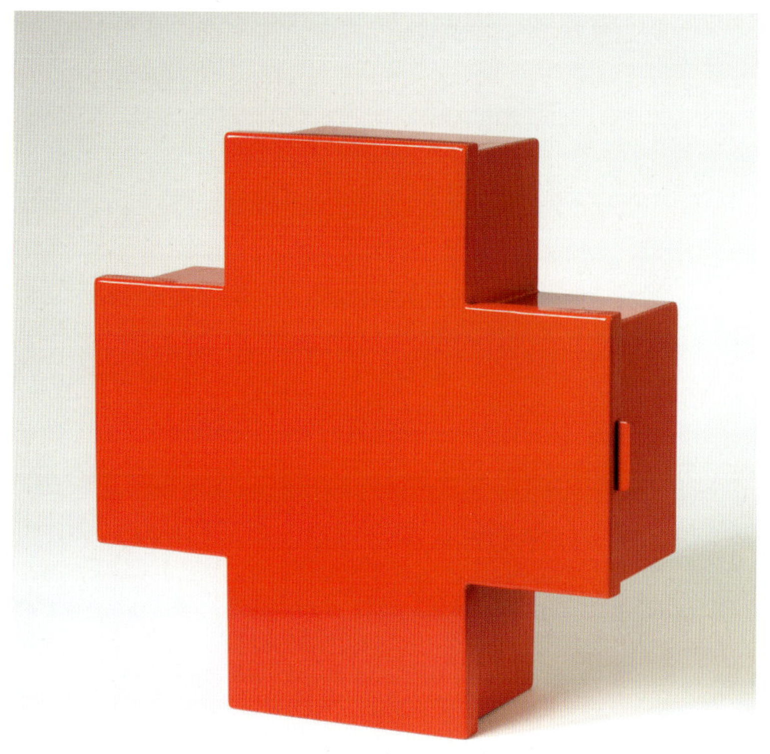

Blood is the essence of life. HIV/AIDS strikes at the heart of existence: age, ethnicity, gender and sexuality make no difference to infection. In 1993, two years after the red ribbon was adopted as a symbol of support for people with HIV, Eclipse Enterprises published a pack of trading cards to improve understanding of the crisis (opposite). In 2009, the jeweller Solange Azagury-Partridge launched a special edition of her 'Hotlips' ring (above left) for Product (Red), an initiative that works with Global Fund to eliminate AIDS on the African continent.

Beliefs that good health was stimulated by red were challenged in China by the Cultural Revolution; but folk art was encouraged under the regime, and papercuts became tools of the Communist state. This example from 1964 (right) promotes the 'barefoot' doctors who provided treatment in rural areas.

Thomas Ericksson designed this medicine cabinet (above right), commissioned by Cappellini in 1992 for the *Progetto Ogetto* (Project Object) collection. Simply named 'Help', it references the Red Cross, which universally offers neutral assistance in disaster and war. Its bright logo calls out: here is succour; here is hope and health.

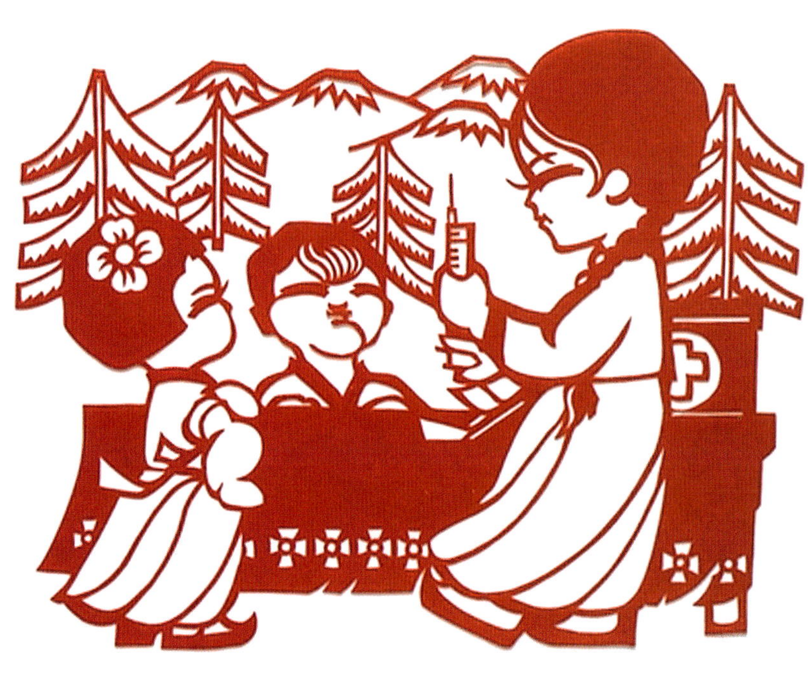

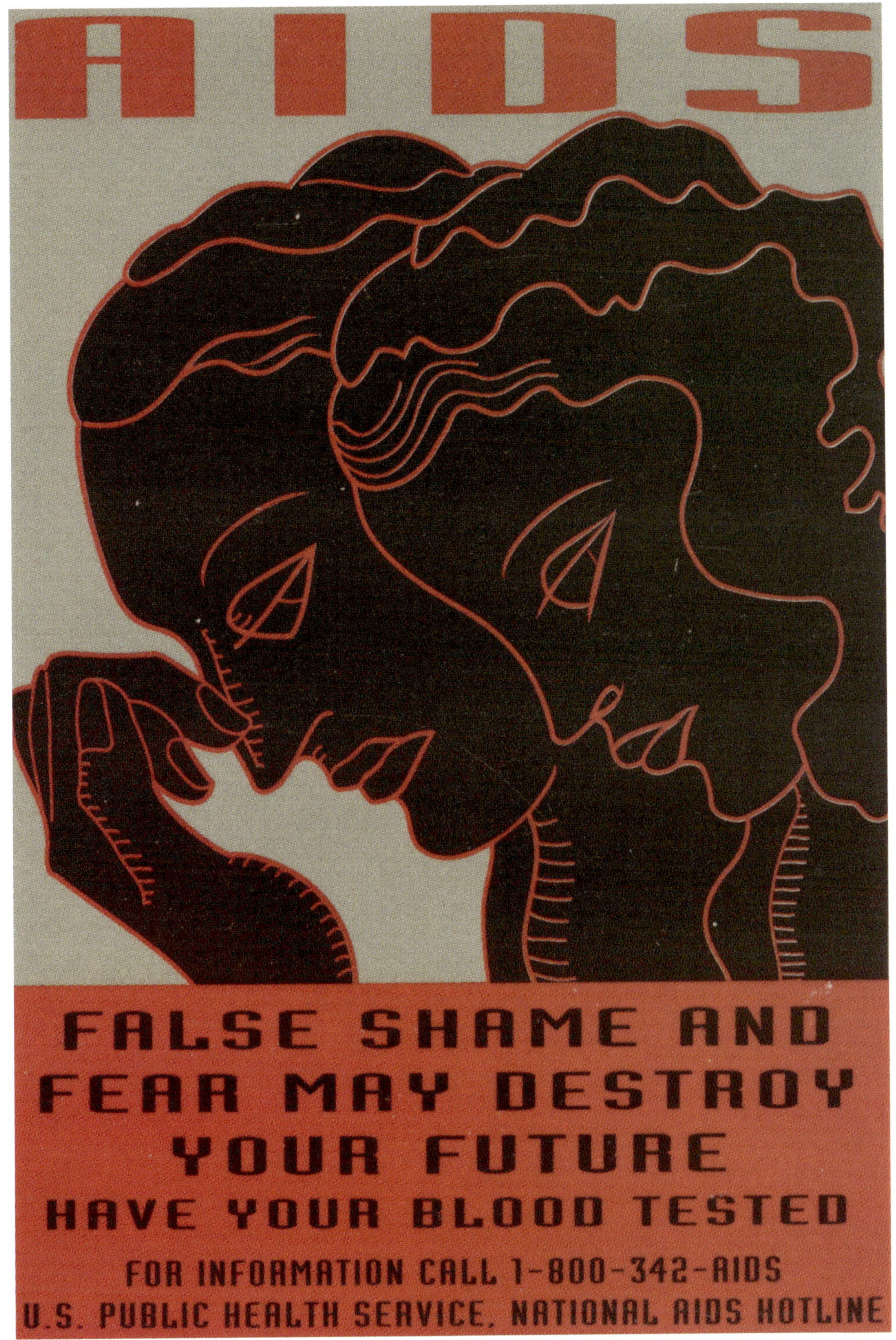

AIDS
FALSE SHAME AND
FEAR MAY DESTROY
YOUR FUTURE
HAVE YOUR BLOOD TESTED
FOR INFORMATION CALL 1-800-342-AIDS
U.S. PUBLIC HEALTH SERVICE, NATIONAL AIDS HOTLINE

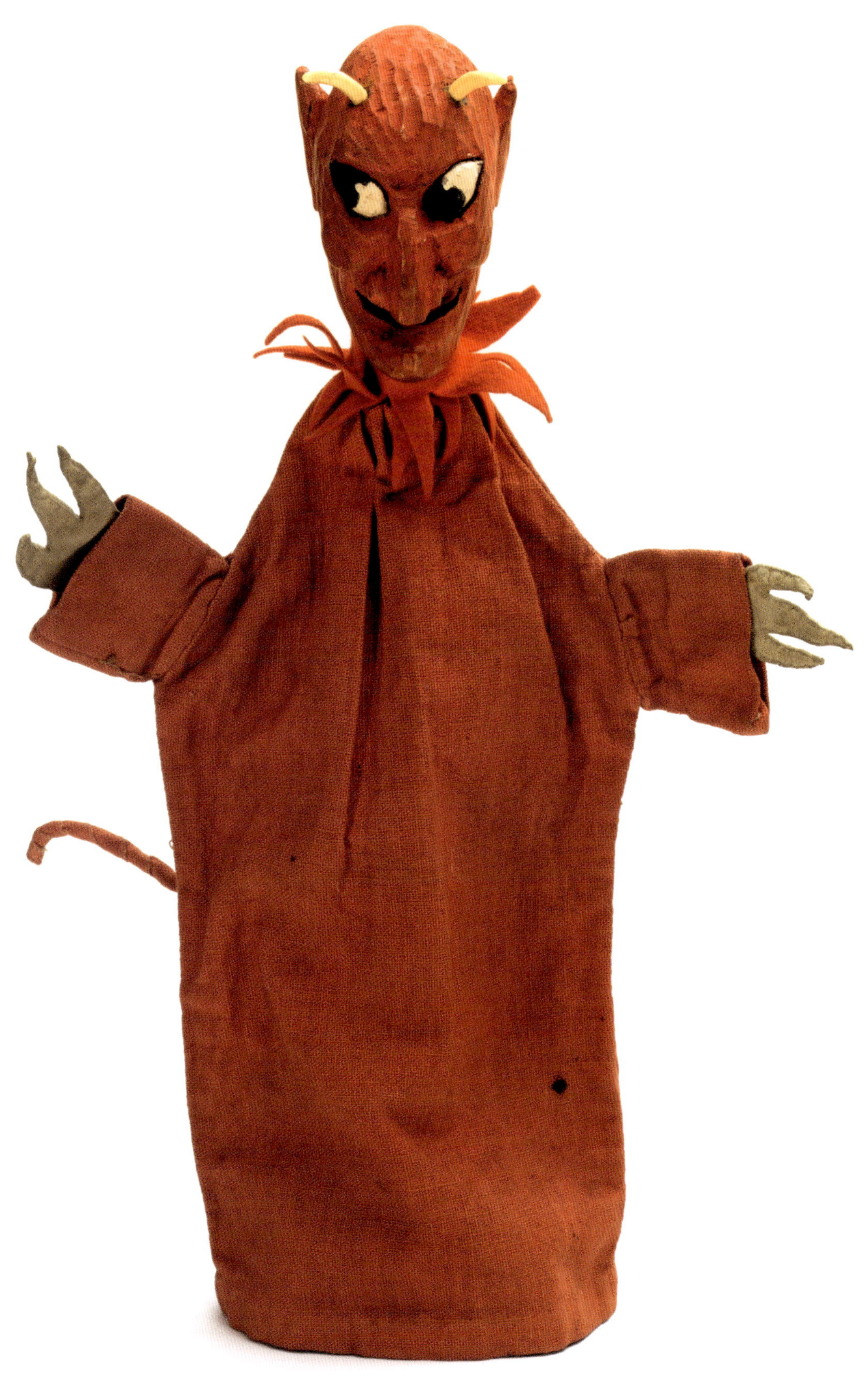

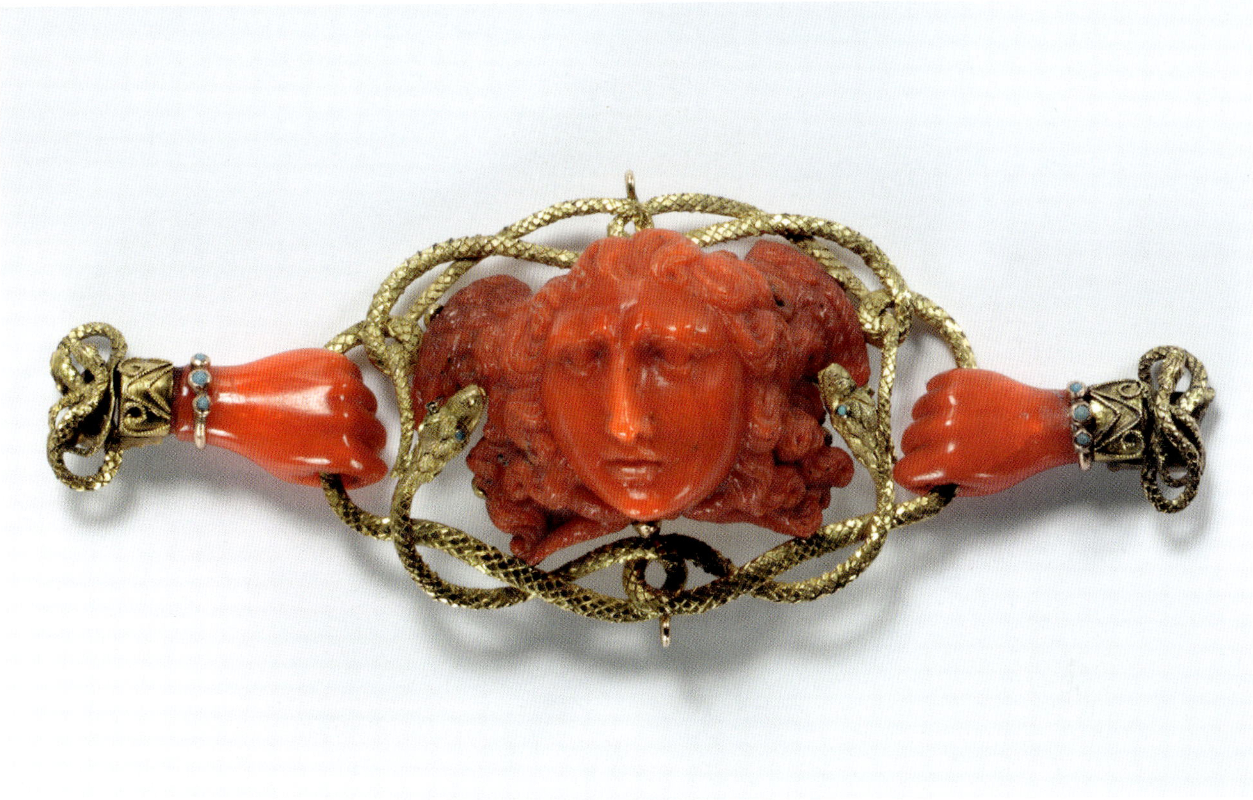

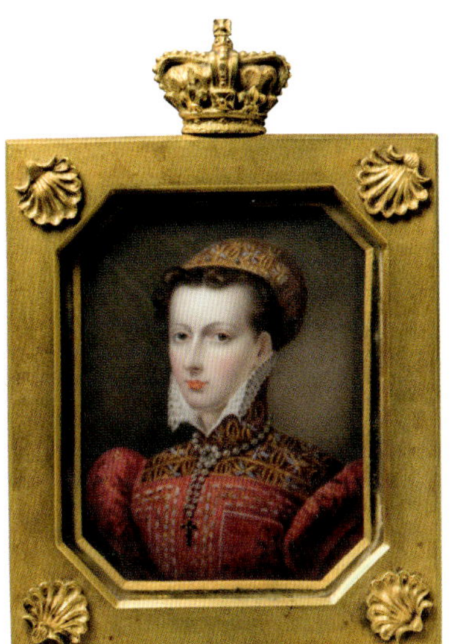

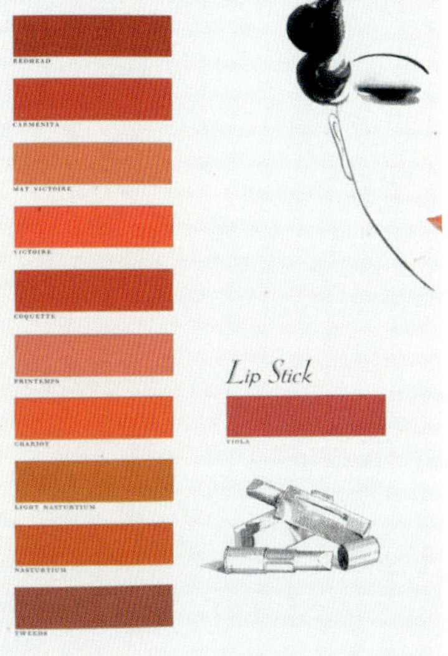

Imagery of the devil, such as Walter Wilkinson's puppet from 1920 (opposite), borrows from many traditions, including red as the colour of evil. In this portrait miniature by Denis Brownell Murphy (1804; far left), Mary Queen of Scots wears red, possibly in reference to the warm red undergarments she wore to her execution in 1587 for plotting to assassinate Elizabeth I in 1567. For those inclined to label her 'witch', their hue may have suggested her sorcerous impulses, rather than her bravery.

Elizabeth I herself believed that lip rouge had life-saving powers. Today, lipstick in any shade of red – eleven of which are shown in Elizabeth Arden's 1930s booklet 'Cosmetic Harmony' (left) – may empower its wearer, while coral amulets, such as this mid-19th-century Italian bracelet clasp (above), have protected expectant mothers and newborns since antiquity. The carved Medusa alludes to coral's mythical origins, when blood from her severed head dripped into the sea. Killed by Perseus, in one version of the Greek myth Medusa was transformed into a monster after being raped by the god Poseidon.

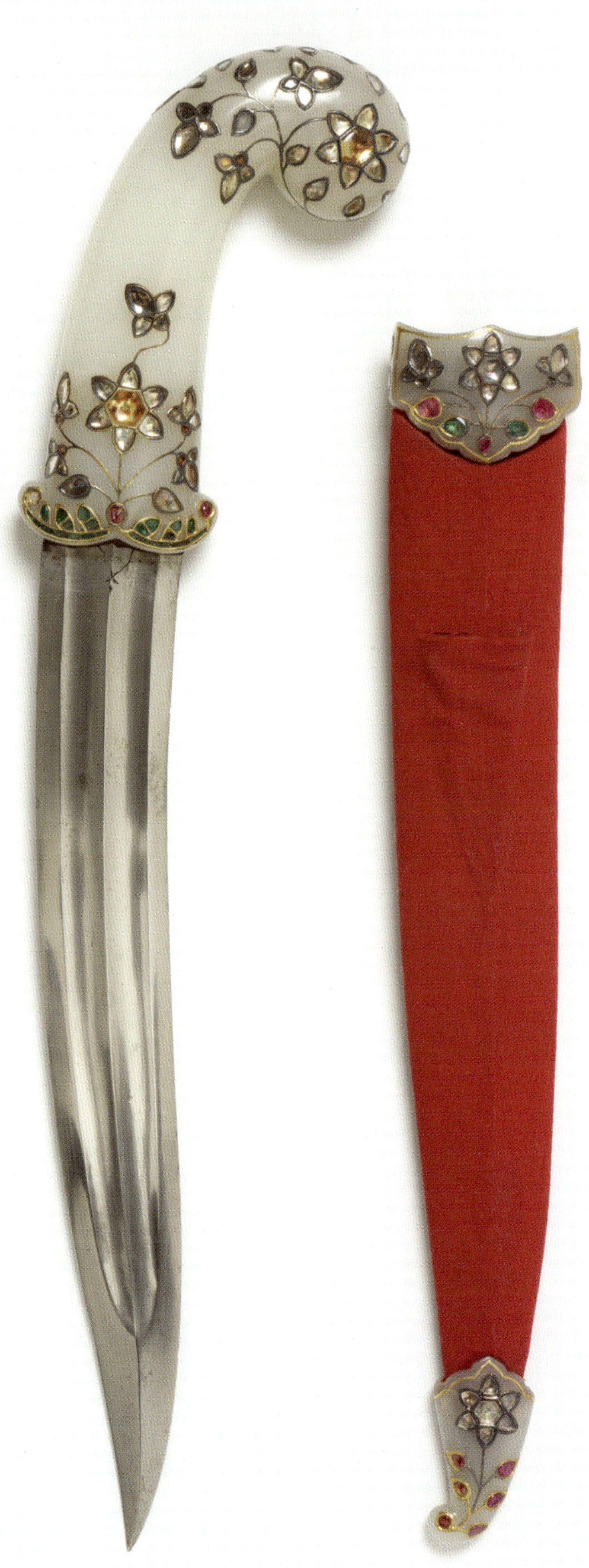

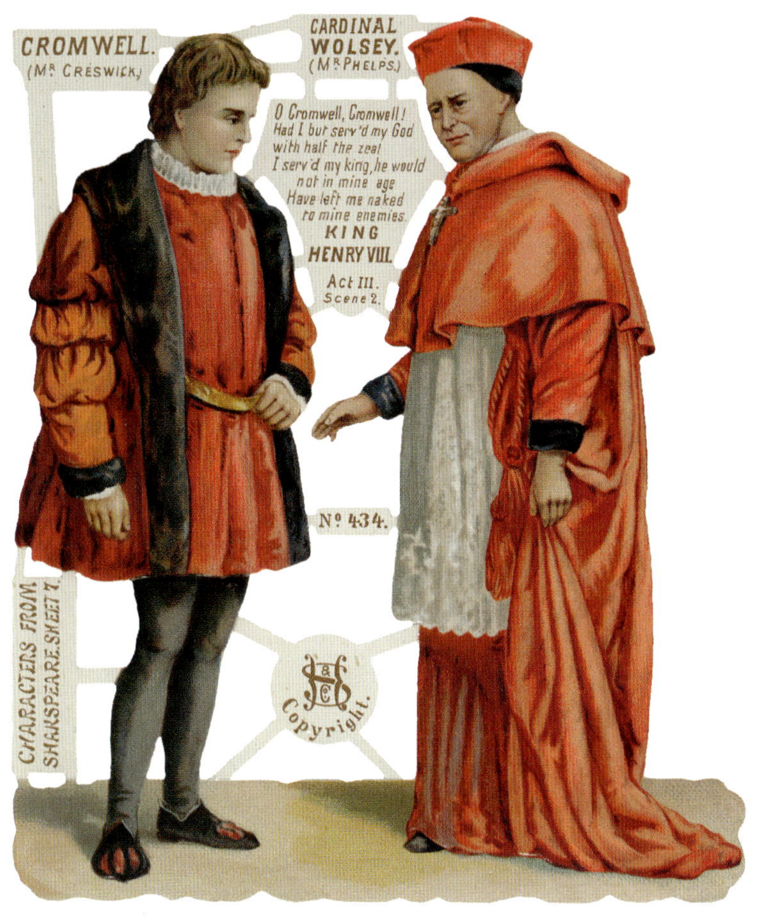

The scarcity of the raw materials once needed for red pigments made the colour a luxury for the privileged few. Red signalled the presence of power. Exquisite furniture such as this 16th-century folding chair (below right), decorated with carved cinnabar-red lacquer, conveyed the majesty of the imperial court of China's Ming dynasty. In India, emperors of the Mughal dynasty recognized loyal service with bejewelled ornamental daggers. The red scabbard of this 18th-century example (opposite) complements the rubies.

In England, Tudor sumptuary laws restricted the wearing of crimson to the elite. This chromolithograph from 1890 (left) depicts Henry VIII's most influential ministers: Thomas Cromwell's crimson doublet signifies his rising position at court, and Cardinal Wolsey's robes are the trappings of his office. Hunting rights also came from the king, and hunt masters wore the scarlet royal livery. This is possibly the origin of traditional scarlet hunting coats such as this one (below left) from the early 19th century, still a potent status symbol.

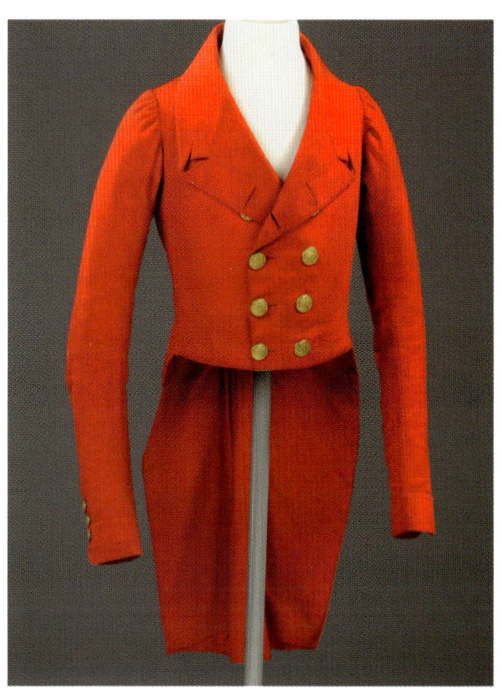

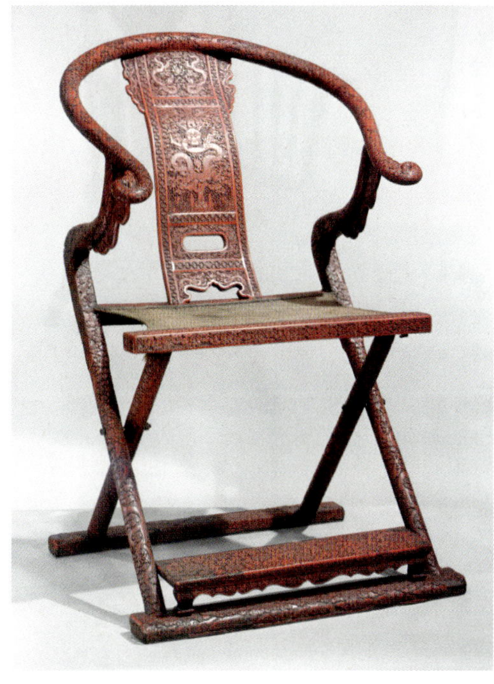

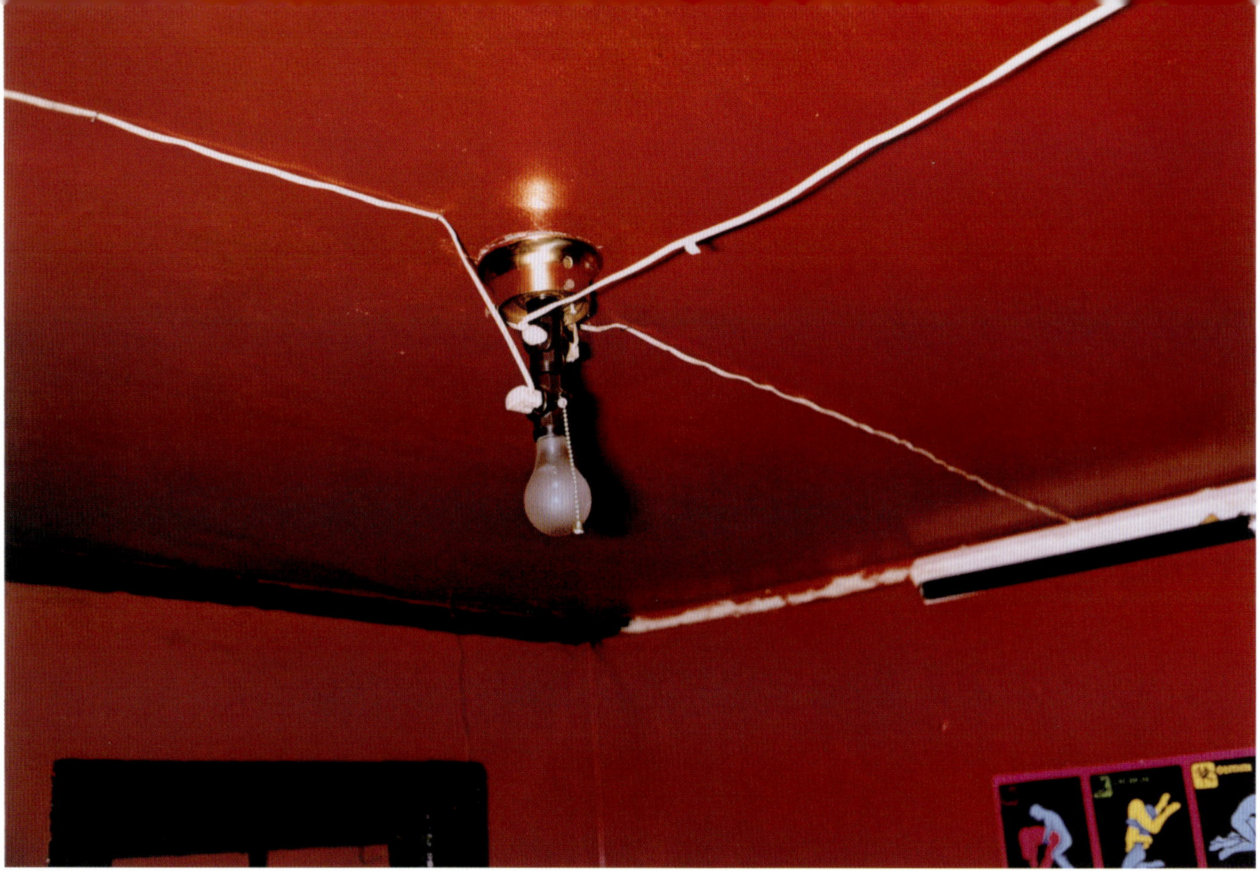

In *Untitled* (c. 1973; above), we
see a room with claret walls. The
suffocating hue reflects the seediness
that permeates William Eggleston's
photograph. Despite the focus on the
ceiling light, the eye is drawn to the
image's shady peripheries: explicit
pictures, half-obscured, stimulate the
viewer's speculations as to what may
be happening outside the frame.

This poster, depicting the cautionary
tale of Little Red Riding Hood, was
designed by John Hassall to advertise
a pantomime in about 1898. The story
has been interpreted as a metaphor for
sexual awakening, the colour of Little
Red Riding Hood's cloak representing
the menstrual blood of an adolescent
girl deceived and savaged by a 'big
bad wolf'. This story was a reality for
young maidservant Elizabeth Parker,
who embroidered her trauma into this
extraordinary sampler (opposite) in
about 1830. After leaving a kind family
for a supposedly better position,
Elizabeth instead suffered 'cruelty too
horrible to mention' and was 'thrown
down stairs' for trying to avoid her new
master's 'wicked design'.

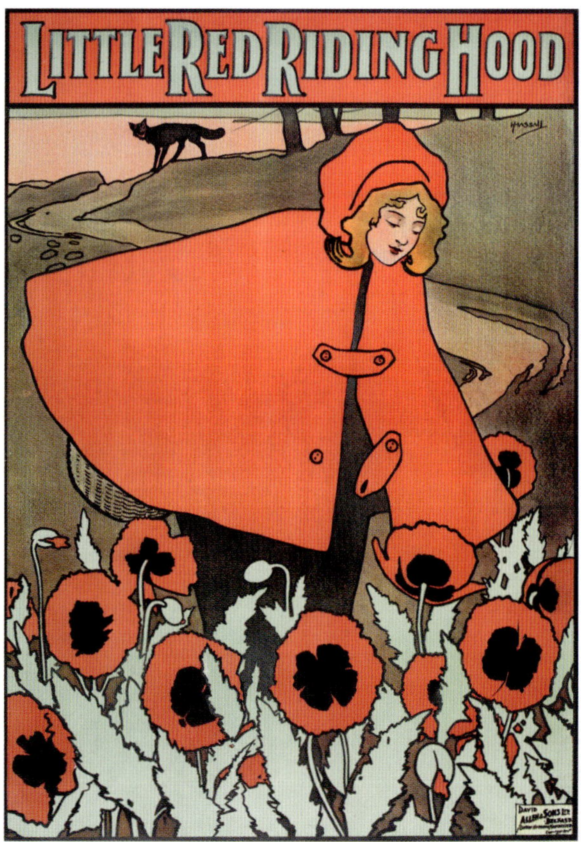

fathers occupation was a labourer for the Rt Hon the Earl of A. my Mother kept the Rt H
to render a comfortable living for their family which were eleven in number William Samuel Mary —
nd admonition of the lord as far as lay in their power always giving us good advice and wishing us
which we were to incounter with this world wishing us at all times to put our trust in god t
end But at the early age of thirteen I left my parents to go and live with Mr and Mrs P. to
ce until this day but like many others not knowing when I was well of in fourteen months I le
there cruel usage soon made me curse my Disobedience to my parents wishing I had taken —
cruelty to horrible to mention for trying to avoid the wicked design of my master I was throw
er told my friends what had happened to me they thinking I had had a good place and good —
with Col P Catsfield kitchenmaid where I was well of but there my memory failed me and my
d me in the care of my parents and sent for Dr W. who soon brought me to know that I was
en her advice to follow the works of darkness For I acknowledge being guilty of that great si
rthy Gentleman Dr W he came to me in the year 1829 he said unto me Elizabeth I understand
you do when you come before that great God who is so good to you he will say unto you —
epared for the Devil and his Angels For the impression it has made on my mind no tongue can
or surely I never felt such impressions of awe striking cold upon my breast as I felt when Dr —
onounced by an offended God But my views of things have been for some time very different
youth And above all I have felt the stings of a guilty Conscience for the great Disobedience
affliction but my affliction is a light affliction to what I have deserved but the Lord has —
e for repentance For blessed be God my frequent schemes for destroying myself were all —
went to stay with Mrs Welham she being gone out one day and left me alone soon after
the Lord let live surely never no one had such thoughts as me against the Lord and I arose
I retire into the most remotest part of the wood and there execute my design and that —
mad career for seeing the Bible lay upon the shelf I took it down and opened it and the first
was tempted of satan I read it and it seemed to give me some relief For now and not till —
able condition I have brought myself into by my sins for now do I see myself lost and undo
ndition But the only object I have now in view is that of approaching death I feel assured —
can I do to be saved what can I do to be saved from the wrath of that God which my
wretch that I am who shall deliver me from the body of this death that I have been —
and kneel before the Lord my maker oh with what confidence can I approach the mercy
use to address the Lord my maker pardon mine iniquity pardon mine iniquity O Lord for —
en the secret desires of me thine unworthy servant O Lord I pray the Look down with
to the Lord to turn my wicked Heart the Lord has heard my prayer the Lord has give
nds For while the lamp holds on to burn the greatest sinner may return Life is the seaso
r is none its rapid course can stay The Living know that they must die But ah the dead
n their hatred and their love is lost Their envy's buried in the dust By the will of God a
whenever my thoughts do from the stray And lead me Lord to thy blest fold That I th
and punish me but as my Father to pity and restore me For I know with the O Lord no
sin and misery For since my earthly Physician has said he can do no more for me in the w
e to cast me of in thy displeasure Forgive my sins my folly cure Grant me the help I nee
me take me O kind shepherd take me a poor wandering sinner to thy fold Thou art Lord
r to rise again O God keep me from all evil thoughts The little hope I feel that I shall ob
never knew anything like happiness till now O that I may but be saved on the day of Jud
in until Dr W. remind me of my wickedness For with shame I own I returned to the

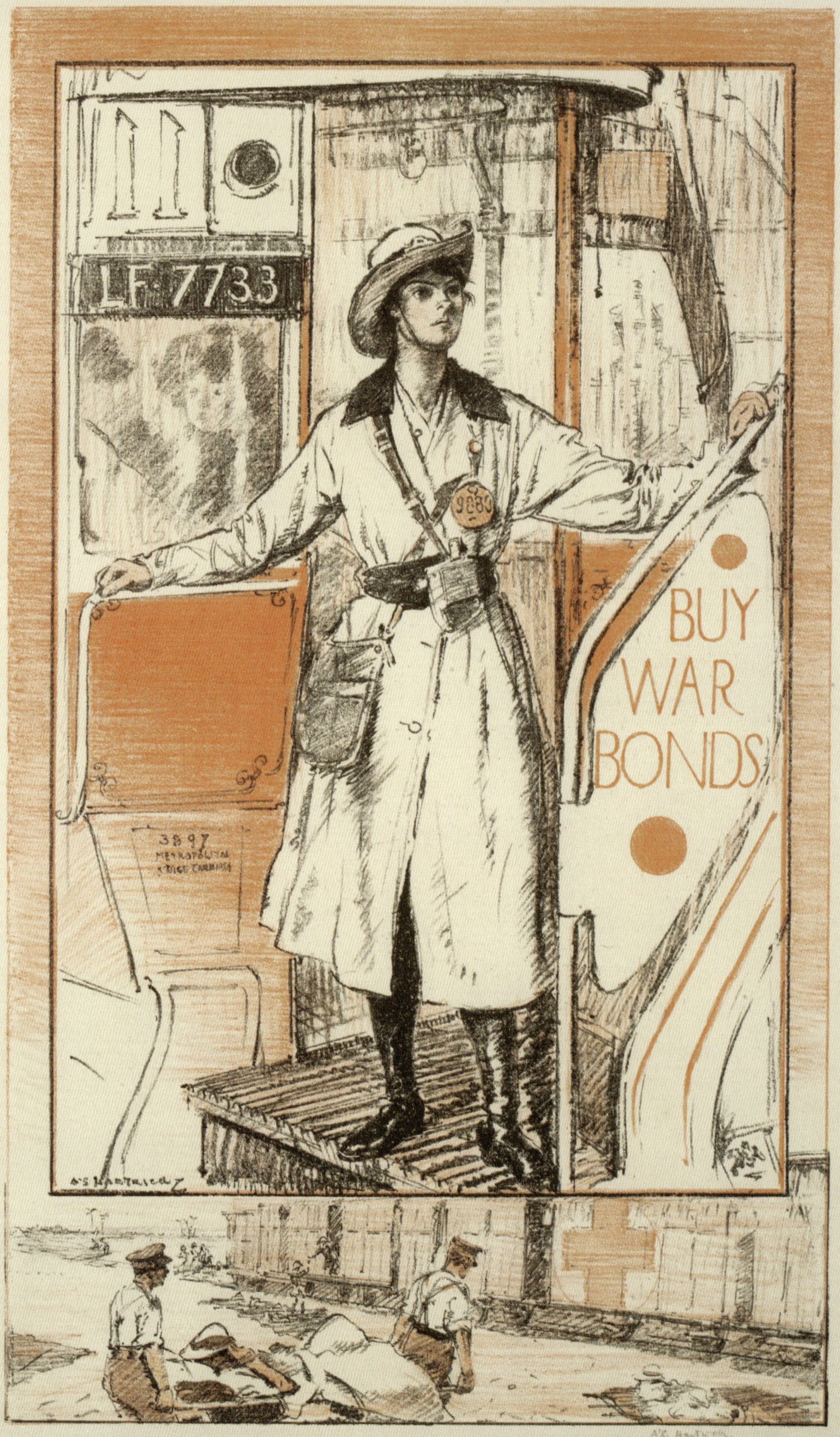

LF·7733
BUY
WAR
BONDS

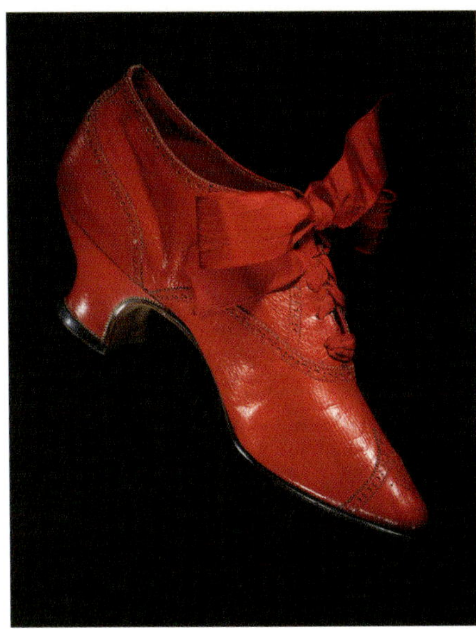

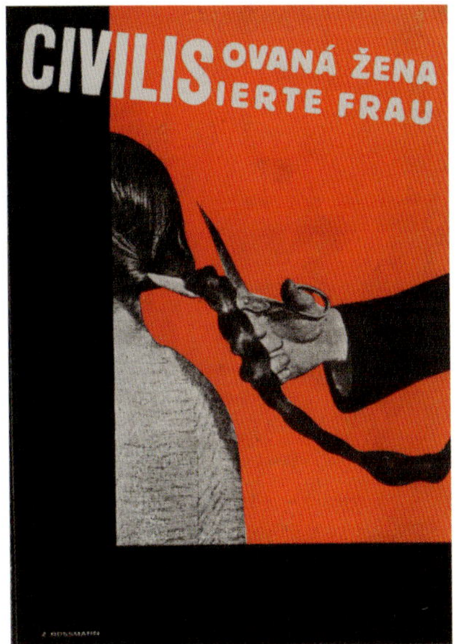

Sensible clothing and trousers were worn by working women during the First World War, as shown in the lithograph by Archibald Hartrick (opposite), depicting a bus conductor. This was one of a series of prints from 1917 intended to encourage women to volunteer for jobs in sectors formerly reserved for men. Middle-class women had been employed prior to 1914, and smart, practical attire such as these ruby leather shoes made by Hook, Knowles & Co. in 1900 (above left) indicate the pre-war emergence of independent women: strong and ready for anything. At the *Civilisovaná žena* (*Civilized Woman*) exhibition in Brno, Czechoslovakia, in 1929, Bozena Hornekova liberated women from skirts by presenting elegant everyday trousers for all. Bobbed hair was also stylish, convenient and, initially, a brave decision, as suggested by the cover for the catalogue (above right).

It certainly took courage to climb into early motor cars and drive at speed, but her chic cherry-red outfits may have helped inspire Jill Thomas to hit 120 mph. This portrait (right), taken by the innovative photographer Madame Yevonde in 1938, celebrates the record-breaking racing driver all in red.

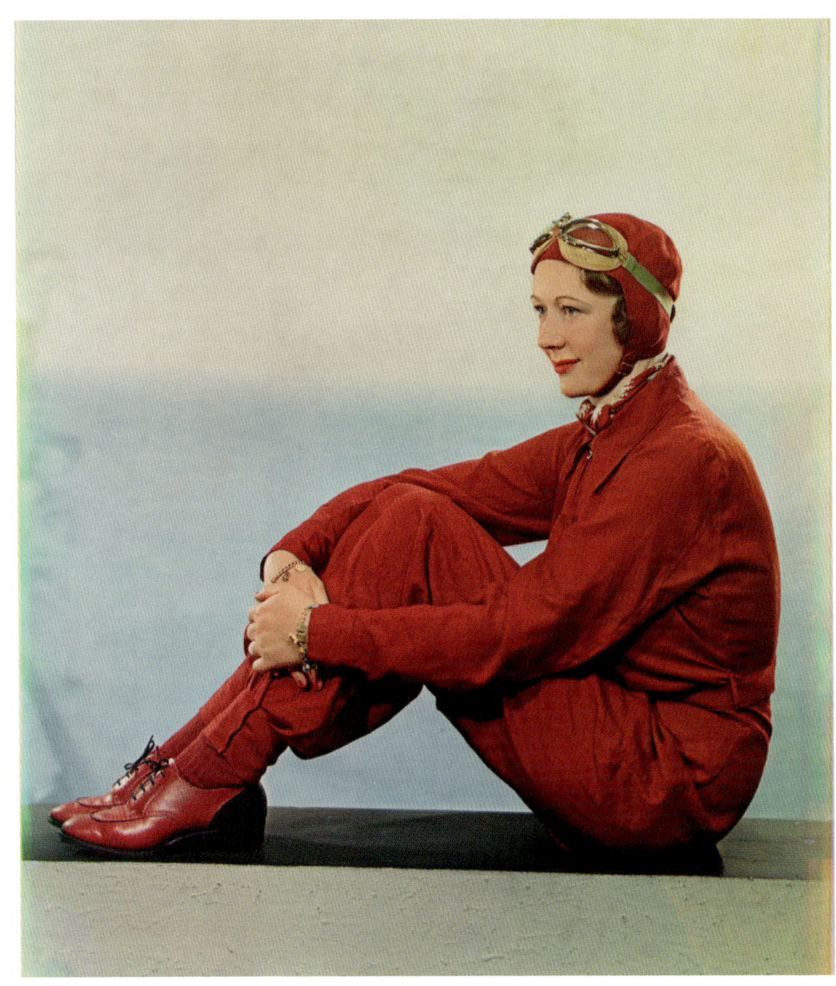

The bright red sari of this courtesan, painted by Nibaran Chandra Ghosh (right), highlights her voluptuous sensuality, captured in the bold brushstrokes typical of Kalighat paintings. Originally depicting Hindu deities, these were produced as devotional images for pilgrims, then as souvenirs for European tourists. They also portrayed aspects of daily life, satirizing the complexities of the colonial experience.

In the print below from the portfolio *To Catch a Whiteman by his Manifesto*, a series of experimental typography and concrete poems made by Dom Sylvester Houédard and his students at the Bath Academy of Art in 1967, the poem is shaped like two shoeprints. The syncopated rhythm and red typeface amplify words that echo fetish, appropriation and oppression. These footsteps dance through blood.

Chris Ofili's *Afro Lunar Lovers* (2003; opposite) unites the glamour of romantic stereotypes with the green, black and red palette of Black Nationalism to evoke a dream of a place where racial hatred no longer exists. As Ofili observes, 'Love is a blissful state, but it's not a utopia.'

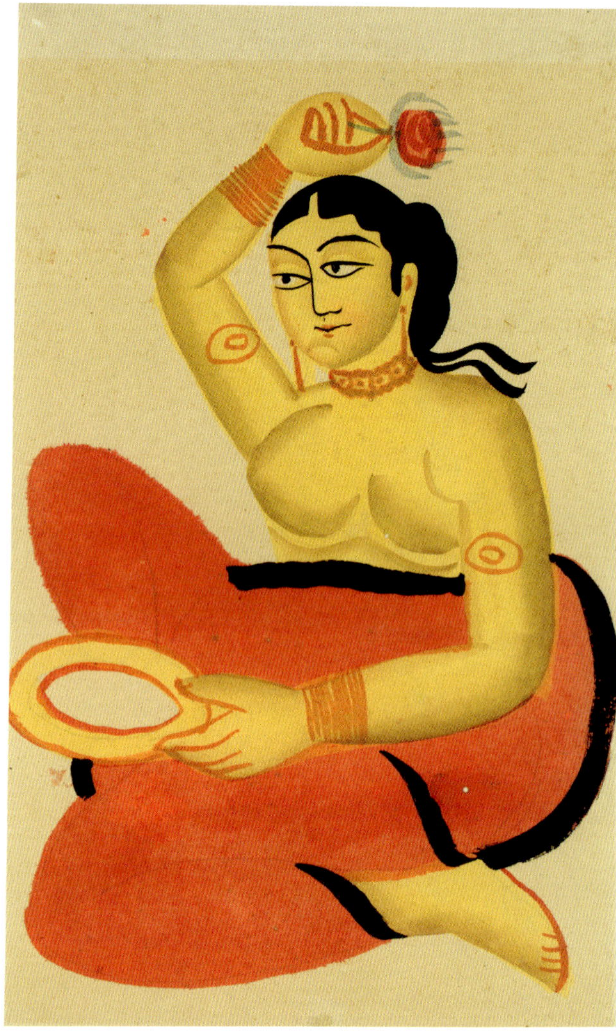

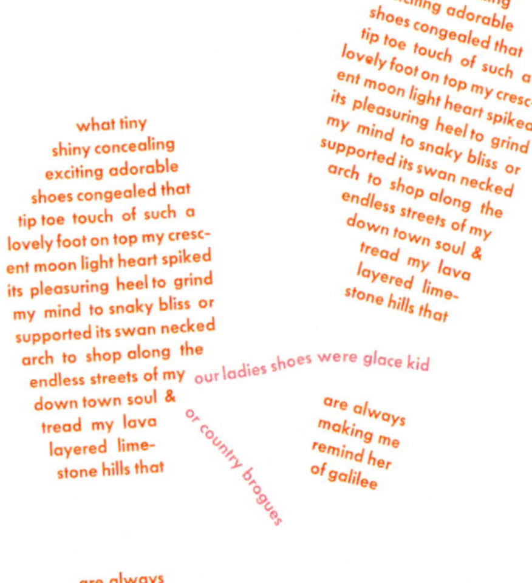

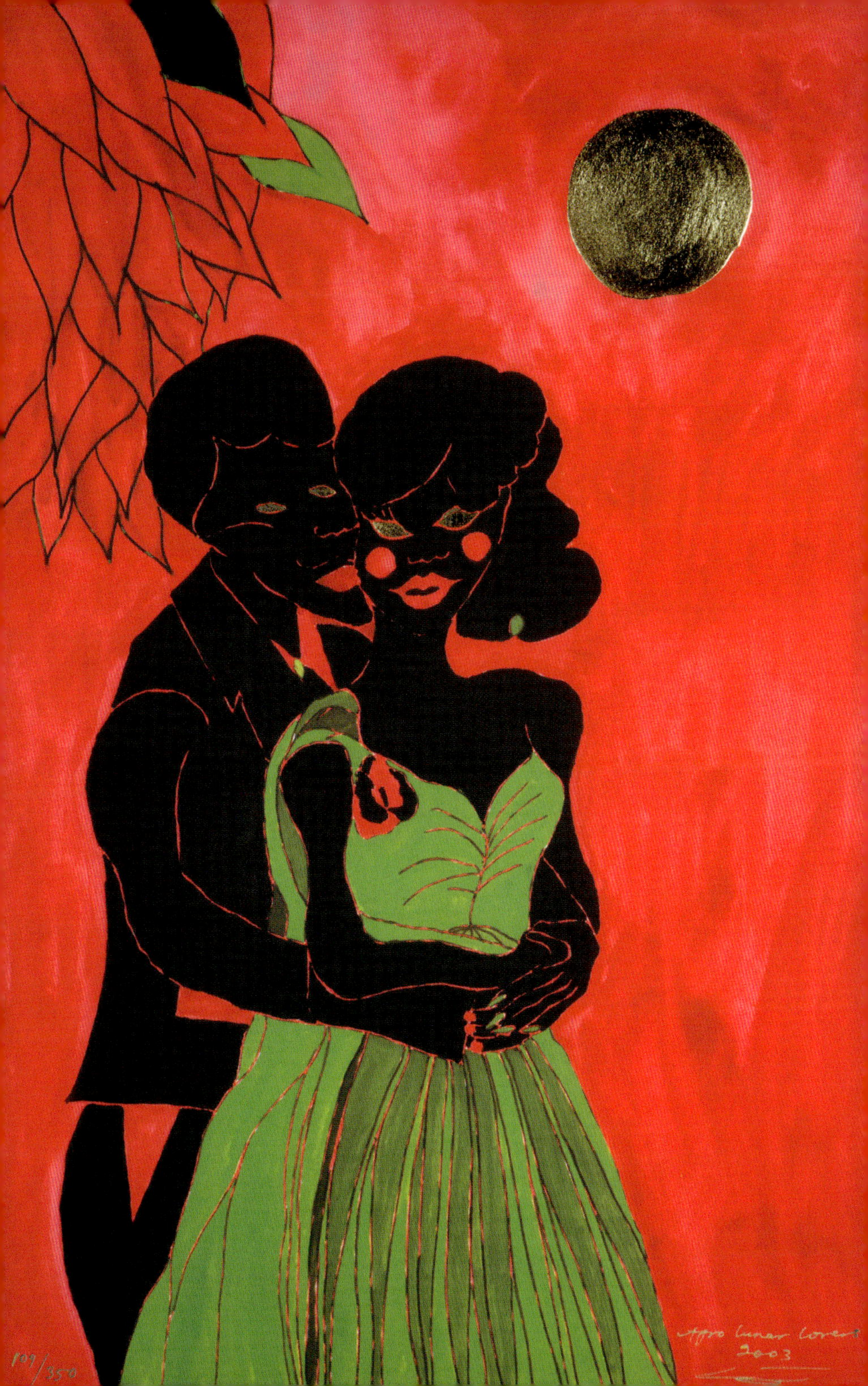

109/350
Afro Lunar Lovers
2003

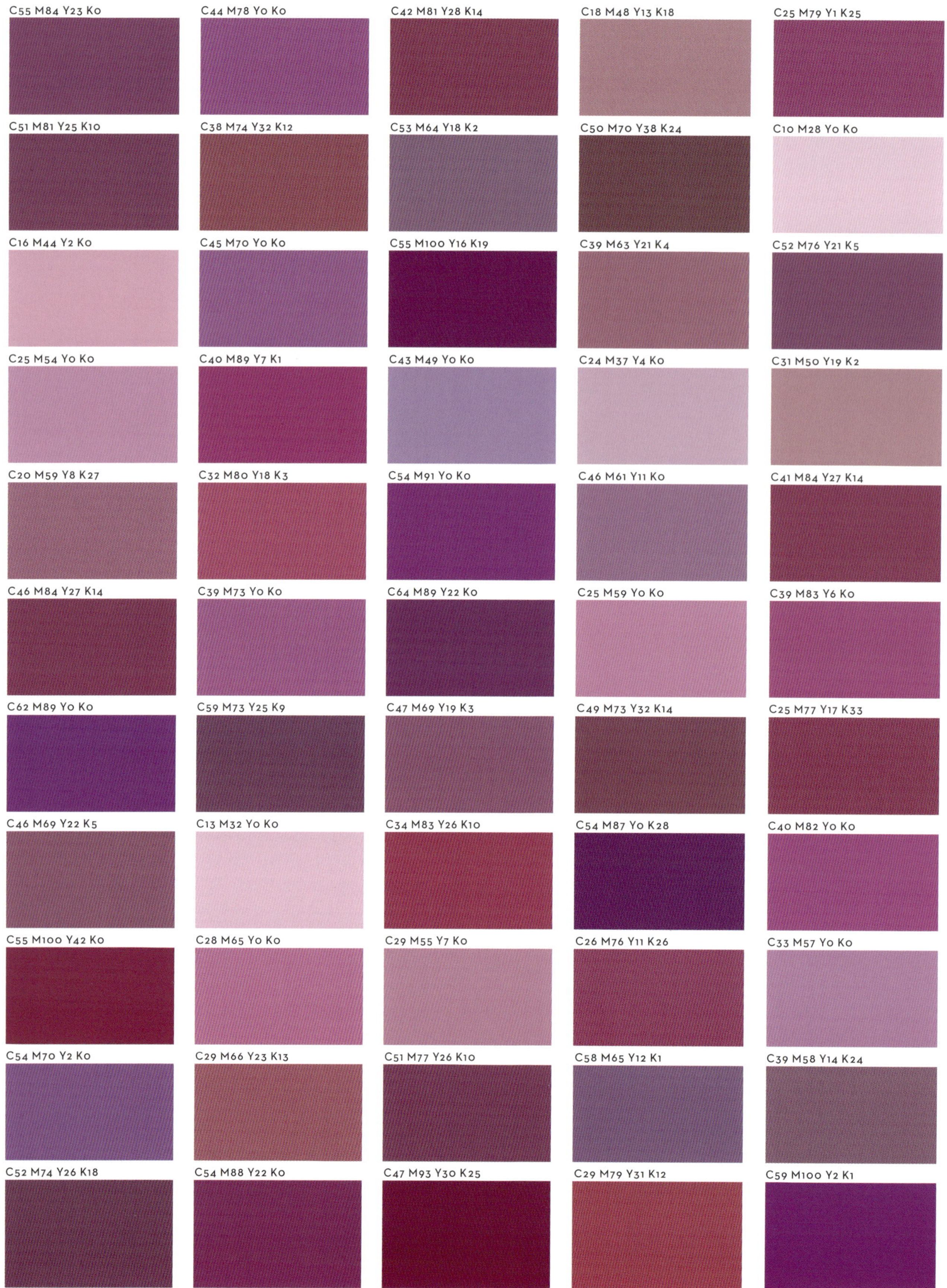

PURPLE

When the British suffragette movement chose purple for one of their three campaign bands, they were reclaiming the colour of royalty, dignity and most of all, power. Purple's association with power can be traced back thousands of years and across the globe, from the Mediterranean basin to the Japanese archipelago. In part this association came from its beauty – Plato named it the most beautiful hue – but more importantly from its rarity. Before the existence of synthetic dyes, the difficulty in procuring purple materials, from pigments to stone, made it both incredibly expensive and highly prized. A rare colour in the natural world, purple was forbidden to common people; from the Byzantine Empire to the Chinese Tang dynasty, the use of purple was restricted by law. Once synonymous with imperial power, the colour – imbued with the symbolism of purity and dignity – would over time be reimagined as a colour of protest and subversion.

The earliest form of purple pigment (*purpura*) used in the west was discovered in 1600 BC, off the Mediterranean coast of Lebanon. Tyrian purple, named after the Phoenician seaport of Tyre, came from the tiny glands of murex seashells. The colour they produced was an iridescent crimson-wine tone inclining to black, not the mauve or amethyst hues that have come to represent purple today. Harvesting the molluscs was an enormous task; it took around 250,000 shells to make one ounce of dye – just about enough for one dress or toga. It was the Phoenicians who perfected the process. Taken from the Ancient Greek, the name literally means 'purple land'.

Labour-intensive and rare, purple dye became the preserve of the elites, and in a world where dyes were mostly used for textiles, the most prized were saved for silk. Constantine I, the first Christian Roman Emperor, was remembered in the *Historia Augusta* as wearing a purple silk robe: 'some heavenly angel of God, his bright mantle shedding lustre like beams of light'. In Christianity, purple was considered a colour of light and associated with purity. In the Old Testament those clad in purple were revered figures, such as priests and virtuous women. Purple's connection to virtue was not limited to the Christian world. In Japan during the Asuka period (603–47), a system was established whereby officials at the imperial court were ranked according to the six Confucian virtues. A person's rank was determined by merit and personal achievement. Different shades of purple are believed to have been preserved for the highest ranks, deep purple being for the most virtuous.

Praise for purple reached its zenith under the Roman and Byzantine Empires, where the colour became synonymous with power. Alexander the Great decked both himself and his court with the colour, even referring to his courtiers and high officials as *purpurati*. Pliny the Elder understood its ethereal qualities: 'It brightens every garment, and shares with gold the glory of the triumph.' But according to him, purple also brought vice: 'moral corruption and luxury spring from no other source in greater abundance than from the genus shell-fish'. The desire for purple led to severe laws permitting its use. The Roman Emperor Nero had people sentenced to death for wearing the colour without permission. Four hundred years later, when the western Roman Empire fell, the manufacture of purple ceased in Europe and the colour became the preserve of the imperial family of Byzantium. The craze for purple extended to staining parchment used for the creation of important documents, such as the Gospels. This tradition, known as *Codex purpureus*, was renewed in the west during the Renaissance, in recognition of the status of the colour (see p. 165).

In Japan, deep purple (*murasaki*) was deemed a forbidden colour and restricted to high-level officials and the imperial family. Much like the harvesting of the murex seashells, producing purple in Japan was a difficult process, as it had to be extracted from the delicate purple gromwell plant. In China, the importance of purple has changed dramatically over time. Prior to the Tang dynasty (AD 618–906), purple was among the secondary ranking colours, reserved for clothing the lower body and the lower classes. Under the rule of the Tang, purple rose up the ranks to become a colour suitable for imperial robes (reserving yellow as the most exclusive colour). With the Chinese and Byzantine empires engaged in trade along the silk routes, it is possible that purple's newfound popularity in the Chinese court was the result of contact between the two empires. For those in the Byzantine Empire, purple was so intimately tied to power that when an heir to the throne was born during his father's lifetime, he was named *Porphyro gennetos* – born in the purple. A metaphor for royal blood, this also referred to the tradition of cladding the walls of birthing chambers in a purple stone known as porphyry.

Porphyry is a lustrous crimson-purple stone quarried from the Red Sea mountains of eastern Egypt. Its name is derived from Tyrian '*purpura*'. The stone itself varies in tone from black to crimson red, but the purple variety of porphyry, known as Imperial porphyry, is found only in eastern Egypt. Imperial porphyry, like Tyrian pigment, was reserved for the most prestigious commissions, such as the Hagia Sophia cathedral in Constantinople (now Istanbul). An igneous rock, porphyry is extremely hard to carve and took immense labour and skill to both procure and shape. To add to the mystery of this impossibly difficult stone, knowledge of the exact location of the mountain range (*Mons Porphyrites*) was lost for nearly a thousand years after the quarries were abandoned in about AD 350–450. It wasn't until the first decade of the fifteenth century that the site was uncovered by the Tuscan Jacopo d'Angelo, who translated Ptolemy's *Geografica* from Greek into Latin, thereby revealing the approximate location of the mountains, east of the river Nile. The exact position of the quarries only came to light in the nineteenth century.

When knowledge of the *Mons Porphyrites* was lost, the only porphyry in circulation was from the ancient world, making the purple stone a prestigious commodity. Fragments of porphyry came to medieval Europe from the eastern Roman Empire. When its capital, Constantinople, fell in 1204, its sacred and civic buildings were sacked. The precious stones that had decorated their rooms made their way into Europe through trade ports such as Venice. In Venice's St Mark's Basilica statues and columns of ancient stone from Constantinople adorn the facades and interior. Of all the stone that was plundered, porphyry was the most prized, and was the chosen material for decorating the interior of the Doge's chamber. The association between power and porphyry was so tightly bound that when the merchant Medici family rose to become Grand Dukes of Florence during the Renaissance, they used this ancient stone as material support for their newfound power. Commissioning family portraits carved in the stone once reserved for sculptures of the imperial family supported their claim as rulers of the city.

Naturally occurring purple is expressed in a range of hues from blue-purple to red-purple. This variation comes not only from the different natural resources used to produce purple dye but also from the dyeing process. When knowledge of Tyrian purple and the process of its production were lost in the mid-1400s, dyers tried to re-create its hues with vegetable and plant-based combinations. In late Medieval Europe purple dyes were made by combining madder (a perennial plant), cochineal or kermes (scale insects) with vagello, a blue dye based on indigo. It was this process that was used to produce the purple garments worn by the cardinals of the Roman Catholic Church, as decreed by Pope Paul II in emulation of Imperial Rome. Thread dipped in both colours combined to produce a purple known in Italy as *paonazzo*. For hundreds of years dyers and merchants alike searched for the secret of the colour purple. Hopeful discoveries of the origin of purple dye appeared across Europe. One such was recorded in 1689 by William Cole. In a declaration of the discovery of '*Purpura Anglicana*' on the west coast of England, Cole declared that the shellfish had the 'durable Tincture of the Ancient, Rich, Tyrian Purple'.

By 1856 the search for Tyrian purple was over. That year, an eighteen-year-old chemistry student, William Perkin, made an accidental discovery that completely transformed synthetic dyes. While experimenting with coal tar in the hopes of producing a synthetic alternative to quinine, a remedy for malaria, Perkin made a reddish powder. With the addition of aniline, the powder became a crude black product that could be used as a dye. The colour he discovered was not Tyrian purple, despite his initial attempt to brand it as such, but instead a brilliant lilac that he named 'mauve'. It was the lustrous quality of the dye that was so popular. Almost overnight the new vibrant tones, previously unavailable on the market, gained vast popularity. The process Perkin discovered enabled the production of an array of colours (2,000 artificial dyes, in fact) but it was purple that had its greatest moment – so much so that in 1859 the satirical journal *Punch* described the purple craze as 'Mauve Measles'.

As with all fashions, that for mauve waned, and with it the frivolity associated with the colour. Four years after the death of her beloved husband Prince Albert in 1861, Queen Victoria set a new standard by graduating from a full black dress to a mauve one. According to the rigidly prescribed etiquette of the period, after two years a mourner could wear what was known as a half-mourning dress, predominantly black but flourished with purple bows and trims (see pp. 172–3). Purple was once again a colour of dignity.

Green, white and purple became the party tricolour of the Women's Social and Political Union in their fight for women's right to vote in the UK (p. 177). 'Purple', Emmeline Pethick-Lawrence later declared, 'is the royal colour .... It stands for the royal blood that flows in the veins of every suffragette, the instinct of freedom and dignity'. White stood for purity, and green for hope. During the campaign to 'Give Women the Vote!', these three bands entered people's lives in a huge variety of ways. Depending on the individual and how brave they were feeling, they could either clad themselves entirely in an outfit of green, white and purple, such as those styled by Louisa Folkard, or show support with a smaller token. Sashes, buttons and motor scarfs were designed and sold in support of the movement. As a colour of female protest, purple has endured. Feminist groups such as Sisters Uncut continue to adorn their placards with the shade of female liberation.

By the 1960s, deep purple mixed with acid green had gained a different kind of popularity, as colours representative of the psychedelic and counter-culture movement. Political protests swept the western world as people fought for civil rights, spoke out against social injustice, and reconsidered the ethics of war. In this new age of freedom, psychedelia was combined with a fascination for eastern mysticism to produce new genres of music and art. Graphic design responded to the social revolution and the movement's identity became associated with an exuberant use of colour; psychedelic purple was a mixture of fluorescent magenta and blue. Once representative of the elite establishment, purple had been claimed as a colour of social liberation and free expression. In March 1967, Jimi Hendrix, the American guitarist and singer-songwriter, released 'Purple Haze', a song filled with mind-altering lyrics. Of all the tones, purple was the one that Hendrix imagined when he wrote the line 'You got me blowin', blowin' my mind'.

Under Roman and Byzantine Imperial rule, purple was highly sought after and reserved for elite subjects. In the 4th century, the sarcophagus of St Helena, mother of Emperor Constantine, was made entirely from porphyry. This fragment (right), depicting the head of a warrior, possibly formed part of the tomb's decoration. Purple stones such as amethyst were also used to depict imperial and sacred figures, such as this tiny statuette of a Roman Empress (c. 300–400; opposite, right), or this cameo of St Theodore (c. 1100; below left). Forbidden to most, the imperial family clad themselves and their palaces in the colour. Woven silks, such as this fragment from 12th- to 14th-century Byzantium (opposite, left), were dipped in murex dye. When the Grand Duke of Florence, Cosimo I de' Medici, wanted a set of family portraits, he emulated the imperial tradition and commissioned relief portraits in porphyry. The expert sculptor Francesco Ferrucci del Tadda carved this portrait of Cosimo I in 1570 (below right).

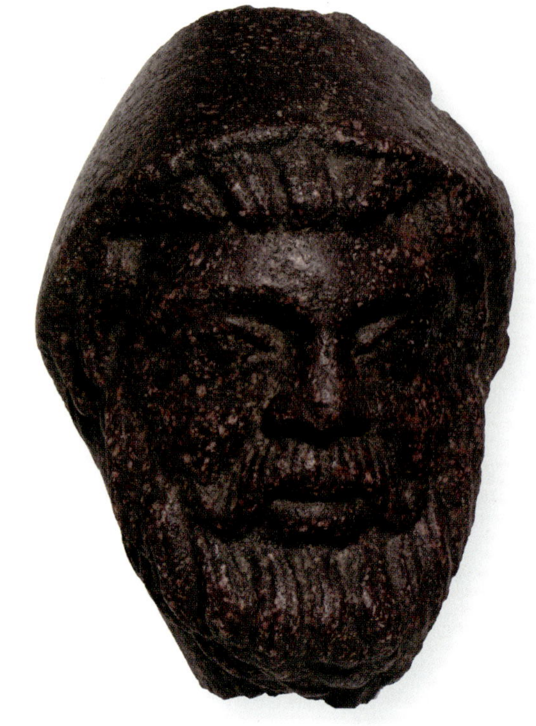

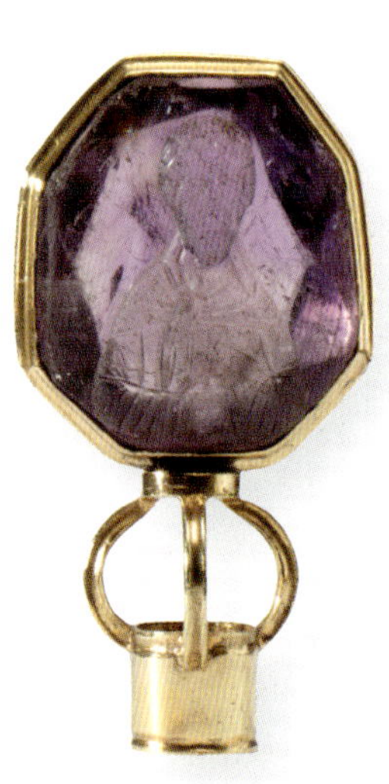

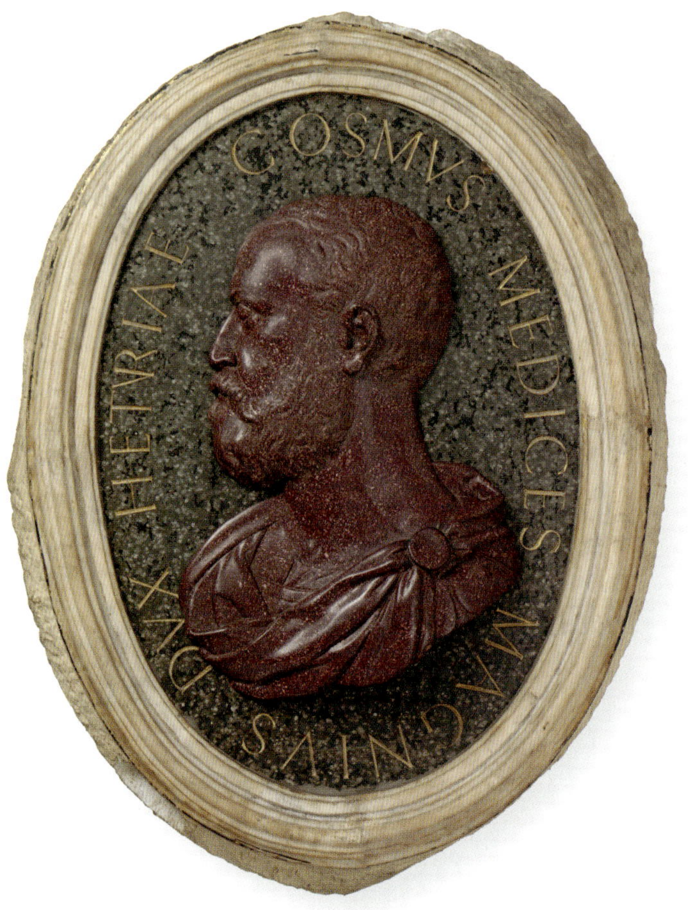

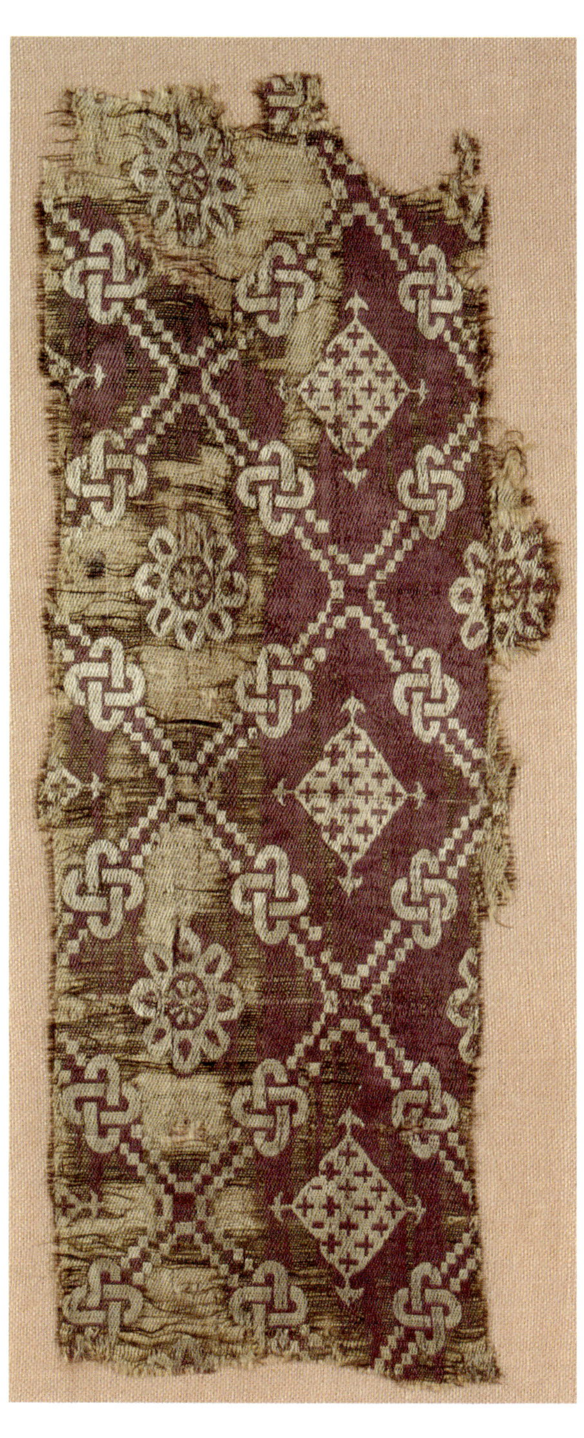

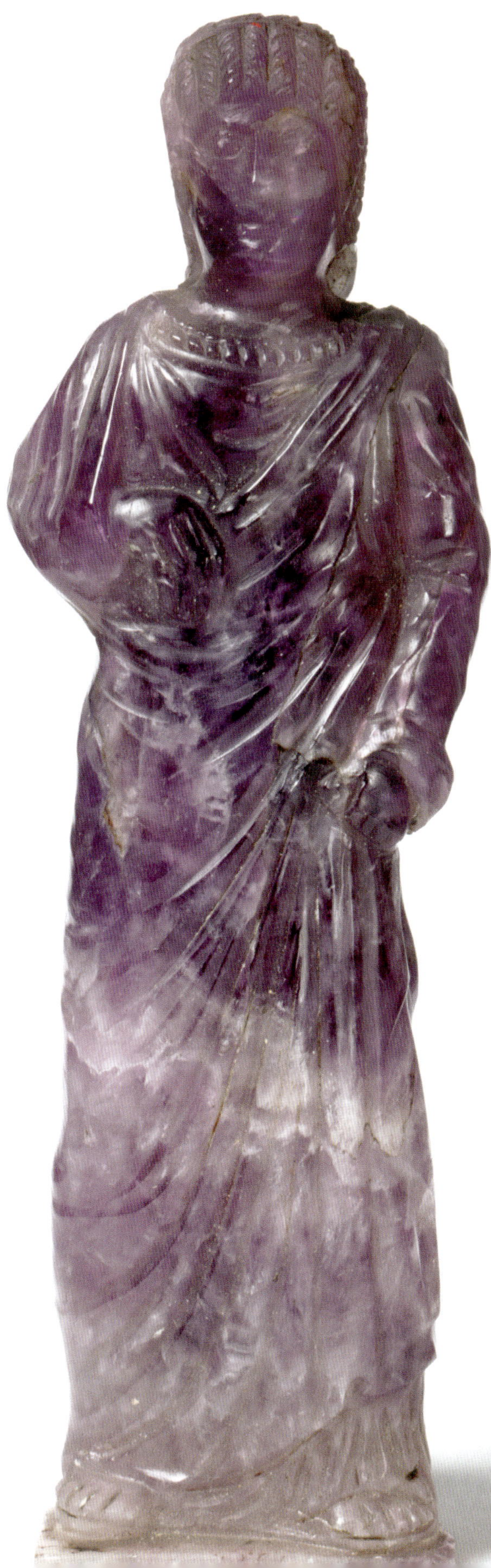

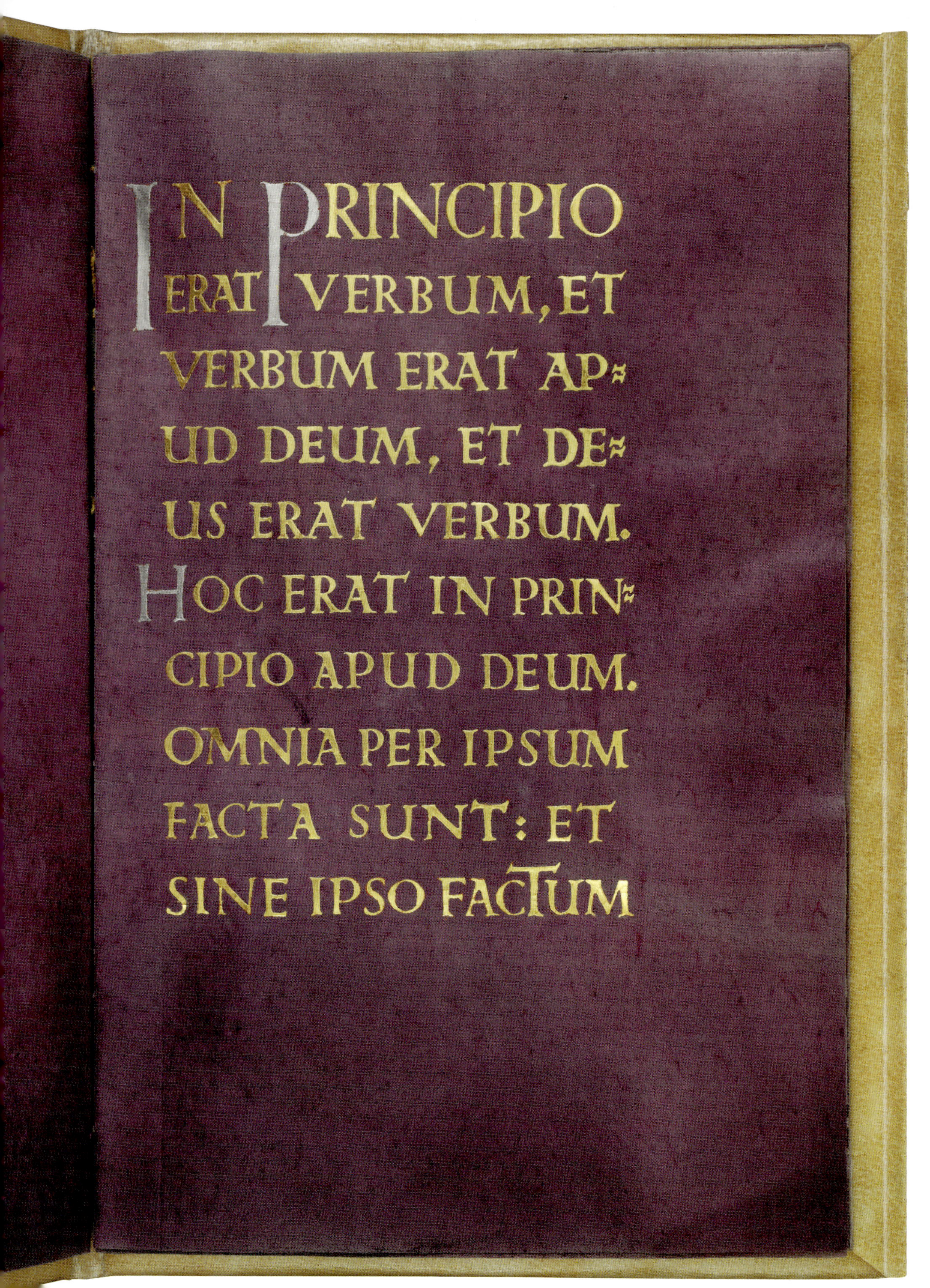

IN PRINCIPIO
ERAT VERBUM, ET
VERBUM ERAT AP-
UD DEUM, ET DE-
US ERAT VERBUM.
HOC ERAT IN PRIN-
CIPIO APUD DEUM.
OMNIA PER IPSUM
FACTA SUNT: ET
SINE IPSO FACTUM

In this highly decorated copy of Francesco Petrarch's *Sonnets and Triumphs*, made in Padua (1463–4; right), the scribe Bartolomeo Sanvito revived the Late Classical tradition of staining parchment purple. To announce the start of the *Triumphs*, Sanvito chose a crimson-purple ground for the illuminator's brushed-gold depiction of the Triumph of Love. An expensive process, purple stain was only used for a few choice pages and the most prestigious commissions. Letters were then inscribed in gold or silver, heightening the drama of the page and the luminosity of the words. In celebration of this tradition, in 1903 the revivalist calligrapher Graily Hewitt stained every page in this manuscript (opposite), containing the opening verses of the Gospel of St John (I, 1-14), purple. Part of a different tradition of manuscript decoration, this initial 'R' (below) uses the same complementary palette of gold and purple. Introducing the word *Resurrexit* (He is risen), it probably comes from a 15th-century Netherlandish choir book.

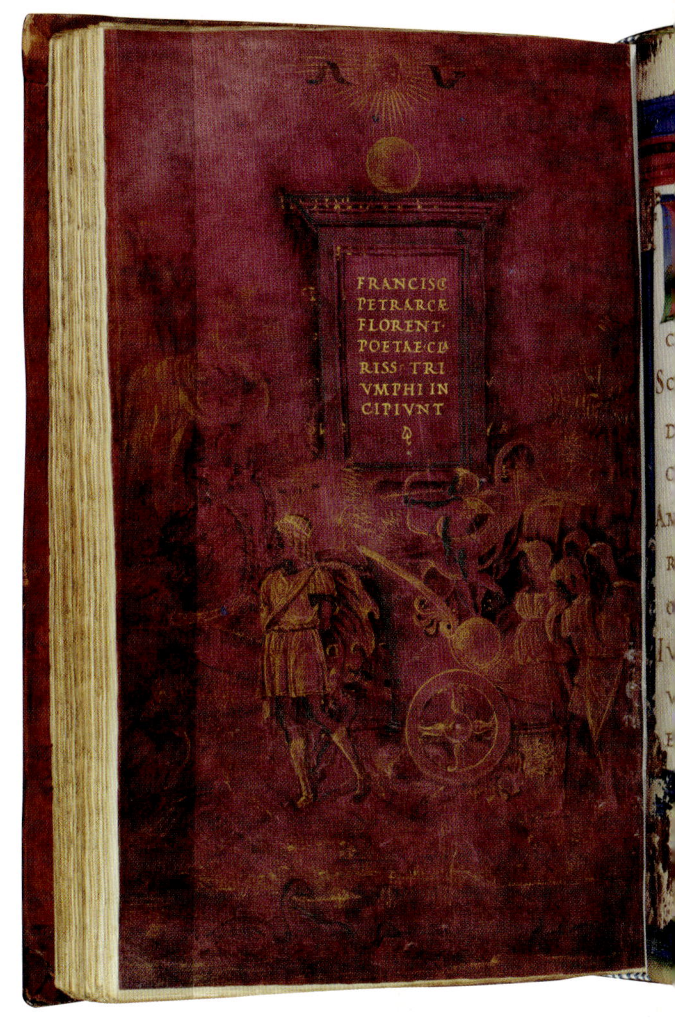

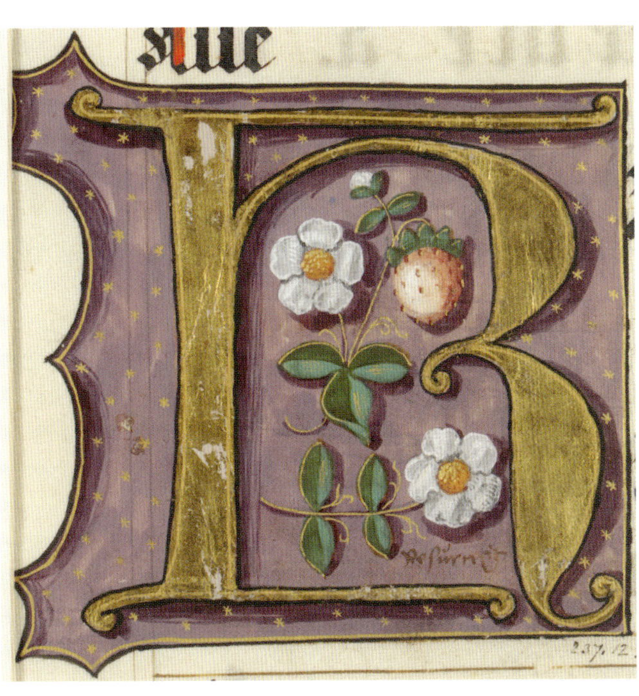

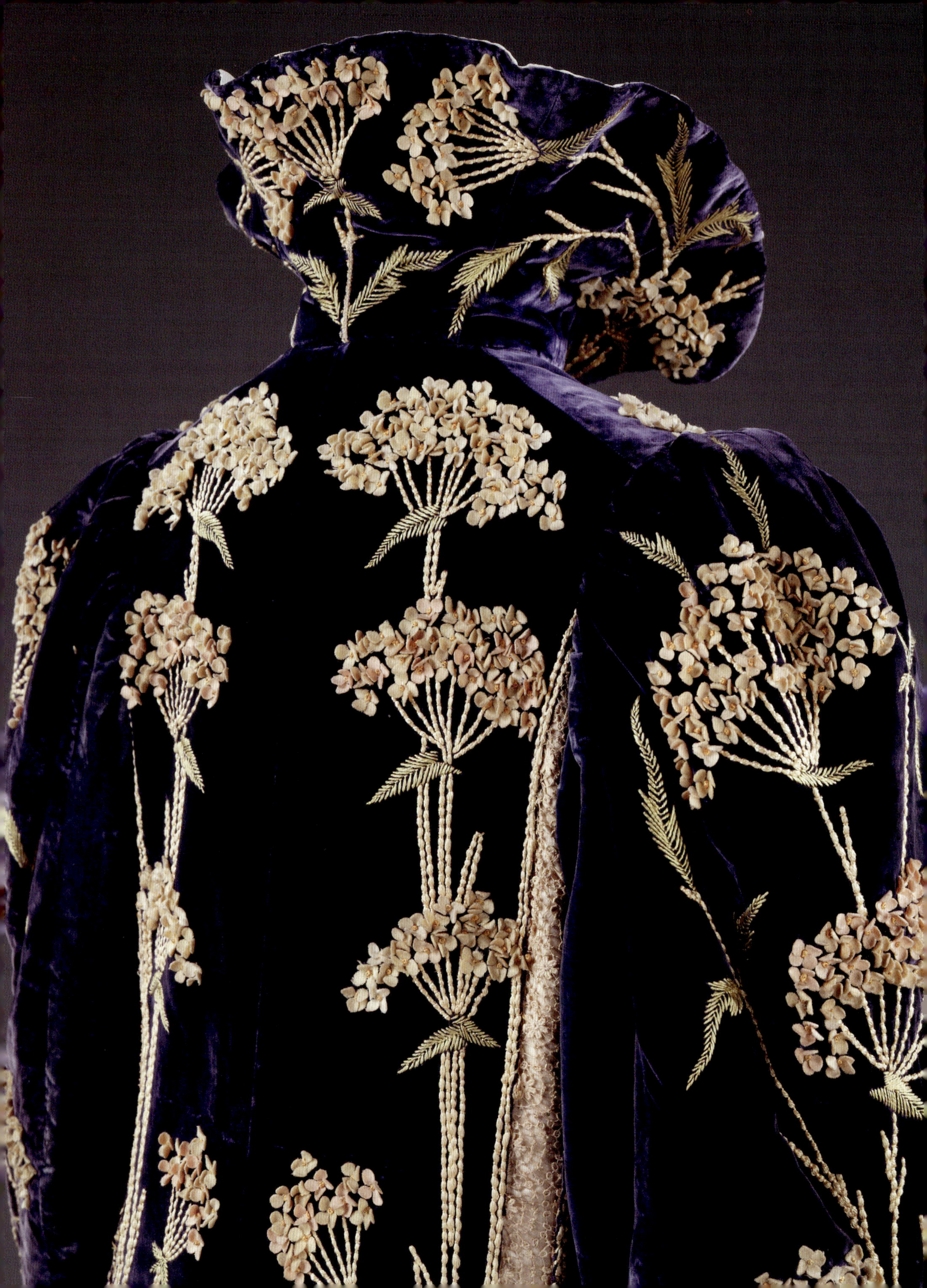

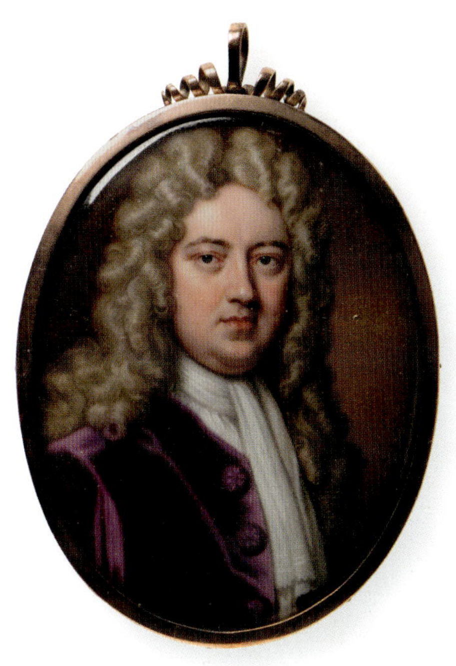

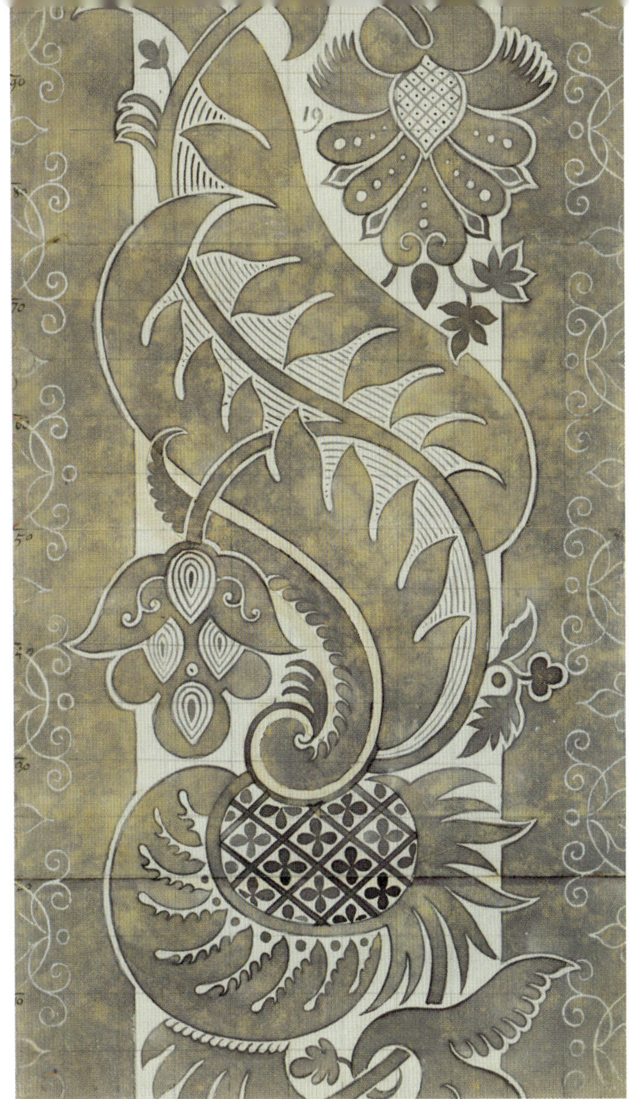

Owing to its imperial origins, purple is synonymous with luxury and decadence. Made by the royal upholsterer John Casbert in 1661, this lavish chair of state (right) was intended as a throne for the Archbishop of Canterbury during the coronation ceremony of King Charles II. Its luxurious gold and silver-fringed purple velvet upholstery denoted the authority of the sitter. In this portrait miniature by Christian Friedrich Zincke (c. 1715; above left), the sitter himself, possibly Admiral George Churchill, was depicted in an outfit appropriate for a gentleman: a mauve velvet coat with a white cravat. Like velvet, silk has long exploited the richness of purple dye, as seen in this extravagant design by James Leman (c. 1711–12; above right). At the turn of the 20th century, purple velvet still represented luxury, as this dramatic floor-length coat (opposite) shows. Hand-embroidered with silk sprays, it was made and retailed by one of London's most exclusive department stores, Marshall & Snelgrove.

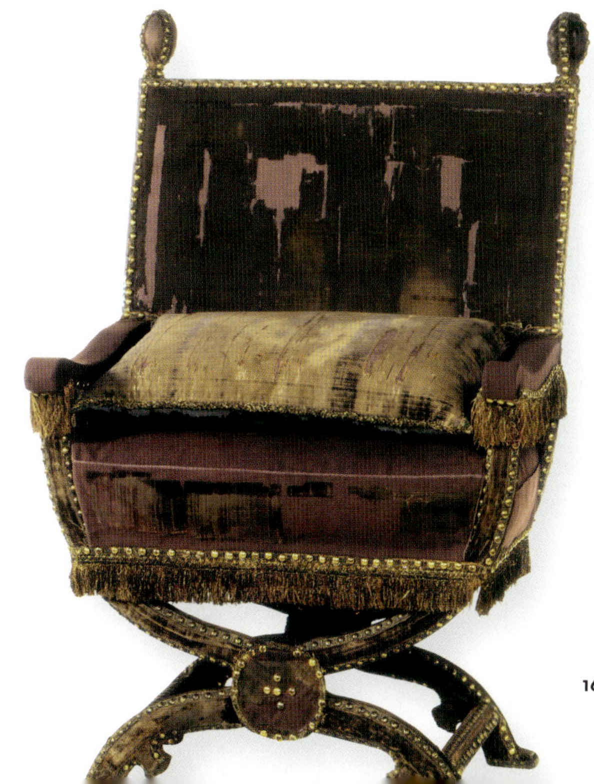

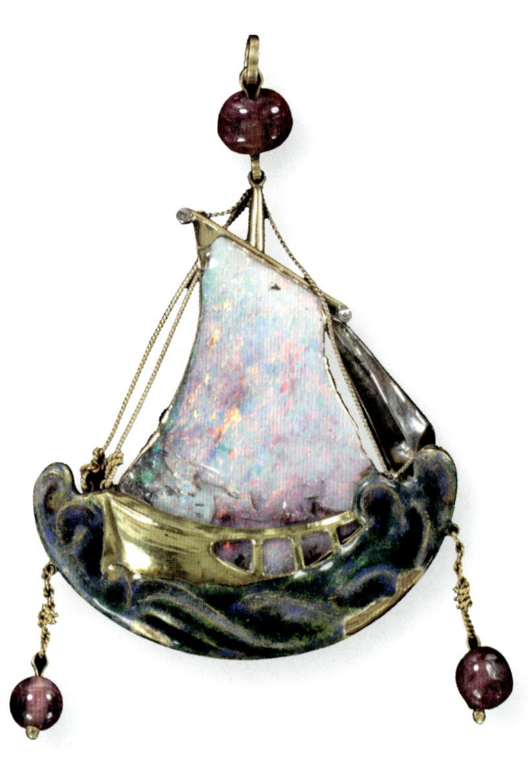

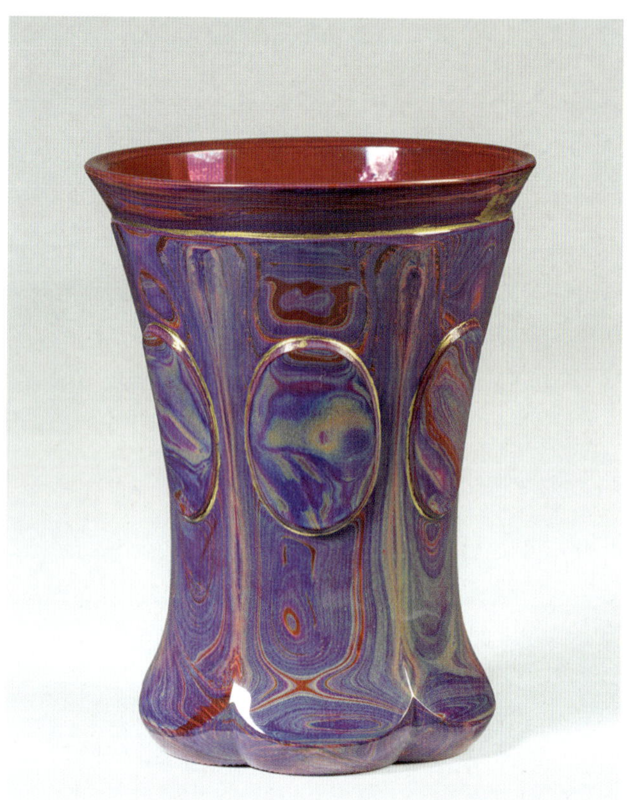

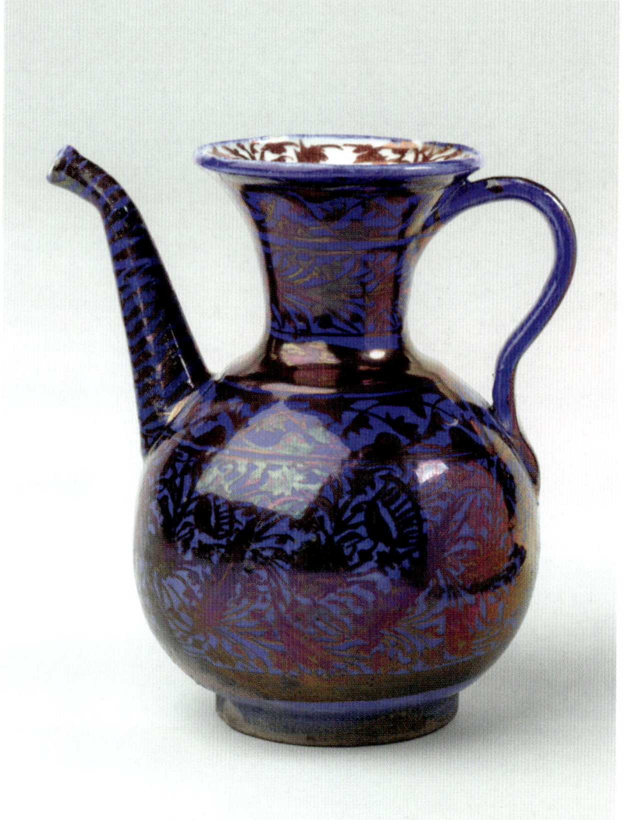

Purple is a secondary colour, a mixture of red and blue. This detailed study of an iris by Jacques Le Moyne de Morgues (1575; opposite) beautifully reproduces the purple spectrum, with petals in shades from magenta to indigo. The way the colours are mixed can produce a wonderful array of effects. The flecks of pink, blue and purple in the opal 'sail' of C.R. Ashbee's boat pendant (c. 1903; above left) create a stunning natural iridescence. This gemstone effect was mimicked by the makers of Lithyalin glass in Bohemia by applying metallic glazes to plain-coloured glass. In this example from the mid-19th century (above right), a purple glaze has been applied to a red base and delicately swirled by hand. Similarly, the decoration on this 17th-century ceramic ewer from Iran (right) was applied in red lustre glaze over the top of a plain blue base, to create a luminous purple pattern.

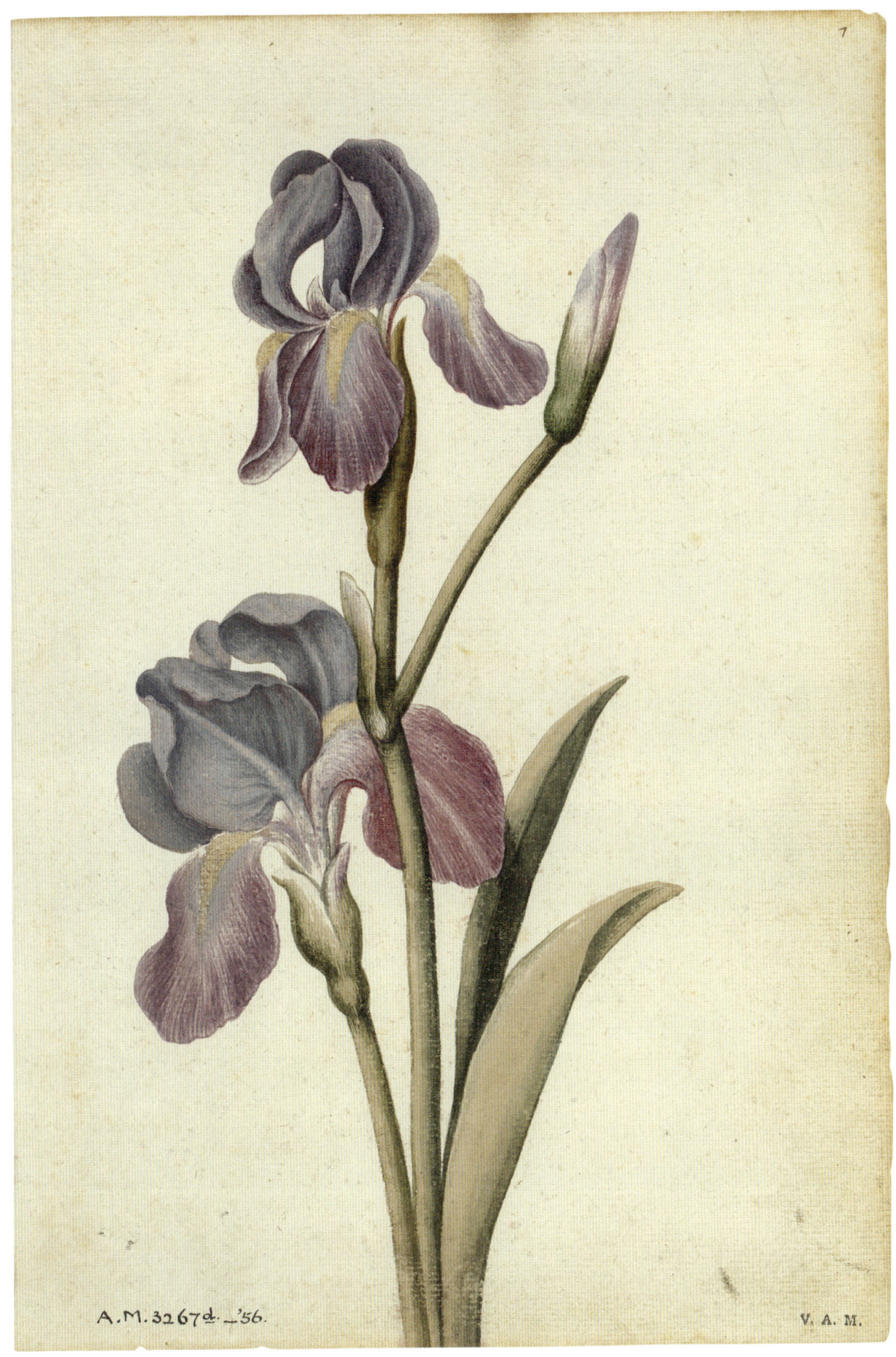
A.M.3267d.-'56.
V. A. M.

Following the discovery that Ancient Greek buildings were originally polychrome, designers travelled across Europe and the Middle East in search of inspiration. Buildings such as the Hagia Sophia in Constantinople, decorated with ornate mosaics and bold colours, urged them to rethink the neutral tones of Regency architecture. This watercolour study by artist Arthur Henderson (opposite, bottom right), who visited the Hagia Sophia in 1898, captures the marbled purple tones of the porphyry pillars. A revived taste for the ancient stone can be seen in this pair of decorative ionic columns (right and opposite, left). Made in England in the mid-19th century, they playfully combine amethyst and porphyry. Owen Jones introduced purple into his interior schemes. His wallpaper design from around 1860 (below) combined a stylized Islamic-inspired pattern with tones of purple, red and grey, while in his design for a music room (c. 1850; opposite, top right) the exclusively purple walls were a bold contrast to the room's classical proportions.

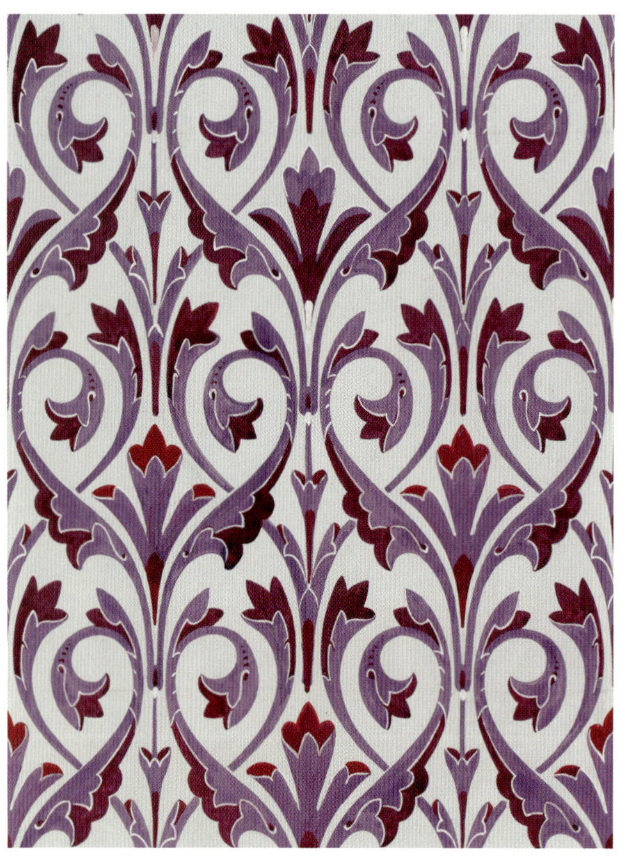

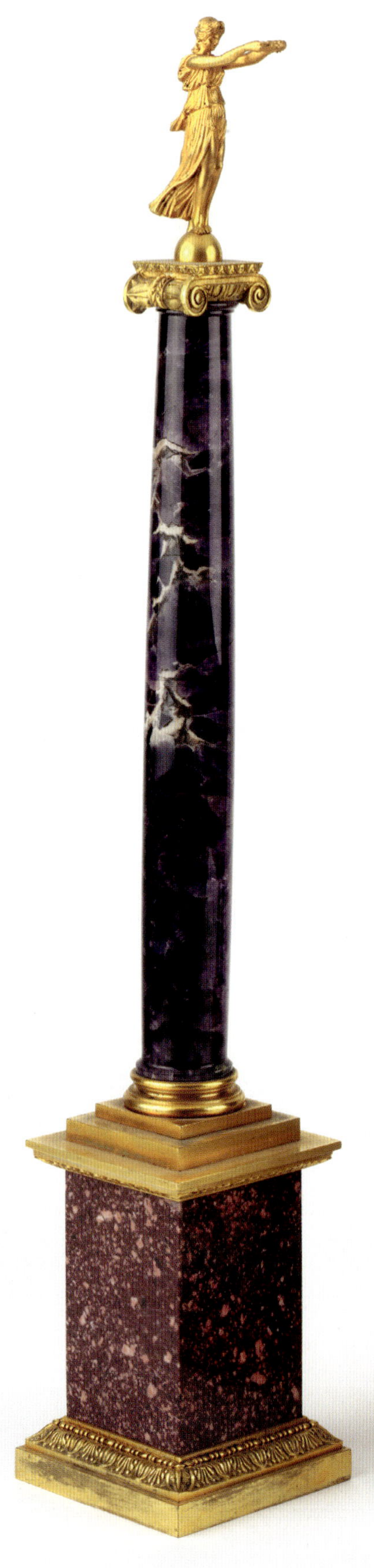

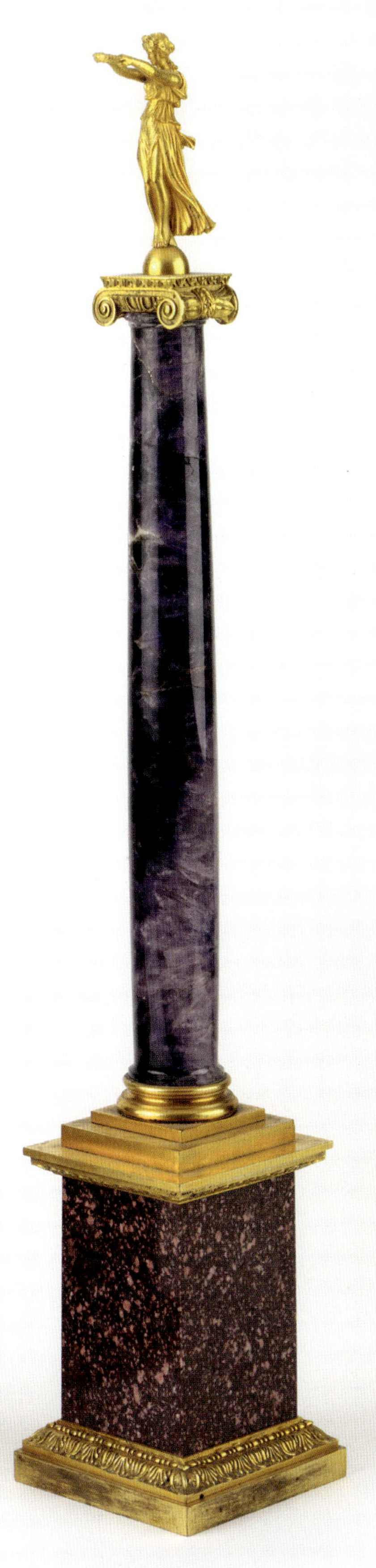

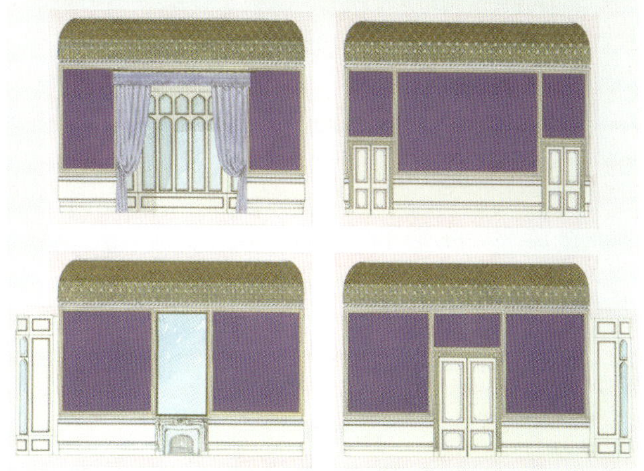

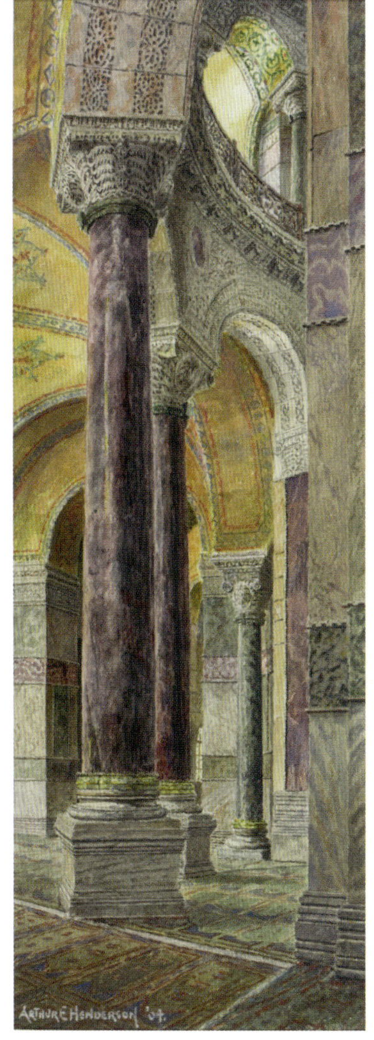

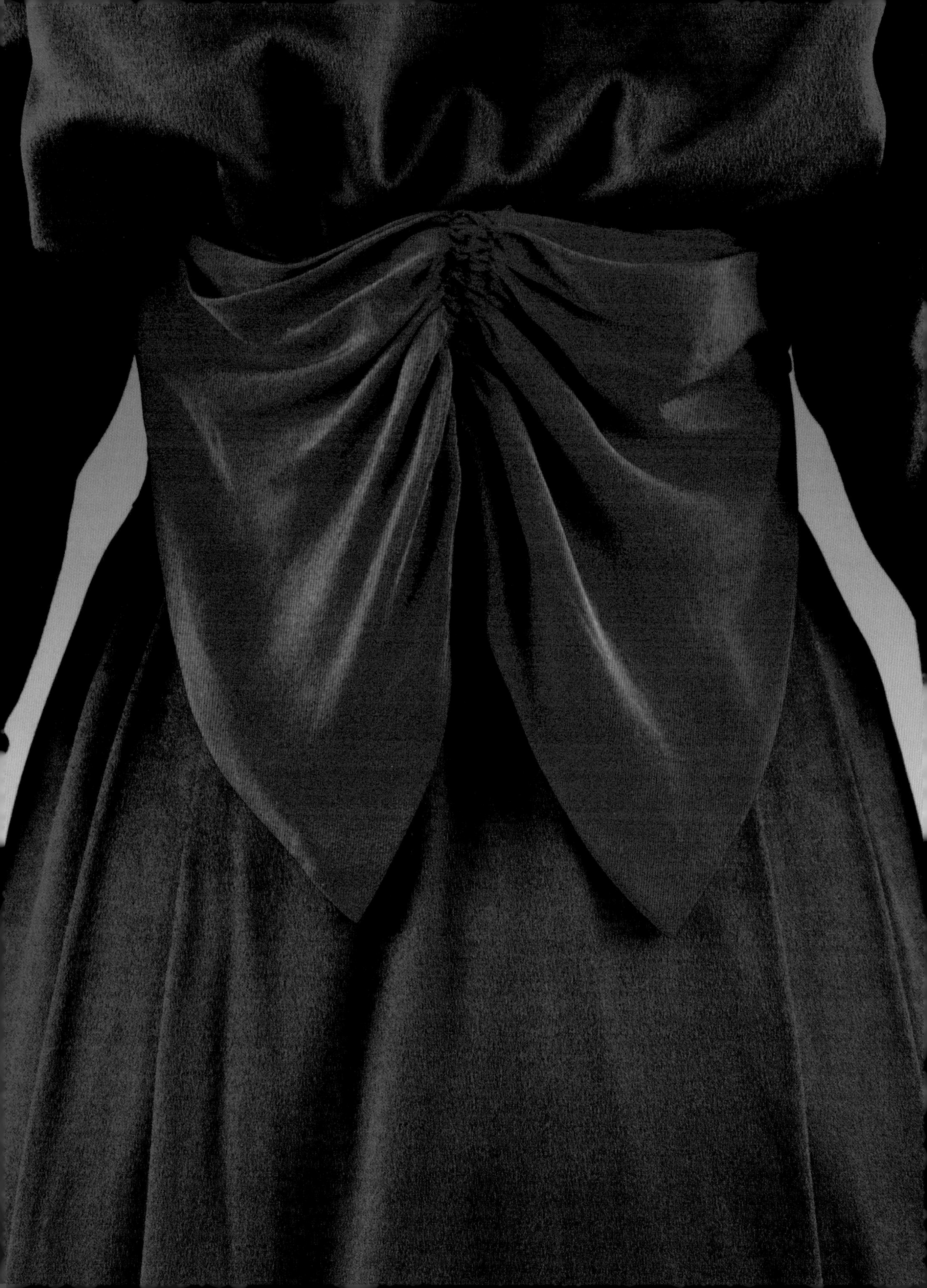

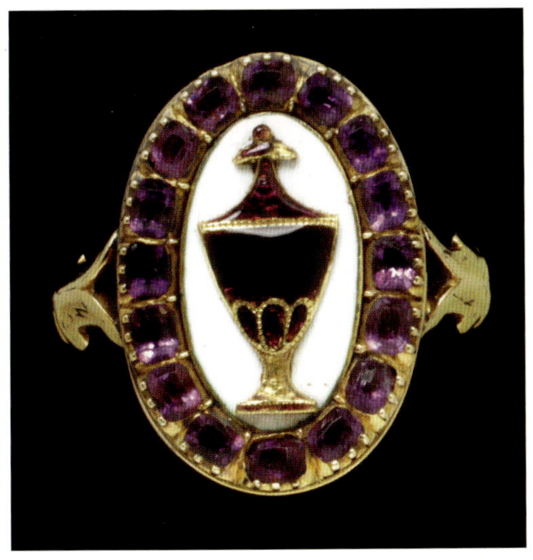

Following the example set by Queen Victoria after the death of Prince Albert in 1861, the practice of wearing mourning dress became prevalent in Britain. There were also several phases of mourning. After a year of dressing entirely in black, a widow could introduce one of three colours – white, grey or purple – into her clothing. Dresses such as this one, designed by John Redfern around 1913 (opposite), coupled black sobriety with touches of colour – here, a sumptuous purple silk-crêpe sash.

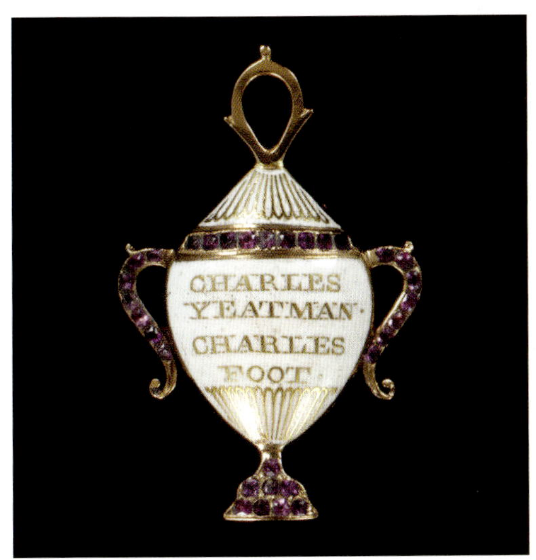

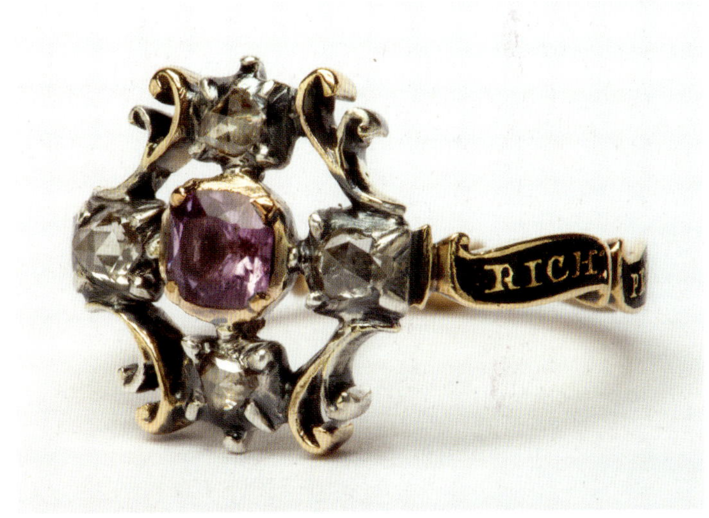

These 'half-mourning' colours were already popular for memorial jewellery. From the early 17th century, commemorative rings were given to the family and friends of the deceased to remember them by. Made in England between the mid-18th and early 19th century, the three rings and pendant on this page were designed for such a purpose. They combine enamelled gold surfaces with amethyst pastes and touches of other gemstones. Each piece is inscribed with the name of the deceased and decorated with funerary motifs such as urns.

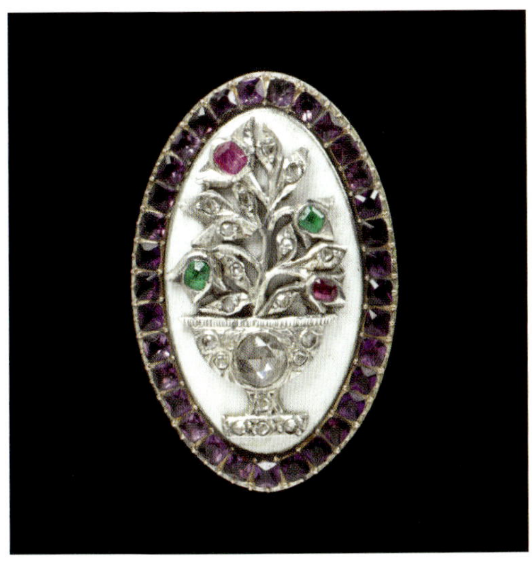

Purple's association with power and
wealth has meant that, historically,
objects in this regal hue were
aspirational for most. But the plentiful
amethyst has always been more
affordable than other, rarer gemstones.
Its striking natural purple is cleverly
used to resemble bunches of grapes
in this exquisite pair of earrings from
the mid-1800s (below). In the 19th
century, purple was finally produced
commercially. In the age of steam-
powered factory production, William
Henry Perkin's discovery of synthetic
dyes in 1856 brought the colour to a
mass market. Thread, buttons and trims
could all be dyed; notably this dress
from 1873 (opposite) does not have a
contrasting stitch or trim. Shopping
became a leisure activity, and in 1875
Liberty's department store opened,
specializing in goods imported from Asia
and north Africa and patterned textiles.
This silk scarf (1923–30; right), with its
Indian-inspired paisley 'Ring and Stripe'
pattern, is typical of the affordable
luxury offered by the London store.

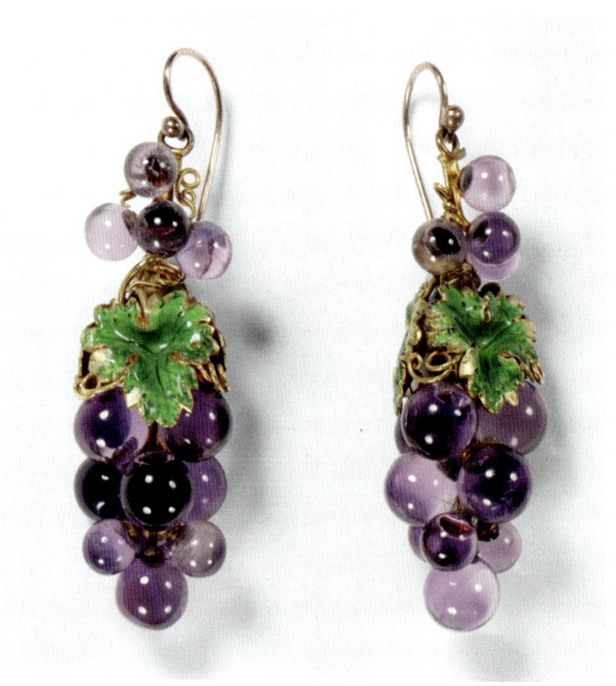

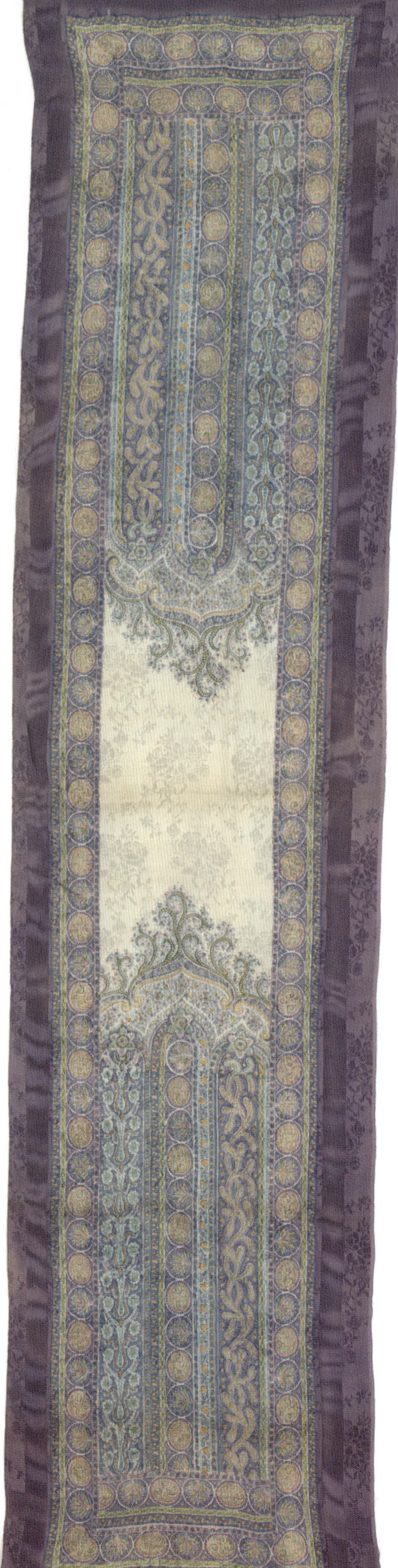

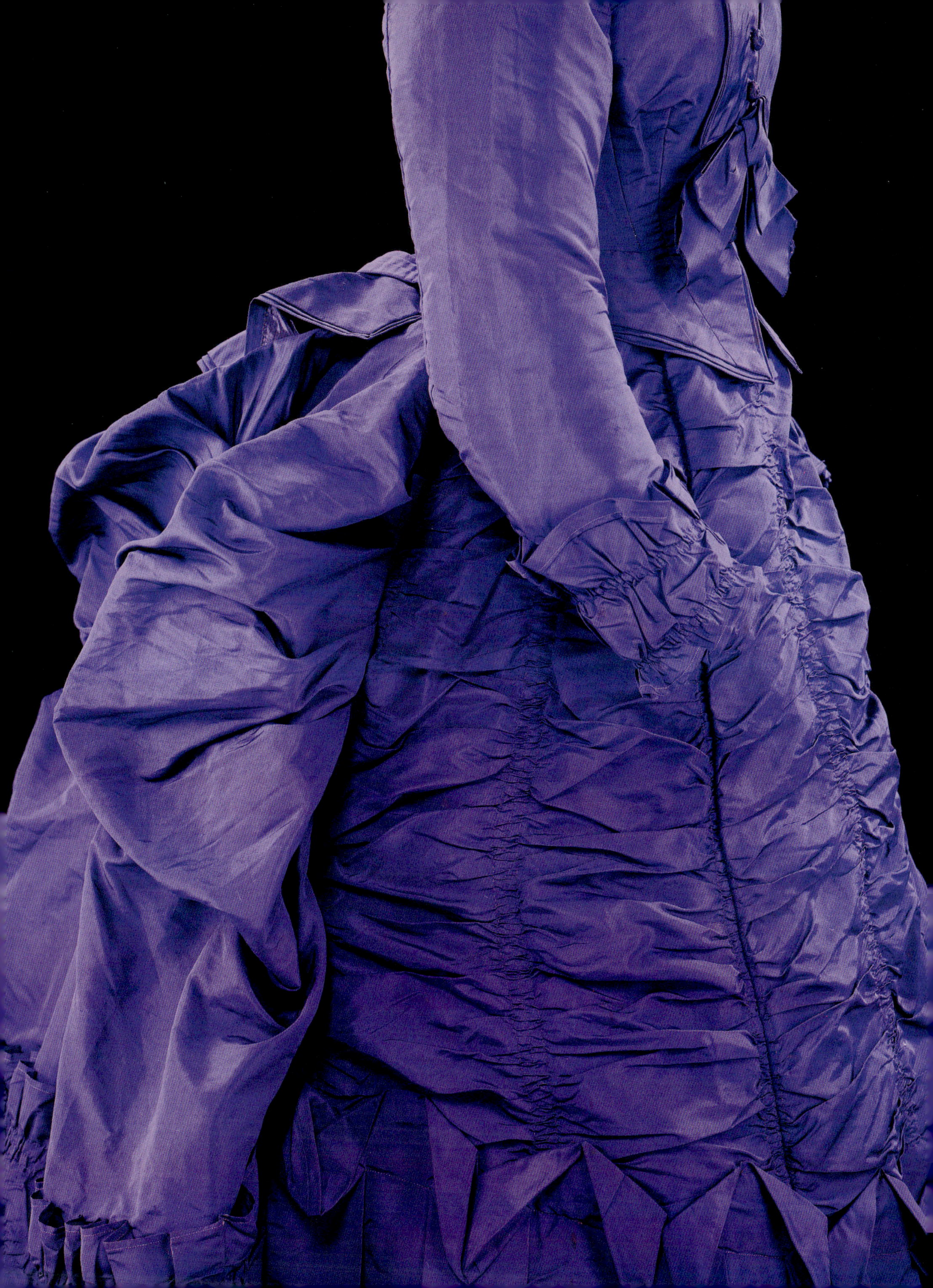

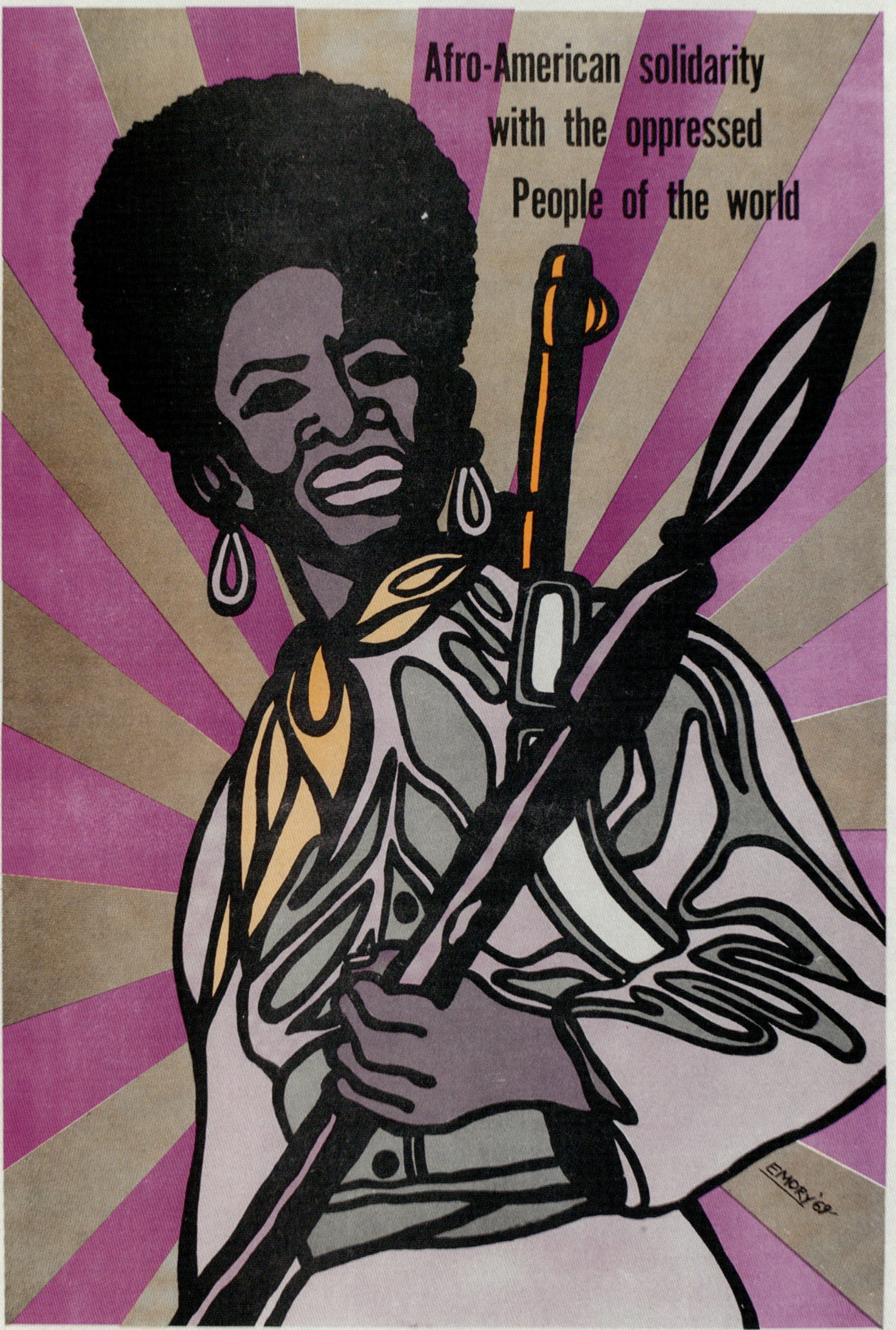

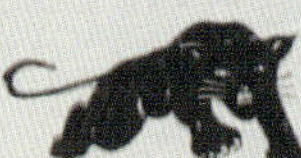

Afro-American solidarity
with the oppressed
People of the world
EMORY '69
Revolutionary art by
Minister of Culture
EMORY
Ministry of Information
Box 2967, Custom House
San Francisco, CA 94126

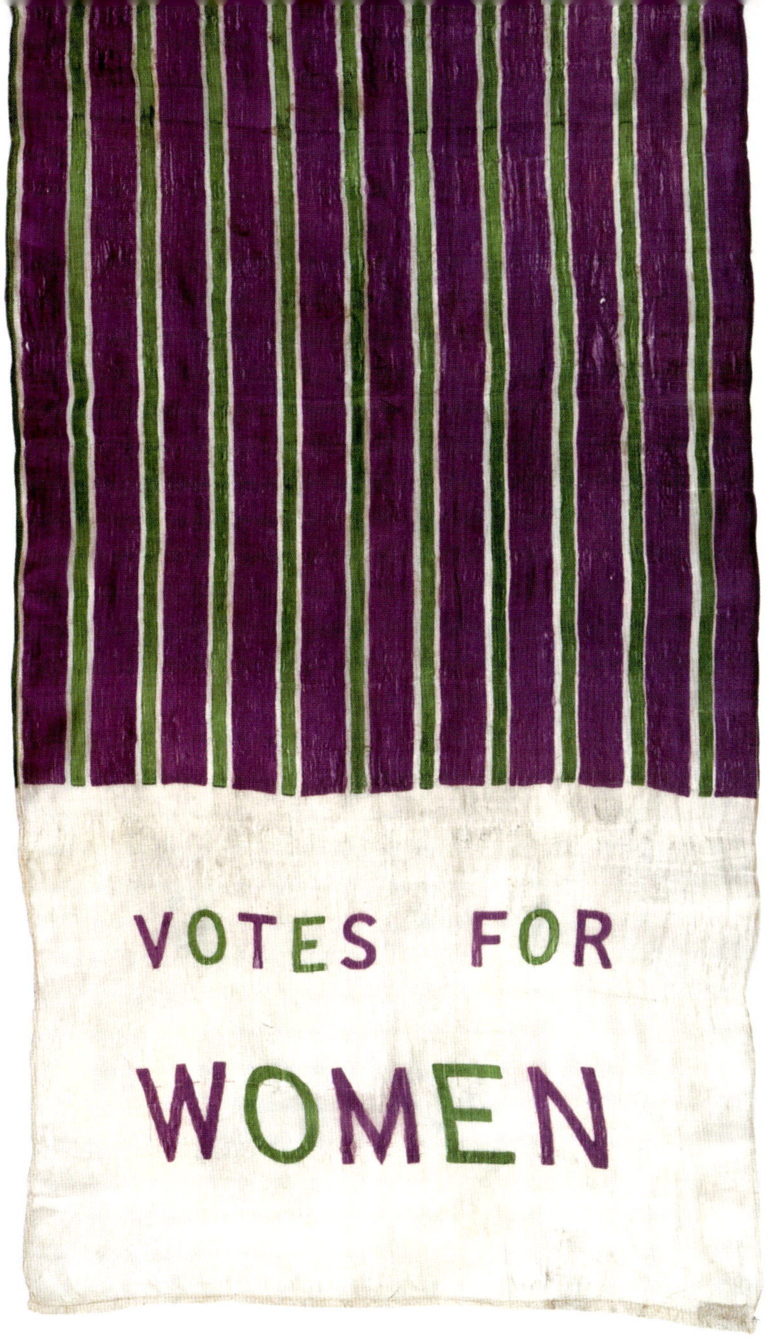

The eye-catching boldness of purple makes it a strong choice for use in protest graphics. It is used to dramatic effect by Emory Douglas in this poster for the Black Panther Party (1969; opposite). The emanating lines of regal purple and gold transform this freedom fighter into a warrior queen. The Black Panthers formed in the USA in 1966 as a response to police brutality in Black communities, and Douglas was their Minister of Culture. His bold style and punchy colours could be inexpensively reproduced to create maximum impact.

In Britain, the Women's Social and Political Union made purple synonymous with their cause by asking their members 'to wear the colours', making them instantly identifiable. It has been said that the group chose green, white and purple (or violet) for merchandise such as this silk driving scarf (c. 1910; left) because the first letter of each represented 'Give Women Votes'. But the slogan was not commonly seen on banners, so this may just be poetic hindsight.

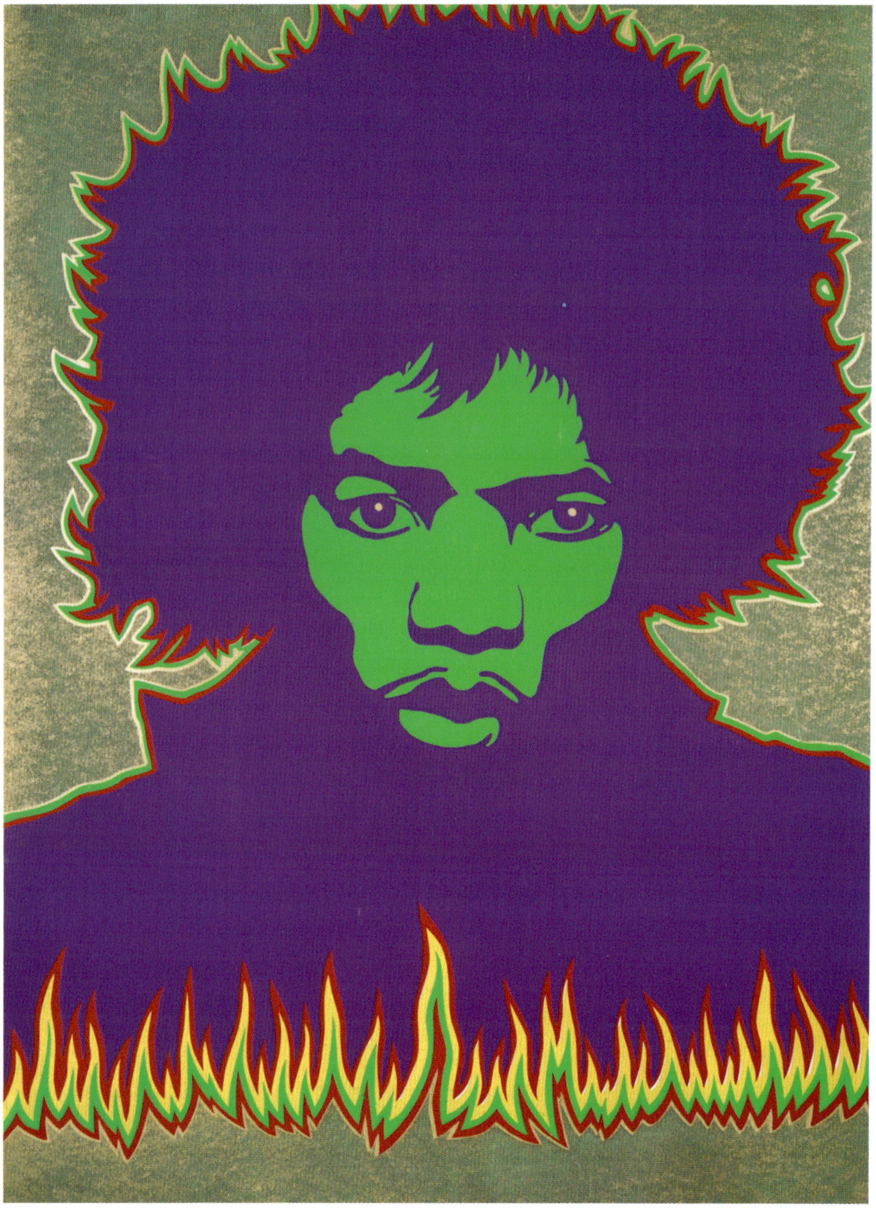

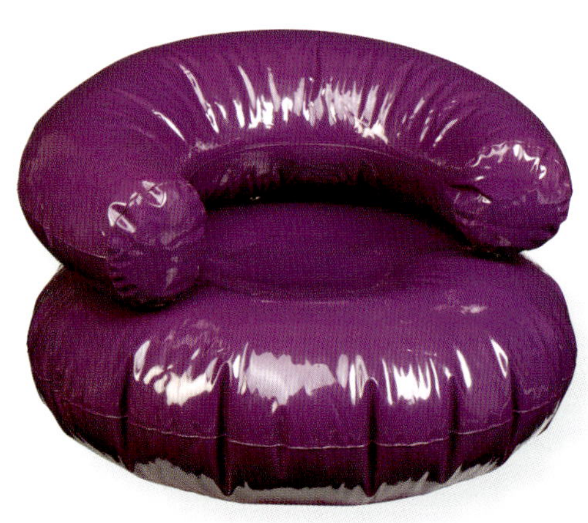

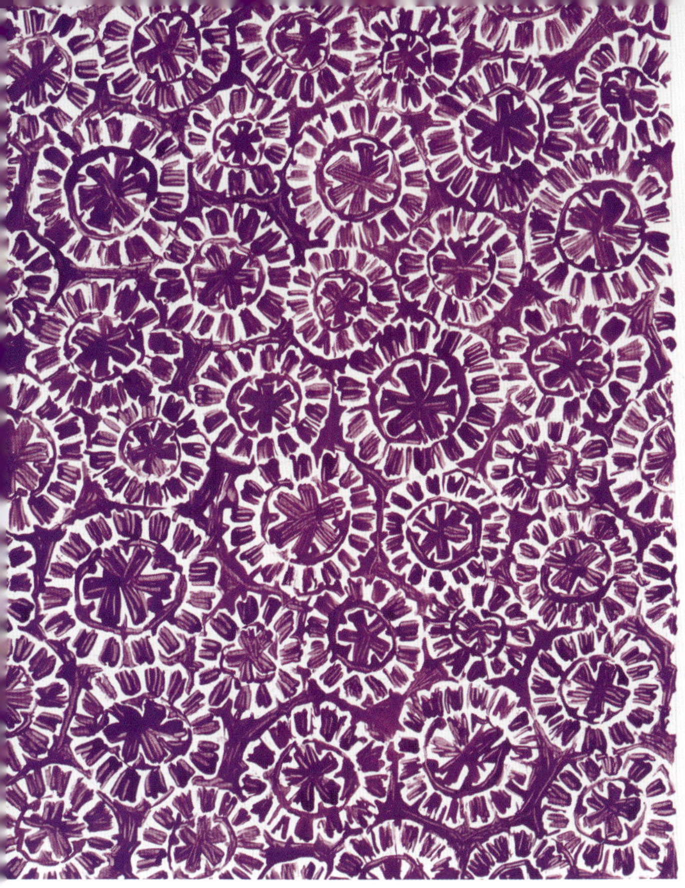

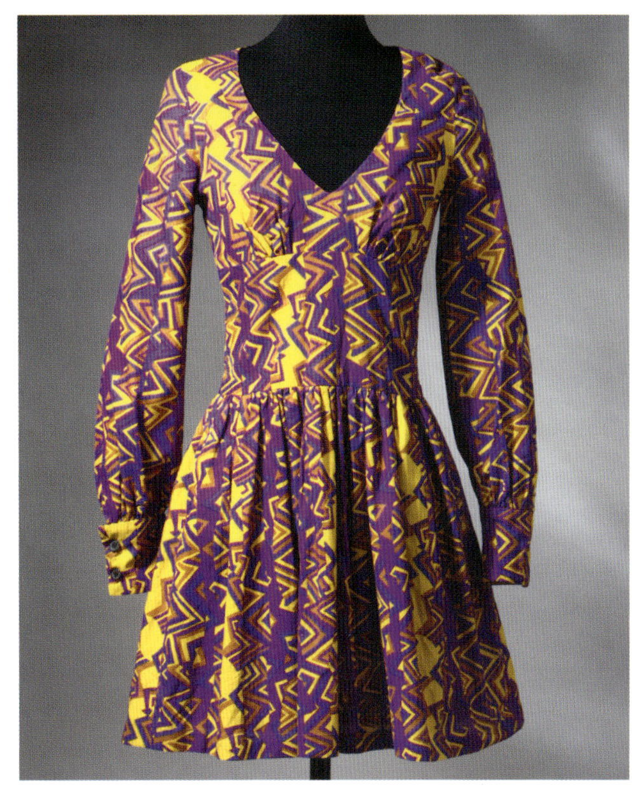

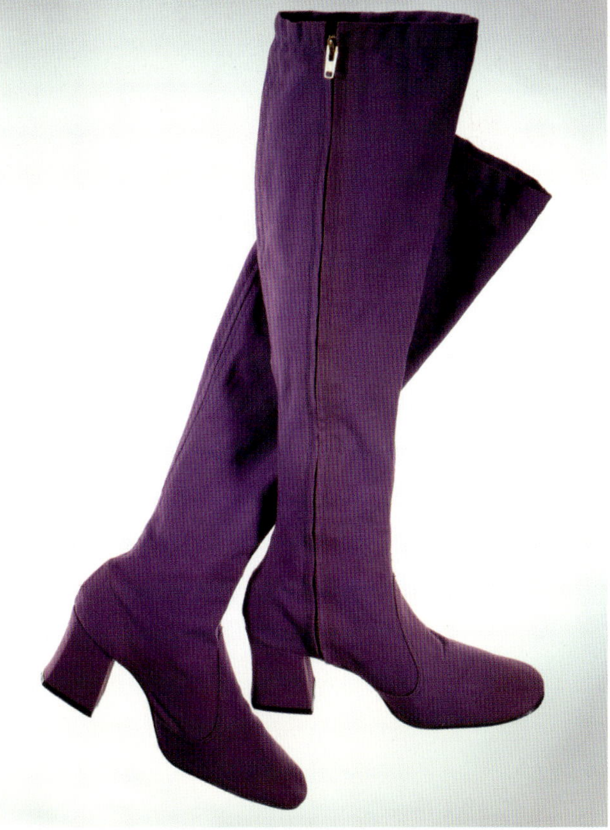

'Purple Haze' is one of Jimi Hendrix's best-known songs, so it seems appropriate that Larry Smart turned Hendrix's hair into a flaming purple afro for this psychedelic poster of 1967 (opposite, top). The psychedelic 1960s were a time of social and artistic change, heavily influenced by drugs. Artists and designers used jarring colours from opposite ends of the spectrum, like the purple and yellow of this Biba minidress (1967; above right), and swirling patterns, as in this textile design by Mary Yonge (1970; above left), to create 'visual vibrations' like those experienced on an acid trip. The counter-culture youth were rebelling against their parent's buttoned-up traditions. Dresses were shorter and boots, such as this bright purple pair by Biba (1969; right), were higher. Even furniture had a futuristic twist. Inflatable chairs made from modern plastics, such as this one designed by Quasar Khanh (c. 1968; opposite, bottom), could be blown up or deflated on a whim, and came in an array of bold sweet-shop colours.

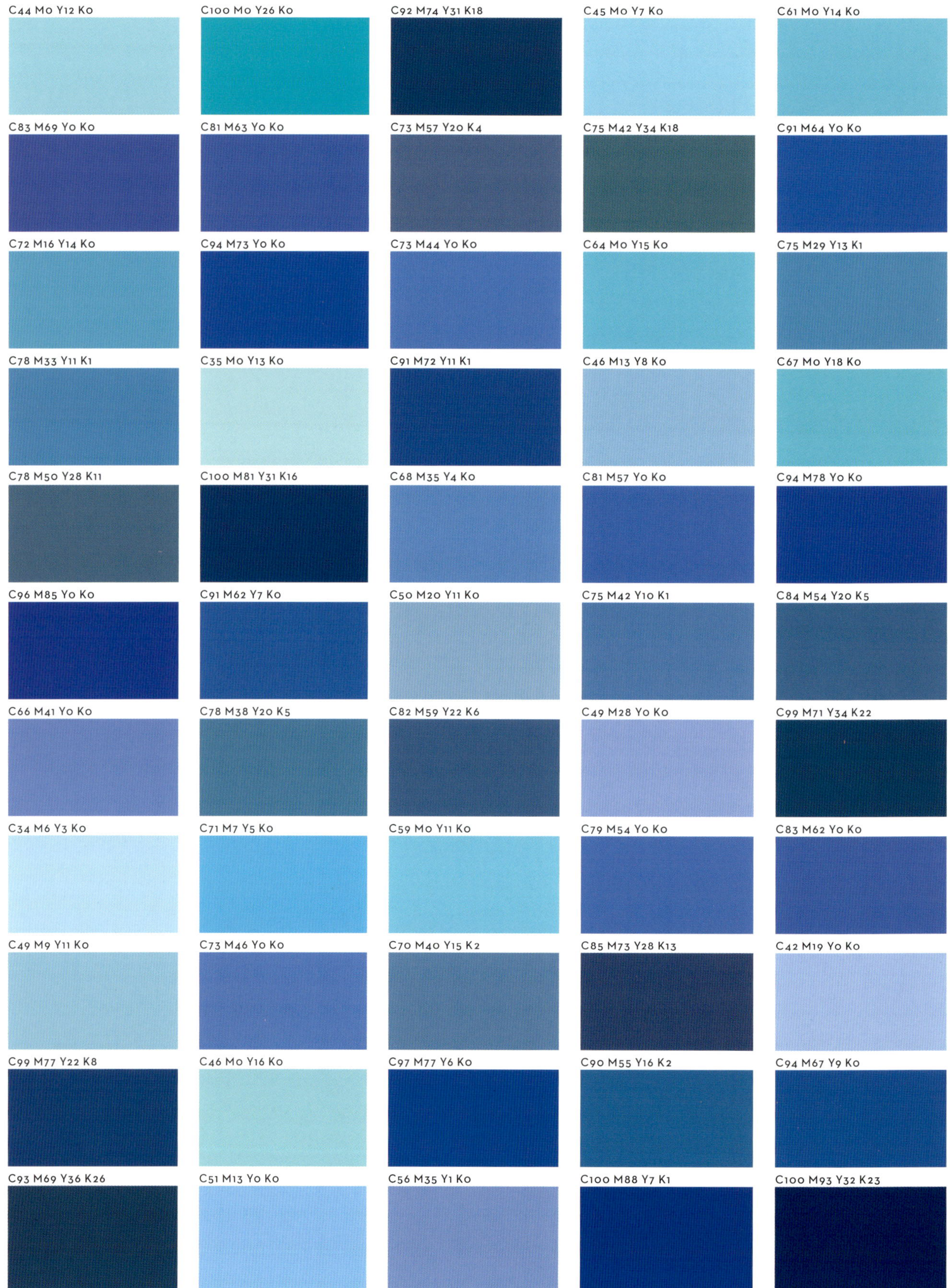

C44 M0 Y12 K0
C100 M0 Y26 K0
C92 M74 Y31 K18
C45 M0 Y7 K0
C61 M0 Y14 K0
C83 M69 Y0 K0
C81 M63 Y0 K0
C73 M57 Y20 K4
C75 M42 Y34 K18
C91 M64 Y0 K0
C72 M16 Y14 K0
C94 M73 Y0 K0
C73 M44 Y0 K0
C64 M0 Y15 K0
C75 M29 Y13 K1
C78 M33 Y11 K1
C35 M0 Y13 K0
C91 M72 Y11 K1
C46 M13 Y8 K0
C67 M0 Y18 K0
C78 M50 Y28 K11
C100 M81 Y31 K16
C68 M35 Y4 K0
C81 M57 Y0 K0
C94 M78 Y0 K0
C96 M85 Y0 K0
C91 M62 Y7 K0
C50 M20 Y11 K0
C75 M42 Y10 K1
C84 M54 Y20 K5
C66 M41 Y0 K0
C78 M38 Y20 K5
C82 M59 Y22 K6
C49 M28 Y0 K0
C99 M71 Y34 K22
C34 M6 Y3 K0
C71 M7 Y5 K0
C59 M0 Y11 K0
C79 M54 Y0 K0
C83 M62 Y0 K0
C49 M9 Y11 K0
C73 M46 Y0 K0
C70 M40 Y15 K2
C85 M73 Y28 K13
C42 M19 Y0 K0
C99 M77 Y22 K8
C46 M0 Y16 K0
C97 M77 Y6 K0
C90 M55 Y16 K2
C94 M67 Y9 K0
C93 M69 Y36 K26
C51 M13 Y0 K0
C56 M35 Y1 K0
C100 M88 Y7 K1
C100 M93 Y32 K23

BLUE

For centuries, blue has been a popular colour in the west: Navy blue, Republican blue, the colour of business, of trust, authority, sobriety and the rational. The English language gives us the uplifting phrase 'blue-sky thinking', in which anything is possible. But the colour is also widely associated with melancholy, i.e. 'having the blues', a term dedicated to a whole subculture and musical genre. In many languages, however, the identification of blue as a unique colour has tended to postdate other hues, such as black, white, red, yellow and green. The Ancient Greeks, for example, would have classified blue as a variant of green. A notable exception is the Ancient Egyptians, for whom the colour had divine associations and who created the first synthetic blue-coloured pigment. 'Egyptian blue', also known as calcium copper silicate, has been identified on artefacts dating from about 2500 BC.

Early natural blue pigments were made from the copper mineral azurite or lapis lazuli, the latter a deep-blue coloured stone interspersed with white and golden veins that has been highly prized since antiquity. When ground and purified into a pigment it is known as ultramarine. In Christian Europe, the cultural status of this striking hue is personified by the Virgin Mary, who was increasingly depicted clothed in blue from the twelfth century onwards. The popularity of wearing blue spread to the depiction of other high-ranking historical and religious figures, such as the posthumous portrait of the French King Louis IX, who was canonized in 1297. By the second half of the twelfth century the French royal arms had taken the shape of gold fleur-de-lys on a blue ground – and thus the trend for royal blue commenced. The Virgin's blue, meanwhile, stood for mourning and the divine, as powerfully exemplified by the 'Virgin of Sorrows' (see p. 187). The Virgin's blue cloak is likely derived from lapis lazuli. Originating from Afghanistan and Iran (the two main suppliers for the European market) as well as Siberia, China, Tibet and South America, lapis lazuli, and thereby ultramarine, was immensely costly, equal to gold due to its distant origin, laborious refinement process and the intense colour it could produce. These elements combined to make a shade fit for the highest authorities – meaning, in medieval Europe, the church and the state.

Beyond the parameters of Christianity lie further links between the colour blue and divinity. The Hindu deity Krishna, who is known as the 'dark one' or 'black one', is generally depicted blue-skinned (see p. 187). There are several thoughts as to the origin and symbolism of Krishna's blue skin. According to the lexicographer Monier Monier-Williams, writing at the end of the nineteenth century, the colours blue and black were used interchangeably in Hindu culture. We also see this tendency in pre-sixteenth century Europe, where the quality and availability of black and blue colourants seems to have determined a preference for one or the other. A passage in the Bhagavata Purana, an important and sacred Hindu text, on the other hand, suggests that the complexion reflects Krishna's personality 'dark blue like a rainy cloud' (as translated by G.V. Tagare). Yet a third explanation may be that Krishna is an avatar of Vishnu, worshipped by many Hindus as the supreme god, who is also known as blue-skinned. Scholars have also suggested symbolic associations with darkness (or dark blue), to include blue as 'the colour of infinity, of space'.

The power of the colour blue to present the immaterial, the void and the vastness of space led the French artist Yves Klein towards his blue period. Klein's blue (known as International Klein Blue or IKB), mixed in collaboration with Parisian paint supplier Edouard Adam, is neither negative or positive, but rather a study in the pictorial sensibility of pure colour. In his lecture at the Sorbonne in Paris in 1959, Klein said 'in the realm of the blue air more than anywhere else one feels that the world is accessible to the most unlimited reverie,' explaining that to him, blue, unlike other colours, 'has no dimensions, it is beyond dimensions'. He famously quoted the French philosopher Gaston Bachelard, saying 'first there is nothing, next there is a depth of nothingness, then a profundity of blue'. It is perhaps apt to say that IKB, at one and the same time, holds the promise of being everything and nothing.

In stark contrast to Klein's philosophical blue is the scientific discovery of the blueprint. Today the term is widely used for engineering and architectural drawings, but it originates in Sir John Herschel's discovery of the cyanotype in 1842. A cyanotype – the original blueprint – is made by placing an object on a sheet of paper covered with light-sensitive iron salts and leaving it exposed to light. The exposed area turns blue, its brightness depending on exposure time and light intensity, while the covered area remains uncoloured. The blue colour was derived from a synthetic pigment known as Prussian blue, which had been discovered sometime between 1704 and 1706. The composition, initially a secret, was identified by a third party and published in 1724, making the colour widely accessible. European artists applied it to their canvases; Japanese artists to their woodblock prints.

The fact that Prussian blue entered Japan during its 220-year isolation period seems a testament to the colour's global success; during the seventeenth and eighteenth centuries the Dutch and Chinese both had a limited trading monopoly, and either could have brought the pigment into the country. It had certainly been shipped to China via the East India Company by 1775. Prussian blue was in high demand. John Gray, Archdeacon of Hong Kong, noted that 253,000 lbs were imported in 1810/11 – and yet East India Company records show that, from the mid-1820s, demand ceased completely. A factory is believed to have been set up by the Chinese, who by that time had identified the recipe for Prussian blue, making the country self-sufficient and capable of export.

Just as Prussian blue had moved from west to east, so blue-and-white porcelain had moved from east to west only a few centuries prior. The city of Jingdezhen in south-east China was the first large-scale manufacturing centre of such wares. Large quantities of porcelain had been produced there since the eleventh century, while the use of cobalt blue pigment was introduced in the thirteenth century by the Mongols. The process of painting with a cobalt blue compound onto white porcelain, which was subsequently glazed and fired, was tricky, highly skilled work. The crisp porcelain and captivating designs produced in China took the luxury market of seventeenth- and eighteenth-century Europe by storm. Potters throughout Europe, notably in Delft, attempted to imitate it. One of the earliest and most successful styles to come out of Britain was the 'Willow' pattern (see p. 201).

Seeking to identify an item of today that is highly coveted, mass-produced and distributed worldwide, we might look to fashion and particularly to the most ubiquitous of garments: a pair of blue denim jeans. Denim, a hardwearing cotton cloth in a twill weave with a white weft and a blue warp thread, was first used to make rivet-reinforced trousers – jeans – intended for workmen, farmers and cowboys in the nineteenth century. Since then, the garment has grown into a unisex wardrobe staple across socio-economic spheres. Jeans' cultural connotations have included Americanization, pop culture and a plethora of subcultures and youth rebellions; they are simultaneously a highly branded fashion item, and brand-less.

Blue jeans get their colour from synthetic indigo, which came onto the market at the end of the nineteenth century and quickly crushed the global trade in natural indigo. The production of blue dyes had historically depended on woad, a herb belonging to the mustard family, or plants of the indigofera family. Woad was cultivated in temperate climates from England to Spain, and was traded across Europe and exported as far as Byzantium and the Middle East between the thirteenth and seventeenth centuries. But this industry was gradually outdone by the growing import trade in indigofera, favoured as it produced a stronger dye. It was also cheaper, generally relying on forced labour. A global trade in indigo intended for European consumption developed from the late sixteenth century, with indigo plantations in India as well as French and Spanish colonies in the Caribbean and Central America, followed by North American exports in the second half of the eighteenth century and colonial India in the nineteenth century. All shades of blue can be made from indigo, though the process, in the words of William Morris, is 'a ticklish job, and requires … more experience than other dyeing processes'. This, however, did not dissuade him, and he spent many years perfecting his dyeing techniques.

The perception of blue as a unifying colour is evident in its frequent use in flag design during the latter half of the twentieth century. Unions including the United Nations (UN) and its subsidiaries, the European Union (EU) and the North Atlantic Treaty Organization (NATO) all emerged as a consequence of the devastation brought about by the Second World War, and all chose bright blues as their distinctive colour. Also during the twentieth century, several western countries redesigned their national uniforms. From the postal service to police forces, sailors and soldiers, the predominate colour of uniforms shifted from black to shades of dark or mid-blue. In *Blue: The History of a Colour*, Michel Pastoureau traces the move of this new, uniform blue into civilian wardrobes. But the connotations of safety and respectability are fairly recent ones. Before the twentieth century, blue, and particularly navy blue, had a rollercoaster ride of symbolic associations, jumping from one camp to its diametric opposite on several occasions. Blue was originally the uniform colour of the king's guard in France. When these soldiers changed sides at the start of the French Revolution, they continued to wear their blue uniform while fighting the royal regime as the Parisian National Guard. Such jumps back and forth between liberal and conservative, establishment and anti-establishment continued throughout the nineteenth century, leaving behind a jumbled history of politics and uniforms. During the American War of Independence, the colonies subverted the British Union Jack, using the same colours for their flag. Sympathizers in France adopted them as colours for freedom, and wore them ahead of the French Revolution, even at court.

From the twelfth century to today, blue has made a journey from a costly, luxurious colour, reserved for the holiest and highest of figures, to a popular colour that belongs to us all.

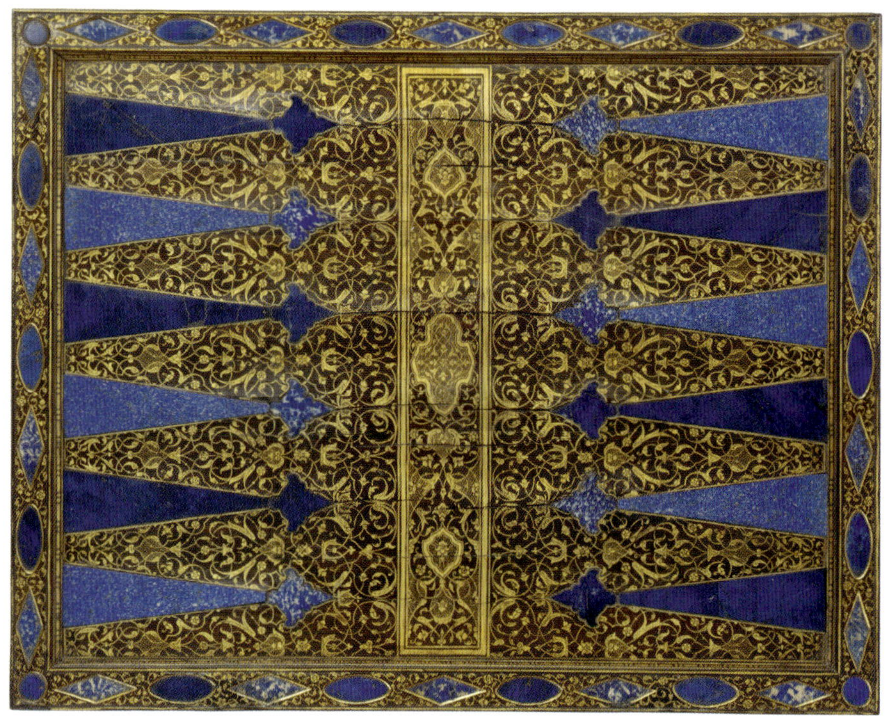

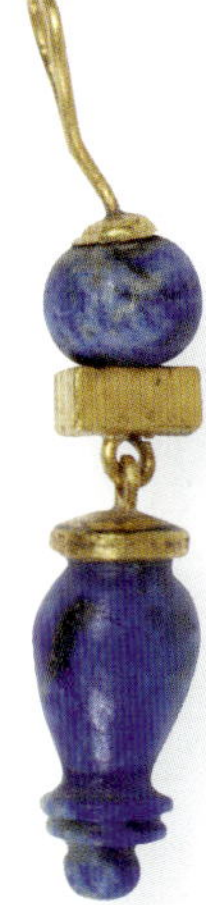

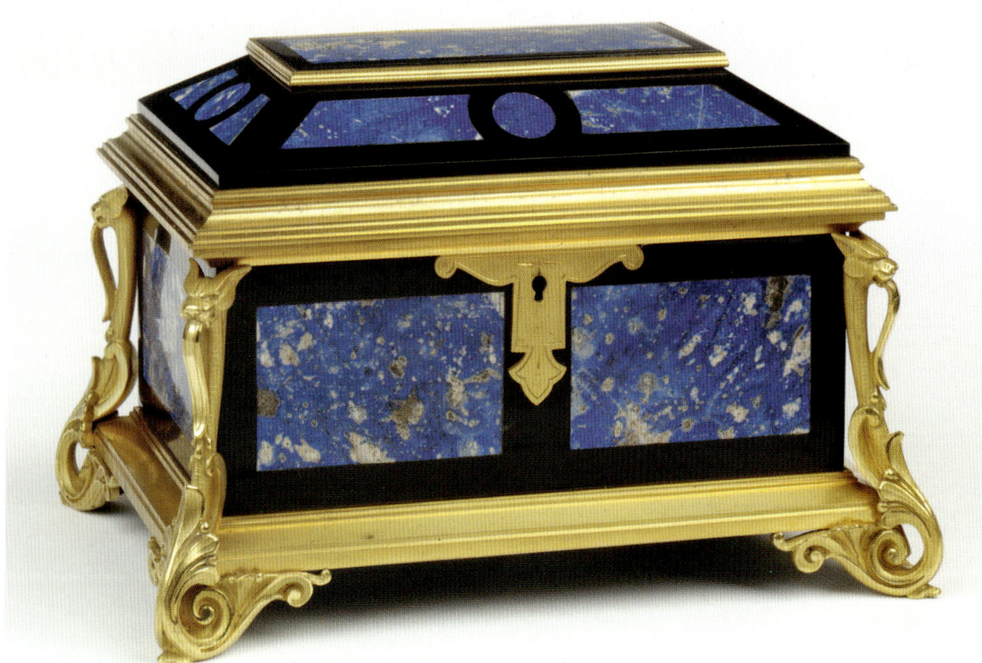

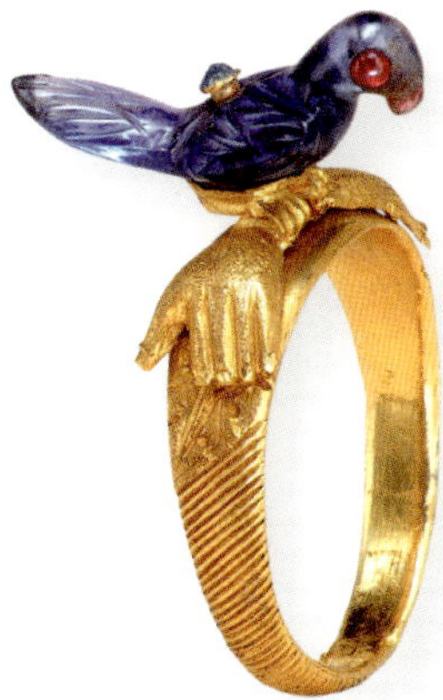

The difficulty and expense of extracting or creating blue materials elevated the colour's status among those keen to demonstrate their wealth and taste. Richard Sackville, the subject of this miniature painting by Isaac Oliver (1616; right), had a reputation as a 'licentious spendthrift'. He clearly spared no expense on his portrait, which uses three different expensive blue pigments, including ultramarine for his ostentatious blue stockings.

The lapis lazuli used in this Roman drop earring (opposite, top right) was mined probably in Afghanistan, beyond the furthest reaches of the empire. Slabs of lapis lazuli, with their sparkling seams of pyrite, were used to create opulent objects such as this 19th-century casket by Jean-Pierre-Alexandre Tahan (opposite, bottom), and this 16th-century Venetian game board (opposite, top left), in which three shades of lapis contrast with rosewood and gold. Sapphire is another of the most sought-after gemstones, valued for its hardness and intense blue colour. A single sapphire was carved into a bird for this beautiful Indian ring from the 1850s (above), set with ruby eyes and a garnet beak.

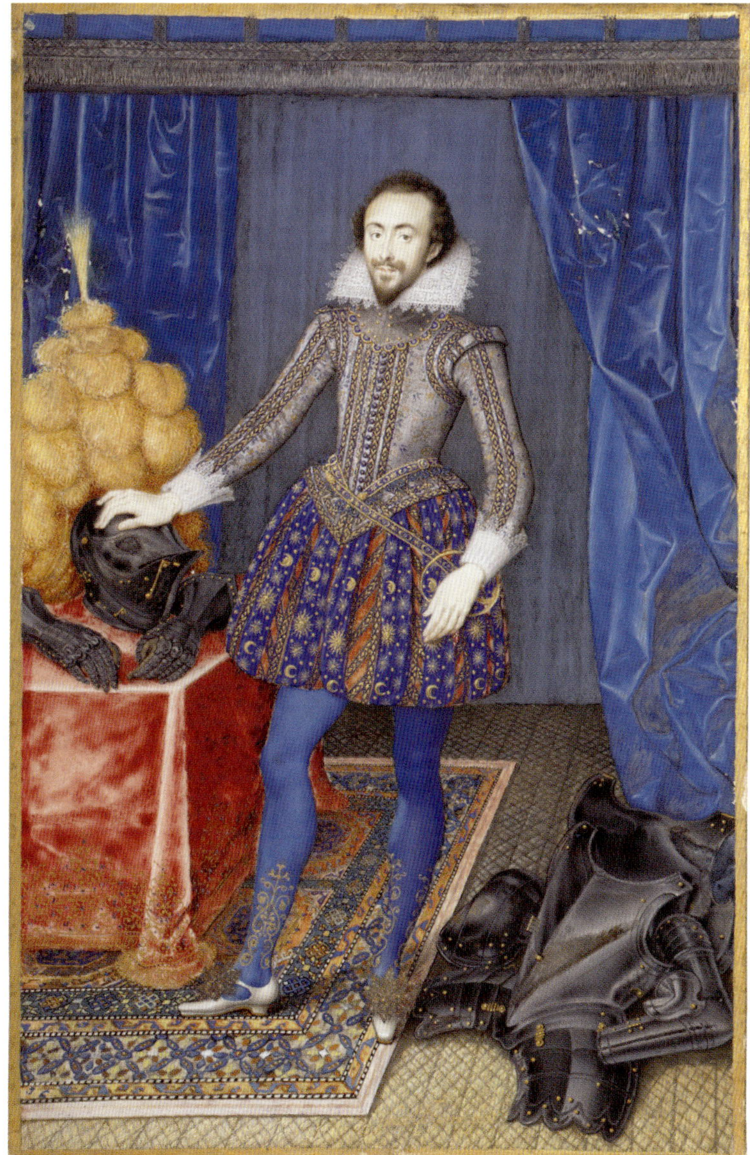

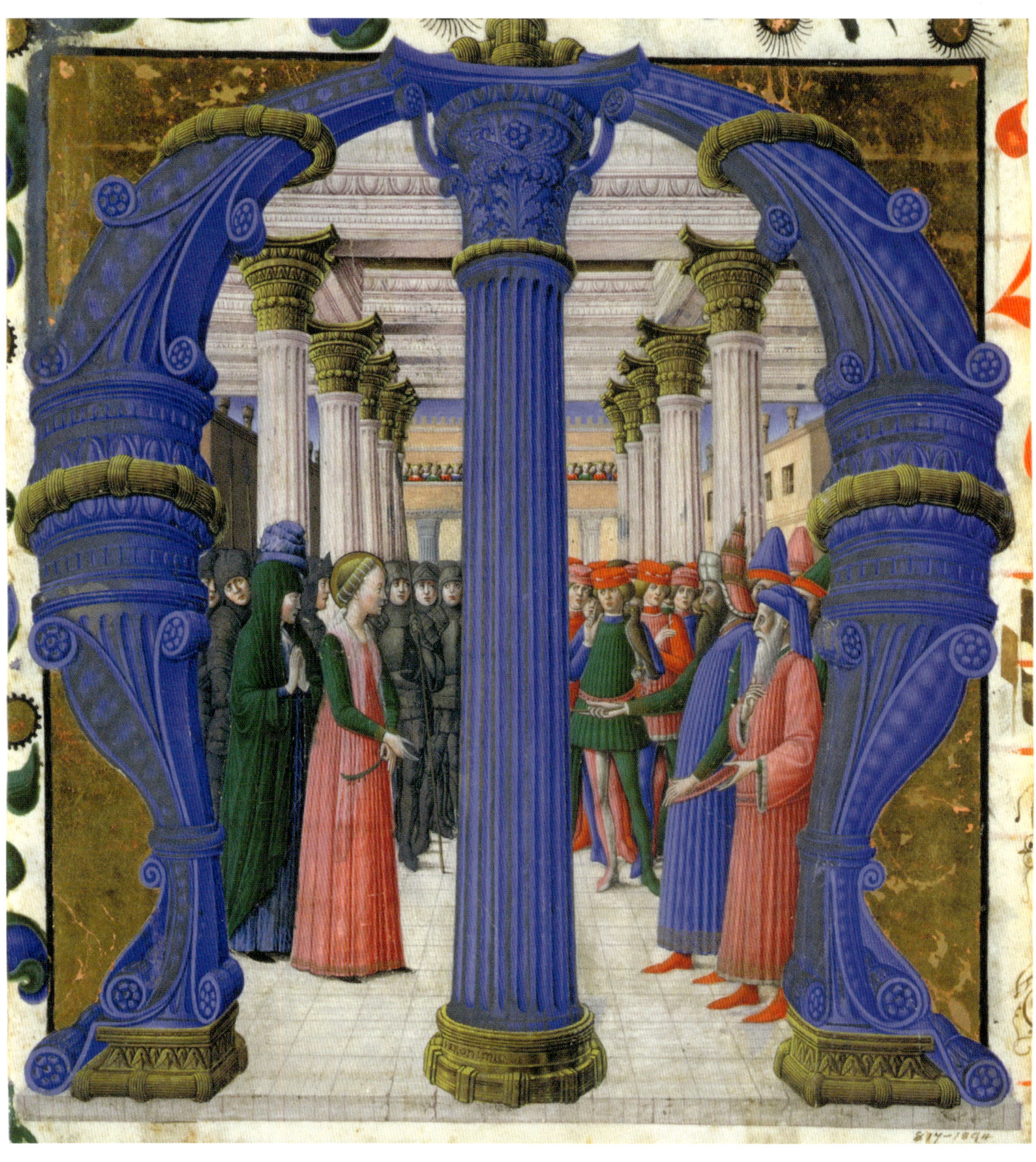

186

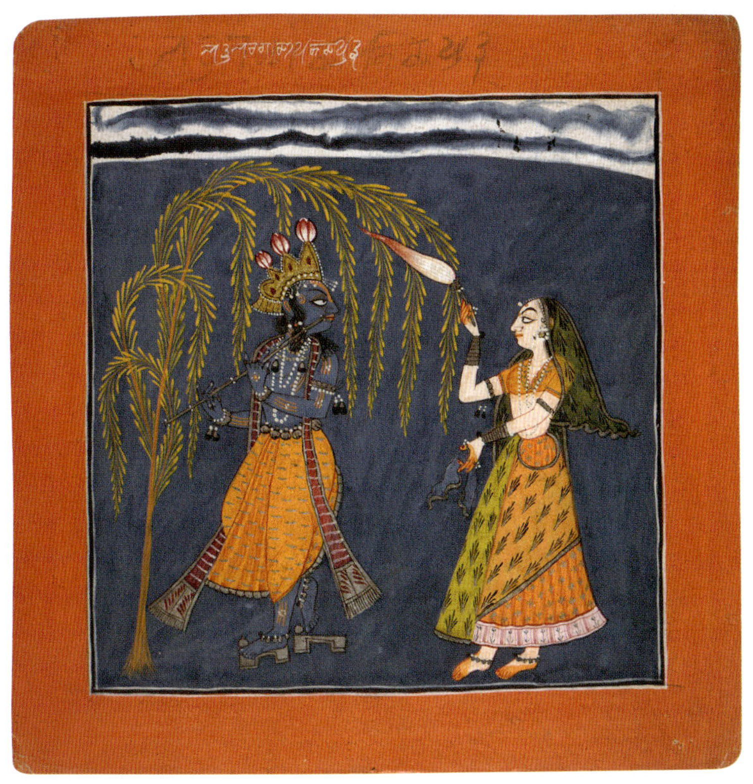

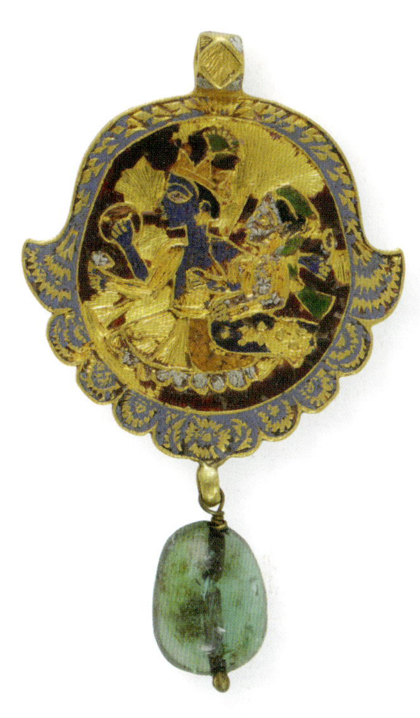

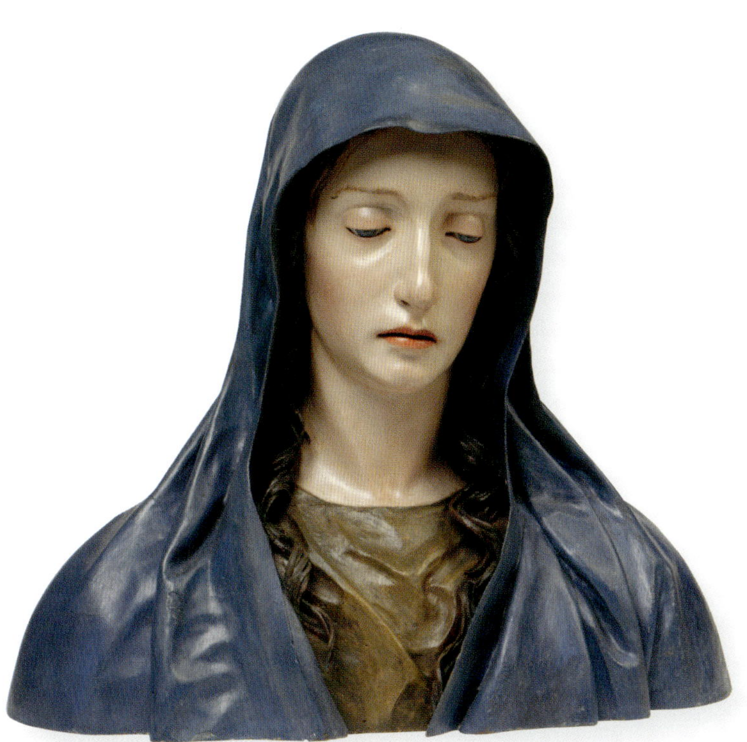

As the colour of the sky, and by association Heaven, blue features prominently in religious iconography. The Virgin Mary, Queen of Heaven in the Christian faith, is traditionally dressed in blue, symbolizing her holiness and purity. A Spanish pinewood bust (c. 1680–1700; left), attributed to José de Mora, represents her as the 'Virgin of Sorrows'. The blue paint on the veil may have been coloured with precious lapis lazuli and coated with fine glass powder to sparkle in candlelight. Lazurite, the blue mineral contained in lapis lazuli, was used along with azurite and indigo in the ultramarine blue of this initial letter 'M' from an Italian choir book, illuminated by Girolamo da Cremona (c. 1470; opposite). The Hindu god Vishnu and his avatar Krishna are often depicted as blue-skinned, as in this *ragamala* painting (c. 1700–10; above left). Krishna plays a flute, illustrating the improvisational musical mode *lahula raga*. Krishna appears again, with his consort, Radha, picked out in blue enamel on this 20th-century gold amulet (above right).

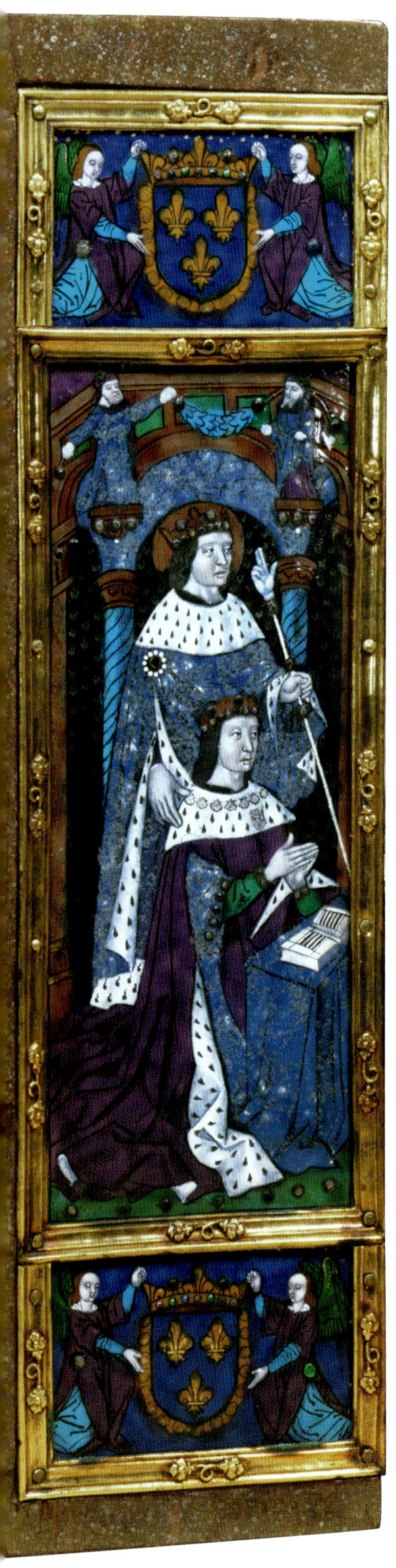

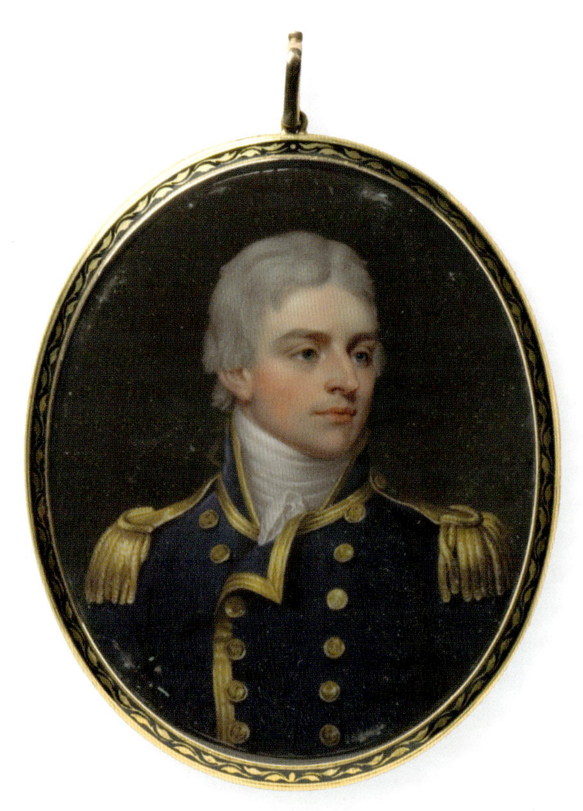

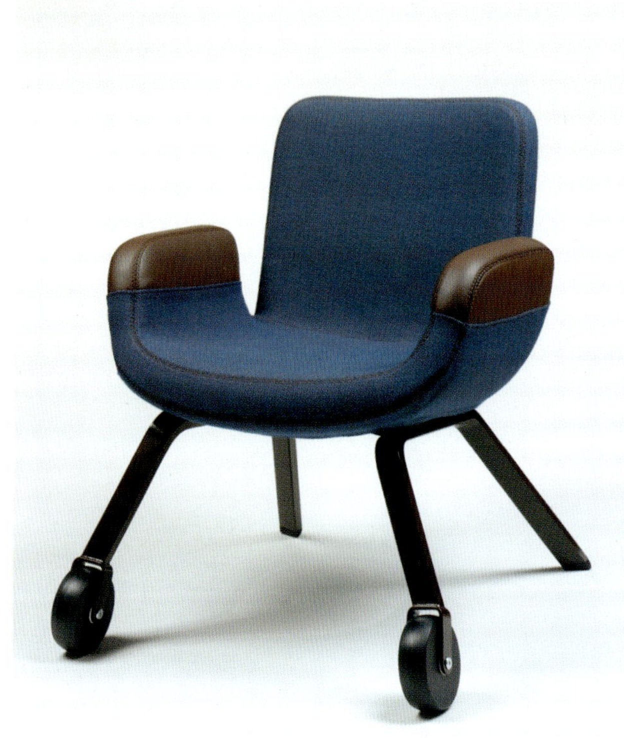

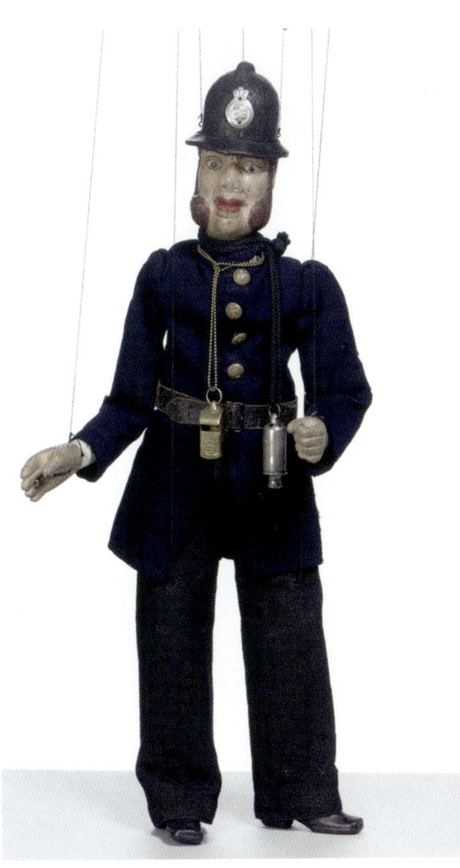

Blue communicates authority and dignity. A side panel from a Limoges enamel triptych of the Annunciation (1498–1514; opposite, left) depicts King Louis XII of France with his patron saint Louis IX, symbolically associating the blue sacred to the Virgin Mary with the monarch's divine right to rule. The British Royal Navy and police forces chose practical dark blue, in contrast to the Army's red. In this enamel portrait miniature (1806; opposite, top), Captain John Whitby wears the uniform of the Royal Navy, which gave its name to the colour 'Navy blue'. The blue uniform of this policeman, above, a stock character from the Tiller marionette theatre troupe (made 1870–90), embodies security and authority. Uniforms have also inspired civilian menswear such as this double-breasted woollen coat (1815–20; right), making blue a fashionable and respectable colour. Hella Jongerius designed this blue chair (2013–14; opposite, bottom right) for the delegates' lounge at the United Nations, a comfortable, secure space intended to inspire trust and cooperation.

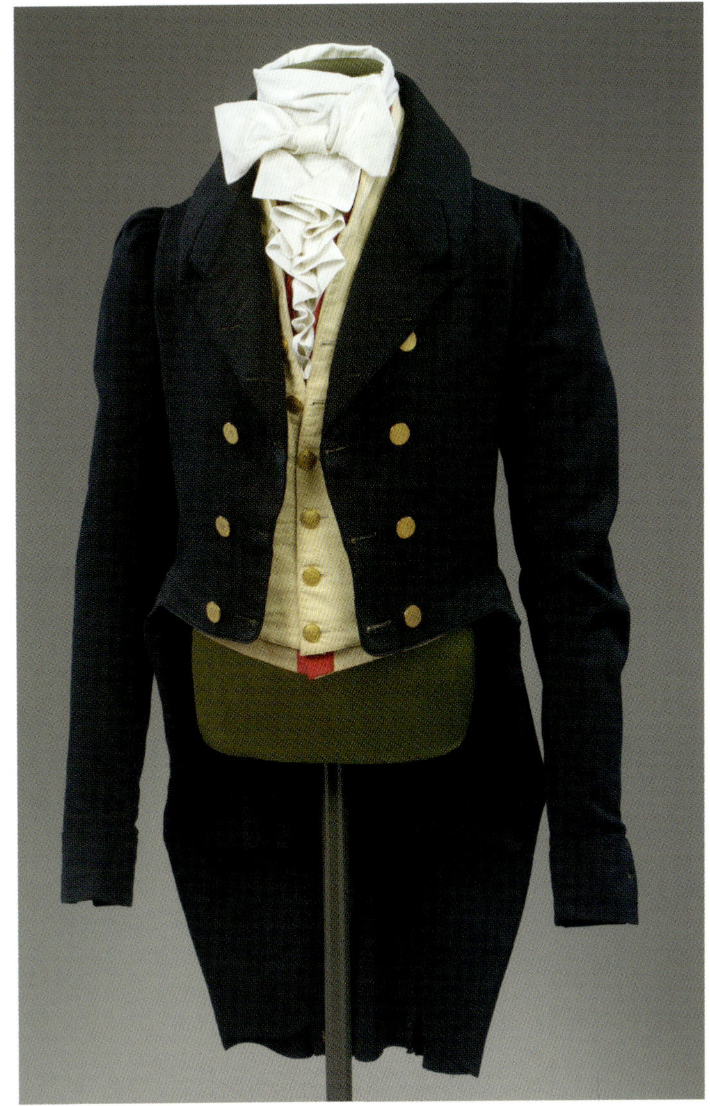

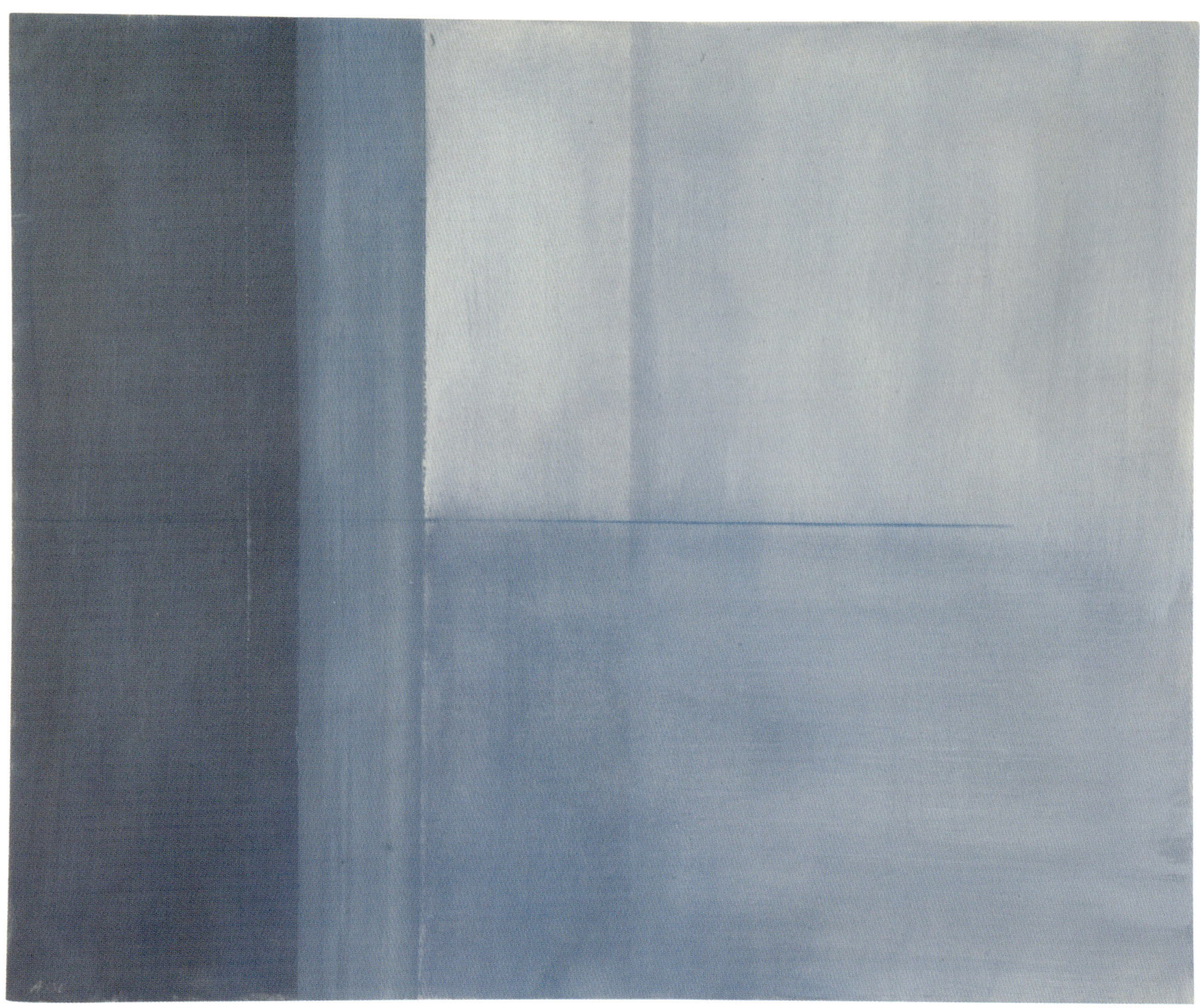

Blue evokes serenity and calm. In
her oil painting *Ligne Bleu* (1969;
above), Geneviève Asse has arranged
harmonious tones of blue, which for
her is 'the colour of silence, of dreams
and of endless space'. The colour of sky
and water, blue is intimately connected
to landscape. The tranquility of John
Constable's oil sketch *Buildings on
rising ground near Hampstead* (1821;
overleaf) is enhanced by a blue sky
illuminating the countryside, reflected
in the pool in the foreground and
on the distant horizon.

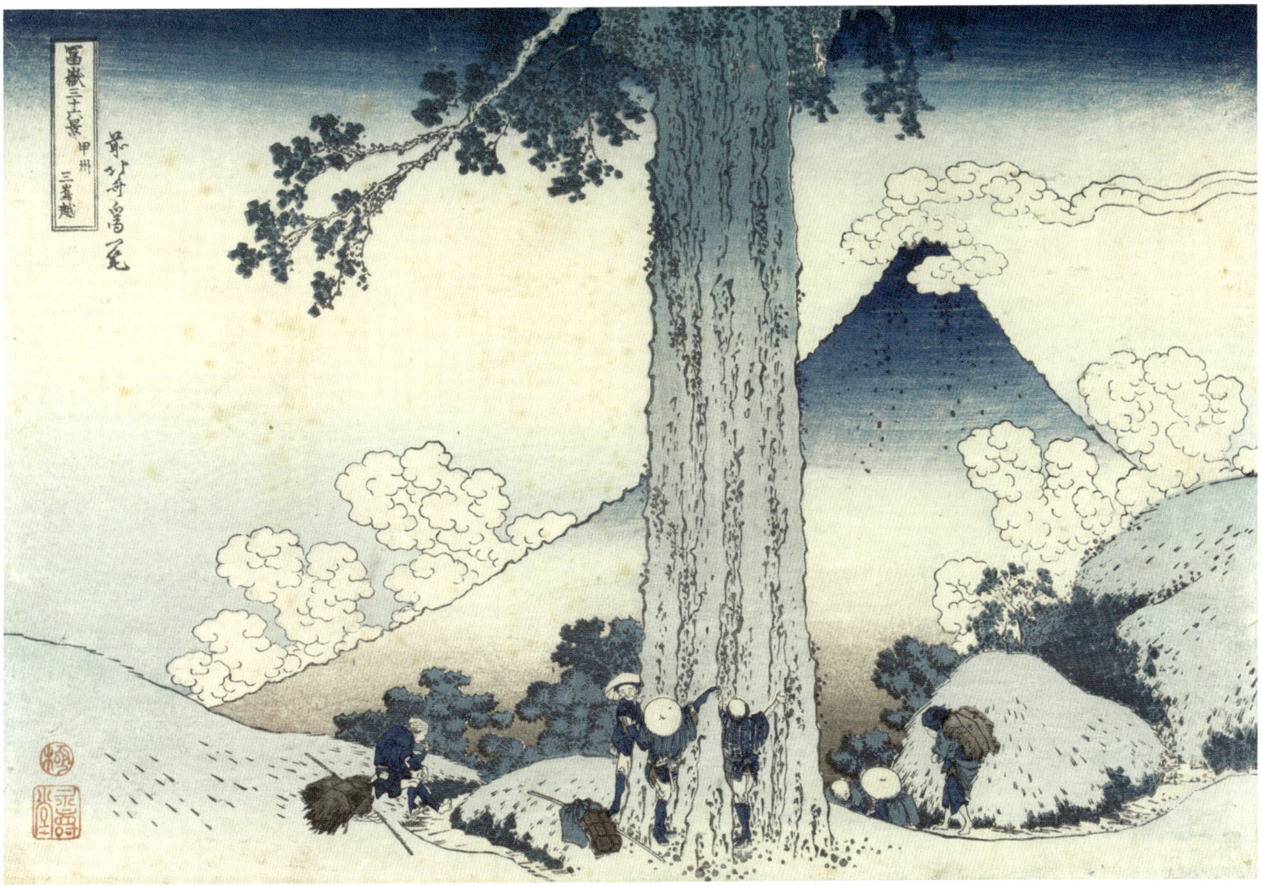

Glowing through the landscape, indigo blue conveys light, depth and atmosphere in Shihoko Fukumoto's linen hanging *Morning Mist* (2006; left). A mountainous landscape softly emerges from the haze, echoing the mountain motif of Katsushika Hokusai's woodblock print *Mishima Pass in Kai Province* (1831; above), from his series *Thirty-six Views of Mount Fuji*. The artist used precious Prussian blue pigment to convey the majestic tranquillity of the scene.

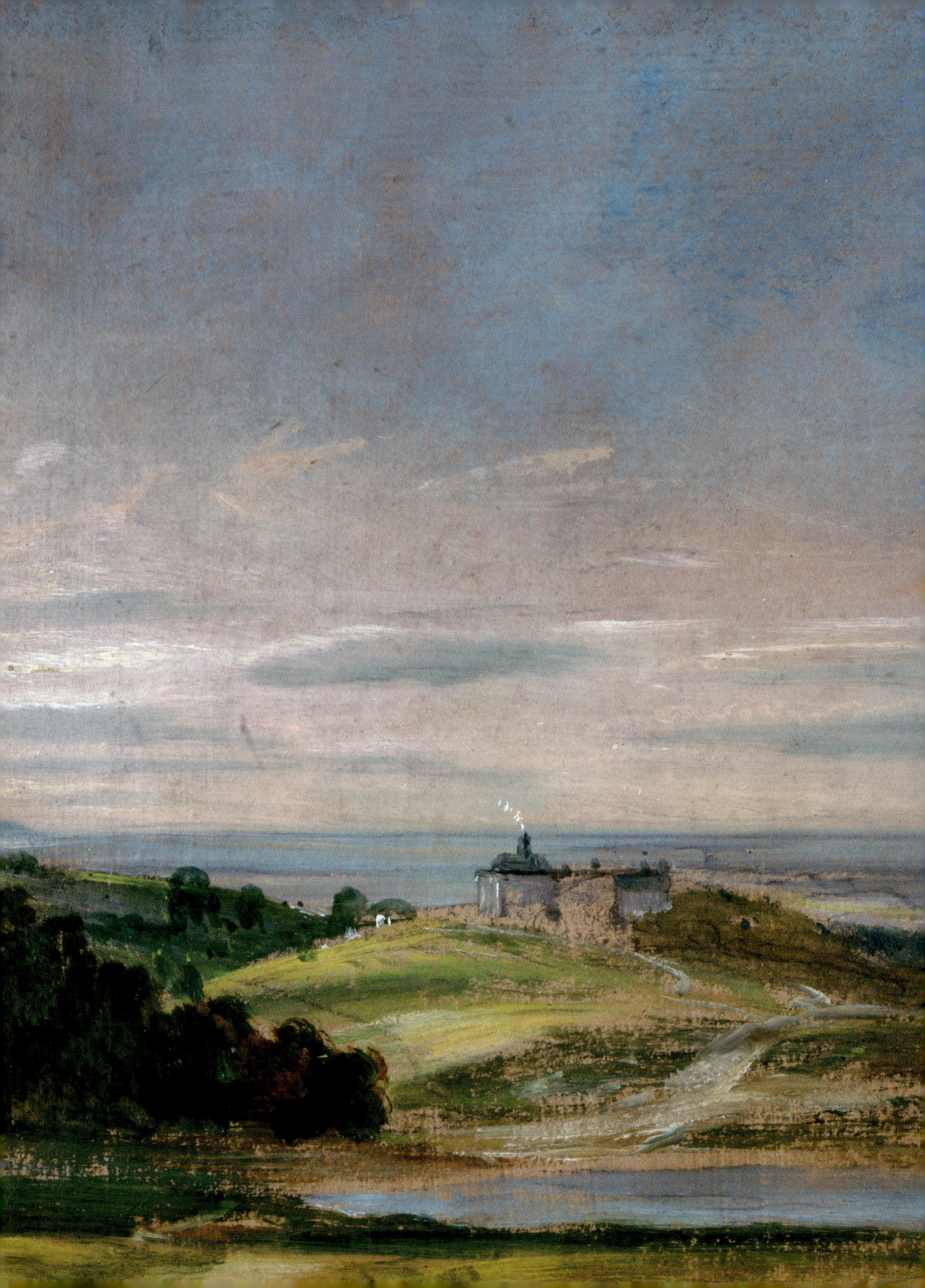

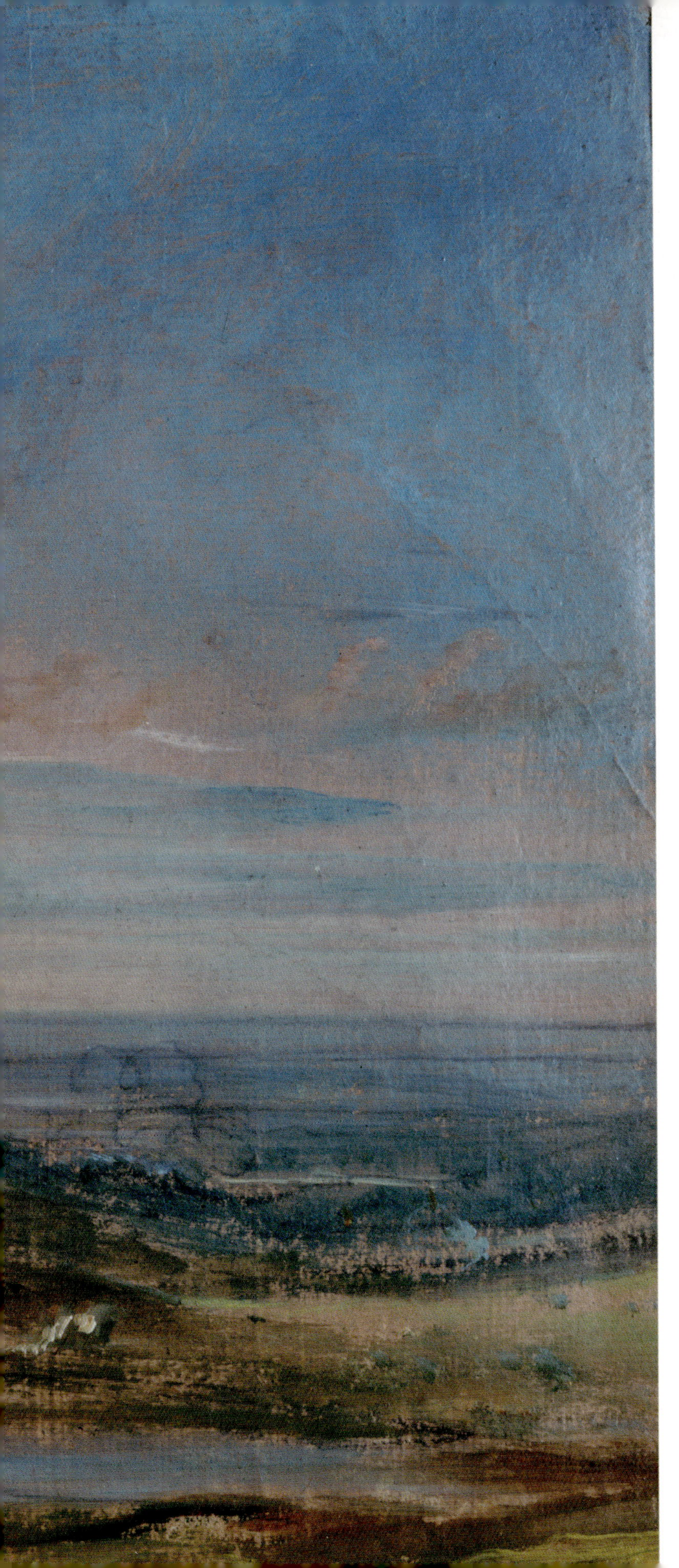

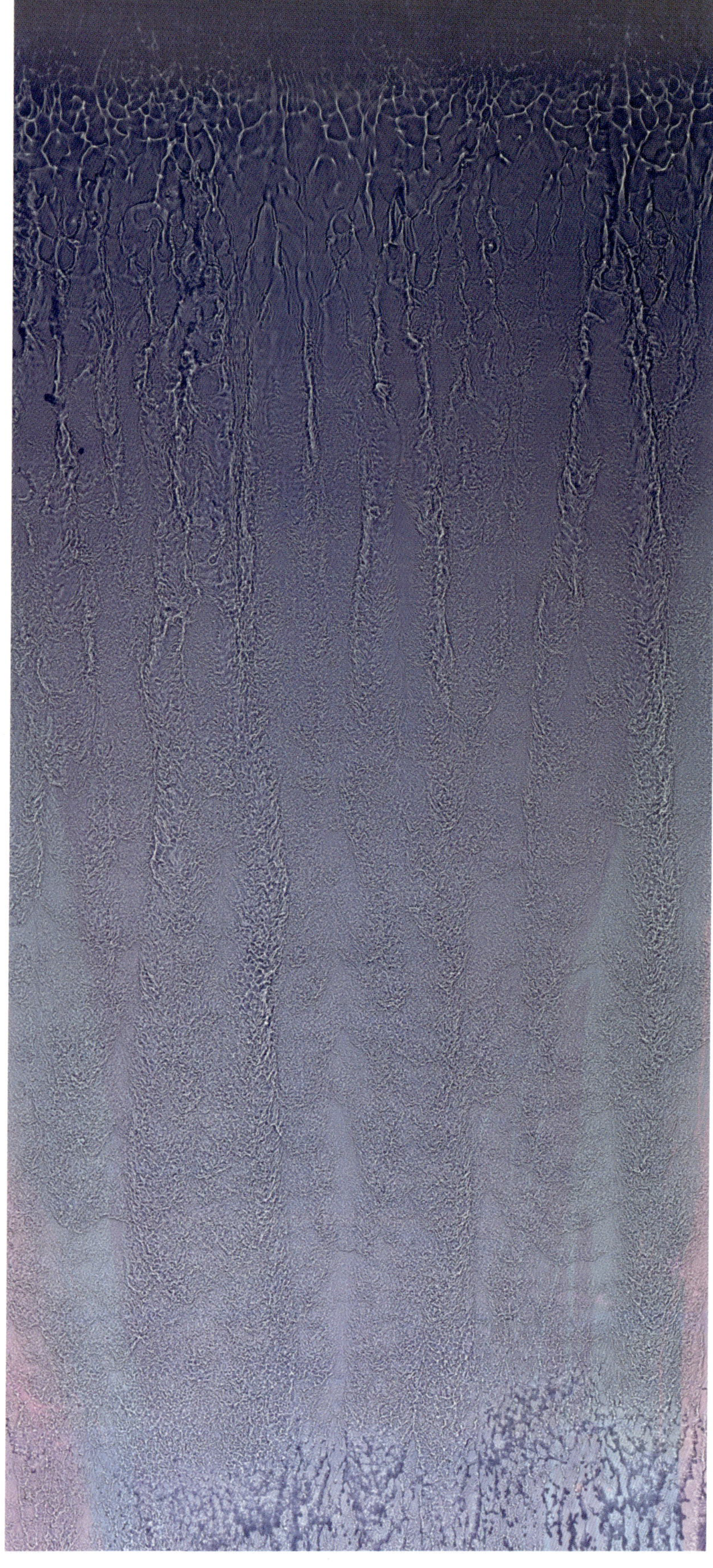

Mysterious and untameable, water has long attracted and inspired artists. Susan Derges's photogram *River Taw* (1997; left) captures the movement of cascading water over the surface of photographic paper laid out underwater, at the bottom of a waterfall. This Japanese blue-and-white porcelain dish from the Edo period (1615–1868; opposite, top right), moulded and shaped like a seashell, is painted in underglaze blue. It re-creates the restless movement of the sea's currents and tides, forming waves and whirlpools among the rocks. In contrast, Qu Leilei's *Fish* dish (1984; opposite, top left) uses cobalt blue on a black glaze to suggest the darkness of the seabed, littered with the skeletal remains of ocean life. The fabulous unknown sea creatures of Jules Verne's novel *Twenty Thousand Leagues Under the Sea* (1870) inspired the swirling forms of Stephen Webster's 'Fighting Fish' bracelet (2009; opposite, bottom), cast in dark blue titanium and set with black spinels, white diamonds and blue sapphires.

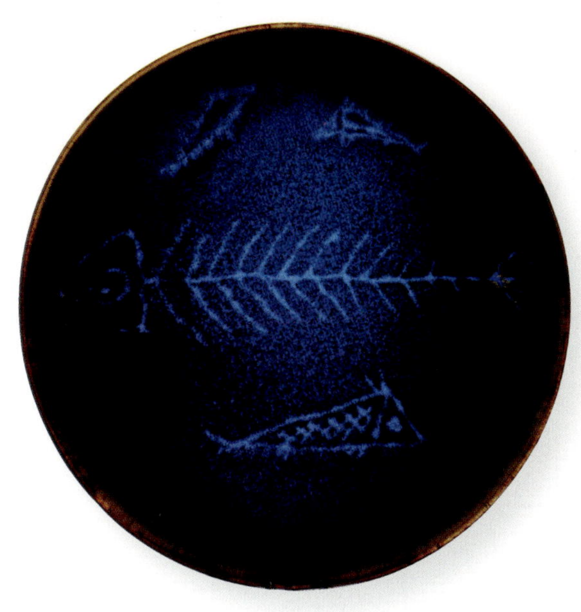

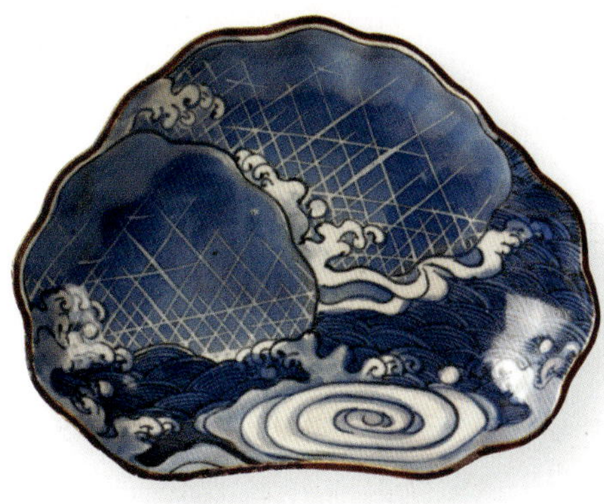

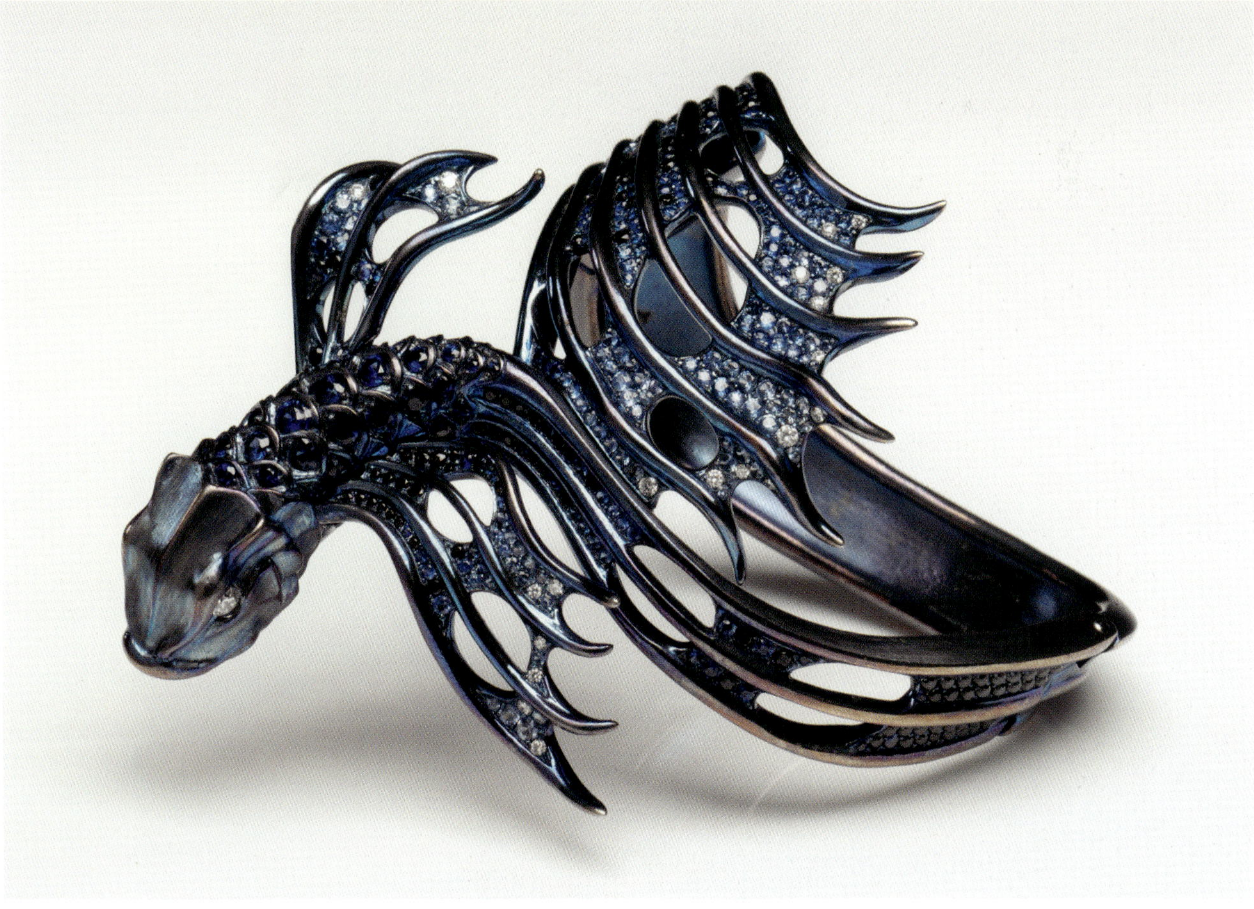

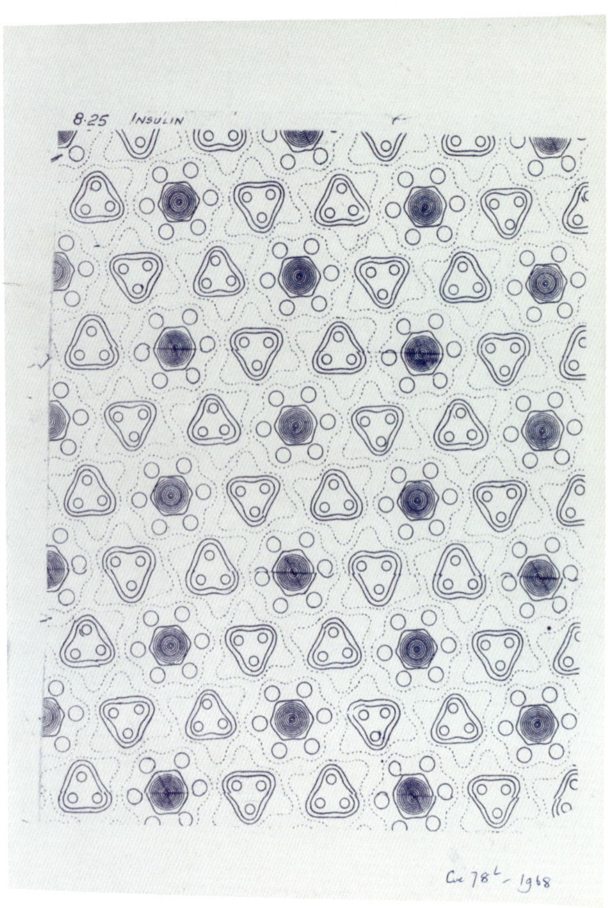

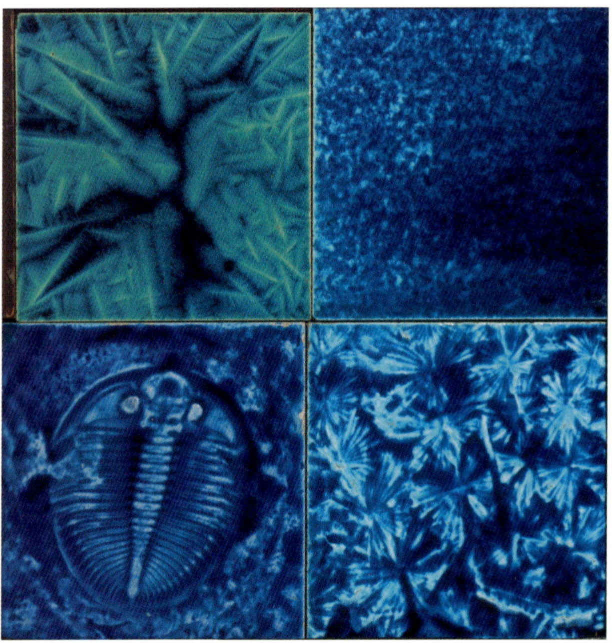

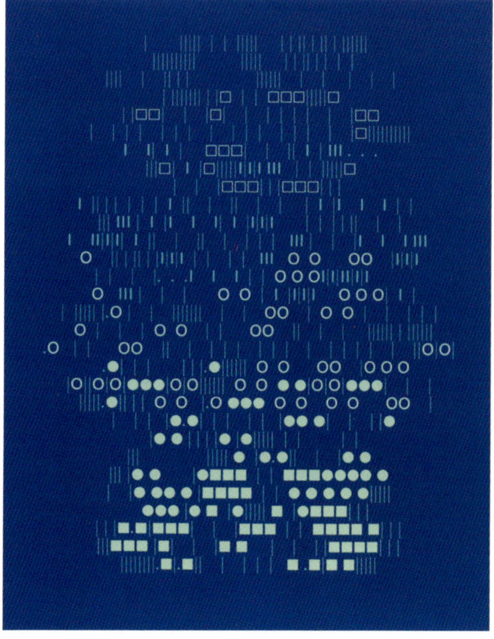

Blue is considered a cool, rational colour, and has a strong association with science, chosen by many scientific, medical and technology companies for their logos and advertisements. Anna Atkins's cyanotype of a poppy, made in about 1854 (opposite) combines scientific precision and accuracy with artistic beauty. Light-sensitive chemicals create the contrast between clean white lines and a rich, Prussian blue background. These unusual 19th-century tiles (below left) were produced by British manufacturers Maw & Co., and reflect George Maw's passion for geology, depicting trilobites and crystals coloured with iridescent blue glazes. The print *Insulin* (left) is based on X-ray crystallography, which enabled images to be made of the arrangement of atoms within molecules. For the Festival of Britain of 1951, designers used these patterns as inspiration, translating the spare scientific diagrams printed in blue into more colourful designs for wallpaper and textiles. Aaron Marcus's print *Evolving Gravity* (1972; below right) was created on a computer using the Fortran programming language. The pattern of symbols on a dark blue background suggests constellations in the night sky, but also recalls computer screens.

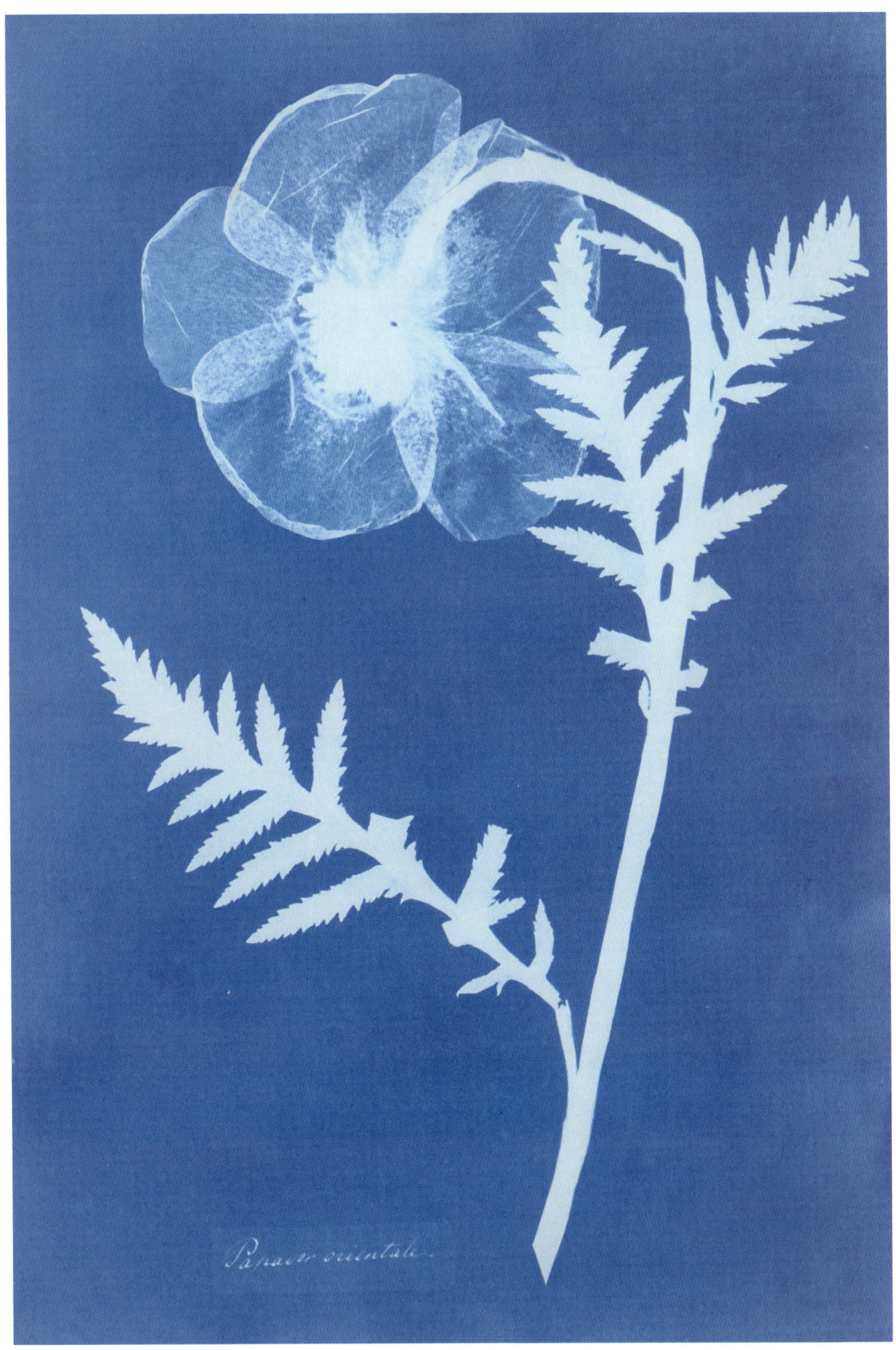

Papaver orientale.

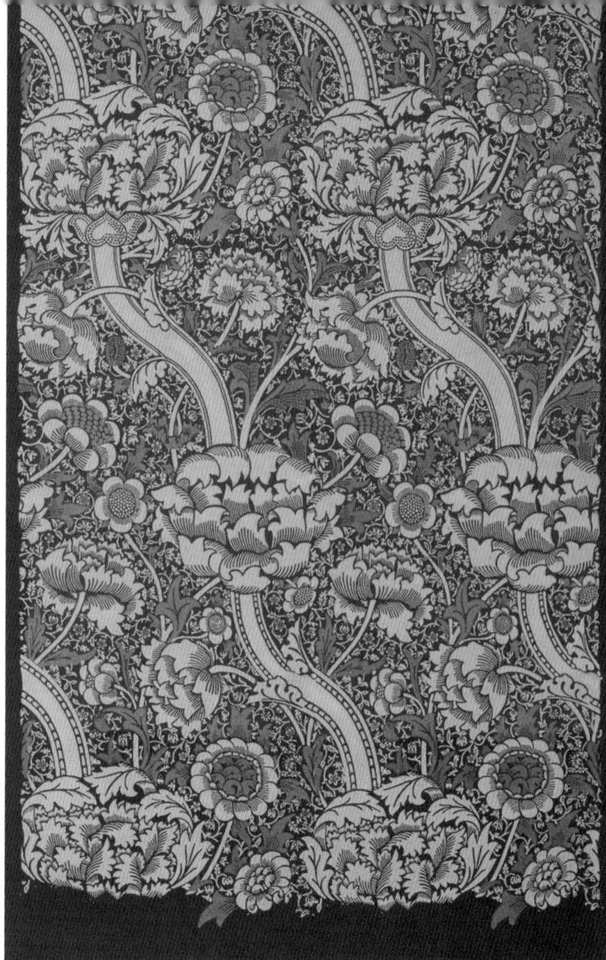

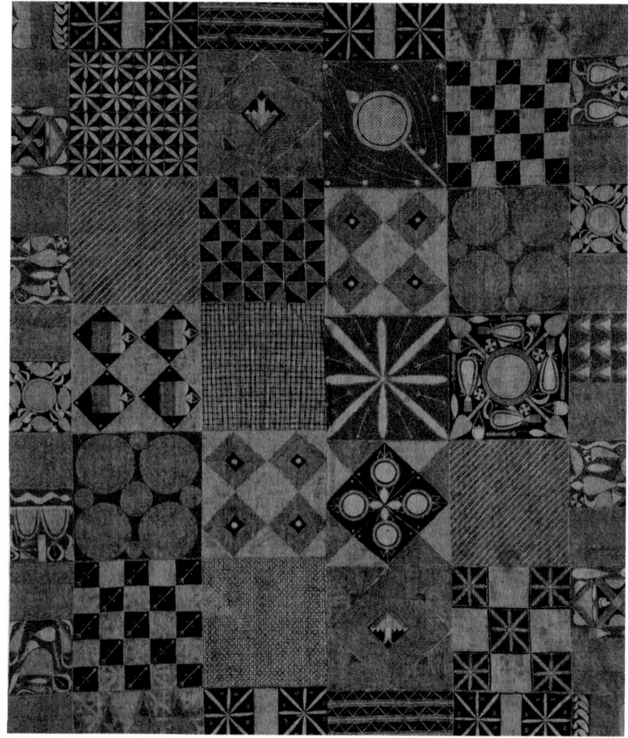

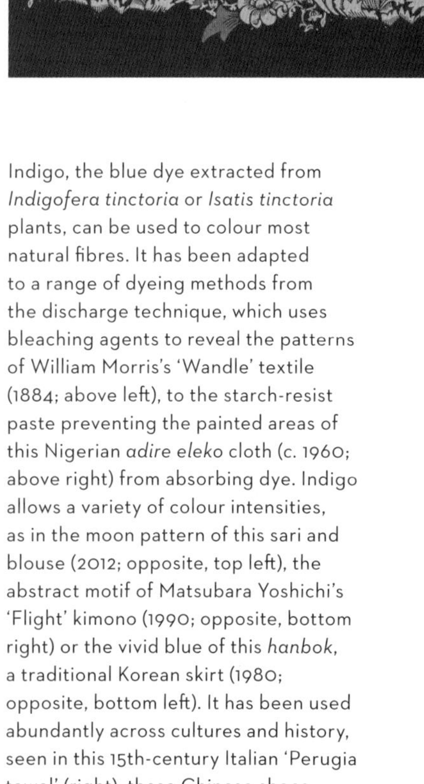

Indigo, the blue dye extracted from *Indigofera tinctoria* or *Isatis tinctoria* plants, can be used to colour most natural fibres. It has been adapted to a range of dyeing methods from the discharge technique, which uses bleaching agents to reveal the patterns of William Morris's 'Wandle' textile (1884; above left), to the starch-resist paste preventing the painted areas of this Nigerian *adire eleko* cloth (c. 1960; above right) from absorbing dye. Indigo allows a variety of colour intensities, as in the moon pattern of this sari and blouse (2012; opposite, top left), the abstract motif of Matsubara Yoshichi's 'Flight' kimono (1990; opposite, bottom right) or the vivid blue of this *hanbok*, a traditional Korean skirt (1980; opposite, bottom left). It has been used abundantly across cultures and history, seen in this 15th-century Italian 'Perugia towel' (right), these Chinese shoes for bound feet (1850–1950; opposite, centre right), and this pair of English gloves (1951; opposite, top right).

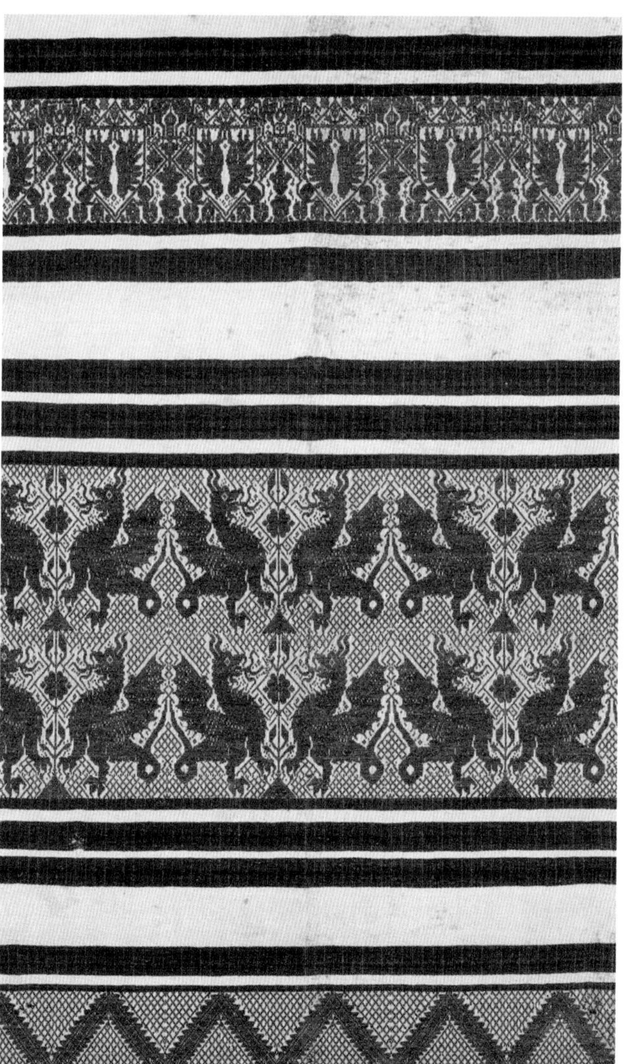

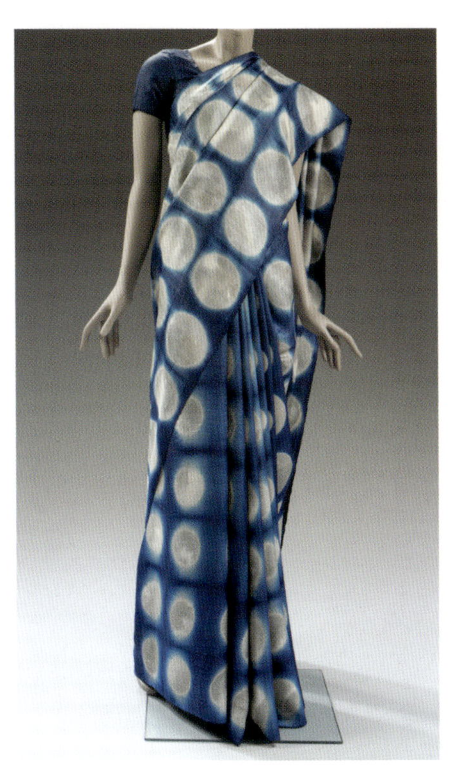

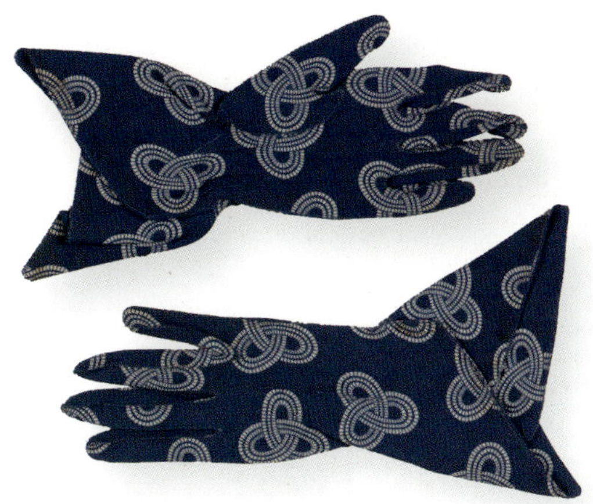

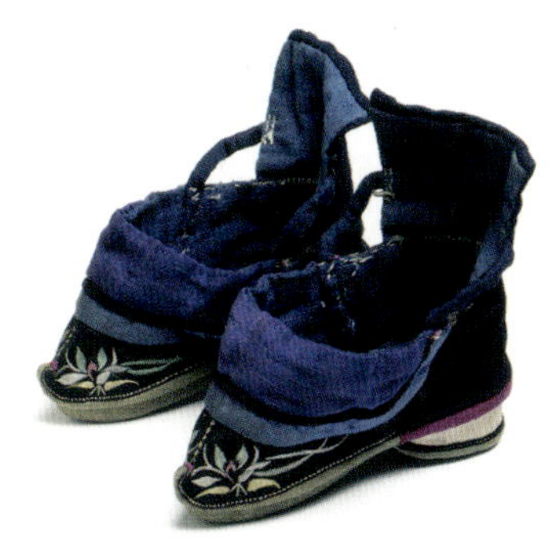

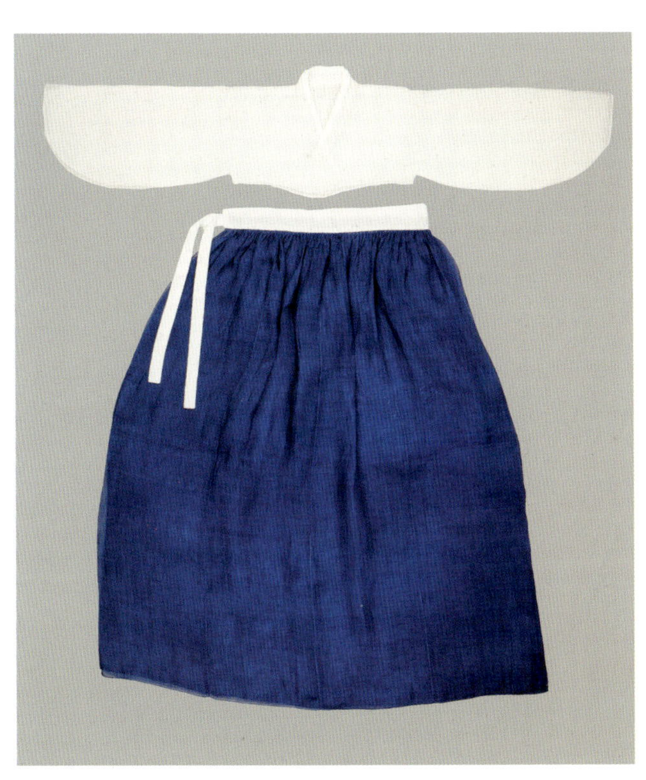

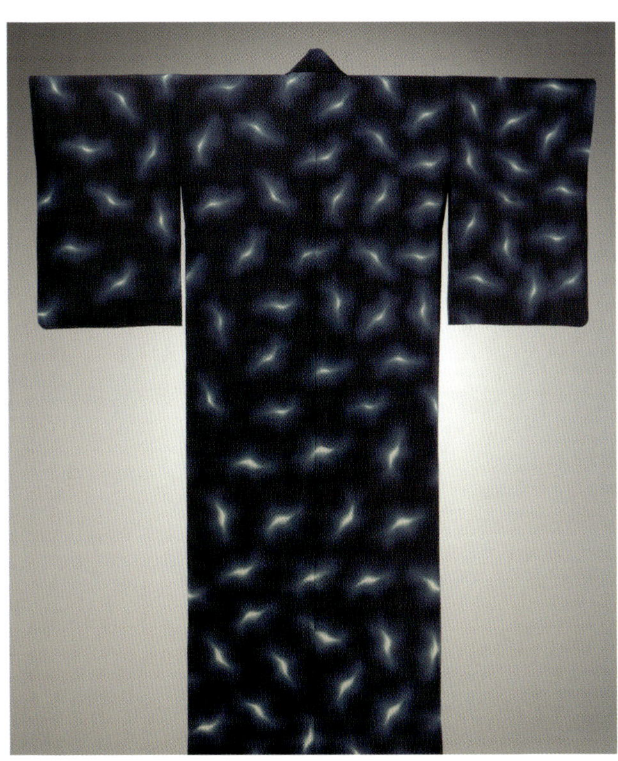

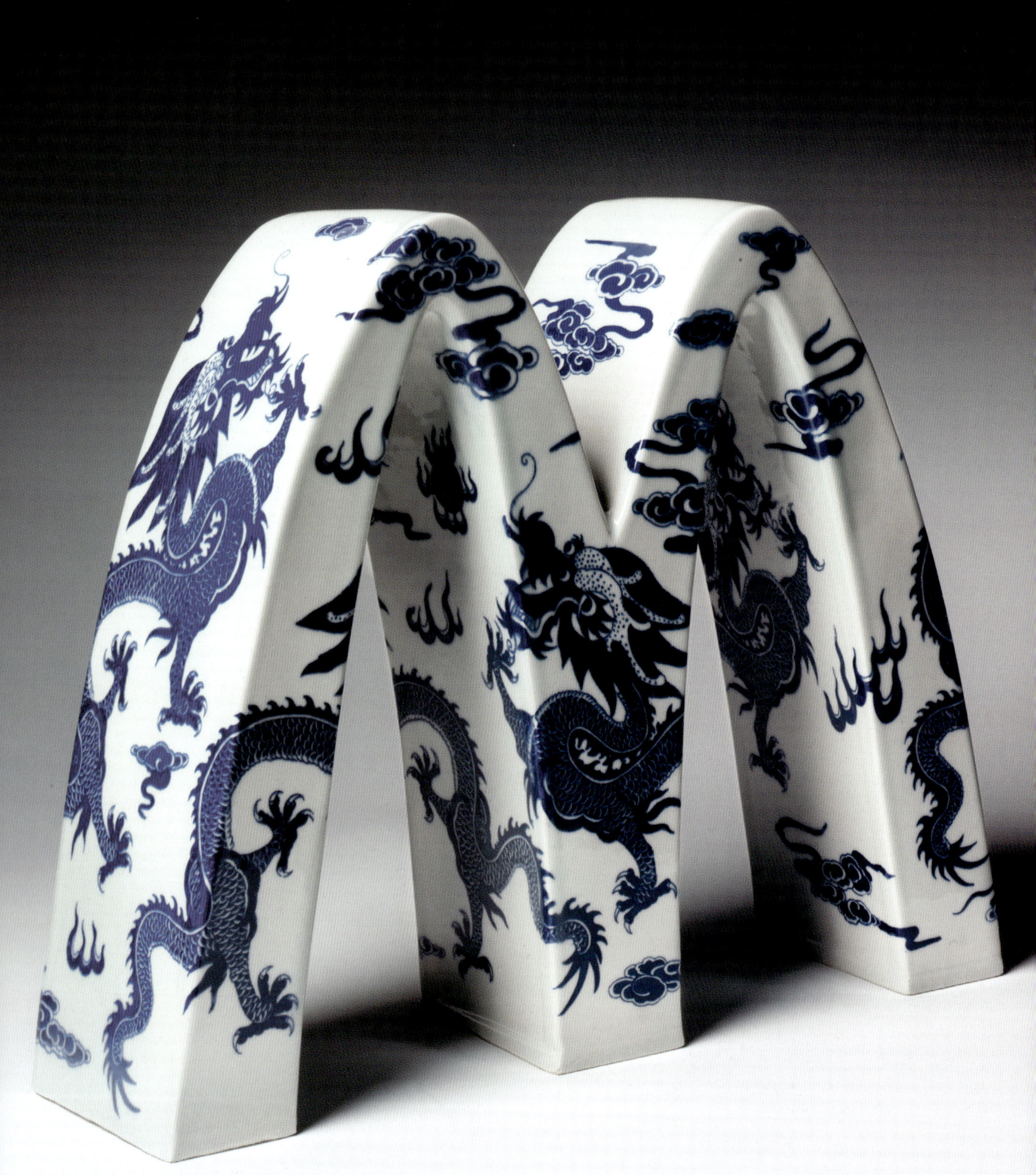

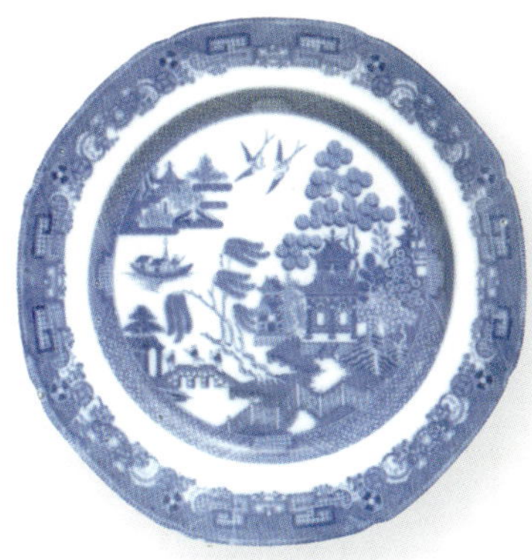

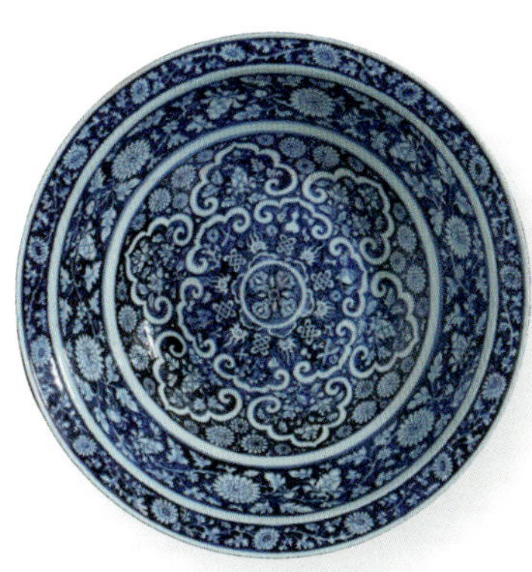

The simplicity and elegance of blue-and-white pottery has crossed continents and centuries. It originated in China, with vessels such as this bowl (1426–35; bottom right) from Jingdezhen, the major production centre for blue-and-white wares from the 14th century onwards. Combining white Chinese porcelain with cobalt from Persia, the designs were instantly popular, made for the Chinese Imperial family and exported around the world in patterns and shapes adapted for local markets. This 17th-century chocolate cup and saucer (centre right) were made for export to Europe, while the 14th-century bowl with a Persian-style flower design (above) was exported to the Middle East. Other countries began to make their own versions. Dutch Delftware such as this tulip vase (above right) flourished in the 17th century, and the British willow pattern seen on this plate (top) was made in Staffordshire from the early 19th century. This style of blue-and-white is still instantly recognizable; in 2007 Li Lihong combined traditional decoration with the McDonald's symbol for his ceramic work *McDonald's #1* (opposite), which explores themes of globalization and cultural exchange.

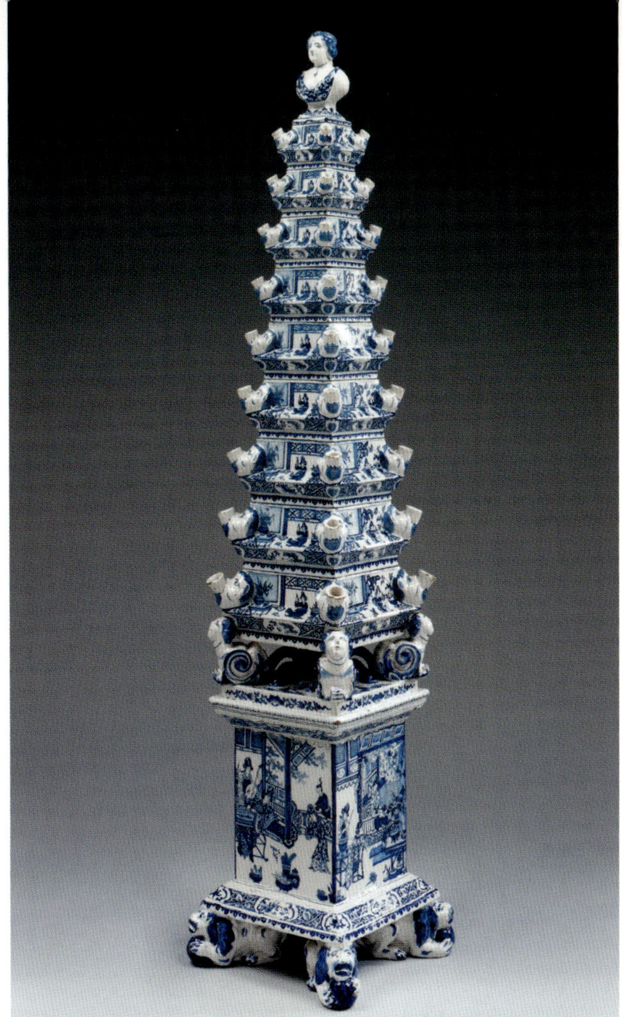

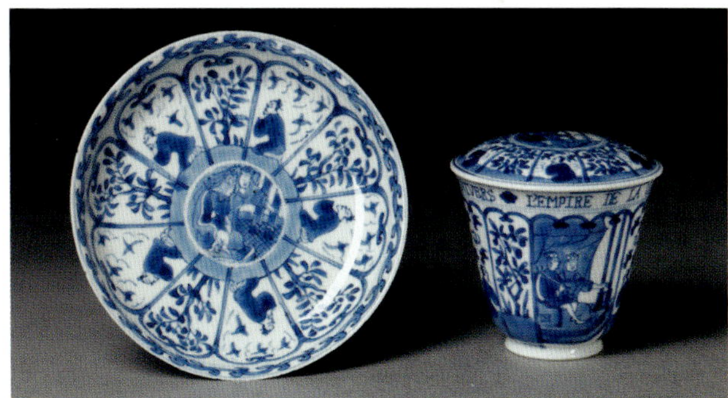

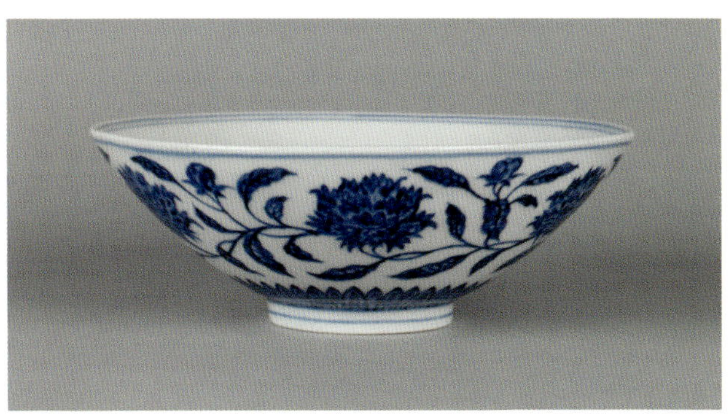

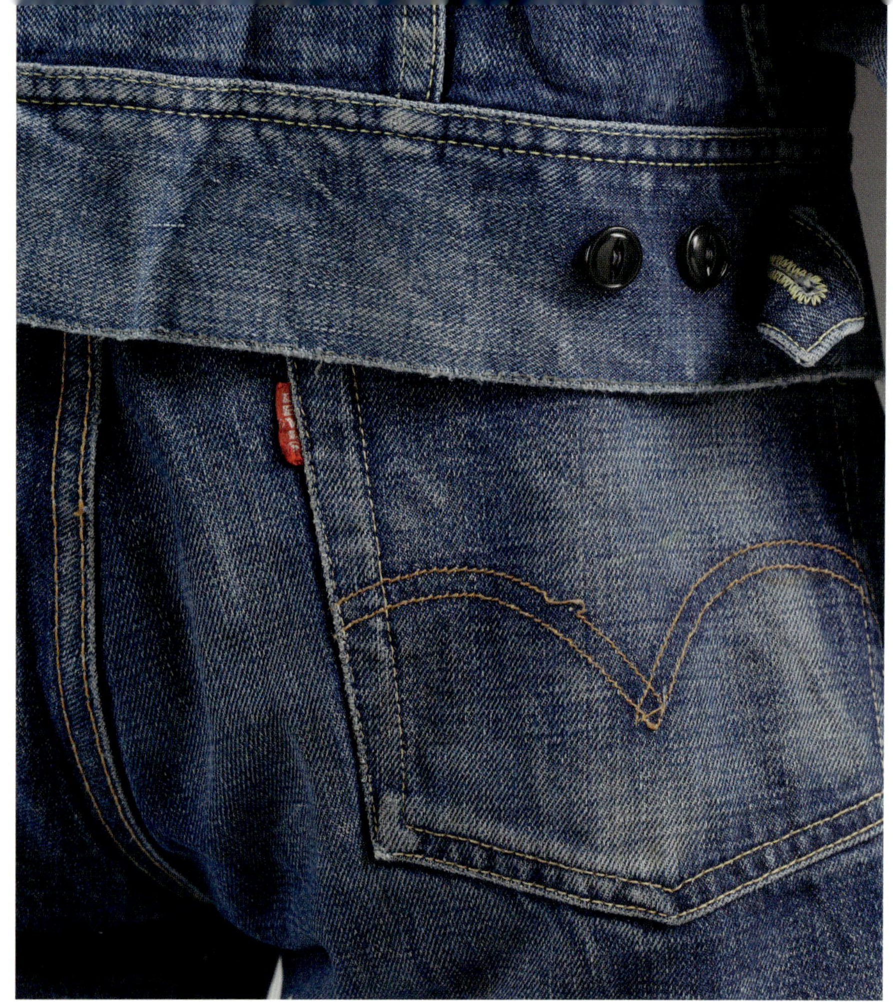

Blue is the colour of many practical, everyday things. Denim jeans, originally designed as workwear, were coloured with indigo dye. Synthetic dyes in a variety of colours have replaced natural indigo, but the blue jeans in this 1970s ensemble (left) remain a fashion staple. From Alec Issigonis's sketch for the Mini car (1956; opposite, top) to David Bowie's scrawled lyrics for Ziggy Stardust, the use of the humble blue Biro is ubiquitous. More personal than black, a blue pen is also recommended to distinguish handwritten signatures on printed documents.

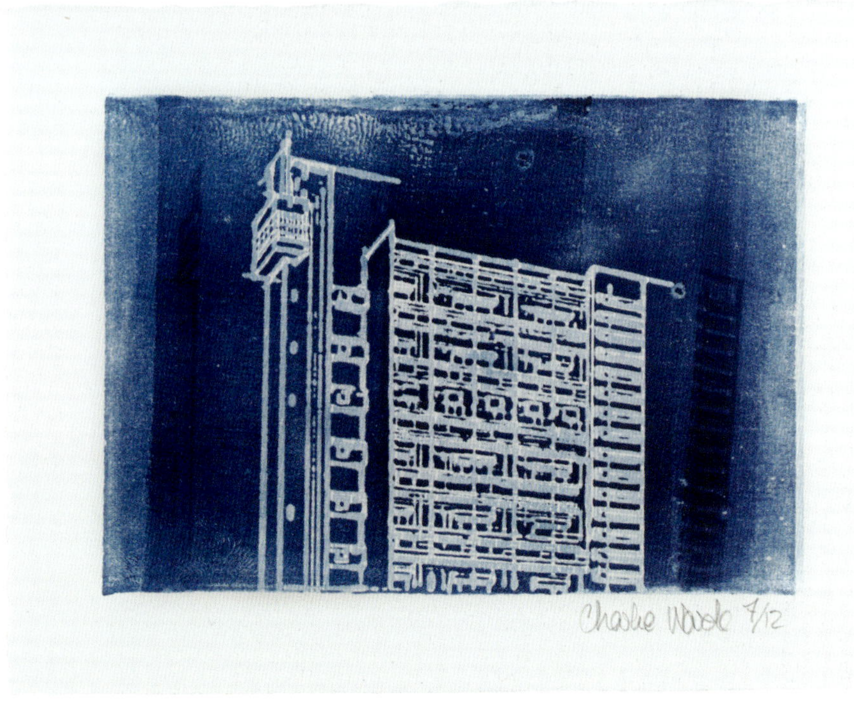

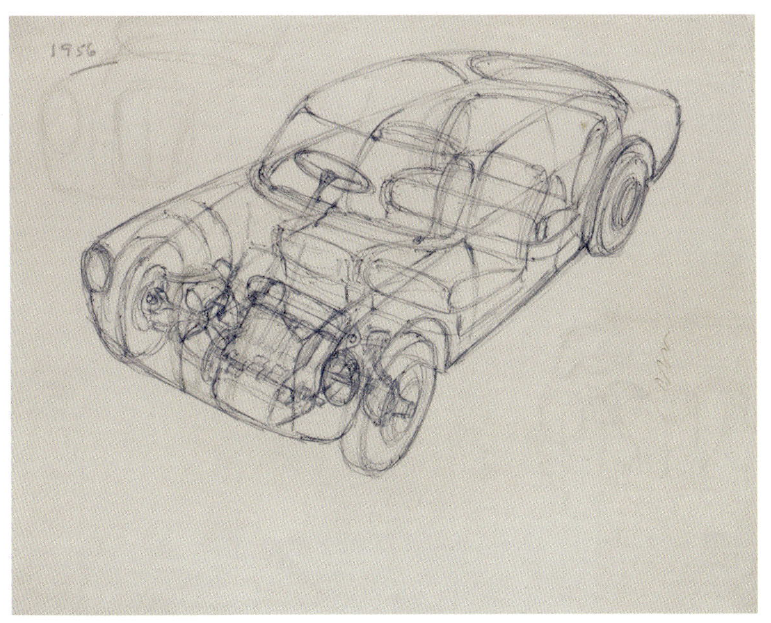

A blueprint is a type of contact print used to copy technical drawings, such as this 1939 design, below, for the 'Isokon' bookcase. The 'Isokon' was designed to fit Penguin paperback books, which in the mid-20th century were sold for sixpence each, intended to bring literature to the masses. Charlie Warde's *Prometheus* (2012; opposite, bottom) is a series of 228 etchings in the style of an architectural blueprint, depicting London's iconic Trellick Tower. In the egalitarian spirit of post-war social housing in Britain, Warde gave most of the prints away to the tower block's residents.

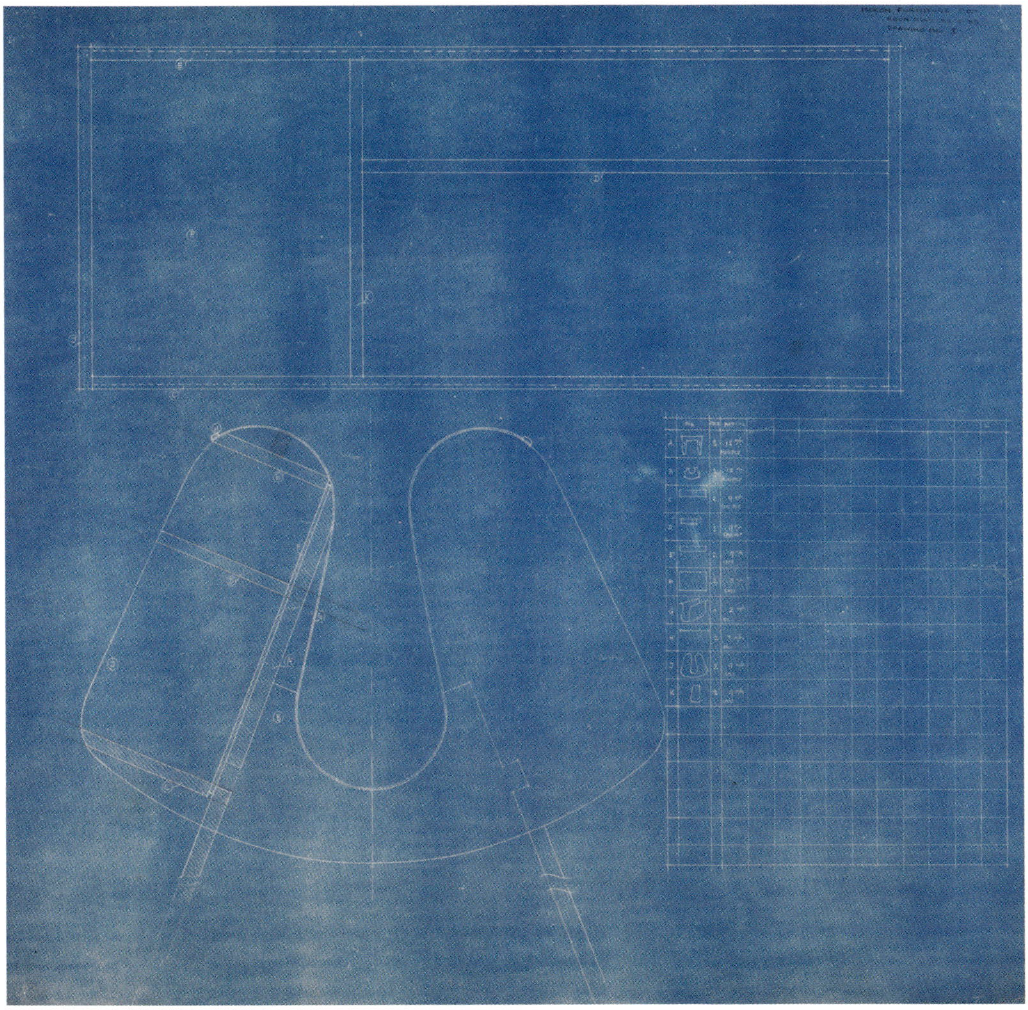

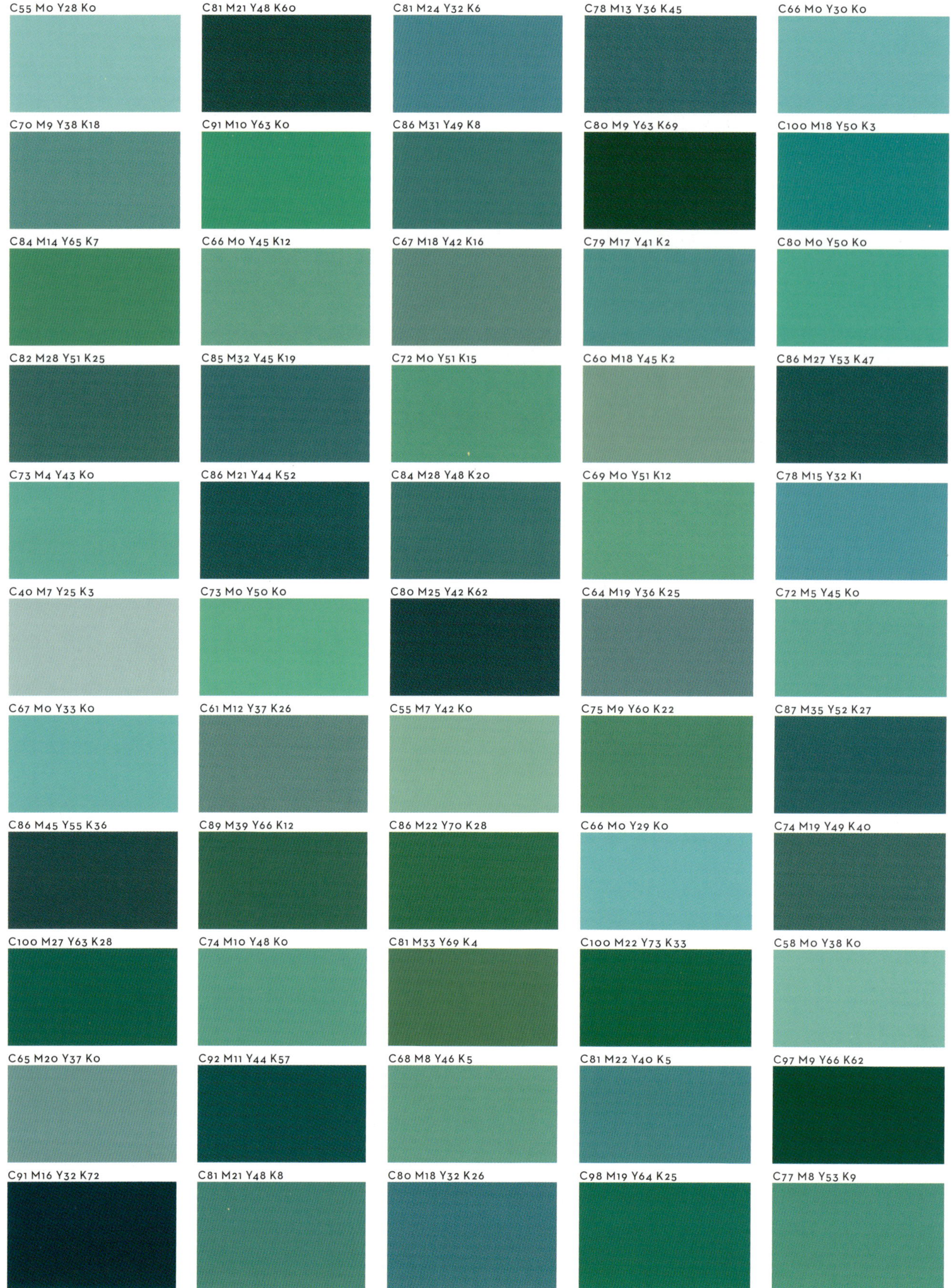

C55 M0 Y28 K0
C81 M21 Y48 K60
C81 M24 Y32 K6
C78 M13 Y36 K45
C66 M0 Y30 K0
C70 M9 Y38 K18
C91 M10 Y63 K0
C86 M31 Y49 K8
C80 M9 Y63 K69
C100 M18 Y50 K3
C84 M14 Y65 K7
C66 M0 Y45 K12
C67 M18 Y42 K16
C79 M17 Y41 K2
C80 M0 Y50 K0
C82 M28 Y51 K25
C85 M32 Y45 K19
C72 M0 Y51 K15
C60 M18 Y45 K2
C86 M27 Y53 K47
C73 M4 Y43 K0
C86 M21 Y44 K52
C84 M28 Y48 K20
C69 M0 Y51 K12
C78 M15 Y32 K1
C40 M7 Y25 K3
C73 M0 Y50 K0
C80 M25 Y42 K62
C64 M19 Y36 K25
C72 M5 Y45 K0
C67 M0 Y33 K0
C61 M12 Y37 K26
C55 M7 Y42 K0
C75 M9 Y60 K22
C87 M35 Y52 K27
C86 M45 Y55 K36
C89 M39 Y66 K12
C86 M22 Y70 K28
C66 M0 Y29 K0
C74 M19 Y49 K40
C100 M27 Y63 K28
C74 M10 Y48 K0
C81 M33 Y69 K4
C100 M22 Y73 K33
C58 M0 Y38 K0
C65 M20 Y37 K0
C92 M11 Y44 K57
C68 M8 Y46 K5
C81 M22 Y40 K5
C97 M9 Y66 K62
C91 M16 Y32 K72
C81 M21 Y48 K8
C80 M18 Y32 K26
C98 M19 Y64 K25
C77 M8 Y53 K9

TURQUOISE

The word turquoise began its life describing a mineral. Variously also known as aquamarine, cyan, robin's-egg blue and sky stone, turquoise actually comes in a range of shades, with mottles and veins varying from dark blue to almost white. Over time, its name began to be used to describe the mineral's colour more generally, and today refers to a whole range of hues lying between blue and green. For this reason, identifying the colour can be highly subjective, and what one person sees as turquoise another might see as instead blue or green – recently illustrated by debates in Britain over exactly which colour Queen Elizabeth II wore to the 2019 Opening of Parliament ceremony, and the political meanings behind the choice.

Historically, because of its rarity, the mineral turquoise was highly prized. Turquoise requires specific geological conditions to form – arid highlands, in areas of highly weathered rock, close to the interface with the water table. The largest pockets typically occur alongside or near gold and copper deposits, as it is in fact formed through the weathering and oxidation of other minerals. Turquoise's value was historically, therefore, closely linked with trade and resource control. The English word turquoise is believed to derive from French *turquois*, 'of or from Turkey', indicating the route by which the mineral historically entered Europe.

The appeal of the mineral turquoise is global, and stretches back into antiquity; it has been mined for millennia. In Iran, the starting point for the European turquoise trade, deposits were discovered on Ali-Mersai mountain near Nishapur. Consumers regarded this turquoise as of the highest quality due to its high copper content; 'Persian blue' is still a name occasionally given to the colour. The Ancient Egyptians intensively exploited the mountains of the Sinai Peninsula, and in China the largest historic mines were in the highlands of Hubei province. Together, these three areas were the principal historical sources for turquoise across Africa, Asia and Europe. Artefacts such as beads attest to the transfer of the mineral across trade routes for thousands of years – at least 5000, in fact, as demonstrated through turquoise jewellery found on the mummy of a queen of the 1st dynasty Egyptian Pharaoh Djer. On the other side of the world, the people of the Americas also made use of turquoise, with mining sites known from Chile, Mexico and the southern United States. These sources were extensively utilized by a range of North, Meso- and South American native cultures.

As a visible display of wealth, turquoise has long been inlaid into jewellery and other portable objects. A particularly well-known illustration of this principle comes from Shakespeare, where in *The Merchant of Venice*, Shylock's prized possession was a ring inlaid with turquoise. Across Europe, the increased importation of Iranian turquoise from the sixteenth and seventeenth centuries made such items increasingly common.

Because of the historical value and relative rarity of turquoise, many cultures instead looked for ways of emulating the stone and its bright colour in other materials. Several ancient societies derived pigments: in Mesoamerica, for example, 'Mayan blue' was derived from indigo. Artificial substances were also created to replicate turquoise itself. The first and best-known instance of this comes from Ancient Egypt, where a more readily-available substitute, today known as faience, was developed as early as the 5th millennium BC.

Faience was used for many of the thousands of amulets and *shabtis* now found in museum collections worldwide (see pp. 220–1). Composed of a silica (ground quartz or sand), alkali (typically natron or plant ash) and lime mixed with water, it formed a paste that could be shaped. Copper oxide, added either to the main material or as a layer on the surface, reacted when fired to give the finished product a rich blue-green colour. Although easier to source than actual turquoise, and ultimately an imitation of a precious stone, faience was not regarded as a 'lower-class' material. The Ancient Egyptian word for faience, *tjehnet* ('dazzling') speaks to the esteem in which it was held. Indeed, due to the transformative nature of its production, faience was considered to have unique ritual properties of its own. There are plentiful examples of faience items made for an elite, even royal milieu.

As the above examples demonstrate, the mineral turquoise was not the only historical source of turquoise as a colourant. As was the case for the Egyptians, the most commonly exploited material was copper oxide. This was especially utilized in the case of ceramics, where the tradition of glazing vessels blue-green spans back millennia across much of Asia (see pp. 208–9). Because access to turquoise as a colour was not solely dependent on access to the mineral itself, symbolic meanings have developed around the colour turquoise more generally, even in areas where the mineral is unknown. In 1915, Joseph Pogue penned *The Turquoise*, a complete compendium of the locations of turquoise mines, its minerology and its cultural significances; these meanings show striking commonalities worldwide.

Understandably, turquoise is seen foremost as a colour of water and sky. In Ancient Egypt, the colour turquoise – and by extension the material faience – were closely associated with the life-giving Nile, and therefore concepts of rebirth and regeneration. This is best seen in burial contexts, where a wide range of funerary goods were made in faience.

Owing to its celestial connotations, the colour turquoise appears frequently in Islamic art, most famously the dazzling blue-green tilework of mosques and mausoleums across Iran and Central Asia. Victorian designers who turned to the aesthetics of Islam, such as Owen Jones and William De Morgan, likewise made heavy use of the colour

in their work (see pp. 218–19). In Mesoamerica, turquoise also held celestial associations. To both the Toltecs and later Aztecs, turquoise was a 'sky stone', related to the Sun, meteors and fire – the final association potentially because the strongest and most intense part of a flame is blue. It was the colour associated with warriors, the colour of royal paraphernalia and the stone of the God of fire, 'Turquoise Lord'.

Another shared belief surrounding turquoise, held particularly in relation to the stone itself, is in its protective or healing properties. Variations of these ideas include that a turquoise object worn by its owner will change colour to warn of impending sickness; that turquoise stones will break if their owner is in danger; or that they will protect the owner from falls, especially from horseback. Turquoise has historically been particularly associated with horse-riders for this reason. There may actually be some geological grounding for the idea that turquoise gems can 'change' colour, as long-term contact with skin oils and light exposure do indeed discolour turquoise, especially paler stones.

The perceived healing qualities of turquoise have long attracted scholarly attention. Medieval European lapidaries discussed the protective qualities of the stone, particularly to guard against poison. Bernardus Caesius's 1636 handbook *Mineralogia, sive Naturalis philosophiae thesauri* included a comprehensive list of the medicinal properties commonly ascribed to turquoise. The Cambridge scholar Thomas Nicols's 1652 *A Lapidary or History of Precious Stones* claimed that turquoise strengthened the sight and renewed the bond between man and wife. The French gemologist Tavernier visited Iran in the seventeenth century to see the turquoise mines there for himself.

Turquoise – *yu* – is especially highly valued in Tibetan culture, and alongside coral is perhaps the most popular gemstone for use in jewellery or embellishing metal objects. Much of the turquoise used in the country was historically sourced from China or Iran, although small deposits are known in Tibet itself. Documents recording its significance are known from as early as the seventh to ninth centuries. As well as being precious, turquoise was linked to concepts of the supernatural and protection. Among various attested practices, offerings of turquoise were presented to demons in payment for averting sickness, while folklore held that swallowing turquoise could cure poisons and, in common with medieval Europe, that a turquoise in contact with poisonous substances would change colour.

These beliefs are perhaps a reason why turquoise was often inlaid in other portable objects such as swords and knives – again an association with good luck and fortune, this time in a military context. For the Apache nations of southwestern America, affixing turquoise to a bow would afford greater accuracy. In Iran, as well as being a colour of Heaven, it holds connotations of fortune; its Farsi name, *firuzeh*, means 'victory'. In around 1300, Muhammed Ibn Mansur wrote that 'if one sees a turquoise early in the morning, he will pass a fortunate day … the turquoise helps its owner to victory over his enemies, protects him against injury and makes him liked by all men.'

In the nineteenth and twentieth centuries, new fashions developed around turquoise. In contrast with its historical value, the mineral itself became less prized, and today it is one of the least expensive gemstones. In America, the development of rail links and subsequent gold rush led to the discovery and exploitation of numerous new turquoise mines, still in use today; in 1980 it was estimated that 200 mines were active across the southwestern states. Turquoise jewellery became a favoured souvenir for tourists to sites such as the Grand Canyon. Mines were also discovered and exploited in Australia. Industrial-scale mining has vastly increased the market supply of turquoise, especially lower-quality stones, and therefore its original connotations of luxury and rarity have been lost. Synthetic substitutes have also become more readily available. Historically, in the absence of turquoise, turquoise-coloured glass or odonto-lite, fossil ivory stained blue-green, could serve as substitutes. Today, a dyed white mineral called howlite is also commonly used. The perceived apotropaic qualities of turquoise have persisted, however, and continue today in New Age thinking, where it is both a gemstone of healing and a birthstone for December, believed to symbolize the virtue of 'truth'.

Despite the changing value of the mineral, from the nineteenth century new ideas developed around the colour more generally. Turquoise was increasingly selected as a colour for sentimental jewellery, associated with forget-me-not flowers and therefore particularly appropriate for love tokens (see p. 215). It was a popular gift for bridesmaids, often in the form of a turquoise dove; those at Queen Victoria's wedding were gifted turquoise brooches shaped like the Saxe-Coburg eagle.

The colour turquoise has also increasingly been adopted by advertising and commerce. Psychologically, turquoise supposedly encourages calmness and relaxation, in part due to its marine associations. Combined with its historical connotations of luxury and opulence, it has been an obvious colour for manufacturers and retailers seeking to communicate those qualities. Most famously, 'Tiffany Blue' was developed by Tiffany jewellers in 1837, appearing on the cover of their first 'Blue Book' catalogue in 1845 and remaining key to the company's advertising ever since. In the 1920s, the discovery of Tutankhamun's tomb and its untouched treasures spawned another craze for turquoise, bringing the story full circle.

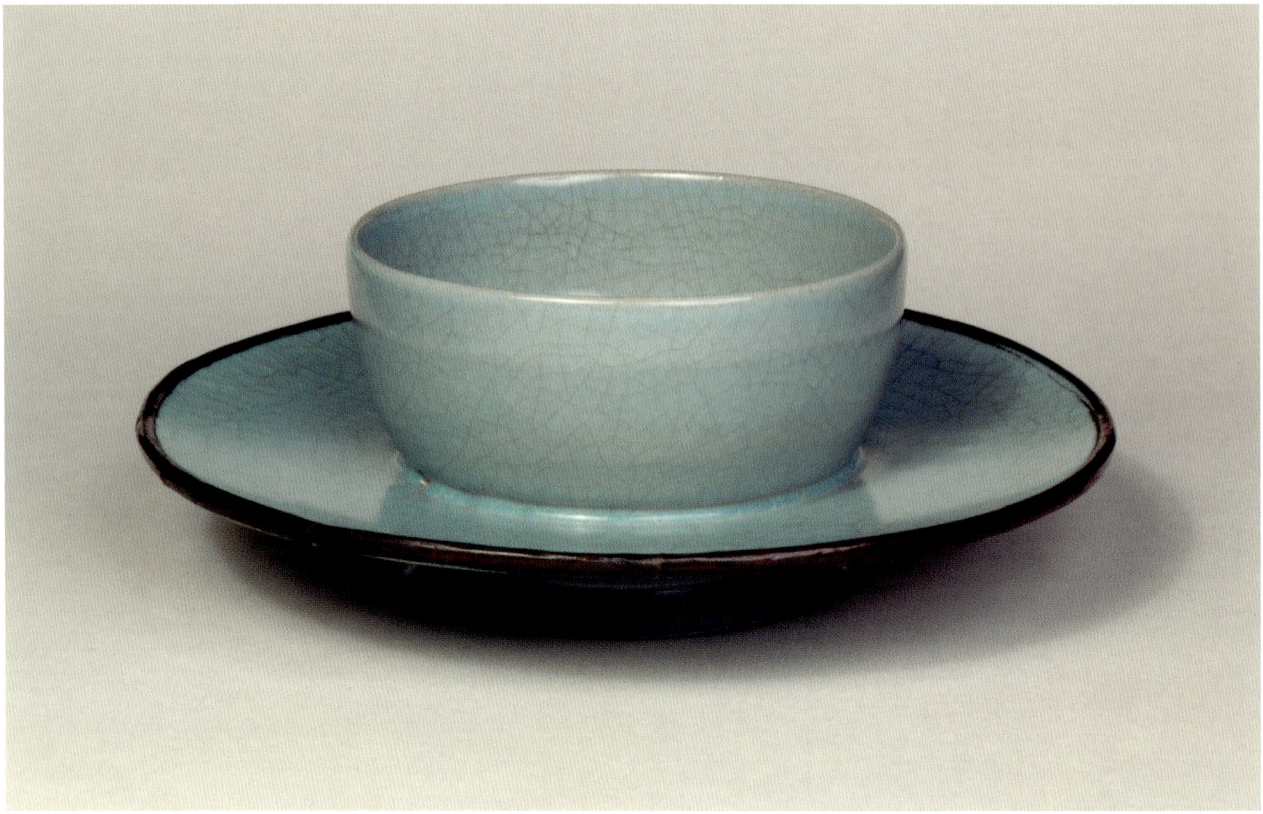

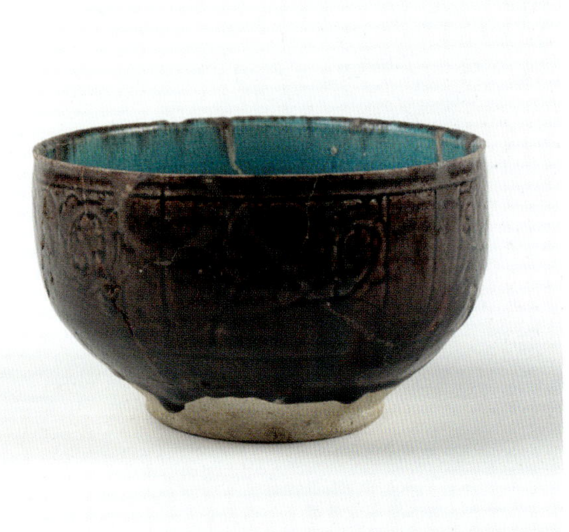

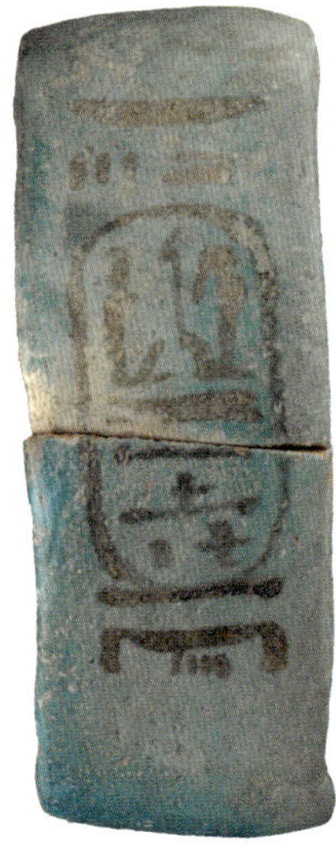

In many cultures, the colour turquoise was associated with the sky, the heavens or water. The Ancient Egyptian goddess Hathor, 'Lady of Turquoise', was the patron of mining sites; shrines to her have been discovered filled with votive offerings from the miners, such as this bracelet fragment in turquoise-coloured faience (left). In the medieval Islamic world, especially Iran, turquoise was associated with the heavens, and domes and tombs were furnished with turquoise tiles, such as this 11th-century example (opposite).

The practice of glazing ceramics blue-green using copper oxide dates back millennia. This 12th-century Iranian bowl (far left) also has an exterior glazed purple with manganese. Glazing vessels made them more impermeable, and the glossy finish suggested the appearance of costly metal. The ru-ware bowl (also 12th-century) above is a prized imperial porcelain, made for less than a century in China. The pale, delicate colour is described in medieval writings as akin to the colour of sky after rain.

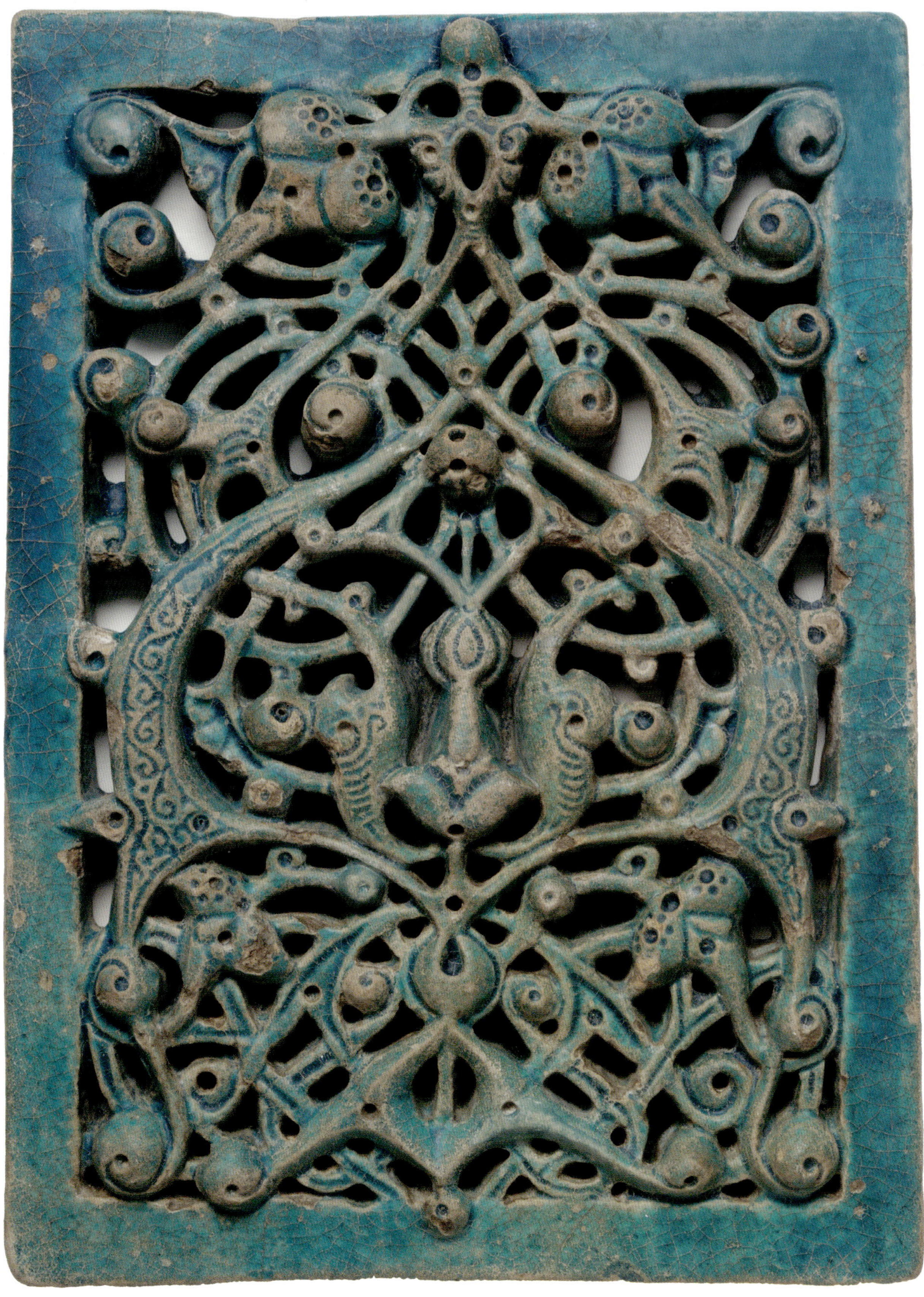

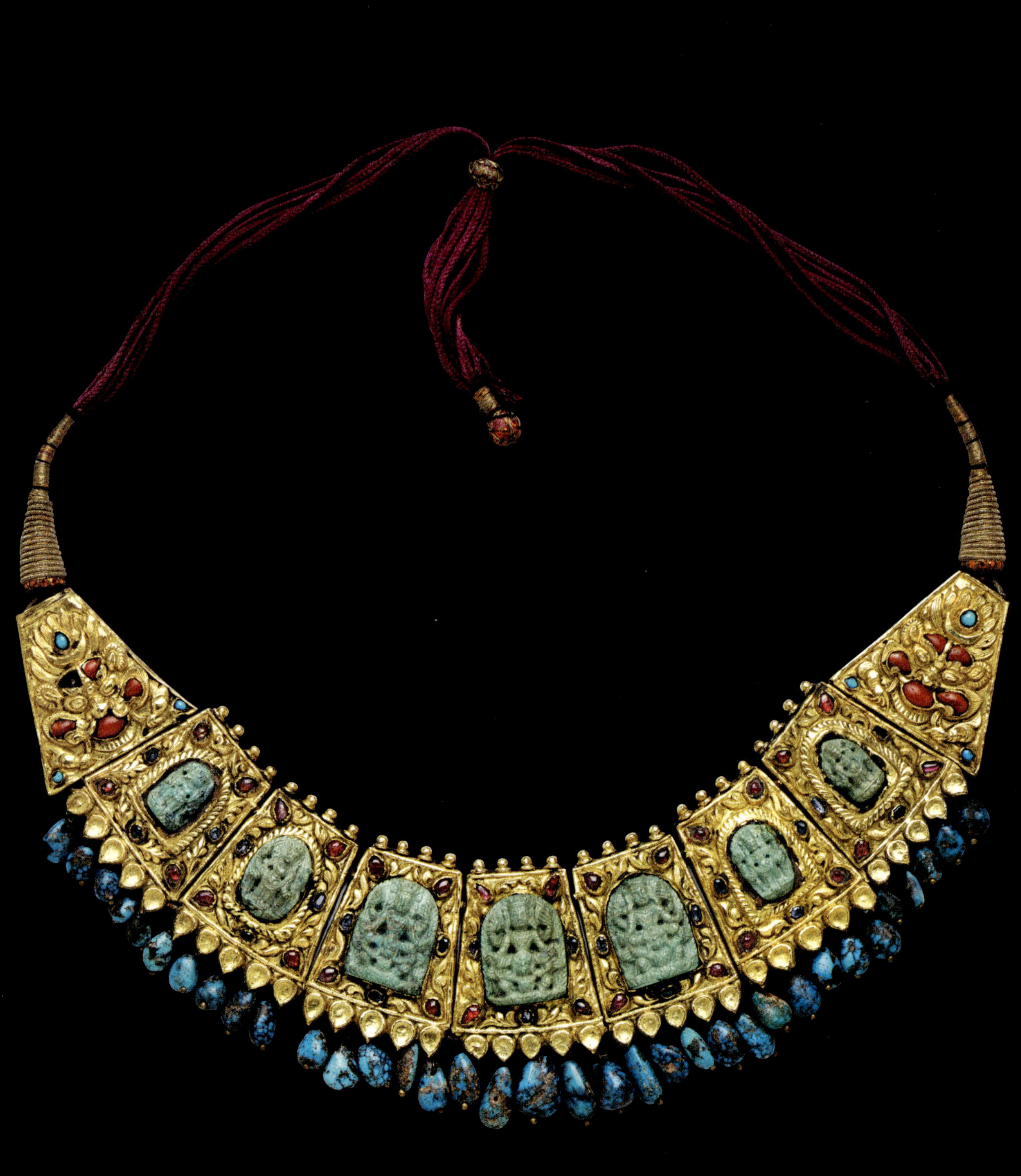

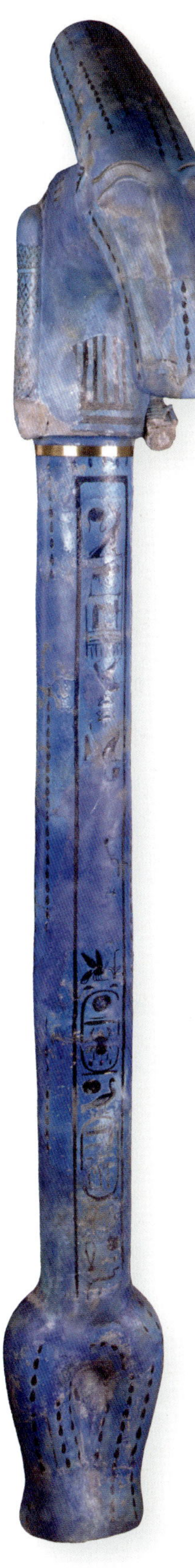

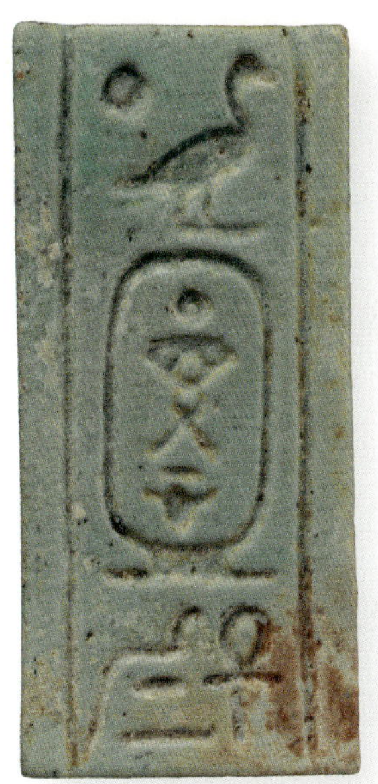

Turquoise is often associated with divinity, and especially deities linked to the sky or heavens. On the far left is the largest known example of ancient faience, a ritual *Was* sceptre (the Egyptian hieroglyphic symbol for power), in turquoise faience with black decoration painted in manganese. It was dedicated to a temple of the god Seth by Pharaoh Amenhotep II. The faience plaque (left) formed part of a royal foundation deposit placed by Pharaoh Apries – himself a living deity – to commemorate the inauguration or expansion of a temple or state building.

The 19th-century ceremonial necklace (*tikma*; opposite) would have been worn by women of the Kathmandu valley, Nepal. The pale inset turquoises are carved with representations of Vishnu, the Hindu god of protection and preservation, on his eagle mount Garuda. A contemporary example of turquoise as the colour of the divine, this brooch by jewellery designer Kevin Coates (below) depicts a seraph, the highest rank of angel, surrounded by a turquoise-coloured titanium border.

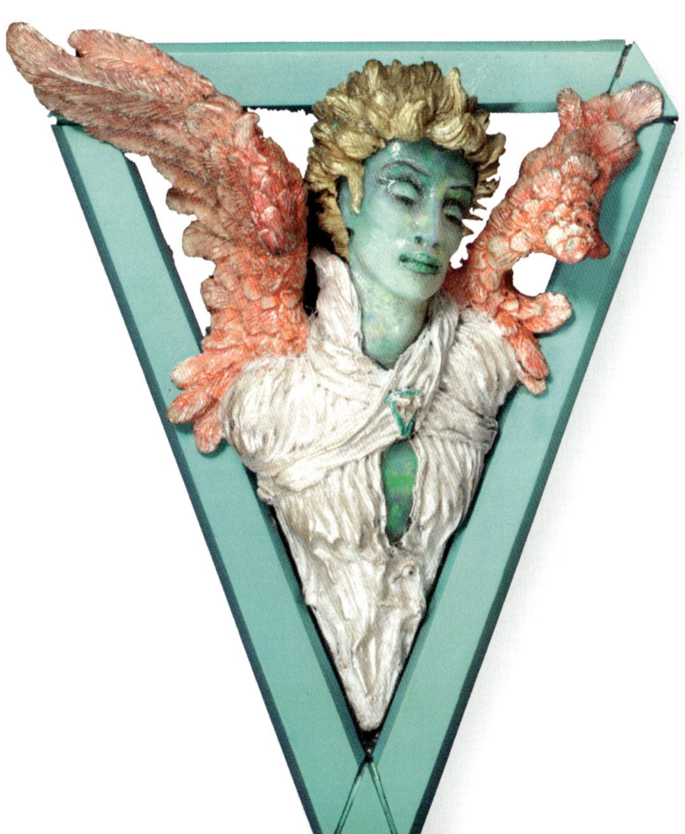

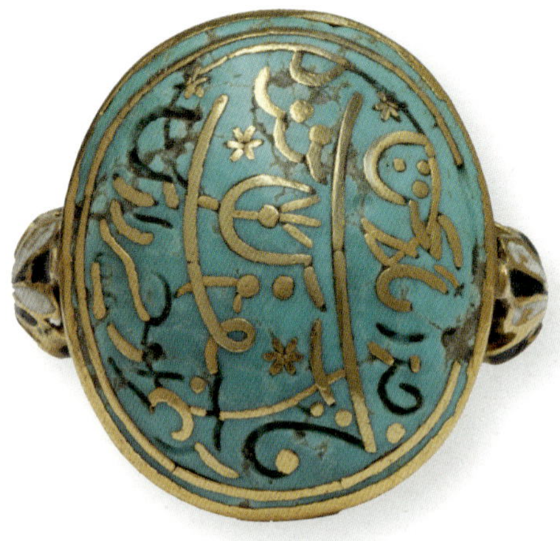

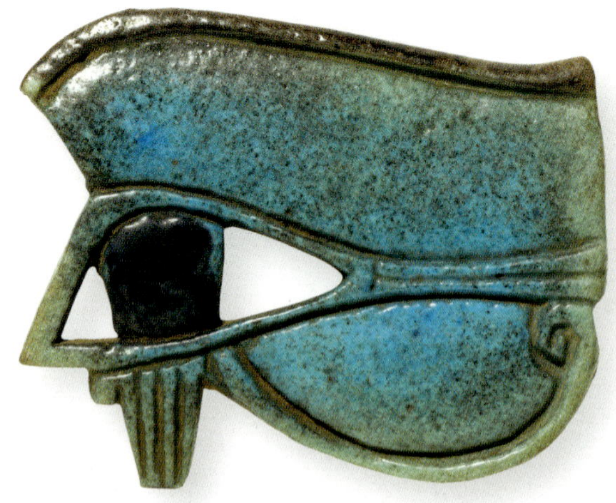

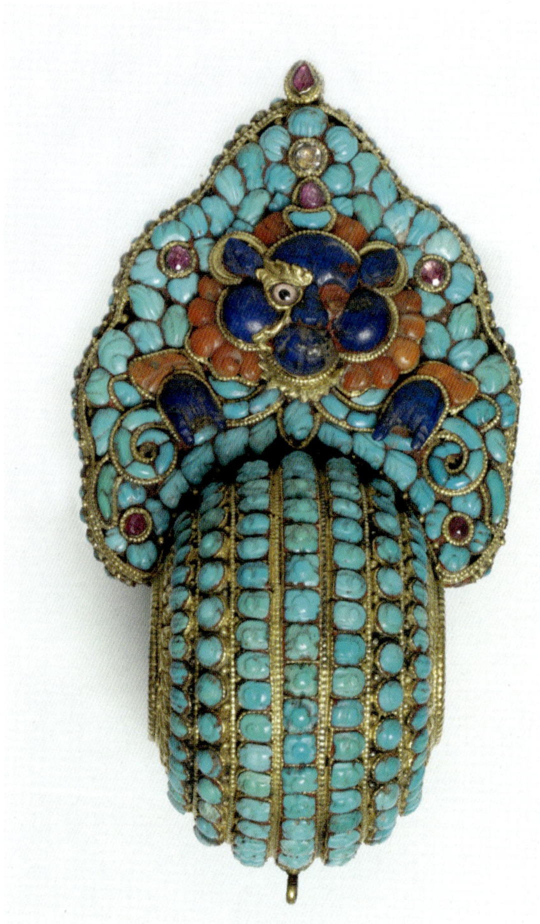

Turquoise is considered an apotropaic – protective – colour, and objects containing or coloured turquoise have often been worn for personal protection. To enhance the stone's natural protective qualities, Islamic turquoise jewellery might include religious or protective phrases. This 17th-century European ring (above left) imitates that principle with a pseudo-inscription emulating Arabic script, inlaid in gold.

The Blue Beryl, a 17th-century Tibetan medical treatise, lists seven types of turquoise by colour. The most vibrant were regarded as 'living' and therefore had life-giving properties. These ceremonial objects (left and opposite) from the 18th or 19th century, an earring and an amulet box (*jantar*) – often used to hold prayers or other protective tokens – both bear a mythical *Chepu*, or monster mask.

In Ancient Egypt, because the colour turquoise was associated with rebirth, it was an ideal colour for funerary goods such as amulets, intended to assist the deceased on their journey to the afterlife and service them there. Amulets such as this one in the form of the Eye of Horus (c. 1075–945 BC, above right) were also worn in life, to protect the bearer on Earth.

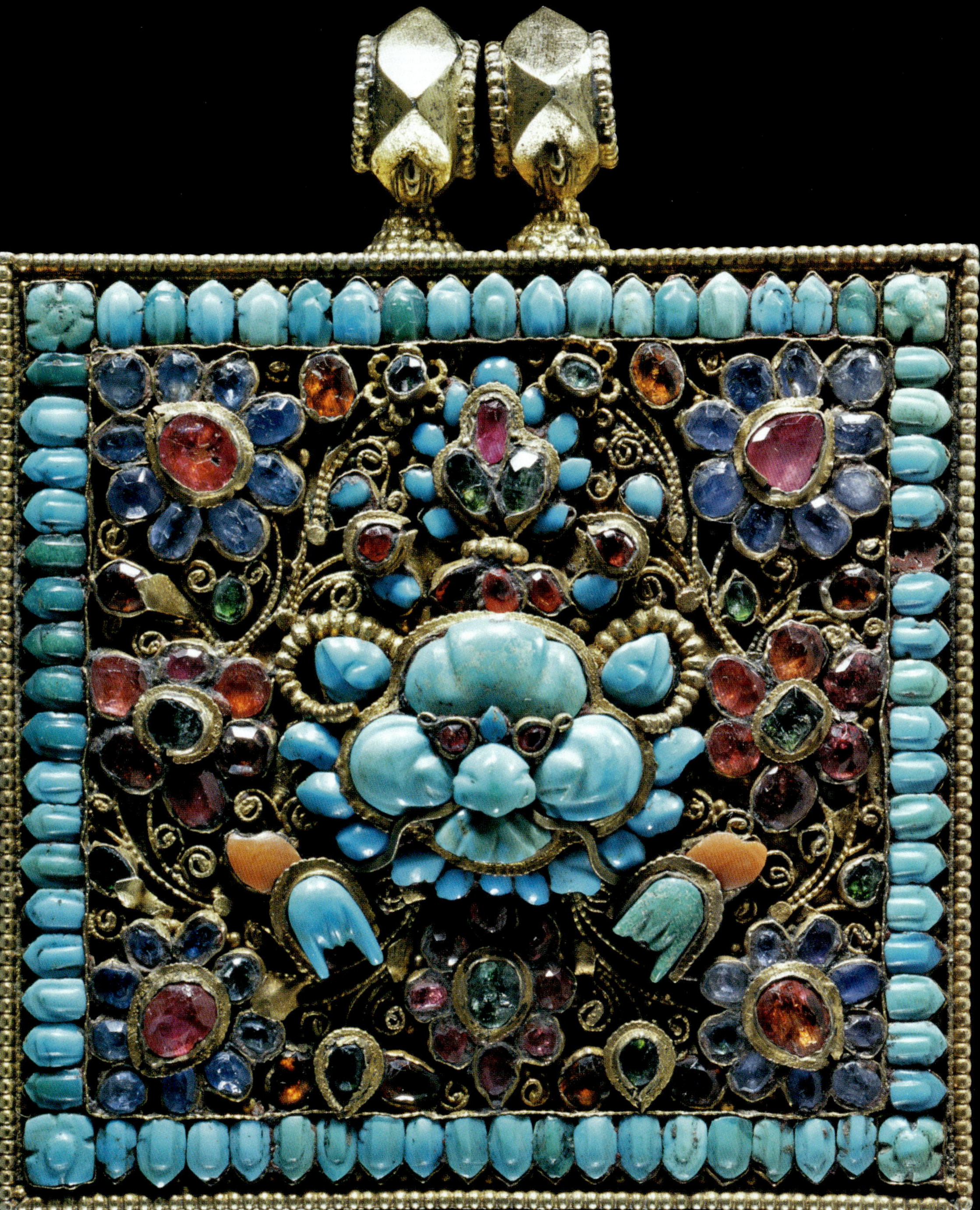

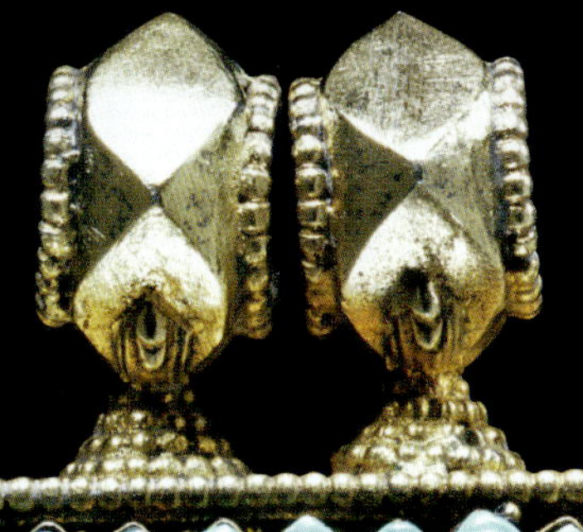

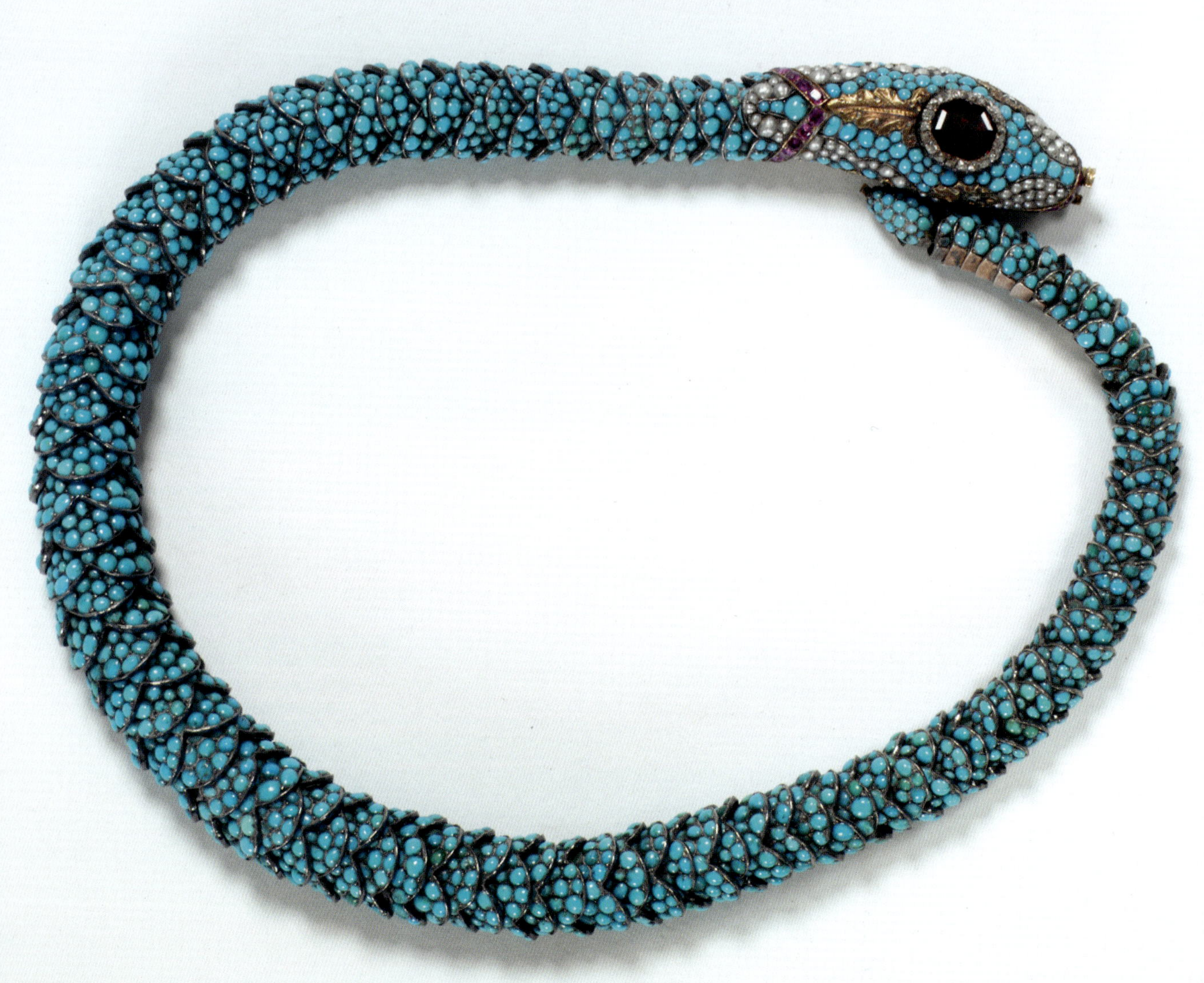

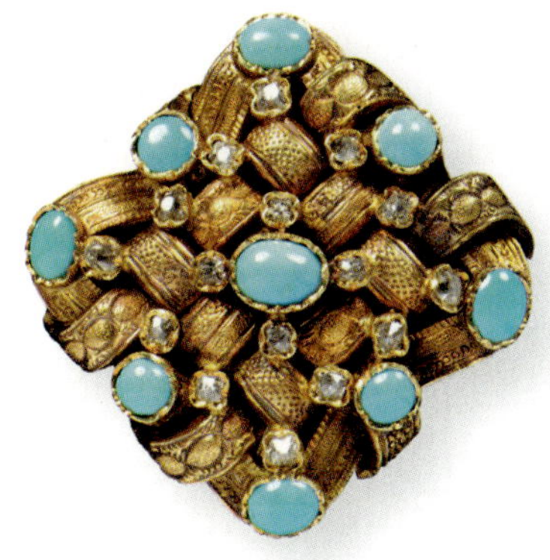

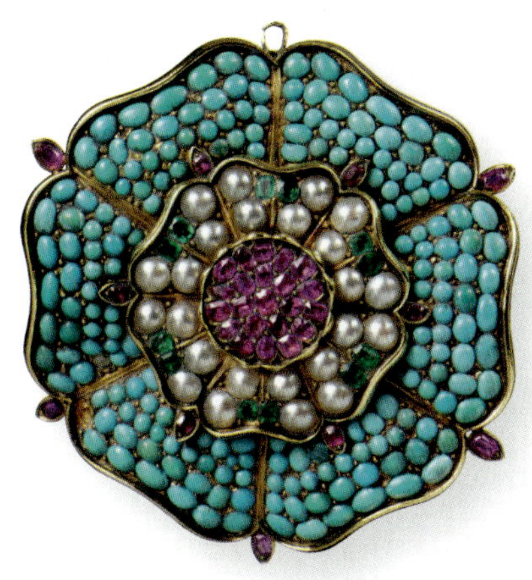

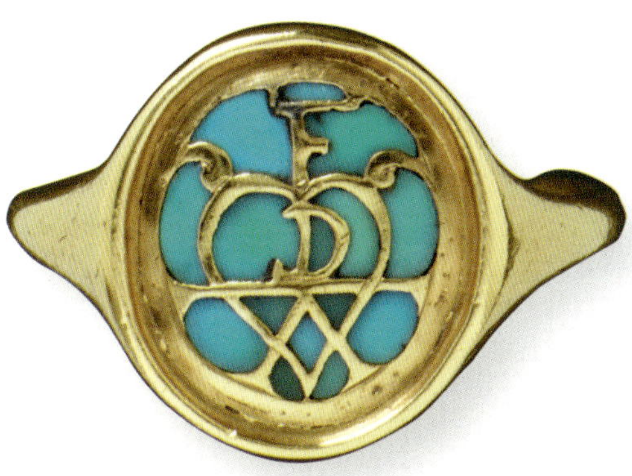

In the Victorian language of flowers, the turquoise forget-me-not symbolized true love. It therefore became a common theme for sentimental jewellery – especially love tokens – in the mid-19th century. A particularly interesting example is this serpent necklace depicting a snake eating its own tail, the ancient *ouroboros* symbol (opposite). Individual nodules of turquoise have been pavé-set into the body, an effect resembling scales. Similar to floral love tokens, the unending circle may have represented eternal love. Two other lavish items of 19th-century English jewellery are a gold brooch in the form of a Tudor rose (above left), set with turquoise, rubies, emeralds and pearls, and another set with diamonds and particularly bright turquoises (top left). The turquoise bezel of an earlier, 16th-century German ring (left) is set with a finely cut gold monogram of the letters 'FDA' and a heart, and probably records a marriage.

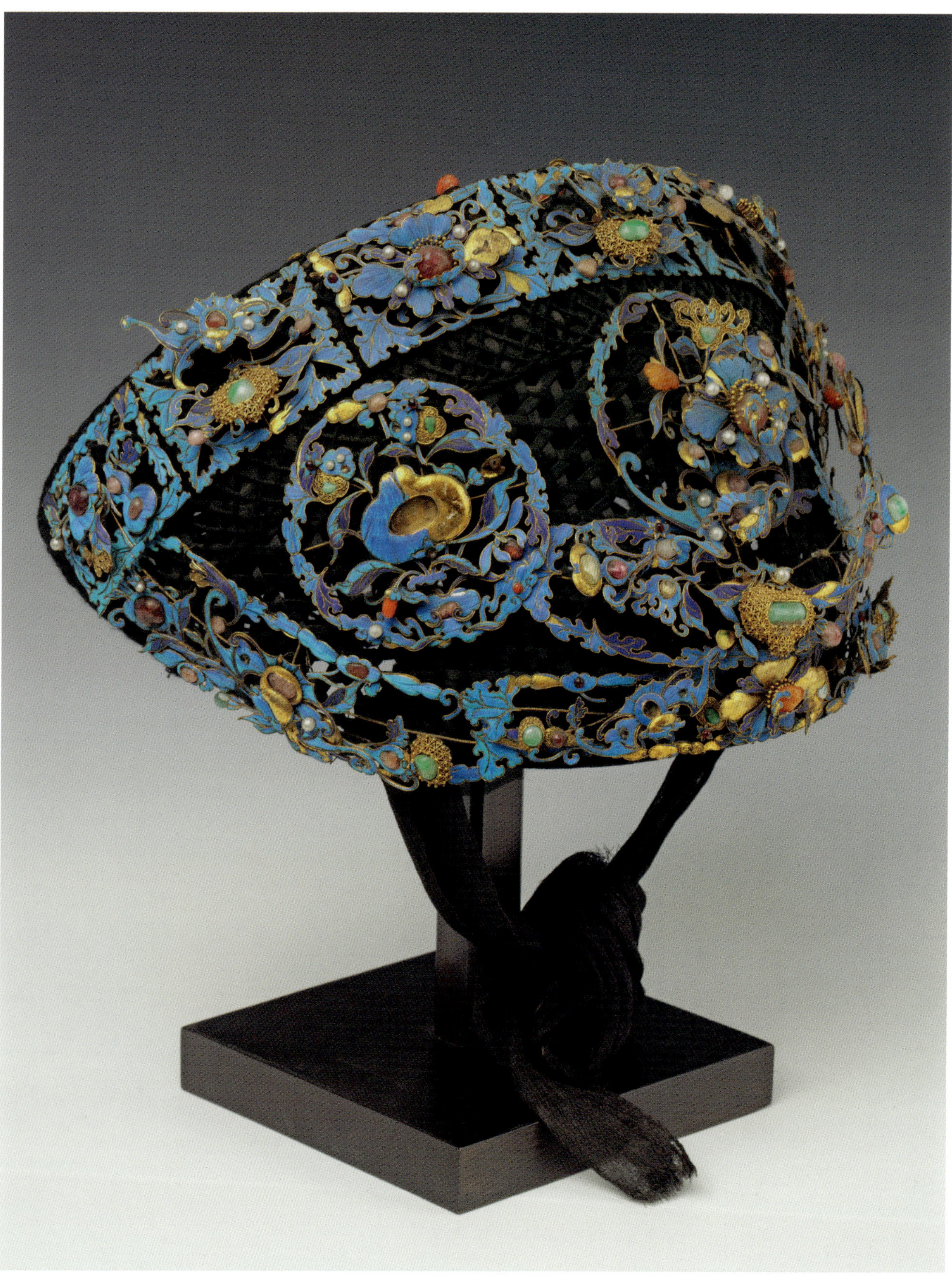

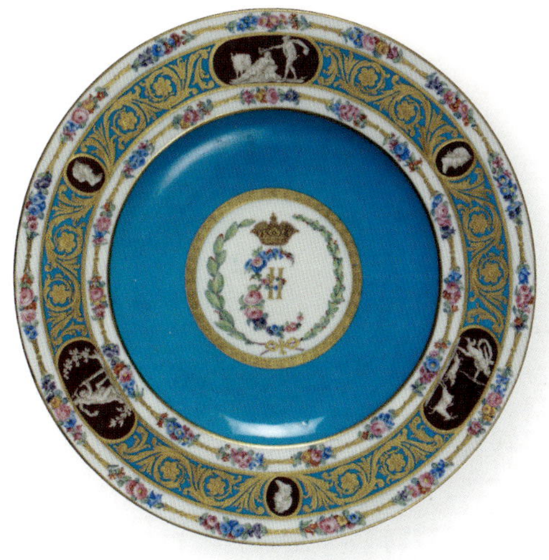

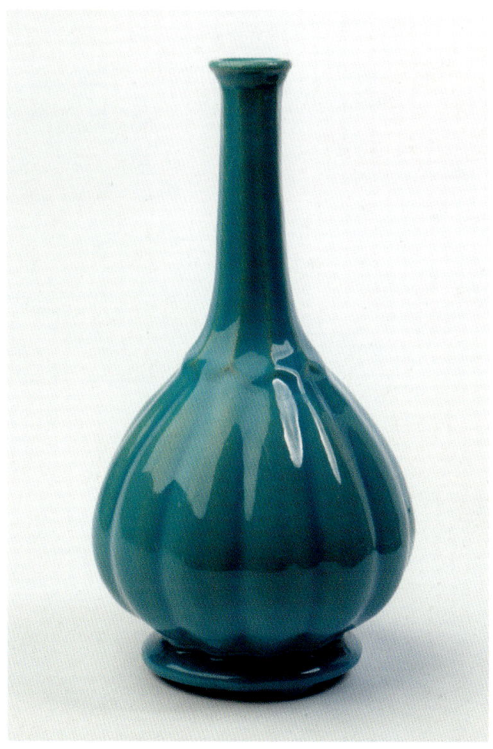

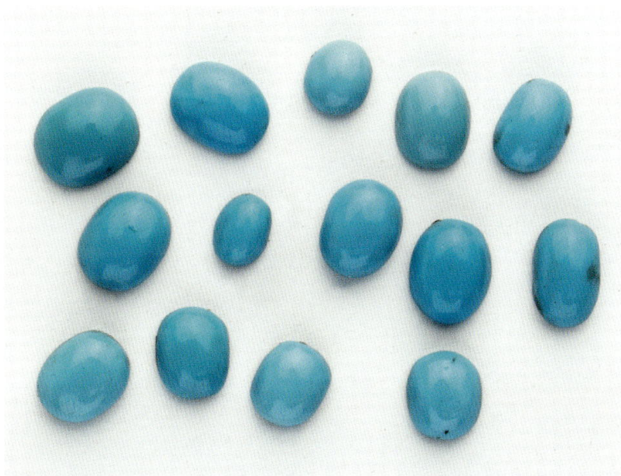

Turquoise for inlay was historically cut *en cabochon* – shaped and polished, but not faceted – as were artificial turquoise substitutes such as this coloured glass from India (c. 1850; left). Boxes covered in turquoise, such as this snuffbox (c. 1820; below left), appear to have been particularly popular in 19th-century Russia. This soup plate (above left) is from one of the most expensive porcelain services ever made at the French porcelain factory Sèvres, commissioned by Catherine the Great, Empress of Russia, in 1776.

Large numbers of Longquan celadon wares from China were traded to the Middle East between the 13th and 15th centuries. Islamic production centres responded by creating imitation pieces with turquoise and green glazes. The carved lobes on this 17th-century bottle (above right) may also imitate the shape of Chinese bottles. The 'Phoenix Crown' headdress (opposite) represents another Chinese use of turquoise colouring, being richly decorated with kingfisher feathers and precious stones. Historically, such crowns were the exclusive preserve of the Empress, although by the 19th century they were also worn by noblewomen.

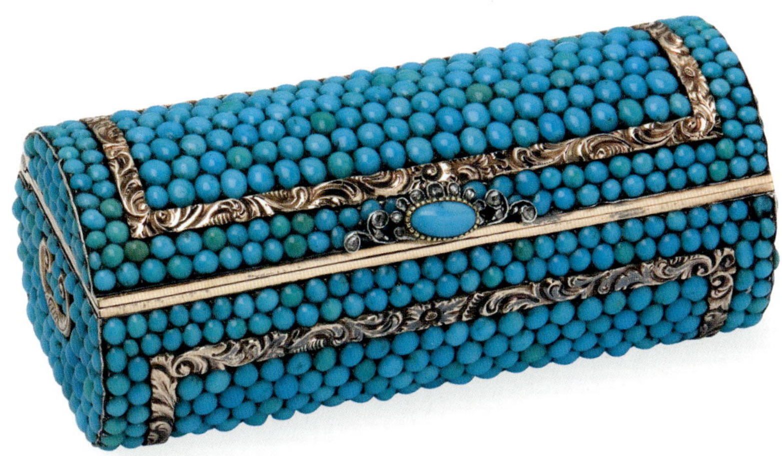

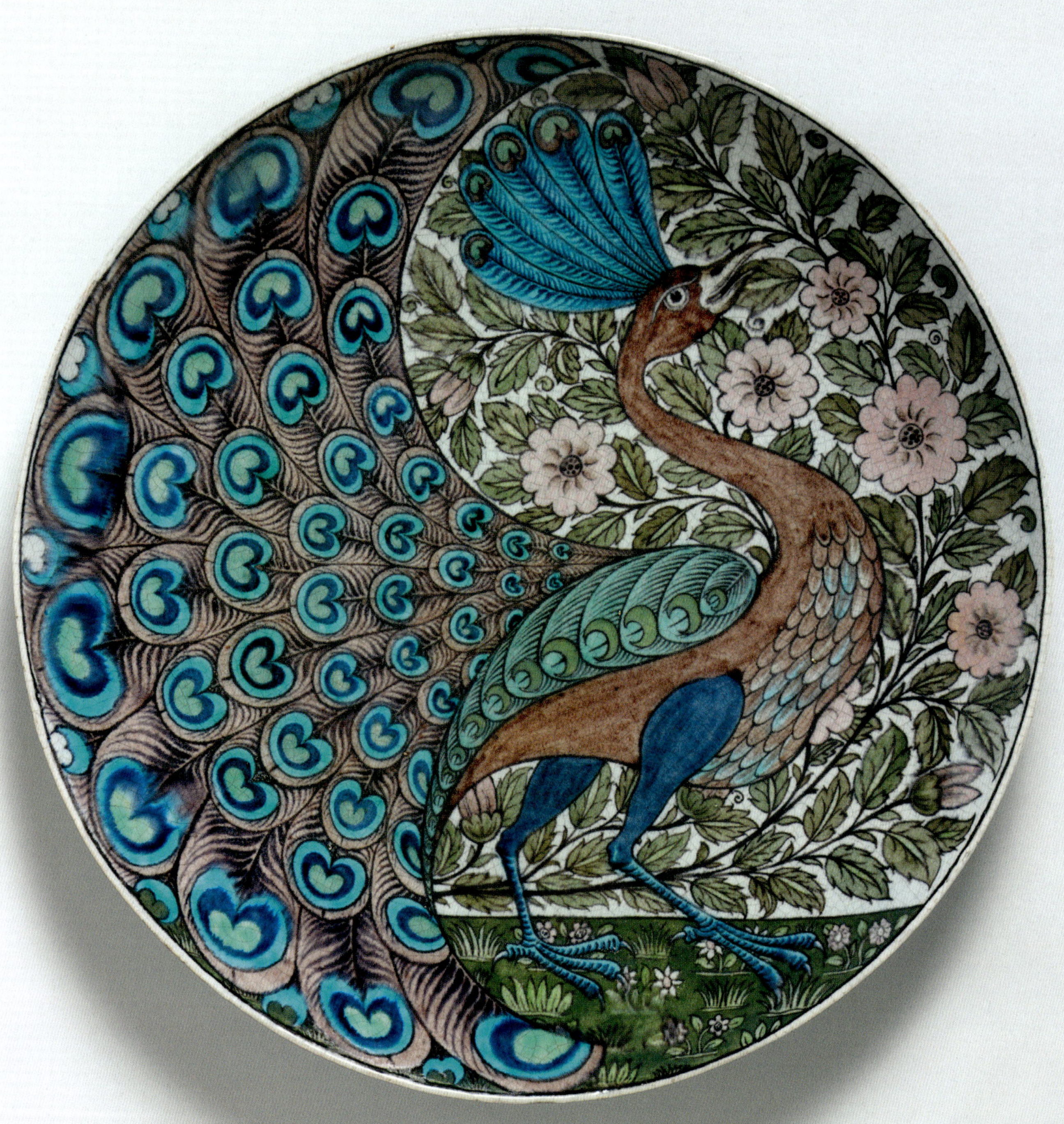

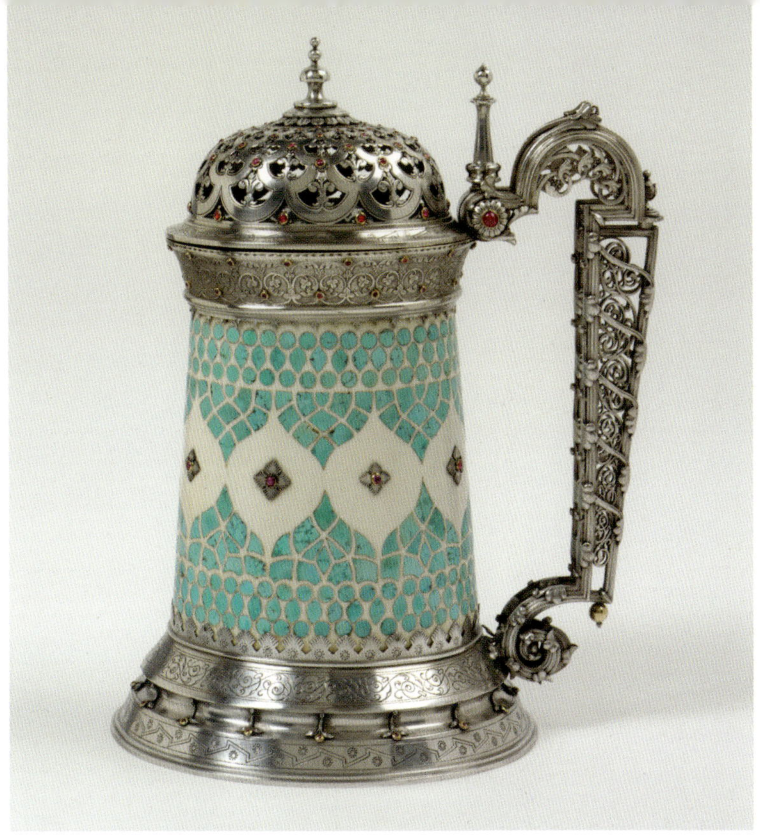

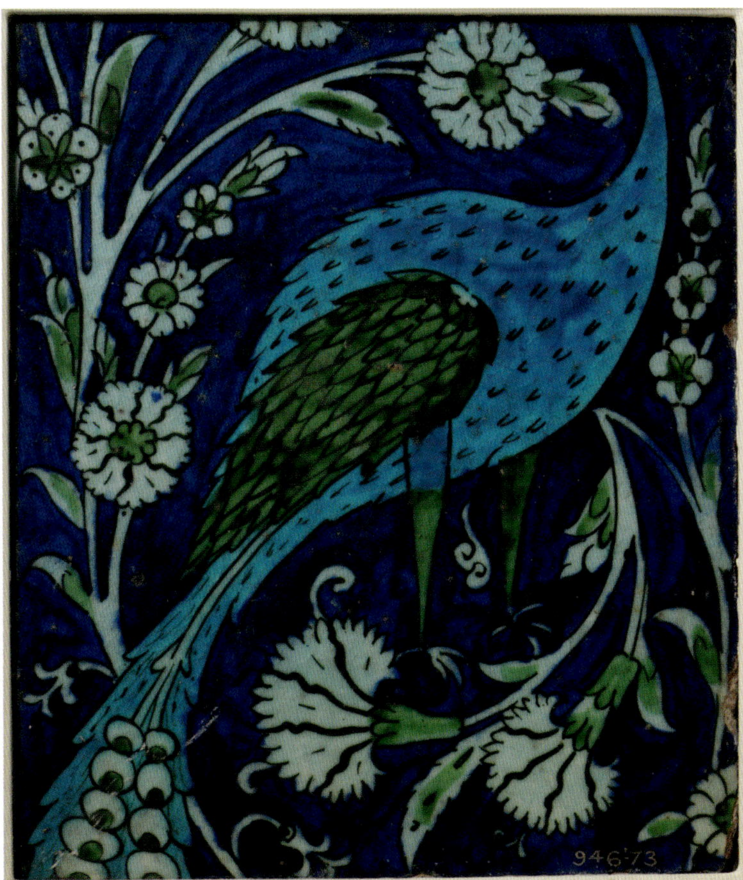

Victorian designers took heavy inspiration from Islamic arts and crafts, and turquoise, or 'Persian blue', formed a core element of their Orientalist colour palette. Tiles from Turkey and Syria, brought back to furnish houses and collections, provided first-hand sources for designers. The 16th-century Syrian tile on the left has a vibrant palette of cobalt blue, turquoise, black and sage green itself derived from Turkish Iznik tilework, and a central design of a peacock. A plate made by William De Morgan (c. 1888–9; opposite) shows a close parallel, with turquoise featured heavily as a spot-colour. The peacock was a particularly important motif to Arts and Crafts designers, and thus tiles such as these were attractive sources.

The tankard above, made by French designer Frédéric-Jules Rudolph in 1855, demonstrates the synthesis of world styles that characterized 19th-century design. Its shape relates to Renaissance forms and the handle draws from early medieval ironwork, but the colours and design of the body are inspired by Middle Eastern or Indian art.

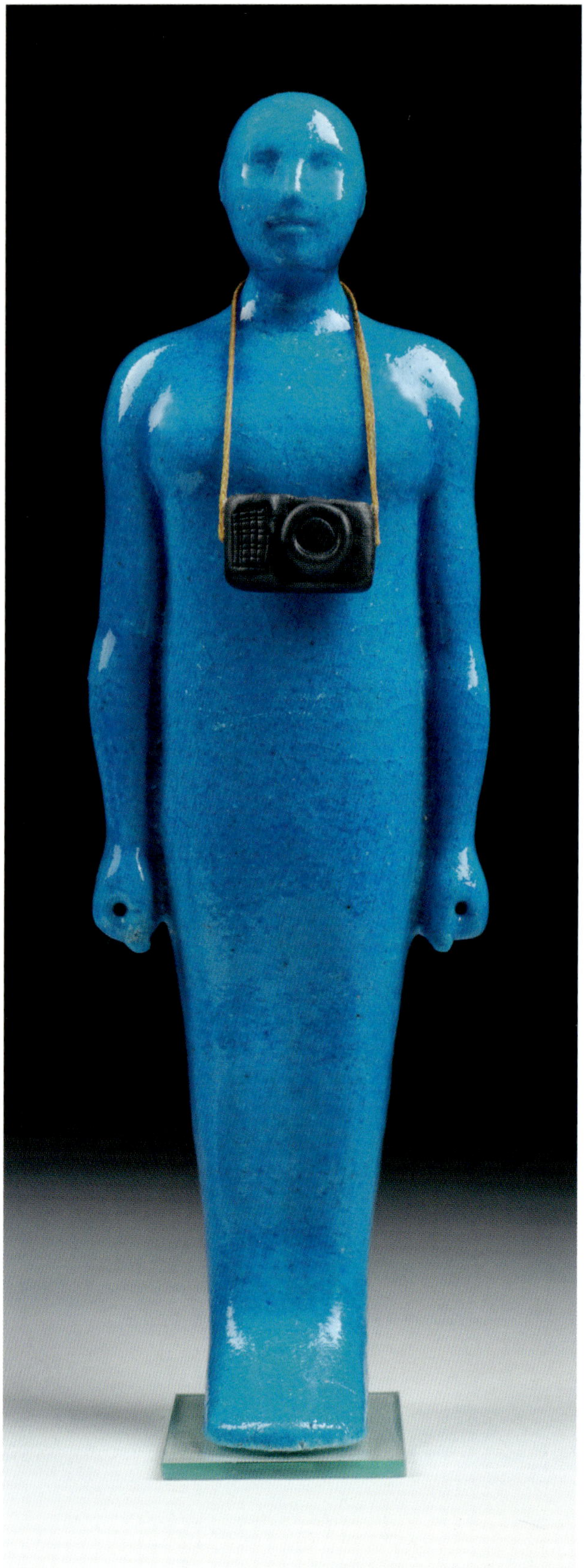

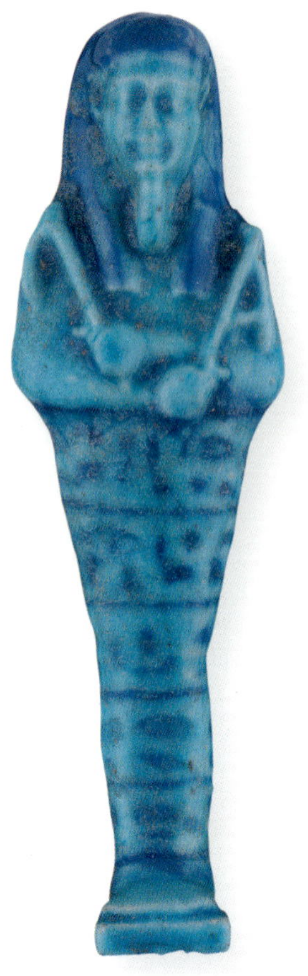

In Ancient Egypt, *shabti*s were typically of turquoise faience; this example (above) is particularly complicated, with an inscription in purple-blue glaze. Zahed Taj-Eddin's *Nu shabtis* (2014; left) are inspired by ancient colours and techniques. *Shabtis* were designed to serve the dead in the afterlife; Taj-Eddin's have awoken in a world with no afterlife, and have chosen to join modern society.

Popular interest in Ancient Egypt increased in the 19th century. This late 19th-century ring (opposite, above left) is inspired by ancient scarabs such as this example (opposite, above right), which is made not of faience but blue-glazed steatite. The discovery of Tutankhamun's tomb in 1922 sparked another worldwide craze for Egypt in art and design. The colours gold and turquoise became synonymous with the boy king, and jewellery and fashion tapped into the craze. This Cartier box (opposite, bottom) is a particularly high-end example.

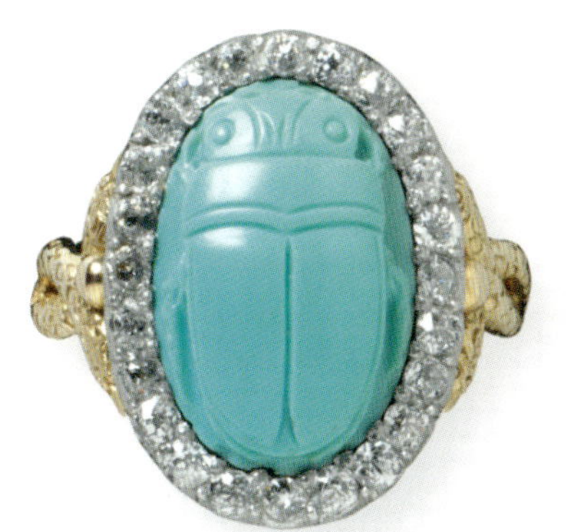

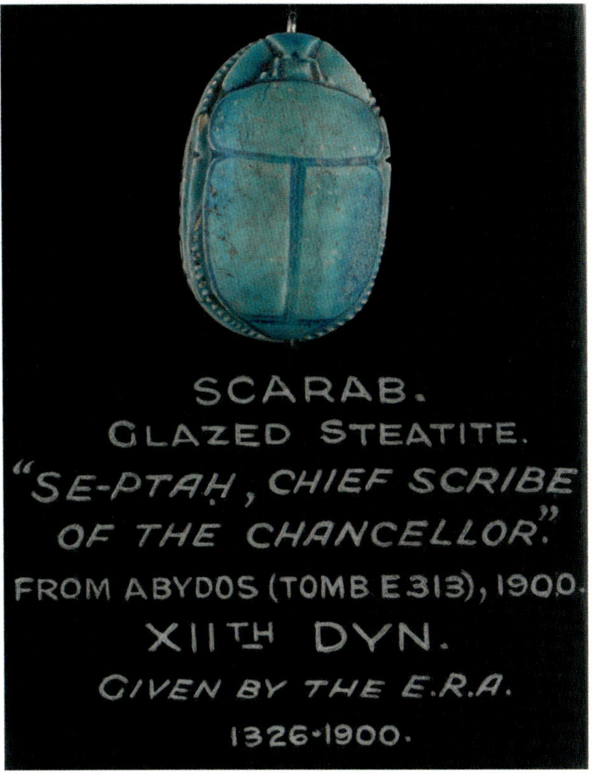
SCARAB.
GLAZED STEATITE.
"SE-PTAH, CHIEF SCRIBE
OF THE CHANCELLOR".
FROM ABYDOS (TOMB E313), 1900.
XIITH DYN.
GIVEN BY THE E.R.A.
1326·1900.

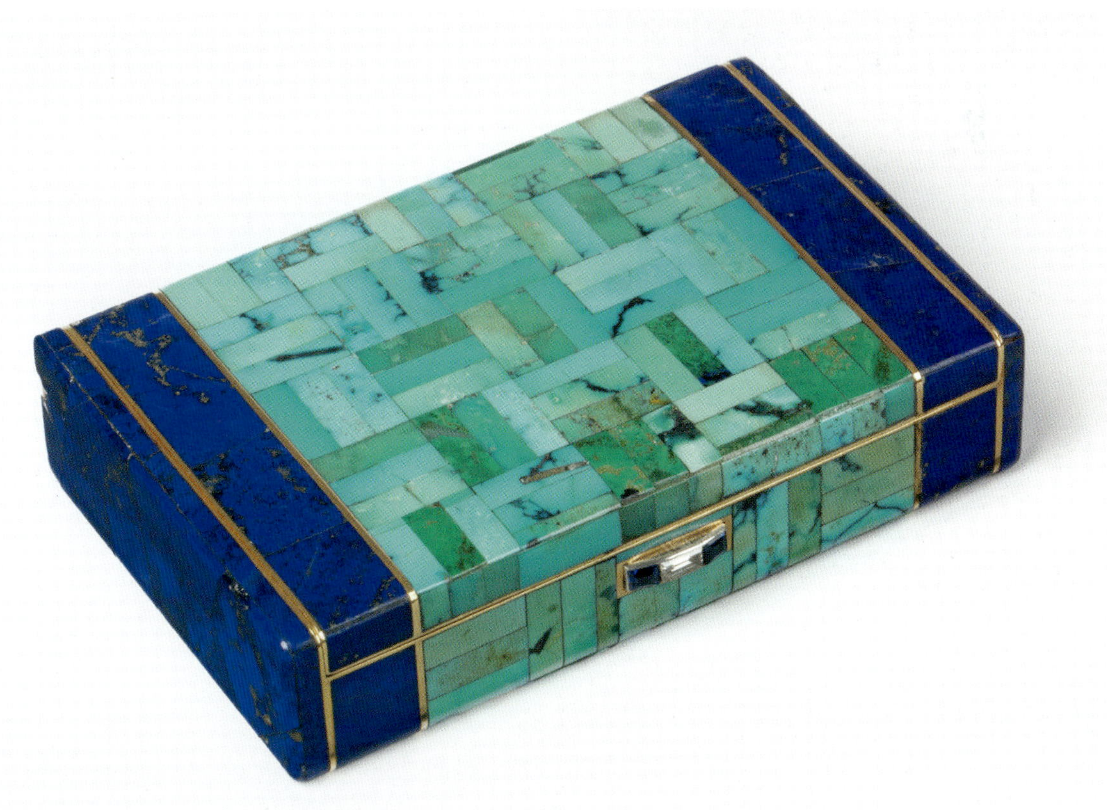

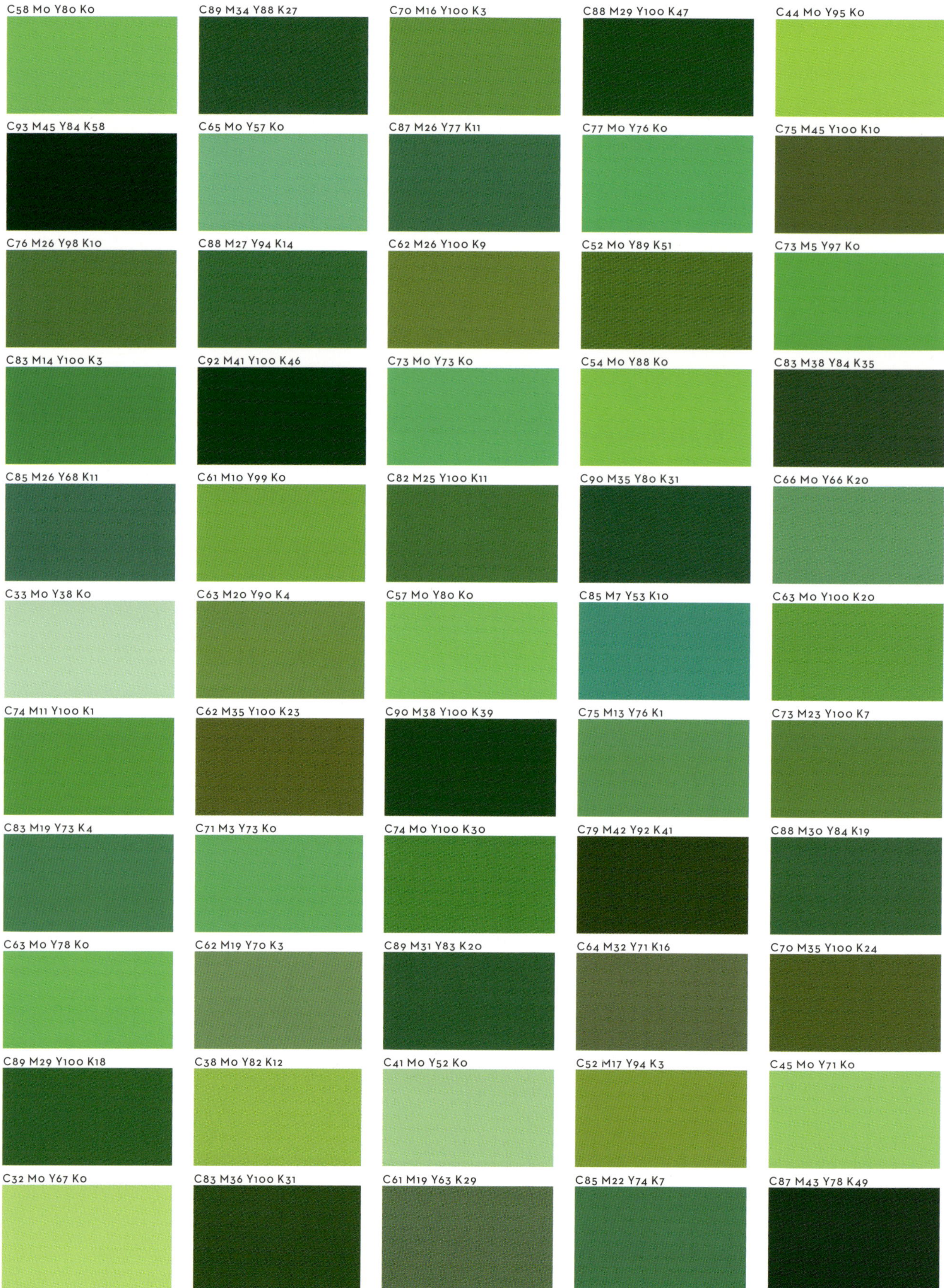

GREEN

Today green is widely associated with nature, the environment and sustainability. But the history and cultural symbolism associated with the colour is much more complex. In Europe, green has been the colour of love and luck but also of envy, poison and devilry.

Puzzlingly, despite its abundance in nature green is a very challenging colour to reproduce. On the artist's palette, it is a secondary colour produced by mixing yellow and blue. The same principle is applied when creating natural dyes, using blue woad or indigo and yellow weld. It is notoriously difficult to produce natural green dyes that are consistent. They fade very easily, as the dye from the yellow weld plant is incredibly light sensitive; this explains why blue, rather than green, foliage may appear in old tapestries and other textiles. During the Middle Ages, the dyeing industry was strictly regulated in some European countries, limiting the mixing of green dyes. This was due to a combination of guild interests and a dislike for what was believed to be the inherent demonic and alchemical properties associated with the production of green dye.

By contrast, the Islamic world has found green to be consistently positive. The Prophet Muhammad showed a preference for the colour, and it is the colour of the dome built over his tomb in Medina. In the Qur'an green is mentioned a number of times, including a description of the fine silks and brocades worn by the people of Paradise. It is conceivable that the positive association with green in the Islamic world spurred the trend for importing, and later imitating, a particular type of Chinese green ceramics. In 1171, a sultan by the name of Saladin sent such wares as a gift to the Sultan of Damascus. In Europe,

the colour of these wares were given the name 'celadon'. Characterized by a greenish-grey glaze resembling light-coloured nephrite jade, a precious and auspicious material in Chinese culture, these wares were highly sought after both within and beyond Chinese borders. Celadon is a tricky term, as there is no singular criteria for it. Present-day classification may be judged by factors such as the colour, glaze or particular type of ware. The range of glaze shades run from a transparent olive green to opaque bluish-green, and is dependent on factors such as the kiln atmosphere. Celadon had reached south-east Asia and the Middle East before it came to Europe. The Iranian fritware dish on p. 229, which dates between 1450 and 1550, demonstrates the long-standing admiration for and desire to imitate celadon.

Moving below the surface of the earth, beyond the roots of trees and other plants, we find many more stunning greens. Valuable minerals have provided the artist, stone carver and jeweller with an abundance of creative opportunity. Gemstones such as emerald may be cut into sparkling jewellery, while semi-precious stones such as jade, bowenite and malachite may be carved into decorative objects or even monumental works such as the malachite vase on p. 240, measuring over 2 metres (83½ in.) tall. This vase was exhibited alongside its pair by the Russian Government at the Great Exhibition of 1851 in London's Hyde Park. It was made to a fashionable design known as the 'Medici', named after the notoriously wealthy Florentine dynasty, and was displayed as an impressive example of Russian craftsmanship and a luxurious celebration of the country's mineral wealth. Vases of a similar design, made in a variety of materials and sizes, were very popular at the time; but here the link between green, wealth and good fortune seems to resonate particularly.

Ironically, although green has been imbued with these positive connotations, their complete opposites – feelings of envy, jealousy and desire so easily prompted by the wealth and luck of others – may also be associated with the colour. Shakespeare famously draws the link between green and envy in his play *Othello*, in which the tragic hero, who strangles his wife, Desdemona, for imagined adultery, is warned about giving in to the 'green-ey'd monster' of jealousy that will be his eventual downfall. Desire and jealousy bring destruction, it would seem. Certainly, we are increasingly aware of this as regards humanity's relationship to nature: our desire for its beauty and resources has seen us mimic, consume and exploit it to the point of extinction.

Our growing awareness of humanity's impact on nature is changing the way we think about consumption. A twenty-first-century response to an advertisement placed on 16 October 1867 in the *Public Ledger and Daily Advertiser*, reporting a single shipment of 25,000 wing cases from the jewel beetle (*Buprestidae*), may differ dramatically to contemporary attitudes. Indian fabrics embellished with jewel beetle-wing cases became popular export products for the European market in the nineteenth century. Examples were displayed at the Great Exhibition of 1851 and in Britain it became fashionable to embellish dresses and cloth with jewel beetle-wing cases in decorative patterns, as seen on p. 239. Subsequently, huge shipments of jewel beetle wings allowed dressmakers in Britain to copy the technique. The wings are attractive for their iridescence; their shiny, light-reflective surface, together with the silver-gilt metal thread used in *zardozi* embellishments, would have given a glowing, glistening quality to any garment. Beetle wings can change their colour over time, moving away from shimmering emerald green to a blue-violet iridescence not unlike the colours of an oil spill.

In 1775, the Swedish scientist Carl Wilhelm Scheele made a chance discovery of a synthetic green pigment that would come to influence fashion, commerce and health in Europe throughout the nineteenth century. Quick to capitalize on his discovery, the pigment, known as Scheele's green, was set into production and used in wallpapers, fabrics and colour pigments for artists and the food industry. The vibrance of Scheele's green proved a great commercial success. Variations of this brilliant colour were developed during the nineteenth century, promising fashionable status, wealth and conquest with names such as Paris green, emerald green and imperial green. The common denominators in production of these greens were copper and arsenic – but the vibrant shades were so fashionable that the small matter of their poisonous nature was long trivialized.

The matter of poisoning by arsenic wallpaper entered public debate in the nineteenth century. Interior designer and social activist William Morris of Morris & Co. was, like many, puzzled by the fact that only some people were affected. A scientific explanation was offered in 1891 by Italian medical scientist Bartolomeo Gosio. He suggested that a poisonous gas would vaporize from arsenic wallpapers only when exposed to damp conditions.

Arsenic was also present in the millinery and artificial flower-making trades, where workers were especially vulnerable to arsenic poisoning, experiencing symptoms ranging from painful skin sores to excruciating deaths. Arsenic was used as a pesticide for plumage, and pigments containing arsenic were used to colour foliage in the quest to produce fanciful trimmings and headdresses. These industries were the focus of a number of medical inquiries, which helped, at long last, to pave the way for legislation by the end of the century. Yet the legacy of green as a source of bad luck lives on in the haute couture industry. In her book *Fashion Victims: The Dangers of Dress Past and Present* (2015) fashion historian Alison Matthews David notes that in a 2005 documentary on the fashion house Chanel, the première main Madame Dominique states 'seamstresses don't like green'.

The appearance of pigments containing copper and arsenic can prove useful to the dating of a work, as the case of a medieval-style manuscript illumination depicting Susannah and the Elders (p. 226) shows. The artistic style and historic representation used in the illumination, especially Susannah's pose, which copies that of Botticelli's

Birth of Venus, do not make sense. If the illumination was in fact medieval, it would have been made at least a century before Botticelli painted his iconic Venus in the mid-1480s. Here, scientific analysis, in particular that of the colour green, was instrumental in sorting fact from fiction. Tests showed that 'None of the traditional medieval pigments (green earth, verdigris, malachite, atacamite and the other copper chlorides, brochantite, etc.) was detected … only Scheele's green and emerald green were found'. In other words, the illumination of Susannah surrounded by lush foliage is not medieval. Instead it is thought to be the work of the 'Spanish Forger', a prolific but little-known individual believed to have been active in the late nineteenth and early twentieth centuries.

Arsenic was just one problematic ingredient used in the quest for ever-newer and more desirable green goods. Recipes for glass and glazes containing the radioactive metal uranium, which had been discovered in 1798 by the German chemist Martin Heinrich Klaproth, were developed during the nineteenth century. For glass, the result was typically wares ranging in shades from yellow to green, with a fluorescent glow when exposed to ultraviolet light. Although it seems likely that uranium glass recipes were developed by multiple glassworks at the same time, it is nonetheless often the glassmaker Josef Riedel who has the (now dubious) honour of being credited as among the first to successfully produce it. He famously called his green uranium glass Annagrün (see p. 229) and the yellow Annagelb, in honour of his wife, Anna. Green glass in itself was nothing new. In several European languages the shade 'bottle green' testifies to a long-standing association between the colour and material; but how this came about is difficult to pinpoint. Research certainly suggests that substances kept in coloured glass bottles may be either better preserved or more likely spoiled depending on the colour of the glass. In mid-seventeenth century Europe a very dark green or brown glass termed 'black glass' was discovered through coal-fired furnace production. The dark, light-excluding glass was found to be ideal for storing wine.

More recently, green has become the champion colour of things considered to be good and healthy. It is the dominant colour in the ecology flag, adverts for Earth Day and recycling signage. It has been adopted by political parties, federations and activist groups across the globe advocating for environmental legislation, from Greenpeace to Die Grünen. In *The Secret Lives of Colour* (2018), Kassia St Clair argues that green first became the response colour to environmental awareness in America, from whence it spread. The awakening moment was a disastrous oil spill in Santa Barbara, California, in 1969. As always, design and manufacture was quick to catch on. Dark olive and avocado shades joined the moodboard of the 1970s, infiltrating homes and colouring everything from electrical goods to clothing. Fresher tones eventually came into fashion, but the essential colour and symbolism remains the same. If the story of green tells us anything, it is perhaps our ability to embrace opposing ideas about one and the same thing. We are quick to forget, to renew and reconfigure cultural and symbolic meanings. Fickle as we are, one wonders when green will once again fall out of favour – as Project Runway presenter and supermodel Heidi Klum reminds us, 'in fashion, one day you're in, the next day you're out.'

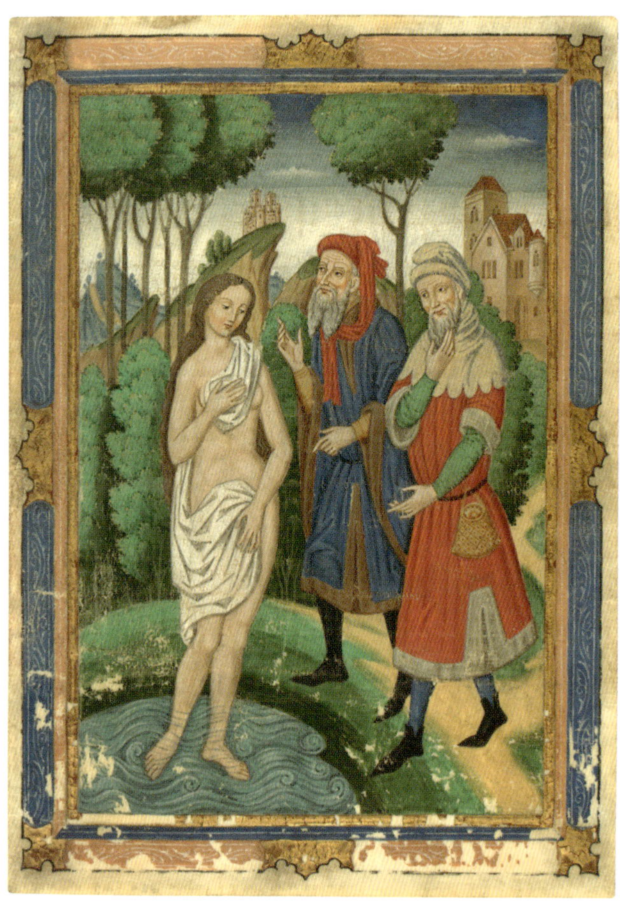

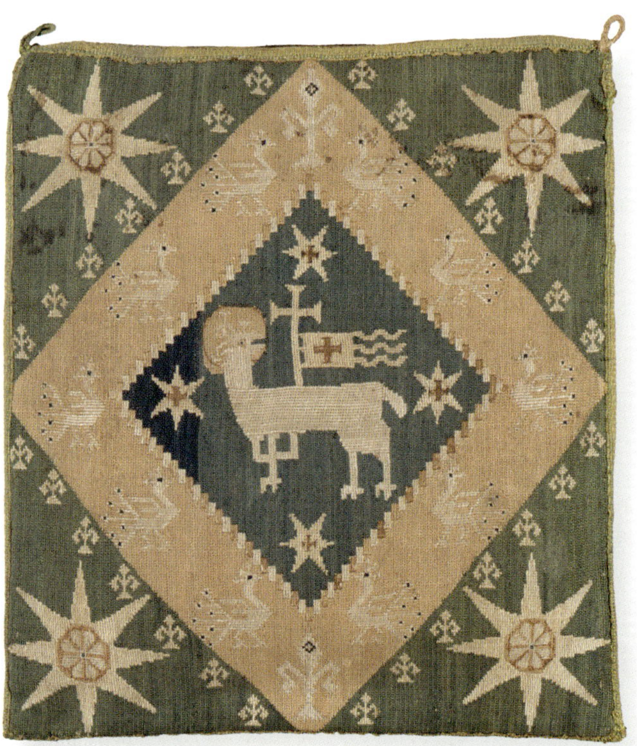

Historically, green was seen as a fleeting colour. Dyed by dipping fabric in natural blue and then yellow plant dyes, green cloth inevitably faded through exposure to sunlight, as seen in this English burse (left), embroidered with coloured silks and edged in green braid, made between 1290 and 1340. In contrast, the floral pattern on Mrs Garrick's painted silk dress (c. 1735–65; opposite) remains, the lasting green pigment made from malachite. Woven and painted in China for the European market, the silk's design reflects British rococo taste interpreted by Chinese craftsmen of the Qianlong period, from British textile samples supplied by the East India Company.

This leaf of an apparently medieval illuminated manuscript, 'Susannah and the Elders' (above left), is now known to be a fake created by the 'Spanish Forger' in about 1900. The forgery was exposed by the maker's use of more resilient green pigments only discovered after 1778.

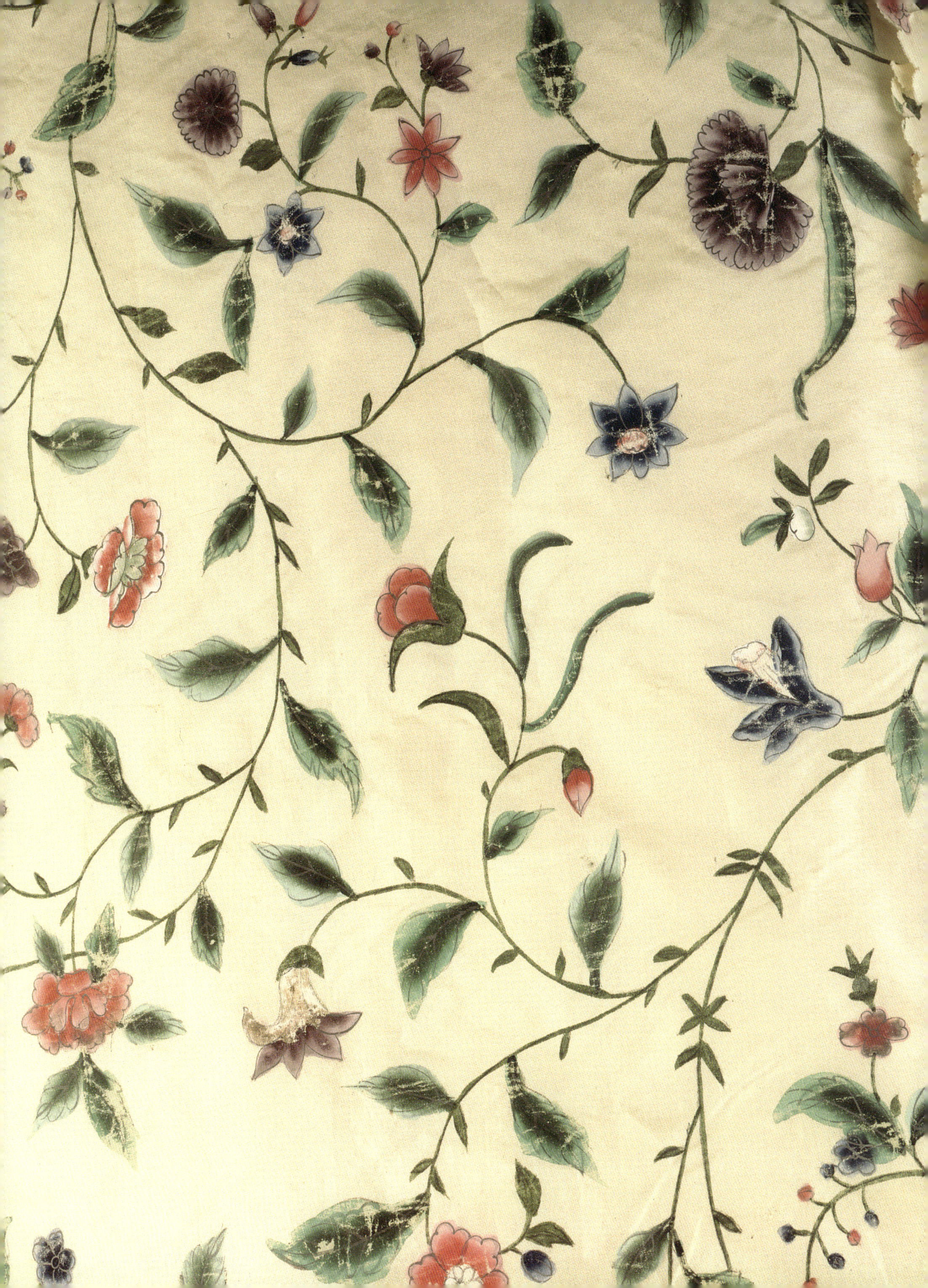

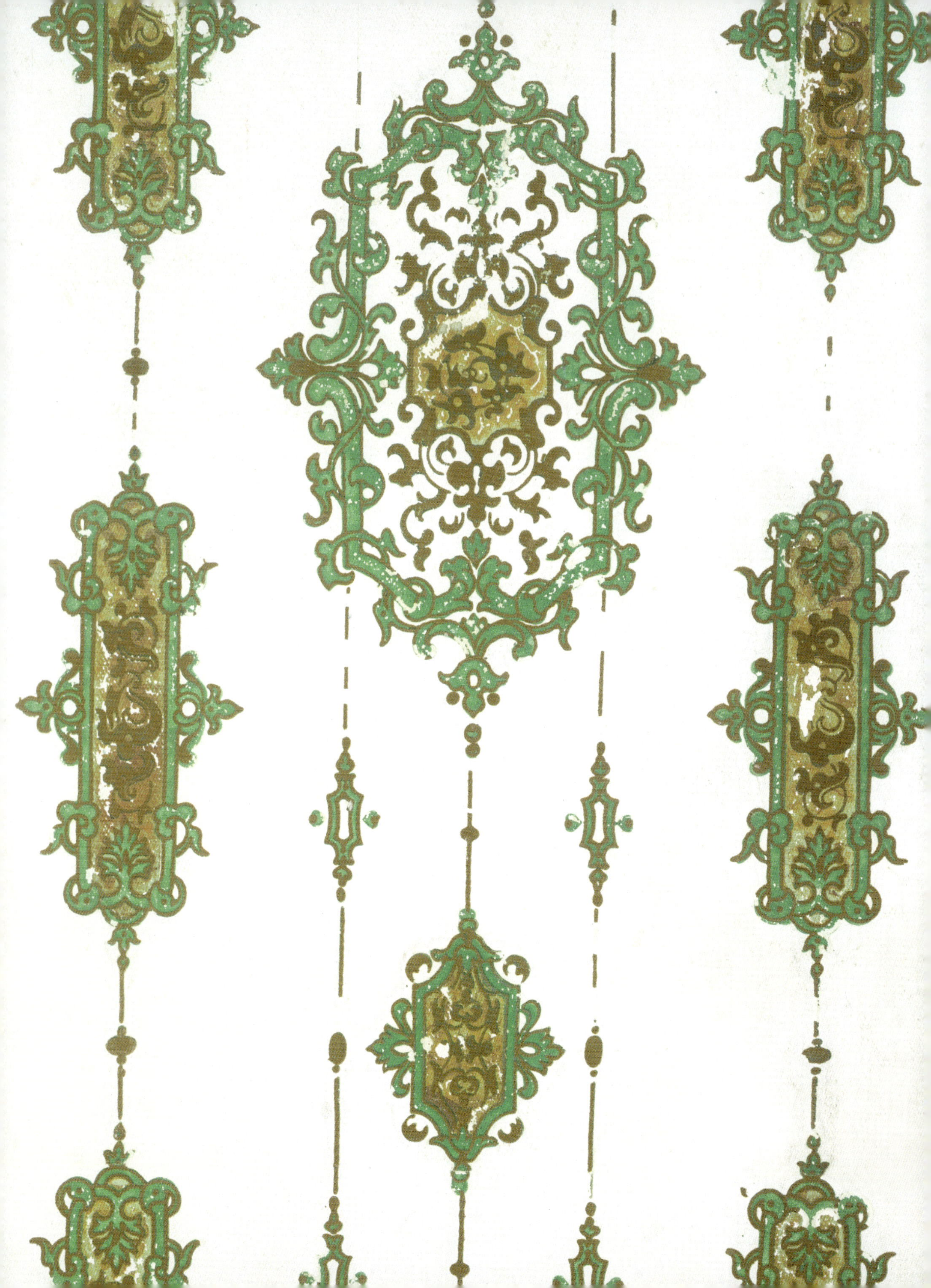

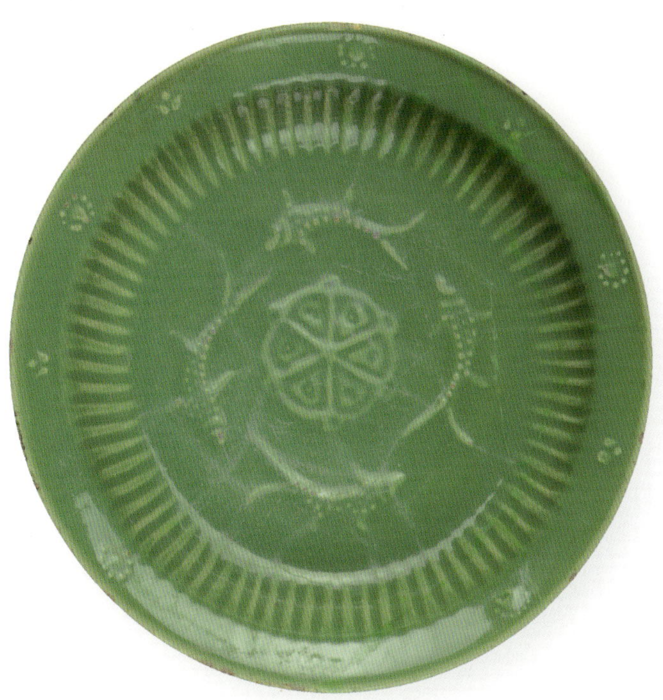

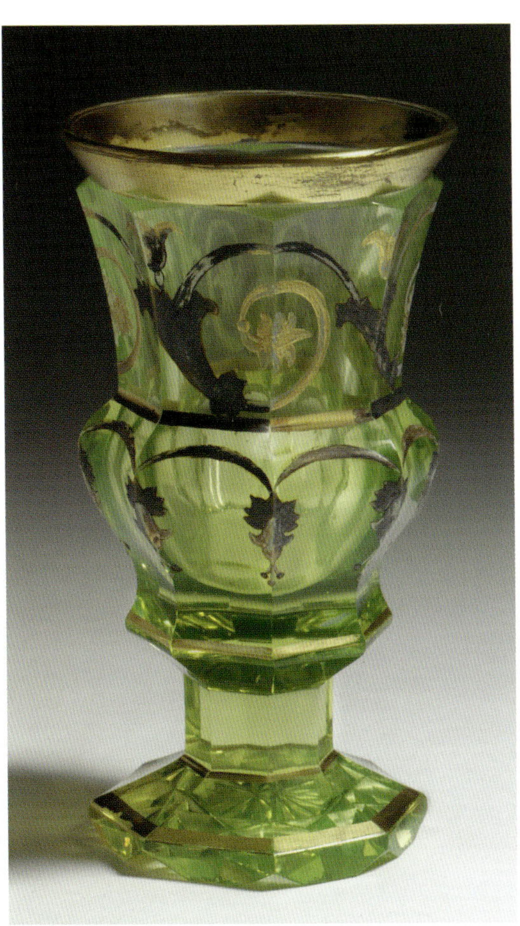

Green-glazed porcelain ceramics imported from China were much prized in the Middle East during the 14th and 15th centuries, as they were believed to change colour in the presence of poison. This fritware dish (above) with moulded relief fish decoration was made in Iran between 1450 and 1550, in imitation of 14th-century Chinese celadon or Longquan ware. Fritware was developed by Middle Eastern potters to challenge the import of Chinese porcelain.

In 19th-century Europe, green's protective associations were inverted as the poisonous nature of pigments such as Scheele's green (copper arsenite) and fluorescent green Annagrün glass (radioactive uranium) became known. Scheele's green, discovered by Carl Scheele in 1775, was vibrant in colour and relatively inexpensive. It was common in 19th-century household decoration, such as this arabesque pattern wallpaper (opposite) from Cranford House in Scheele's green with brown flock, before its devastating effects were known. This Annagrün glass goblet (left), the glass recipe containing radioactive uranium, was probably created by Josef Riedel at his Isergebirge glassworks between 1835 and 1845.

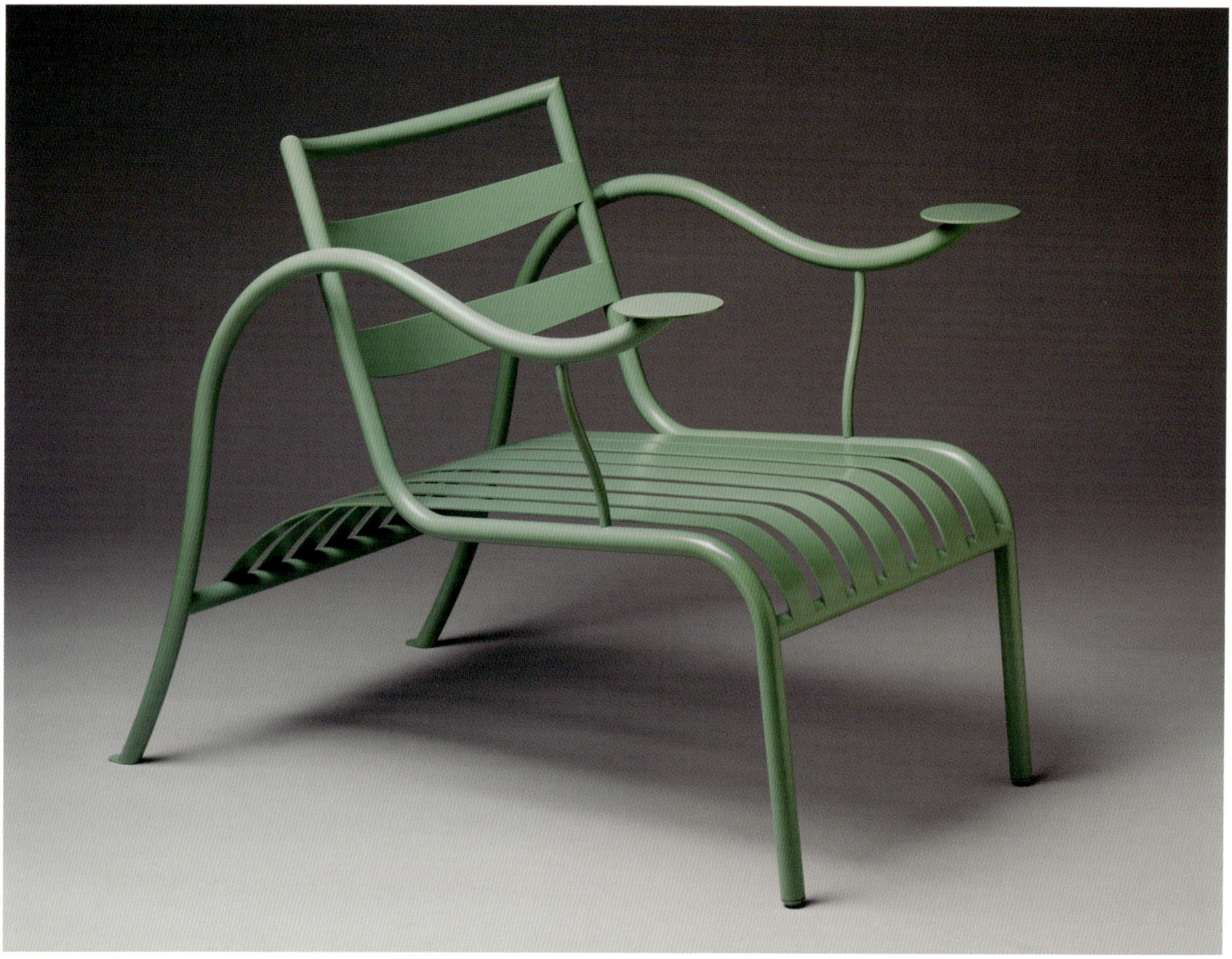

Green's association with flourishing gardens promotes feelings of calm and equilibrium. Designed by Jasper Morrison, the 'Thinking Man's Chair' (c. 1986; above), with its powder-coated green steel frame and reclining form, beckons you to take a contemplative moment, preferably outdoors. In tune with the 'back to nature' trend for indoor plants in the 1970s, 'Lily Pond' (right), a printed cotton furnishing fabric designed by Mary Oliver in 1976 for British firm Heal's, brings the outside into the home. The lily pads and flowers – associated with enlightenment in Buddhism – are reduced to a series of halftone leaf-green dots for the 'photo-print' design. Equally, 'celadon' glazed wares elicit a sense of tranquil beauty. Subtle colour variations can be found, from misty blue and grey-greens to the earthy hue of this 14th- or 15th-century Chinese pear-shaped stoneware bottle (opposite).

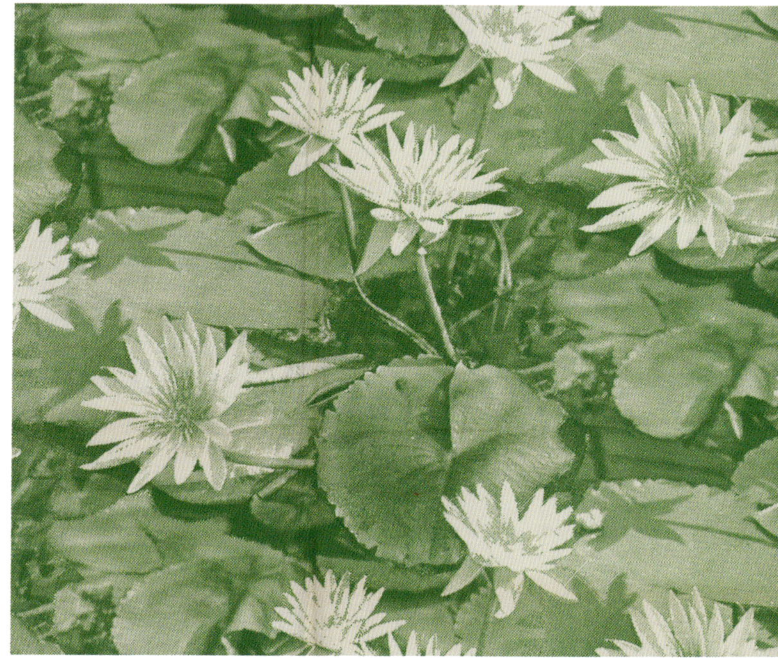

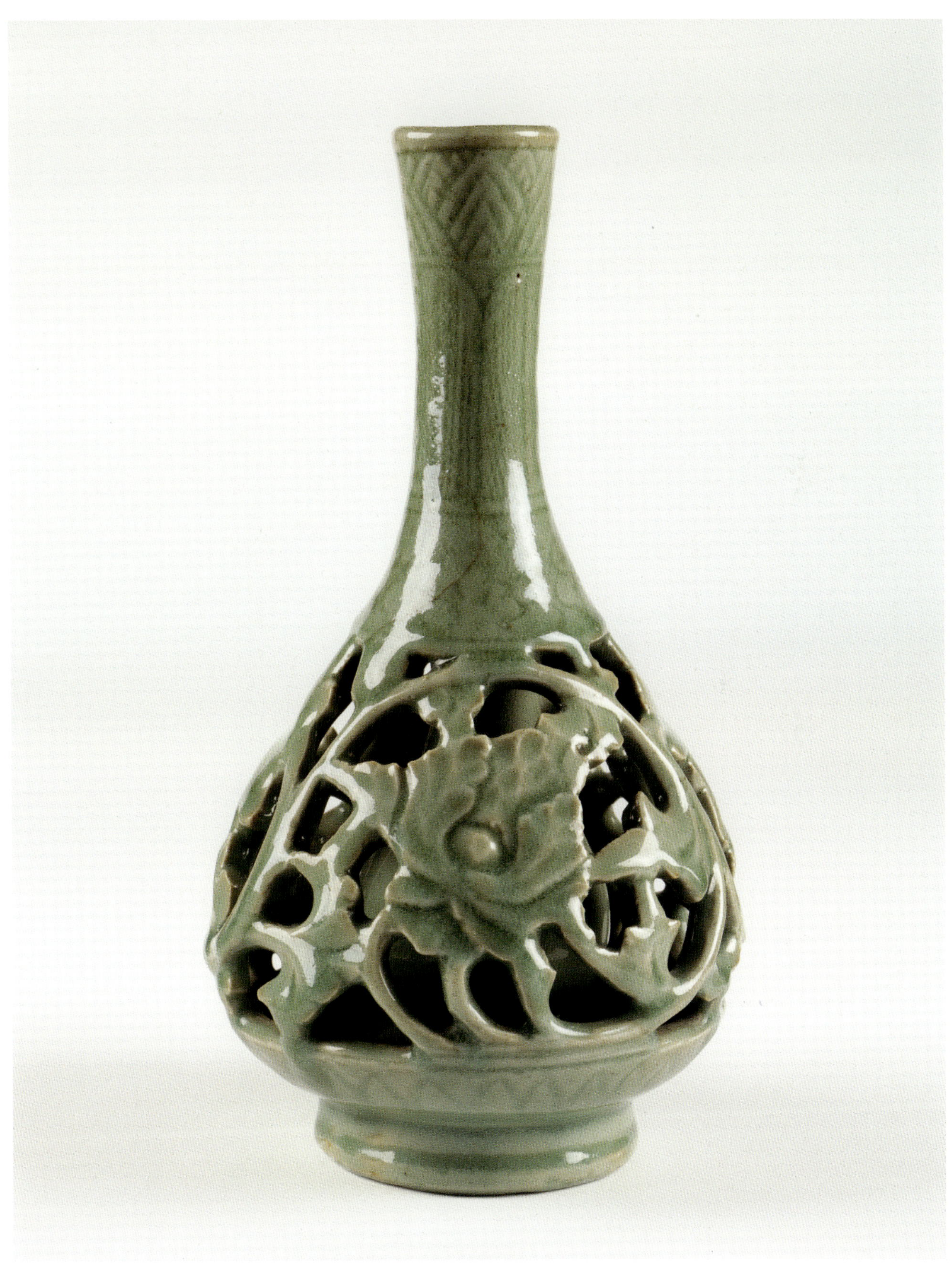

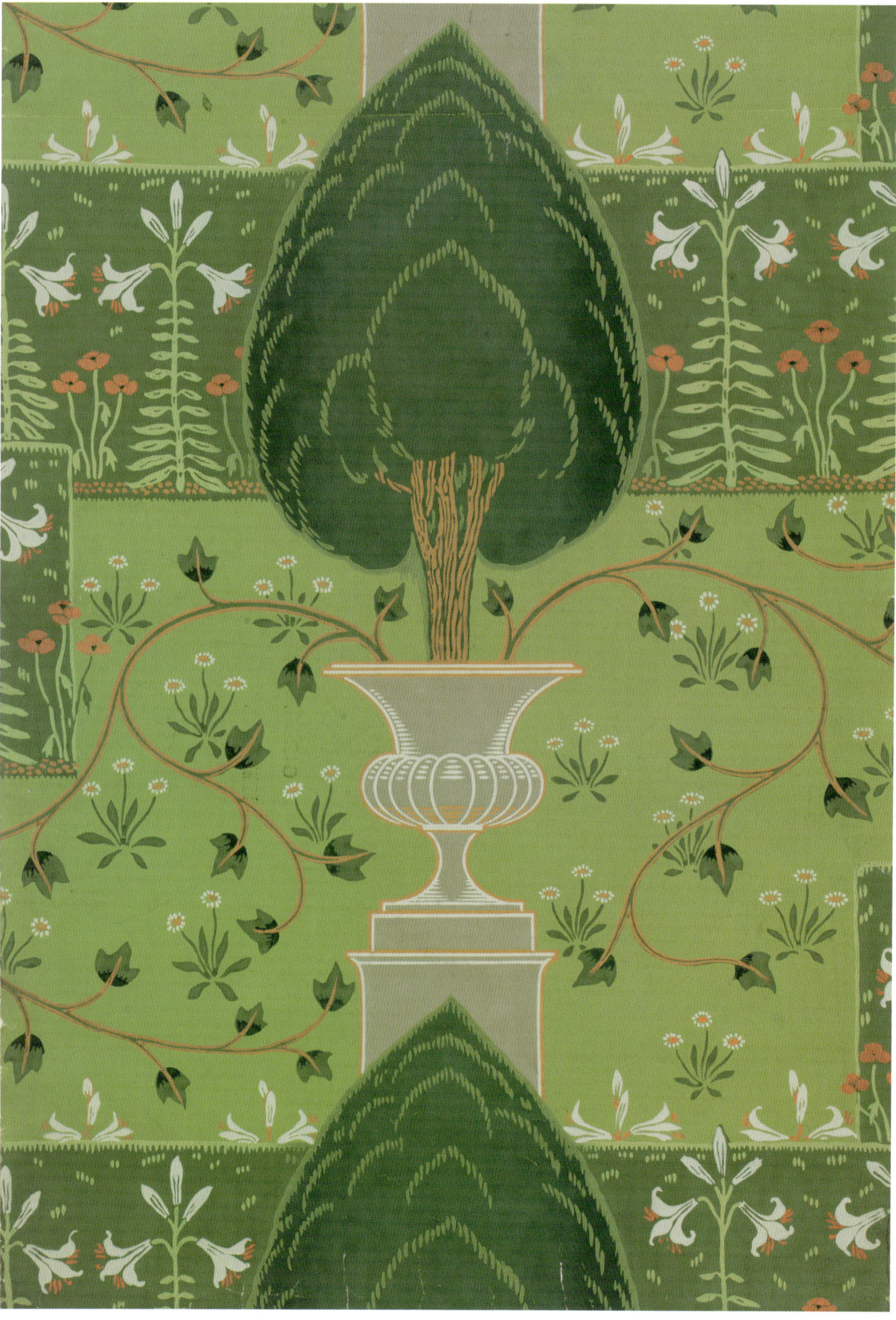

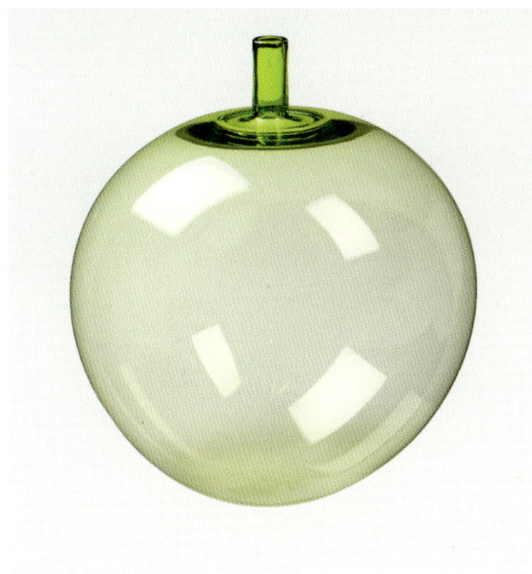

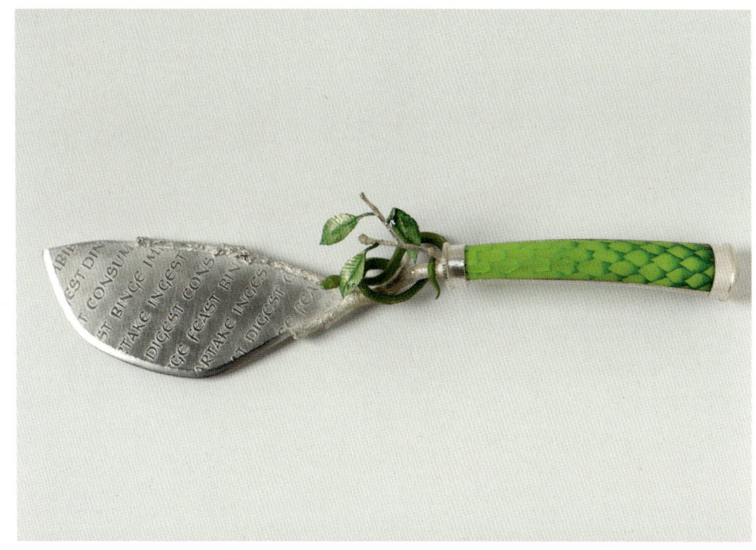

Entitled 'The Formal Garden', this wallpaper by Walter Crane (1904; opposite) depicts an ordered garden design, the pattern repeat consisting of a tree and planter surrounded by scrolling foliage, poppies and white lilies; a paradise untouched by the wilder side of nature. Reminiscent of the temptation of Eve in the Garden of Eden, a coiled tree-snake lurks within the branches that grasp the handle of an Arts and Crafts-inspired silver server made by Harlan W. Butt in 2004 (above right). The blade is etch-imprinted with bold block lettering that entices the user to 'partake, consume, ingest, digest, binge', and the green handle, graduating to a shocking lime shade, brings the piece crashing into the 21st century. The beguiling apple-shaped form of Ingeborg Lundin's hand-blown glass vase (c. 1957; above left) is also beset by an element of danger in its apparent fragility. Equally delicate is the mould-blown glass bottle (right) made in Iran between the 11th and 13th centuries. The semi-transparent glass carries an Arabic inscription that asks for 'blessing, good fortune [and] happiness to the owner', green being a colour associated with Paradise in Islam.

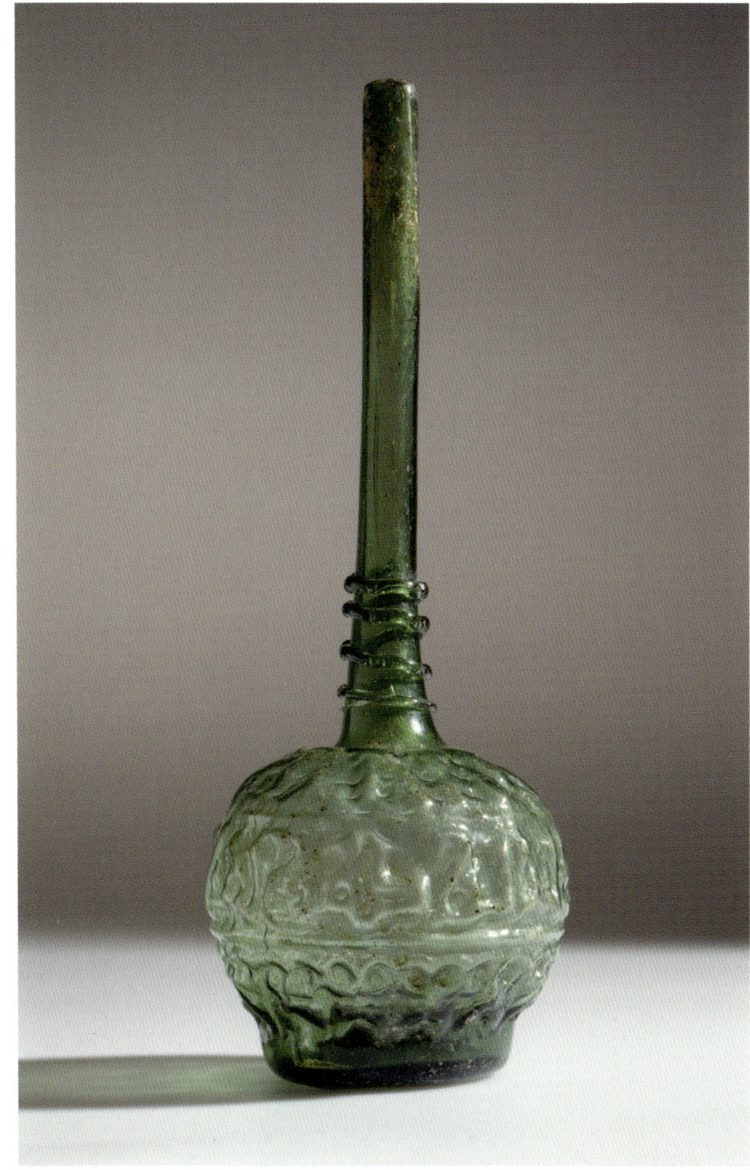

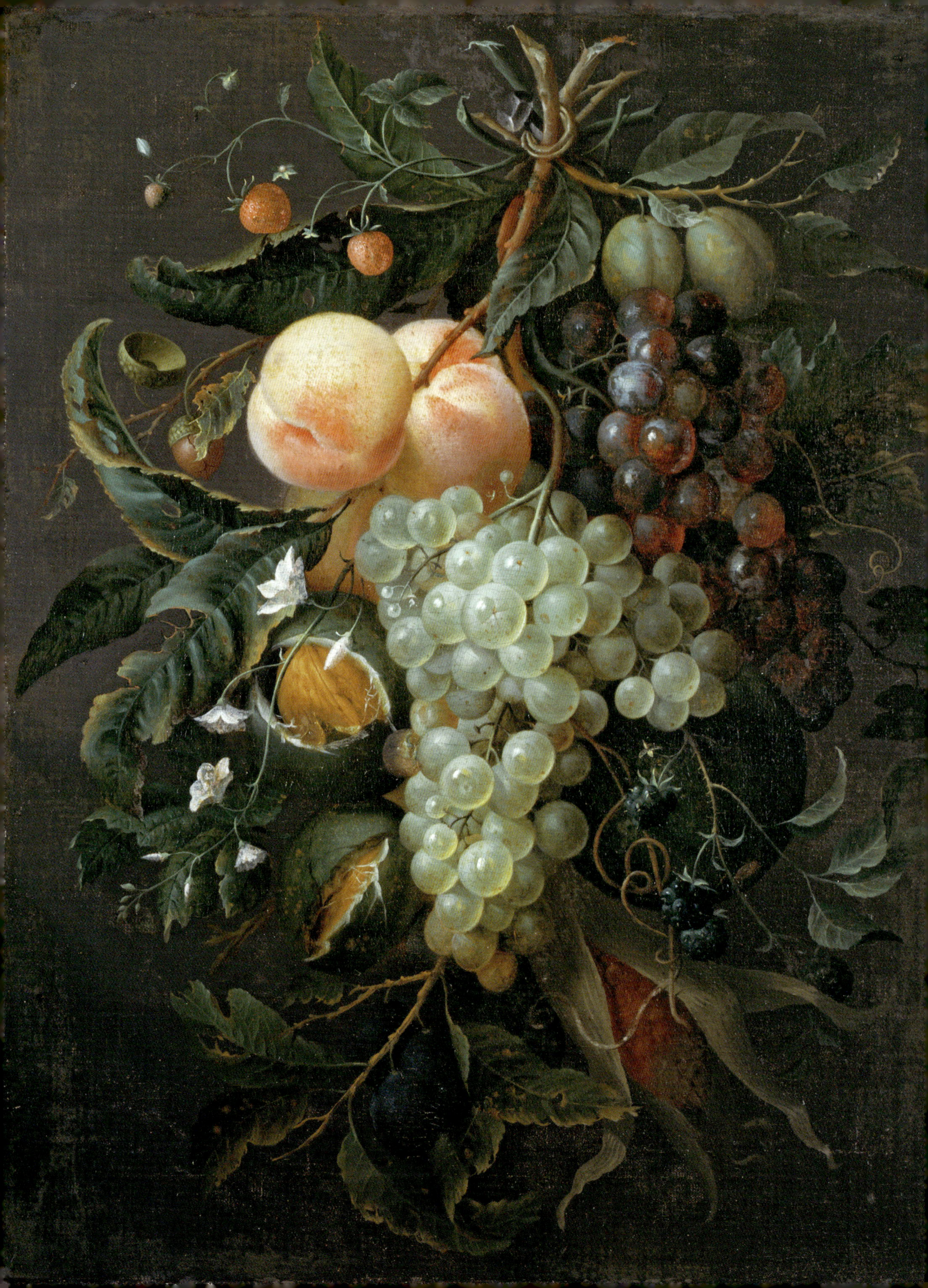

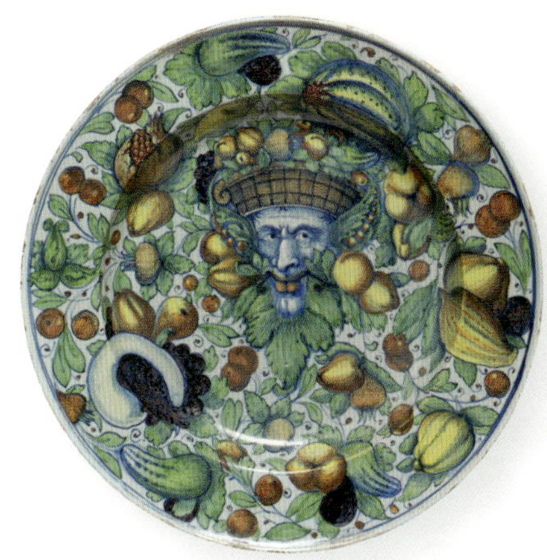

In the west, decorative greenery is linked to the joys of spring, romance and a new cycle of life. Green holds a special place as a life-giving force in nature; the green pigment chlorophyll absorbs light and generates energy for plants through photosynthesis. A creature of excess, the face of a satyr emerges from an abundance of leaves and vegetables on this unusual mid-16th-century Venetian dish (above), while the leaves of a sycamore tree frame the dryad-like figure of Jane Morris in Dante Gabriel Rossetti's *The Day Dream* (1880; right). The density of green tones highlights the ruby-red lips of the subject and the pink and white sprig of honeysuckle she holds, a symbol of the bonds of love for Victorians and perhaps a veiled reference to the passionate affair between painter and sitter.

In Pieter Gallis's mid-17th-century oil painting *Festoon with Fruit, Corn, Nuts and Flowers* (opposite), green grapes are used as a counterbalance to the red fruits. This is likely suggestive of the water and blood from St John's account of the wounding of Christ on the cross and the resurrection.

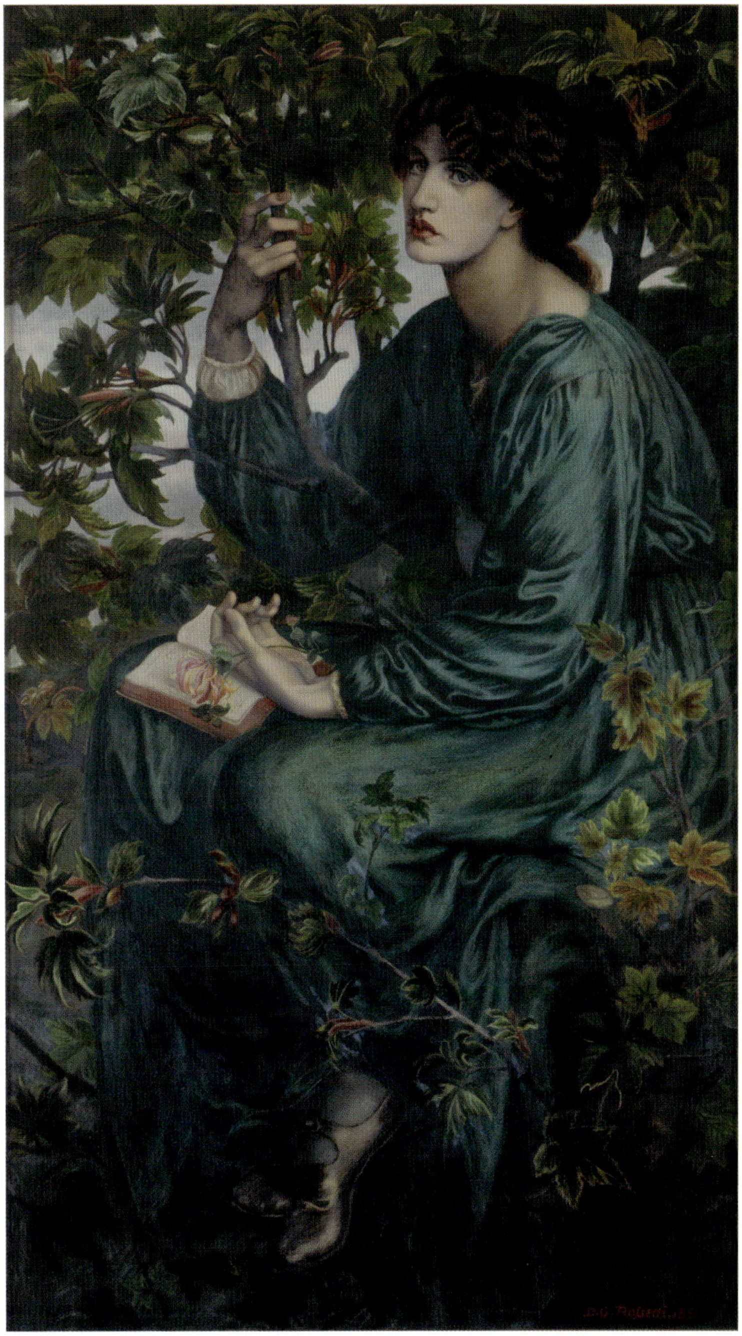

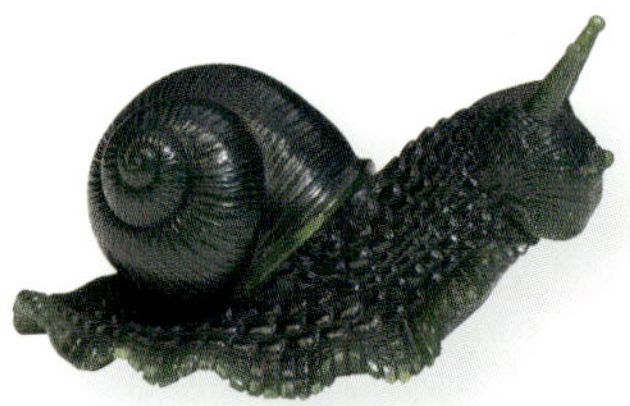

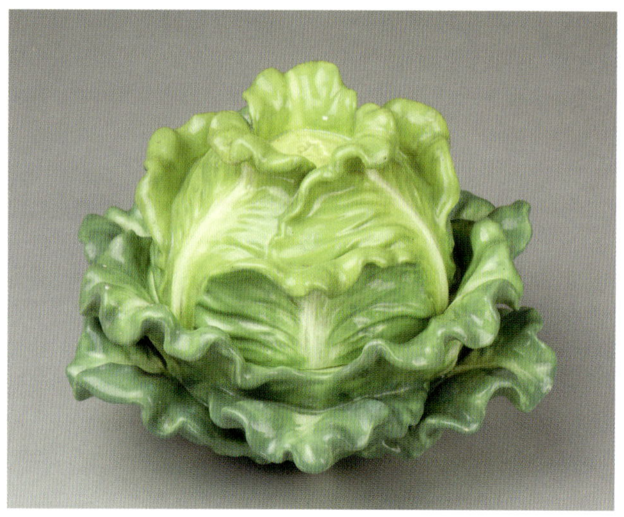

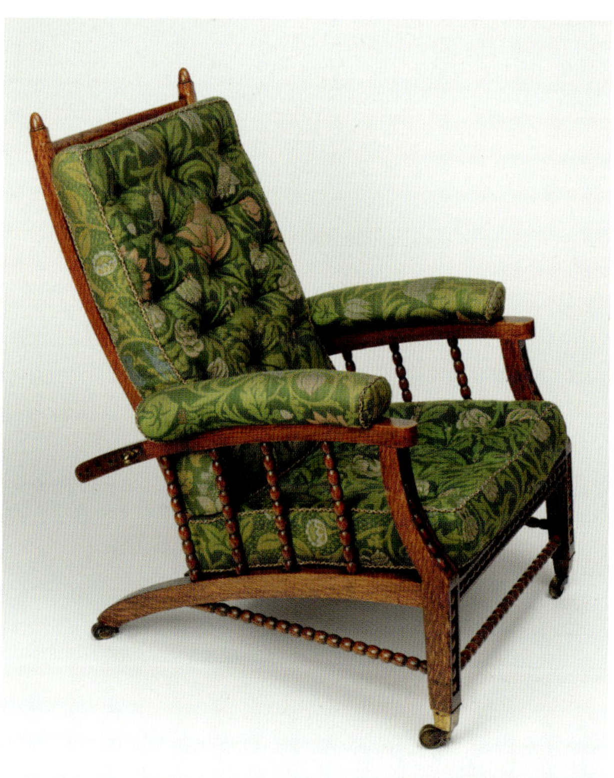

The 19th-century designer William Morris was greatly inspired by the British countryside. The willow was one of his favourite motifs for wallpapers and textiles. In 'Willow Bough' (opposite), a block-printed wallpaper from 1887, the undulating forms create a sense of depth against the sky-blue background. Morris's 'Violet and Columbine' design, in which varied blooms complement rich greens, also covers the cushions of Webb's vernacular armchair (1883–1900; below left) to create a rural idyll inside the home. Inspired by Japanese kimono, this mid-18th-century British banyan (below right) with a botanical damask pattern on heavy green silk similarly brings the outside in. It was designed to be worn over stays and petticoats around the house in the mornings and evenings.

Meanwhile, a nephrite jade snail carving (above left), part of a range of imitation animal 'netsuke' created by Fabergé at the turn of the century, and a cabbage-shaped porcelain tureen and cover (c. 1830–70; left), invite the wonders of the garden or allotment inside.

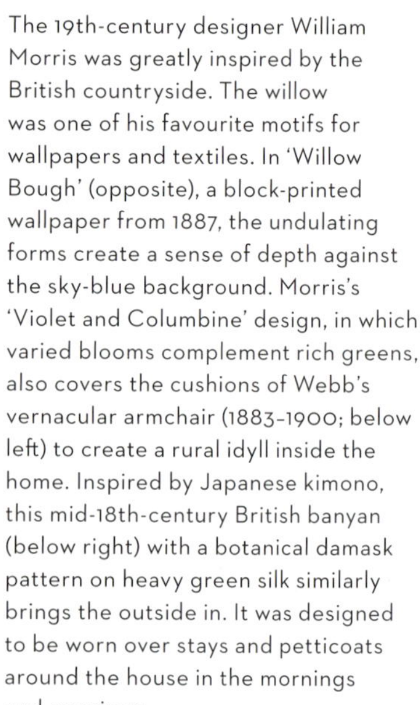

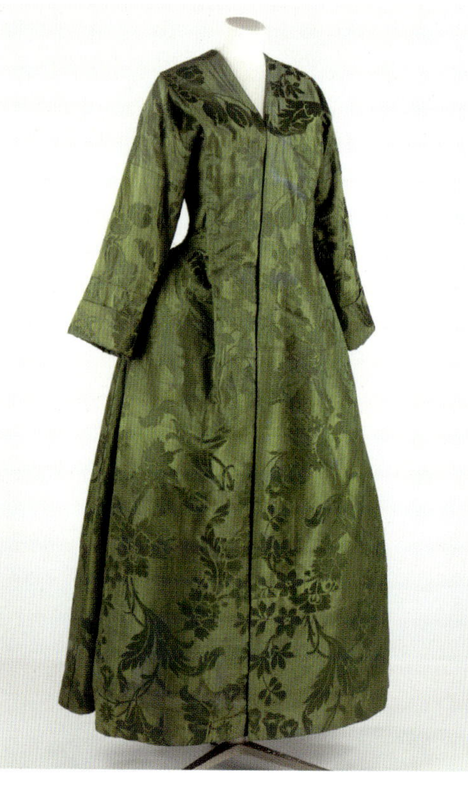

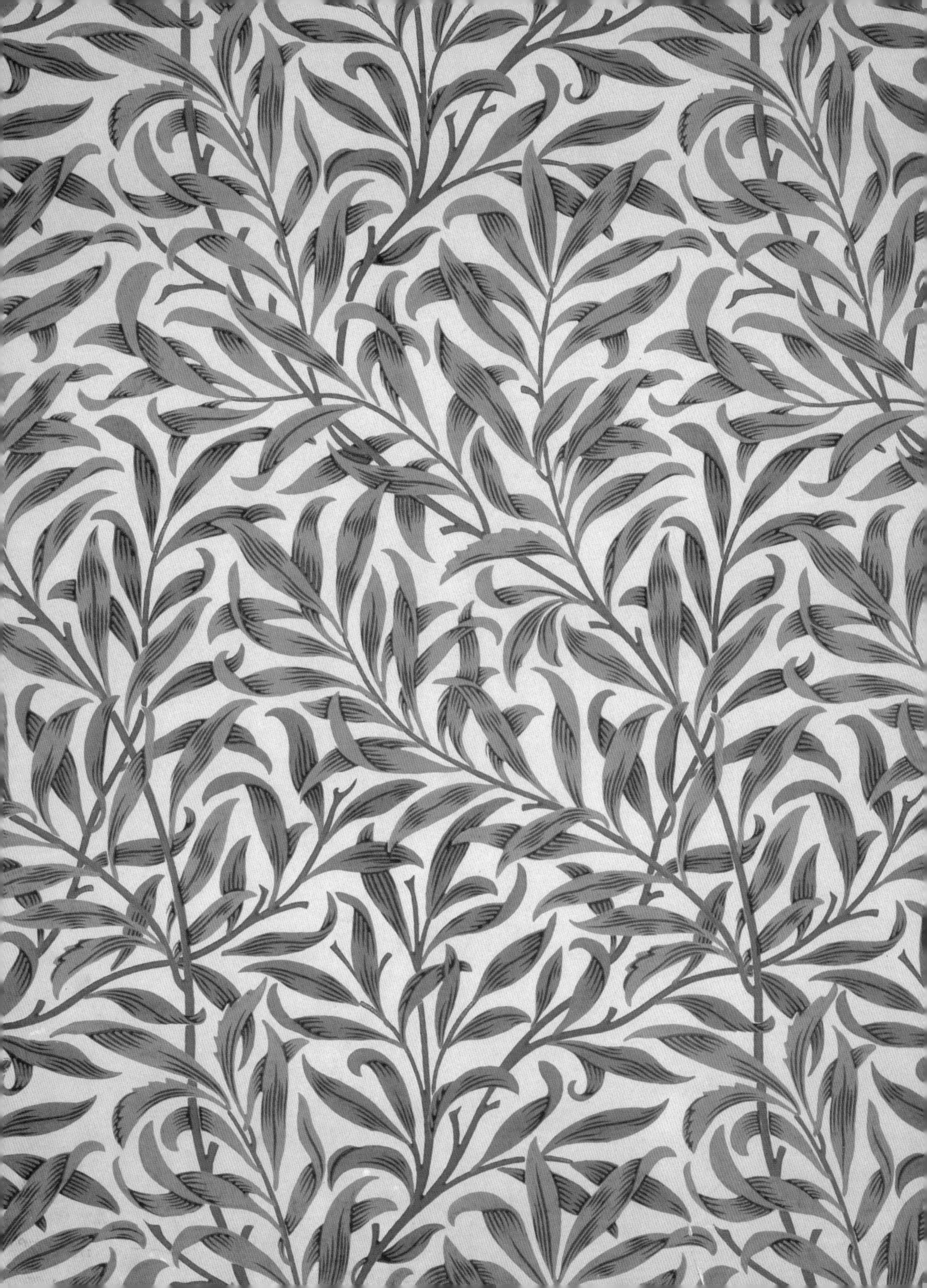

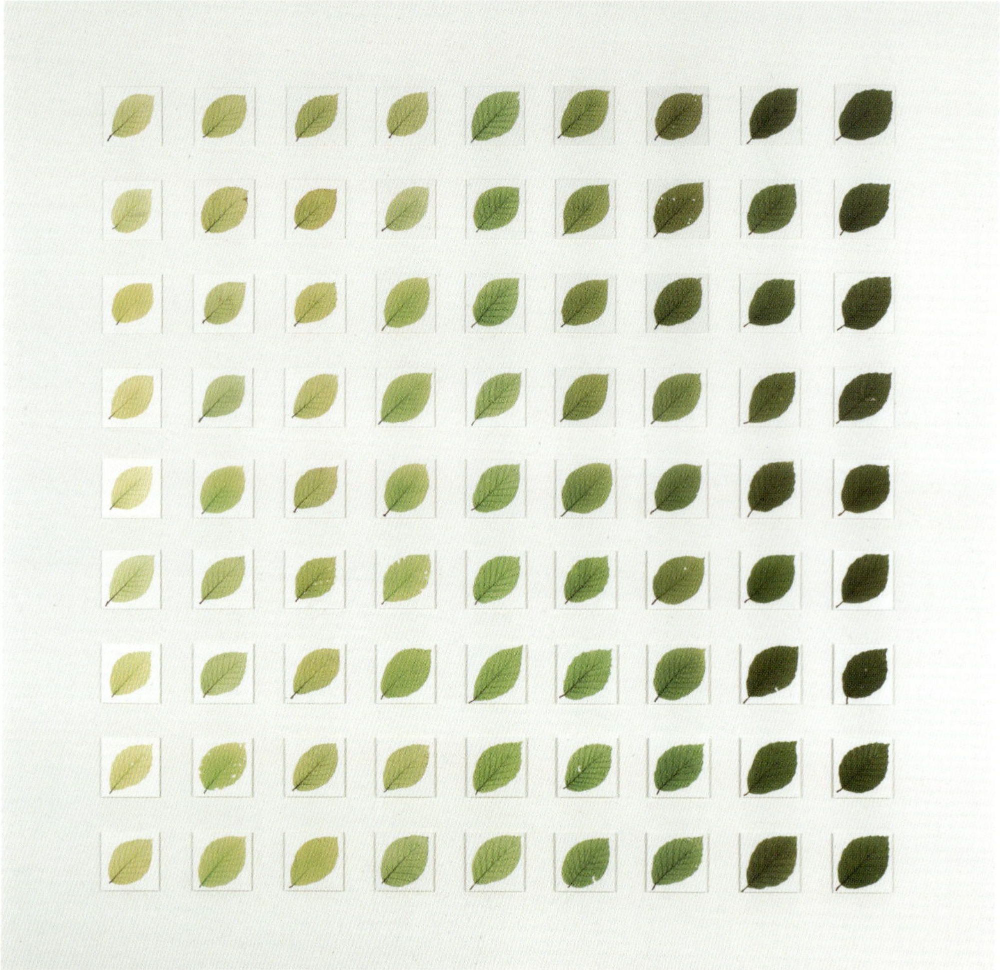

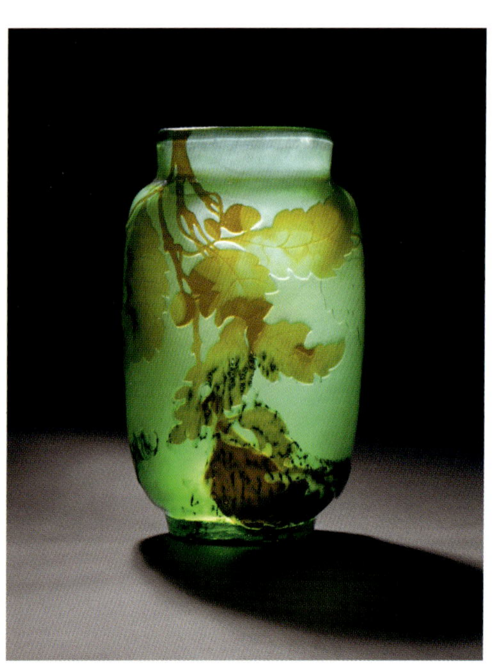

Breathing in the Beech Wood, Homeland, Dartmoor, Twenty-Four Days of Sunlight (2004; above), cameraless photography by Garry Fabian Miller, draws a comparison between plants' accumulation of light-absorbing chlorophyll and photography, also reliant on the power of light. Luminous green materials create a similarly energizing effect in E.C.M. Gallé's translucent glass *Oakleaf* vase (c. 1895; left), which evokes the dappled light of the forest. Light also illuminates the unbacked enamel of this late 19th-century spoon from Norway (opposite, bottom left), an example of the *plique-à-jour* technique.

jewel beetle-wing embroidery, as on this dress from Britain (1868–9; opposite, bottom right), was introduced to Europe from India. The iridescent, individually applied wings, outlined with couched gold wire, also decorate this piece of muslin (opposite, top), probably made in India during the 19th century.

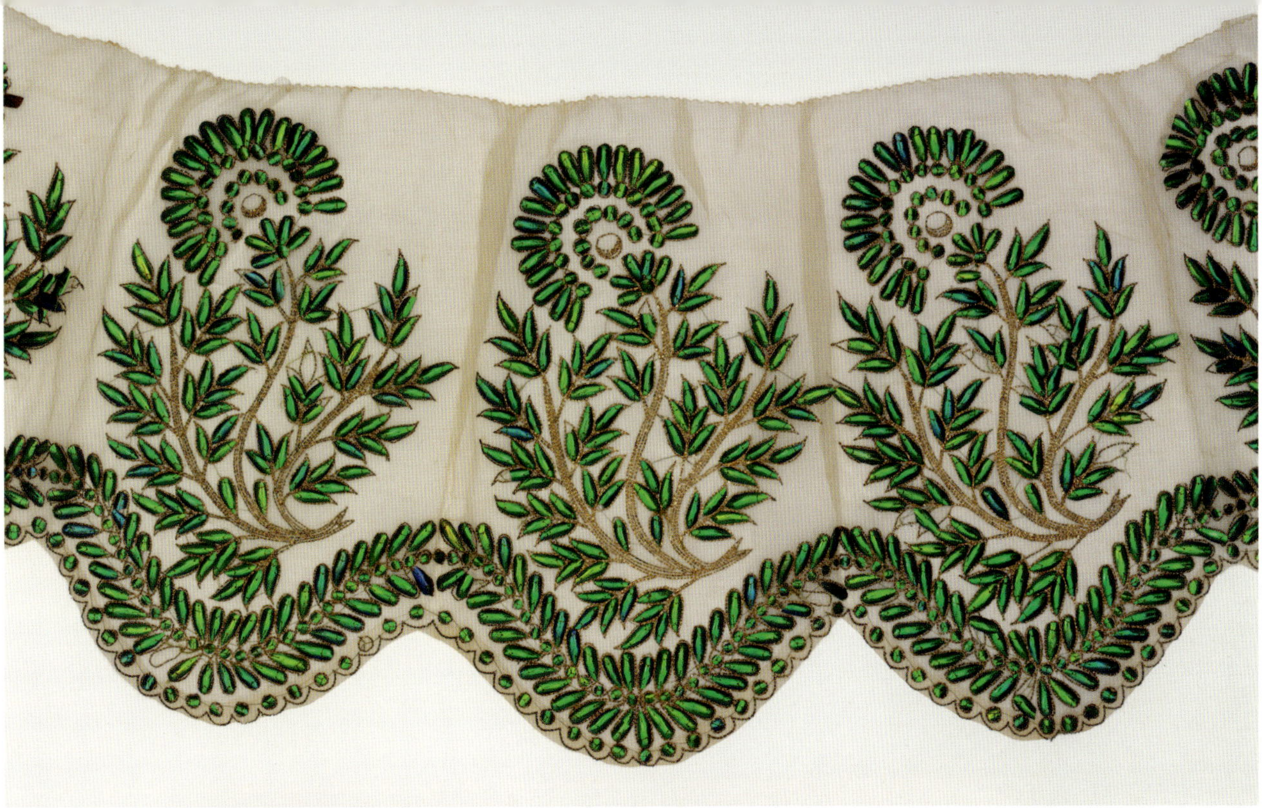

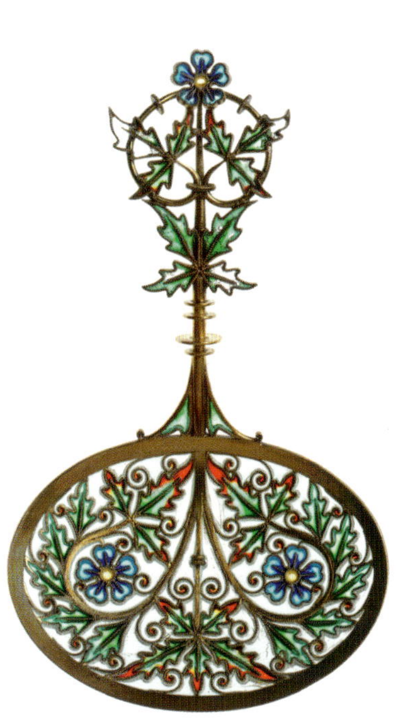

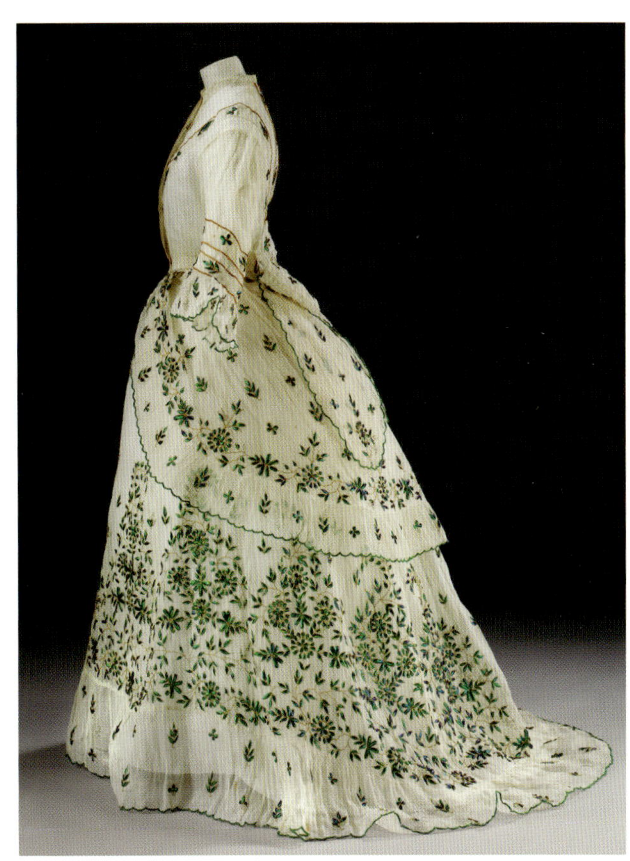

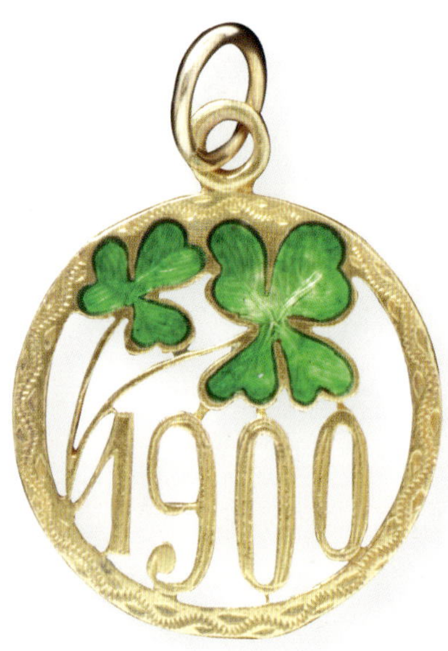

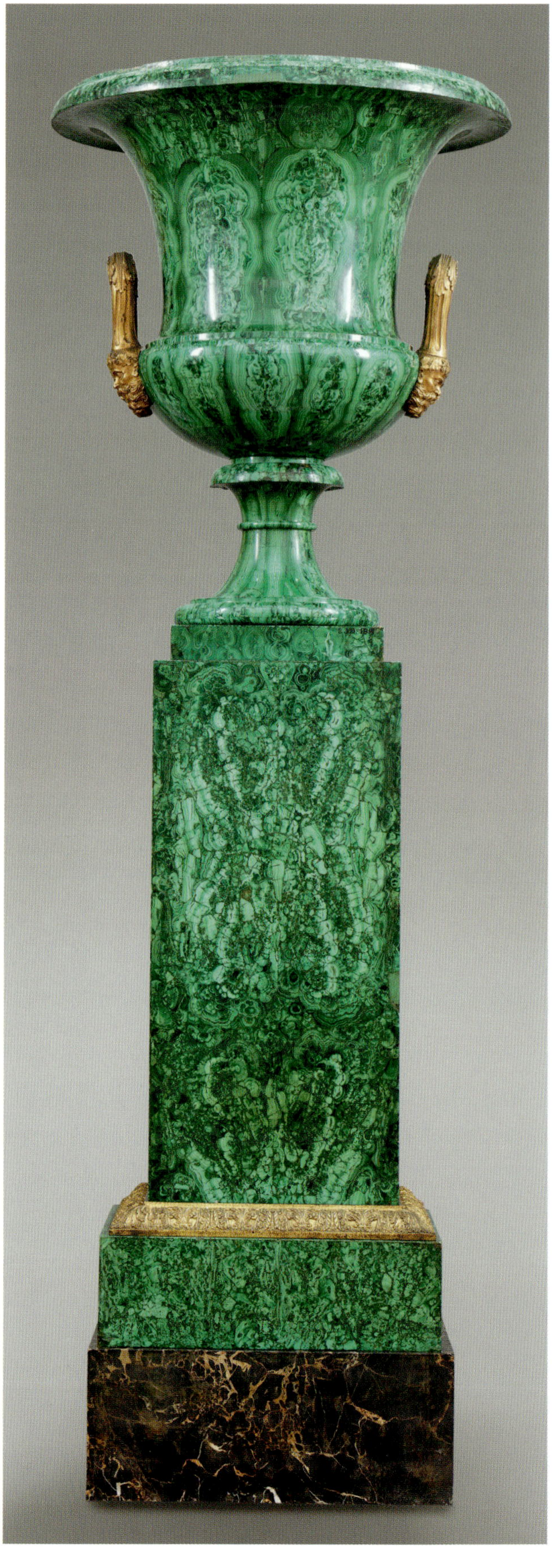

Green is often thought of as the colour of good luck. Malachite is a green mineral especially associated with wealth and power. This 'Medici'-style malachite vase (right), produced between 1820 and 1840, was one of pair exhibited by Russia at the Great Exhibition of 1851, proclaiming Russian wealth and power. The green four-leaf clover is a traditional symbol of luck and good fortune. This gold pendant decorated with enamelled four-leaf clovers (above) was intended to bring the wearer good luck at the dawn of the 20th century.

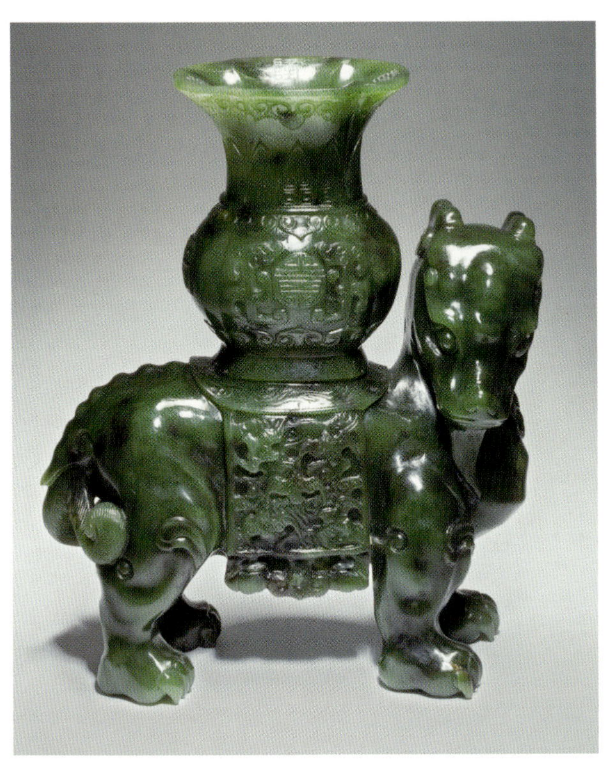

This Chinese *yongchang* vase of spinach-green jade (left) represents a mythical animal called a *tianlu*. Dating from the Qianlong period (1736–95), it symbolizes strength, wisdom and fidelity. Green emeralds are associated with Venus, Roman goddess of love, and symbolize both love and fidelity. The emerald and diamond necklace and earrings below were a wedding present from Napoleon Bonaparte and his wife Joséphine to their adopted daughter, Stéphanie de Beauharnais, in 1806.

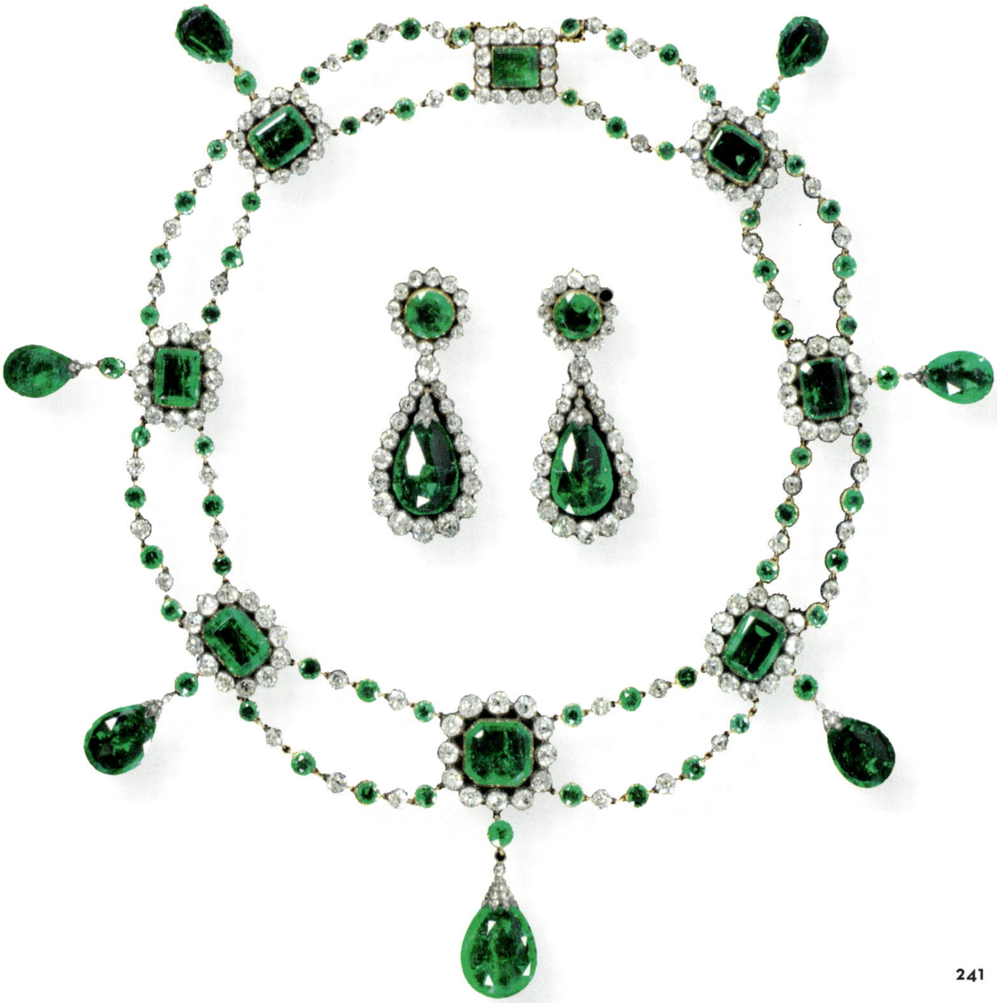

The colour green is often associated
with the commons – cultural and
natural resources accessible to all –
and the figure of the 'everyman'. A.W.N.
Pugin's colour scheme in the Palace
of Westminster, the seat of Britain's
government, used green in the House
of Commons, in contrast with the royal
red used in the House of Lords. His
wallpaper design for the Houses of
Parliament (1848; below) was inspired
by medieval woven silk textiles. In 2015,
the artist Grayson Perry collaborated
with FAT Architecture on the creation
of 'A House for Essex'. Designed for
the exterior of the building, this green-
glazed ceramic tile (opposite) depicts a
nude woman with a large belly standing
in a Romanesque arch. Like much of
the decoration for the house, it is
dedicated to Julie, a fictional Essex
'everywoman'. The screen-printed
green banknotes (2018; right) are part
of the art project *Bank Job*, by Hilary
Powell and Dan Edelstyn, which aimed
to raise money to buy out privately
owed debt in London's E17 postcode.
The notes feature the faces of four
people involved in local services.

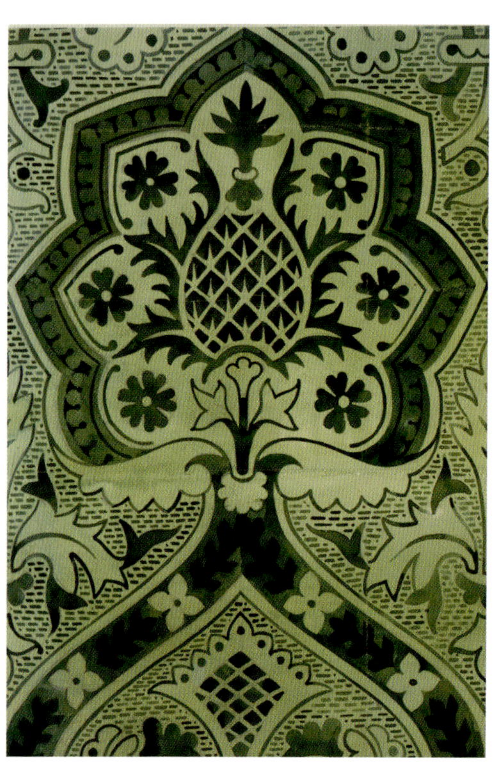

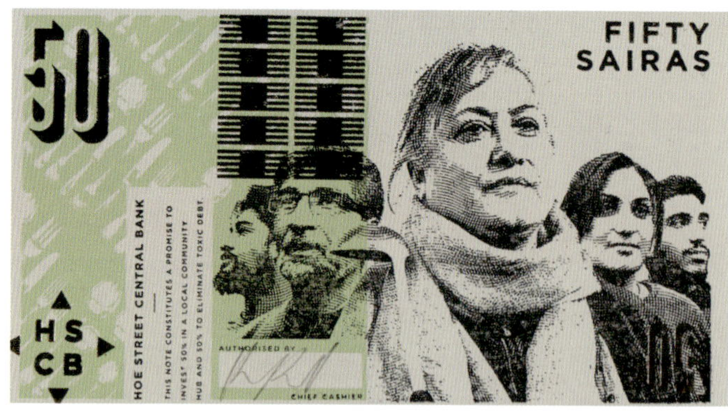

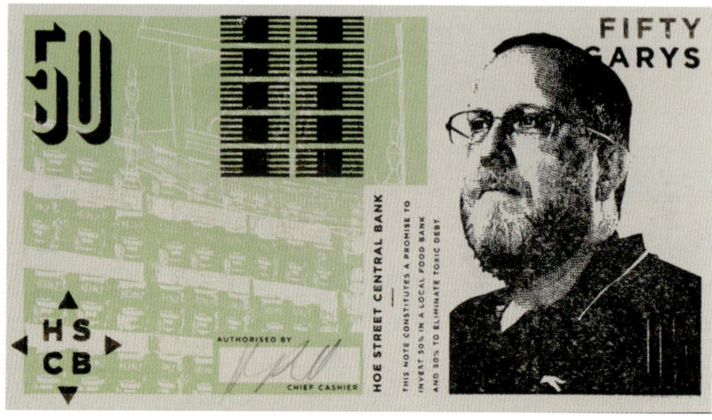

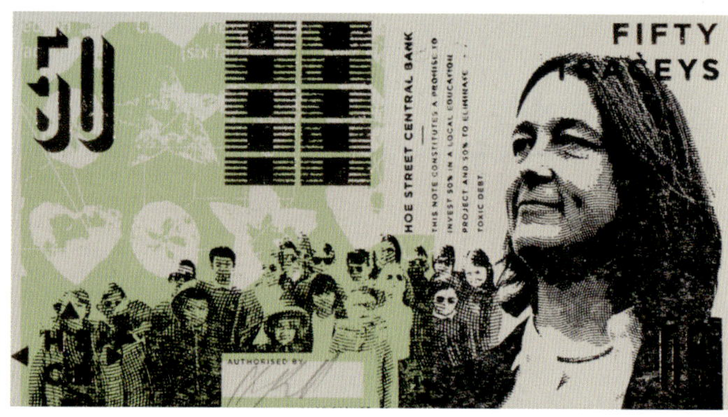

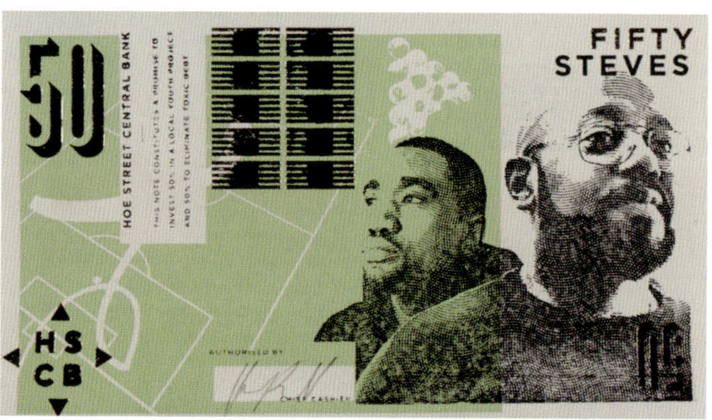

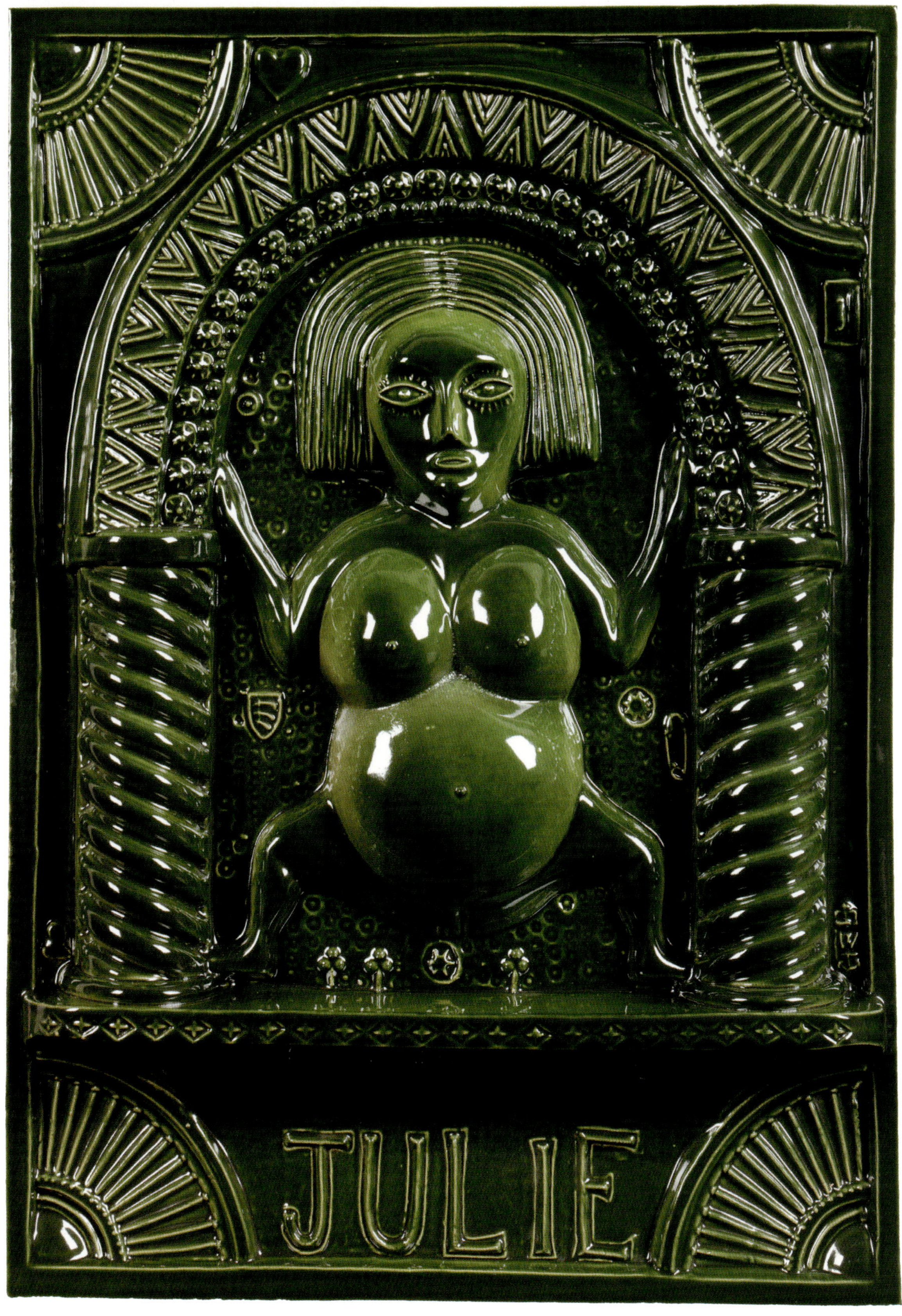

JULIE

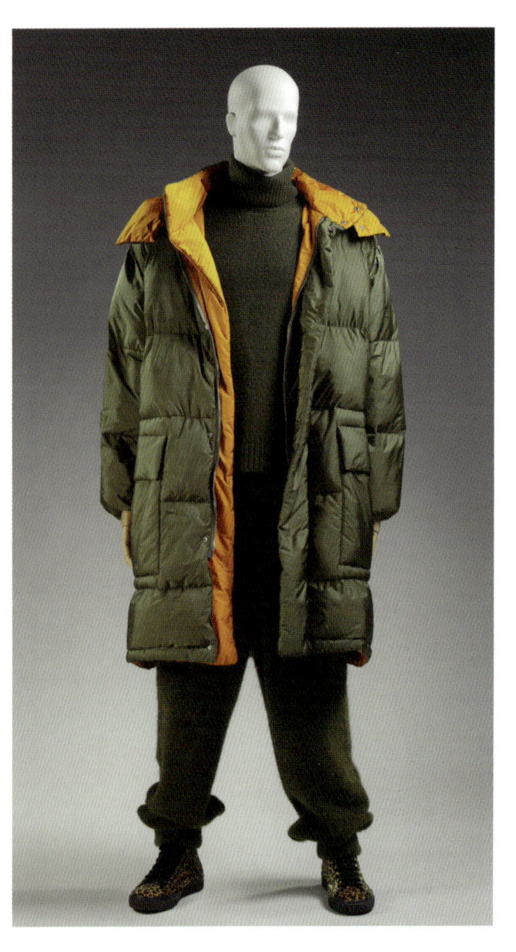

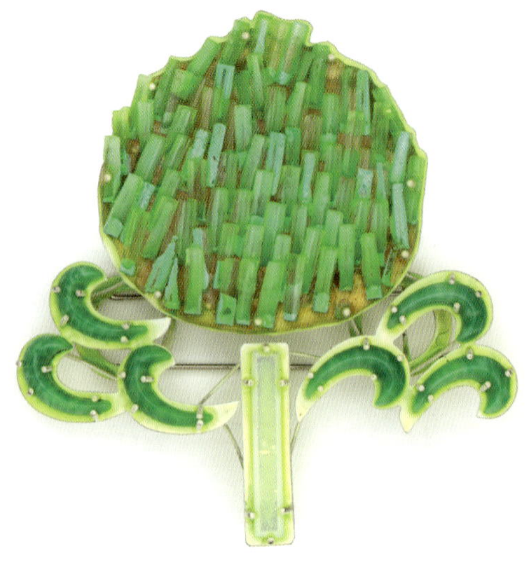

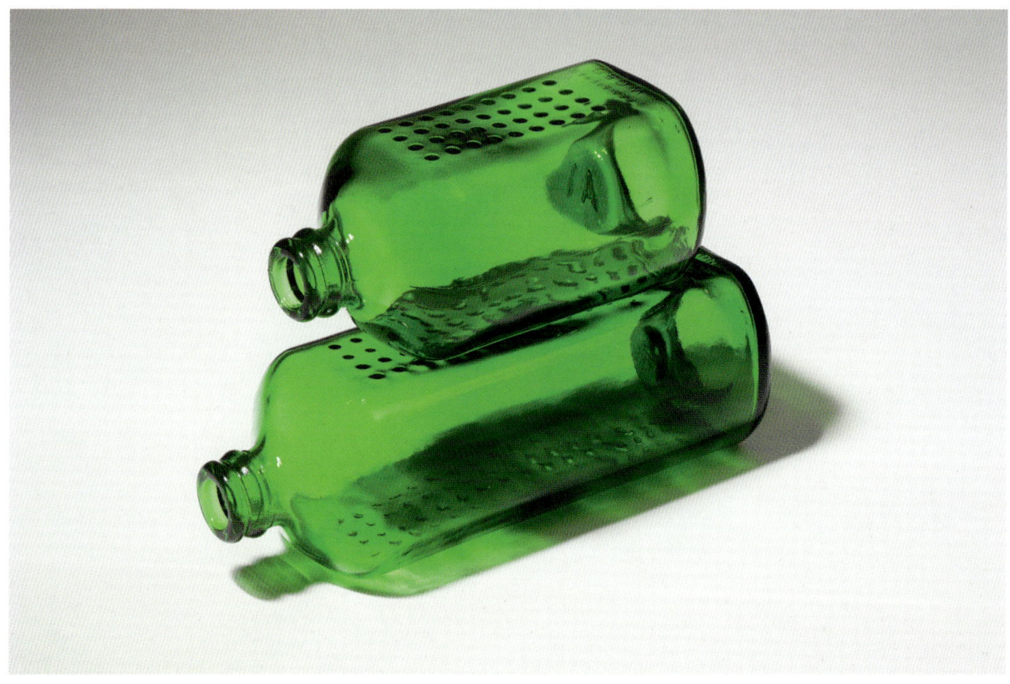

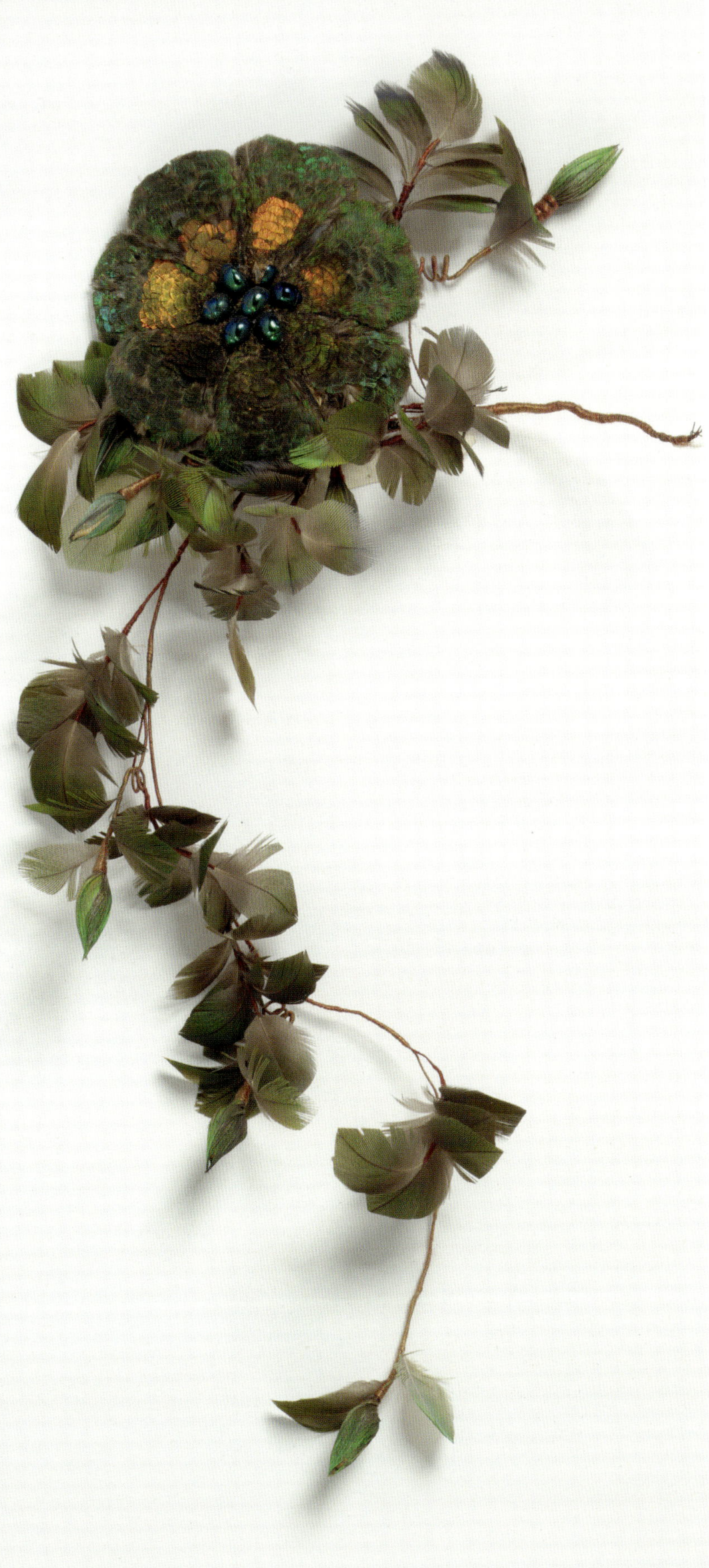

In the 20th century green became the colour of environmental and sustainability movements. The Anti-Plumage Bill (1921), banning the use of exotic birds in fashion following a campaign concerned with wildlife preservation, would have outlawed the manufacture of goods such as this flower-spray hat decoration (left), which is made of hummingbird and green parrot feathers (1870–90).

Helen Britton's 'Green Flower' brooch, made in 2004 (opposite, top right), incorporates recycled materials including green glass for the bloom and leaves. She describes this as 'a new opportunity, a chance to sing again or to sing at last'. Frustrated by bottles he saw littered on beaches, Alfred Heineken asked John Habraken to design a 'brick that holds beer' that could be reused for construction. The result was an interlocking green glass bottle: the WOBO (World Bottle) in 1963 (opposite, bottom). Never commercially produced, it is nonetheless seen as a revolutionary example of recycling. This menswear outfit in olive green (opposite, top left), designed by Stella McCartney in 2017, is made from recycled nylon, cashmere and polyester. McCartney's fashion label focuses on sustainable materials, and the use of the colour green echoes this ideal.

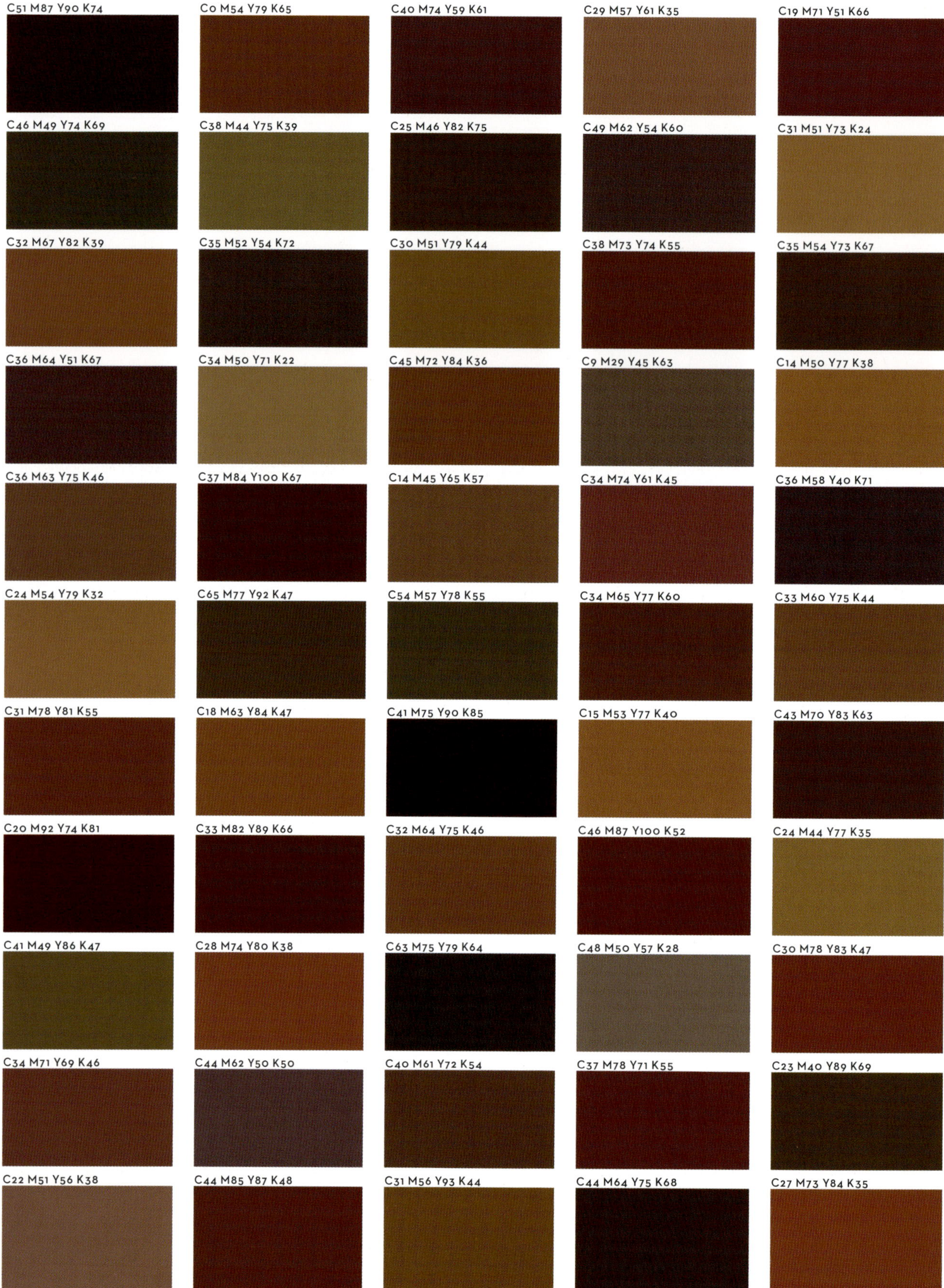

C51 M87 Y90 K74
C0 M54 Y79 K65
C40 M74 Y59 K61
C29 M57 Y61 K35
C19 M71 Y51 K66
C46 M49 Y74 K69
C38 M44 Y75 K39
C25 M46 Y82 K75
C49 M62 Y54 K60
C31 M51 Y73 K24
C32 M67 Y82 K39
C35 M52 Y54 K72
C30 M51 Y79 K44
C38 M73 Y74 K55
C35 M54 Y73 K67
C36 M64 Y51 K67
C34 M50 Y71 K22
C45 M72 Y84 K36
C9 M29 Y45 K63
C14 M50 Y77 K38
C36 M63 Y75 K46
C37 M84 Y100 K67
C14 M45 Y65 K57
C34 M74 Y61 K45
C36 M58 Y40 K71
C24 M54 Y79 K32
C65 M77 Y92 K47
C54 M57 Y78 K55
C34 M65 Y77 K60
C33 M60 Y75 K44
C31 M78 Y81 K55
C18 M63 Y84 K47
C41 M75 Y90 K85
C15 M53 Y77 K40
C43 M70 Y83 K63
C20 M92 Y74 K81
C33 M82 Y89 K66
C32 M64 Y75 K46
C46 M87 Y100 K52
C24 M44 Y77 K35
C41 M49 Y86 K47
C28 M74 Y80 K38
C63 M75 Y79 K64
C48 M50 Y57 K28
C30 M78 Y83 K47
C34 M71 Y69 K46
C44 M62 Y50 K50
C40 M61 Y72 K54
C37 M78 Y71 K55
C23 M40 Y89 K69
C22 M51 Y56 K38
C44 M85 Y87 K48
C31 M56 Y93 K44
C44 M64 Y75 K68
C27 M73 Y84 K35

BROWN

In his introduction to *Painting as a Pastime* (1948), Winston Churchill pronounces his affinity for bright colours, writing 'I cannot pretend to feel impartial about the colours. I rejoice with the brilliant ones, and am genuinely sorry for the poor browns.' Sensible and drab, warm and earthy, despite Churchill's swift dismissal of the colour, brown belies easy interpretation. Celebrated for its warmth and richness, it just as easily calls to mind wastage, filth and dreariness. For Samuel Johnson in his dictionary of 1775, 'brownstudy' was the act of 'gloomy mediations'. Brown is unfiltered and organic, the colour of wood, clay and earth, but it is also non-spectral, the product of mixing other colours together. In art and design, brown is celebrated for its aesthetic properties, but it also plays a supporting role, giving form, depth and tone.

Brown has been used consistently to signify utility and everydayness. It is sober, sensible and lacks sophistication – so the adage 'no brown in town' tells us. The brown dye of the habits worn by nuns and monks of various orders speaks to vows of humility and poverty, unadorned and simple. In a comparable way, the 1950s uniform of the 'Brownies' girlguiding organization demonstrates modesty and practicality, the value of stepping away from one's own needs for the sake of others. In the history of dress, different hues of brown have also carried specific connotations. Russet, a reddish-brown colour, was used to describe a type of cloth that was worn by country folk and the poor. In his *Life of Theocritus*, for example, John Dryden describes the charming 'clownishness' of 'a fair Shepherdess in her Country Russet, talking in a Yorkshire Tone' (*Sylvæ*, 1685). But though Dryden patronized his rural shepherdess, brown has also been used to signal glamour and sumptuousness; the perfect partner to lustrous gold. The colour of many widely used materials, it is often chosen for its beauty – a wooden marquetry cabinet, a leather-bound book, an agate piece of jewellery. The striking and inventive presentations of these brown materials celebrate the hues of the natural world.

Where there is naturalness and authenticity, so follows imitation. Designers have often sought to re-create the browns that occur in nature to lend an object a sense of history, to deal with declining supply or to show off technical innovation. Tortoiseshell remains the subject of much imitation. Treasured for its dappled appearance, it has been used for thousands of years, the earliest examples of tortoiseshell work dating to pre-dynastic Europe. It was popular in ancient Greece and Rome, in Europe from at least the fifteenth century and Japan since the seventeenth century. Ieyasu Tokugawa, *shōgun* (ruler) of Japan in the early 1600s, is known to have had a pair of eyeglasses with a tortoiseshell – *bekko* – frame that fuelled an early trend for the material. From the eighteenth century onwards, the hawksbill sea turtle, from which the material was derived, was highly prized and hunted almost to extinction. In the mid-eighteenth century in Staffordshire, English makers sought to mimic its striking mottled effect by treating the lead glaze on earthenware with different oxides. This came to be known as 'tortoiseshell ware'. In the 1960s, the scarcity of real tortoiseshell and an eventual ban on 'turtling' and the international trade in turtle shell led to a rise in plastic imitations that could be used for glasses, for which tortoiseshell patterns have proven enduringly popular, as well as other small items such as boxes and buttons.

Beyond tortoiseshell, in fashion brown has had the capacity to traverse the old and new, the established and the trendy. The writer Gertrude Stein was described by her partner Alice B. Toklas as 'a golden brown presence' in her memoir *What is Remembered*, and was portrayed as such by Picasso in 1905–6. Stein would have embodied this fully in her specially designed haute couture brown velvet suit, embellished with sequins and tassels by Pierre Balmain, hailed as the doyen of the 'New French Style' (see p. 252). In fact, in 1946 Toklas wrote the accompanying text to the designer's summer collection, 'A New French Style: Eight Models from Pierre Balmain', in which brown escaped the shadows of wartime utility. Treading the line between tradition and invention, in the 1970s John Michael's brown suits allowed young men to look fashionable but 'neither brash nor brazen' according to Geoffrey Aquilina Ross, the first men's fashion editor for *Vogue*, in *The Day of the Peacock: Style for Men 1963–1973* (2011). The 1970s also saw brown's popularity skyrocket beyond clothing, with the earth tones widely used in interior decor chiming with the hippy culture and increasing environmental consciousness of the era. In US magazine *House Beautiful*'s survey of popular paint colours, 'earthy brown' is the colour of 1970–1, with walls a paler shade of 'sandy beige' by 1978.

While trends come and go, brown bears a sense of permanence and history. Great Britain, among other countries, uses brown signage to direct people to heritage sites and natural attractions. It is also the colour used to describe areas of land designated for redevelopment, known as brownfield sites. This term often refers to derelict parts of the urban landscape or those that have been cleared following commercial use. Brown in this instance signifies something stripped back to its essential nature, ripe for regeneration. Like green, brown is also used to connote land on maps, each colour signifying the terrain and type of landscape. The UK's Ordnance Survey maps use brown to indicate contours and inclines – the steeper the hill, the closer the lines. These patches of brown designate the highest points of the land furthest from the sea, which is rendered in blue.

In other contexts, brown signifies waste and degradation. It often suggests something that is 'turning over', rotting or disintegrating into the very ground from which it came. Brown evokes dust and grease, dried blood and faeces. Indeed, many artists have experimented with excrement in their work, from Piero Manzoni's *Artist's Shit* (1961) to Chris Ofili's elephant dung paintings. Even Picasso is said to have exploited the particular qualities of this human by-product. Designers too have found ways of working with excrement. The Museum of Shit in Lombardy has started to produce household products made from Merdacotta®, a new kind of composite earthenware made from cow dung and clay, bringing together an ancient form of manufacturing with twenty-first-century technology. Other designers have invented entirely new materials from different kinds of brown waste. Berlin-based product designer Julian Lechner has created an innovative new product called Kaffeeform, which is made from used coffee grounds, biopolymers, starch, cellulose, wood, natural resins, waxes and oils. Lechner sources his coffee grounds from local coffee shops and companies, exploiting the potential to create sustainable products from readily available waste. Chemical engineer Silio Cardona, meanwhile, has developed Maderón, a wood-like material composed of resin and ground almond shells, a waste product of the Spanish almond industry. Innovations such as these provide designers with a new vehicle for experimentation, the materials' colour subtly referencing sustainability.

Alongside these new inventions, brown is the colour of some of the oldest pigments used in artistic practice. The different hues of these materials often depend on the method of production and quantities of the constituent parts. Umber, for example, is an earth pigment that varies in depth and richness depending on the amounts of iron oxide and manganese oxide present. It is named for the location of its early extraction, the mountainous region of central Italy, Umbria; its Italian name is *terra d'ombra*. In Giorgio Vasari's biography of Agnolo Gaddi in his *Lives of the Most Eminent Painters, Sculptors, and Architects* (1550), he notes the recent discovery of umber, though similarly composed earth browns were used at least as long ago as the Neolithic period, for cave paintings. Untreated, the pigment is known as raw umber, but when heated the colour becomes more intense and is referred to as burnt umber.

Brown pigments are often hard to distinguish from one another due to their subtle variations. Old Master drawings in sepia and bistre have regularly fallen prey to this confusion. Bistre, made from boiling the soot from burnt wood, has been in use since the European Middle Ages. It gained its name, however, only in the sixteenth century, and was not widely used until the eighteenth century, when it became a popular pigment for watercolour and wash drawings. It varies in hue from yellow-brown to a deep blackish brown depending on the type of wood used and its concentration when mixed with water. Sepia, produced from the dried ink sacs of the cuttlefish or squid, seems to have been introduced by Professor Jacob C. Seydelmann in Dresden, Germany, in the late eighteenth century, and became widely used in the nineteenth century. Some brown pigments became so well associated with an artist's work that they were named after them. Cologne or Cassel earth became known as Van Dyck (or Vandyke) brown in honour of the Flemish painter's frequent use of the pigment.

Even when combined with other colours, brown has long given artists the capacity to accentuate the tone and three-dimensionality of their subject. During the 1640s, miniaturists adopted a 'sad-coloured' style by painting the background of their portraits with brown watercolour, giving them an 'extreme noble severity of treatment' according to Murdoch, Murrell, Noon and Strong in *The English Miniature* (1981). Samuel Cooper adopted this style in 1657 when painting his portrait miniature of Sir William Palmer, using brown tones to heighten the contrast between light and dark, or chiaroscuro, perhaps under the influence of the Dutch painter Rembrandt.

Churchill may have felt 'genuinely sorry for the poor browns', but from the practical to the luxe, the prevalence of this colour in art and design speaks to both its evocative power and ongoing utility.

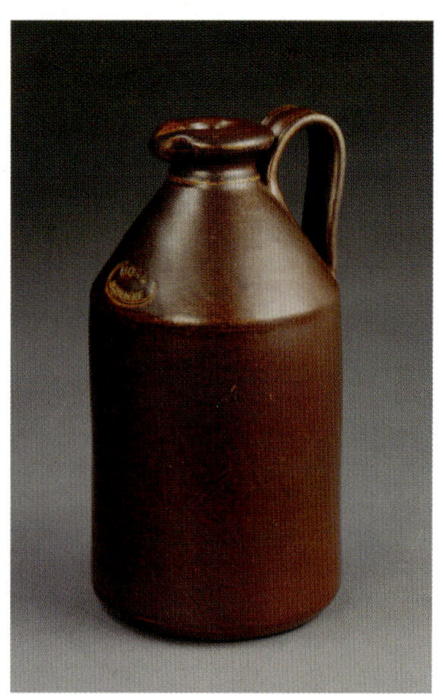

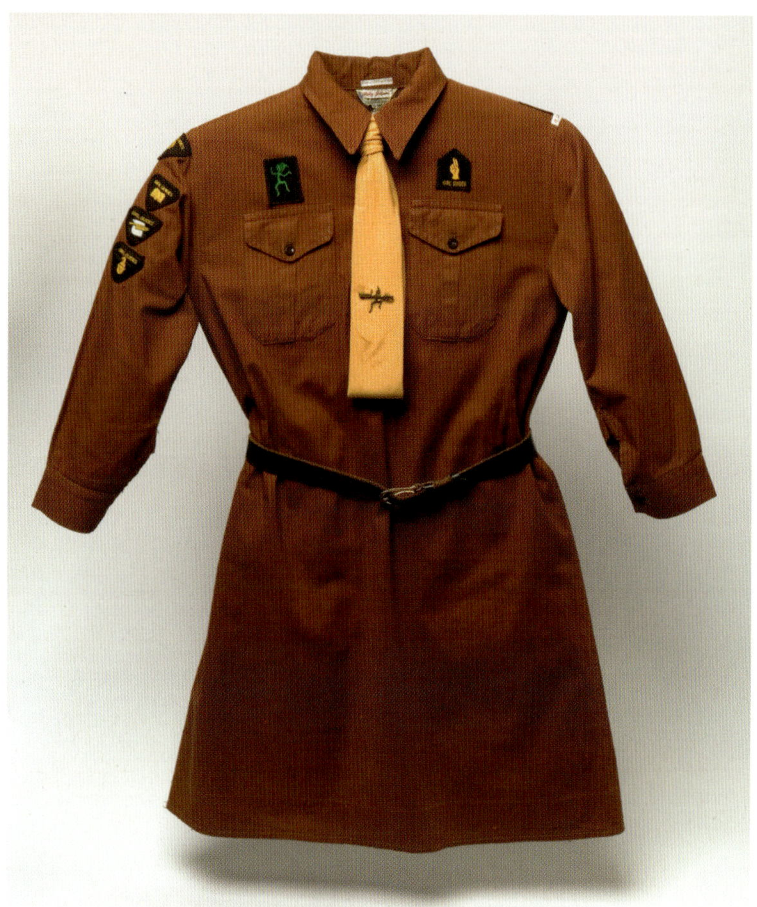

Brown is often considered a demure and sensible colour. Brown shoes such as these men's brogues from the 1940s or 1950s (below right) are not for dress suits or parties. The brown habits of Capuchin nuns embody their humble focus on the internal religious life; this 19th-century figure (opposite) is one of a set of fifty dressed to represent the outfits worn by different Catholic religious orders. This 1960s uniform (above right) belongs to the Brownie section of the Girl Guides, who take their name from ancient British folklore about brown sprites that secretly complete chores while householders sleep. Brownie 'law' states 'a Brownie Guide thinks of others before herself'. Brown is a practical shade for a uniform, and is often also the default in uncoloured wares and textiles. This stoneware bottle (above) from the Moira pottery in the Midlands, England, was produced in 1981, but could easily be from 150 years earlier. The simple, brown, salt-glazed form unashamedly claims utilitarian chic by copying plain stoneware storage bottles from the 18th and 19th centuries.

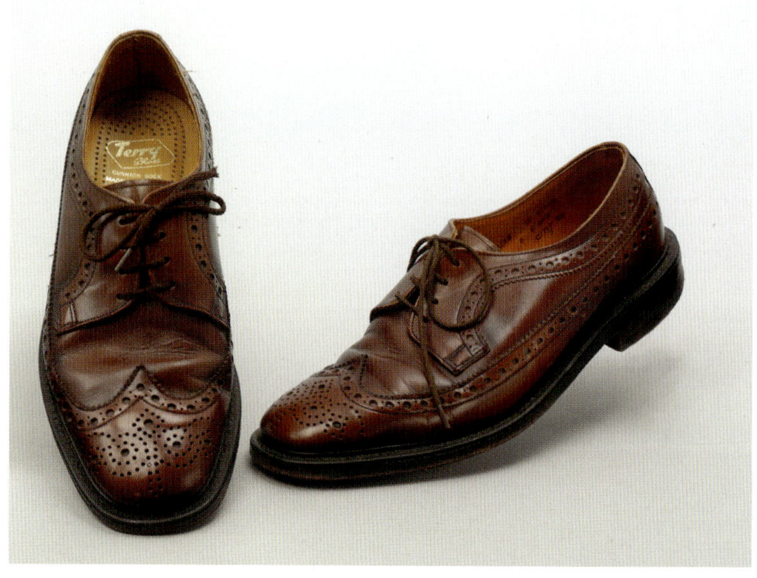

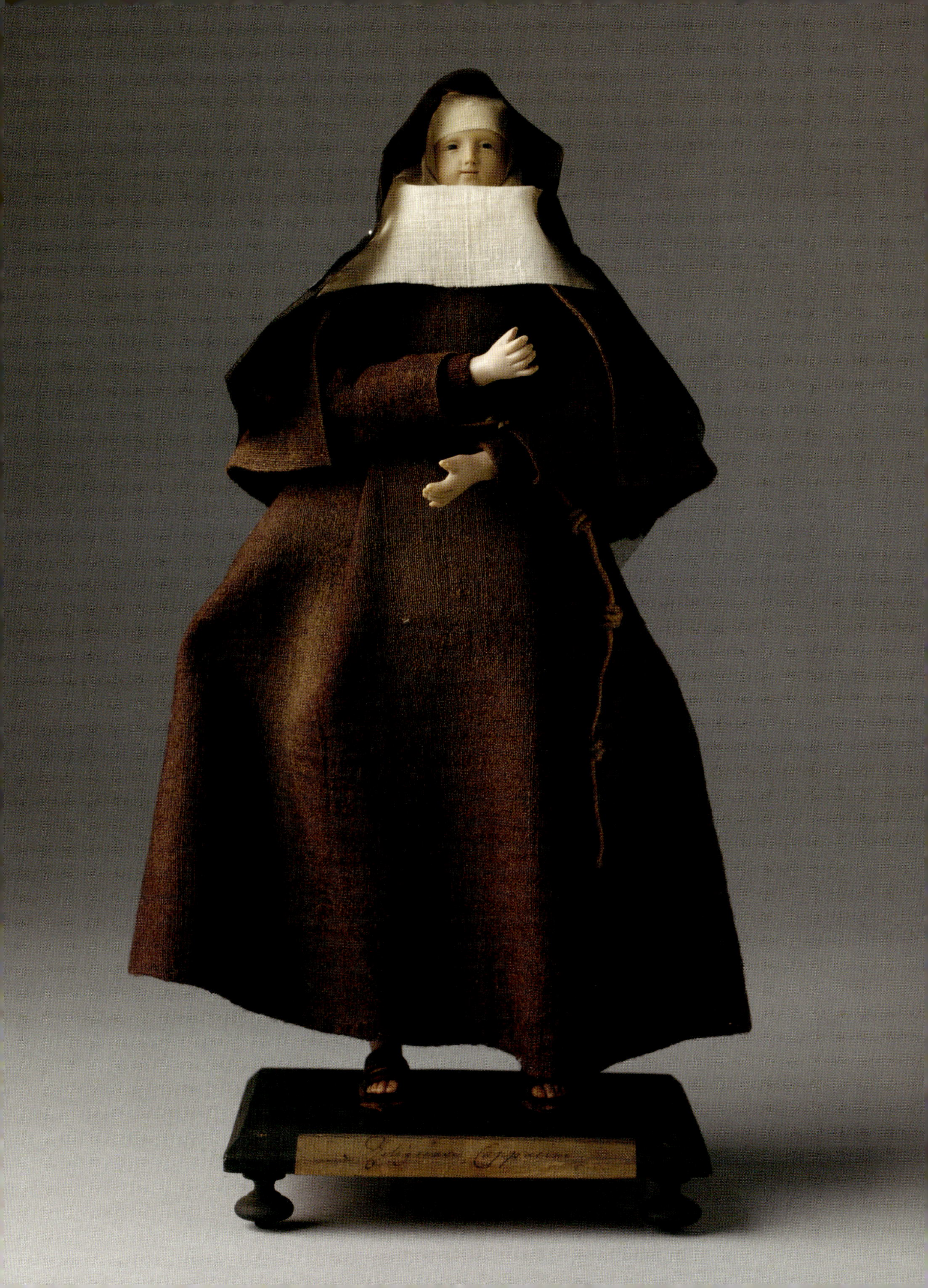

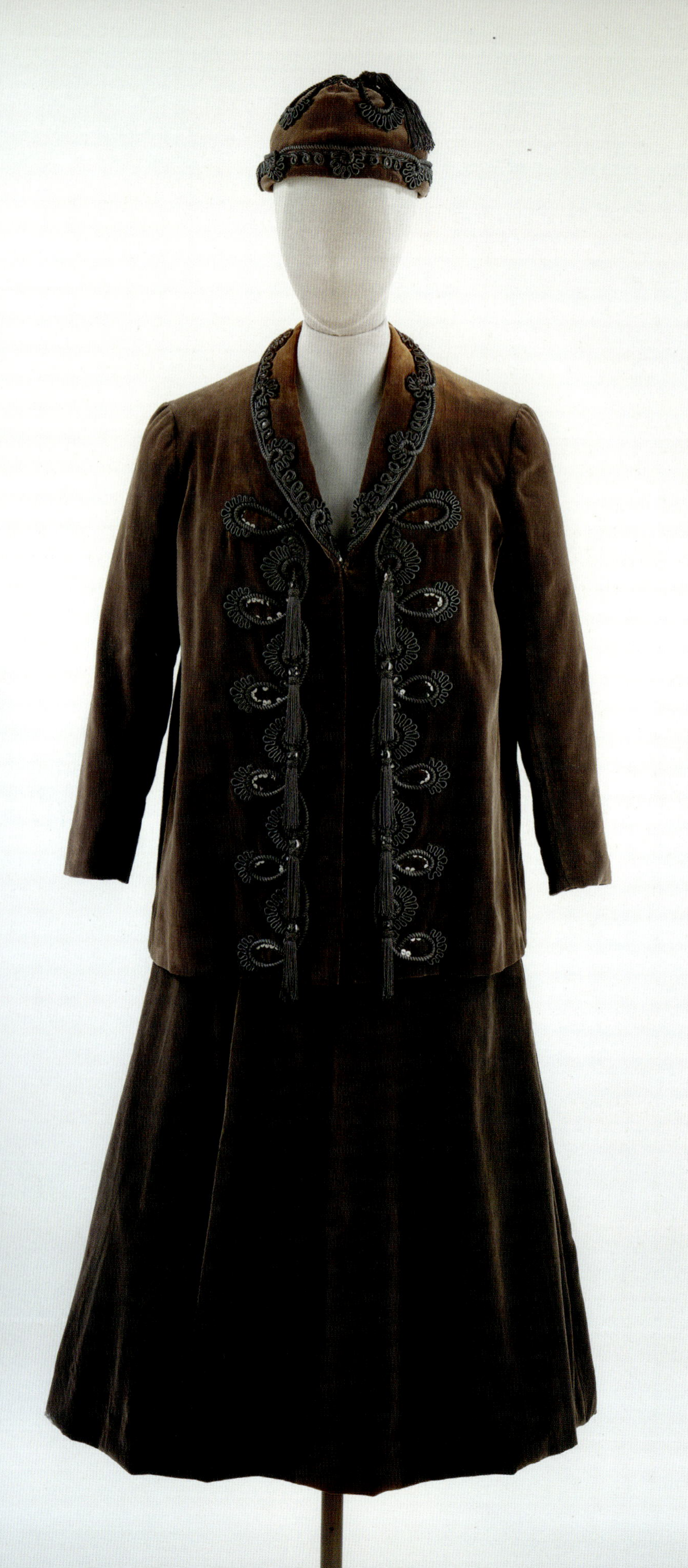

In 1754, the British cabinetmaker Thomas Chippendale published a book of his furniture designs titled *The Gentleman and Cabinet Maker's Director*. It was a huge success, and his furniture, such as this chair (1755–70; opposite, bottom left), became fashionable in homes throughout Britain, making 'Chippendale' the first English furniture style not named after a monarch. In France, the French cabinetmaker André-Charles Boulle made tortoiseshell popular by inlaying it with delicate brass motifs, as on this exquisitely detailed box (1710–15; opposite, bottom right). Boulle furniture remained fashionable across Europe until the 19th century.

Brown was transformed from sensible to haute couture by Pierre Balmain in this suit made for Gertrude Stein from 1945–6 (left), but it was not until the 1970s that the colour gained mainstream popularity across all areas of design. This suit by John Richmond (1970; opposite, top right) has the decade's signature flares and wide lapels, while the design of this brown mug (1972; opposite, top left) by the Clappison, Dadd and Hornsea Pottery was endorsed by the British Design Council.

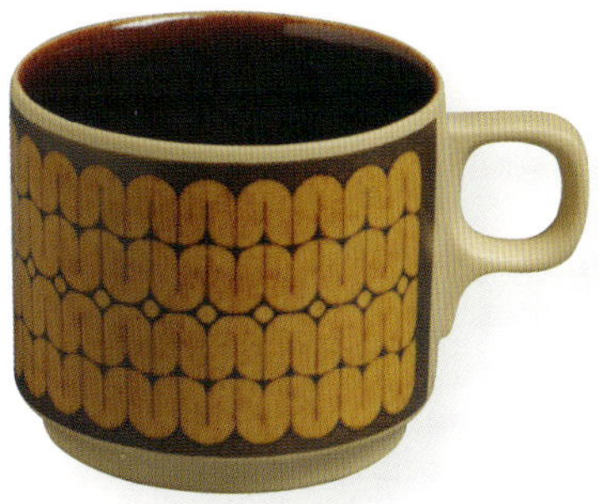

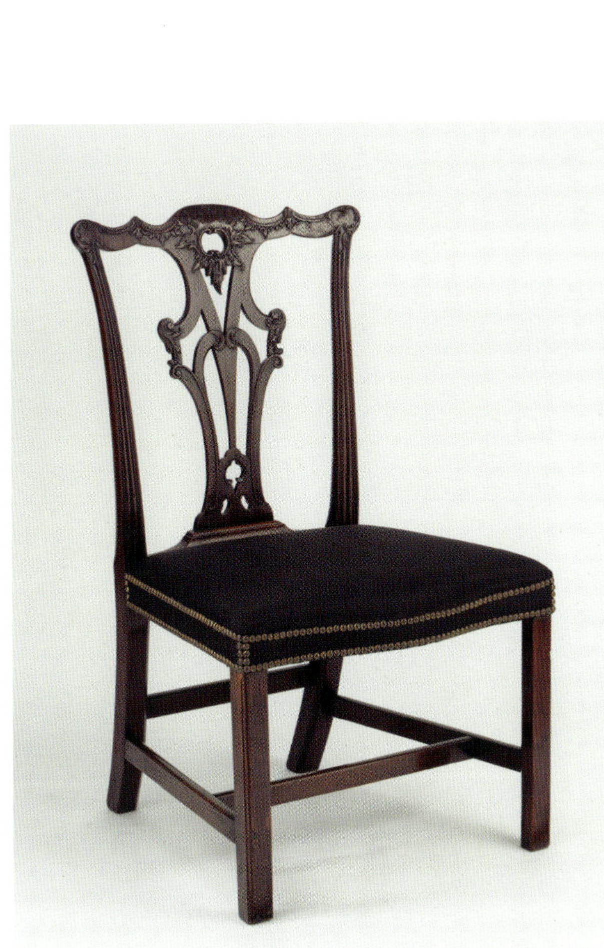

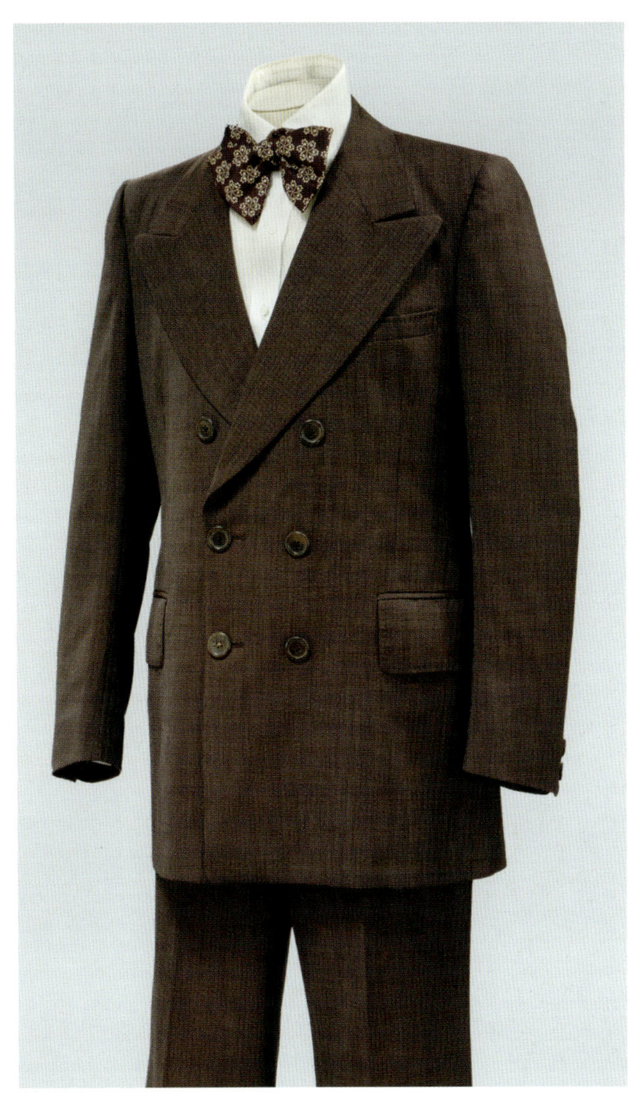

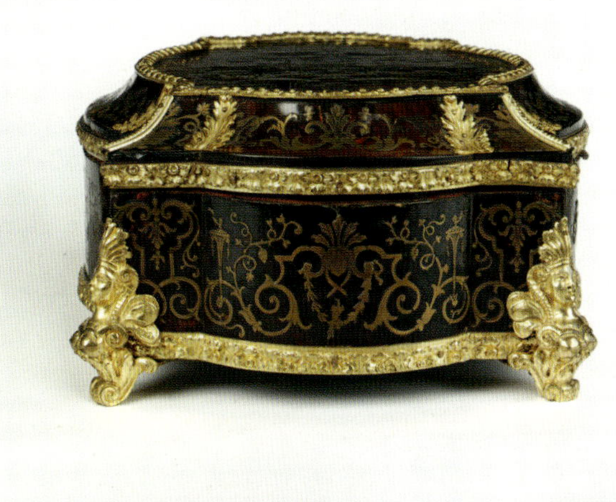

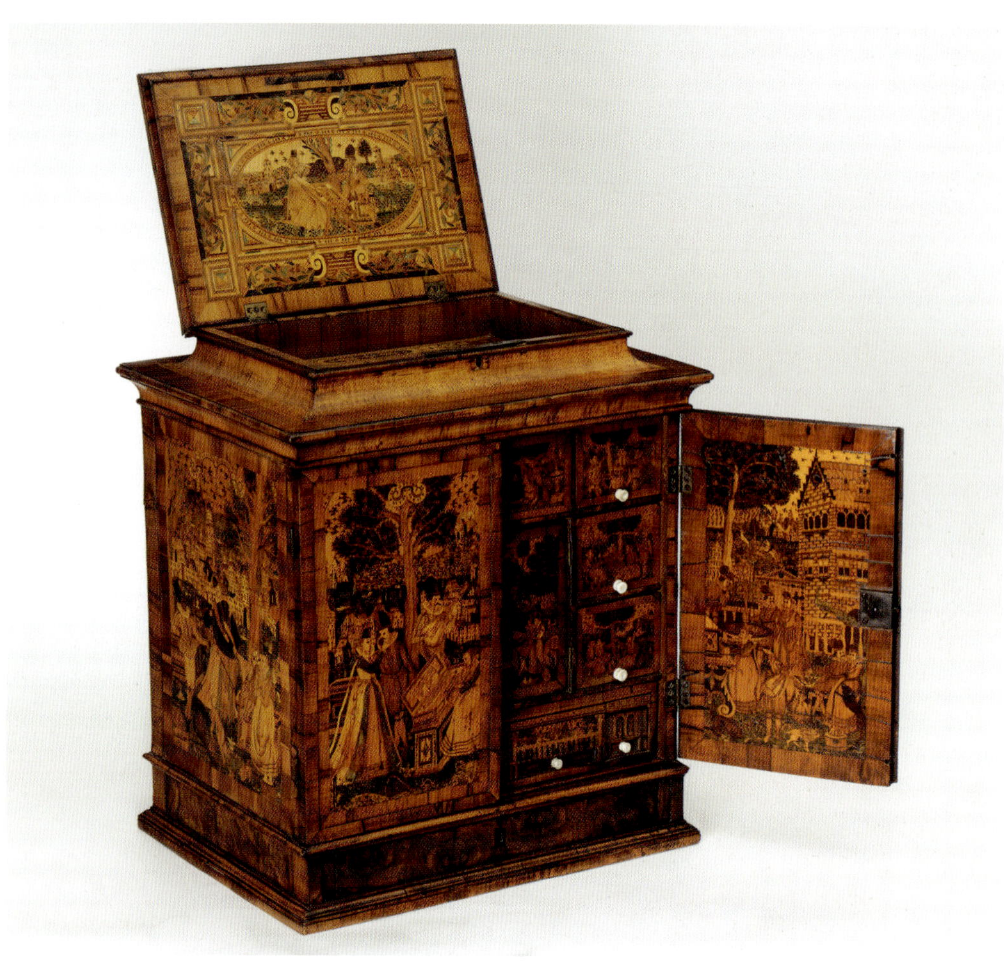

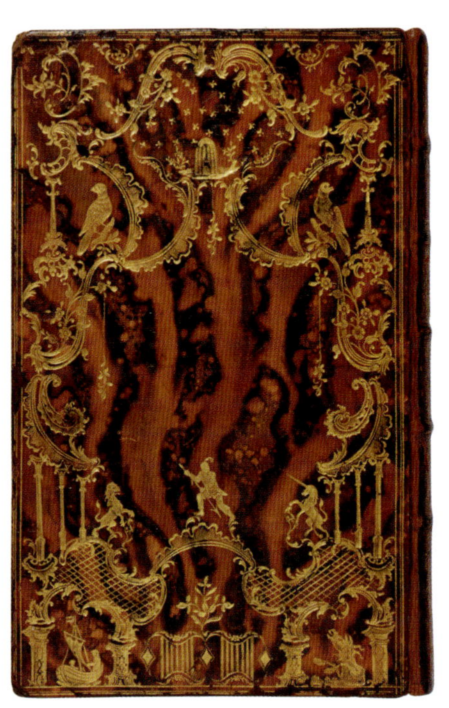

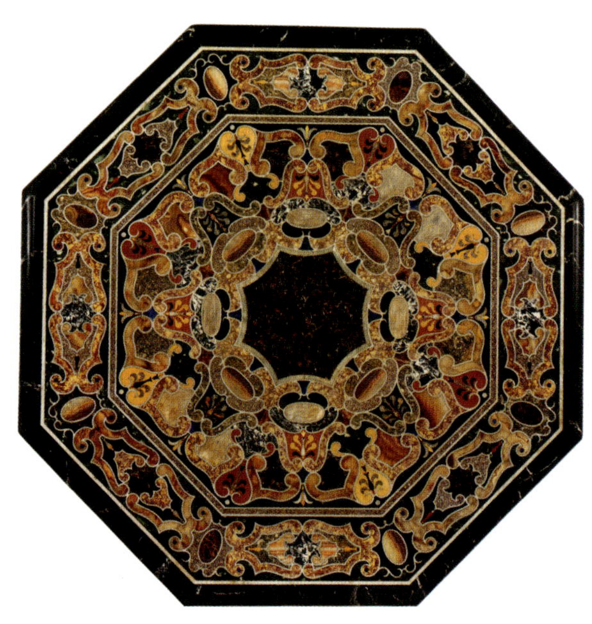

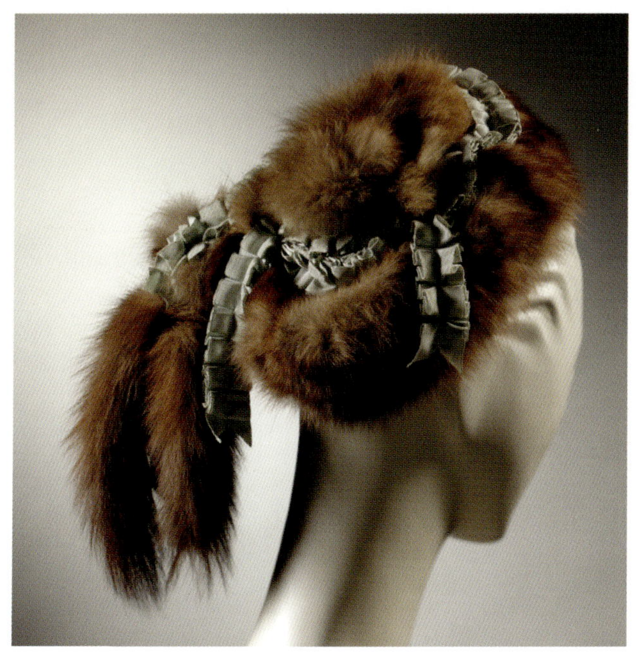

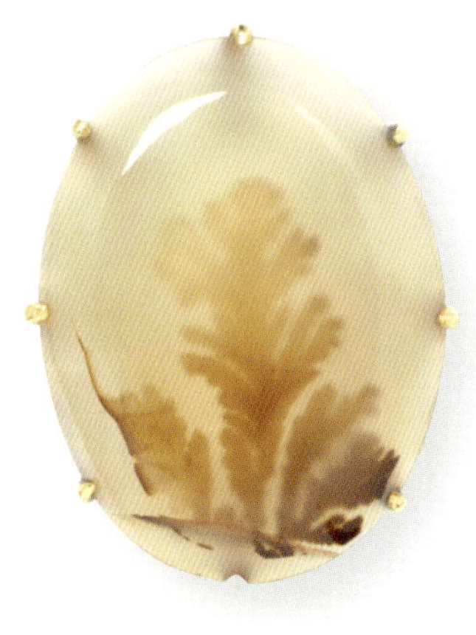

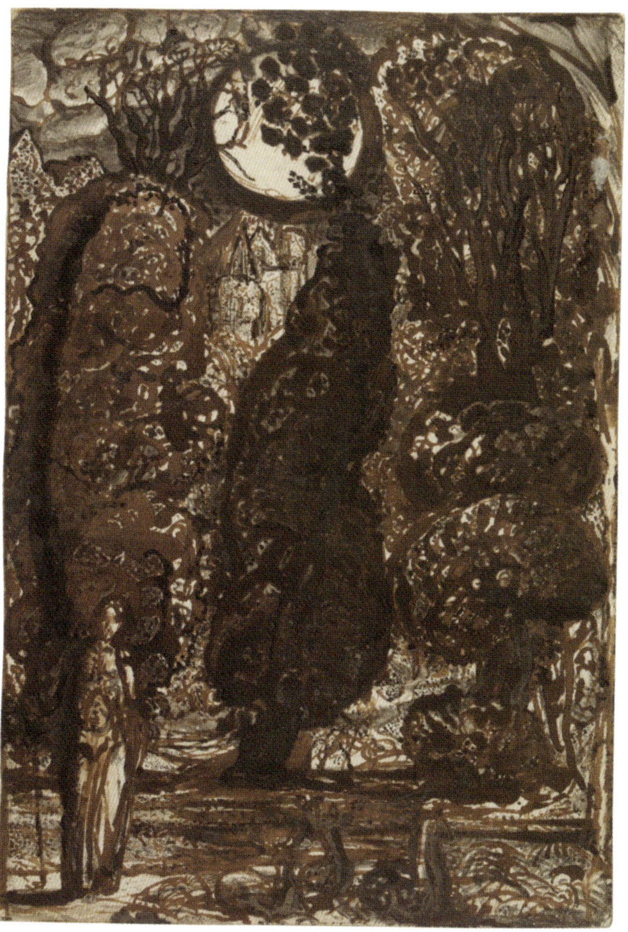

We rarely think of brown when considering gemstones, but moss agate has stunning natural forms and luminosity. The brown pattern in the stone of this 19th-century ring (above right) looks like a delicate leaf set in amber. It takes little embellishment to turn beautiful natural browns into luxurious objects. A frame of gold tooling brings out the warm tones and dramatic pattern of this leather binding by J.E. Baumgarten (c. 1770; opposite, bottom left), while a ribbon trim elevates a fur hat to high fashion (c. 1897; above left). Natural browns become fine art in this Italian *pietra dura* table (opposite, bottom right) and German marquetry cabinet (opposite, top), both dating from the late 16th century. Different types of the same material – stone for the table and wood for the cabinet – have been pieced together like intricate puzzles, to produce the beautifully detailed surface imagery seen here. For his *Nocturnal landscape with full moon & deer* (c. 1829; left), Samuel Palmer chose the softer, tonal qualities of brown washes rather than harsh blacks to represent the natural world.

Natural materials are often finite and expensive, and working with them frequently requires specialist skills. But there are many ingenious ways to mimic their qualities. This ceramic tortoiseshell-ware sauce boat (c. 1750; bottom right) was produced by adding manganese oxide to the lead glaze before firing. Papering a wall with marble-effect paper such as this 19th-century British example (right) is not only economical, but can also be installed without the need for a stone mason. This radio (1933; below) is moulded from Philips's own version of the plastic Bakelite, Philite, which allowed for mass production.

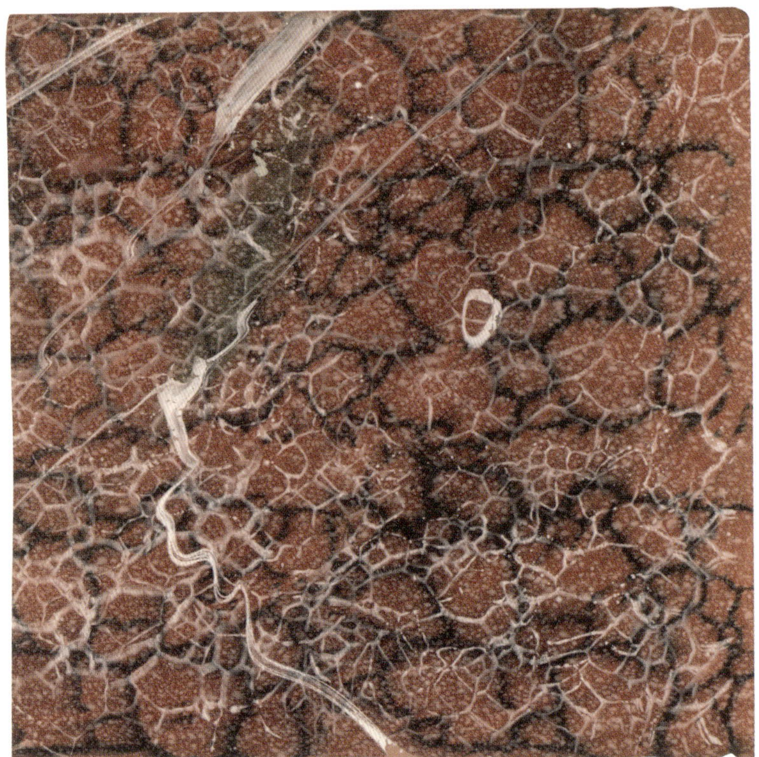

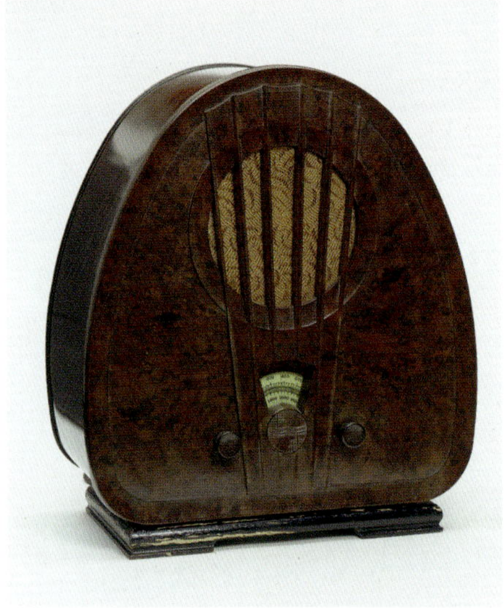

Leather is harder-wearing than plastic, but the buyer of these shoes (1960s, below left) would have cared more for the fashion statement than the longevity of their purchase. Maarten Baas's 'Plastic Chair in Wood' (2015; opposite) turns this idea upside down: the immediately recognizable cheap, mass-produced plastic chair is in fact wooden, and painstakingly crafted by carpenters in China.

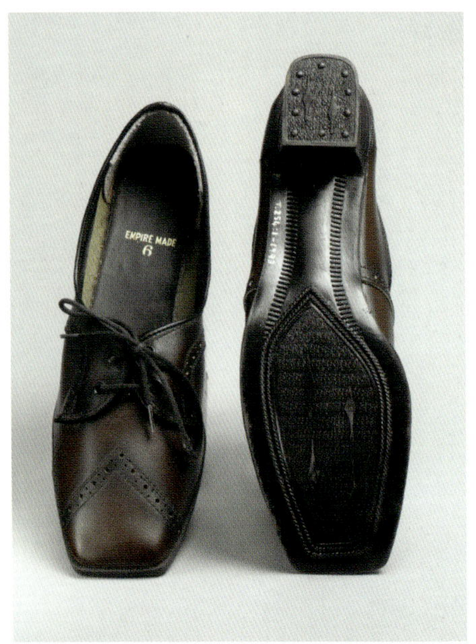

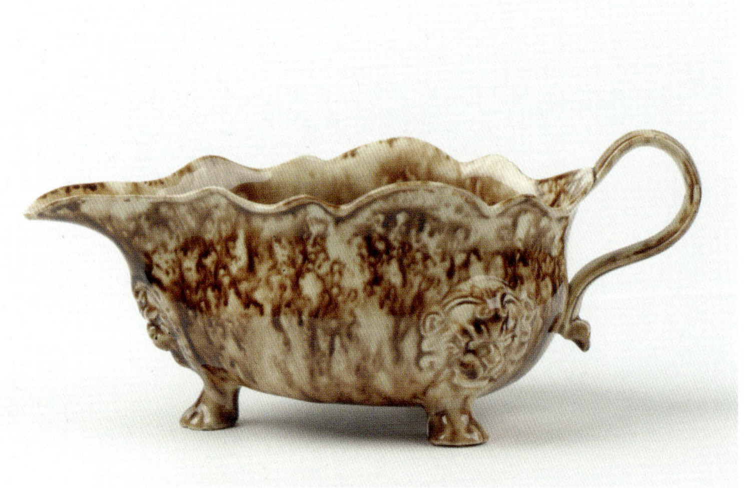

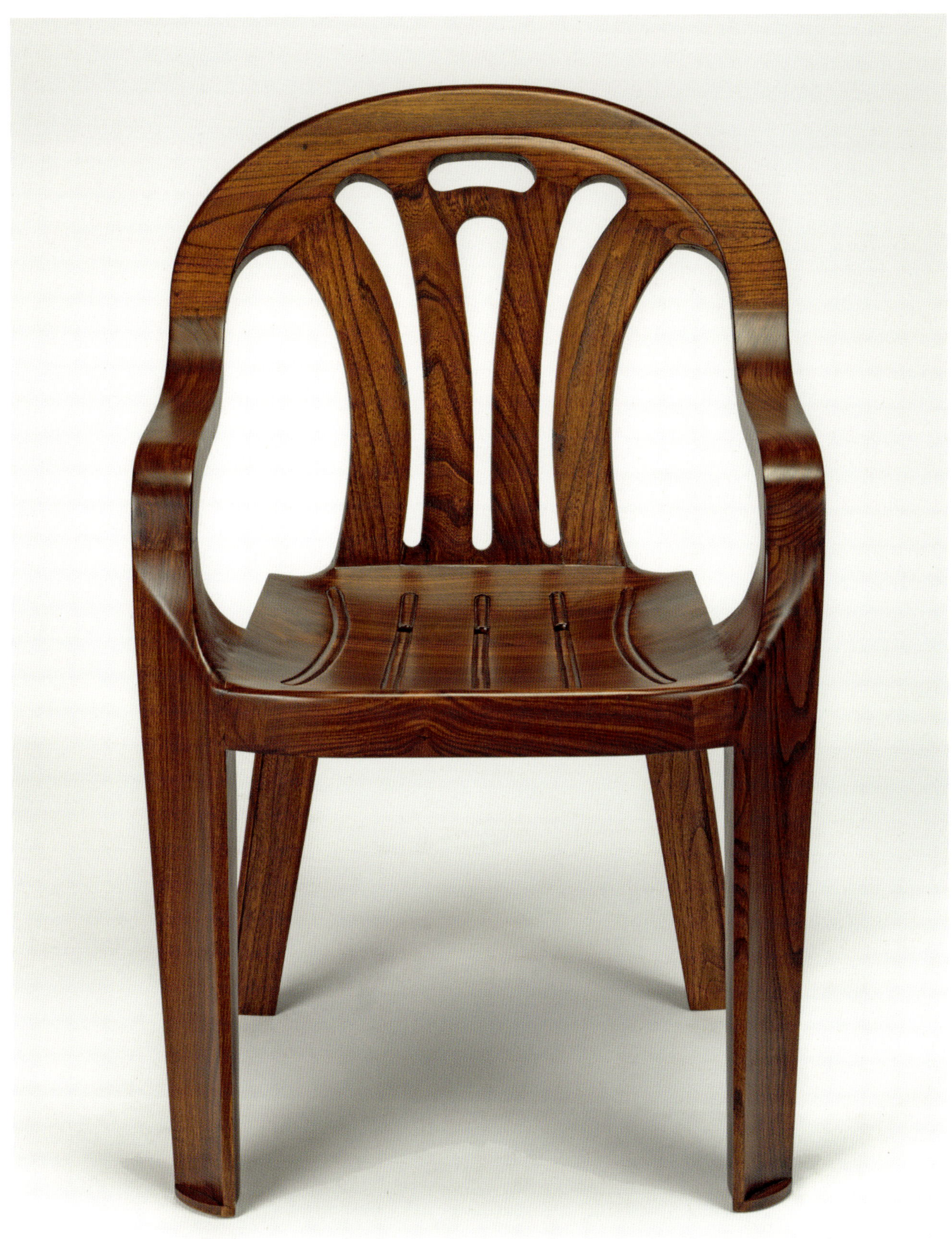

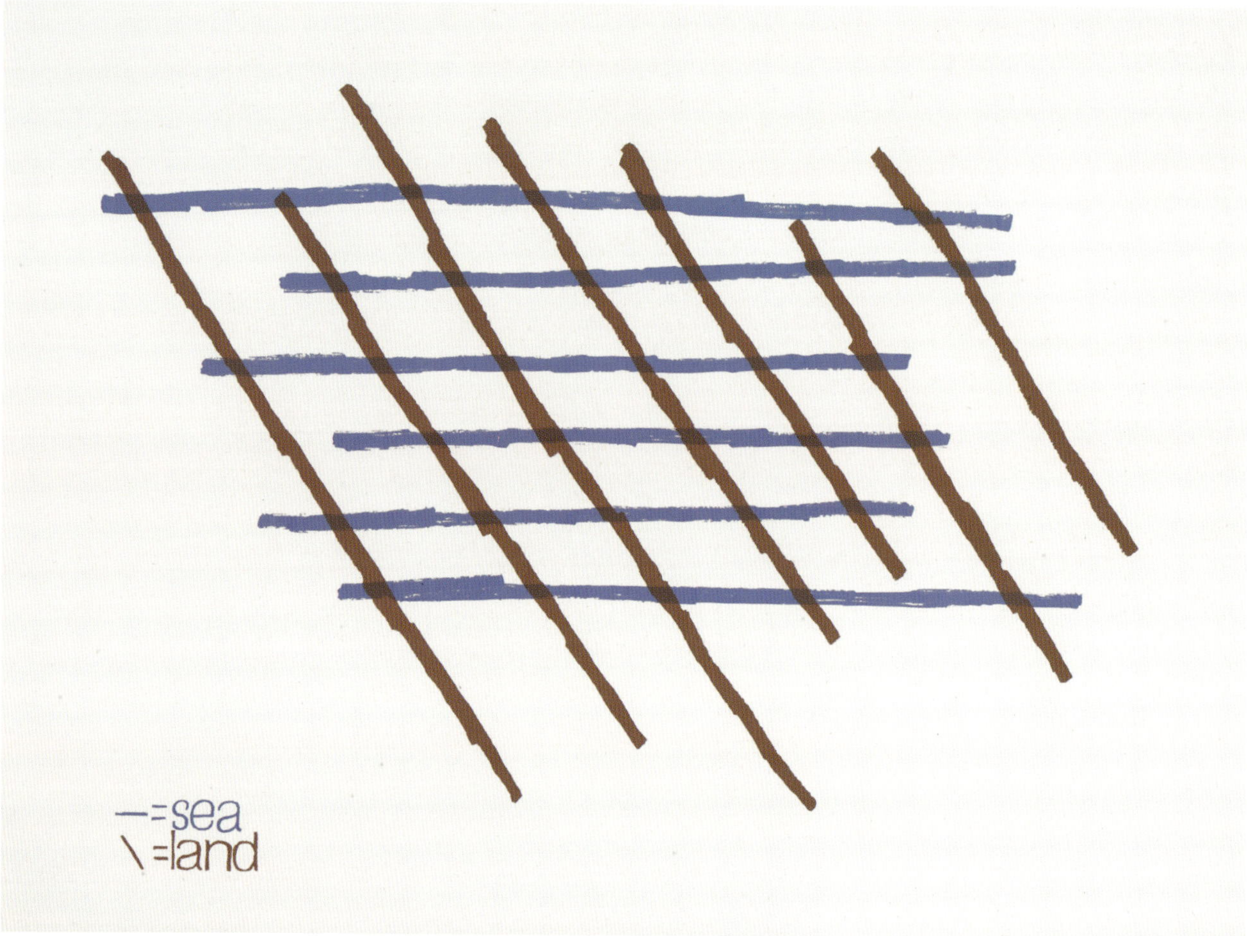

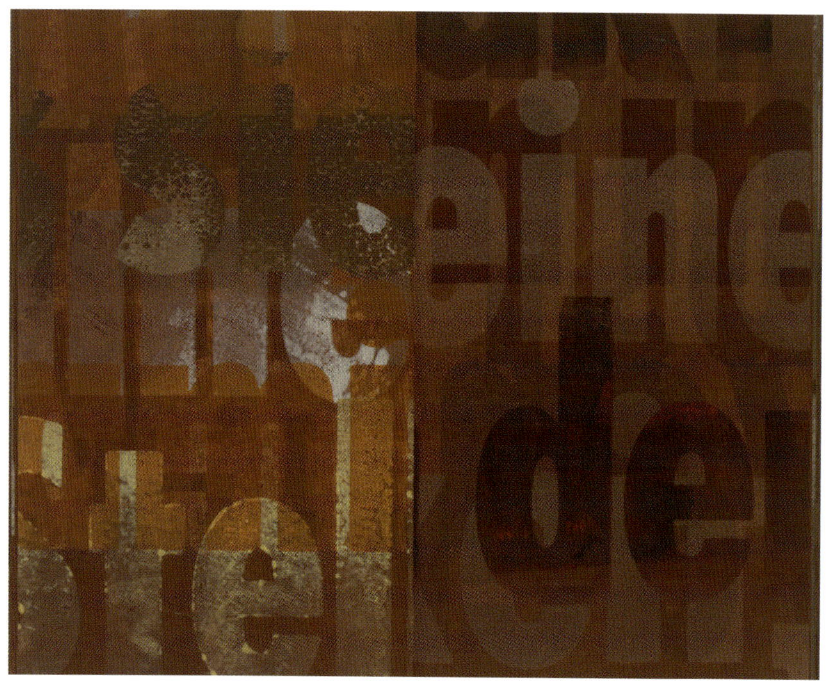

Brown has a fundamental connection with soil and the earth. In his print *Sea/Land* (1967; above), Ian Hamilton Finlay effectively uses simple brown lines as a visual shorthand for the land. Perhaps these are the furrows of a ploughed field. John Constable puts a brown background behind his *Studies of Two Ploughs* (1814; opposite, top) to suggest the soil that they will turn.

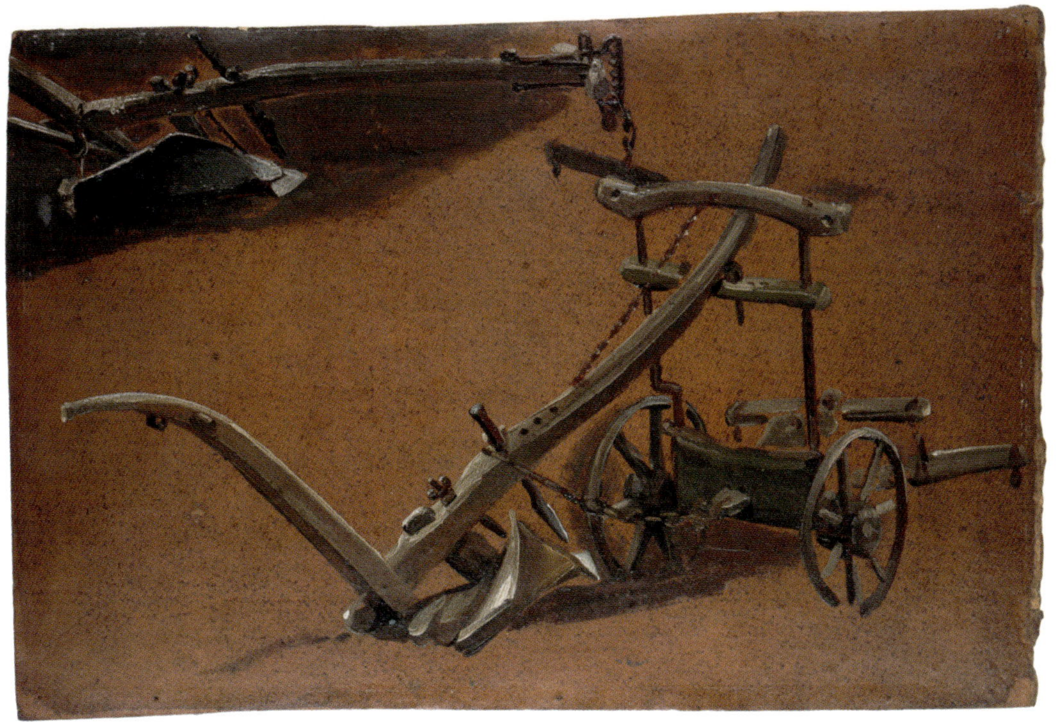

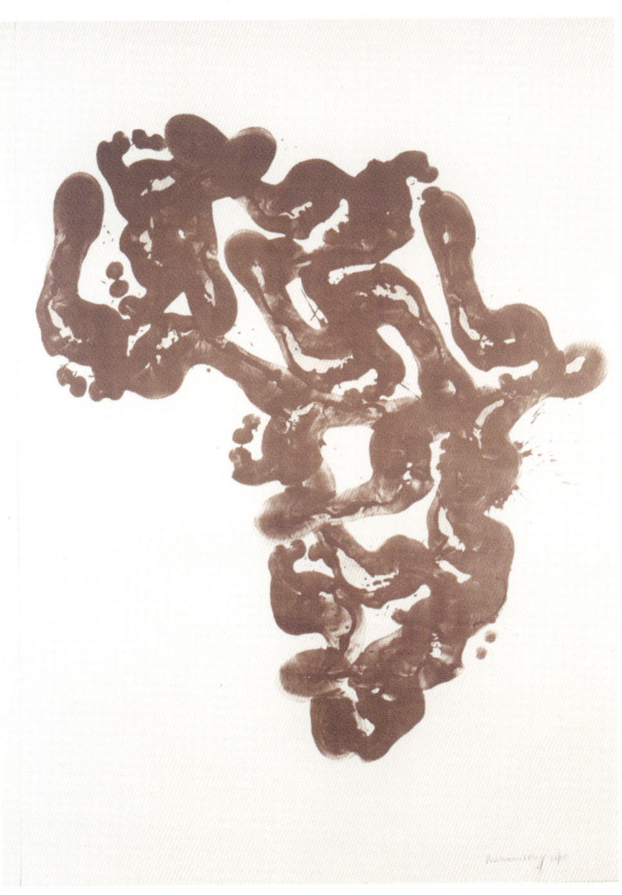

The artist's book *Erde* (*Earth*) (2006; opposite, bottom) was produced by Ines von Ketelhodt as part of a project with Peter Malutzki. Over ten years the pair published fifty books as an encyclopaedia, *Zweite Enzyklopädie von Tlön* (*Second Encyclopedia of Tlön*). Representing the letter E, the brown paper of Erde invokes the earth that it represents. This is overlaid with letterpress type in terracotta, grey and green, to create a landscape in text. Richard Long makes this link between brown and the earth explicit in *Africa Footprints* (1986; left) by marking out the land of the African continent in muddy footprints.

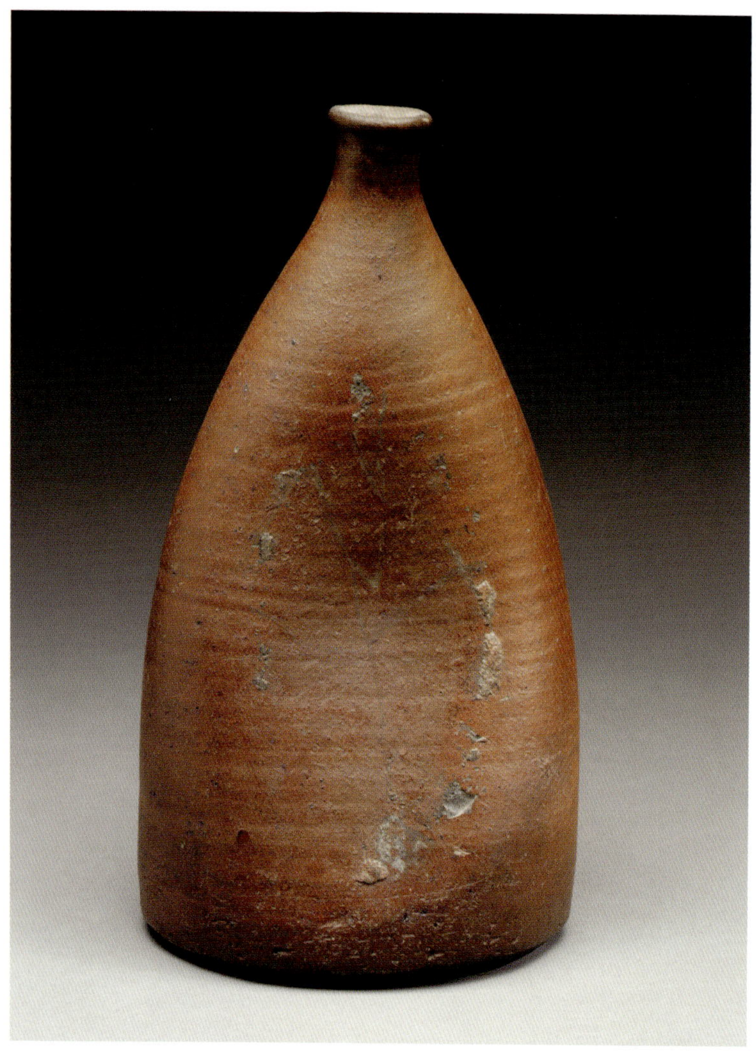

To make this Japanese Bizen-ware bottle (1700–1850; left), clay was taken directly from the ground and worked by hand. The colour and patina were produced in the kiln during firing. This faithfulness to natural materials and processes gives the object an understated elegance that has come to be highly prized in a world that feels increasingly dominated by mass-production and technology. Bryan Newman takes these two opposing concepts and subtly brings them together in his hand-modelled sculptural piece *Houses with Motorway* (1973; opposite). The natural earthiness of the stoneware contradicts the very urban concrete tower blocks and encroaching bypass. Richard Notkin's *The Double Cooling Towers Teapot no.10* (1984; below left) addresses this anxiety directly. Made in the traditional style of Chinese Yixing stoneware, the pot is unglazed to emphasize the beauty of the clay. But this natural simplicity is juxtaposed with an intricately detailed mushroom cloud knob and painfully jagged handle, highlighting humanity's self-destructive abstraction from nature.

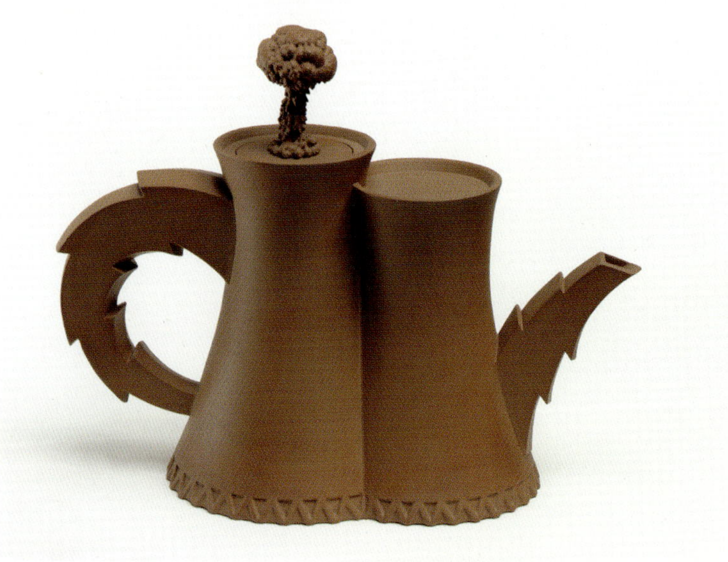

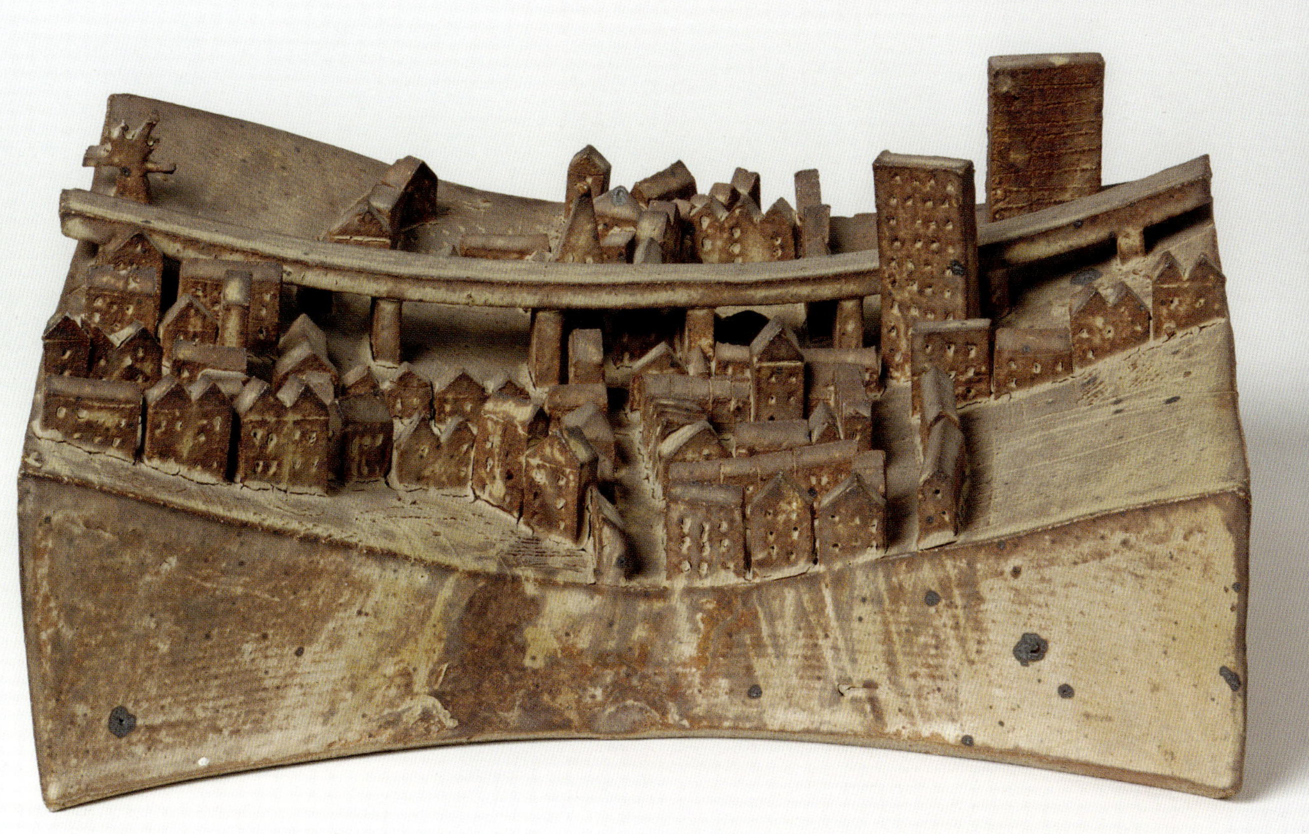

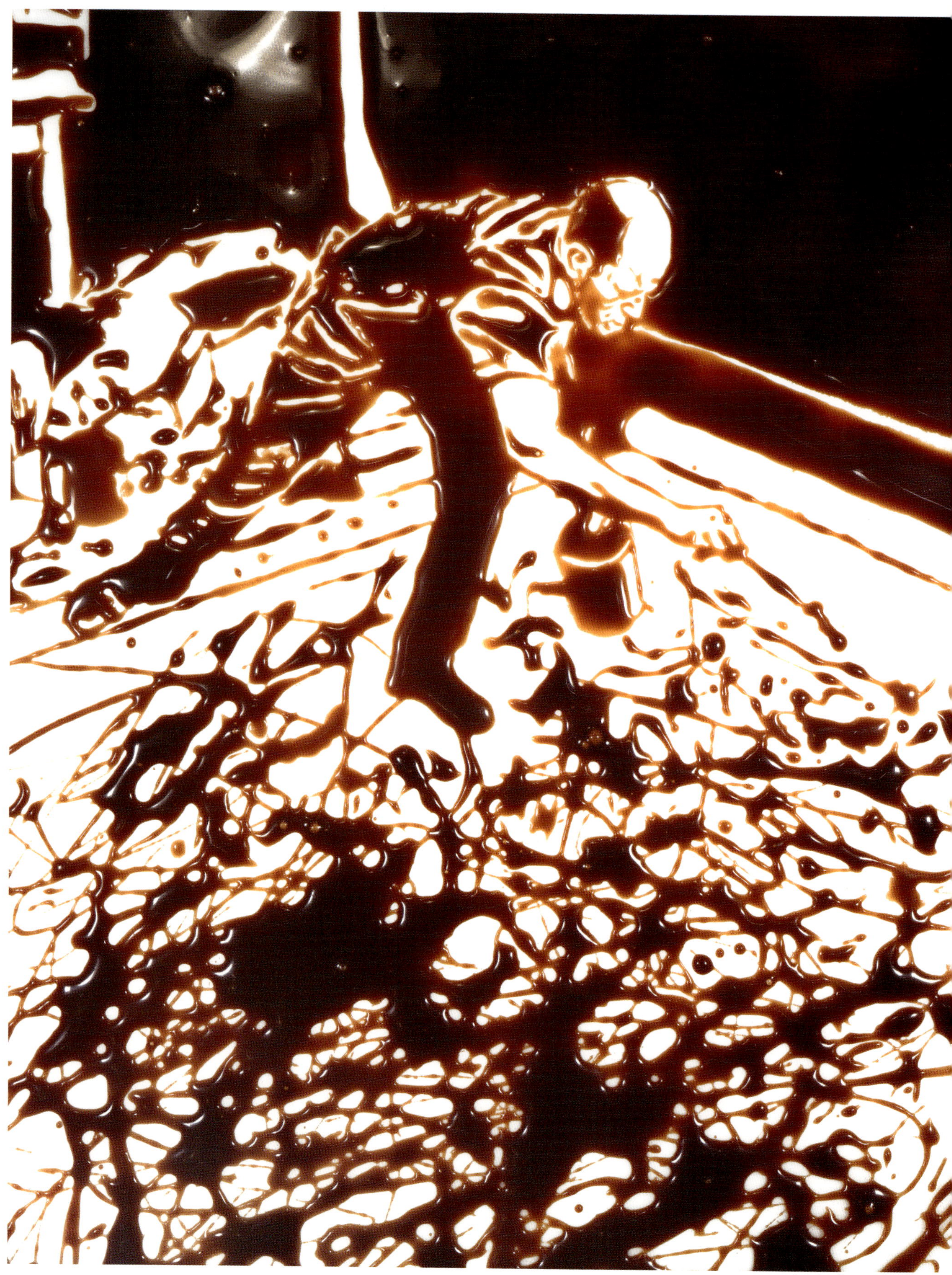

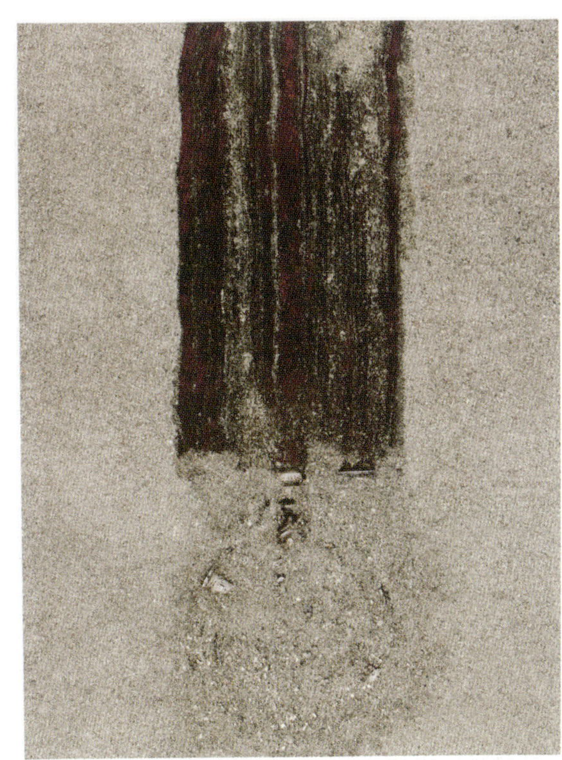

Brown is the colour of decay, rotting matter and bodily fluids. This waistcoat from the 1780s (right) bears a dramatic splash of blood from a duel wound, which has turned brown with age. These associations have also been used by artists to provoke debate. Blood stains and dirt replace the ribbon and obscure the medal in this print from Peter Kennard and Cat Picton Phillips's *Award* series (2004; above right). The portfolio was made to express their anger over the invasion of Iraq in 2003, and comprises fifteen prints of medals which have been degraded or destroyed.

The artist Vik Muniz invites viewers to think about the physical value of artworks by creating images from unusual materials including dust, rubbish and food. In his *Pictures of Chocolate* series, Muniz used Bosco chocolate syrup to re-create famous images, which worked particularly well in replicating Jackson Pollock making a drip painting in *Action Photo I (After Hans Namuth)* (1997; opposite). Muniz captured these chocolate artworks in large-scale photographs for display, leaving the original drawings to decay and disintegrate.

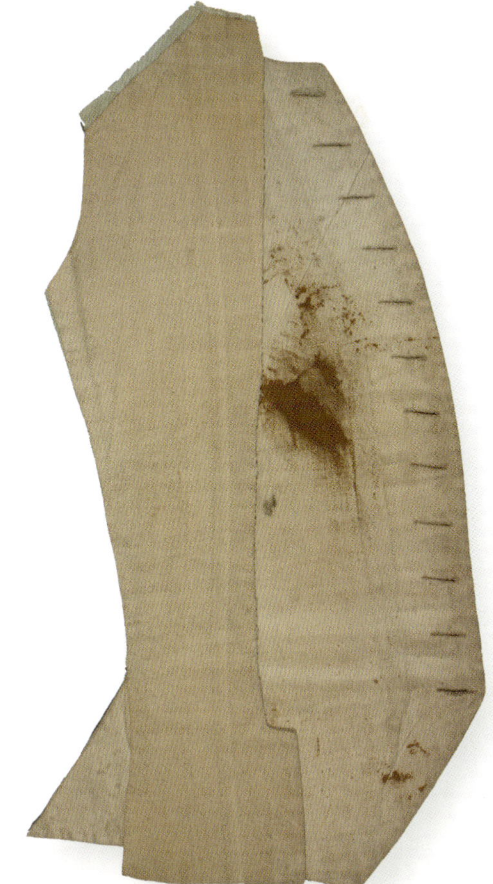

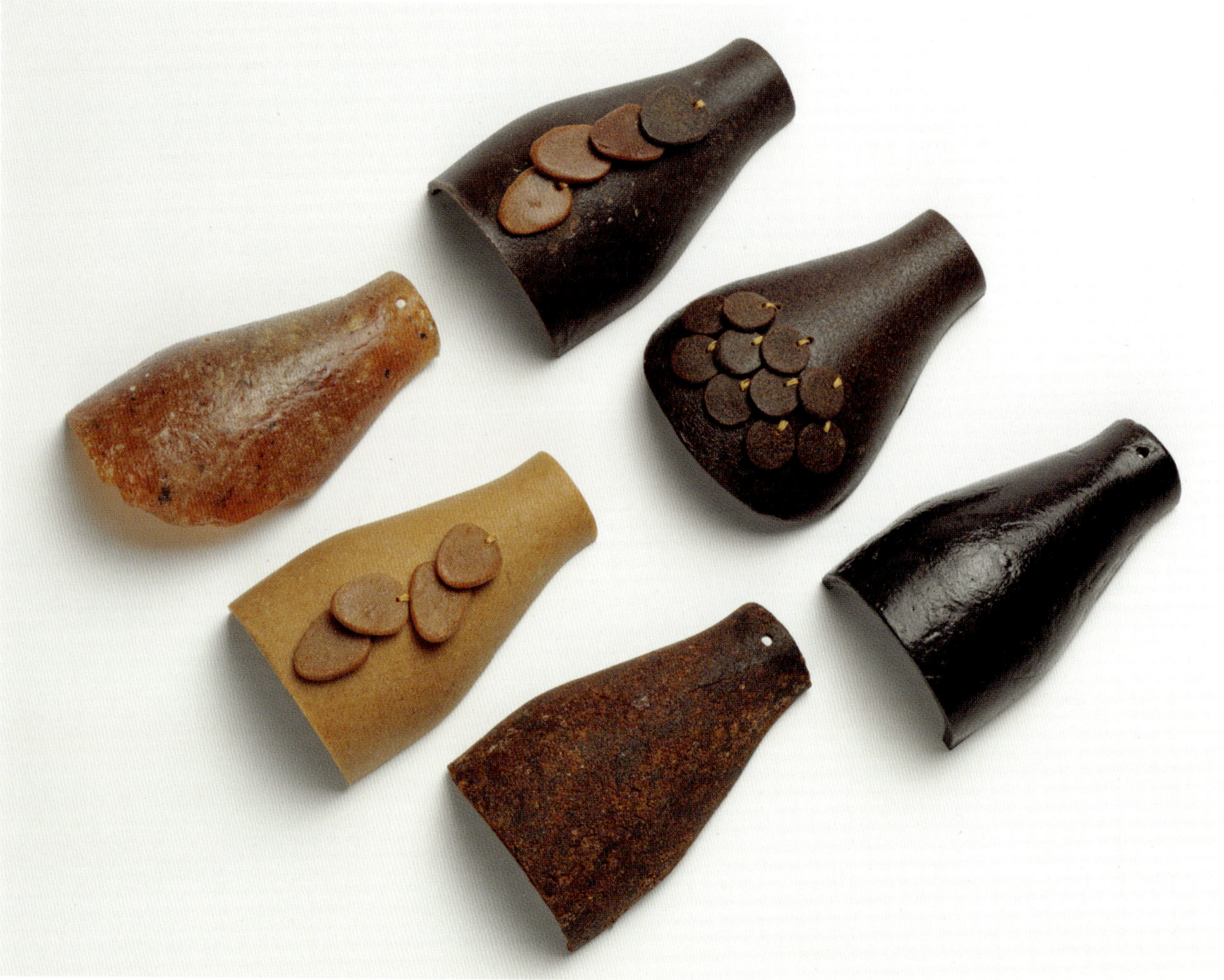

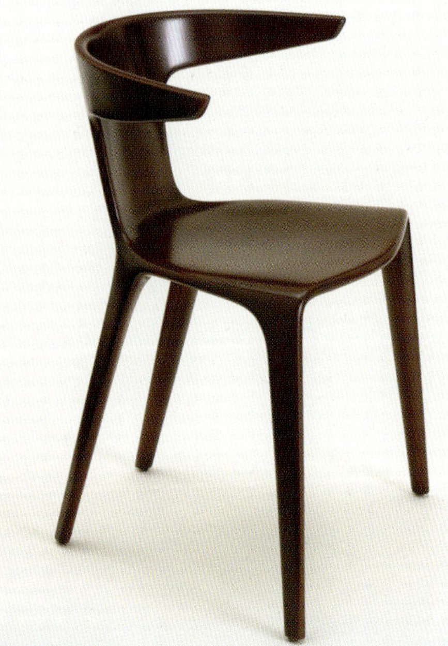

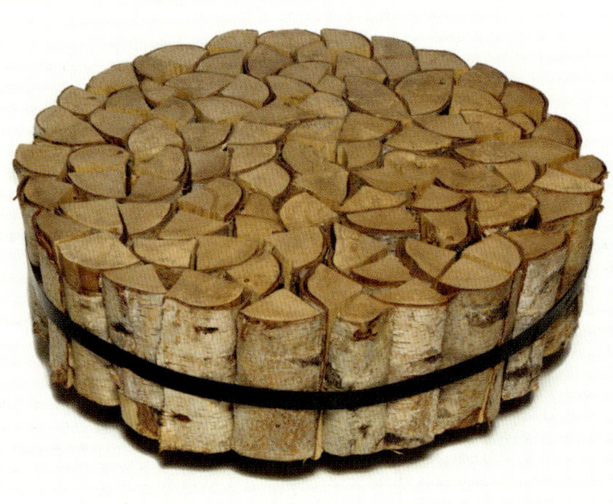

Brown's associations with nature and waste make it a very 'green' colour. The design of this Body Shop bag by Frances Myers (1990; right) conveys an environmental message by making a virtue of its plain brown paper construction and proudly declaring 'THIS BAG IS MADE FROM RECYCLED PAPER'. But recycled brown does not have to be plain or humble, and raw materials have produced highly sophisticated objects. The elegant 'Rothko' chair (1996; opposite, bottom left) by Alberto Lievore is made from ground almond shell waste, while the refined simplicity of Fredrikson Stallard's 'Table#1' (2002; opposite, bottom right) depends entirely on the natural beauty of silver birch logs. John Cage turned recycling into fine art with his suite of *Wild Edible Drawings* (1990; below right). Created from foraged ingredients such as milkweed, cattail and hibiscus, Cage wanted to produce beautifully textured papers that could be recycled as food. Studio Formafantasma also used natural materials when exploring sustainable and biodegradable plastics. Using ingredients such as shellac and natural rubber, in 2011 they created polymers with similar properties to synthetic plastics. The surprising results (opposite, top) are similar in appearance to the first plastic, Bakelite.

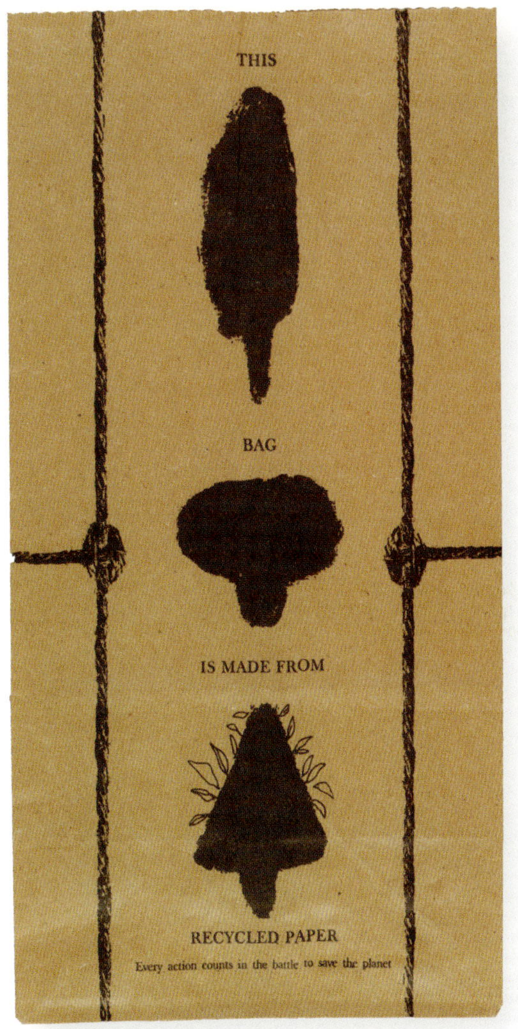

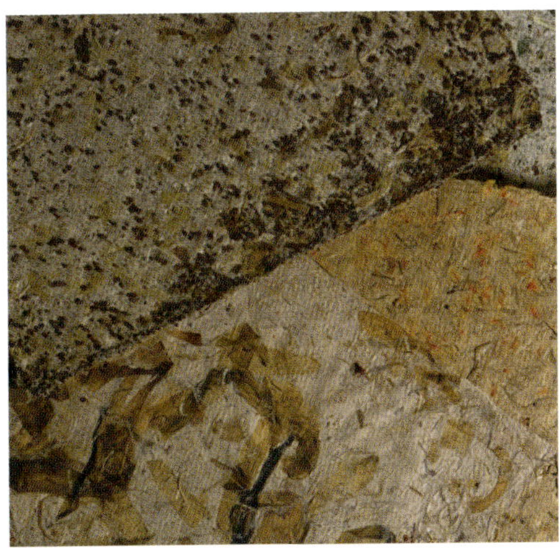

Brown is an important colour in the
artist's palette. Preparatory sketches
are often made in *brunaille,* or brown
monochrome, such as this one for an
Antwerp altarpiece (1619–20; opposite,
top left) by Peter Paul Rubens. The
lack of colour places the focus on
composition and form. The carved
detail of this small wooden sculpture
(c. 1500; below right), probably from
the Netherlands, needs no additional
pigment; the use of unadorned wood is
fitting as part of a sequence narrating
the Legend of the True Cross. On a
grander scale, Auguste Rodin's full-sized
Age of Bronze (c. 1880–1914; below left)
is a refined take on Classical Greek
bronze statuary.

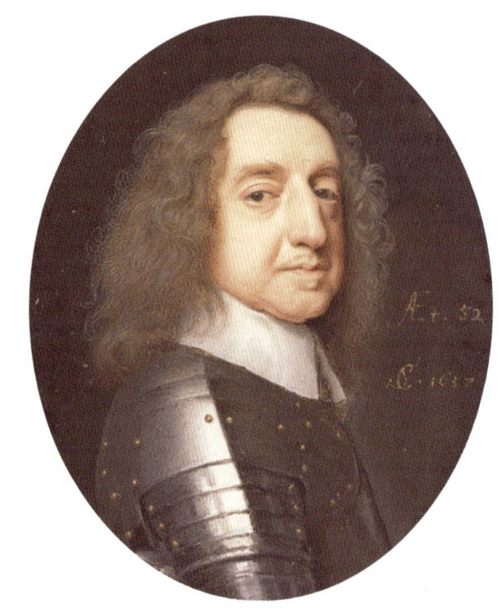

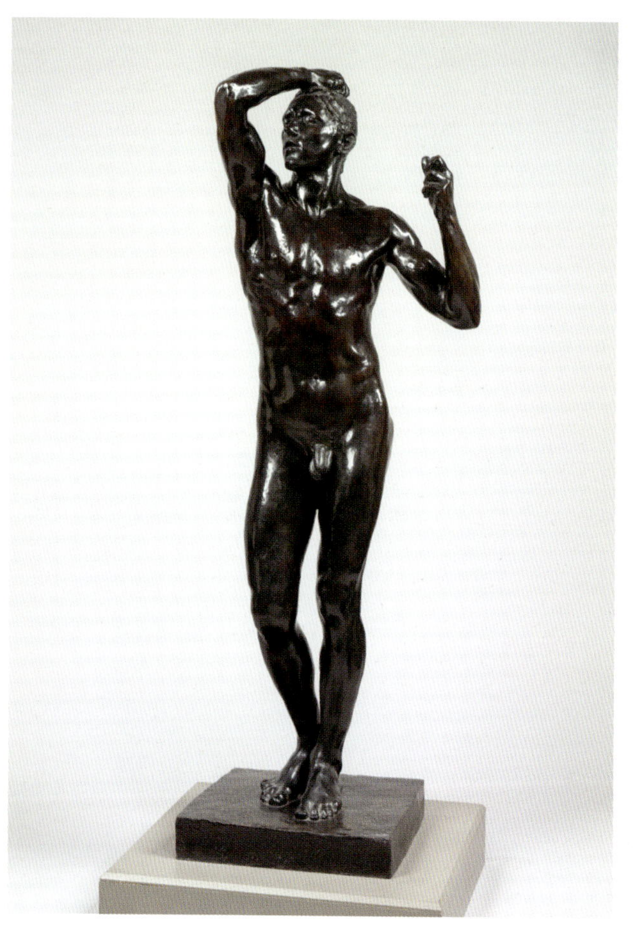

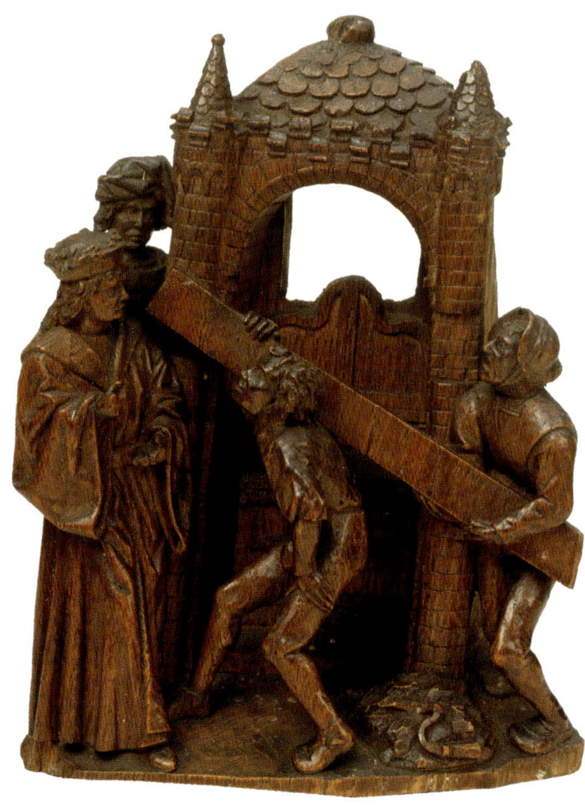

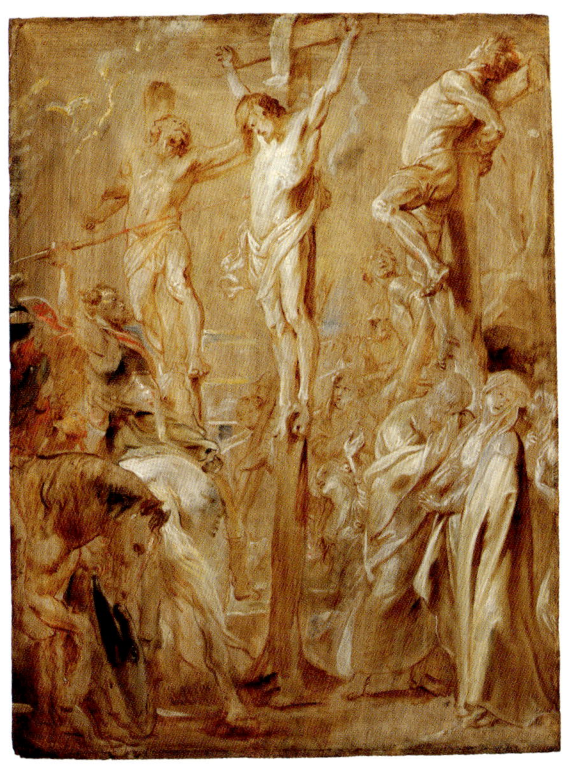

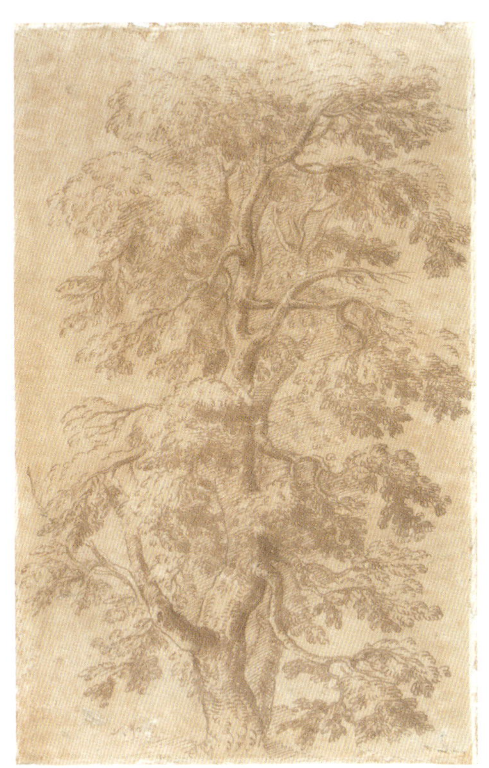

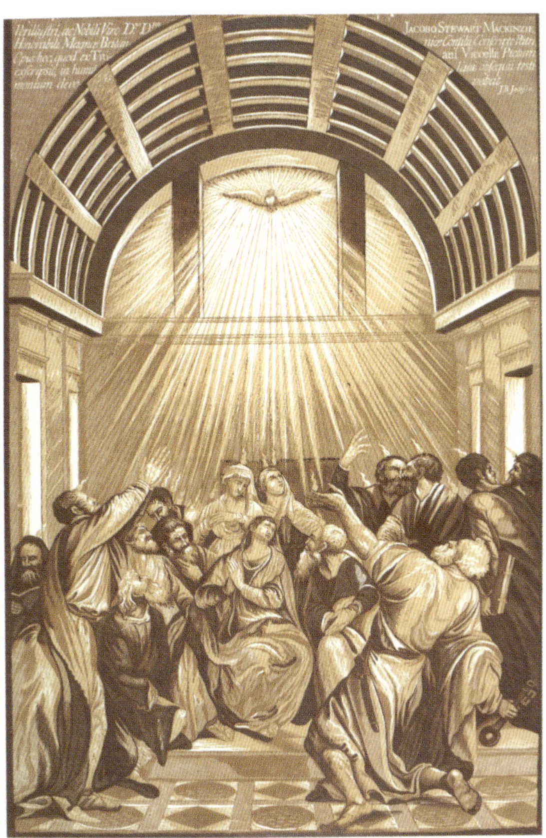

Sombre brown is also a popular choice for chiaroscuro, which uses the contrast between light and shade to create dramatic relief effects, as seen in this print depicting the divine light, *The Descent of the Holy Ghost* (c. 1745; left), by John Baptist Jackson. Similarly, the dark brown background of this miniature (1657; opposite, top) by Samuel Cooper brings into sharp relief the finely drawn features of Sir William Palmer. This 17th-century study of a tree (above right), possibly by the Italian Baroque painter Salvator Rosa, has been delicately rendered in pen and ink with a bistre wash – a brown pigment made from the soot of burnt beechwood and commonly associated with Old Master drawings.

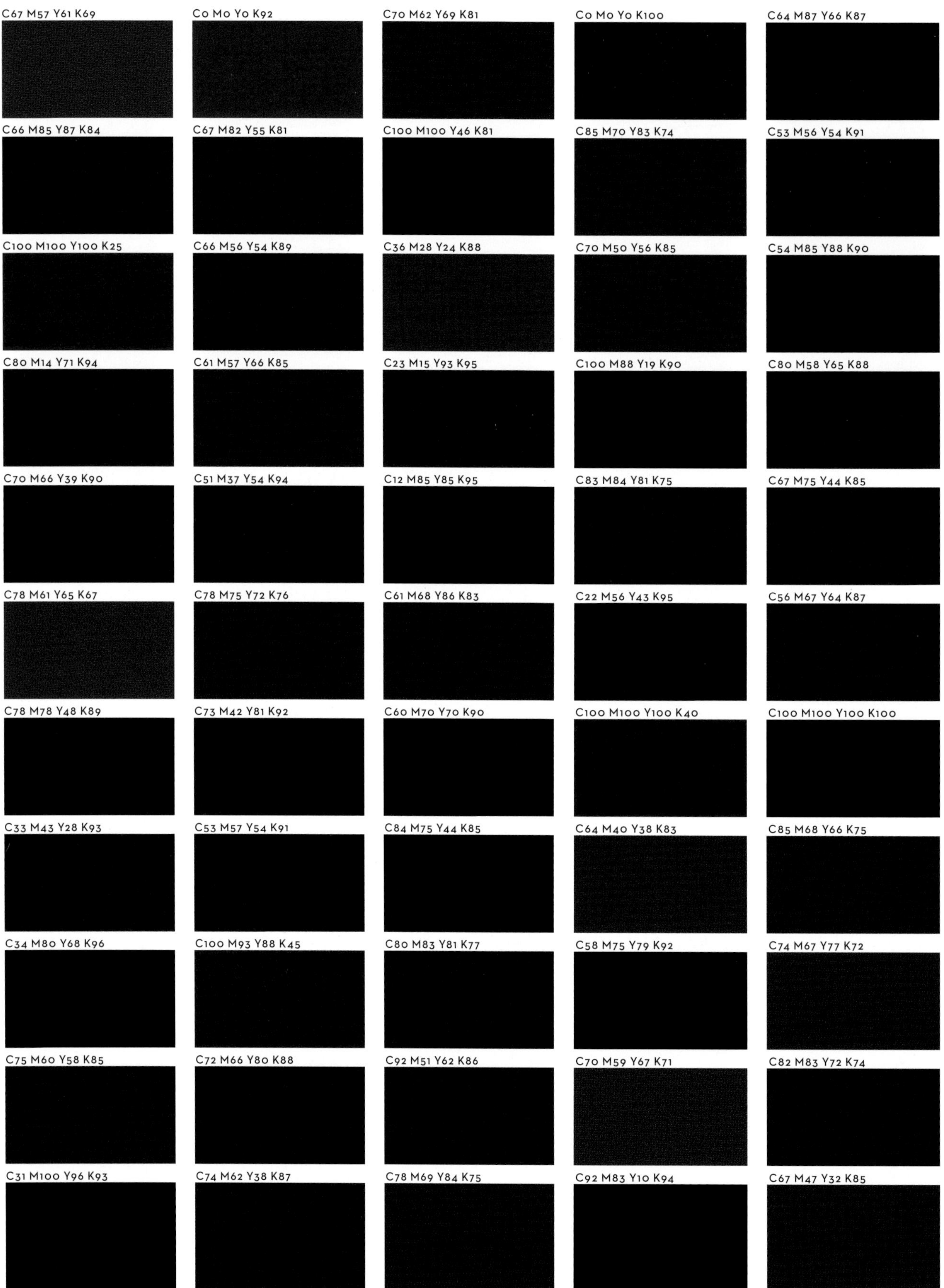

C67 M57 Y61 K69
C0 M0 Y0 K92
C70 M62 Y69 K81
C0 M0 Y0 K100
C64 M87 Y66 K87
C66 M85 Y87 K84
C67 M82 Y55 K81
C100 M100 Y46 K81
C85 M70 Y83 K74
C53 M56 Y54 K91
C100 M100 Y100 K25
C66 M56 Y54 K89
C36 M28 Y24 K88
C70 M50 Y56 K85
C54 M85 Y88 K90
C80 M14 Y71 K94
C61 M57 Y66 K85
C23 M15 Y93 K95
C100 M88 Y19 K90
C80 M58 Y65 K88
C70 M66 Y39 K90
C51 M37 Y54 K94
C12 M85 Y85 K95
C83 M84 Y81 K75
C67 M75 Y44 K85
C78 M61 Y65 K67
C78 M75 Y72 K76
C61 M68 Y86 K83
C22 M56 Y43 K95
C56 M67 Y64 K87
C78 M78 Y48 K89
C73 M42 Y81 K92
C60 M70 Y70 K90
C100 M100 Y100 K40
C100 M100 Y100 K100
C33 M43 Y28 K93
C53 M57 Y54 K91
C84 M75 Y44 K85
C64 M40 Y38 K83
C85 M68 Y66 K75
C34 M80 Y68 K96
C100 M93 Y88 K45
C80 M83 Y81 K77
C58 M75 Y79 K92
C74 M67 Y77 K72
C75 M60 Y58 K85
C72 M66 Y80 K88
C92 M51 Y62 K86
C70 M59 Y67 K71
C82 M83 Y72 K74
C31 M100 Y96 K93
C74 M62 Y38 K87
C78 M69 Y84 K75
C92 M83 Y10 K94
C67 M47 Y32 K85

BLACK

If you find yourself drawn to darkness, you are not alone. While society sometimes fears, shuns or looks askance at those shrouded in darkness, the colour black has captivated and inspired artists and designers throughout history. Their works celebrate the beauty and power of black as intense and flawless; the colour of supernatural mystery, sombre dignity, unsettling rebelliousness. Black can be both solid and shadow.

Creation stories often begin with the appearance of light within a boundless darkness. In the absence of visible light, black appears as both an absence of colour, and the only colour. Black and white, dark and light, night and day, evil and good – whereas white has been associated historically with light, life, goodness and purity, black has been widely used to symbolize evil, danger and death. Artists such as Rembrandt, Goya and especially Caravaggio employed a potent device known as chiaroscuro – Italian for 'light-dark' – to enhance dramatic or portentous scenes. Often, a divine light illuminates the pure, while sinners are marginalized, in spiritual and visual darkness.

The dramatic relationship between darkness and light was captured in a new and awe-inspiring way with the invention of photography, literally 'drawing with light', in the nineteenth century. Using sunlight and shadows to imprint images onto paper, photography has the curious ability to capture the insubstantial.

Darkness can make people feel fearful. Across many cultures, wickedness, the supernatural and sinister forces have hidden in its shadows. It is the colour of the Devil – the prince of darkness – and those who practise his 'black arts', especially witches, hailed by Shakespeare's Macbeth as 'you secret, black, and midnight hags!' The subject of much paranoia in the European Middle Ages and beyond, these sinister characters were often a source of fascination for artists. Traditionally, they inhabit the shadows of night, dressed in darkness. In the Romantic period a cultural obsession arose around sinister supernatural occurrences, with writers such as Goethe penning poems recounting tales of witchcraft and creating troubled characters who dabbled in the supernatural (see pp. 288–9).

Often seen as otherworldly, black animals hold a talismanic place in the imagination. The mysterious darkness of crows and ravens has granted them mythic status in many cultures. Their habit of scavenging their food from corpses has linked them to the realm of the dead, while the birds' stark black plumage seems like a mourning outfit, not out of place in a graveyard or haunted ruin. In mythology from America to Scandinavia, these birds act as a conduit between the earthly and spiritual worlds. They are sometimes lost souls, messengers from the other world, companions of gods, artful tricksters or shapeshifters. They have also made their mark in literature with, among others, Edgar Allan Poe's *The Raven* (1845).

Black cats, meanwhile, with their nocturnal ways, have been demonized as a companion of witches and the devil. Seen as harbingers of bad luck, in medieval Europe black cats were sometimes slaughtered. In Britain in 2018, the RSPCA released statistics that showed that black or black and white cats take the longest to rehome, perhaps suggesting that these superstitions still linger. But their elegance and artfulness has also seen a number of artists succumb to their charms. An engaging feline peers out from a poster to welcome patrons to the cabaret 'Le Chat Noir', a famed Paris nightclub of the late nineteenth century. 'Le Chat

Noir' also epitomizes the freedom and excitement to be found under cover of darkness; nightclubs are just one of the many entertainments, from the uplifting to the risqué, to be found after dark.

Unlike cats and other nocturnal animals, humans are not natural inhabitants of the dark; exciting for some, for others the blackness of night is strange and unsettling, full of the unknown and the dangerous. The Greek goddess Nyx, the shadowy personification of night, begets discomfiting children such as Apate (deceit) and Thanatos (death), but also the Oneiroi (dreams). Inspiration can be found when willing eyes adjust to the depths of night. The darkness of night was especially alluring for the writers of Gothic fiction in late eighteenth- and early nineteenth-century Europe. In novels such as Ann Radcliffe's *The Mysteries of Udolpho* (1794) the night is crowded with macabre adventures and strange dreams; tormented souls may lurk in the gloom, the familiar becomes unfamiliar and imperceptible things haunt the shadows.

Also in the eighteenth and nineteenth centuries, day was turning to night as the Industrial Revolution darkened the sky. The black of industry is dirty, choking and polluting. Named after the soot and stifling black smoke of heavy industry, the Black Country is an area of the West Midlands that was one of the most industrialized parts of Britain in the nineteenth and early twentieth centuries. Craig Oldham's *In Loving Memory of Work* (2015) on p. 278 is a provocative, mournful tribute to the coal mining industry, which declined dramatically in Britain in the mid- to late twentieth century. Oldham uses coal dust particles in his contemporary print, a carbon-based material like those that have enabled artists to draw and create in black for thousands of years.

In the 1760s, Josiah Wedgwood unearthed his own new darkness from fire, when he created a black stoneware ceramic. His black basalt ware was made to imitate pure volcanic basalt rock, a form of cooled lava that was prized in the ancient world for sculpture and vessels. The intense heat of a high-temperature firing process transformed his reddish clay to an alluring black. Enamoured of his dark discovery, Wedgwood declared: 'Black is Sterling and will last forever'.

Just as black can symbolize the eternal void, the nothingness before Creation, it can also be an essential instrument of the act of creation itself. Charcoal, carbon from burnt wood and the sooty deposits from flames were among the earliest and blackest drawing and writing materials. A simple black ink mark on white communicates thoughts and ideas. In Zen Buddhism, the making of a calligraphic mark can be a spiritual, meditative act.

Reversing the prominence of black on white, Aubrey Beardsley ignored fellow artist Walter Sickert's warning against drawings where there was more black than white, and revelled in making work in which black was the dominant colour, decadent and stylish. The intense, sooty blackness of a mezzotint makes it distinctive among printing techniques. The prepared printing plate, with its worn down, pitted surface, allows the maximum uptake of ink, which when printed creates a rich, soft depth to the dark areas and subtle shifts in tonality. An exquisite contemporary example is Judith Rothchild's study of pears on p. 272.

Trees have been a rich source of naturally dark materials: ebony and jet are formed from wood, and lacquer from tree sap. Ebony and lacquer are rare and sought after products of species native to Asia and Africa, while jet originates from long-hidden primordial forests. Ebony is a dense, black hardwood that can be polished to a smooth finish. Examples of carved ebony have been found in Ancient Egyptian tombs. Initially imported to Europe by Dutch travellers from India and Africa in the sixteenth century, its rare, velvety beauty made it the perfect material for creating luxury furniture, musical instruments and games pieces. As a result of unsustainable harvesting, many ebony species are now threatened.

Another dark, natural treasure is the gleaming, lustrous sheen of lacquer. The process of collecting resin from the east Asian lacquer tree and transforming it into a hard, smooth, high-gloss coating for objects began thousands of years ago in China and Japan. These exquisite black artefacts became a global phenomenon from the sixteenth century, as trade brought them to the west, and Chinese and Japanese lacquer makers began to produce certain wares in forms and patterns specifically for export.

The black gemstone jet is formed over centuries, as wood decays under pressure into fossilized carbon. During the medieval period it was believed to have medicinal and magical properties, demonstrated by its static charge if rapidly polished.

It was carved into distinctive, dark, protective amulets and rosary beads or pilgrim badges. Its dusky hue, which could be matt black or polished to a shine, gained it favour as a material for mourning jewellery, particularly in the Victorian era, which strictly forbade colour or sparkle during the long grieving period. Jet complemented the conspicuous gravitas of Victorian mourning dress. In grief, life loses joy and colour; black is worn on the outside to mirror the melancholy felt inside, but there is beauty and grandeur in it too.

The solemnity of black also makes it a desirable colour for those rejecting society. In many cultures and religions black is worn to display piety, modesty and penitence, chosen by those who set themselves apart for a life of poverty and contemplation. Originally clothed in undyed garments, the austere Benedictine monks elected to dress in black from the ninth century; this became a recognized symbol of their high level of spiritual rigour.

For much of human history, creating a rich and durable black fabric was a thorny task: dark blues and greys were poor alternatives, as black dyes quickly faded. Only from the late Middle Ages did opulent black clothing become obtainable in Europe. Dyeing methods were developed using iron deposits or scarce and expensive oak galls (tumours growing on oak trees), producing a heightened black colour that kept its pristine darkness. These new, striking fabrics were only for those who had the riches to acquire them, and thus black became a signifier of luxury and power, worn by princes and wealthy citizens showing off their status.

In the twentieth century Coco Chanel was among several re-inventors of timeless style for women. Black became a chic colour to wear for a wide variety of occasions: a sophisticated, practical and authoritative black suit could be an everyday working wardrobe, while Chanel's little black dress became a cocktail-party staple.

The colour black in fashion is also associated with oppositional forms of dress that set an individual or group apart. Flattering, dramatic yet serious, rebellious black was worn by the tall, brooding Romantic heroes of the nineteenth century to project their aloof, sombre, masculine 'cool' of affected indifference. Leading actors donned an 'inky cloak' and 'customary suits of solemn black' to play Shakespeare's Hamlet, while writers such as Percy Bysshe Shelley and George Sand sat for portraits all in black. The diarist Anne Lister was infamous for her striking and unconventional appearance, dressing only in black, and often male, clothes. Their dissenting pose has appealed equally through the ages to the artistic, the romantic radicals and the anti-bourgeois. On the one hand it inspired an idea of elegant understatement, while on the other, heralded a kind of alternative fashion of nonconformity. The predominately black 'existentialist uniform' of post-war left-bank Paris – casual yet serious – would go on to inspire the clothes of the culturally rebellious beatniks in the US. As a statement, black has become the colour of the outsider; the wearer of a black leather jacket marks themselves out as a rebel. Setting the wearer apart from the crowd, black in fashion also draws nonconformist groups together, becoming the garb of choice for heavy metal fans and anarchists in the late twentieth century.

It is Goths, however, that have perhaps taken the colour black and its attributes most closely to their hearts. This subculture, which arose in the 1980s around the Gothic rock music scene, has adopted a midnight-hued style and aesthetic, and delights in all the elements of black: the supernatural, otherworldly, romantic, the creative and dramatic, the macabre and the melancholy. Goths are among many who have found inspiration in the beauty and mystery of black.

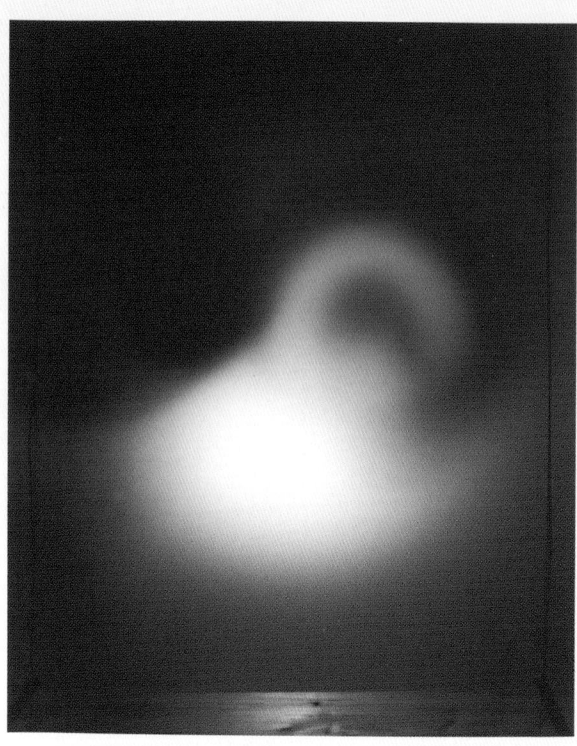

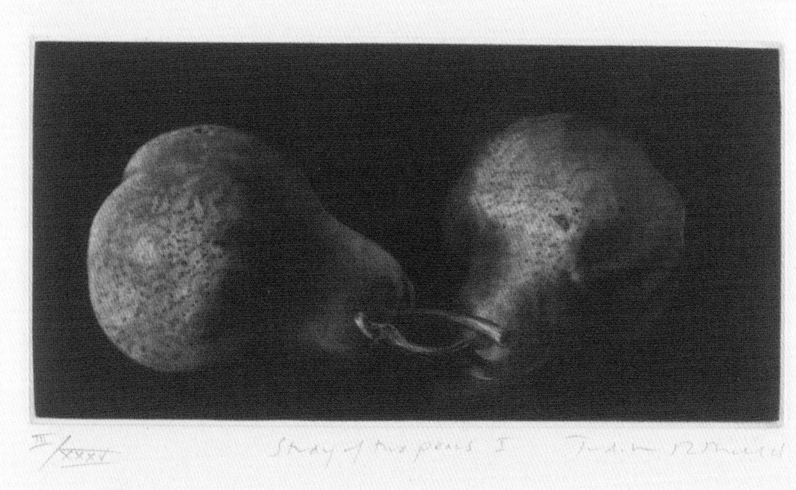

Without light, there is absolute darkness. Despite their gloom, artists have long explored the shadows and the light that reaches through them. In Paul Nash's print *The Void* (1924; above left), heavy black ink vividly imagines the primordial darkness in the Bible, before God decreed 'let there be light'. The play between light and shadows revealed in the photographic process is considered by photographer Tess Hurrell in her series *Redrawing Light* (2007–8; above right).

A *memento mori* is a reminder of the darkness that swallows all living things in death; Judith Rothchild's velvety mezzotint *Study of Two Pears I* (2003; left) exposes the sensual fleshiness of the fruit surrounded by shade. Rembrandt van Rijn extensively reworked his drypoint print of the Crucifixion (opposite) in 1660, intensifying the dramatic darkness of the shadows of ignorance and sinfulness surrounding the crucified Christ, who is illuminated with divine light.

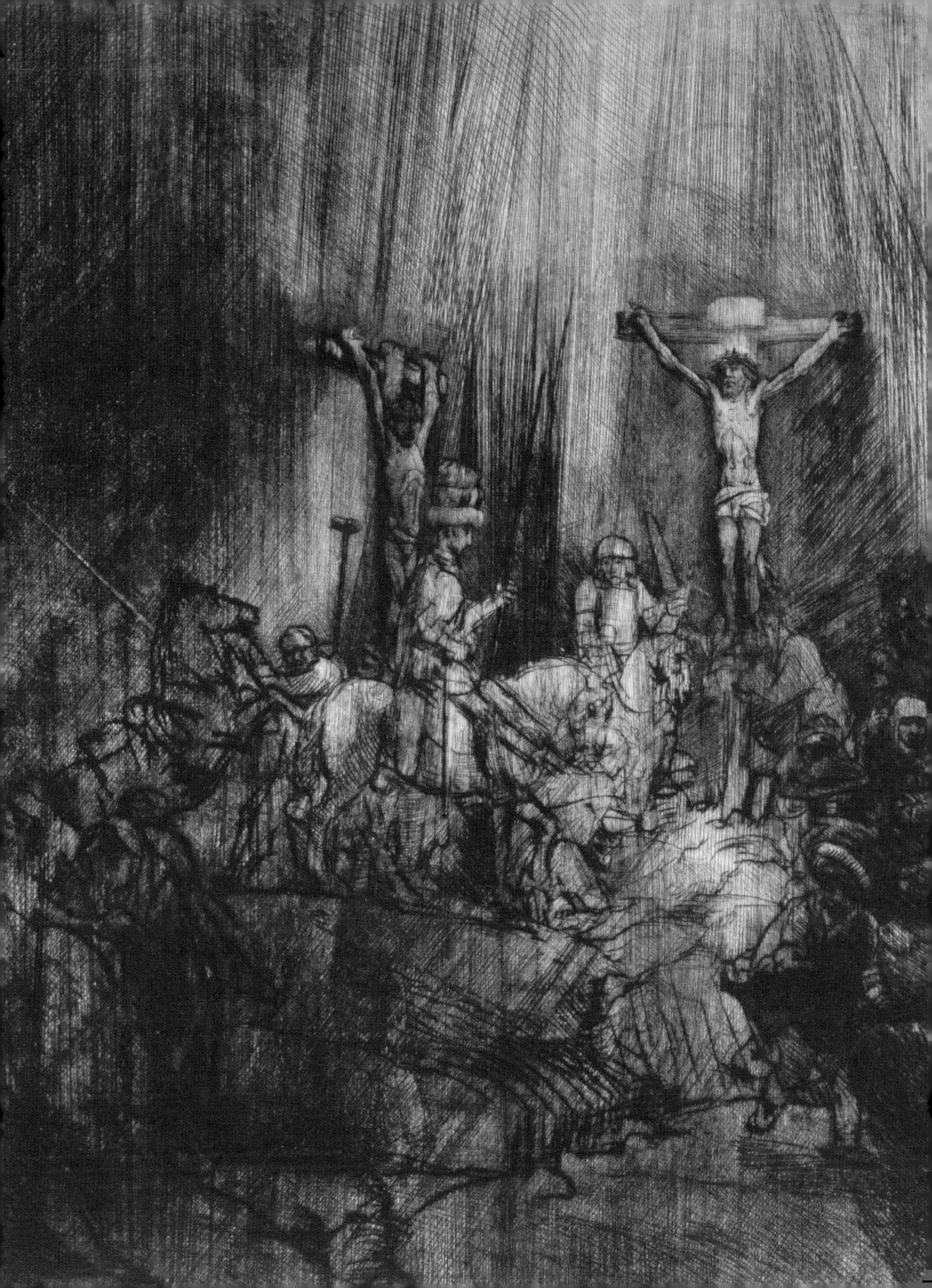

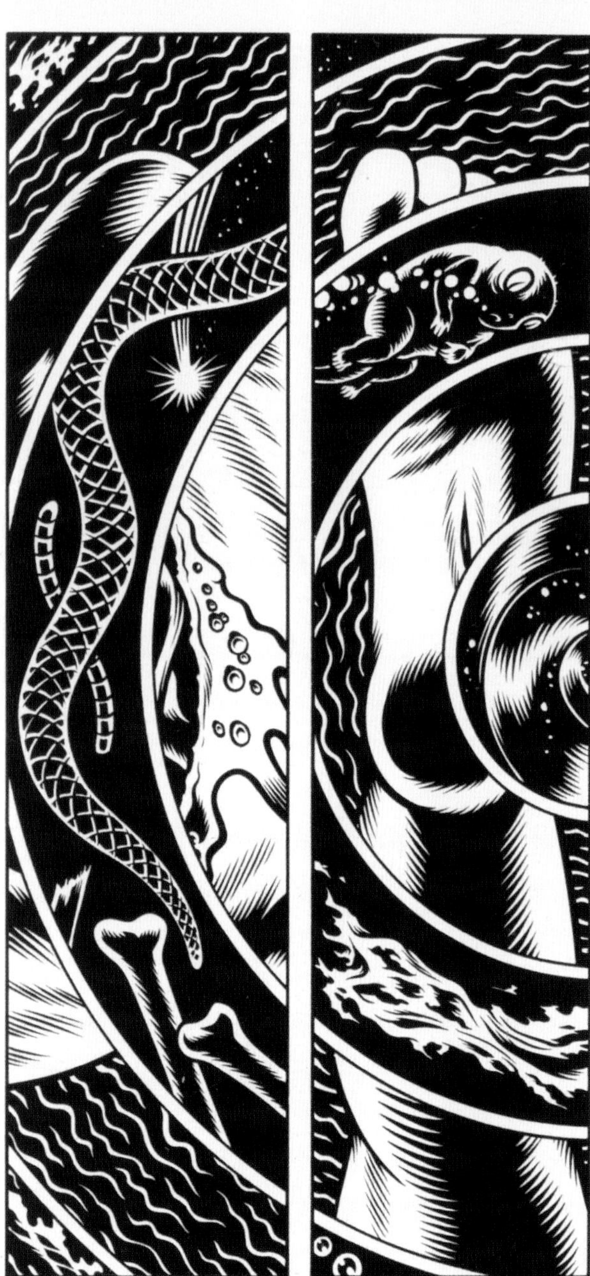
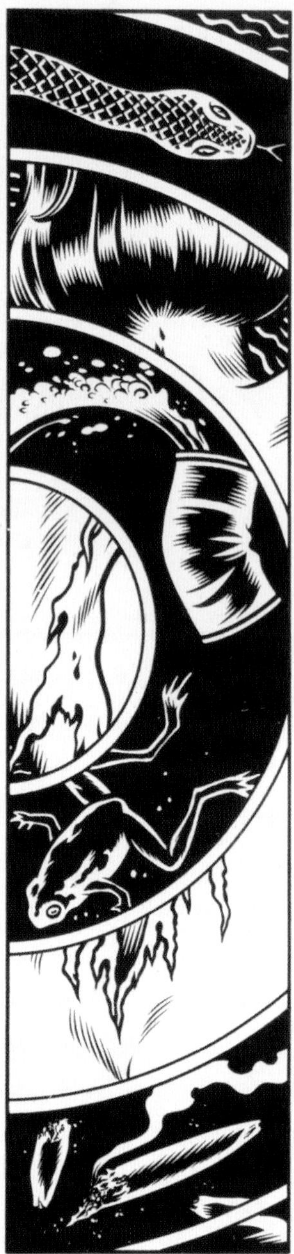
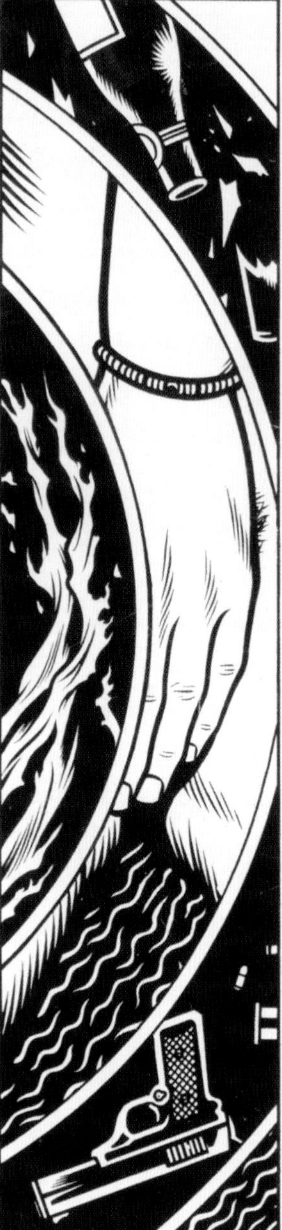

...AND I COULD FEEL MYSELF FALLING FORWARD, TUMBLING DOWN INTO NOTHINGNESS.

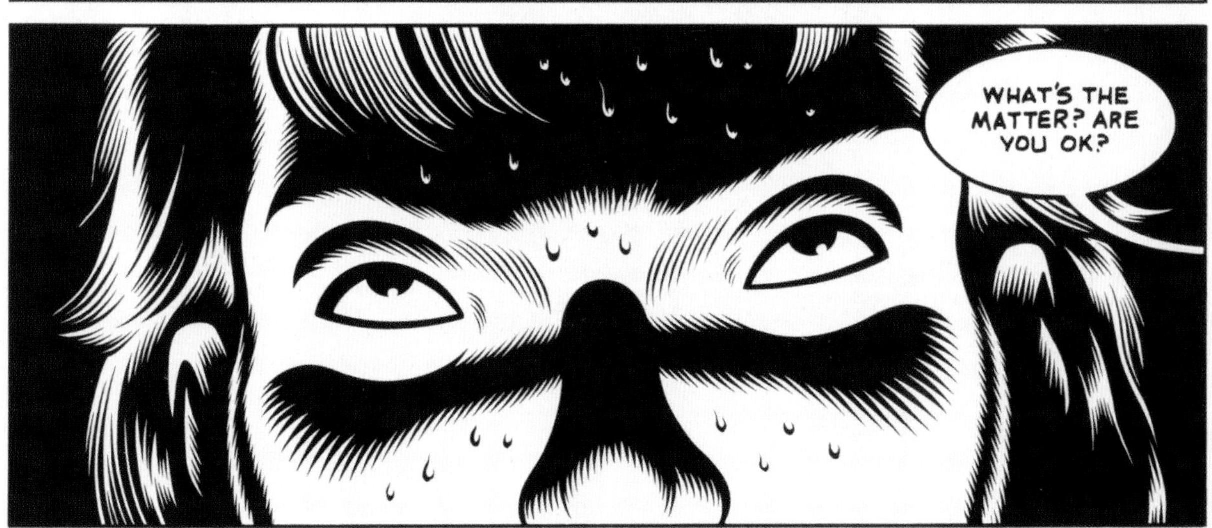

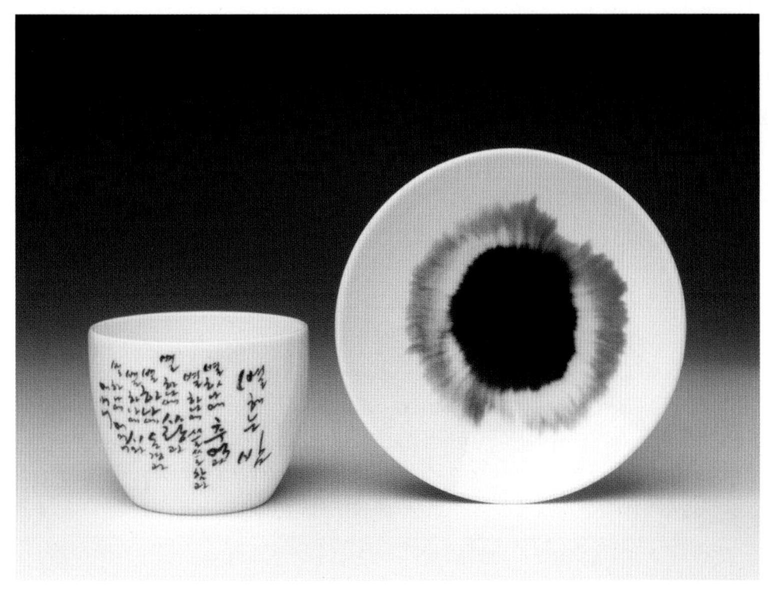

For centuries, black ink has been used to capture thoughts and ideas. For his poem *Celebration of Hangul (a Korean alphabet)* (2008-9; left), Lie Sang-bong has forgone paper for white bone china. In a similarly unorthodox use of the pigment, Alexander Cozens drew his compositions almost unconsciously, as in this example of his 'blot' drawings (1750-86; below), which he worked up into landscapes curiously devoid of the colours of nature. Charles Burns's comics, such as *Black Hole* (1995-2005; opposite), are influenced by 1960s American horror magazines, published in black and white to circumvent 'Comics Code' censorship. Burns take things deeper, viscerally and psychologically. His crisp black inks are no longer a necessity but an aesthetic: in the literal darkness of his pages lurk nightmarish themes of alienation and sexual anxiety.

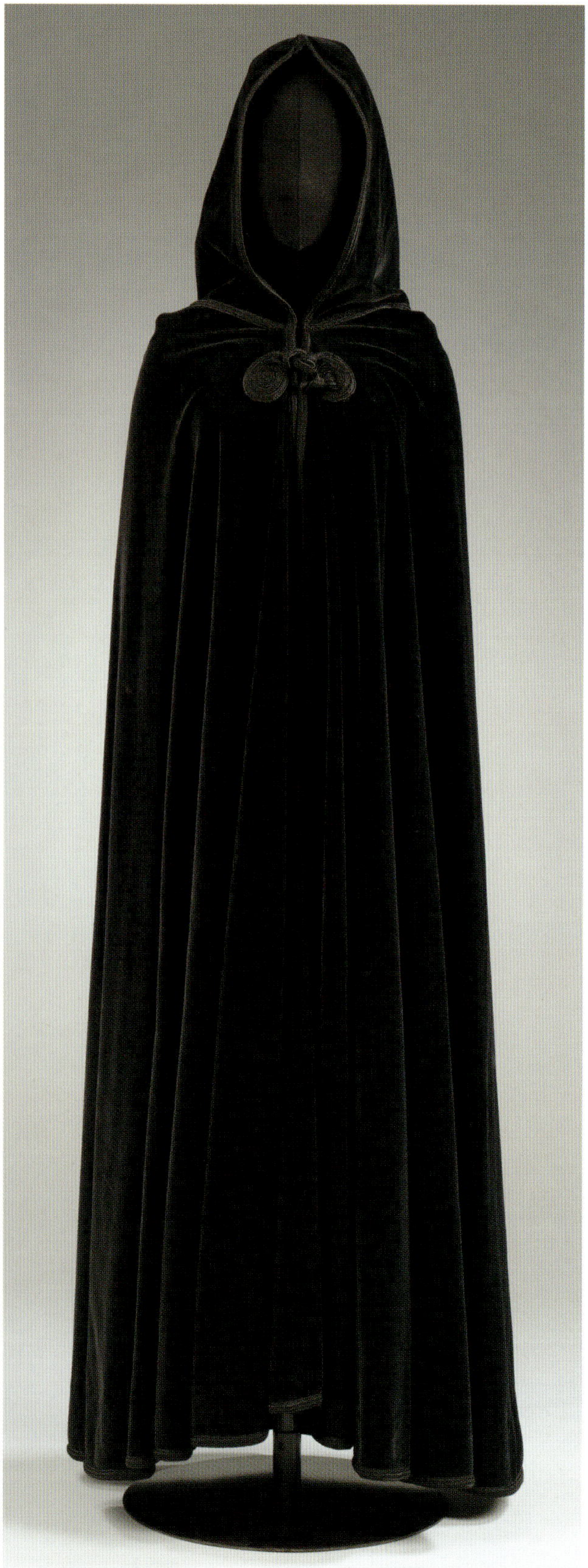

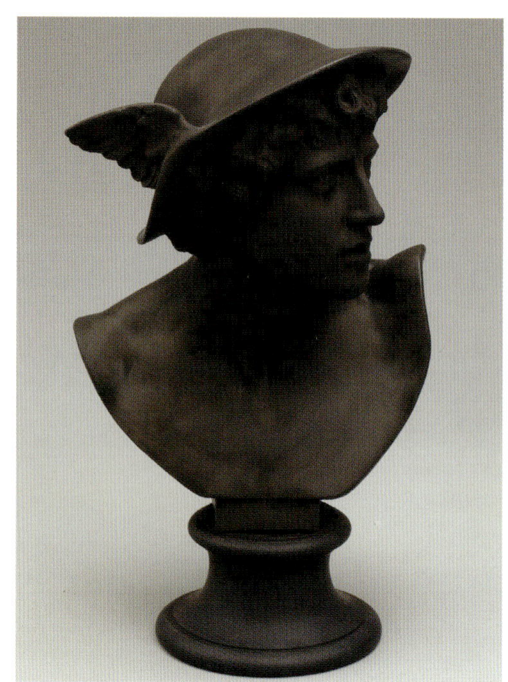

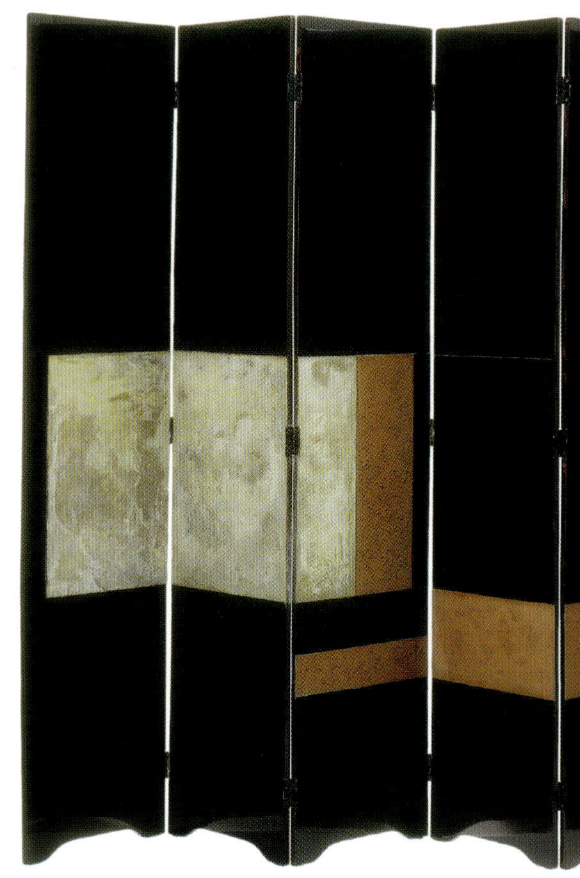

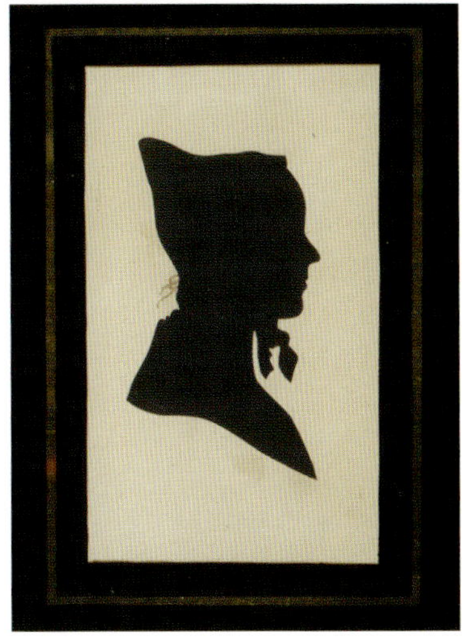
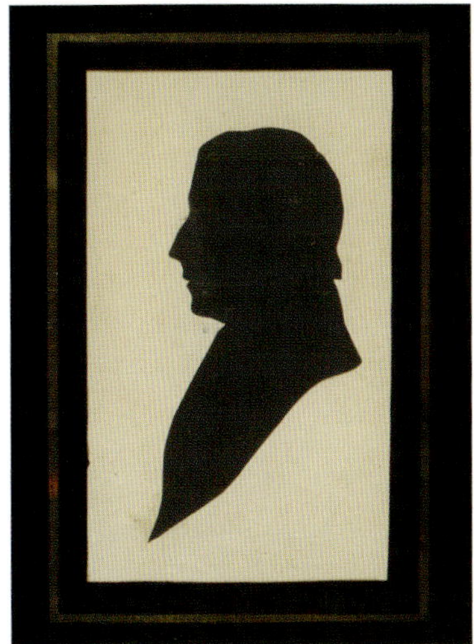

The density of black can create a strong, luxurious silhouette. Fashion designer Zhor Sebti's heavy velvet hooded cape (1970–80; opposite, left) seems both solid and insubstantial as a shadow. Shadows were a popular form of portraiture in 19th-century Britain – this facing pair are the profiles of husband and wife William and Jane Miller (c. 1850; left). Positioned by a lamp, the sitter's silhouette was traced onto paper, which was then blackened using lampblack (a pigment made from soot) to resemble a captured shadow or 'shade'.

Responding to the 18th-century love of Greek and Roman art, Josiah Wedgwood manufactured stoneware to imitate the dark materials beloved of the Classical world. Here, the god Mercury is depicted in his 'black basalt' (1780–1800; opposite, top right). Also prized for its rich, dark colour, ebony from Africa or east Asia was favoured for luxury furniture in the 17th century, including the sturdy but beautiful Endymion cabinet (1630–50; below). In the 20th century, designer Eileen Gray used the traditional Japanese technique of lacquering to create this sleek, black Modernist screen (c. 1923; left).

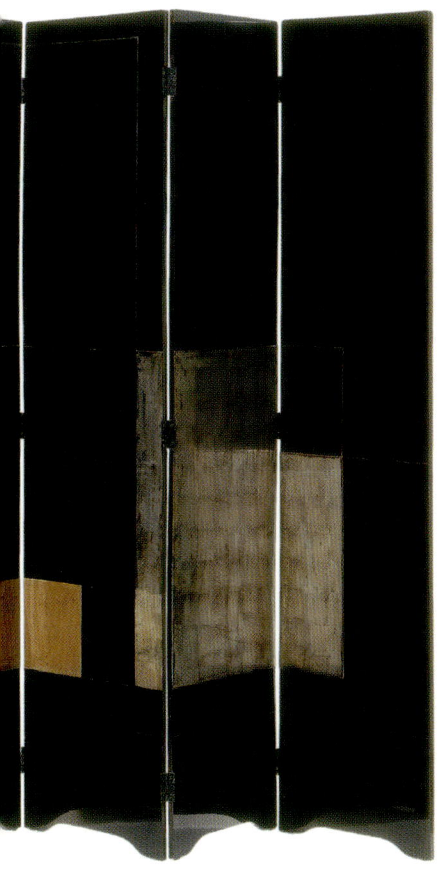

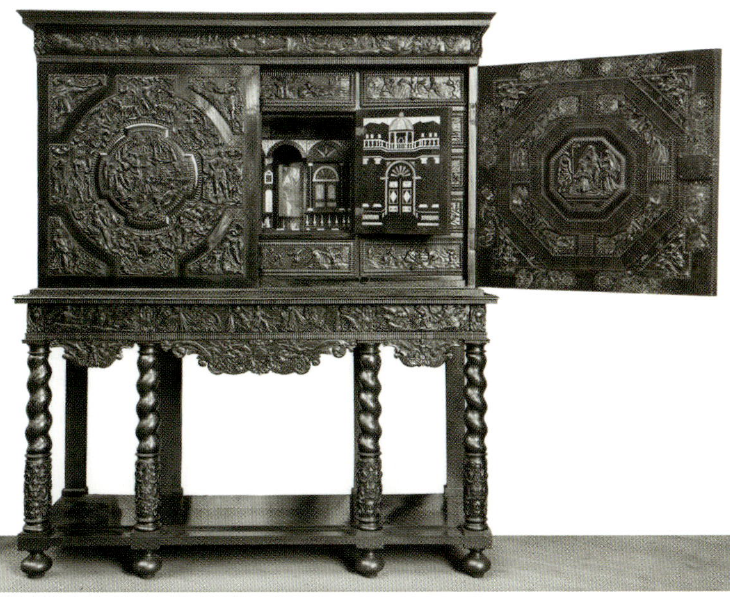

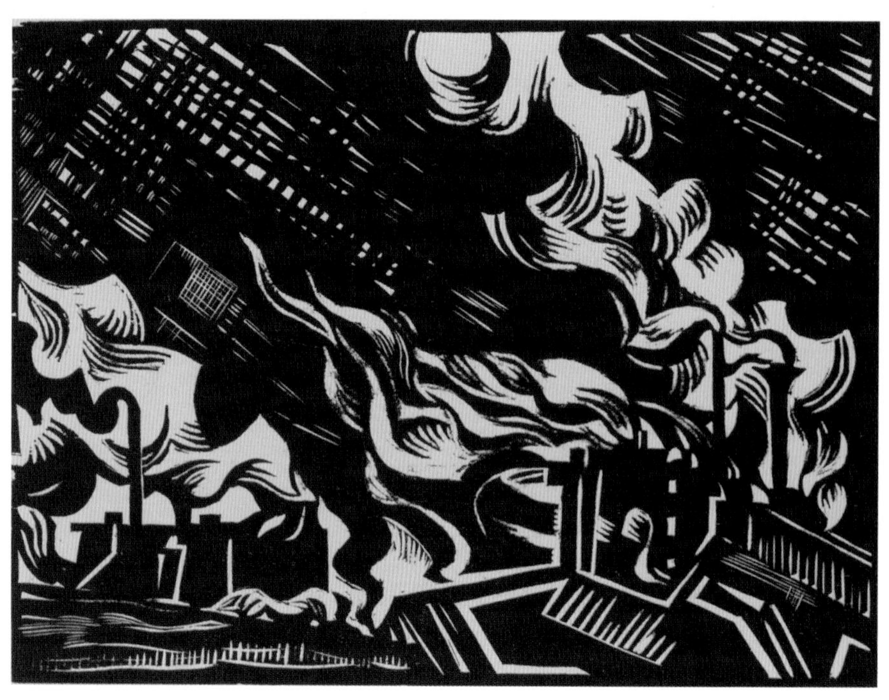

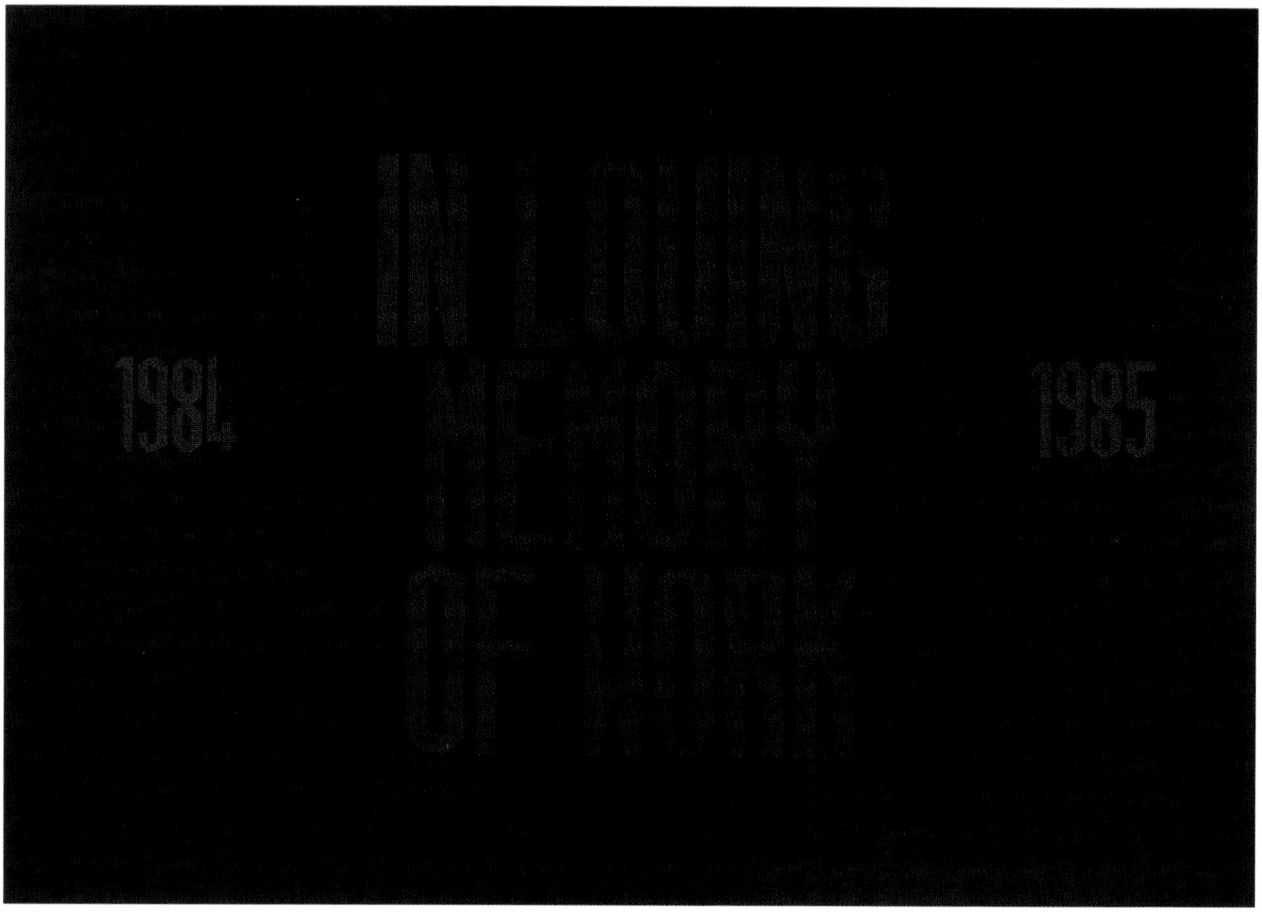

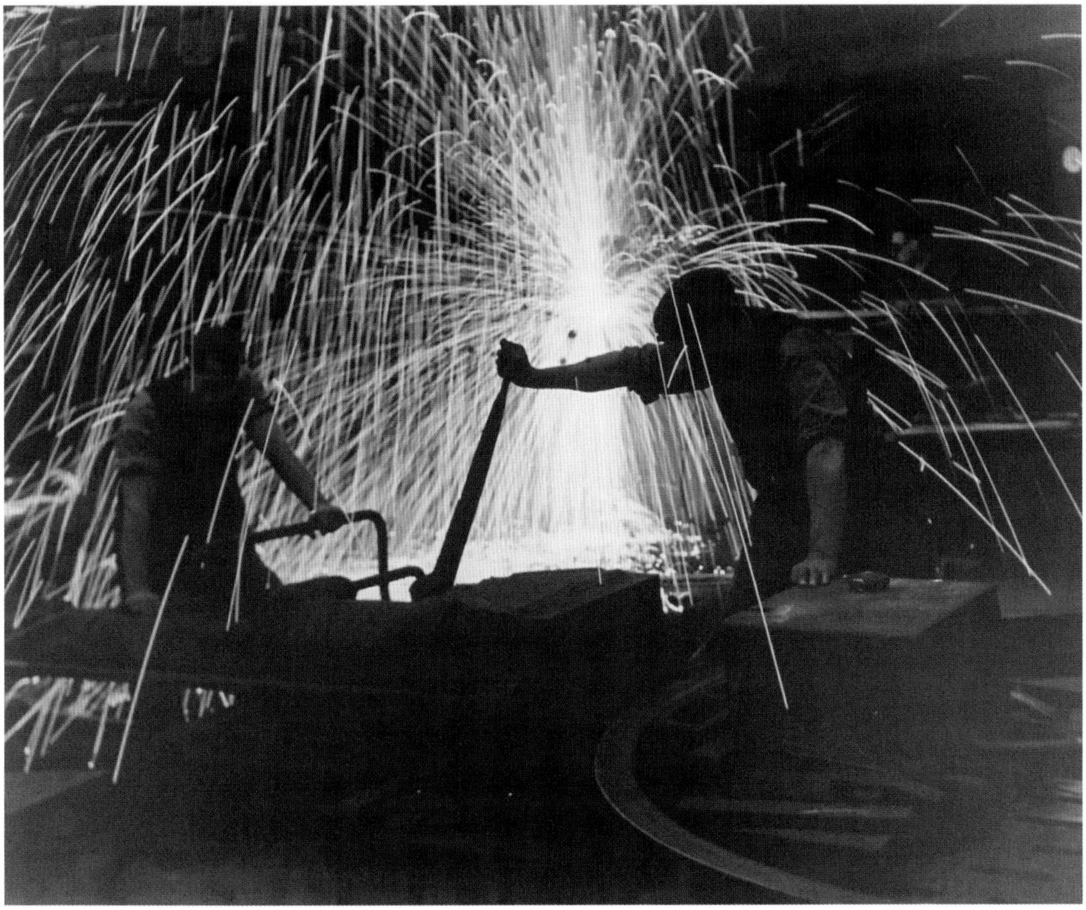

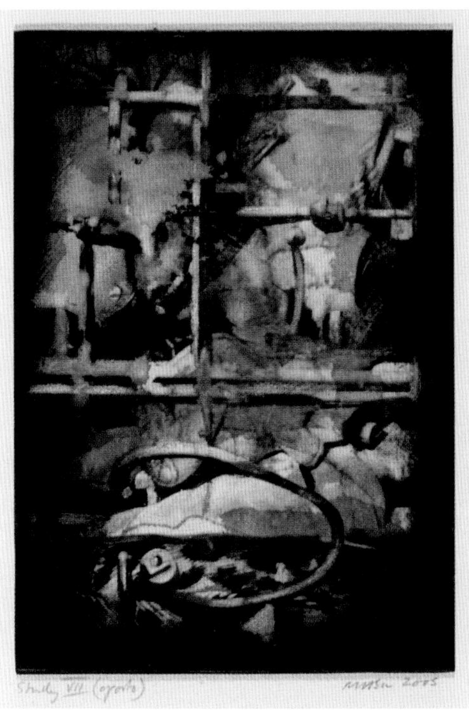

Industry can be hard, dirty work; but it has also inspired remarkable works of art. Maurice Broomfield's dynamic black-and-white photograph of G.A. Harvey & Co., Greenwich Metal Works, Woolwich Road, London (1952; above) captures a powerful spark of creation amid the gloom of manufacturing. The thick, choking smoke of the factories that dominated the English Midlands in the 19th and early 20th century is pictured in Edward Wadsworth's dark, congested print *Black Country* (1921; opposite, top). Craig Oldham goes a step further, printing on black paper using coal dust from the pits in Barnsley where his family worked for his print *In Loving Memory of Work* (2015; opposite, bottom), which references the death of the mining industry and the decline of the towns that supported it. Robert Mason used a combination of dark materials to create his *Study VII (Oporto)* (2005; left). Industrial elements, rendered in soft charcoal and dense crayon, emerge from the darkness.

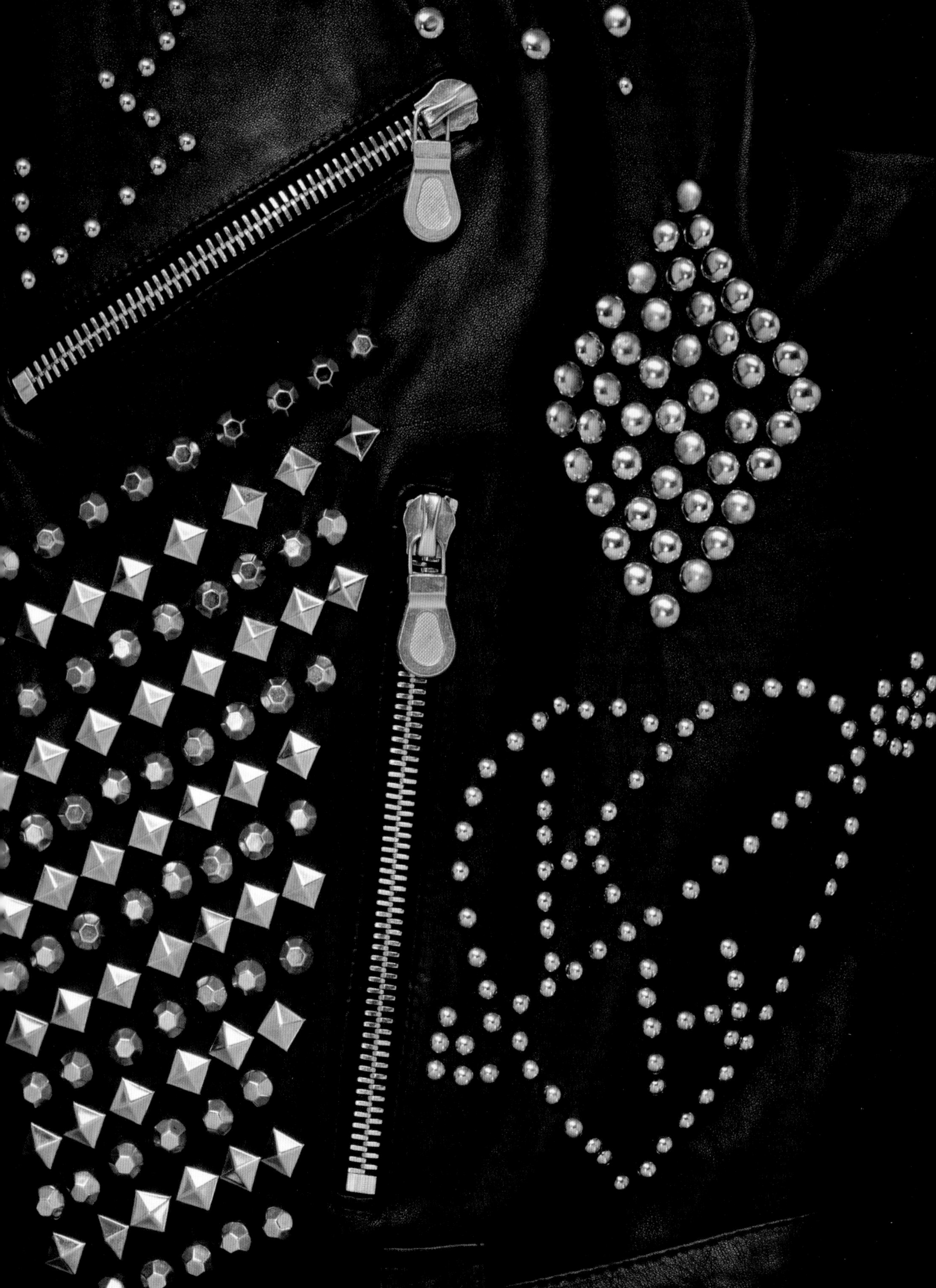

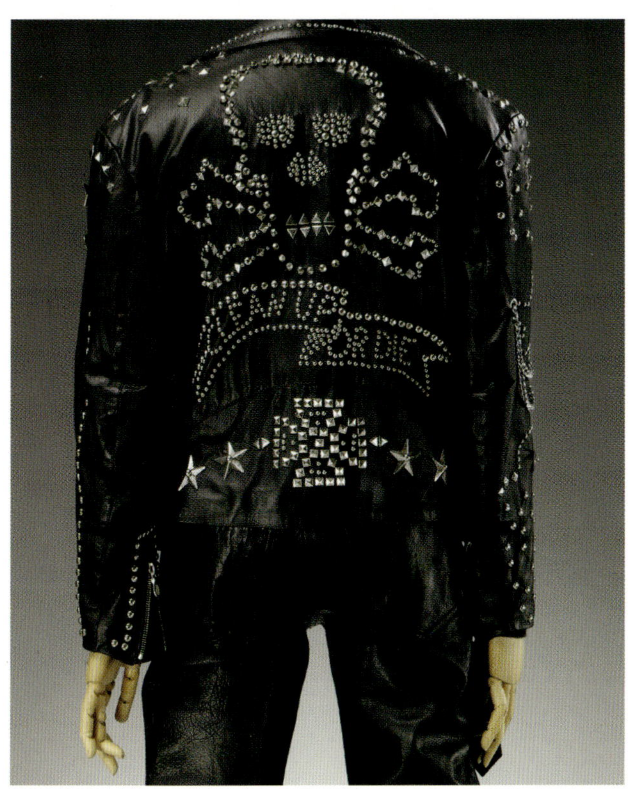

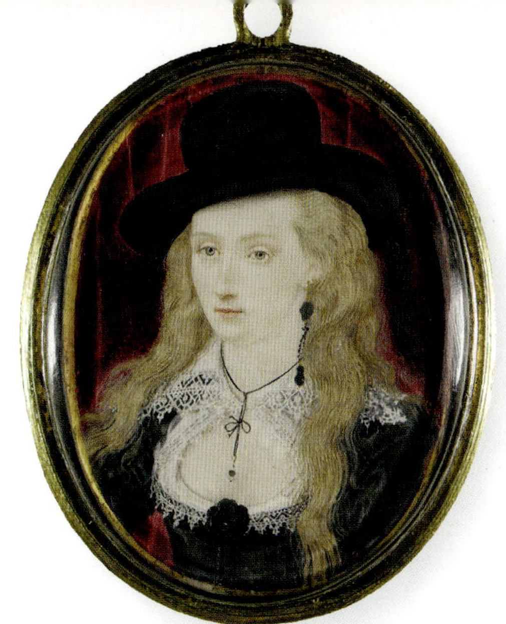

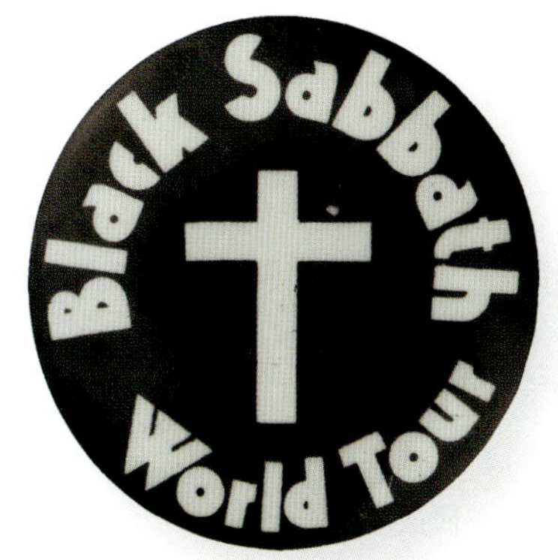

A black outfit is often a symbol of difference and defiance. Black boots were a staple part of a 1980s Goth's dark wardrobe. In this British example from 1984–6 (below right), the Victorian-style boots are embellished with metal buckles that hint at a harder, punkier character. Similarly, heavy metal band Black Sabbath's music and aesthetic provocatively references dark themes such as the occult, horror and insanity. A stark black-and-white badge (1972–3; centre right) commemorates their tour.

In contrast, fashion designer and eco-activist Katharine Hamnett played with the rebellious symbol of a black leather jacket when creating her 'Clean up or Die' collection (1990; opposite and above). The menacing metal studs spell out a message that threatens ecological catastrophe rather than teenage angst. Another intriguing black outfit is worn by the woman in this portrait miniature by Isaac Oliver (c. 1605–25; above right). Although not dissimilar to a black riding outfit, her unusual, large gentleman's hat, loose hair and daringly low-cut neckline seem provocative rather than practical.

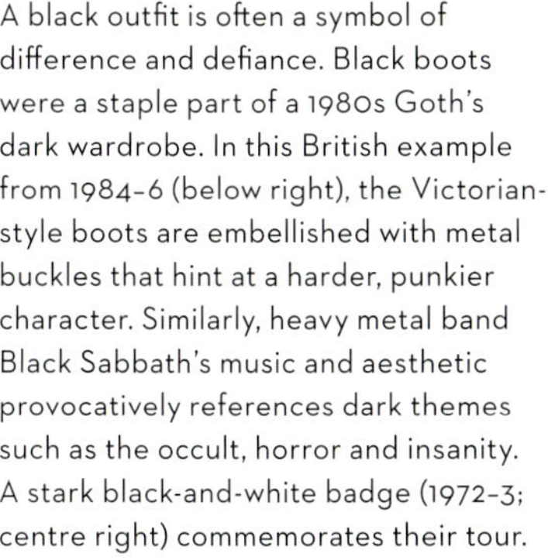

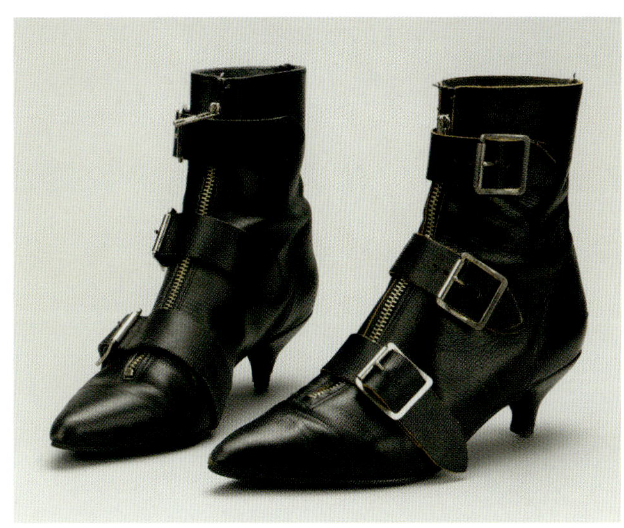

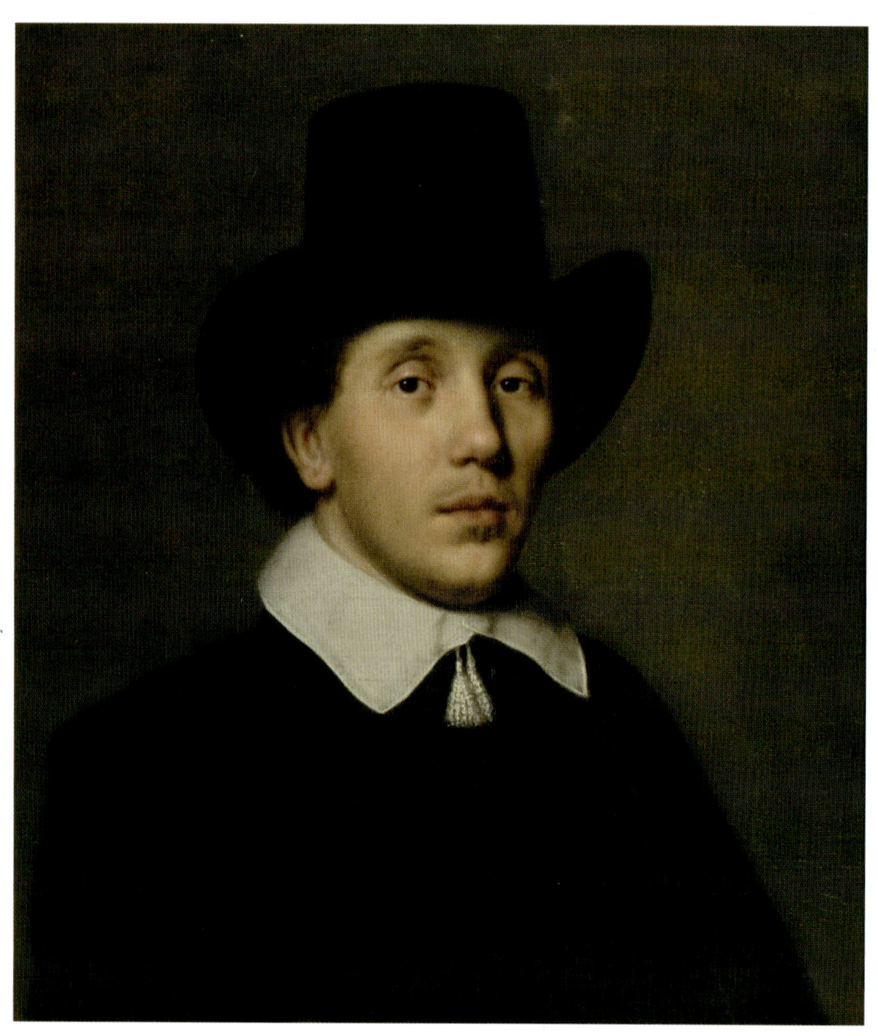

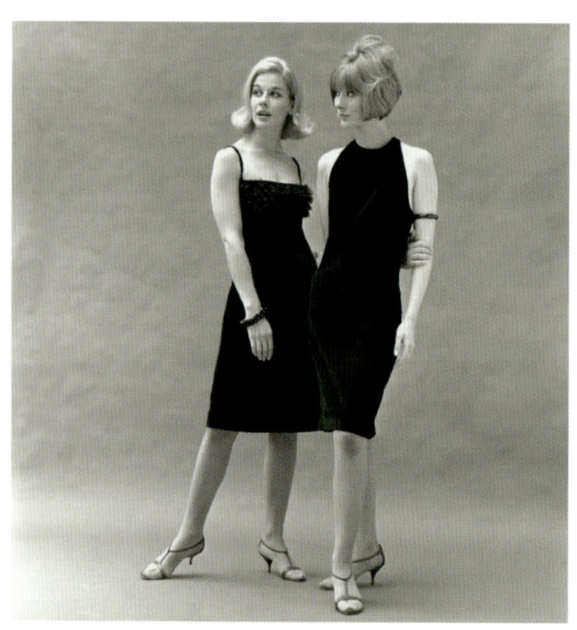

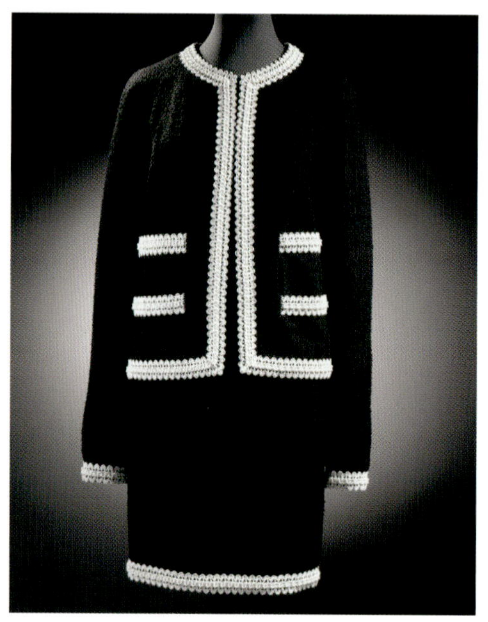

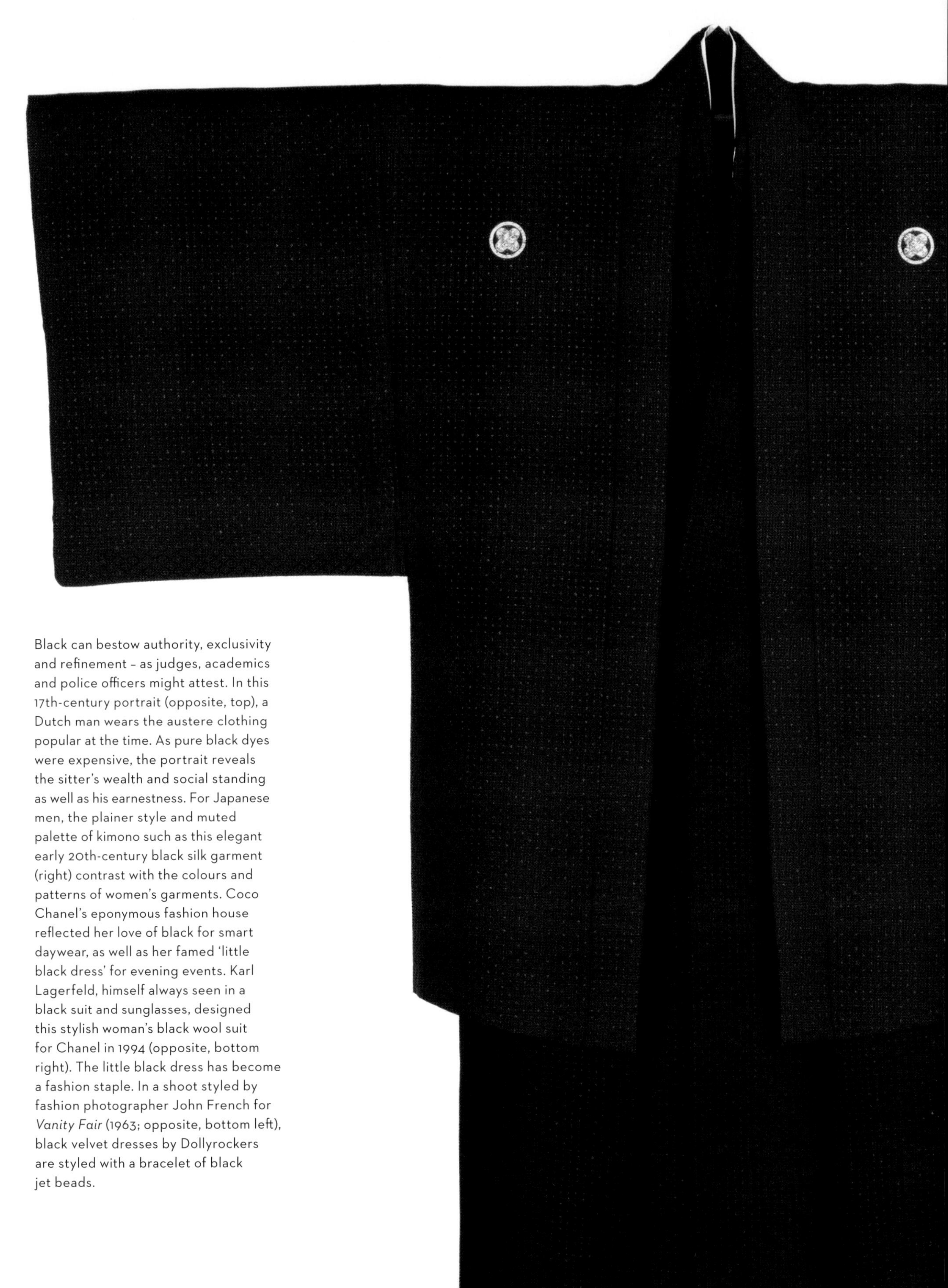

Black can bestow authority, exclusivity and refinement – as judges, academics and police officers might attest. In this 17th-century portrait (opposite, top), a Dutch man wears the austere clothing popular at the time. As pure black dyes were expensive, the portrait reveals the sitter's wealth and social standing as well as his earnestness. For Japanese men, the plainer style and muted palette of kimono such as this elegant early 20th-century black silk garment (right) contrast with the colours and patterns of women's garments. Coco Chanel's eponymous fashion house reflected her love of black for smart daywear, as well as her famed 'little black dress' for evening events. Karl Lagerfeld, himself always seen in a black suit and sunglasses, designed this stylish woman's black wool suit for Chanel in 1994 (opposite, bottom right). The little black dress has become a fashion staple. In a shoot styled by fashion photographer John French for *Vanity Fair* (1963; opposite, bottom left), black velvet dresses by Dollyrockers are styled with a bracelet of black jet beads.

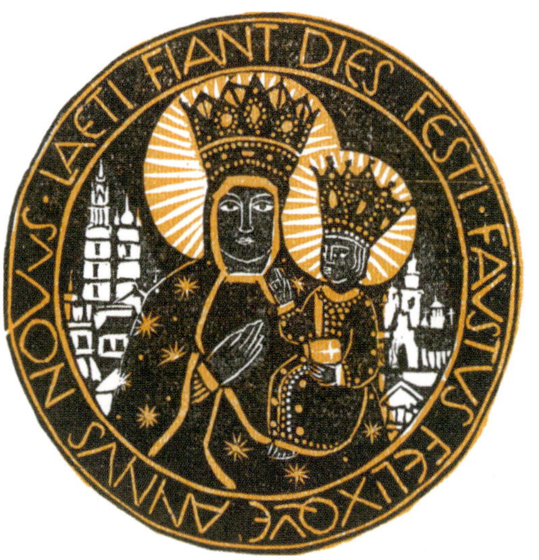
LAETI FIANT DIES FESTI · FAUSTUS FELIXQUE ANNUS NOVUS

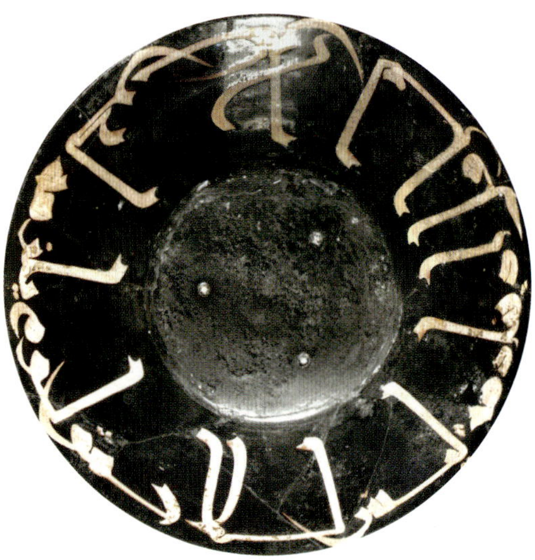

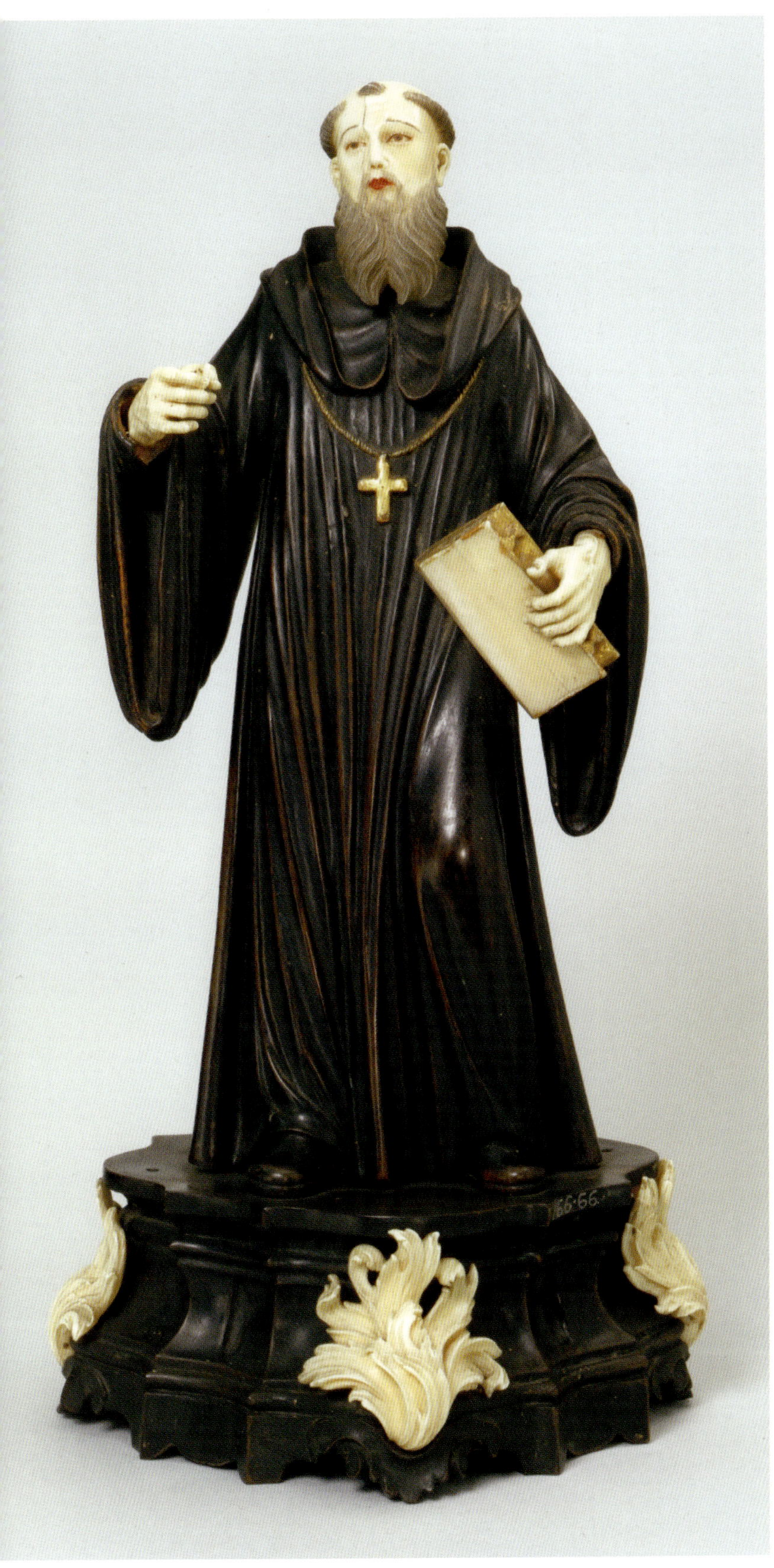

The austere nature of black has seen the colour adopted to signal piety. Originally of various colours, the Kiswah, the silk cloth that covers the Kaaba, Islam's most sacred pilgrimage site, in the Great Mosque, Mecca, has been exclusively black since the 13th century. This Egyptian example was made in about 1918 (opposite, top). The cloth is also decorated in black, with inscriptions from the Qur'an.

The Arabic motto on this austere 10th-century Iranian black bowl (opposite, bottom right) warns 'the fool never receives the reproaches he deserves, but the wise man does who keeps him company'. To mark the wise and pious path they chose, Benedictine monks wore dark, sober clothing and were known as the 'black monks' – ebony is used to re-create the habit on this 18th-century statuette (left). The Black Madonna of Częstochowa, depicted here by Jewish artist Wiktoria Gorynska in this wood engraving from 1938 (opposite, bottom left), is revered in Poland and looked to in times of national crisis.

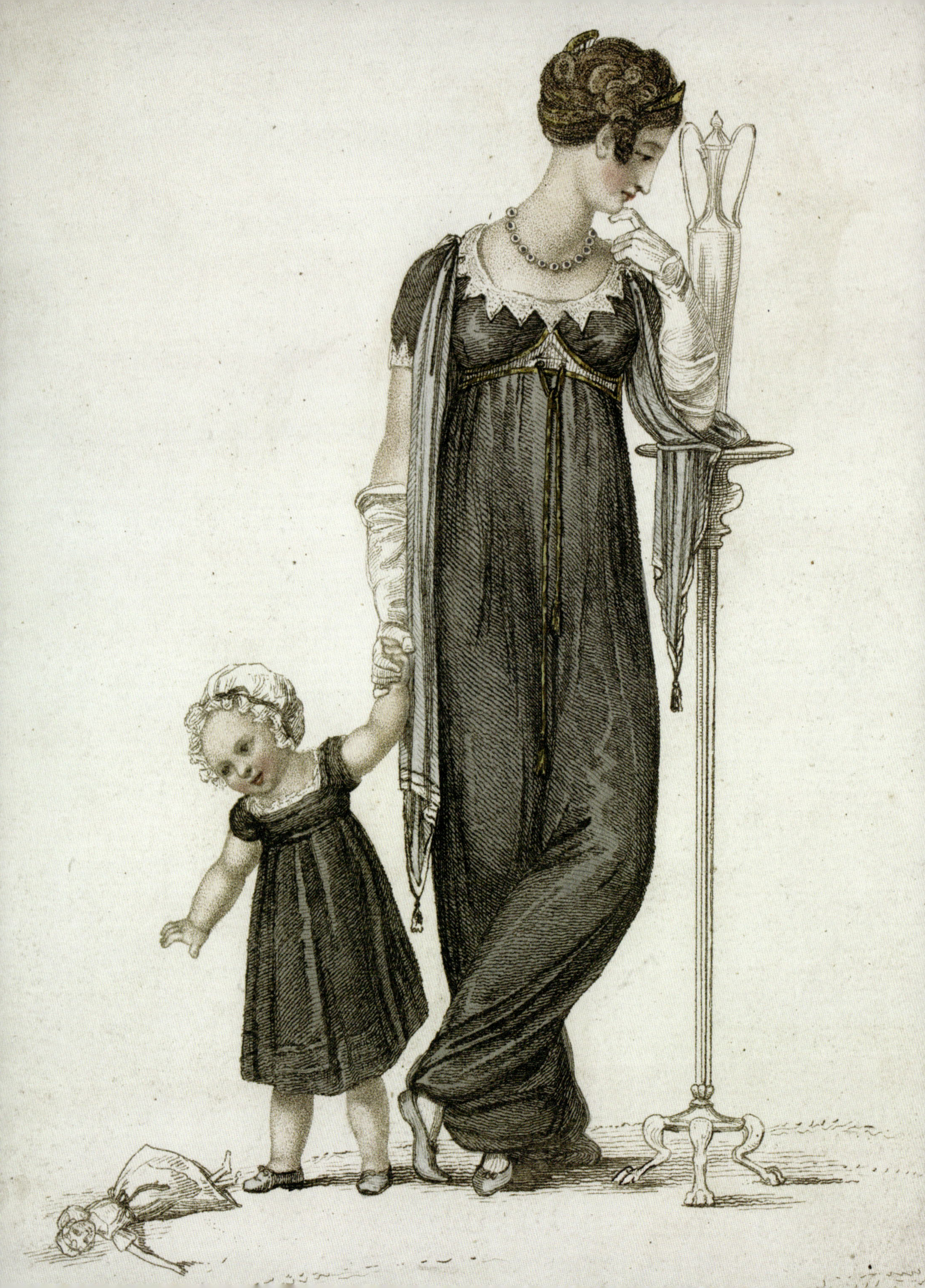

Black is traditionally worn for mourning in many cultures. An empire-line mourning dress in a fashion plate (1809; opposite) demonstrates how to grieve stylishly; the child stretching out for an unreachable doll is a poignant metaphor for death. This child's mourning garment (below left) from about 1882 was made for a two-year-old to wear for the funeral of her grandmother. In the late 19th century, mourning could last for many months. The whole family would dress in subdued colours, and even stationery would show the sender's grief. Jewellery would also be black; jet was especially beloved of Queen Victoria herself, desolate after the death of her husband Prince Albert. It takes great skill to carve jet, and the sober decorations traditionally featured motifs from nature or Christianity. This piece from the 1870s (below right) is probably Whitby jet from Yorkshire, where most of the jet in England was sourced. In Dante Gabriel Rossetti's illustration for Edgar Allan Poe's *The Raven* (1848; right), the grieving lover is disturbed by the 'ebony bird ... ghastly, gaunt, and ominous.' Ravens are traditionally seen as intermediaries between the living and dead; here, the ghostly figure of Lenore floats between narrator and bird.

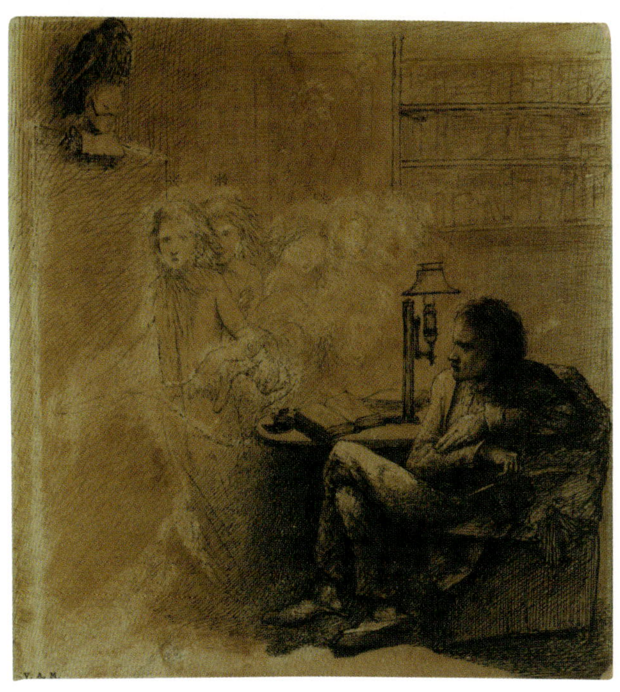

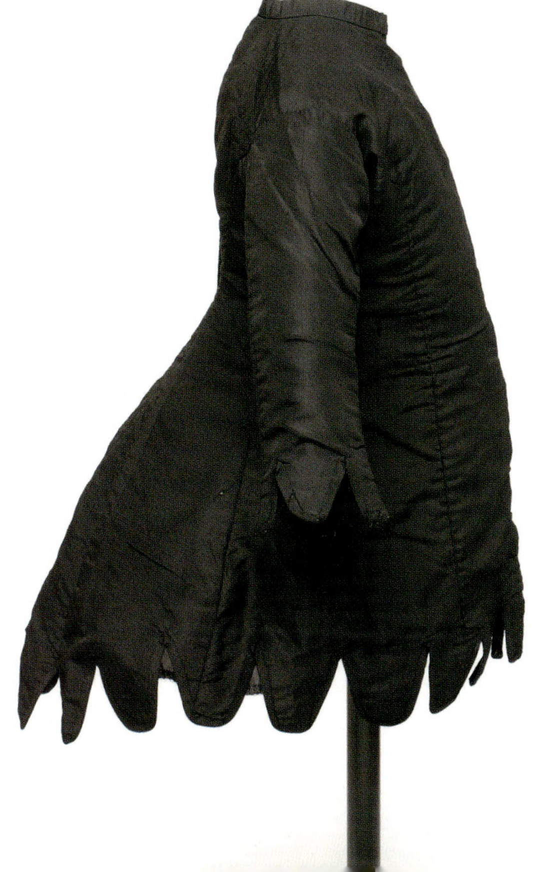

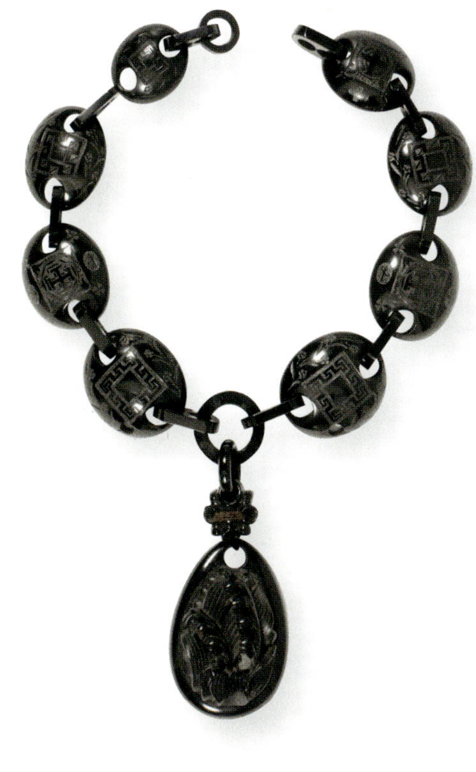

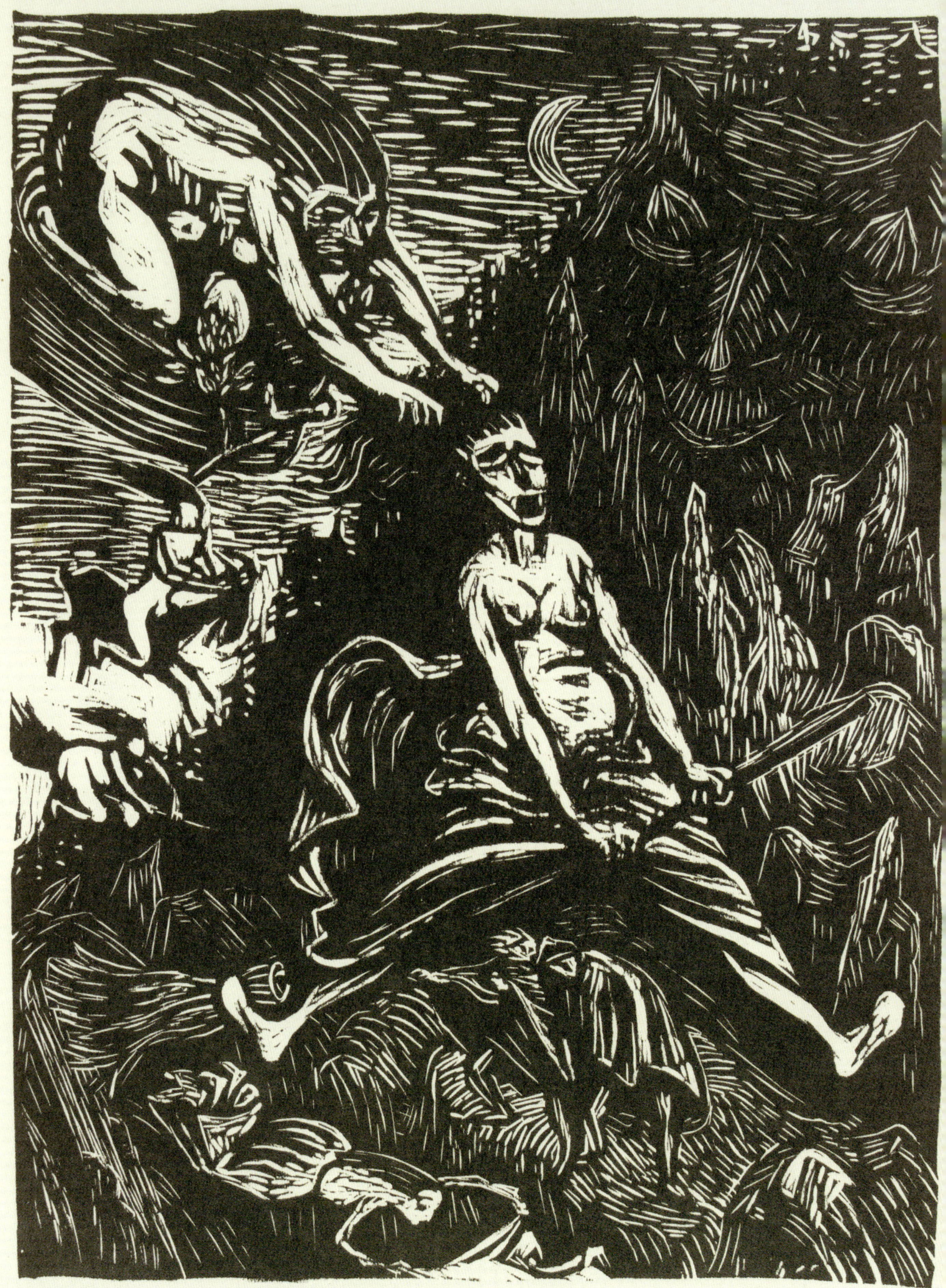

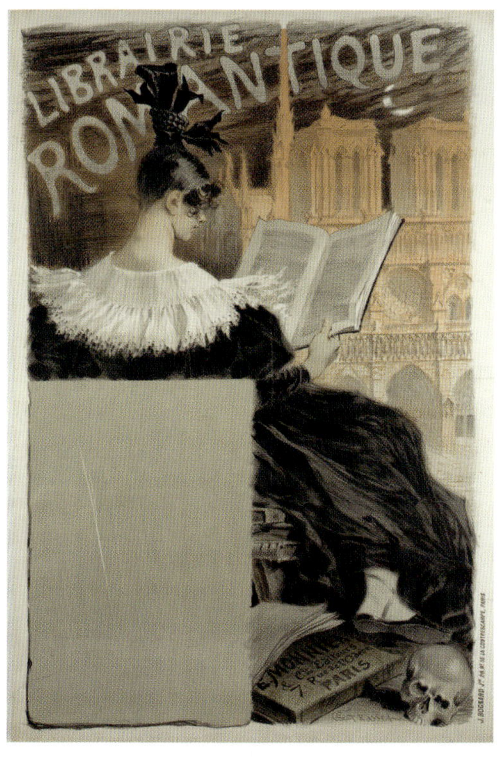

Gothic horror emerged from the shadows in the 19th century. Eugène Grasset's *Librairie Romantique* poster (1887; far left) includes tropes of the literary genre: the church of Notre Dame at night; a skull. The black-clad woman avidly reads a novel, to be advertised in the blank space. Ernst Barlach's bold, black woodcut of 1922 (opposite) depicts the menacing, unruly darkness of *Hexenritt (witches' ride)*, a riotous gathering in which witches ride broomsticks and goats. Gothic tales unfolded in dark and mysterious castles such as Neuschwanstein, as shown in this dramatic mezzotint (1913; below right), *The Mad King's Castle*, by Percival Gaskell. A great lover of the Gothic, Horace Walpole commissioned black chairs based on medieval windows (left) for his Strawberry Hill House, London. Designed by Richard Bentley and made in 1777, the chairs were painted black to imitate ebony. Jo Gordon dyed unusually long feathers raven black to give her 'Kiss of Death Bonnet' (1994; below left), a disquieting reimagining of a traditional poke bonnet, a darkly menacing, inscrutable aspect.

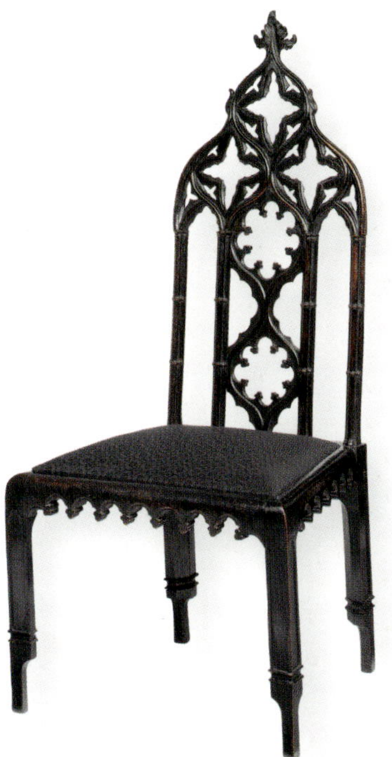

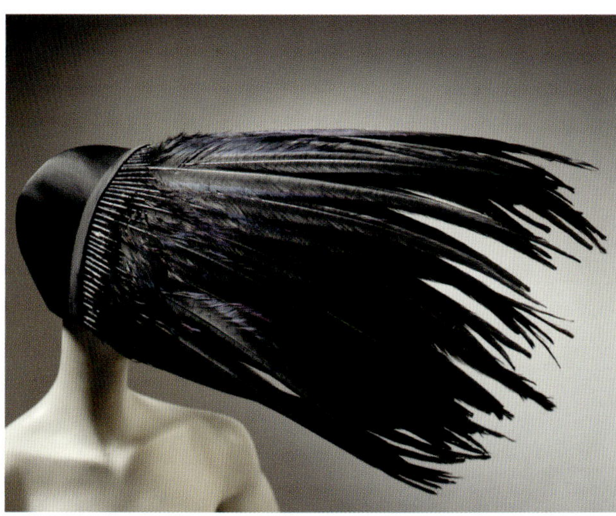

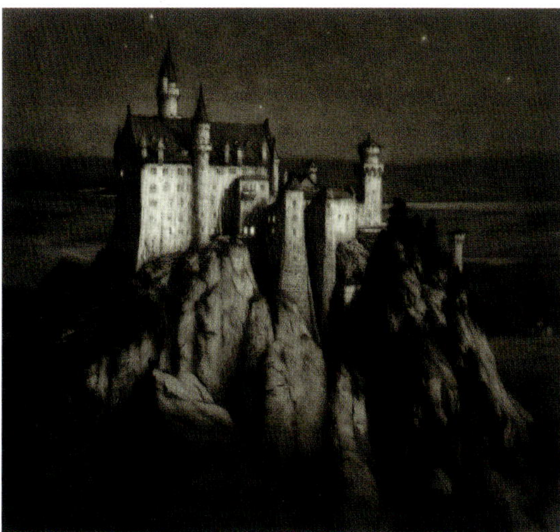

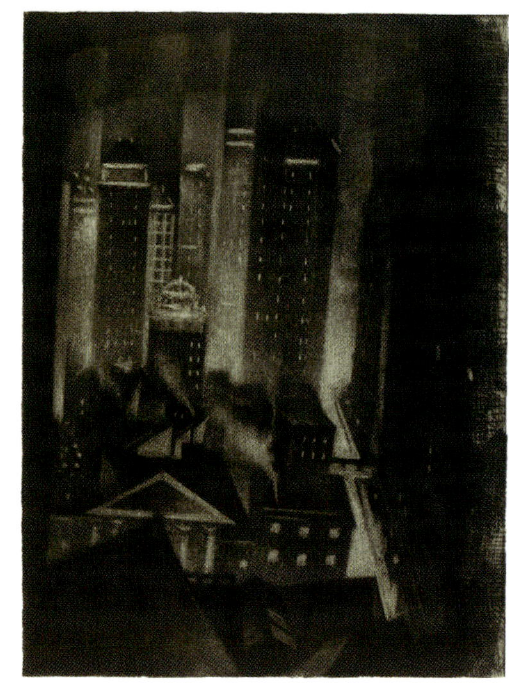

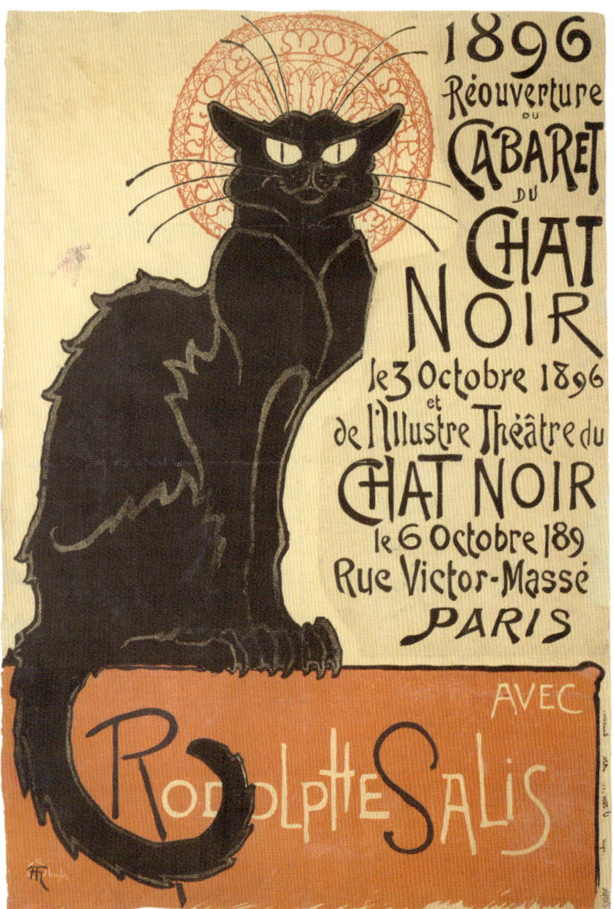

The darkness of night offers a perfect backdrop for revelries and reveries. The sleek finish of an early 20th-century black top hat made in London (above left) signifies the glamour of a night out, perhaps to the theatre. Aubrey Beardsley used large areas of black ink to portray a darkly clad audience watching Wagner's *Tristan and Isolde* in *The Wagnerites* (1894; opposite). The intense black of the image gives the scene an atmosphere of intimacy and decadence. A night out could also provide more scandalous entertainments at 'Le Chat Noir' cabaret, Paris, which reopened in 1896 and featured edgy, satirical performances. Theophile-Alexandre Steinlen created an iconic image for the avant-garde club in the form of a darkly streetwise feline (left). The darkness of night in C.R.W. Nevinson's early 20th-century cityscape *New York, Night* (above right) is punctuated by the glow from buildings, cars and streetlights, but the inky mezzotint gives the scene a foggy, distorting aspect, rendering it mysterious and lonely despite the lights.

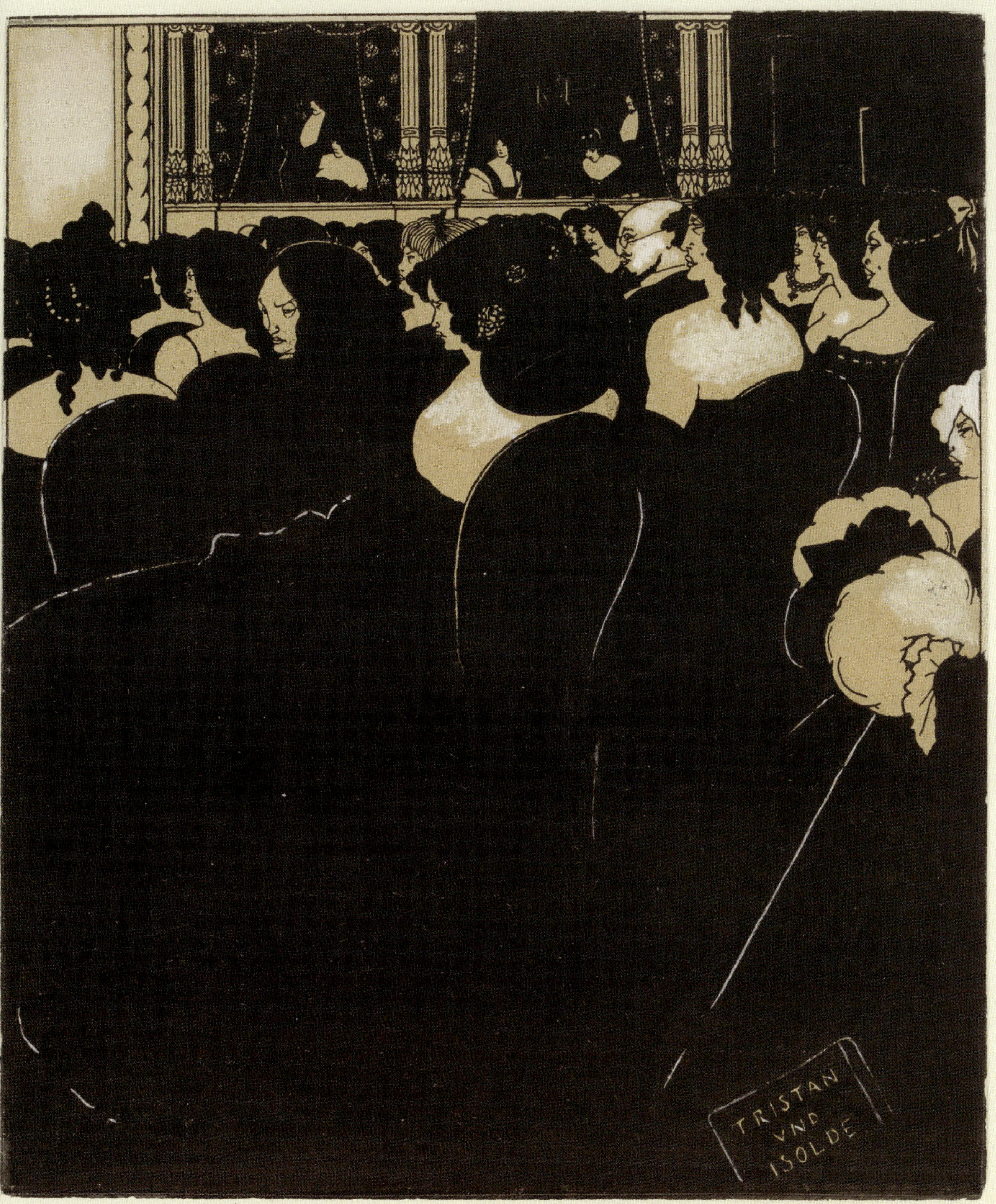

TRISTAN
VND
ISOLDE

BIBLIOGRAPHY

General

Sean Adams, *The Designer's Dictionary of Colour* (London, 2017)

Josef Albers, *Interaction of Color* (New Haven, 1953; new edn 2013)

David Batchelor, *The Luminous and the Grey* (London, 2014)

— (ed.), *Documents of Contemporary Art: Colour* (London, 2008)

—, *Chromophobia* (London, 2000)

Patrick Baty, *The Anatomy of Colour: The Story of Heritage Paints and Pigments* (London, 2017)

Julius Bryant, *Designing the V&A: The Museum as a Work of Art (1857–1909)* (London, 2017)

Ros Byam Shaw, *Spectrum: Heritage Patterns and Colours* (London, 2018)

David Coles, *Chromatopia: An Illustrated History of Colour* (Melbourne, 2019)

Gary Evans, *The Story of Colour: An Exploration of the Hidden Messages of the Spectrum* (London, 2017)

Jonathan Faiers, *Colours in Fashion* (London, 2016)

Victoria Finlay, *The Brilliant History of Colour in Art* (Los Angeles, 2014)

—, *Colour: Travels through the Paintbox* (London, 2007)

Rutherford J. Gettens and George L. Stout, *Painting Materials – A Short Encyclopaedia* (New York, 1966)

Derek Jarman, *Chroma: A Book of Colour* (London, 1995)

Susan Kay-Williams, *The Story of Colour in Textiles: Imperial Purple to Denim Blue* (London, 2013)

Alexandra Loske, *Colour: A Visual History* (London, 2019)

Eoberts Panzanelli (ed.), *The Colour of Life: Polychromy in Sculpture from Antiquity to the Present* (Los Angeles, 2008)

Michel Pastoureau, *The Colour of our Memories* (Cambridge, 2012)

Stella Paul, *Chromaphilia: The Story of Colour in Art* (London, 2017)

Kassia St Clair, *The Secret Lives of Colour* (London, 2016)

Patrick Syme, *Werner's Nomenclature of Colours: Adapted to Zoology, Botany, Chemistry, Minerology, Anatomy and the Arts* (1814; new edn London, 2018)

Anne Varichon, *Colours: What they Mean and How to Make them* (New York, 2006)

White

Katherine Ashenburg, *The Dirt on Clean: An Unsanitized History* (Toronto, 2007)

Kathleen M. Brown, *Foul Bodies: Cleanliness in Early America* (New Haven, CT & London, 2009)

Sarah Bond, 'Whitewashing Ancient Statues: Whiteness, Racism and Colour in The Ancient World', *Forbes Online*, 27 April 2017 <https://www.forbes.com/sites/drsarahbond/2017/04/27/whitewashing-ancient-statues-whiteness-racism-and-color-in-the-ancient-world/#4b23595875ad>

Catherine L. Howey, 'Dressing a Virgin Queen: Court Women, Dress, and Fashioning the Image of England's Queen Elizabeth I', in *Early Modern Women: An Interdisciplinary Journal 4* (Autumn 2009), pp. 201–8

Courtney Humphries, 'Have we Hit Peak Whiteness?, *Nautilus*, 30 July 2015 <http://nautil.us/issue/26/color/have-we-hit-peak-whiteness>

Courtney Humphries, 'How White Came to Be Synonymous With Clean and Good', *Nautilus*, 4 August 2015 <http://nautil.us/blog/how-white-came-to-be-synonymous-with-clean-and-good>

Leander Kahney, *Jony Ive: the genius behind Apple's greatest products* (London, 2013)

Herman Melville, *Moby-Dick; or, The Whale* (London, 1851)

Michel Pastoureau, *Black: The History of a Colour* (Princeton, NJ, 2009)

William H. Monroe, 'An Early Gothic French Ivory of the Virgin and Child', in *Art Institute of Chicago Museum Studies 9* (1978), pp. 6–29

Margaret Talbot, 'The Myth of Whiteness in Classical Sculpture', *The New Yorker Online*, 29 October 2018 <https://www.newyorker.com/magazine/2018/10/29/the-myth-of-whiteness-in-classical-sculpture>

Lou Taylor, *Mourning Dress: A Costume and Social History* (London, 1983)

Grey

G.K. Chesterton, 'The Glory of Grey', in *Alarms and Discursions* (London, 1910)

James Abbot McNeill Whistler, transcript of 'Mr Whistler's Ten O'Clock', a lecture at Prince's Hall, London, 1885 <https://www.whistler.arts.gla.ac.uk/miscellany/tenoclock/>

Alexandra Harris, *Weatherland: Writers & Artists Under English Skies* (London, 2015)

Yellow

Jordanna Bailkin, 'Indian Yellow: Making and Breaking the Imperial Palette', *Journal of Material Culture 10/22* (2005), pp. 197–214

Susanna Brown (ed.) *Horst: Photographer of Style* (London, 2014)

Lucia Burgio, Michelle Shulman and Michael Wheeler, 'Materials and Techniques of Kalighat Paintings: Pigment analysis of nine paintings from the collections of the Victoria and Albert Museum', *Journal of the Institute of Conservation 34/2* (2011), pp. 173–85

Rosemary Crill (ed.), *The Fabric of India* (London, 2015)

Chander Vishwa Ohri, *The Technique of Pahari Painting* (Delhi, 2001)

Michel Pastoureau, *Yellow: The History of a Colour* (Princeton, NJ and Oxford, 2019)

Orange

Clarissa Hyman, *Oranges: A Global History* (London, 2013)

John McPhee, *Oranges: a History of Citrus* (London, 2016)

Isaac Newton, *Opticks: or, A Treatise of the Reflexions, Refractions, Inflexions and Colours of Light* (London, 1704)

'Orange colour clash set for court', *BBC News*, 20 February 2005 <http://news.bbc.co.uk/1/hi/business/4281845.stm>

Gill Saunders, *Orange and Lemons: Fruit Wrappers from the Victoria & Albert Museum* (London, 1985)

Jessica Stewart, 'The History of the Color Orange: From Tomb Paintings to Modern-Day Jumpsuits', *My Modern Met*, 21 February 2019 <https://mymodernmet.com/history-color-orange/ >

Pink

Valerie Steele, *Pink: The History of a Punk, Pretty, Powerful Colour* (London, 2018)

Red

Yvonne Baby, 'Portrait de l'Artiste: Interview with Yves Saint Laurent at the Metropolitan New York', *Le Monde*, 8 December 1983

Ruth Bottomley, *Chinese Papercuts: A Selection* (Singapore, 1994)

Amy Butler, *A Perfect Red: Empire, Espionage and the Quest for the Colour of Desire* (London, 2005)

Edwina Ehrman, *Undressed: A Brief History of Underwear* (London, 2015)

Jessica Harrison-Hall, *Ming: 50 Years That Changed China* (London, 2014)

Erika Janik, *Apple: A Global History* (London, 2011)

Lisa Jardine, 'A Point of View: the power of wearing red', *BBC News Magazine*, 19 September 2014 <https://www.bbc.co.uk/news/magazine-29240820>

Christy Lange, 'Love in a Red-Hot Climate', *The*

Observer, 15 June 2003 <https://www.theguardian.com/theobserver/2003/jun/15/featuresreview.review>

Carmella Padilla and Barbara Anderson, *A Red Like No Other: How Cochineal Colored the World* (New York, 2015)

Sophie Page & Marina Wallace, *Spellbound: Magic, Ritual and Witchcraft* (Oxford, 2018)

Michel Pastoureau, *Red: The History of a Color* (Princeton, 2017)

Helen Perrson, *Shoes: Pleasure and Pain* (London, 2015)

Sarah Schaffer, 'Reading our Lips: the history of lipstick regulation in western seats of power', 2006 <http://nrs.harvard.edu/urn-3:HUL.InstRepos:10018966>

'Shades of doubt and shapes of hope: Colors in Iranian culture', *Tehran Times*, 21 February 2012 <https://www.tehrantimes.com/news/396974/Shades-of-doubt-and-shapes-of-hope-Colors-in-Iranian-culture>

Annemarie Schimmel, *The Empire of the Great Mughals: History, Art and Culture* (London, 2006)

Suhashini Sinha, *Kalighat Paintings: from the Collection of the Victoria and Albert Museum, London, and Victoria Memorial Hall, Kolkata* (Ahmedabad and London, 2011)

Jan Stuart, 'Chinese Red', 2 September 2016 <https://www.freersackler.si.edu/red/>

Victoria and Albert Museum, Exhibition Administration file, 1998–1999: *The Shape of Colour: Red* (held at The Lighthouse, Glasgow): V&A event - 50 Reds, V&A Archive ref. A0553

Purple
Suzanne B. Butters, *The Triumph of Vulcan: Sculptors' Tools, Porphyry, and the Prince in Ducal Florence* (Florence, 1996)

Elizabeth Crawford, '"Our readers are careful buyers": Creating Goods for the Suffrage Market', in *Suffrage and the Arts: Visual Culture, Politics and Enterprise*, ed. Miranda Garrett and Zoë Thomas (London, 2019), pp. 117–36

Kenneth Florey, 'English Suffrage Badges and the Marketing of the Campaign', in *Suffrage and the Arts: Visual Culture, Politics and Enterprise*, ed. Miranda Garrett and Zoë Thomas (London, 2019), pp. 137–56

Simon Garfield, *Mauve: How One Man Invented a Colour that Changed the World* (London, 2000)

Jon Savage, 'All Together Now?', in *You Say You Want a Revolution? Records and Rebels 1966-1970*, ed. Victoria Broackes and Geoffrey Marsh (London, 2016)

Mary Schoeser, *Silk* (New Haven, CT & London, 2007)

Blue
Amanda Game, 'Vital Communities', in *Porcelain City Jingdezhen* <http://researchonline.rca.ac.uk/610/49/PDF_of_Porcelain_City_Catalogue.pdf>

B.N. Goswamy and A.L. Dallapiccola, 'Visions of the Dark Lord', in *Krishna: The Divine Lover, Myth and Legend through Indian Art*, ed. B.N. Goswamy, A.L. Dallapiccola and Walter Spink (Bombay, Calcutta, Delhi & Madras, 1982)

Yves Klein, transcript of a lecture at the Sorbonne, Paris, 1959 <http://theoria.art-zoo.com/sorbonne-lecture-yves-klein/>

L.E. Mengoni, 'Jingdezhen: an Enduring Legacy in Porcelain Production', in *Porcelain City Jingdezhen* <http://researchonline.rca.ac.uk/610/49/PDF_of_Porcelain_City_Catalogue.pdf>

William Morris, 'Dyeing as an Art', in *The Decorator and Furnisher* 19/6 (March, 1892), pp. 217–18

Museum of Fine Arts Boston, *Blue: Cobalt to Cerulean in Art and Culture* (New York, 2015)

R.C. Nash, 'South Carolina indigo, European textiles and the British Atlantic economy in the eighteenth century', in *The Economic History Review* 63/2 (May 2010), pp. 362–92

Michel Pastoreau, *Blue: The History of a Color* (Princeton, NJ and Oxford, 2018)

Aaron Sidder, 'Earliest Evidence of Indigo Dye Found at Ancient Peruvian Burial Site', *Smithsonian Magazine*, 2016 <https://www.smithsonianmag.com/smart-news/earliest-evidence-indigo-dye-found-ancient-peruvian-burial-site-180960477/>

Ganesh Vasudeo Tagare (tr.), 'The Bhāgavata Purāa, Part IV', in *Ancient Indian Tradition and Mythology* 10 (Delhi, 1978)

Turquoise
J. Clarke, *Jewellery of Tibet and the Himalayas* (London, 2004)

Florence Dunn Friedman, *Gifts of the Nile: Ancient Egyptian Faience* (New York, 1998).

R.J. King, 'Turquoise', in *Geology Today* 18/3 (2002), pp. 110–14

Arash Khazeni, *Sky Blue Stone: The Turquoise Trade in World History* (California, 2014)

Joe Dan Lowry and Joe P. Lowry, *Turquoise: The World Story of a Fascinating Gemstone* (Layton, UT, 2010)

Karl A. Taube, 'The Symbolism of Turquoise in Ancient Mesoamerica', in J.C.H. King, Max Carocci, Caroline Cartwright, et al (eds), *Turquoise in Mexico and North America: Science, Conservation, Culture and Collection* (London, 2012), pp. 117–34

Green
Mary O. Bogard, 'Coloured Glass in Pharmacy', in *Pharmacy History* 26/1 (1984), pp. 20–7

Lucia Burgio, Robin J.H. Clark and Richard R. Hark, 'Spectroscopic Investigation of Modern Pigments on Purportedly Medieval Miniatures by the "Spanish Forger"', in *Journal of Raman Spectroscopy*, 17 July 2009 <www.interscience.wiley.com>

Alison Matthews David, *Fashion Victims: The Dangers of Dress Past and Present*, (London, 2015)

Derek C. Davis, *English Bottles & Decanters 1650–1900* (London, 1972)

Edwina Ehrman, '1800–1900', in *Fashioned from Nature* (London, 2018), pp. 62–105

Lucinda Hawksley, *Bitten by Witch Fever: Wallpaper & Arsenic in the Victorian House* (London, 2016)

Reino Liefkes (ed.), *Glass* (London, 1997)

Susan North, *18th-Century Fashion in Detail* (London, 2018)

Lauren Osmond, 'Investigating the Microstructural Changes in Jewel Beetle Elytra on Textiles', 2019, unpublished research report submitted to Queen's University

Michel Pastoureau, *Green: The History of a Color* (Princeton, NJ and Oxford, 2014)

'Celadon' <https://www.gotheborg.com/glossary/celadon.shtml>

Black
Diana Edwards, *Black Basalt: Wedgwood and Contemporary Manufacturers* (Woodbridge, Suffolk, 1994)

John Harvey, *The Story of Black* (London, 2013)

—, *Men in Black*, (London, 1995)

Paul Hodkinson, *Goth: Identity, Style, and Subculture* (Oxford & New York, NY, 2002)

Juan José Junquera and Gilla Evans, *The Black Paintings of Goya* (London, 2003)

John M. Marzluff and Tony Angell, *In the Company of Crows and Ravens* (New Haven, CT, 2005)

Valerie D. Mendes, *Black in Fashion*, (London, 1999)

Michel Pastoureau, *Black: The History of a Color* (Princeton, NJ and Oxford, 2009)

Dale Townshend (ed.), *Terror and Wonder: The Gothic Imagination* (London, 2014)

PICTURE CREDITS

All photographs are © Victoria and Albert Museum, London, unless otherwise stated. For reference, the following list also provides Victoria and Albert Museum accession numbers.

To learn more about the Museum and the objects illustrated in this book, please visit www.vam.ac.uk, where you can search the collection using the V&A accession numbers provided.

t top   b bottom   l left
r right   m middle

Introduction

p. 6 National Art Library, V&A: 38041800703191

p. 9 Given by Elizabeth Howard. T.52-2016

p. 10 P.C. Manuk and Miss G.M. Coles Bequest through The Art Fund. IS.9-1949

p. 12 E.3177:1-2007

p. 14 15170

White

p. 20 T.169-1962 Given by Miss Elizabeth Allen and Mrs Hargrave

p. 21 E.238-1999 Given by Christopher Bucklow © Christopher Bucklow

p. 22 t 622-1882 Bequeathed by John Jones bl 200-1867 br M.97-1917 Bryan Bequest

p. 23 232-1894

p. 24 l T.360-1984 and T.608-1996 r T.260-1976 Given by Miss Hepburne Scott

p. 25 t T.44-1987 Given by the manufacturer b 172-1900

p. 26 T.271-1974 Given by Mrs Alec Hambro

p. 27 tl FE.154-2002 Given by Moe Co. Ltd. tr 900-1864 Given by the Rev. R. Brooke bl 1055-1871 br 7912-1862

p. 28 tl AAD/1979/9 tr W.661:1-4-2001 Given by Adam Carey Courtesy of JVCKENWOOD Corporation b T.111&A-1974 Given by the designer Courtesy André Courrèges patrimoine

p. 29 E.438-1947 Given by Gordon W. Gilkey Courtesy

of the Portland Art Museum Portland Oregon

p. 30 E.1313-2000 Transferred from the British Museum

p. 31 t E.2056-1991 Given by Dr David Segal b M.126-2011 Given by the American Friends of the V&A through the generosity of Patricia V. Goldstein

p. 32 t E.956-1954 Bequeathed by Miss Mary (May) Morris b C.66-1967

p. 33 E.533-2005 Purchased through the Cecil Beaton Royalties Fund © Huang Yan

p. 34 t C.21:12-2009 b FE.115-2009 Supported by the Friends of the V&A © Young Sook Park

p. 35 FE.30-1983 © MIYAKE DESIGN STUDIO

p. 36 E.656-2011 Given by Martin Barnes

p. 37 t E.605-2002 Purchased through the Julie and Robert Breckman Print Fund r C.546-1910 Salting Bequest

p. 38 E.264-2011 Supported by the National Lottery Heritage Fund © Charlie Phillips /www.nickyakehurst.com

p. 39 A.49-1914 Given by Rodin in November 1914

Grey

p. 44 FE.23-2014

p. 45 tl 178-1894 tr RPS.1932-2018 The Royal Photographic Society Collection at the V&A acquired with the generous assistance of the National Lottery Heritage Fund and Art Fund b T.304-2002

p. 46 t C.160&A-1979 © Elizabeth Fritsch bl Circ.257-1976 © Bridget Riley 2020. All rights reserved br E.57-1994 © The Josef and Anni Albers Foundation / Artists Rights Society (ARS) New York and DACS London 2020

p. 47 E.966-1926

p. 48 FE.7-2010 Purchased from Sydney L. Moss Ltd. 12 Queen Street Mayfair London W1J 5PG

p. 49 tl E.3245-1980 © Simon Rendall tr B.370:12-2012 Purchased from G.J. Smith b B.372:1-4-2012 b E.251-1908

p. 50 t M.32-2014 The Louise Klapisch Collection Given by Suzanne Selvi © Dorothy Hogg b M.29-2006 Given by the artist © Axel Russmeyer

p. 51 t M.18-2016 Given by the artist © Ann Carrington b CAI.1061

p. 52 tl M.269-1977 tr M.11-1986 © Kevin Coates ml M.67-2008 Given by the American Friends of the V&A through the generosity of Professor B. Seymour Rabinovitch © Jacqueline Mina OBE mr Circ.451-1963 b Circ.481-1962

p. 53 tr M.561-1926 Lt. Col. G. B. Croft-Lyons Bequest b B.85-2004

p. 54 tl T.45 to B-1942 Given by the Board of Trade bl M.27-1993 br Misc.475-1980

p. 55 l T.40:12-2005 r M.2-2002 Gift of John S. G. Simmons

p. 56 tl T.109-1982 Given by Mrs D.M. Haynes and Mrs M. Clark tr E.232-2015 Given by Brenda Bishop bl M.3-2017 Accepted under the Cultural Gifts Scheme by HM Government from Nicholas Snowman and allocated to the Victoria and Albert Museum 2017 br T.18:1-2-2015 Given by Mrs Fiona McWatters

p. 57 Circ.95B-1947 Given by the manufacturer © Julian Trevelyan for Ascher

p. 58 t E.1882-1992 © Maria Lalic (bl) 320-1891 br Ph.3566-1904 Purchased from the photographer

p. 59 bl P. 101-1920 br P. 9-1949

p. 60 t S.4217-2009 bl E.453-1965 Given by the artist © The Estate of Gertrude Hermes br FE.11-2013

p. 61 E.620-2015 Given by David Potter © The Estate of Leonard Potter

pp. 62-3 E.1517-1905

p. 64 tl E.269-2013 tr M.28-2001 © Jan Yager b E.681:8-2014 Given by East London Printmakers © East London Printmakers.

p. 65 E.998-1979 © Tom Phillips. All Rights Reserved DACS 2020

Yellow

p. 70 t 252-1906 bl C.17&A-1968 br FE.58-2008 Given from the Everts-Comnene-Logan Collection

p. 71 T.753-1950 Bequeathed by W. Llewellyn Jones

p. 72 IM.421-1923

p. 73 l M.32A-1963 Wallis Bequest tl IS.299B-1951 tr M.28-1965 Bequeathed by Miss Estella Canziani br CAI.99 Bequeathed by Constantine Alexander Ionides

p. 74 t 1394-1869 Bequeathed by Rev. Chauncey Hare Townshend bl T.264-1974 Given by her Majesty the Queen br T.426&A-1990

p. 75 l D.902-1908 tr M.14-2006 Given by Joan Hurst through Art Fund

p. 76 L.520-1987

p. 77 tl P. 5-1917 Purchased with the assistance of the Murray Bequest tr A.93-1956 b CIRC.554-1962

p. 78 t CIRC.502-1973 Courtesy Brionvega a division of SIM2 BV International S.r.l. m W.8-2007 © ghyczy.com b T.59:1 2 -1992 © Mary Quant

p. 79 C.71-1979 © Estate of Peggy Angus. All Rights Reserved DACS 2020

p. 80 E.3910-1983 © The Estate of Frédéric Henri Kay Henrion courtesy of Marion Wesel-Henrion

p. 81 t S.793-1990 m T.17:1, 2-2005 Given by Nike © NIKE Inc. bl E.237-2014 Courtesy The Horst Estate br E.379-1989 Given by Kevin Edge © STABILO International GmbH

p. 82 tl IM.88-1930 tr 0782(IS) bl IS.247-1953 Given by the University Museum of Archaeology and Ethnology Cambridge to which the series was presented by Mrs. Western of Langbrookside Havant Hampshire (bm) IS.21:1, 2-2012 br IS.89-1963

p. 83 IS.34-1949 Bequeathed by P. C. Manuk and Miss G. M. Coles through The Art Fund

p. 84 tl W.1-2019 Purchased with support from the National Heritage Memorial Fund Art

Fund and V&A Members © Salvador Dali Fundació Gala-Salvador Dalí DACS 2020 tr T.369&A-1985 © Yves Saint Laurent b 2518(IS)

p. 85 l M.2:1 to 2 -2016 Given by Jacqueline and Jonathan Gestetner © Ute Decker r T.57-1976

p. 86 tl E.57-1892 tr IS.1877-1883l bl T.294&A-1971 br S.1657&A to I -1982 © The Estate of David Walker

p. 87 95-1865

Orange

p. 92 E.1183-1937

p. 93 tl E.1704-1974 Given by Mr Lond-Caulk tr E.2589-1920 b E.734-1949

pp. 94-5 E.545-2001 Given by Karsten Schubert © Anya Gallaccio. All Rights Reserved DACS 2020

p. 96 E.945-2008

p. 97 t RPS.1332-2018 The Royal Photographic Society Collection at the V&A acquired with the generous assistance of the National Lottery Heritage Fund and Art Fund © Courtesy of the Estate of Helen Messinger Murdoch b IS.48:5/A-1956 Gift of Mr. John Goelet

p. 98 t 1013-1886 Bequeathed by Joshua Dixon b C.74-1976 © Fiskars UK Limited

p. 99 CIRC.39-1969 Given by Heal Fabrics Ltd. ©Robin & Lucienne Day Foundation

p. 100 t 513-1870 Bequeathed by John M. Parsons bl 831-1871 br M.520-1924 Bequeathed by Sir Claude Phillips

p. 101 t M.3-2009 Given by Francis Ames-Lewis in memory of Felicity Ashbee b 659-1904

p. 102 T.139&A-1967

p. 103 t CIRC.564-1962 b E.594-1999 Gift of Ruth and Joseph Bromberg in memory of their son Michael © & tm 2020 The Estate of Jean-Claude Forest

p. 104 tl National Art Library V&A: 3804180016831 2 © Belinda Theyre Kennedy tr W.9-2003 Given by British Telecom Ltd. b CIRC.214-1970 ©Ignazia Favata-Studio Joe Colombo

p. 105 t T.96-2018 b B.87-2004

p. 106 E.2-1924 Presented by the Underground Electric Railways Co. of London Ltd. ©Simon Rendall

p. 107 tl S.993-2015 tr E.846-1976 © The Estate of Patrick Caulfield. All rights reserved DACS 2020 b E.2760-1991 © Belinda Theyre Kennedy

p. 108 t E.721-2017 Given by Mark Fox & Angie Wang / Design is Play b W.674-2001 Given by the designers ©Dunne & Raby

p. 109 E.2565-2007 Given by the artist © Ori Gersht

Pink

p. 114 tl C.1194-1917 H.L. Florence bequest tr E.4037-1915 Given by Mr Emslie John Horniman b IS.19-1949 P. C. Manuk and Miss G. M. Coles Bequest through Art Fund

p. 115 FE.149-2002 Given by Moe Co. Ltd.

p. 116 tl S.703-2001 Cyril W Beaumont Bequest bl M.172-1962 Given by Dame Joan Evans br T.298-1974 Given by Mr Vern Lambert

p. 117 E.1405-1979

p. 118 tl T.14&A-1951 Given by Miss C. E. Gallini bl 1317-1869 Bequeathed by the Rev. Chauncy Hare Townshend br 273A-1905 Given by Mr W.G. Gulland

p. 119 E.614-1915 Given by the Underground Electric Railways Co. of London Ltd.

p. 120 t T.355-1985 Given by Miss E. Carlill b 768-1882 Bequeathed by John Jones

p. 121 l T.145-1991 r LOAN:GILBERT.271-2008 © The Rosalinde and Arthur Gilbert Collection on loan to the Victoria and Albert Museum

p. 122 IM.226-1923 Given by Mrs W. H. Charsley

p. 123 tl CIRC.223-1921 tr LOAN:GILBERT.330-2008 © The Rosalinde and Arthur Gilbert Collection on loan to the Victoria and Albert Museum m 168-1874 Bought from the Haliburton Collection b T.149&A-1974 Given by Mrs Loel Guinness

p. 124 MISC.449&1 to 15-1980

p. 125 tl B.8-2016 Given by Lionel Hemsley tr MISC.559:1 2-1986 bl B.382-1993 Given by Ilona Hirsch br B.449-2010 Given by Jennifer Leaver

p. 126 E.970-2010 Supported by the National Lottery Heritage Fund Photograph: Jennie Baptiste, Make-up Artist: Brenda Cuffy, Stylist: Chinyere Eze

p. 127 l T.221&A-1974 Given by Princess Irene Galitzine tr T.368-1976 Given by Mrs. A. Lu br S.803A-1981 Cyril W Beaumont Bequest

p. 128 t T.63-1967 Given by Lady Glenconner © Maison Schiaparelli b T.738-1974

p. 129 T.182-1996 Given by the designer. Courtesy of Philip Treacy

p. 130 l E.166-2011 U-Print Community printshop for the Cardiff Women's Festival. Great Britain, c. 1980s. Exhibited in Greenwich Mural Workshop's 'Printing Is Easy?' exhibition, London, 1986. Given by Greenwich Mural Workshop r CD.5-2017 Given by Song Oh © Jayna Zweiman, Pussyhat Project

p. 131 E.152-2011 Given by Greenwich Mural Workshop

Red

p. 136 FE.32-1982

p. 137 tl T.121:1, 2-2011 © Maiko Dawson tr T.27-1997 Worn and given by Mrs Margaret Stewart. b M.24:12-1993

p. 138 tl MISC.148-1988 tr T.872:1-2000 Given by Agent Provacateur © Agent Provocateur b T.81:1 2-2002 Purchased with Art Fund support and assistance from the Friends of the V&A the Elsbeth Evans Trust and the Dorothy Hughes Bequest © The Estate of Malcolm McLaren

p. 139 S.342-1999

p. 140 E.1127-2012 Art Fund Collection of Middle Eastern Photography at the V&A and the British Museum Courtesy of the artist and Rosenfeld Gallery Tel Aviv

p. 141 l T.22-1925 Given by Mrs George Eumorfopoulos t T.33-1981 b 6773(IS)/A

p. 142 t 664-1907 Given by Mrs. Julia C. Gulland bl 335-1870 br C.913-1936

p. 143 C.10:1 to 6-2015 ©Paul Cummins

p. 144 E.1286-2004 Gift of the American Friends of the V&A Gift to the American Friends by Leslie Judith and Gabri Schreyer and Alice Schreyer Batko

p. 145 t M.20-2005 Gift of the Whiteley family b E.1050-2003 Purchased through the Julie and Robert Breckman Print Fund © Courtesy of Ralph Steadman

p. 146 tl M.22-2008 Given by Solange Azagury-Partridge © Solange Ltd tr W.4-2000 Given by Cappellini © Courtesy of Cappellini, Design by Thomas Ericksson br FE.234-1992

p. 147 E.140-1997

p. 148 S.261-1998 Given by the British Puppet and Model Theatre Guild

p. 149 t M.36-1961 Given by Mrs K. E. Sargent bl LOAN:GILBERT.234-2008 © The Rosalinde and Arthur Gilbert Collection on loan to the Victoria and Albert Museum br National Art Library at the V&A: 3804180055494l Acquired from Elizabeth Arden, December 1937

p. 150 3467(IS) to 3467A/(IS) Transferred from the India Museum in 1879

p. 151 t S.64-2008 Given by the British Theatre Museum Association bl T.100-2003 Purchased with Art Fund support and assistance from the Friends of the V&A, and a number of private donors br FE.8-1976 Given by Sir Harry Garner and Lady Garner

p. 152 t PH.247-1981 © Eggleston Artistic Trust Courtesy Eggleston Artistic Trust and David Zwirner b E.391-1921 Given by Mrs J.T. Clarke

p. 153 T.6-1956

p. 154 E.2339-1918 Given by the Underground Electric Railways Co. of London, Ltd

p. 155 tl T.246:1 to 4/&A-1979 Given by Mr John Tayleur tr National Art Library at the V&A: 3804180072785l bl RPS.3160-2018 The Royal Photographic Society Collection at the V&A, acquired with the generous assistance of the National Lottery Heritage Fund and Art Fund

p. 156 t IS.29-1952 Given by W.G. Archer b E.2907-1995 Courtesy of the Prinknash Abbey Trustees

THE AUTHORS

Authors are credited in chapter order.

Tim Travis
Curator of Prints in the Word & Image Department
Editor; 'Introduction', pp. 6–15

Anna White
Assistant Curator of Designs in the Design, Architecture & Digital Department
'White', pp. 16–19; captions pp. 22–5, 28–9, 32–5

Melanie Lenz
Curator of Digital Art in the Word & Image Department
'White' captions pp. 20–1, 26–7, 30–1, 36–9

Gill Saunders
Senior Curator of Prints in the Word & Image Department
'Grey', pp. 40–3; captions pp. 44–65

Lydia Caston
Assistant Curator of Photographs in the Word & Image Department
'Yellow', pp. 66–9; captions pp. 70–87

Douglas Dodds
Senior Curator of Digital Art in the Word & Image Department
'Orange', pp. 88–91

Nika Narkeviciute
Archive Assistant, Archive of Art and Design in the Word & Image Department
'Orange' captions pp. 92–109

Elisabeth Murray
Curator in the Furniture, Textiles & Fashion Department
'Pink', pp. 110–13

Rachael Chambers
Curator, Clandon Park, National Trust; previously Assistant Curator of Photographs in the Word & Image Department
'Pink' captions pp. 114–31

Deborah Sutherland
Curator of Operations, National Art Library
'Red', pp. 132–5; captions pp. 144–9, 154–6

Matthew Abel
Collections Move Officer, V&A East
'Red' captions pp. 136–43, 150–3

Ella Kilgallon
Curator of Designs in the Design, Architecture & Digital Department
'Purple', pp. 158–61; captions pp. 162–7, 170–3

Juliet Ceresole
Assistant Curator of Designs in the Design, Architecture & Digital Department
'Purple' captions pp. 168–9, 174–9; 'Brown' captions pp. 250–67

Hanne Faurby
Project Curator in the Sculpture, Metalwork, Ceramics & Glass Department
'Blue', pp. 180–3; 'Green', pp. 222–5

Sarah Beattie
Assistant Curator in the Word & Image Department
'Blue' captions pp. 184–7, 196–7, 200–3

Anne-Margaux Illido
Assistant Curator in the Word & Image Department
'Blue' captions pp. 186–95, 198–9

Benjamin Hinson
Assistant Curator, Middle East Section, Asian Department
'Turquoise', pp. 204–7; captions pp. 208–21

Susan M Harris
Factory Project Cataloguer, Word & Image Department
'Green' captions pp. 226–9, 240–5

Frances Willis
Assistant Librarian, National Art Library, Word & Image Department
'Green' captions pp. 230–9

Emily Knight
Assistant Curator of Paintings in the Word & Image Department
'Brown', pp. 246–9

Ruth Hibbard
Curator in the Word & Image Department
'Black', pp. 268–71; captions pp. 272–91

ACKNOWLEDGMENTS

The publishers would like to thank everyone who contributed to the research, writing and production of this book. This project would not have been possible without the enthusiasm, patience and collaboration of a large cross-disciplinary team, headed by the book's unfaltering editor, Tim Travis, who brought everyone together, and Hannah Newell, Development Editor at the Victoria and Albert Museum. Huge thanks are due to the authors for their hard work, creativity and commitment to the book. We would also like to acknowledge the invaluable contributions of Elizabeth James to the chapter on Brown and Anita Nathwani to the chapter on Yellow. Another essential contribution came from Richard Davis and his team at the Victoria and Albert Musem Photography Studio.

We are extremely grateful to the many curators at the Victoria and Albert Museum who made time to advise on the items from the Museum's collection, including: Martin Barnes, Silvija Banić, Ricarda Brosch, Susanna Brown, Katy Canales, Connie Carol Burks, Sau Fong Chan, Zorian Clayton, Judith Crouch, Max Donnelly, Avalon Fotheringham, Catriona Gourlay, Alun Graves, Fuchsia Hart, Nick Humphrey, Rosalie Kim, Jenny Lister, Susan North, Leela Meinertas, Alice Minter, Josephine Rout, Nick Smith, Divia Patel, Clare Phillips, Tim Stanley, Catherine Yvard, and Claire Wilcox. Special thanks to Anna Jackson for her reading of the text. Thanks also to Keith Levett, Director of Savile Row tailors Henry Poole & Co., who advised on the history of hunting coats.

Many thanks are due to the team at Thames & Hudson, including Kate Edwards for her thoughtful copy-editing, Avni Patel for her design work, Kate Thomas for taking the book through production, and to Julian Honer, commissioning editor, and Susannah Lawson for their continued guidance and unwavering support for this project. We are indebted to the team at Here Design for the original concept and design, notably Caz Hildebrand, Alex Merrett, Ainhoa Nicolau and Tae Yang.

INDEX